MENTAL HEALTH
POLICY
AND
PRACTICE
TODAY

Ted R. Watkins
James W. Callicutt

editors

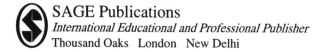

SAGE Publications
International Educational and Professional Publisher
Thousand Oaks   London   New Delhi

For information address:

SAGE Publications, Inc.
2455 Teller Road
Thousand Oaks, California 91320
E-mail: order@sagepub.com

SAGE Publications Ltd.
6 Bonhill Street
London EC2A 4PU
United Kingdom

SAGE Publications India Pvt. Ltd.
M-32 Market
Greater Kailash I
New Delhi 110 048 India

Printed in the United States of America

Library of Congress Cataloging-in-Publication Data

Main entry under title:

Library of Congress Cataloging-in-Publication Data

Mental health policy and practice today / edited by Ted R. Watkins and
James W. Callicutt.
      p.   cm.
   Includes bibliographical references and index.
   ISBN 0-8039-7138-9 (cloth). — ISBN 0-8039-7139-7 (pbk.)
   1. Mental health policy—United States. 2. Mental health
services—United States. I. Watkins, Ted R. II. Callicutt, James
W.
   RA790.6.M442 1997
   362.2'0973—dc21   96-51206

97 98 99 00 01 02 03 10 9 8 7 6 5 4 3 2 1

Acquiring Editor:	Jim Nageotte
Editorial Assistant:	Kathleen Derby
Production Editor:	Sanford Robinson
Production Assistant:	Denise Santoyo
Typesetter/Designer:	Christina Hill
Indexer:	Teri Greenberg
Cover Designer:	Candice Harman
Print Buyer:	Anna Chin

With love, I dedicate my contribution to this book to my dear wife, Ann, and to Frances and Ben, Jack and Susan, Daniel, Raleigh, Evan, and Rachel.

—J.W.C.

To Iva, who departed; to Jessica, who arrived; and to Betty, who sustained me through this process.

—T.R.W.

Contents

Foreword   xi
    Michael M. Faenza

Preface   xv

PART I. INTRODUCTION   1

1. Overview of the Field of Mental Health   3
    James W. Callicutt

2. Institutional and Community Approaches to the
   Provision of Mental Health Services   17
    Vikki L. Vandiver

3. Political Aspects of Mental Health
   Treatment   32
   James I. Martin

4. The Impact of the Courts on Mental
   Health Policy and Services   49
   Brian D. Shannon

5. Personnel: The Professionals and
   Their Preparation   69
   James W. Callicutt and David H. Price

PART II. THE EXPANDING BASE OF KNOWLEDGE IN MENTAL HEALTH   87

6. Neuroscientific Research in
   Mental Health   89
   William H. Wilson

7. Research Into Social Factors in
   Mental Illness   107
   David W. Millard

8. Psychoeducation:
   A Contemporary Approach   129
   Cassandra Simon

9. Self-Help and Advocacy Groups in
   Mental Health   146
   Ted R. Watkins and James W. Callicutt

PART III. MENTAL HEALTH SERVICES TO SPECIAL POPULATIONS   163

10. Mental Health Services to Immigrants
    and Refugees   164
    Muriel Yu

11. Current Perspectives on the Homeless
    Mentally Ill   182
    R. Duane Hopson and Ted R. Watkins

12. Services to the Severely and Persistently
    Mentally Ill   195

    Vikki L. Vandiver

13. Mental Health Services to America's Veterans   209

    David H. Price

14. Mental Health Services to Minority Groups
    of Color   235

    John S. McNeil and Robin Kennedy

15. Women as Mental Health Service Recipients
    and Providers   258

    Theresa Bruno Mulloy

16. Treatment of Children and Adolescents:
    Inpatient and Outpatient Mental Health Issues   274

    Christian E. Molidor

17. Mental Health Services to Older Adults   286

    John S. McNeil and Robert L. Canon

18. The State of Mental Health Services to
    Criminal Offenders   298

    Charles Turnbo and Donald W. Murray, Jr.

19. Mental Health Services to Substance
    Abusers   312

    Ted R. Watkins

PART IV. IMPLICATIONS FOR THE
          21ST CENTURY   327

20. The Influence of Technology on Mental
    Health Services   328

    Albert D. Farrell

21. Mental Health Service Delivery in the
    Age of Managed Care   346

    E. Clarke Ross and Colette Croze

22. Looking Ahead: Issues to Be Resolved   362

    James W. Callicutt and Ted R. Watkins

Name Index   367

Subject Index   379

About the Authors   393

Foreword

This book is being published at a crucial time in the history of America's health movement. I believe the values and skills of mental health policy makers and practitioners are needed in the current U.S. health and human services environment more than at almost any other time. Effective mental health policy and practice is increasingly recognized as fundamental to the success of most of our society's undertakings. From the economic costs of untreated mental disorders in the U.S. workforce, to the highly visible plight of people in every major U.S. city who are homeless and have a serious mental illness, we are realizing the human and economic costs of past neglect.

The designers of mental health policy and services must work to span the boundaries of diverse health and human services systems, and even social institutions. The rapid change in health care and social services that is now taking place in the United States presents formidable new risks to vulnerable populations that are currently underserved in most U.S. communities. *Mental Health Policy and Practice Today* will serve professionals that must face these challenges on behalf of America's children and adults with mental health treatment needs.

At this writing, the United States is undergoing an unprecedented process of refinancing and reorganizing health and human services. With the failure of comprehensive national health care reform in the 103rd Congress, we now have countless reform scenarios taking place in state capitals and local communities across the nation. No area of health care is changing more rapidly than mental health services.

The need to contain costs is promoting the advance of managed care and related efforts to privatize the public mental health systems in many states. The use of managed care arrangements to deliver services to children and adults with the most severe illnesses and long-term care needs is a social experiment that is larger than any change in community mental health since the signing of the federal Community Mental Health Centers Act in 1963. At the same time, the United States is experiencing cutbacks in funding of crucial services and supports to low-income people and people with disabilities through congressional and state legislative action across the country.

We have also learned some important lessons through recent legislative victory. With recently enacted federal legislation, we have taken the first step in reforming the private insurance industry's practices that have traditionally discriminated against mental disorders. The mental health community's lobbying effort to end discriminatory aggregate annual limits and lifetime caps against mental health needs compared with other health care benefits is an example of what can be done through tenacity and coalition building in the public policy arena.

The National Mental Health Association (NMHA), the United States' oldest mental health advocacy movement, has included consumers, family members, and mental health professionals in its ranks since early in this century. NMHA's perspective is that we are now at a crossroads in mental health policy and practice. This time of rapid change and political pressure on public policy and funding streams that support services to people with mental disorders presents great risks to populations that mental health professionals have served and supported over many decades.

No group of American children or adults is more vulnerable in the current environment than those with mental illnesses. The chapters in this book that discuss the current policy and practice issues involved in delivering services to people with mental disorders present extremely important information for our field.

Without mental health policies that provide access to effective services for children and adults with mental health treatment needs, our communities suffer. I believe that many policymakers and practitioners will benefit from this book. However, my colleagues and I at NMHA hope that many readers also will find ways to turn their knowledge about human need and mental health services into advocacy.

I think that the majority of mental health professionals who have worked in the field over time believe that people with mental illnesses have been treated in an appalling way within U.S. society. In a country with the level of wealth and science that exists in the United States, we should have been able to bring many more resources and higher quality to the tasks of community mental health over the last 25 years. Not surprisingly, we pay a huge price for our failures.

What we do see today in U.S. cities are increasing numbers of people with the most severe disorders ending up homeless and in our urban county jails and state prison systems. And it could be said that mental disorders of adolescents have become increasingly criminalized. The current political and public policy culture seems to emphasize punishment and does much less about understanding the mental-health and social-services needs of youth who make up our juvenile justice system rolls. As with other populations, we know a great deal about delivering mental health services to children and families, but we fail miserably in most communities in delivering the goods. Adequate funding and enlightened public policy have just not been there for mental health needs in America.

Mental health policymakers and practitioners need to work in partnership with primary consumers of mental health services, parents of children with emotional disorders, and families of adults with severe and persistent mental illnesses. NMHA's vision is that through these partnerships, mental health professionals will become increasingly skilled and courageous mental health advocates at the local, state, and federal levels.

Michael M. Faenza, MSSW
President and CEO
National Mental Health Association
Alexandria, Virginia

Preface

We have been frustrated in recent years by the difficulty in finding textbooks that reflect the dynamic nature of mental health practice in today's rapidly changing social, intellectual, and political context. Through our teaching of graduate-level mental health courses in policy and practice, we have identified specific areas in which available material seems to be insufficient, dated, or scattered. This book is our solution to the need for timely information on the critical variables in the mental health field today. It covers the state of the field at this time, the cutting edge of research and service, the critically important forces external to the field of mental health that are shaping it, and the population groups in need of special service and policy attention. We conclude the book with a projection of what these factors mean for the future.

The book is divided into four parts. The first provides an overview of the field of mental health, including the extent and costs of mental health problems in the United States, the basic formats for service delivery (i.e., institutional and community structures), the influences of political biases and court decisions on policies and services, and a description of the professional personnel who plan and deliver mental health services. This look at the problem, the agencies that address it (and their contexts), and the personnel in those agencies lays the foundation for the next three sections.

The first two chapters in Part II review the most recent research into both the neuroscientific and the social factors that contribute to mental illness. The timeliness of this material enhances its importance for professional education in any of the mental health disciplines. Accompanying these two research reviews are chapters focusing on psychoeducation, which many believe to be the most significant contribution to the mental health service repertoire in recent years, and self-help and advocacy groups, which are counterbalancing the influence of professional caregivers with that of consumers.

Specific populations within the United States have mental health needs or subcultural characteristics that demand some accommodation by mental health practitioners for effective service. Part III includes chapters on 10 of these populations and explains their special needs and service requirements. Immigrants and refugees often bring histories of trauma with them, and the difficulties inherent in relocation contribute new levels of trauma to compound that which already exists. The homeless have fallen outside the reach of traditional service delivery systems, having been, in many cases, expelled from institutional care and not having a lifestyle compatible with usual outpatient programs. The severely and persistently mentally ill are those who are sometimes said to "resist" treatment because their needs are often greater than our resources or expertise. They continue to be at the center of public and professional concern. The mental casualties of military service have been so numerous that the nation has evolved a system of services, albeit inadequate, for dealing with this unique population. Racial minority groups, excluded from the mainstream of American society in health, have not fared better in mental illness; therefore, consideration of their needs regarding services and policies is in order. An interesting discussion is offered of the implications of gender, not only for clients, but also for the staff of mental health agencies. Children and adolescents and elders also have special needs relating to their stages in the life cycle, and these needs are explored in two chapters. Criminal offenders and substance abusers make up populations that have been ineffectively served in traditional mental health agencies. Much progress is being made through innovations in both policy and practice for these populations.

The chapters in Part IV discuss the changes that will shape the mental health services of the 21st century. Funding shifts to managed care plans and the influence of technology will have far-reaching effects on policy and practice in mental health. In the final chapter, we reflect briefly on the preceding contributions, risk some projections for the future suggested by recent trends, and raise some questions for consideration.

We have been most fortunate to receive the cooperation of an outstanding collection of contributors who represent universities from the East Coast to the West Coast of the United States, plus Oxford, England. The professional positions of our contributors include professorships in degree programs in social work, psychology, psychiatry, public health, public administration, and law, as well as practice positions including regional administrator, psychologist, executive director of a multicounty agency, private psychiatric hospital and clinic practice, executive of a national managed care system, representative of a national association of state mental health executives, and consultant to community and military groups. Many of these individuals add volunteer contributions to their professional efforts, serving on agency boards, speakers' bureaus, and government panels, and working in many other ways to advocate for mentally ill persons and their families. They all have something to say, and we are fortunate to have them share their expertise through their contributions to this book. We are confident that readers will also appreciate the contributors' blend of expertise based on both research and service "in the trenches."

We believe this book will be useful in educational programs in the traditional mental health professions of social work, psychology, psychiatry, and nursing, as well as in specialized courses in such programs as public health, sociology, and public administration. Its focus on the practice implications of policy gives it broad applicability and illustrates the inseparability of these two dimensions of the mental health field.

We also believe that practitioners currently working in mental health will find the broad range of topics informative and stimulating. In a field where workloads are high, resources are always less than we would wish, and rewards are more intangible than spendable, it is sometimes helpful to step back and look at the progress that is being made toward greater understanding and effectiveness. We hope that this volume will facilitate that process.

Acknowledgments

We want to express our appreciation to the many students whose desire to know more about the current reality of the mental health field inspired us to undertake the preparation of this book, to our colleagues at the University of Texas at Arlington who encouraged us, to the contributors who generously shared with us their expertise, and to Jim Nageotte of Sage Publications for his patience and understanding.

Ted R. Watkins
James W. Callicutt

PART I

Introduction

Before we present discussion of today's major issues in the mental health field, we need to provide a foundation of basic information to establish a common frame of reference for the material that follows. We begin with an overview of the field of mental health. In Chapter 1, James Callicutt presents data regarding the prevalence of mental illness in U.S. society, its costs, and how they are borne; he then describes the broad categories of services available for the treatment of mental illness.

In Chapter 2, Vikki Vandiver traces the historic shifts and vacillations of public interest from institutional to community approaches to mental health services, and sets the stage for much of the policy discussion incorporated in later chapters of the book.

Policy and practice do not exist in a vacuum. Political considerations, broadly speaking, color how assessment and treatment are conducted and determine the policies through which services are offered. In Chapter 3, James Martin clearly illustrates these points in relation to the history of services to gay men and lesbians and to women.

Another force that is instrumental in shaping mental health policy and services is the judicial system. Competing interests and perspectives often are studied in courts of law, and the resultant judicial decisions determine the direction of future practice and policy. For example, court decisions have addressed both the right to treatment and the right to refuse treatment. In Chapter 4, Brian Shannon traces the course of judicial law affecting current mental health policy and practices.

In any "game" it is essential to know who the players are. In Chapter 5, James Callicutt and David Price present a wealth of data on the personnel in each of the four traditional mental health professions: social work, psychology, mental health nursing, and psychiatry. The authors discuss the numbers of each of these kinds of professionals in the field, describe the training processes required for entrance to each of the professions, and give demographic data about each profession.

As a whole, the chapters in Part I lead to Part II's presentation of an update on research and practice.

CHAPTER 1

Overview of the Field of Mental Health

JAMES W. CALLICUTT

Today the mental health arena may be likened to a minefield. Rocked by revelations of the scandalous, widespread practices of patient abuse and fraud in private psychiatric hospitals that surfaced in the early 1990s (Sharkey, 1994), anticipating the shock waves of the impact of health care reform and managed health care (Broskowski & Marks, 1992; Corcoran & Bernstein, 1994), and reeling from the problems of homeless mentally ill persons (Grob, 1994; Kuhlman, 1994; Rochefort, 1993; Torrey, 1988), policy makers, service providers, advocates, and service constituencies are negotiating the minefield. This precarious passage is attended by the misery and suffering of casualties among persons with mental illness and their families. Yet the field of mental health is buoyed somewhat by the development of knowledge involving new technologies and interventions related to research advances in the neurosciences and the social sciences, as discussed in other chapters in this volume.

This overview surveys the scarred landscape of the field of mental health, focusing on the broad areas of mental health policy and the mental health service system. Much of the discussion is presented under two major headings: (a) the scope of the problem and (b) how the problem is addressed in the United States.

Mental health service provision is a reflection of mental health policy. Public mental health policy is largely a product of legislative, regulative, and judicial processes—that is, laws, regulations, and court decisions. These processes and their outcomes often reveal competing philosophies, values, and assumptions. Thus the conclusion that there is no unified, comprehensive set of policies that provides clear direction to the field of mental health should not be unexpected.

Kiesler and Sibulkin (1987) make a useful distinction between de jure and de facto public policy: "*De jure* policy is intentional in nature and usually legislated into law. The *de facto* policy is the net outcome of overall practices, whether the outcome is intended or not" (p. 27). Nationally, de jure mental health policy has focused on deinstitutionalization and community-based care emphasizing outpatient services. However, de facto policy has been shaped by the underfunding of community-based programs and resources, leading, in part, to the deluge of homeless mentally ill persons, an unintended negative consequence of deinstitutionalization. Funding provisions of government and private insurance programs that have favored paying for inpatient services rather than outpatient and community-based services have played a prominent part in creating de facto policy. However, as I shall note later in discussing some of the fiscal aspects of the scope of the problem of mental illness, there is a trend toward increased support for community-based services, including case management services (Frank & McGuire, 1994).

Efforts to describe the mental health service system are also met by a host of issues. Perhaps the most basic of these relates to the concept of "system" as embracing the notion of interrelated or interdependent parts forming a unified or organized whole (Anderson & Carter, 1990). Instead of a unified whole, we have a wide array of mental health programs and services that are often fragmented and driven by forces (political, philosophical, professional, and ideological) that may be antagonistic or neutral rather than supportive of the development of an organized, authentic mental health service system. Given the potency of these forces and a reasonable assumption that what exists is a "nonsystem," there is nevertheless a clear recognition that mental health services are provided in a multiplicity of settings under public, not-for-profit, and for-profit corporate auspices, resulting in the existence of a de facto mental health services system (Bevilacqua, 1991; Regier, Goldberg, & Taube, 1978). In essence, then, we have a de facto mental health policy and a companion de facto mental health service system.

The Scope of the Problem

Prevalence in Adults

"The term 'mental health' defies uniform definition. It is vague and imprecise with multiple meanings that differ with the context" (Callicutt, 1987, p. 125). Sometimes *mental health* is used as a euphemism for *mental illness*. In this discussion it is primarily so used. Although there are a variety of models and conceptions dealing with the definition and explanation of mental illness (see Vandiver, Chapter 12, this volume), including Szasz's (1960) contention that mental illness is a myth, there is conventional use of the American Psychiatric Association's (1994) *Diagnostic and Statistical Manual of Mental Disorders (DSM,* currently in its fourth edition) as the standard psychiatric classification reference publication governing much of the field of mental health in the United States. Despite *DSM-IV*'s widespread use, it should be noted that critics have discussed its shortcomings, including the problem of diagnostic reliability (Kirk & Kutchins, 1992).

Also, by way of further clarification, *mental disorder,* a synonym for *mental illness,* is defined by Barker (1995) as

> impaired psychosocial or cognitive functioning due to disturbances in any one or more of the following processes: biological, chemical, physiological, genetic, psychological, or social. Mental disorders are extremely variable in duration, severity, and prognosis, depending on the type of affliction. The major forms of mental disorder include *mood disorders, psychosis, personality disorders, organic mental disorders,* and *anxiety disorder.* (p. 231)

The chapters in this book do not focus on specific diagnostic classifications per se, but rather on broader categories, special populations in terms of policy and service provision.

Mental illness, whether considered a health problem, a social problem, or both, is a problem of immense consequence for the United States. Based on *DSM* classification, estimates of prevalence rates in 1990 (i.e., a measure of the existence of mental illness in the United States at that time) suggest that 40.4 million persons experienced a nonaddictive mental disorder, with an additional 10.9 million persons affected by an addictive disorder (Bourdon, Rae, Narrow, Manderscheid, & Regier, 1994). This translates to a mental or addictive disorder prevalence rate of 28.1% of the adult population: More than one-fourth of the adult population of the United States is suffering from a mental or addictive disorder within any given year.

Prevalence in Children

It is difficult to determine the number of seriously emotionally disturbed children in the United States. Differing definitions and diagnostic criteria make for inconsistencies among databases. In addition, responsibility for service delivery to children with emotional disorders is shared by multiple service systems (e.g., mental health, general health, education, and child welfare agencies). Further, the fact that many children with mental problems are never seen in the mental health system contributes to our inability to answer fundamental questions concerning the number of children with emotional disorders and the extent of unmet need (Hoagwood & Rupp, 1994). Nevertheless, estimates of children with diagnosable mental disorders from community studies, as reported by Hoagwood and Rupp (1994), vary from 17.6% to 22%.

There can be no doubt that the sheer number of individuals affected by mental disorders is impressive. When we consider the emotional and financial impact of mental illness on family members, the direct costs of services, and the less obvious but important costs of lost productivity, we can clearly see a health and social problem of the first order.

Mental Health Expenditures

There are three major sources of funding for mental health services: the federal government, state and local governments, and private sources. Dichotomized into government and private sources, estimated expenditures for 1990 indicate that government funding accounted for $23.6 billion (55.7%) and private funding for $18.8 billion (44.3%), a total of $42.4 billion (Frank & McGuire, 1994). Table 1.1 shows these data, with government funding disaggregated into the payment sources of Medicaid, state and local, the Department of Veterans Affairs (VA), other federal, and Medicare.

Private sources include philanthropic contributions, insurance payments, and out-of-pocket payments. Although most private expenditures are likely to be from private insurance sources, as much as 40-45% may come from individual out-of-pocket payments, as a consequence of the higher rate of cost sharing in mental health as opposed to general medical insurance coverage (Frank & McGuire, 1994).

As displayed in Table 1.1, state and local funding sources ranked second to private sources in 1990 in estimated mental health expenditures of $11.7 billion, 27.5% of the total. In part, this reflects the historical reality of states carrying the responsibility for providing mental health care for persons with serious mental illness and for the poor (Frank & McGuire, 1994; Hudson & Cox, 1991). Although most of the funds controlled by state mental health agencies (SMHAs) continue to go to state mental hospitals, the trend reflects an increase in the allocation of funds to community programs (Frank & McGuire, 1994). However, programs and responsibilities of individual SMHAs vary. Similarly, per capita expenditures diverge, "ranging from a high of $118 in New York to $17 in Iowa, with a national median of $38" (Frank & McGuire, 1994, p. 15).

Medicaid expenditures ranked third in 1990 at $8.1 billion, 19.1% of the total shown in Table 1.1. The critical role played by Medicaid, a federal/state program that varies from state to state, in paying for mental health services for the poor is well established (Frank & McGuire, 1994; Grob, 1994; Kiesler & Sibulkin, 1987; Koyanagi, 1990; Mechanic, 1989). Grob (1994) points out that Medicaid funding provisions have influenced a decline in the number of aged patients in state hospitals and a concurrent substantial increase in mentally ill residents in nursing homes. The consequences of this funding policy of Medicaid provides a dramatic example of how de facto mental health policy is formed.

In addition to the above focus on the more obvious and available data on expenditures for mental health services, it is also germane to identify some less

Table 1.1 Estimated Mental Health Expenditures by Payment Source, 1990[a]

	Dollars (in billions)	*Percentage*
Private sources[b]	18.8	44.3
Medicaid	8.1	19.1
State and local	11.7	27.5
VA	1.5	3.5
Other federal	0.8	1.8
Medicare	1.5	3.5
Total	42.4	100.0[c]

SOURCE: Reprinted from Frank and McGuire (1994, p. 8).
a. Exclusions: 90% of nursing home costs; support costs; administrative portion of block grant.
b. Includes out-of-pocket payments and philanthropy.
c. May not add to 100% due to rounding.

obvious and, to a large degree, hidden costs. In a study of 408 members of the Massachusetts Alliance for the Mental Ill, Franks (1987) found that the mean dollar expense of families in caring for their mentally ill members was $3,311 per year. Also, families devoted an average of 792 hours per year, with most of it provided to caregiving functions for their mentally ill family members. Converting the time spent to a monetary value and adding it to the dollar expenses, Franks found that the sample spent nearly $4 million per year on the care of mentally ill family members. Using prevalence rates for mental illness, Franks projected the statewide estimate of expenditures by families to exceed $50 million.

Add to these expenditures the significant costs of lost productivity (and the related loss of tax revenues) and the human costs of anguish and suffering as well as stigmatization, and factor in the numbers (prevalence) discussed previously, and a profile of the profound scope of the problem of mental illness begins to emerge. We can see both sharp and blurred features.

How the Problem Is Addressed

In this section I provide a general description of mental health service organizations in the United States, which increased from 3,005 in 1970 to 5,284 in 1990 (Redick, Witkin, Atay, & Manderscheid, 1994). I present other trend data and information useful for comparing and contrasting the tendencies to offer inpatient and outpatient services. In addition, I identify and briefly describe an array of mental health service settings involving both traditional and innovative programs, primarily in the specialty mental health sector. Attention is also given to the general health care sector, including the role of private practitioners, both primary care providers and mental health professionals.

Inpatient and outpatient services are the two major components of mental health care. *Inpatient services* refers to 24-hour care in a mental health facility such as a state hospital, private psychiatric hospital, or general hospital providing psychiatric services. *Outpatient services* refers to mental health services provided in clinics or office settings. Partial care, an increasingly important component of care, falls between the two categories of inpatient and outpatient care. Partial care, which includes day treatment services, experienced a more than fivefold increase in the number of additions (admissions and readmissions) to mental health organizations in the United States between 1969 and 1990. What are the trends in these service categories?

Inpatient Services

Around-the-clock care is indicated when an individual is disturbed to the extent that he or she poses a significant threat to self or others (Callicutt, 1987). The number of inpatient residential treatment beds declined from 524,878 in 1970 to 272,253 in 1990, a reduction of 252,625, or slightly more than 48% (Redick et al., 1994). The most dramatic decreases occurred in state and county hospital beds, from more than 400,000 in 1970 to fewer than 99,000 in 1990. Conversely, the most explosive increase in beds was in private psychiatric hospitals, from 4,295 in 1970 to 44,871 in 1990. Major increases in other inpatient categories included nonfederal general hospitals with separate psychiatric services, which expanded from 22,394 to 53,479 in the 20-year span (Redick et al., 1994).

The decrease in inpatient treatment beds is related to the deinstitutionalization movement, an increase in outpatient services, the use of psychotropic medications, and increases in the number of community mental health centers. Also, judicial and legislative decisions as well as funding policy changes in private insurance and public programs that seek to address both cost containment issues and the abuses of some private psychiatric hospitals in their unethical practices related to filling beds without regard to patients' needs for inpatient treatment have resulted in the closing of hospitals, consolidation, and downsizing (Sharkey, 1994).

In terms of length of stay in inpatient facilities, Table 1.2 indicates a median stay of 15 days for 1986. The influence of managed care and the other forces previously mentioned as contributing to the downsizing of many inpatient facilities suggests that the median days of stay will likely have decreased over the past decade. However, the need for prolonged inpatient care will continue for violent patients who are not responsive to currently available treatment technologies and for whom community-based care is not a viable option.

Reductions in the number of psychiatric inpatient beds have seen a coincident decrease in the number of inpatients in all mental health organizations, as depicted in Table 1.2. Despite the dramatic drop in the number of beds in state and county hospitals, these public institutions continue to care for the largest number of inpatients among the various types of mental health organizations listed in Table 1.3. In fact, when combined with the Department of Veterans Affairs (VA medical centers), we see that these government entities

Table 1.2 Median Days of Stay for Persons Terminated (Excluding Deaths) From Inpatient Psychiatric Service, by Race, Sex, Age, Selected Principal Diagnoses, and Type of Inpatient Psychiatric Service: United States, 1986

Patient Characteristics	Inpatient Psychiatric Service					
	Total, All Inpatient Services	*State and County Mental Hospitals*	*Private Psychiatric Hospitals*	*VA Medical Centers*	*Nonfederal General Hospitals*	*Multiservice Mental Health Organizations*
Race and sex						
Total all races	15	28	24	23	11	11
Male	15	27	24	23	9	11
Female	14	30	23	26	12	11
Total white	15	27	25	24	11	11
Male	15	25	26	23	10	11
Female	15	29	24	28	12	12
Total all other races	14	30	17	22	9	9
Male	16	30	17	22	8	11
Female	13	30	20	—[a]	9	—[a]
Age						
Under 18	26	43	43	—	12	—[a]
18-24	12	27	24	22	8	10
25-44	14	28	19	22	10	11
45-64	16	24	21	24	12	10
65 and over	16	43	17	28	15	16
Selected principal diagnoses						
Alcohol-related disorders	8	15	24	22	5	6
Drug-related disorders	16	27	27	21	8	6
Affective disorders	16	33	24	24	13	13
Schizophrenia	19	37	18	23	13	17
Personality disorders	9	9	18	31	7	10
Adjustment disorders	8	9	18	12	7	5
Organic disorders	16	—[a]	17	27	13	10

SOURCE: Reprinted from Manderscheid and Sonnenschein (1992, p. 288). Data are from the 1986 Client/Patient Sample Survey of Inpatient, Outpatient, and Partial Care Programs, Statistical Research Branch, Division of Applied and Services Research, National Institute of Mental Health.
a. Median based on five or fewer sample cases or median has a relative standard error of 50% or higher. Therefore, median not shown because it does not meet standards of reliability.

account for almost half (47.5%) of all inpatients and residential treatment patients at any given time.

Although the number of beds declined between 1970 and 1990, the number of inpatient and residential treatment additions increased, from 1,282,698 in 1969 to 2,035,248 in 1990. The most striking changes in terms of inpatient additions between 1969 and 1990 occurred in state and county hospitals, which dropped from 37.9% of the total to 13.6%. On the other hand, nonfederal general hospitals increased from 7.2% to 20% (Redick et al., 1994). As alluded to earlier, private psychiatric hospitals have experienced turmoil in closings, consolidations, and downsizings that is not adequately reflected in the 1990 data, and more current data are not yet available.

Table 1.3 Number, Percentage Distribution, and Rate[a] of Inpatient and Residential Treatment Additions, by Type of Mental Health Organization: United States, Selected Years, 1969–1990

Type of Organization	1969	1975	1979	1986	1988	1990
Number of inpatient additions						
All organizations	1,282,698	1,556,978	1,541,659	1,891,189	1,996,522	2,035,245
State and county mental hospitals	486,661	433,529	383,323	332,884	303,853	276,231
Private psychiatric hospitals	92,056	125,529	140,831	234,663	381,300	406,522
Nonfederal general hospitals with psychiatric services	478,000	543,731	551,190	849,306	877,398	959,893
VA medical centers	135,217	180,701	180,416	179,964	245,815	198,111
Federally funded community mental health centers	59,730	236,226	246,409	—	—	—
Residential treatment centers for emotionally disturbed children	7,596	12,022	15,453	24,511	23,441	41,588
All other organizations	23,438	25,240	24,037	197,861	167,715	152,900
Percentage distribution of inpatient additions						
All organizations	100.0	100.0	100.0	100.0	100.0	100.0
State and county mental hospitals	37.9	27.8	24.8	18.3	15.2	13.6
Private psychiatric hospitals	7.2	8.1	9.9	12.9	19.0	20.0
Nonfederal general hospitals with psychiatric services	37.3	34.9	35.8	46.7	43.9	47.2
VA medical centers	10.5	11.6	11.7	9.9	12.3	9.7
Federally funded community mental health centers	4.7	15.2	16.0	—	—	—
Residential treatment centers for emotionally disturbed children	0.6	0.8	1.0	1.3	1.2	2.0
All other organizations	1.8	1.6	1.6	10.9	8.4	7.5
Inpatient additions per 100,000 civilian population[a]						
All organizations	644.2	736.5	704.2	759.9	819.1	833.7
State and county mental hospitals	244.4	205.1	172.0	139.1	124.5	113.2
Private psychiatric hospitals	46.2	59.4	63.2	98.0	156.2	166.5
Nonfederal general hospitals with psychiatric services	240.1	257.2	256.7	354.8	359.4	393.2
VA medical centers	67.9	85.5	84.0	75.1	100.7	81.2
Federally funded community mental health centers	30.0	111.7	110.6	—	—	—
Residential treatment centers for emotionally disturbed children	3.8	5.7	6.9	10.2	9.6	17.0
All other organizations	11.8	11.9	10.8	82.7	68.7	62.6

SOURCE: Reprinted from Redick et al. (1994, p. 102). Published and unpublished inventory data from the Survey and Analysis Branch, Division of State and Community Systems Development, Center for Mental Health Services.
a. The population used in the calculation of these rates is the January 1 civilian population of the United States for the respective years.

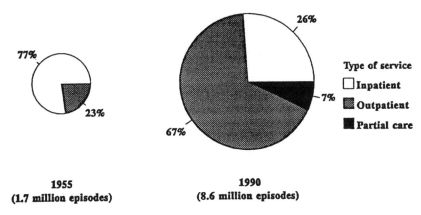

Figure 1.1. Patient Care Episodes in Mental Health Organizations in 1955 and 1990
SOURCE: Reprinted from Redick et al. (1994, p. 83).

Outpatient Services

It has been asserted that outpatient services are the backbone of the mental health system (Callicutt, 1987). More extensive and effective use of outpatient care has both averted admissions to inpatient facilities and shortened inpatient stays. In 1990, there were 3,189 mental health organizations providing outpatient services, an increase from 2,156 in 1970. Interestingly, during the same period the number of organizations providing inpatient services nearly doubled, from 1,734 to 3,430, and those with inpatient services still outnumbered those offering outpatient services (Redick et al., 1994).

The range of outpatient treatment options available includes short-term individual counseling or therapy, medication, group and family therapy, extended supportive treatment, and case management services. These and other services are provided to a wide range of patients reflecting a broad spectrum of mental health problems.

Outpatient service settings include community mental health centers, outreach programs of state hospitals, child and family guidance clinics, outpatient departments of freestanding mental health agencies, and private practice offices of mental health professionals, including psychiatrists, psychologists, and social workers.

In comparing inpatient and outpatient services, there are several significant trends to note. Whereas inpatient additions increased between 1969 and 1990, there was a general pattern of decline in average daily censuses and a decrease in the resident patient rate per 100,000 civilian population from 273 to 93 (Redick et al., 1994). During this same time, the number of outpatient additions almost tripled, from 1,146,612 to 3,004,975, with the addition rate more than doubling, from 576 to 1,231 per 100,000 civilian population (Redick et al., 1994).

Another major trend, reflected in Figure 1.1, is the dramatic increase in patient care episodes from 1955 to 1990 and the conspicuous downward change in the percentage of persons receiving inpatient care with a corresponding increase in the percentage of persons receiving outpatient care. Patient care episodes provides an estimate of the number of people receiving care throughout a given year. Because persons may be admitted to more than one service or the same service more than once during a year, the count is not unduplicated. What is strikingly clear is that the total number of patient care episodes jumped from 1.7 million in 1955 to 8.6 million in 1990, a more than fivefold increase. Again, the growth in percentage and number of outpatient episodes is significant and a product of the same forces responsible for the decline in the number of inpatient beds.

Major Mental Health Settings

Community Mental Health Centers

Primarily as a consequence of the passage of the Mental Retardation Facilities and Community Mental Health Centers Construction Act of 1963 (known as the CMHC Act) and its later amendments, community mental health centers increased in number from 205 in 1969 to 789 in 1980 (Lecca, 1983). However, the Omnibus Budget Reconciliation Act of 1981 during the administration of President Ronald Reagan changed the course of federal support of community mental health centers from direct funding to the provision of block grants to be allocated by the states. Although the federal initiative of providing construction and staffing grants was discontinued, the influence of the funding support that stimulated the development of community mental health centers from 1963 to 1981 continues to be felt. The organization, structure, and funding of community mental health centers varies from state to state, as does the per capita funding of mental health programs from state sources.

The de jure policy of deinstitutionalization affected the development of community mental health centers, which were originally federally mandated to provide five essential elements of service: inpatient, outpatient, and 24-hour emergency services; partial hospitalization; and consultation and education. Subsequent amendments to the CMHC Act of 1963 provided for staffing grants and added service element requirements. These requirements no longer apply, as federal funds come to the states through block grants.

Department of Veterans Affairs

In 1990 the Department of Veterans Affairs provided psychiatric services to veterans at 141 VA medical centers. The number of inpatients at the end of 1969 was 51,696. This figure dropped to 17,233 in 1990. During this same period, the number of outpatient additions rose from 16,790 to 164,143, and partial care additions increased from 3,500 to 19,478. VA medical centers accounted for 10% of the inpatient and residential treatment care episodes and 8% of the 5.8 million outpatient care episodes in all mental health organizations in 1990. (A more detailed discussion of mental services for veterans is presented by David H. Price in Chapter 13 of this volume.)

State and County Mental Hospitals

State hospitals continue to play a vital role in the care of the seriously mentally ill and the poor. State mental health agencies provide planning, policy making, and other functions in addition to direct care services to clients (Lutterman, 1994). In 1993, states operated 256 state hospitals, 22 fewer than in 1980, revealing a general trend of closing hospitals, closing wards, reducing the numbers of beds on wards, and a concurrent shift from state hospital to community-based services (Lutterman, 1994).

Private Psychiatric Hospitals

The number of private psychiatric hospitals increased markedly between 1970 and 1990, from 150 to 462, with all of them providing inpatient care (Redick et al., 1994). In 1990, outpatient services were offered by 176 of these hospitals. Private psychiatric hospitals accounted for only 2.7% of inpatient beds in 1970, but in 1990 they had 44,871 beds, 16.5% of the total of 524,878 for all mental health organizations (Redick et al., 1994). There is a strong likelihood that this trend has reversed since 1990 as the result of several dynamic forces discussed earlier.

Psychiatric Units in General Hospitals

Nonfederal general hospitals with psychiatric units increased from 796 in 1970 to 1,674 in 1990 (Redick et al., 1994). Similarly, the number of inpatient additions increased from 478,000 in 1969 to 959,893 in 1990, and inpatient care episodes rose from 21% of a total of 1.3 million episodes in 1955 to 44% of 2.3 million episodes in 1990. Thus we can see an important trend in the locus of mental health care shifting to nonfederal general hospitals.

Residential Treatment Centers

Residential treatment centers for emotionally disturbed children, which numbered 261 in 1970, nearly doubled to 501 in 1990, also nearly doubling the number of beds, from 15,129 to 29,756. In 1990 these facilities had 27,785 inpatients at the end of the year, up from 13,489 in 1969 and accounting for 12.2% of all inpatient and residential treatment center additions (Redick et al., 1994).

Other Organizations

Freestanding psychiatric partial care organizations and multiservice mental health organizations, which include community mental health centers unless they are part of psychiatric or general hospitals, are included in this category. In 1990 there were 1,490 such organizations, with about one-third providing inpatient services, 1,249 providing outpatient services, and nearly all (1,373) providing partial care services.

Freestanding Psychiatric Outpatient Clinics

The number of freestanding psychiatric outpatient clinics declined from 1,109 in 1970 to 743 in 1990, and the number of outpatient additions decreased from 538,426 in 1969 to 462,147 in 1990, but these facilities cared for 15% of the outpatient care episodes in mental health organizations in 1990 (Redick et al., 1994).

Nontraditional Settings, Innovative Services, and Relationships With Other Human Services/Social Welfare Systems

The preceding discussion has not covered services provided by mental health professionals in private practice settings. Although this is recognized as a significant component of mental health care, systematic service statistics are not available.

Also, the role of primary care clinicians has been recognized, with Regier et al. (1978) observing that 54.1% of persons with mental disorders received services in the primary care/outpatient medical sector. Frequently, primary care clinicians (e.g., general practitioners, family practitioners, pediatricians, and internists) are the sole source of care for persons with mental disorders (Manderscheid, Rae, Narrow, Loch, & Regier, 1993). In this context, Spitzer et al. (1994) have reported on a newly developed procedure designated Primary Care Evaluation of Mental Disorders (known by the acronym PRIME-MD) to assist primary care clinicians in identifying mental disorders. PRIME-MD consists of a 1-page patient questionnaire and a 12-page clinician's evaluation guide used in a structured interview form as a follow-up to positive responses on the patient questionnaire. PRIME-MD shows promise as a useful instrument for identifying mental disorders in both primary care practice and research (Spitzer et al., 1994).

There have long been recommendations about integrating mental health care into the general medical system. Increasingly, the influence of managed health care (discussed by Ross & Croze in Chapter 21, this volume) will exert pressure on the primary care/general medical sector to play an even more active and prominent part in mental health care (Kelleher, Holmes, & Williams, 1994).

Self-help and mutual aid groups, advocacy organizations, and consumer groups will have increasing impacts in the mental health arena (Gartner & Riessman, 1984). An example of a self-help approach to dealing with grief and bereavement is the Widow to Widow program, developed by Silverman (1981). (For further discussion of these topics, see Watkins & Callicutt, Chapter 9, this volume.)

Finally, it should be stressed that mental health services are offered within educational, occupational, and other organizational systems; in primary, secondary, and higher education settings; in the workplace, with booming employee assistance programs; and in jails, prisons, and other correctional settings. (See Turnbo & Murray, Chapter 18, this volume, for a discussion of services to adult criminal offenders.)

I have presented in this chapter an overview of the field of mental health in the contemporary United States. In this survey I have discussed mental health policy and the service system, identifying and briefly covering the scope of the problem of mental disorder and how it is addressed in the United States today.

References

American Psychiatric Association. (1994). *Diagnostic and statistical manual of mental disorders* (4th ed.). Washington, DC: Author.

Anderson, R. E., & Carter, S. (1990). *Human behavior in the social environment: A social system approach* (4th ed.). New York: Aldine De Gruyter.

Barker, R. (1995). *The social work dictionary*. Washington, DC: National Association of Social Workers.

Bevilacqua, J. J. (1991). Overview of state mental health policy. In C. G. Hudson & A. J. Cox (Eds.), *Dimensions of state mental health policy* (pp. 73-83). New York: Praeger.

Bourdon, K., Rae, D., Narrow, W., Manderscheid, R. W., & Regier, D. (1994). National prevalence and treatment of mental and addictive disorders. In R. W. Manderscheid & M. A. Sonnenschein (Eds.), *Mental health, United States, 1994* (CDHHS Publication No. SMA 94-3000, pp. 22-51). Washington, DC: Government Printing Office.

Broskowski, A., & Marks, E. (1992). Managed mental health care. In S. Cooper & T. H. Lentner (Eds.), *Innovations in community mental health* (pp. 23-49). Sarasota, FL: Professional Resource Press.

Callicutt, J. W. (1987). Mental health services. In A. Minahan (Ed.), *Encyclopedia of social work* (18th ed., Vol. E, pp. 125-135). Silver Spring, MD: National Association of Social Workers.

Corcoran, K., & Bernstein, C. A. (1994). Is managed care good for mental health clients? In S. A. Kirk & S. D. Einbinder (Eds.), *Controversial issues in mental health* (pp. 240-251). Boston: Allyn & Bacon.

Frank, R., & McGuire, T. (1994). Health care reform and financing of mental health services: Distributional consequences. In R. W. Manderscheid & M. A. Sonnenschein (Eds.), *Mental health, United States, 1994* (CDHHS Publication No. SMA 94-3000, pp. 8-21). Washington, DC: Government Printing Office.

Franks, D. D. (1987). The high cost of caring: Economic contribution of families to care of the mentally ill (Doctoral dissertation, Brandeis University, 1987). *Dissertation Abstracts International, 48*, 07A1901.

Gartner, A., & Riessman, F. (Eds.). (1984). *The self-help revolution*. New York: Human Services Press.

Grob, G. N. (1994). *The mad among us*. New York: Free Press.

Hoagwood, K., & Rupp, A. (1994). Mental health service needs, use, and costs for children and adolescents with mental disorders and their families: Preliminary evidence. In R. W. Manderscheid & M. A. Sonnenschein (Eds.), *Mental health, United States, 1994* (CDHHS Publication No. SMA 94-3000, pp. 52-64). Washington, DC: Government Printing Office.

Hudson, C. G., & Cox, A. J. (Eds.). (1991). *Dimensions of state mental health policy*. New York: Praeger.

Kelleher, K., Holmes, T. M., & Williams, C. (1994). Major recent trends in mental health in primary care. In R. W. Manderscheid & M. A. Sonnenschein (Eds.), *Mental health, United States, 1994* (CDHHS Publication No. SMA 94-3000, pp. 149-164). Washington, DC: Government Printing Office.

Kiesler, C. A., & Sibulkin, A. E. (1987). *Mental hospitalization: Myths and facts about a national crisis*. Newbury Park, CA: Sage.

Kirk, S. A., & Kutchins, H. (1992). *The selling of DSM*. New York: Aldine De Gruyter.

Koyanagi, C. (1990). The missed opportunities of Medicaid. *Hospital and Community Psychiatry, 41*, 135-138.

Kuhlman, T. L. (1994). *Psychology on the streets: Mental health practice with homeless persons*. New York: Brunner/Mazel.

Lecca, P. J. (1983). Current trends in mental health services and legislation. In J. W. Callicutt & P. J. Lecca (Eds.), *Social work and mental health* (pp. 11-29). New York: Free Press.

Lutterman, T. C. (1994). The state mental health agency profile system. In R. W. Manderscheid & M. A. Sonnenschein (Eds.), *Mental health, United States, 1994* (CDHHS Publication No. SMA 94-3000, pp. 165-187). Washington, DC: Government Printing Office.

Manderscheid, R. W., Rae, D. S., Narrow, W. E., Loch, B. E., & Regier, D. A. (1993). Congruence of service utilization estimates from the Epidemiologic Catchment Area Project and other sources. *Archives of General Psychiatry, 50*, 108-114.

Manderscheid, R. W., & Sonnenschein, M. A. (Eds.). (1992). *Mental health, United States, 1992* (CDHHS Publication No. SMA-92-1942). Washington, DC: Government Printing Office.

Mechanic, D. (1989). *Mental health and social policy* (3rd ed.). Englewood Cliffs, NJ: Prentice Hall.

Redick, R. W., Witkin, M. J., Atay, J. E., & Manderscheid, R. W. (1994). Highlights of organized mental health services in 1990 and major national and state trends. In R. W. Manderscheid & M. A. Sonnenschein (Eds.), *Mental health, United States, 1994* (CDHHS Publication No. SMA 94-3000, pp. 99-125). Washington, DC: Government Printing Office.

Regier, D. A., Goldberg, J. D., & Taube, C. A. (1978). The de facto U.S. mental health services system: A public health perspective. *Archives of General Psychiatry, 35*, 685-693.

Rochefort, D. A. (1993). *From poor homes to homelessness: Policy analysis and mental health care*. Westport, CT: Auburn House.

Sharkey, J. (1994). *Bedlam*. New York: St. Martin's.

Silverman, P. R. (1981). *Helping women cope with grief*. Beverly Hills, CA: Sage.

Spitzer, R. L., Williams, J. B. W., Kroenke, K., Linzer, M., de Gruy, F. V., III, Hahn, S. R., Brody, D., & Johnson, J. G. (1994). Utility of a new procedure for diagnosing mental disorders in primary care. *Journal of the American Medical Association, 272*, 1749-1756.

Szasz, T. S. (1960). The myth of mental illness. *American Psychologist, 15*, 113-118.

Torrey, E. F. (1988). *Nowhere to go*. New York: Harper & Row.

CHAPTER 2

Institutional and Community Approaches to the Provision of Mental Health Services

VIKKI L. VANDIVER

Recent years have seen dramatic changes in the conceptualization, funding, and delivery of mental health services to persons with chronic mental illness (Lefley, 1994). The challenge of these changes is as old as Hippocrates, yet even Hippocrates could not have estimated how volatile mental health care systems would become when he insisted that physicians, at the least, "do no harm." State institutions are closing at an accelerated rate despite the lack of accessible community services to absorb their populations. In many cases, state psychiatric facilities have been downsized and now provide intermediate care, leaving general hospitals to be the primary providers of acute psychiatric care (Hanes, Butz, & Leonard, 1994). Consequently, patients, family members, and mental health professionals have found themselves in the challenging throes of a paradigm shift, from a preponderance of professionally and politically driven services to consumer-directed services.

Society has a lengthy history of experimenting with institutional and community approaches to care for its mental health populations. In this chapter, I first explore the historical development (e.g., of philosophy, public policy, service, and patient characteristics) of institutional and community-based approaches to mental health services. Here, *institutional approach* refers primarily to inpatient care delivered through state hospitals, local general hospitals, and private care settings. In contrast, *community-based approach* refers primarily to care delivered through the outpatient (public) community mental health care service system, such as community mental health centers. The discussion then shifts to three critical issues that have emerged from these approaches: disjointed policies, more severe multiple need patients, and fragmented services. Finally, I outline some current service needs and make some recommendations.

History of Institutional and Community Care in the United States

The history of care for the mentally ill in the United States has shifted dramatically from an institutional focus to community care. Prior to the 1700s, there was no identified group of mentally ill citizens in America. Individuals unable to function in society because of emotional disability were cared for by their families or lived in almshouses and on poor farms. It was not until the mid-1700s that the mentally ill were recognized as having special needs. By 1840, reformers such as Dorothea Dix led crusades to have mentally ill people removed from jails and almshouses and placed in state hospitals. The first state asylum for the mentally ill was established in 1845 in Trenton, New Jersey. These institutions virtually removed the mentally ill from the public eye and public consciousness (Rochefort, 1989). Very quickly, these institutions began to favor treating people with milder disturbances and who came from the wealthier classes of society. Although high success rates were reported with those cases, more troublesome patients were labeled "vulgar" and "abusive" and received treatment that consisted of subduing and physical restraint.

At the same time that state "insane asylums" were being built, community alternatives were used. Examples of these are the cottage plan developed by the Illinois State Hospital at Kankakee and the Farm of St. Anne, which was described in 1855 by John Galt. In 1885, a community boarding program for mental patients was started in Massachusetts.

By the 1900s, mental hospitals were basically custodial; their philosophical approach was that they served to provide refuge for individuals from society and to protect society from the discomfort of having mentally disabled in the community (Shore, 1989). Active treatment for patients was minimal, consisting mostly of occupational therapy. Between 1910 and 1945, state hospitals filled up with severely mentally ill patients who were rejected from other psychiatric hospitals and correctional facilities. Institutional budgets were severely affected by the Great Depression in the 1930s but were increased after World War II, in part owing to the record number of soldiers who received military discharges for psychiatric reasons, which highlighted the extent of mental illness in the population.

Prior to World War II, the federal government had little involvement in mental health programs. The first official piece of federal legislation dealing with mental health care was introduced in 1946, with the passage of the

National Mental Health Act (Public Law 79-487). It provided for the development of the National Institute of Mental Health, the entity that would later direct the development of federally sponsored community mental health centers. However, as state hospital censuses peaked in 1955 at 600,000 residents, it became clear to policy makers that change must occur. Consequently, there was an emphasis on community involvement and community ownership of programs to deal with the overburdened hospital care system. Thus the philosophy of community-based programs was guided by the notion of a comprehensive service delivery system that emphasized services not only to the severely mentally ill, but also to children, families, and adults suffering from the effects of stress (Cutler, 1992). The reality, however, was very different.

Despite an increase in funding that encouraged research on the etiology, treatment, and prevention of mental illness, state hospitals soon began to lose favor with the professional psychiatric community. This, too, was greatly influenced by epidemiological studies that not only suggested a high prevalence of psychiatric impairment but also illustrated that most people reporting distress were functioning in society. By the 1950s, prominent mental health officials were beginning to call for a restructuring of state hospital conditions, often calling them "antitherapeutic facilities" (Rochefort, 1989).

Philosophy of Care

The history of institutional care in the United States was shaped not only by social circumstances but also by philosophical and theoretical positions. Like community care, these forces did not develop separately, but as parallel in social thought. Between 1750 and 1960, at least seven models or theories of care were developed that have driven and shaped the design of institutional services: somatic theory, moral theory, custodial theory, mental hygiene theory, social-environmental theory, biological theory, and community theory.

Between 1750 and 1800, the *somatic* theory of treatment was derived from the notion that the mind is a function of the brain and that mental pathology is related to behavior. The corresponding mode of medical treatment included the use of mechanical restraints, medical purges, chains, whips, and coercion (Brizendine, 1992). By 1800, the *moral* theory of treatment came into vogue; it suggested that a cause of insanity was the onset of advanced civilization. The moral theory argued that an orderly environment and a compassionate staff would counteract the instability of society and restore mental fitness. The mode of treatment was kindness and care. Asylums and mental hospitals were considered to offer effective treatment at the time because they provided shelter and a safe haven from the stresses of everyday life (Rochefort, 1989; Shore, 1989). As hospitals filled rapidly, a *custodial* theory of treatment emerged. Hospitals soon became settings for people who could not get along in society. This resulted in minimal treatment, overcrowding, and a diverse mix of patients with severe symptoms. At the same time, popular opinion was changing about the causes of mental illness. New theories were emerging that attributed the cause of mental illness to genetics and concluded that it was incurable (Rochefort, 1989).

The theory of *mental hygiene* for acute mental illness surfaced in 1909. It stressed childhood and upbringing as the source of insanity. Treatment approaches often focused on patients who displayed mild disorders and were not in asylums or hospitals (Hogan, 1993). This period also witnessed important changes in the treatment of the young mentally ill. Juvenile courts were created that separated young offenders from adults, including youths with mental disabilities. Out of the courts emerged treatment facilities such as the Judge Baker Clinic in Boston. The mental hygiene movement, spearheaded by Clifford Beers and Adolph Meyers, helped set the stage for the modern community mental health era. Eventually, this separation led to the creation of child guidance clinics (Lubove, 1971), the philosophy of which linked attention to sociocultural influences, aftercare, preventive efforts, integrated programs, defined catchment areas, and public education. It was from this emphasis on aftercare and social aspects of mental illness that the profession of psychiatric social work emerged (Lubove, 1971; Shore, 1989).

By the end of World War II, institutional care for mental illness had pervaded the military ranks. Because of the number of soldiers discharged or deferred from active duty due to psychiatric reasons, psychiatry offered the *social-environmental* theory of mental disorder. This theory suggested that mental disorder is influenced by life experiences and socioeconomic factors (Grob, 1991). Also emerging at this time was an emphasis on community and pharmacological treatment. During the 1950s the *biological* theory of mental disease emerged. Severe mental illness was viewed as a central nervous system dysfunction in need of evaluation, diagnosis, and pharmacotherapy (Wilson, 1992). With the advent of neuroleptics, psychiatric care was revolutionized and the deinstitutionalization movement was initiated.

In the early 1960s, the idea of *community psychiatry* emerged. This was the culmination of the development of earlier philosophies that saw social factors as antecedents of social illness, and it asserted that mental disorder is a result of socioeconomic conditions such as poverty, racism, unemployment, and social support. The focus was on the deficit in a person's environment, the need to remove barriers and establish resources. Treatment emphasized intervention at the societal and community level rather than just with the individual (Hogan, 1993).

Public Policy

As theories of mental illness have changed over time, so has the public policy that operationalized them. For example, in line with the custodial treatment of the 1840s, an early policy dealing with caring for the mentally ill can be found in the Oregon's Territorial Statutes of 1843-1844: In 1844, a law was enacted that allowed the indigent insane to be auctioned off to the lowest bidder to be clothed and boarded for one year at state expense (Larsell, 1945). Oregon's response to the needs of the mentally ill was not very different from national trends; clearly, this approach did not speak well for the quality of care of the mentally ill.

In later developments, in 1952 the Committee on Mental Health of the World Health Organization recommended components for a community mental hospital that included outpatient treatment, part-time services, rehabilitation, research, and community education (Shore, 1989). The Mental Health Study Act of 1955 authorized the formation of the Joint Commission on Mental Illness and Health. This commission published the 1961 congressional report *Action for Mental Health,* which provided the background for President Kennedy's programs in mental illness and mental retardation. In 1963, Congress passed the Community Mental Health Centers Act, which called for the construction of mental health centers in defined geographic catchment areas (Shore, 1989).

During the 1980s, the care of persons with severe mental illness became a priority for public mental health policy makers, despite the conservative political climate of the Reagan years. The ensuing result was an entrepreneurial response from private and public providers that led to an unprecedented development of new forms of institutional and community-based services. Perhaps the most striking aspect of public policy at this time was the shifting of legislation from federal to state responsibilities. The State Comprehensive Mental Health Services Plan Act of 1986 (Public Law 99-660) built on the Community Support Program base by calling for each state to prepare a detailed plan for the care of individuals with serious mental illness that would involve consumers of mental health services, as well as their families and advocates, in the planning process (Koyanagi & Goldman, 1991). Consequently, Medicaid created the case management option, which was supported by advocates for persons with developmental disabilities as well as advocates for the mentally ill.

These policy shifts were not without controversy. There has been little agreement in U.S. society about where the responsibility for care lies. Hollingsworth (1994) argues that care for the mentally ill has historically had a strong state component. As the federal government has reduced its role in favor of state responsibility, states have appointed local mental health authorities to assume responsibility for the funding and development of services for the chronically mentally ill. Some states have integrated long-term institutions (e.g., state hospitals) into their communities, but others have not. Thus there are many different approaches to creating community-based services that have been structured by the political economies of individual states rather than planned, thoughtful, or empirically based service planning.

Services

In the broadest sense, an *institution* is a bundle of supports and services that are typically delivered at a fixed location. It is a comprehensive provider that offers nutrition; social support; and medical, dental, and psychiatric treatment (Surles, 1994). During the era of therapy based on the moral theory of mental illness (between 1750 and 1800), the goal of treatment services was to return the patient to control of him- or herself. The emphasis on service delivery began with the enhancement of the total environment of the patient.

Institutions of the 1880s through 1940s were known to provide treatment using various forms of hydrotherapy, restraints, and cranial surgery, but progressive changes in science, medication, and public policy brought about new treatment approaches. Yet, for many patients caught in the "mental hygiene" movement, therapy was restricted to occupational therapy or tasks related to maintaining the institution itself. Examples include repair work, sewing, furniture making, and working in the hospital kitchen or laundry (Rochefort, 1989). Between 1910 and 1930, services were developed in response to observations of World War I battlefield casualties who displayed what was first called "war neurosis" (Shore, 1989). Thomas Salmon, who visited battlefields to study this phenomenon, is credited with developing a model of short-term crisis intervention emphasizing immediate treatment close to the stressful situation (Shore, 1989).

From 1938 to the 1950s, electroconvulsive therapy was a major, if not frequently the only, biological treatment for mental illness (Hay, Peterson, Endler, Spiro, & Mills, 1992). The most influential time in the development of mental health services occurred at the close of World War II. Given that approximately 40% of all service-related discharges were for mental illness, the high prevalence rate was probably influential in the early development of the notion of the therapeutic community (Katz, 1989). The first partial hospital program in the United States was established at Yale University in 1948 (Katz, 1989).

As deinstitutionalization and diversion of clients from state hospitals proceeded, it became obvious that if clients were to have any services, organizations based in the community would have to provide them (Hollingsworth, 1994). Early legislation emphasized that these programs were to be comprehensive, coordinated, of high quality, and available to the total population (Cutler, 1992). However, many community-based programs were unable to provide the desired services (Hollingsworth, 1994). This was partly due to a lack of evidence to determine what constituted effective treatment for discharged mentally ill clients. The most popular program format was partial hospitalization, or day program. Clinicians and program planners found that many recently discharged people had little knowledge of how to structure their days, nor did they possess the skills to negotiate community reintegration. Consequently, partial hospitalization programs were established to fill this gap. Offered in the community and staffed by professionals and paraprofessionals, partial hospitalization programs were designed to offer a therapeutic milieu that could be used to provide structure, skill building, social support, and medication monitoring. Partial hospitalization programs set the stage for the development of day programs, such as transition programs for inpatients, rehabilitation day programs, educational and growth-oriented day programs, and social clubs. One of the most notable day programs is Fountain House, established in 1940 and credited as one of the early models for what is today referred to as the *psychosocial rehabilitation* program model (Cutler, 1992).

Outcome studies indicate that partial hospitalization and day programs constitute an effective therapeutic modality and cost-effective treatment for approximately two-thirds of patients with major psychiatric disorders (Cutler, 1992; Katz, 1989).

Although innovative models were in place, community mental health programs lacked adequate trained staff to deal with chronic mentally ill populations. Professional staff members often had received their training in clinical psychotherapy, which was irrelevant to the needs of this population. Clinicians were often skilled as family therapists and did not see the importance of social skills training, case management, home visits, and prevocational training, which are critical to chronically mentally ill persons (Cutler, 1992).

The locus of care changed as discharged patients exchanged state hospital beds for nursing home beds and adult foster homes (Johnson, 1994). Deinstitutionalization fueled the development of new businesses that were rapidly created in response to the new purchasing capacity represented by social security entitlement (Surles, 1994). Cottage industries known as adult homes and single-room occupancy apartments or hotels developed as places of residence for those who had no families. The Medicaid program funded general hospitals and specialty outpatient clinics, but they were minimally coordinated with the traditional mental health system (Surles, 1994). During the 1970s and 1980s, community general hospitals began to increase their capacity to provide emergency and acute psychiatric care.

Patient Characteristics

Despite the optimistic and paternal intentions of early models of care, the patients who made up most institutional care facilities were from the low-income sectors of society. Between 1850 and 1900, the patient populations in most facilities were made up of paupers, immigrants, criminals, mentally retarded persons, alcoholics, and the aged (Rochefort, 1989). This trend continued well into the 1950s, with the additional inclusion of persons with epilepsy, drug users, and war veterans (Surles, 1994). Patients in the 1960s tended to be older and had lived in the state system for long periods; many were also people who had criminal histories.

In spite of a massive increase in community services between 1960 and 1975, many client groups continued to be underserved. These included racial and ethnic minorities, the urban poor, migrant and seasonal farmworkers, women, Vietnam veterans, the deaf, the physically disabled, and children, adolescents, and adults with chronic mental illness (Cutler, 1992).

Critical Issues in Institutional and Community Care

As a result of the historical trends in social thought, public policy, and services, the picture today of mental health care is very different from in the past. Once, state institutions were responsible for 99% of patient care (English & McGarrick, 1989). Today, state hospitals provide less than 50% of patient care, owing to the move toward decentralization of patient care to community facilities, including smaller institutional settings. In the era of downsizing, state and community hospitals are offering short-term stabilization, brief models of treatment using fewer beds, and more complicated and restrictive funding mechanisms. As a result of these changes, the field of mental health care today faces at least three critical issues: disjointed policies; increased numbers of severe, multiple-need patients; and fragmented services.

Disjointed Policies

The challenge of providing care and treatment for persons with chronic mental illness is restricted more by political forces than by technological forces. For the most part, public policy on mental illness has been as disjointed as the services it has sought to organize. At one level, policies that encourage the provision of community-based services do little to establish realistic funding mechanisms. Medicaid and private insurance do not provide for long-term, prevention-oriented care. At another level, when funding for community services has been brought to more equitable levels, clinical training has not been in place. Consequently, community-based mental health services must deal with funding practices that encourage "rationing" of some kind (e.g., capitation programs) as well as trying to hire clinicians who are interested in working with this population (Lefley, 1994; Menninger, 1989).

Public policy will most likely continue in its campaign to emphasize health promotion and health education practices, thus continuing to place the onus for change on the individual and not the structure of the system. As Gruenberg (1986) notes, persons with chronic mental illness will continue to need unified community and hospital services, whereas the current direction of public policy has been to add more and more diverse treatment elements and different treatment personnel. Examples include community general hospital psychiatric units, mental health center outpatient units, nursing homes, halfway houses, quarterway houses, patient advocates, patient management teams, psychologists, sociologists, and social workers.

Increased Numbers of
Severe, Multiple-Need Patients

Currently, there are more than 2 million chronically mentally ill individuals in the United States. Of these, 150,000 have been hospitalized for longer than a year; many others reside in nursing homes (Katz, 1989). The data suggest that these patients reflect an increase in cases involving substance abuse overlaying mental disorders. There is an extended-care population that is made up of young male schizophrenic patients, female schizophrenic patients of all ages, and older females with organic mental disorders (Katz, 1989).

Problems posed by clients in the 1980s and 1990s were more variable and intractable than estimated by the optimistic policy makers of the 1960s who favored deinstitutionalization. Consequently, services are now more tailored to the numbers of persons who present with multiple problems, including homelessness, sexual and physical abuse, substance abuse, HIV positive/AIDS, and tuberculosis (Bourgeois, 1994).

Moreover, contact between mentally ill persons and the criminal justice system has increased. Between 30% and 40% of the general prison population suffers from psychiatric or addictive disorders, and many prisoners remain undiagnosed and untreated. (For further discussion of mental health services to prisoners, see Turnbo & Murray, Chapter 18, this volume.) Most community-based service systems have had to cope with providing considerable crisis care to new clients and considerable continuing care to established (or chronic) patients (Gruenberg, 1986).

Fragmented Services

State hospital census records show increases in drug- and alcohol-affected patients, homeless patients, and medically fragile mentally ill patients. Consequently, inpatient units are converting general units to short-stay specialty units (e.g., for treatment of substance abuse). These acute care services are often mixed with chronic care and rehabilitation services. Acute care has not totally replaced the need for long-term care, but long-term care approaches are shifting to community sites that are meant to provide the least restrictive settings, although in reality they often provide more restrictive settings (e.g., jails). This shift has resulted in ineffective case coordination, inadequate resource development, and inappropriate care.

From 1963 (the date of the first community mental health legislation) to the present, the number of community mental health centers has grown to more than 800. Currently, the mental health service delivery system is being increasingly taxed by the demands placed on it by deinstitutionalized chronic patients, young adult chronic patients, the homeless mentally ill, HIV and physically disabled mentally ill patients, and substance-abusing patients. Even in communities that have adequate service networks, these individuals are difficult to maintain in traditional community-based programs (Katz, 1989). Consequently, new and innovative approaches are needed to complement the changing profile of the person with chronic mental illness.

Hoge, Davidson, Griffith, Sledge, and Howenstein (1994) describe four service delivery strategies that are used to address service fragmentation: (a) case management, (b) assertive community treatment, (c) use of local mental health authorities, and (d) new financing strategies. Case management is designed to facilitate access to existing services by having one key individual (a case manager) assess the client's needs, establish the client's links with resources, and monitor community services to the client (Vandiver & Kirk, 1992). Assertive community treatment is designed to supplant fragmented and uncoordinated office-based services by using multidisciplinary teams to provide community or home-based services. Local mental health authorities use a systems approach to monitor organizational, professional, and fiscal accountability. New financing strategies such as capitation programs and single-point entry are designed to remedy the lack of fiscal incentives for cost-efficient performance. All of these service strategies, however, are incomplete because they address only subsets of problems in the current system of care. Of continuing concern are the numbers of patients, their needs, and their limited ability to participate or engage in services available to them. In summary, these issues point to numerous service needs for people with chronic mental illness who are involved in institutional and community services.

Service Needs and Recommendations

Institutional and community approaches need to function as natural partners in the delivery of services to the chronically mentally ill. How and where these services are developed and delivered are constantly changing. What does not change, however, is the number of individuals who need the linkage between hospitals and community care systems. The key to a successful partnership is for both institutional and community-based care systems to agree to collaborate on providing core services, in spite of many states' efforts to dismantle state-funded long-term hospitals.

As a consequence of disjointed policies, increasing numbers of severe and multiple-need patients, and fragmented services, there are six service needs that are generally unmet in the present structure of services: housing, medication, open-ended community support services, family caregiver intervention, clinical therapy services, and access to short-term hospitalization.

Housing

Housing is an essential aspect of care for severely mentally ill adults (Bachrach, 1994). Unfortunately, housing placements are often made based on availability rather than as part of an integrated treatment plan. Attempts to provide housing currently often consist of removing undomiciled mentally ill persons from the streets or shelters and placing them in conventional housing units without regard to social support networks, access to shopping, or transportation sites (Bachrach, 1994). To avoid incompatible housing arrangements, institutions and community-based services need to collaborate to create new resources to provide an array of long-term, short-term, transitional, and crisis residences (Bachrach, 1994). Institutions and community service providers should work together to link their mutual consumers to settings that will result in successful placements in housing that the individuals can return to subsequent to any necessary short-term hospitalization.

Medication

Since the advent of neuroleptics in the 1950s, medication has been an integral component of comprehensive care for clients who move in and out of hospital- and community-based programs. Data on neuroleptic use with people with chronic mental illness indicate fewer hospital stays, longer community tenure, and increased quality of life (Meltzer, Burnett, & Bastani, 1990). Within the past decade, community programs have had to work more closely with hospital systems to continue certain patients on newer drugs. For example, clozapine, recognized as an efficacious medication in the treatment of schizophrenia, has been a major drug that has presented problems with cost and monitoring. Medication trials are often initiated in the controlled environment of the hospital, but the expense of clozapine (at about $7,500 per year, compared with $1,000 for other neuroleptics) has restricted its community-based use. Large-scale payers such as Medicaid and private insurers are skeptical about the expense of clozapine treatment (Reid, Mason, & Toprac, 1994). According to Reid et al. (1994), the Texas mental health system allocates $5,000 per patient per year for clozapine prescribed in state hospitals and $9,000 per patient per year for clozapine prescribed in community-based care. Yet only about 40% of outpatients who take the medication are eligible for Medicaid, which pays only 63% of the cost. The remainder of the cost must be picked up by the patient, his or her family, or the community mental health system. This raises the ethical dilemma attached to the prescription of medications that may be clinically efficacious in institutional settings but completely unaffordable and therefore unavailable in community-based settings.

One way the problem of such prohibitive costs could be resolved is through a universal health care system with a single-payer model that eliminates marketplace rationing based on ability to pay. The current political climate does not suggest that this will be forthcoming in the near future, however. A second, and perhaps more politically acceptable, solution would be to place a user's fee on therapists' licenses. Every renewal would be tagged with a small surcharge, say $5.00, which would be targeted to cover excessive mental health care costs for use by indigent patients on clozapine. Although this approach is used in some states to cover particular programs (e.g., California places a fee on marriage licenses to cover divorce mediation), I know of no state that has instituted such an approach for mental health services.

Open-Ended Support Programs

Open-ended, non-time-limited support programs have long been recognized as an integral component of consumer-oriented mental health services. An issue that has been raised by many participants in formal psychosocial rehabilitation programs is that current therapy models emphasize clinician dominance over client needs, with the consequence being chronically dependent patients (Fisher, 1994). Consumer groups recommend that mental health programs build a system of support services that emphasizes attitudinal and environmental changes and promotes choice and control of services by the people who are receiving them (Fisher, 1994).

Family Caregiver Interventions

Historically, mental health professionals have maintained distant relationships with the families and family caregivers of those suffering from mental illness. When these persons have been involved, interventions have often taken the form of blaming and/or assigning guilt to family members for the illness (Riesser & Schorske, 1994). However, new relationships are being forged as families become full partners in interactions with mental health professionals. (For more on the changing relationship between clients' families and mental health professionals, see Watkins & Callicutt, Chapter 9, this volume.) Riesser and Schorske (1994) suggest that families may benefit from having a menu of service and setting options from which to choose (e.g., agency and home-based consultation, psychoeducation, support groups, respite care, and referral and linkage). Lefley (1994) recommends that state systems mandate that all mental health institutions and agencies that receive public funds offer family education on mental illness, psychotropic medications, and illness management strategies. In this way, family services can become driven by quality assurance rather than dollar reimbursement.

Clinical Therapy

Despite the efforts of clinicians to use treatment approaches that are effective and affordable, and that utilize known principles of practice (Vandiver & Kirk, 1992), the whole diagnostic system is based on an illness model, not on health or on how well an individual functions. Wylie (1994) is particularly critical of the current system; he argues that, despite our most sophisticated technology of care and assessment, there is a lack of accountability and few incentives for mental health professionals to determine the relative effectiveness of one treatment over another or the quality of care by one provider or psychiatric center versus another. Wylie asserts that clinicians have the chance to be at the forefront of an innovative public health effort, to participate in educating people and changing the popular perceptions of health care to a more integrated vision that takes into account the whole person, body and mind. Institutions and community-based programs should participate in interdisciplinary cross-training that brings together the strengths of professionals, paraprofessionals, and consumers. Many consumer groups recommend the use of a health-promotion model in which individuals define their own needs and are active collaborators in the process of maintaining health (Fisher, 1994). Wylie (1994) lays out specific recommendations regarding how clinical care could be delivered through community- or hospital-based approaches. These include measuring specific problems and indicating specific treatments for resolving specific problems and identified impairments. In other words, the clinician should demonstrate the level of impairment, the intensity of treatment, and the expected length of treatment in each case. From this perspective, it will no longer be acceptable to work generally on, say, self-esteem. Further, consumer-run services that emphasize self-help models are effective complements to standard clinical therapy.

Access to Short-Term Hospitalization

People with chronic mental illness may at times benefit from the intense and structured services that only a hospital setting can provide. An issue that occurs for many clients and service providers is that discriminatory insurance practices create barriers to clients' obtaining adequate mental health care. One study in Texas found that of those clients with the highest need, the mental health system served only a minority; the majority of those with chronic mental disorders and who were considered dangerous had never been hospitalized (Reid et al., 1994). Of this sample, only 25% with major affective disorders and schizophreniform spectrum disorders had ever been in a psychiatric hospital. The explanations ranged from distrust of services with a medical emphasis to intolerance of bureaucratic services. Current policy makers favor creating community-based, short-term, crisis-oriented hospital programs. In contrast to the rural asylums of yesteryear, these facilities need to be located in the urban community, preferably in local neighborhoods. The goals would be to stabilize the patient and to facilitate his or her readjustment to the community as quickly as medically possible.

Conclusions

At present, the mental health services that are available through institutional and community programs are changing rapidly, driven by fiscal needs, public policies, changing patient populations, and a peculiar dismantling of service delivery systems (Lefley, 1994). These changes necessitate cooperative and collaborative relationships between institutional approaches to care (e.g., state hospitals, community general psychiatric units, nursing homes, and foster care settings) and community-based approaches to care (e.g., peer and family case management, mobile crisis teams, drug and alcohol programs, and case management teams).

To reduce the disjointedness of current policies, mental health professionals need to do more than just develop services aimed at individual behavioral change—they must also engage in collective action for social change (Israel, Checkoway, Schulz, & Zimmerman, 1994). In order to address the severe, multiple-need client, mental health professionals should continually ask, What constitutes *mental health*? How can community and institutional systems facilitate the provision of health-oriented services? Israel et al. (1994) suggest that in order to respond to their clients' needs given today's fragmented services, mental health professionals must think simultaneously in both personal and structural ways; otherwise, they may risk losing sight of the simultaneous reality of both. If they focus only on the crisis management of the individual, they risk privatizing by rendering personal the social and economic underpinnings of poverty and powerlessness. Conversely, if they focus only on structural issues, they risk ignoring the immediate pain caused by the powerlessness of people who are mentally ill. Chronically disabled patients benefit from the care of a unified clinical team that is able to blend inpatient and outpatient services and to mobilize the community's social services and special residency resources as needs change (Gruenberg, 1986).

A call for partnership in the sensitive and logical development of institutional and community-based approaches to mental health services can be heard in the poignant words of Lilly Wallar, an Australian aboriginal woman: "If you are here to help me, then you are wasting your time. But if you care because your liberation is based on mine, then let us begin" (quoted in Labonte, 1994, p. 268).

Ironically, the currents shifts in institutional and community services are reminiscent of days gone by. If we think back to the era of treatment based in the moral theory of mental disorder (1750-1800), we can appreciate what thinkers were trying to achieve: values of equality and an understanding that mental illness is caused by life stresses and societal circumstances. Contemporary views indicate that not much has changed, except that the asylum where patients came to escape from harmful environmental factors is now a return to the threatening streets, crowded shelters, and jails, and to a mental health care system that is uncertain.

References

Bachrach, L. (1994). Residential planning: Concepts and themes. *Hospital and Community Psychiatry, 45,* 202-203.

Bourgeois, P. (1994). Crossing places: A community-based model for acute care. *Journal of the American Association of Partial Hospitalization, 1*(1), 61-70.

Brizendine, L. (1992). The Devon asylum: A brief history of the changing concept of mental illness and asylum treatment. In P. J. Fink & A. Tasman (Eds.), *Stigma and mental illness* (pp. 59-72). Washington, DC: American Psychiatric Press.

Cutler, D. (1992). A historical overview of community mental health centers in the United States. In S. Cooper & T. H. Lentner (Eds.), *Innovations in community mental health* (pp. 1-22). Sarasota, FL: Professional Resource Press.

English, J. T., & McGarrick, R. G. (1989). The economics of psychiatry. In H. I. Kaplan & B. J. Sadock (Eds.), *Comprehensive textbook of psychiatry* (5th ed., Vol. 2, pp. 2074-2082). Baltimore: Williams & Wilkins.

Fisher, D. B. (1994). Perspectives: Health care reform based on an empowerment model of recovery by people with psychiatric disabilities. *Hospital and Community Psychiatry, 45,* 913-915.

Grob, G. N. (1991). *From asylum to community: Mental health policy in modern America.* Princeton, NJ: Princeton University Press.

Gruenberg, E. M. (1986). Mental disorders. In J. M. Last (Ed.), *Public health and preventive medicine* (12th ed., pp. 1341-1384). Norwalk, CT: Appleton-Century-Crofts.

Hanes, L. D., Butz, J. M., & Leonard, J. H. (1994). A quality improvement program in a state hospital during a period of downsizing. *Hospital and Community Psychiatry, 45,* 929-930.

Hay, D., Peterson, G., Endler, N., Spiro, H., & Mills, M. J. (1992). The stigma of electroconvulsive therapy: A workshop. In P. J. Fink & A. Tasman (Eds.), *Stigma and mental illness* (pp. 189-203). Washington, DC: American Psychiatric Press.

Hogan, W. (1993). *A case study approach to evaluating deinstitutionalization: The Oregon 365 plan.* Unpublished master's thesis, University of Oregon, Eugene.

Hoge, M. A., Davidson, L., Griffith, E., Sledge, W. H., & Howenstein, R. A. (1994). Defining managed care in public-sector psychiatry. *Hospital and Community Psychiatry, 45,* 1085-1089.

Hollingsworth, E. J. (1994). Falling through the cracks: Care of the chronic mentally ill in the United States. In J. R. Hollingsworth & E. J. Hollingsworth (Eds.), *Care of the chronically and severely ill: Comparative social policies* (pp. 145-172). New York: Aldine De Gruyter.

Israel, B., Checkoway, B., Schulz, A., & Zimmerman, M. (1994). Health education and community empowerment: Conceptualizing and measuring perceptions of individual, organizational and community control. *Health Education Quarterly, 21,* 163-172.

Johnson, A. B. (1994). Has deinstitutionalization failed? Yes. In S. A. Kirk & S. D. Einbinder (Eds.), *Controversial issues in mental health* (pp. 215-219). Boston: Allyn & Bacon.

Katz, S. E. (1989). Hospitalization and the mental health service system. In H. I. Kaplan & B. J. Sadock (Eds.), *Comprehensive textbook of psychiatry* (5th ed., Vol. 2, pp. 2083-2089). Baltimore: Williams & Wilkins.

Koyanagi, C., & Goldman, H. H. (1991). The quiet success of the national plan for the chronically mentally ill. *Hospital and Community Psychiatry, 42,* 899-905.

Labonte, R. (1994). Health promotion and empowerment: Reflections on professional practice. *Health Education Quarterly, 21,* 253-268.

Larsell, O. (1945). History of care of insane in the state of Oregon. *Oregon Historical Quarterly, 46,* 295-326.

Lefley, H. (1994). Future directions and social policy implications of family roles. In H. P. Lefley & M. Wasow (Eds.), *Helping families cope with mental illness* (pp. 343-357). Geneva: Harwood Academic Publishers.

Lubove, R. (1971). *The professional altruist.* New York: Atheneum.

Meltzer, H. Y., Burnett, S., & Bastani, B. (1990). Effects of six months of clozapine treatment on the quality of life of chronic schizophrenic patients. *Hospital and Community Psychiatry, 41,* 892-897.

Menninger, W. W. (1989). The chronically mentally ill. In H. I. Kaplan & B. J. Sadock (Eds.), *Comprehensive textbook of psychiatry* (5th ed., Vol. 2, pp. 2090-2098). Baltimore: Williams & Wilkins.

Reid, W., Mason, M., & Toprac, M. (1994). Savings in hospital bed-days related to treatment with clozapine. *Hospital and Community Psychiatry, 45,* 261-263.

Riesser, G. G., & Schorske, B. (1994). Relationships between family caregivers and mental health professionals: The American experience. In H. P. Lefley & M. Wasow (Eds.), *Helping families cope with mental illness* (pp. 3-26). Geneva: Harwood Academic Publishers.

Rochefort, D. A. (1989). *Handbook on mental health policy in the United States.* Westport, CT: Greenwood.

Shore, J. H. (1989). Community psychiatry. In H. I. Kaplan & B. J. Sadock (Eds.), *Comprehensive textbook of psychiatry* (5th ed., Vol. 2, pp. 2063-2066). Baltimore: Williams & Wilkins.

Surles, R. C. (1994). Has deinstitutionalization failed? No. In S. A. Kirk & S. D. Einbinder (Eds.), *Controversial issues in mental health* (pp. 221-225). Boston: Allyn & Bacon.

Vandiver, V., & Kirk, S. (1992). Case management for persons with schizophrenia. In K. Corcoran (Ed.), *Structuring change* (pp. 72-92). Chicago: Lyceum.

Wilson, W. (1992). Psychiatric education in the state hospital: A current approach. *Community Mental Health Journal, 28,* 51-60.

Wylie, M. S. (1994, March). Endangered species. *Networker,* pp. 20-33.

CHAPTER 3

Political Aspects of Mental Health Treatment

JAMES I. MARTIN

Both the diagnostic process in mental health and the manner in which mental health treatment is formulated and delivered are political. Although this is always important, it is of particular concern when the focus of professional attention is on people who are devalued by society. In this chapter, I will first consider the political aspects of diagnosis and then the political aspects of treatment. I will begin by focusing on the psychiatric diagnosis of homosexuality as a particularly good example of the political use of mental health classification. I will then examine the diagnosis of women's "madness" and the classification of mental disorders in other minorities, showing how all vulnerable groups are subject to the same political dangers in this process. I will then turn to some of the larger political debates regarding the classification of mental disorders, and to the political issues involved in the delivery of mental health treatment to gay men and lesbians, women, and other minorities. Finally, I will discuss a model of affirmative treatment of vulnerable populations.

Politics and Diagnosis

Politics and the Diagnosis of Homosexuality

Several authors have described in detail the process by which the American Psychiatric Association (APA) declassified homosexuality as an official mental illness in 1973 (Bayer, 1981; Conrad & Schneider, 1980; Robitscher, 1980). Some people hailed this change in nomenclature as a humanitarian act serving social justice, whereas others criticized it as being nothing more than a reaction to special interest group pressure. The classification and declassification of homosexuality as a mental illness by the American Psychiatric Association is important for several reasons. First, because of psychiatry's sanctioned position of leadership in the definition and treatment of mental disorders, the APA's decisions tend to influence the other helping professions, including psychology and social work. In 1975 the American Psychological Association followed the APA's lead in stating that homosexuality per se is not associated with any impairment or mental illness (Conger, 1975). Two years later, the National Association of Social Workers' Public Social Policy Statement on Gay Issues strongly criticized any form of discrimination based on sexual orientation (Hidalgo, Peterson, & Woodman, 1985).

Second, the APA's official book of nomenclature, the *Diagnostic and Statistical Manual of Mental Disorders (DSM)*, is accepted by most third-party payers, who require its use by any mental health professionals desiring reimbursement for services. Third, medicine is the most prestigious profession in the United States, and physicians are increasingly seen as experts on every area of human life (Conrad & Schneider, 1980), leading some critics to warn of the rise of the "therapeutic state" (Lasch, 1979). Psychiatrists, as medical professionals, share this great social power. Their opinions tend to be highly influential throughout society at large. Finally, the declassification of homosexuality as a mental illness has taken away one justification for the unequal treatment of gays and lesbians, the justification of illness.

Change in the Psychiatric Profession

Successive editions of the *Diagnostic and Statistical Manual of Mental Disorders* provide evidence of the changes that have occurred in psychiatry's official view of homosexuality. *DSM-I* (American Psychiatric Association, 1952) classified homosexuality as one of the "sexual deviations" under the category of "sociopathic personality disturbance." *DSM-II* (American Psychiatric Association, 1968) moved the sexual deviations, including homosexuality, to the category of "personality disorders and certain other non-psychotic mental disorders." In *DSM-III* (American Psychiatric Association, 1980), homosexuality no longer appeared as a diagnosis. Instead, appearing under the new category of "psychosexual disorders," the diagnosis of "ego-dystonic homosexuality" was reserved for people for whom their gay/lesbian sexual orientation was a source of significant distress. With *DSM-III-R* (American Psychiatric Association, 1987), all references to homosexuality, ego-dystonic or otherwise, were removed.

These changes in the treatment of homosexuality as a diagnostic entity indicate gradual changes in the views of psychiatrists toward people who are gay or lesbian. In general, many psychiatrists' views of homosexuality began to be influenced in the early 1970s by the testimonies of gay men and lesbians who complained of therapeutic mistreatment and demanded support for their civil rights. Not all people urging the APA to change its official view of homosexuality were outside the profession. One gay psychiatrist testified at the 1972 APA convention, wearing a mask to maintain his anonymity. Other leaders in psychiatry, such as Judd Marmor (1965), argued that there is nothing inherently pathological about homosexuality.

In addition, there had been increasing research supporting nonpathological views of gays and lesbians. The Kinsey studies found that homosexual behavior was far more widespread in U.S. society than many people realized (Kinsey, Pomeroy, & Martin, 1948; Kinsey, Pomeroy, Martin, & Gebhard, 1953). Psychologist Evelyn Hooker (1957) found that psychiatrists could not discriminate a group of homosexual men from a similar group of heterosexual men on the basis of their projective test results, suggesting that being homosexual does not necessarily indicate the presence of psychopathology. Views of homosexuality as pathological were criticized as unscientific, based primarily on moralistic assumptions about sexual behavior and gender roles.

In December 1973, after considerable debate and lobbying by those on both sides of the issue, the APA Board of Trustees voted to replace the official diagnosis of homosexuality with what was to become ego-dystonic homosexuality in *DSM-III*. In other words, homosexuality would no longer be considered a mental disorder; however, conflict over one's homosexuality would be. By the time *DSM-III-R* was published in 1987, the diagnosis of ego-dystonic homosexuality had rarely been used or studied. It was also found that gays and lesbians in the United States frequently experienced a phase involving conflict over their sexual orientation, suggesting that such conflict is a normative process rather than a pathological one.

Critiques of Nomenclature Changes

There was significant support for the pathology view of homosexuality prior to 1973, and the nomenclature changes were hotly debated. Dissent came especially from psychoanalysts, most notably Irving Bieber and Charles Socarides. Bieber maintained that male homosexuality is inherently pathological, stemming from aberrant childhood experiences, especially involving mothers who are too close or possessive and fathers who are too distant (Bieber et al., 1962). Socarides (1970) argued for psychoanalysis as the treatment of choice for homosexuality. Both Bieber and Socarides believed that the pathology view was scientific, grounded in years of psychoanalytic experience.

Debate continued within psychiatry after the vote of the APA Board of Trustees in 1973, and advocates for the pathology view of homosexuality forced a referendum of all APA members on the issue in 1974. However, the results of this referendum ratified the change in nomenclature. Many laypersons were horrified to see that decisions about the psychopathology or normality of homosexuality were so blatantly political, determined by a mere vote of psychiatrists. What they apparently did not realize was that both the classification and the diagnosis of all mental disorders are highly political.

Politics and the Diagnosis of "Women's Madness"

The diagnosis of psychopathology in women provides another illustration of the political aspects of psychiatric nomenclature. In the preparation of *DSM-III-R,* the American Psychiatric Association Work Group to Revise *DSM-III* entertained proposals for several new diagnostic categories with particular relevance to women: late luteal phase dysphoric disorder, paraphilic rapism, and self-defeating personality disorder.

Late luteal phase dysphoric disorder was proposed as a "pattern of clinically significant emotional and behavioral symptoms that occur during the last week of the luteal phase and remit within a few days after the onset of the follicular phase [of the menstrual cycle]" (APA, 1987, p. 367). These symptoms included affective lability, fatigue, irritability, and changes in appetite. The proposed disorder was essentially what many people call premenstrual syndrome. Although critics did not dispute that symptoms such as these occur in some women, they did attack the psychiatric establishment for attempting to psychopathologize a normal biological process, adding to the perception that being female is somehow abnormal (Pugliesi, 1992).

Paraphilic rapism, later called *paraphilic coercive disorder,* was proposed as a persistent pattern associating "intense sexual arousal or desire, and acts, fantasies, or other stimuli involving coercing or forcing a non-consenting person to engage in oral, vaginal or anal intercourse" (Halpern, 1986, p. 1). This classification represented an attempt to label as mentally disordered the perpetrators of rape, but it was deleted from the final version of *DSM-III-R.* Halpern (1986) notes that a similar classification, sexual assault disorder, was proposed during the development of *DSM-III,* and that it was deleted only after his own strenuous objections and those of several women's groups were voiced. Critics such as Halpern argued, both in 1977 and in 1986, that rape is a criminal act, and that it should remain so. Medicalizing rape would lead to further minimization of the "wrongfulness of the perpetrator's conduct" (Halpern, 1986, p. 3) and would perpetuate the notion that women who are victims of rape are somehow responsible for it.

Self-defeating personality disorder, originally called *masochistic personality disorder,* was proposed as a pattern in which a "person may often avoid or undermine pleasurable experiences, be drawn to situations or relationships in which he or she will suffer, and prevent others from helping him or her" (APA, 1987, p. 373). This proposed diagnostic category was criticized for promoting the belief that women are masochistic. Critics were especially concerned that the diagnosis would be used to explain the behavior of women who remain in abusive relationships. That is, instead of seeking to understand the multiple environmental obstacles preventing many women from leaving abusive relationships, this diagnosis would explain the plight of such women by calling them sick, and therefore would make them responsible for their continued abuse (Caplan, 1987).

Rosewater (1985) illustrates how problems similar to those identified by Caplan may already occur with existing diagnostic categories by showing how the behavioral dynamics of physically abused women may be similar to behavioral criteria for schizophrenia or borderline personality disorder. Battered women with symptoms such as delusions, blunted affect, social withdrawal, and deterioration in social and occupational functioning may thus be erroneously diagnosed with schizophrenia. If they present with symptoms such as self-damaging impulsive behaviors, unstable and intense interpersonal relationships, and inappropriate expression of anger, they may be erroneously diagnosed with borderline personality disorder.

Ussher (1991) notes that "madness" has been synonymous with femininity at least since Victorian times. Women are more likely than men to report feeling distressed. They are much more frequently referred to, and seen by, mental health professionals than are men. Depression, anxiety, and eating disorders are far more frequently diagnosed in women than in men. According to Ussher, societal prescriptions for female behavior predispose women to think of themselves as "mad" at the same time they predispose the mental health establishment to treat women for their "madness." The feminist argument against psychiatric nomenclature, according to Ussher, is that the concept of "madness" is used to control women, and especially women's anger, in order to maintain a patriarchal society.

There has been considerable research into gender differences in the prevalence of depression, which is far more frequently diagnosed in women than in men. In a review of this body of research, Pugliesi (1992) notes that genetic traits, hormones, and social roles have all been examined as possible explanations. However, she also highlights Showalter's (1985) criticism of the undergirding conceptions of mental health and mental illness as fundamentally gendered. Pugliesi observes that women may indeed suffer psychological distress more frequently or intensely than do men, but this suffering is not necessarily equivalent to mental disorder, a concept laden with "patriarchal values and assumptions" (p. 60). She describes a feminist approach to mental health research and treatment that seeks to understand the social positions of women and their inherent stresses as causes for their distress. Traditional psychiatric nomenclature is avoided in this approach.

Politics and the Diagnosis of Other Minorities

Some writers have also criticized the mental health establishment for institutional racism (De La Cancela & Sotomayor, 1993; Wade, 1993). Wade (1993) notes that racial bias may occur in the diagnosis of mental disorders, citing previous research by Jenkins-Hall and Sacco (1991), Jones (1982), and Teichner, Cadden, and Berry (1981). In particular, Wade observes that African Americans and Hispanics being admitted to state mental hospitals are more likely than whites to be diagnosed with schizophrenia. Fernando (1988; quoted in Wade, 1993) claims that the diagnosis of schizophrenia is particularly susceptible to sociopolitical influence, because it concerns an individual's thinking patterns. Thus beliefs, attitudes, and perceptions that diverge from those of the majority may be labeled disordered.

Racial/ethnic differences in admissions to mental health institutions have been studied by a number of researchers. In a review of this body of research, Halpern (1993) has made observations that are similar to those made by feminist critics of psychiatric nomenclature. First, measures of mental disorder generally use a majority (based on race or ethnicity) standard that is inherently biased against minority group members. Second, labeling someone with a psychiatric diagnosis may cause the source of that person's distress to be ignored. This may occur because some diagnoses, particularly schizophrenia, suggest internal, biological, causes. However, interactive and stress-diathesis models of schizophrenia explain this disorder as *both* internally and environmentally caused. Although an underlying biological vulnerability is acknowledged, symptoms occur in reaction to stressful life events (Lieberman et al., 1984). For minority group members, stressful life events are likely to be associated with societal oppression. When mental health professionals diagnose minority group members with schizophrenia without attention to the sources of stress in the structure of society, they help to maintain the social status quo.

Politics and the Concept of Mental Disorder

As the debates over psychopathology in gays and lesbians, women, and racial/ethnic minorities illustrate, there is much disagreement over what constitutes a mental disorder. Also, sociopolitical forces are highly salient in determining what should be considered a mental disorder. As Klerman (1987) notes, "All clinical diagnosis and classification systems are based as much on social values and judgments as upon scientific data" (p. 3). Because psychiatric diagnoses are social constructions, they should not be reified. Nevertheless, psychiatric classification does serve a variety of purposes, as identified by Kirk and Kutchins (1992):

1. It allows for financial reimbursement for services.
2. It provides a rationalization for therapeutic interventions.
3. It can advance a political agenda.

Financial Reimbursement for Services

Agencies and individuals providing mental health services must assign their clients approved diagnostic labels in order to receive third-party payments. If they want to stay in business, they have to know which labels are reimbursable, to what extent, by which insurance companies. Kirk and Kutchins (1988) found that 25% of a sample of social workers in mental health practice reported frequent overdiagnosis of clients in order to receive insurance reimbursement. Others writers have found similar trends among other mental health practitioners (Sharfstein, Gutheil, & Stoddard, 1983). The *DSM-III* (APA, 1980) diagnosis of post-traumatic stress disorder was created, at least in part, so that practitioners could provide reimbursable mental health services to veterans of the Vietnam War who were experiencing serious mental health problems (Scott, 1990).

In addition to the profit motive, agencies and individuals in mental health practice are motivated to help their clients. In Kirk and Kutchins's (1988) sample of clinical social workers, 55% reported frequently assigning reimbursable individual diagnoses to clients even though nonreimbursable family problems were more significant. Through the practitioner's use of deliberate misdiagnosis, distressed clients might receive services that would be otherwise unavailable. For instance, without an official diagnosis of post-traumatic stress disorder, specialized services might not have been developed for Vietnam veterans with combat-related trauma.

Rationalization for Therapeutic Interventions

The existence of an official psychiatric diagnosis suggests a therapeutic goal and, therefore, an intervention. When homosexuality was an official *DSM-II* (APA, 1968) diagnosis, the logical goal suggested by that diagnosis was the elimination of homosexual behavior, thoughts, and feelings. When ego-dystonic homosexuality was an official *DSM-III* (APA, 1980) diagnosis, the logical goal was the elimination of the client's distress about his or her homosexual behavior, thoughts, and feelings. After homosexuality was removed from the list of official mental disorders, there was no longer any logical therapeutic goal indicated by a person's homosexual orientation. According to Kirk and Kutchins (1992), some psychiatric diagnoses are more helpful than others for guiding therapeutic intervention. Most notably, prescription of lithium is indicated when a diagnosis of bipolar disorder is made. Prescription of an antipsychotic medication is a likely indication when a diagnosis of schizophrenia is made. However, many diagnoses provide little direction for appropriate intervention.

Advancement of a Political Agenda

As Kirk and Kutchins (1992) note, psychiatry's steady expansion of the number of sanctioned diagnostic categories reflects the profession's political agenda. That is, the greater the number of diagnostic categories, the larger the domain of medical/psychiatric intervention. Others have described this process as the "medicalization" of deviance (Conrad & Schneider, 1980). In other words, behaviors deviating from the social norm that used to be defined as "immoral" or "criminal" are increasingly defined as "sick." Societal views of homosexual behavior illustrate this process. Condemned as immoral by Western religions since at least the 13th century (Boswell, 1980), homosexual behavior was punished within the domain of the church. However, responsibility for punishment was gradually transferred from the church to the state. "Criminalization" of homosexual behavior was especially apparent in the United States during the early part of the 20th century, when many harshly repressive laws were passed. Around the time of World War II, psychiatry began to promote the idea of homosexuality as an illness (Conrad & Schneider, 1980). This idea has now become so accepted throughout U.S. society that many people do not even realize its recency. As Conrad and Schneider (1980) note, the declassification of homosexuality as a mental disorder was a rare instance of demedicalization. In general, the domain of medicine/psychiatry has been ever expanding, now including problems previously not considered to be medical, such as juvenile delinquency, marital conflict, and drug abuse.

Robitscher (1980) describes how other political agendas may be advanced through the use of psychiatric classification. The diagnosis of schizophrenia was applied to political dissidents in the former Soviet Union, where diagnostic characteristics included "reformism" and a "parasitic life style" (p. 320). A dissident might be hospitalized for years if given this diagnosis. Even in the United States, people such as Martha Mitchell and Daniel Ellsberg, who held dissident views and had the potential to threaten the power of government officials, have been neutralized by being labeled mentally disordered. Perhaps less ominous but more pervasive throughout society, mental health professionals now often help determine whether individuals seeking employment should be hired, through the administration of increasingly common diagnostic tests.

Issues in the Definition of Mental Disorder

According to Robitscher (1980), a lack of scientific basis for psychiatric nomenclature gives diagnosticians a great deal of power. Others have written at length on the weaknesses in current definitions of mental health and mental disorder. Wakefield (1992) states that the authors of *DSM-III-R* devoted their primary attention to increasing the reliability of diagnostic categories, neglecting their validity. As a result, the manual's basic conceptual validity, or its ability to discriminate disorders from other negative conditions, is weak. According to Wakefield, the *DSM-III-R* definition of mental disorder was guided by two principles. First, to be considered a mental disorder, the condition must have negative consequences for the individual experiencing the disorder. Second, the condition must be a dysfunction, defined by Wakefield as "a condition in which some internal mechanism is not functioning in the way it is naturally designed to function" (p. 233). Unfortunately, *DSM-III-R* inadequately operationalized dysfunction as a statistically unexpected, or deviant, response.

> The most basic problem with the definition is that there are many statistically deviant conditions that cause distress and other harms but that are not dysfunctions. In the mental realm, selfishness, cowardice, slovenliness, foolhardiness, gullibility, insensitivity, laziness, and sheer lack of talent are a few examples of the types of inner misfortunes and failings that can cause harm and that can be statistically deviant either in the nature of the response or in the response's intensity without being classifiable as disorders. The dysfunction requirement is supposed to distinguish disorders from other internally caused harms to which

human beings are subject, and the unexpectability requirement does not succeed in drawing the same distinction. (Wakefield, 1992, p. 238)

The substitution of the *dysfunction* concept with the *unexpectable response* concept illustrates the medicalization of deviance previously mentioned, because deviant responses are simply equated with disorder. Diagnostic categories that do not sufficiently distinguish between dysfunctions and other internal conditions causing harm (as described above), or between dysfunctions and external causes of harm (such as poverty or discrimination), allow the diagnostician to make judgments about people that are highly subject to bias. As Loring and Powell (1988) caution, psychiatric diagnosis will always be subjective, even when objective criteria are used. These authors note that the "trend toward seeking consistent operational definitions is both understandable and admirable, but a false sense of confidence in objective measures can be dangerous when it ignores the possibility of bias (or misperception) and when it helps to maintain that bias through both treatment and statistical reports" (p. 19).

Politics and Treatment

Politics and the Treatment of Homosexuality

As the preceding discussion of the diagnosis of homosexuality might suggest, there has been a great deal of conflict over the manner in which mental health services have been delivered to gays and lesbians. As long as homosexuality was considered a mental disorder, mental health practitioners routinely attempted to eradicate same-sex behavior, feelings, and thoughts in their gay and lesbian clients. Duberman (1991) eloquently recounts how he was misled about being able to change his sexual orientation, exploited, and humiliated in individual and group psychotherapy. Because therapy reinforced his existing self-doubt and self-hatred, it took many years for him to realize that his therapists were not helping him. The behavior of Duberman's therapists was often grossly unethical, and heterosexist beliefs blinded friends and fellow group members to his victimization. Johanns (1978) recounts a history of psychiatric hospitalizations, including a year and a half at a New Jersey state hospital, during her adolescence. Her presenting problems were depression and drug abuse, but her root problems were related to her being a lesbian: loneliness, self-doubt, and victimization by peers. She was treated with medication and electroshock therapy.

Since the 19th century, physicians and mental health practitioners have apparently felt justified in exploiting, abusing, and torturing their distressed gay and lesbian clients. Treatment of same-sex desire in men has included the use of female prostitutes, electric shocks, toxic chemicals, and injections of animal organ extracts, estrogen, and testosterone. Similar desires in women have been treated with chemicals such as cocaine and injections of strychnine. Castration, lobotomy, cauterizations, and other surgical procedures have been performed on both men and women, in whom metrazol was also used to induce grand mal seizures. In spite of these attempts to change the sexual orientation of gay and lesbian individuals, there is virtually no evidence that such change has ever been accomplished (Murphy, 1992).

That evidence notwithstanding, some psychotherapists continue to claim that they are able to accomplish sexual orientation conversion. Kronemeyer (1980) maintains that homosexuality is a personality disorder based on learned responses to painful childhood experiences, despite the fact that there is no empirical evidence to support his claim. In particular, he attributes the development of homosexuality to a "frustrating and non-nurturing mother-infant relationship" (p. 13). He states that his belief in the pathology of homosexuality is based on his clinical experience with clients. Also referring to homosexuality as a "disabling neurosis" (p. 9), Kronemeyer calls for sympathy and understanding toward its "victims." His prescription for them consists of "syntonic therapy," which includes both movement and talking techniques designed to free the client's energy for growth. He especially encourages clients to identify and express their rage toward their mothers.

More recently, Nicolosi (1991) has claimed to have developed an effective treatment for sexual orientation conversion of male "nongay homosexuals," or men with same-sex desires but without identification with a gay community or culture. Nicolosi asserts that "the gay life-style" (p. 13) can never be healthy, and that same-sex relationships are doomed to failure because gay identities revolve around sex. According to Nicolosi, male homosexuality is caused by an inadequate father-son relationship. Nicolosi explains "reparative therapy" as a talking therapy in which clients are encouraged to control their same-sex attractions, form friendships with male heterosexuals, and develop their sense of masculinity. Weinrich (1993) criticizes Nicolosi for ignoring the preponderance of research evidence that has refuted the pathology of homosexuality and points out the serious flaws in Nicolosi's logic and in his treatment model.

Although some therapists have claimed success in accomplishing sexual reorientation in clients, critics have attacked all aspects of these claims. For example, Haldeman (1994) notes that the "fixed, behavior-based model of sexual orientation assumed by almost all conversion therapists may be invalid" (p. 222). Murphy (1992) notes that many clients who have reported successful change of their sexual orientation have had bisexual histories. Haldeman also points out that sexual orientation involves not only behavior but also fantasy, sense of identity, and internalized sociocultural expectations. Therapists who assert that they have changed clients' sexual orientations simply because their same-sex sexual behaviors have ceased are making spurious claims. In addition, therapists claiming success have generally relied on client self-reports or, in the case of Bieber et al. (1962), therapist reports as the only measure of change. Finally, accounts of sexual reorientation generally lack long-term follow-up (Haldeman, 1994).

Haldeman (1994) questions the ethics of psychologists who practice sexual orientation conversion therapy, given the absence of empirical evidence for its effectiveness and its potentially damaging effects. Some professionals, such as Kronemeyer (1980) and Nicolosi (1991), have argued that gays and lesbians who wish to change their sexual orientation should be able to receive services directed toward that goal—that it should be a matter of voluntary, personal choice. However, critics have charged that people's desires to change their sexual orientation cannot be considered truly voluntary in light of the crushing social oppression of gays and lesbians in U.S. society. In other words, complying with clients' desires to reduce their distress by changing their sexual orientation blames the victims for their oppression (Murphy, 1992).

One particularly onerous characteristic of sexual orientation conversion therapies is their predatory nature. Both Kronemeyer and Nicolosi stress that client motivation is critical for treatment success. Although this statement would be true for any treatment or goal, in the case of sexual reorientation it means that those individuals who are most vulnerable are considered the best targets. To illustrate, Nicolosi (1991) comments that men with few same-sex experiences are the best candidates for successful treatment. To that end, he recommends that affirmative counseling services should not be available to gay adolescents, lest they encourage youngsters to form gay identities. Clients who are most distressed about being gay or lesbian may have had a great number of negative life experiences related to their sexual orientation, including abuse, stigmatization, and humiliation. They may lack sufficiently supportive relationships with family members and friends. They may not have experienced the beneficial effects of involvement in a community of people like themselves. Preying on clients' vulnerability to further one's own social or political views is clearly unethical practice, and the fact that this has been condoned by some shows how easily mental health treatment can be used for political purposes.

Politics and the Treatment of Women

The treatment of women is no less politically charged than the treatment of gays and lesbians. Throughout the centuries, women whose behavior has deviated from social norms have been considered immoral, mentally ill, or practitioners of witchcraft. They have been burned at the stake, drowned, or incarcerated. Women have been subject to clitoridectomy and lobotomy, insulin and electroshock therapy, and of course psychotropic medication. Psychoanalysts have accused them of penis envy. Psychotherapists have sexually assaulted them. Individual and family therapists have routinely blamed them for the pathology of their children (Ussher, 1991).

Chesler (1990) charges that the mental health professions are patriarchal institutions that do not support women who challenge expectations that females should be passive, dependent, and emotional. She adds that male mental health professionals tend to show little interest in learning about incest, rape, or wife beating, issues with particular significance for many women. Women who report that they have been sexually abused or victims of incest as children are sometimes greeted with skepticism or disbelief. Adult women who return to their abusing husbands or boyfriends because they have no other source of financial support, or because they fear they will be murdered, are sometimes labeled resistant to treatment. Women are sometimes told they are crazy if they fantasize about running away from their husbands and children. In contrast, according to Chesler, feminist therapists do not view as mentally ill women who "have full-time careers, are lesbians, refuse to marry, commit adultery, want divorces, choose to be celibate, have abortions, use birth control, have an 'illegitimate' baby, choose to breastfeed against expert advice, or expect men to be responsible for 50% of the child care and housework" (p. 319). Chesler calls for the establishment of a Feminist Institute of Mental Health and Healing to improve the quality of mental health services available to women.

Sheppard (1991) notes that involuntary hospitalization of women is used by general practice physicians in the British mental health system in a discriminatory manner. That is, women are referred by general practitioners for involuntary hospitalization, which may include forced use of medication, at a higher rate than are men. Sheppard attributes this difference to physicians' overemphasis on individual malfunctioning and their lack of attention to the social and economic problems that may be the cause of women's symptoms. As a result, a woman experiencing severe symptoms of anxiety and depression as a result of an abusive marriage might be admitted to a hospital and forced to take psychotropic medications against her will.

At the same time that critics such as Chesler and Sheppard point out that women's behavior, thoughts, and feelings are often inappropriately psycho-pathologized, Mowbray, Herman, and Hazel (1992) charge that women who do have serious mental illnesses have been largely ignored by mental health research. These authors note that previous research has found a higher percentage of women in the chronically mentally ill population (Ashbaugh, Leaf, Manderscheid, & Eaton, 1983) but a lower percentage of women in the populations of state and county psychiatric hospitals (Mowbray & Benedek, 1988). They add that a lack of research on women with serious mental illnesses has led to overgeneralization and stereotyping of the needs of these women.

Politics and the Treatment of Other Minorities

De La Cancela and Sotomayor (1993) argue that psychotherapists who treat African Americans for psychological problems without attending to the social, political, and economic oppression affecting this group are perpetuating racism. Behaviors that might be acceptable or understandable for European Americans are often considered unacceptable or pathological for African Americans. This argument is similar to those advanced by feminists and gays/lesbians; women and members of minorities are judged according to white, male, heterosexual standards. People are blamed for their own oppression, and the mental health system works in conjunction with the legal and criminal justice systems to maintain the status quo.

According to Wade (1993), minority-race recipients in the United States have not benefited from community-based mental health services as much as have white recipients. Compared with white recipients, minority-race recipients are more likely to be treated as inpatients in state hospitals. One reason for this situation, according to Wade, is that the needs of African Americans and Hispanics were not taken into consideration when community-based services were developed. Parron (1982) identifies four issues associated with the underservice, or inappropriate service, of minority group members needing mental health services:

1. Services are not located where minority group members can access them.
2. Services are too expensive.
3. Services do not take into account the unique needs of minority group clientele.
4. Service providers are not accountable to minority group communities or their representatives.

Solomon (1982) argues that the mental health system has mistakenly been based on an assumption that its underlying theories are universally applicable. However, members of ethnic minority groups may have mental health problems that are different from those of the Anglo middle class, which has been used as the model for most mental health treatment. Solomon advocates an empowerment model for mental health practice with minority clients, a model that attends to the "social or emotional problems created or exacerbated by one's membership in a stigmatized group" (p. 89). De La Cancela and Sotomayor (1993) recommend that practitioners focus on minority recipients' strengths, rather than their deficits, as one way to reduce institutional racism in the mental health system.

Affirmative Mental Health Treatment

In advancing his case for "reparative therapy" for gay men, Nicolosi (1991) argues that proponents of therapeutic approaches that affirm a client's gay sexual orientation put their own politics above the mental health needs of their clients. In other words, he charges that gay-affirmative therapy is a political, rather than therapeutic, process. Because Nicolosi assumes that heterosexual orientation, culture, roles, and values are inherently superior, he also assumes that his position is not political. It is this very ethnocentrism that has provided the theoretical basis for the mistreatment of gay men and lesbians. Similarly, male and Anglo ethnocentric attitudes have provided the rationalization for the mistreatment of women and non-Anglo minorities. In reality, there are political aspects to all mental health treatment simply because people, and their problems, exist in a sociopolitical environment that defines both mental health and mental illness. Whether or not they are addressed, these aspects of treatment exert important, yet sometimes subtle, effects on clients.

Mental health practitioners can choose to be agents of the social status quo, "peddling therapeutic control in the name of personal liberation" (Szasz, 1991, p. 24), or they can choose to empower their clients. The former choice makes therapists enforcers of social oppression, a choice considered unethical among all the mental health professions. According to Solomon (1982), empowerment involves interventions designed to reduce clients' "powerlessness stemming from the experience of negative valuation and discrimination" (p. 89). This approach acknowledges the environmental, social, economic, and political factors involved in the causation or maintenance of clients' problems. It counteracts the inappropriate personalization, or individualization, of people's problems. Gay/lesbian-affirmative therapy and feminist therapy are two models of mental health treatment that involve client empowerment.

According to Hall (1985), gay/lesbian-affirmative therapists avoid reinforcing the devaluing messages that are issued from heterosexist society. They accept their clients' sexual orientations, whatever they might be. They do not encourage clients to change their orientations. Affirmative therapists do not accept the idea that an individual's sexual orientation is a mental health problem in and of itself. However, they may work with clients to identify and solve problems that are related to sexual orientation. For instance, gay/lesbian clients may experience a lack of support from their families of origin or friends, discrimination at their place of employment, or fear of violence in their neighborhoods. They may feel alienation from their churches and disenfranchisement from their government. Experiences such as these may lead to, exacerbate, or maintain such mental health problems as anxiety, depression, and low or unstable self-esteem. Likewise, ethnic minority-affirmative and feminist therapists acknowledge the devaluing messages inherent in the culture in which their clients live, and they work toward disentangling their clients' internal distress from the social oppression in which it may be rooted.

Issues of sexual orientation, gender, race, and ethnicity intersect for many clients, and truly affirmative practice requires practitioners to attend to the special needs, and sources of oppression, having to do with all of them. As women, lesbians face social expectations for behavior that differ markedly from those of gay men. Many African American gay men and lesbians must maintain a precarious balance between their identification with a racist gay community and a heterosexist African American community, both of which are critical sources of support. As Greene (1994) points out, the meaning of sexuality, an individual's role in the family and community, and gender expectations may differ from culture to culture. Overgeneralizations about minorities such as gays and lesbians, Latinas and Latinos, Asians, African Americans, and Native Americans may predispose therapists to therapeutic bias and empathic failure with their clients. Greene notes that practitioners "must develop a sense of the unique experience of the client with respect to the importance of their ethnic identity and sexual orientation and the need to establish priorities in an often confusing conflict of loyalties" (p. 250).

An affirmative approach to mental health practice necessarily involves attention to clients' support networks. For women and members of stigmatized minorities, support networks are important buffers against societal oppression. Crocker and Major (1989) note that individuals obtain self-esteem benefits from identifying with the stigmatized group to which they belong. Other research has found that people who live in close proximity to a network of ethnically similar others are less likely to experience mental health problems (Halpern, 1993). Affirmative practitioners must explore the extent to which their clients identify, and engage, with other people like themselves. Helping them to identify more fully, engage more actively, and develop sources of support with members of their own group is likely to be an important therapeutic task.

References

American Psychiatric Association. (1952). *Diagnostic and statistical manual of mental disorders.* Washington, DC: Author.

American Psychiatric Association. (1968). *Diagnostic and statistical manual of mental disorders* (2nd ed.). Washington, DC: Author.

American Psychiatric Association. (1980). *Diagnostic and statistical manual of mental disorders* (3rd ed.). Washington, DC: Author.

American Psychiatric Association. (1987). *Diagnostic and statistical manual of mental disorders* (3rd ed., rev.). Washington, DC: Author.

Ashbaugh, J. W., Leaf, P. J., Manderscheid, R. W., & Eaton, W. (1983). Estimates of the size and selected characteristics of the adult chronically mentally ill population living in U.S. households. *Research in Community and Mental Health, 3,* 3-24.

Bayer, R. (1981). *Homosexuality and American psychiatry: The politics of diagnosis.* New York: Basic Books.

Bieber, I., Dain, H. J., Dince, P. R., Drellich, M. W., Rifkin, A. H., Wilbur, C. B., & Bieber, T. B. (1962). *Homosexuality: A psychoanalytic study.* New York: Basic Books.

Boswell, J. (1980). *Christianity, social tolerance, and homosexuality.* Chicago: University of Chicago Press.

Caplan, P. J. (1987). The name game: Psychiatry, misogyny, and taxonomy. *Women and Therapy, 6,* 187-200.

Chesler, P. (1990). Twenty years since *Women and madness:* Toward a feminist institute of mental health and healing. *Journal of Mind and Behavior, 11,* 313-322.

Conger, J. (1975). Proceedings of the American Psychological Association for the year 1974: Minutes of the Annual Meeting of the Council of Representatives. *American Psychologist, 30,* 620-651.

Conrad, P., & Schneider, J. W. (1980). *Deviance and medicalization.* St. Louis: C. V. Mosby.

Crocker, J., & Major, B. (1989). Social stigma and self-esteem: The self-protective properties of stigma. *Psychological Review, 96,* 608-630.

De La Cancela, V., & Sotomayor, G. M. (1993). Rainbow warriors: Reducing institutional racism in mental health. *Journal of Mental Health Counseling, 15,* 55-71.

Duberman, M. (1991). *Cures: A gay man's odyssey.* New York: Dutton.

Fernando, S. (1988). *Race and culture in psychiatry.* London: Croom Helm.

Greene, B. (1994). Ethnic-minority lesbians and gay men: Mental health and treatment issues. *Journal of Consulting and Clinical Psychology, 62,* 243-251.

Haldeman, D. C. (1994). The practice and ethics of sexual orientation conversion therapy. *Journal of Consulting and Clinical Psychology, 62,* 221-227.

Hall, M. (1985). *The lavender couch.* Boston: Alyson.

Halpern, A. (1986, May). Paraphilic coercive disorder: Old sewage in new pipes? *Newsletter of the Psychiatric Society of Westchester.* (Available from the Psychiatric Society of Westchester, 107 Purchase Street, Purchase, NY 10577)

Halpern, D. (1993). Minorities and mental health. *Social Science and Medicine, 36,* 597-607.

Hidalgo, H., Peterson, T. L., & Woodman, N. J. (1985). *Lesbian and gay issues: A resource manual for social workers.* Silver Spring, MD: National Association of Social Workers.

Hooker, E. (1957). The adjustment of male overt homosexuals. *Journal of Projective Techniques, 21,* 18-31.

Jenkins-Hall, K., & Sacco, W. P. (1991). Effect of client race and depression on evaluations by white therapists. *Journal of Social and Clinical Psychology, 10,* 322-333.

Johanns, K. P. (1978). They tried to cure me of lesbianism. In K. Hefner & A. Autin (Eds.), *Growing up gay* (p. 37). Ann Arbor, MI: Youth Liberation.

Jones, E. E. (1982). Psychotherapists' impressions of treatment outcome as a function of race. *Journal of Clinical Psychology, 38,* 722-731.

Kinsey, A. C., Pomeroy, W. B., & Martin, C. W. (1948). *Sexual behavior in the human male.* Philadelphia: W. B. Saunders.

Kinsey, A. C., Pomeroy, W. B., Martin, C. W., & Gebhard, P. H. (1953). *Sexual behavior in the human female.* Philadelphia: W. B. Saunders.

Kirk, S. A., & Kutchins, H. (1988). Deliberate misdiagnosis in mental health practice. *Social Service Review, 62,* 225-237.

Kirk, S. A., & Kutchins, H. (1992). *The selling of DSM: The rhetoric of science in psychiatry.* New York: Aldine De Gruyter.

Klerman, G. L. (1987). Is the reliability of DSM-III a scientific or a political question? *Social Work Research and Abstracts, 23*(4), 3.

Kronemeyer, R. (1980). *Overcoming homosexuality.* New York: Macmillan.

Lasch, C. (1979). *The culture of narcissism.* New York: W. W. Norton.

Lieberman, R. P., Marshall, B. D., Jr., Marder, S. R., Dawson, M. E., Nuechterlein, K. H., & Doane, J. A. (1984). The nature and problem of schizophrenia. In A. Bellack (Ed.), *Schizophrenia: Treatment, management, and rehabilitation* (pp. 1-34). Orlando, FL: Grune & Stratton.

Loring, J., & Powell, B. (1988). Gender, race, and DSM-III: A study of the objectivity of psychiatric diagnostic behavior. *Journal of Health and Social Behavior, 29,* 1-22.

Marmor, J. (1965). Introduction. In J. Marmor (Ed.), *Sexual inversion: The multiple roots of homosexuality* (pp. 1-24). New York: Basic Books.

Mowbray, C. T., & Benedek, E. P. (1988). *Women's mental health research agenda: Services and treatment of mental disorders in women* (Women's Mental Health Occasional Paper). Rockville, MD: National Institute of Mental Health.

Mowbray, C. T., Herman, S. E., & Hazel, K. L. (1992). Gender and serious mental illness: A feminist perspective. *Psychology of Women Quarterly, 16,* 107-126.

Murphy, T. F. (1992). Redirecting sexual orientation: Techniques and justifications. *Journal of Sex Research, 29,* 501-523.

Nicolosi, J. (1991). *Reparative therapy of male homosexuality: A new clinical approach.* Northvale, NJ: Jason Aronson.

Parron, D. L. (1982). An overview of minority group mental health needs and issues as presented to the President's Commission on Mental Health. In F. U. Munoz & R. Endo (Eds.), *Perspectives on minority group mental health* (pp. 3-22). Washington, DC: University Press of America.

Pugliesi, K. (1992). Women and mental health: Two traditions of feminist research. *Women and Health, 19,* 43-68.

Robitscher, J. (1980). *The powers of psychiatry.* Boston: Houghton Mifflin.

Rosewater, L. B. (1985). Schizophrenic, borderline, or battered? In L. B. Rosewater & L. E. A. Walker (Eds.), *Handbook of feminist therapy: Women's issues in psychotherapy* (pp. 215-225). New York: Springer.

Scott, W. J. (1990). PTSD in DSM-III: A case in the politics of diagnosis and disease. *Social Problems, 37,* 294-309.

Sharfstein, S. S., Gutheil, T. G., & Stoddard, F. J. (1983). Money and character disorders: Or how to get the recalcitrant third party and the impossible patient to pay your bills. In M. Zales (Ed.), *Character pathology: Theory and treatment* (pp. 196-215). New York: Brunner/Mazel.

Sheppard, M. (1991). General practice, social work, and mental health sections: The social control of women. *British Journal of Social Work, 21,* 663-683.

Showalter, E. (1985). *The female malady: Women, madness, and English culture, 1830-1980.* New York: Pantheon.

Socarides, C. W. (1970). Homosexuality and medicine. *Journal of the American Medical Association, 212,* 1199-1202.

Solomon, B. B. (1982). A theoretical perspective for delivery of mental health services to minority communities. In F. U. Munoz & R. Endo (Eds.), *Perspectives on minority group mental health* (pp. 85-91). Washington, DC: University Press of America.

Szasz, T. (1991). Psychiatry and social control. *Humanist, 51*(1), 24-25, 34.

Teichner, V., Cadden, J. J., & Berry, G. W. (1981). The Puerto Rican patient: Some historical, cultural and psychological aspects. *Journal of the American Academy of Psychoanalysis, 9,* 277-290.

Ussher, J. (1991). *Women's madness: Misogyny or mental illness?* Amherst: University of Massachusetts Press.

Wade, J. C. (1993). Institutional racism: An analysis of the mental health system. *American Journal of Orthopsychiatry, 63,* 536-544.

Wakefield, J. C. (1992). Disorder as harmful dysfunction: A conceptual critique of DSM-III-R's definition of mental disorder. *Psychological Review, 99,* 232-247.

Weinrich, J. D. (1993). Therapy terminable and interminable: "Non-gay homosexuals" come out of the closet [Review of *Reparative therapy of male homosexuality: A new clinical approach*]. *Journal of Sex Research, 30,* 291-295.

CHAPTER 4

The Impact of the Courts on Mental Health Policy and Services

BRIAN D. SHANNON

Judicial decisions by various state and federal courts throughout the United States have had significant impact on the provision of mental health services to persons suffering from mental illness. Indeed, court decisions have profoundly affected mental health treatment and policy in a variety of areas. This chapter examines a number of those court cases in several areas of law. In particular, it focuses on certain significant legal decisions and their impacts on policy and services with respect to the following matters: the civil commitment process, an individual's right to treatment, an individual's right to refuse treatment, a mental health professional's potential liability to patients or third parties, the involvement of individuals suffering from mental illness in the criminal justice system, and the extent of coverage of serious mental illness by private insurance. Moreover, this chapter is primarily intended to introduce the reader to some of the important cases in these areas. It is by no means an exhaustive study of the topics, and there are also many other important issues in the field of mental health law beyond the scope of this chapter. On the other hand, this chapter discusses a variety of important case determinations regarding certain key issues that have had substantial impact on the delivery of mental health services in the United States.

The history of the overlap of law and mental health in the United States is tied closely to involuntary commitment issues. In the early days of this nation, the purpose of commitment of persons with mental illness was for detention, not treatment or therapy (Spring, LaCoursiere, & Weissenberger, 1989). The apparent intent of confinement in asylums was primarily to insulate the rest of society from persons with mental illness due to fear of possible violence (Spring et al., 1989). As Perlin (1994) has observed, however, in the mid-1800s a Massachusetts decision placed limits on the use of the commitment process by stressing that the state's power to order commitment should be tied either to care and treatment or to protection from harm (*In re Oakes,* 1845-1846). Spring et al. (1989) postulate that the subsequent development of American law as it relates to persons with mental illness has been dependent on such factors as (a) medical knowledge (or the lack thereof) about mental illness, (b) the level of interest by the political community in taking responsibility for treatment and care of persons with mental illness, and (c) awareness within the legal profession of the realities of mental illness. These factors certainly continue to play a role today with respect to judicial attitudes about law and psychiatry. The remainder of this chapter focuses on a sampling of modern cases and their impacts on mental health services with regard to the areas described above.

Court Decisions Affecting Court-Ordered Mental Health Services

A psychiatrist and author who once headed St. Elizabeth's Hospital in Washington, D.C., has observed that "the most common of the legal and ethical dilemmas posed by people with schizophrenia is if and when to hospitalize them against their will" (Torrey, 1988b, p. 315). The same could be said for persons suffering from other serious mental illnesses. There is often a great deal of tension between the wishes of family members and health care professionals to treat a person's mental illness and the ill individual's stated or perceived desires not to receive treatment. Unfortunately, the very organ of the individual's body most affected by the mental illness—the brain—may also be strongly averse to receiving care, regardless of whether the refusal to seek treatment is based on rational or irrational beliefs. Every state has enacted some type of statute to authorize involuntary commitment of persons suffering from serious mental illness who have declined or not sought voluntary treatment. Because these statutes permit commitment in certain situations, often contrary to the patient's stated wishes, legal disputes have played a large role in the shaping of the present state of such civil commitment legislation.

In the modern era, *Lessard v. Schmidt* (1972) represents one of the first cases to raise serious questions about a state's civil commitment statute. Indeed, in *Lessard* a federal district judge struck down the then-existing Wisconsin civil commitment law, which had permitted involuntary commitment upon a court's finding that a person was both mentally ill and a proper subject for custody and treatment (*Lessard,* 1972, p. 1093). The court took the view that citizens have a constitutionally protected liberty interest not to be confined against their will without due process of law. To that end, the court opined that due process requires the state to demonstrate that the individual poses a danger to self or others before commitment can be allowed. Correspondingly, the court instructed that this dangerousness criterion should be demonstrated by a showing of some "recent overt act, attempt or threat to do substantial harm to oneself or another" (*Lessard*, 1972, p. 1093). Perlin (1994, p. 28) notes that *Lessard* was the "forerunner" of many similar challenges to various state civil commitment laws, all of which have generally required some showing of dangerousness to support a commitment.

The U.S. Supreme Court gave greater weight to this dangerousness analysis a few years later in *O'Connor v. Donaldson* (1975). Although the case relates to "right to treatment" issues discussed below, the Court in *O'Connor* also opined that constitutional due process forbids the confining of someone involuntarily who is nondangerous and capable of surviving outside a hospital setting (p. 576). Thus, subsequent to *O'Connor*, states have had no real basis to maintain indefinite commitments absent proof that a patient continues to meet commitment criteria. Correspondingly, most commitment statutes today "confer on the individual charged with responsibility for treatment the authority to release the civilly committed patient from the institution without further intervention by the court" (Spring et al., 1989, p. 388). Problems still occasionally arise, however. For example, in *Texas Department of Mental Health and Mental Retardation v. Petty* (1992, p. 681), the state of Texas was found liable for money damages for having kept a woman committed for more than 50 years whose treatment was limited merely to custodial care. The case has prompted the state to amend its commitment laws to require annual commitment review hearings for the small segment of the hospital population subject to long-term commitment.

Another important case involving the requirements for civil commitment relates to the burden of proof necessary to permit commitment. In *Addington v. Texas* (1979), the U.S. Supreme Court rejected the use of a "preponderance of evidence" standard in civil commitment cases. The preponderance standard is typically employed in most civil litigation and requires the party with the burden of proof to provide evidence to demonstrate that the facts alleged are more likely than not to be true. In *Addington*, the Court concluded "that the individual's interest in the outcome of a civil commitment proceeding is of such weight and gravity that due process requires the state to justify confinement by proof more substantial than a mere preponderance of the evidence" (p. 427). The Court declined, however, to find that the criminal law standard of proof—demonstrating guilt of an offense beyond a reasonable doubt—should apply to a civil commitment proceeding. Instead, the Court reasoned that some middle level of burden of proof should be required to balance the rights of the individual and the interests of the state—a showing of "clear and convincing" proof (*Addington*, 1979, p. 432).

Cases requiring a showing of dangerousness or a heightened burden of proof have been criticized for ignoring the very real treatment needs of persons who may be seriously mentally ill, yet who might not meet the narrow commitment criterion of posing an immediate danger to self or others (Isaac & Armat,

1990). The narrower the grounds for commitment, the greater the potential for individuals with serious mental illness not to receive treatment. Additionally, many states have now enacted commitment statutes that permit commitment only upon a showing of a danger to self or others as demonstrated by recent overt acts. On the other hand, as Brooks (1989) has observed, not all courts have viewed the "dangerousness" standard in terms of violence or physical injury directed at the person with mental illness or others (as in *Lessard v. Schmidt,* 1972, and its progeny). Thus, in *State ex rel Hawks v. Lazaro* (1974, p. 123), the Supreme Court of West Virginia determined that the dangerousness standard is broad enough to encompass the prospect for hospitalization in situations in which symptoms of persons' mental illness might lead to possible death through slow starvation or lack of care.

Not unlike the West Virginia court in *Lazaro,* a federal judge presiding in Alabama has taken the position that a showing of actual violence is not a prerequisite of commitment (*Lynch v. Baxley,* 1974). Instead, the court in *Lynch* opined that the dangerousness requirement may also be met by proof that a person's mental illness involves self-neglect or care posing a real and substantial threat of substantial harm (p. 391). Generally consistent with the analysis in cases like *Lazaro* and *Lynch,* some states have enacted civil commitment statutes that are somewhat broader than the norm. For example, in Texas the legislature has allowed commitment not only upon a showing of danger to self or others, but also upon proof that without immediate intervention, the individual could suffer severe deterioration—perhaps to the point of being a danger to self or others. Texas also permits a judge to employ either inpatient or outpatient commitment.

Regardless of the legal tests employed for civil commitment, court decisions over the past two decades have decidedly narrowed the possible grounds for involuntary hospitalization. As described below, these and other court decisions have also had impacts on the nature of treatment required and made available.

Court Decisions Regarding the Right to Treatment

In *Wyatt v. Stickney* (1971), which Perlin (1994) has described as "one of the most influential mental disability cases ever filed" (p. 175), a federal court found that the Alabama state mental health facility was providing woefully inadequate care. The court declared that "the purposes of involuntary hospitalization for treatment purposes is *treatment* and not mere custodial care or punishment" (*Wyatt,* 1971, p. 784). This is consistent with the U.S. Supreme Court's later determination in *O'Connor v. Donaldson* (1975), discussed above, that the state cannot continue to hold a person with mental illness who no longer meets commitment criteria. *Wyatt* was much more sweeping, however, and related to the poor quality of the Alabama facilities. To remedy the problems with the hospital, the judge in *Wyatt* gave the state 6 months to establish an adequate treatment program. When the state failed to do so in a satisfactory manner, the court pursued the matter further. Thereafter, the court conducted an extensive hearing, which subsequently resulted in the parties' stipulating to a broad array of treatment conditions to provide an acceptable overall treatment program (*Wyatt*, 344 F. Supp., 1972, p. 376). The plan was very sweeping and set forth standards for patients' rights as well as providing rules and minimums for the full range of hospital conditions (Perlin, 1994, p. 178).

The patients' rights spelled out in the *Wyatt* decision touched on a variety of treatment issues. These included the right to be free from medication that is excessive or unwarranted and a right to informed consent before the use of more invasive procedures, such as electroconvulsive treatment (*Wyatt*, 344 F. Supp., 1972, p. 380). One of the most important matters spelled out in the decision was that patients should "have a right to the least restrictive conditions necessary to achieve the purposes of commitment" (*Wyatt*, 344 F. Supp., 1972, p. 379). This was not novel. For example, the court in *Lessard v. Schmidt* (1972, p. 1097) had not only discussed the need for considering a person's potential for dangerousness as part of the commitment process, it had also been critical of the state's failure to consider "less restrictive alternatives" to hospitalization. *Wyatt*, however, addressed the issue head-on by spelling out a specific right to treatment in the least restrictive alternative setting. The court also called for individualized treatment plans for patients. The decree in *Wyatt* (344 F. Supp., 1972, pp. 379-381) addressed other specific patient rights as well, including such personal liberties as the rights to vote, drive, contract, and marry, and also the right to receive compensation in exchange for any voluntary labor and certain therapeutic labor.

In sum, *Wyatt* is a judicial decision that greatly influenced the delivery of mental health services across the nation. It spurred other similar suits in a variety of states, such as *Davis v. Watkins* (1974) in Ohio and *R.A.J. v. Miller* (1984) in Texas. For example, in *Davis* the court developed standards for treatment at Ohio's Lima State Hospital that tracked much of the *Wyatt* opinion verbatim. That court also went beyond *Wyatt* in defining the least restrictive treatment setting to require "the minimum limitation of movement or activity of a patient or resident necessary to provide reasonable assurance that his [or her] dangerousness would not constitute a significant risk to others and in which treatment or habilitation continues to the fullest extent possible" (*Davis*, 1974, p. 1203). Similarly, in *R.A.J.* the court required many of the same treatment initiatives as in *Wyatt* but also created limits on the use of the state hospital system for the placement and treatment of mentally retarded persons and persons with dual diagnoses of retardation and mental illness (*R.A.J.*, 1984, pp. 1316-1318).

Outside the court system, *Wyatt* also caused many states to overhaul their legislation relating to appropriate treatment in state facilities for persons with mental illness (Perlin, 1994). Often these legislative actions were motivated by pending lawsuits or the threat of similar litigation.

Although *Wyatt* and its progeny resulted in substantial positive changes in the delivery of treatment in state mental facilities, these changes, when coupled with more restrictive commitment laws, also resulted in a migration of patients out of the hospital setting. Critics have suggested that cases such as *Wyatt* and *O'Connor* spurred massive deinstitutionalization (Isaac & Armat, 1990). As Stone (1987) has described, the census of state mental hospitals fell by more than 80% in the years following these court decisions. Today, only a small percentage of the overall patient populations at state mental hospitals are persons who have been residents there on a long-term basis. As the state facilities began to reduce in size, the goal was for those people leaving the hospitals in need of a continuity of care to be able to obtain needed treatment in community-based mental health centers. The community-based care available did not keep up with the demand, however (Stone, 1987). Because of the smaller census in the state facilities, states spent less money on these facilities, but often these cost "savings" did not follow patients back into the community. Stone (1987) and Torrey (1988a) have addressed how the combination of deinstitutionalization and the lack of adequate community care have resulted in large numbers of homeless mentally ill in this country who receive little if any mental health treatment.

Although *Wyatt* is representative of a number of cases asserting a right to treatment in an institutional setting, there has been far less litigation with respect to the states' responsibilities to provide care to persons with serious mental illness in the community. As a matter of federal constitutional law, "arguably, where there is no restraint of liberty through institutionalization, there is no state obligation to provide substantive services" (Spring, LaCoursiere, & Weissenberger, 1994, p. 129). As Spring et al. (1994) have described, one alternative approach to this inability to succeed with constitutional claims has been for a court to interpret state statutes broadly to mandate community-based care and treatment. Thus, in *Arnold v. Department of Health Services* (1989), a state court in Arizona gave a broad reading to that state's own laws to find that the Arizona legislature had mandated that state and county governments provide mental health care in the community to persons with chronic mental illness. Although the state legislature had appropriated insufficient funding to operate such community-based care as residential treatment and other outpatient programs, the court in *Arnold* (1989) construed the state's and counties' responsibilities under general indigent health care legislation to include obligations to provide community mental health services to indigent persons with chronic mental illness. The next generation of litigation concerning individuals' rights to treatment for serious mental illnesses should follow the lead of *Arnold* and focus on treatment needs in the community. As Stone (1987) has observed, "Full development of the wide range of community-based care is essential not only for those who will not benefit from short-term involuntary treatment, but also to take care of the treated patients when they return to the community [from the hospital]" (p. 30).

Court Decisions Regarding the "Right" to Refuse Treatment

Today's research has revealed that serious mental illnesses are generally treatable diseases of the brain. Often, the primary treatment involves the administration of psychotropic medications. Although many patients are helped substantially by these drugs, problems can arise. Perlin (1994) has identified certain issues related to such drug treatment: Not all patients necessarily benefit from these drugs, some patients may be overmedicated for purposes of control rather than treatment, and many of these drugs have a variety of side effects. Because of such concerns, litigation has been pursued to permit patients to refuse treatment. This section largely focuses on cases involving medication. With respect to other, more intrusive treatments, such as psychosurgery, electroconvulsive therapy, and aversion conditioning, courts and legislatures have generally required some type of patient consent (Spring et al., 1989). Litigation over medication issues has been far more contentious.

As the U.S. Supreme Court discussed in a different context in *Youngberg v. Romeo* (1982), just because someone has been committed under proper procedures does not deprive that person of all substantive liberty interests. A few years earlier, in *Rennie v. Klein* (1978), a federal court determined that the "fact that the patient is dangerous in a free society may give the state power to confine, but standing alone it does not give the power to treat involuntarily" (p. 1145). In *Rennie* (1978, p. 1134), an involuntary patient at a New Jersey state mental hospital complained about various side effects from medication administered during his hospitalization. The court determined that absent an emergency situation, a patient had a constitutional right to refuse unwanted medication. Upon such a refusal, the court ruled further that some type of due process hearing would be necessary to ascertain whether the recommended medication was warranted. The court subsequently entered an additional ruling calling for an independent review of any contested medication decisions by a neutral decision maker (*Rennie,* 476 F. Supp., 1979, p. 1308). On appeal, a federal appeals panel limited the procedures required upon a patient's refusal of medication to those contained in an existing informal state policy that called for review by a facility's medical director and consultations by the treating physicians with outside medical experts (*Rennie,* 634 F.2d, 1981, pp. 848-851).

Somewhat contemporaneously with *Rennie,* in *Rogers v. Okin* (1979) a federal court in Massachusetts also held in favor of a right to refuse medication. The court in *Okin* took the view that committed patients should be presumed to be "competent to make decisions with respect to their treatment in non-emergencies" (p. 1364). On appeal, the federal court of appeals largely agreed with the trial court in *Okin* that a patient has a constitutional right to refuse the imposition of psychotropic medication, but the appeals court took the view that a qualified state physician should weigh the interests involved in deciding whether medication should be administered as part of determining a patient's competence to make treatment decisions (*Rogers v. Okin,* 634 F.2d, 1980, pp. 656-657). On the other hand, the appeals court in *Okin* appeared to treat the right to refuse medication as more absolute than did the appellate court in *Rennie.*

The Supreme Court of the United States then had an opportunity to consider an appeal of the *Okin* case in *Mills v. Rogers* (1982). In *Mills,* however, the Court did not reach the question of whether a patient has a constitutional right to refuse medication. Instead, the Court ducked the issue by remanding the case to the court of appeals for further consideration in light of a Massachusetts state case. In *In re Richard Roe III* (1981), the Supreme Court of Massachusetts had determined that a committed patient has the right to refuse medication under the provisions of the Massachusetts Constitution. A state is free to create or recognize greater liberties under its state constitution than may be available under the federal constitution (*Mills,* 1982, p. 300). Because the *Okin* case had arisen as a challenge to treatment decisions in Massachusetts, the Supreme Court in *Mills* felt constrained to remand the case for further consideration of the relevant provisions of the Massachusetts Constitution (*Mills,* 1982, p. 306). Later proceedings both in the lower federal courts and in the Supreme Court of Massachusetts resulted in determinations that patients do have a right to refuse medication and that adversarial judicial hearings are required (under Massachusetts law) for administering medication (Spring et al., 1989).

The U.S. Supreme Court has never held that there is an absolute right for an involuntary patient to refuse medication. Instead, that refusal—in a non-emergency situation—generally implicates a right to have the facility's medication decision reviewed. States have taken two approaches to these reviews. Some, like Massachusetts in light of *Okin,* have mandated judicial proceedings to determine whether an individual is incompetent to make medical treatment choices. Other states have created procedures calling for a right of review by higher-level medical authorities within the hospital, as was the case in *Rennie.* In Texas, for example, a federal court at one point upheld this type of internal review process in *R.A.J. v. Miller* (1984), but the state legislature recently changed the law to require judicial determinations of incompetence for making treatment decisions except in emergency situations.

There has been much criticism of the so-called right to refuse medication. Isaac and Brakel (1992) have posited that civil libertarian attorneys who pursued these cases were largely opposed to commitment. Accordingly, they operated under the view that if persons committed to the hospitals could not be treated, the underlying basis for their commitments would be gone. Cases and legislation creating the right to refuse treatment are indeed perplexing. A necessary underpinning of the right to refuse treatment is the belief or presumption that an individual who meets commitment criteria is still generally competent to make medical choices about treatment. If the person is truly ill enough to satisfy the commitment criteria (and is not seeking treatment voluntarily), it is questionable whether the individual can truly be in a position to give informed consent about medication. Torrey (1988b) describes one survey that found that only 13% of state hospital patients with chronic schizophrenia understood that they were mentally ill at that time. If the very reason for commitment is to get help for an ill individual, it is ironic that further proceedings may still be necessary to enable actual treatment for the person. Isaac and Brakel (1992) are more blunt in suggesting that "involuntary hospitalization without involuntary treatment is a sham, turning commitment into a police operation and hospitalization into incarceration" (p. 118). On the other hand, once a patient's illness has become stabilized by medication, there may be a greater likelihood that the person can be in a position to engage in an informed dialogue about further treatment. As more brain research is accomplished and better medications with fewer side effects are developed, perhaps the debate involving treatment choices and volatile issues concerning the refusal to take medication will be tempered.

Court Decisions Affecting the Potential Liability of Mental Health Professionals

Mental health care professionals and treatment facilities are potentially liable to patients and third parties in a variety of contexts. As in other medical fields, malpractice suits are always possible—although traditionally there have been proportionally fewer malpractice claims filed against psychiatrists than are filed against other types of physicians (Perlin, 1994). Malpractice claims against psychiatrists, other mental health professionals, or facilities may take on a variety of forms, however, and have involved such diverse matters as patient abuse or neglect, improper sexual activities, improper medication or other treatment, and proceeding improperly without informed consent (Perlin, 1994).

The potential for liability to patients because of malpractice poses genuine concerns for professionals in the mental health field, but these considerations have been somewhat overshadowed in recent years by the expansion of possible liability to third parties. Historically, professional liability was limited to matters relating to the contractual relationship between the health care professional and the patient (Reisner & Slobogin, 1990). In recent years, however, the courts have moved away from these traditional limits on professional liability to allow suits by third parties. In the past two decades, it is clearly these third-party lawsuits that have generated much discussion and debate in the area of mental health law. Spring et al. (1989) have asserted that "few areas in the mental health field are as controversial as the duty the mental health professional owes to persons outside the therapeutic relationship" (p. 195). The seminal case involving the potential of liability to third parties is *Tarasoff v. Regents of University of California* (1976).

Tarasoff involved a graduate student who killed a young woman whom he had dated at an earlier time. Some 2 months prior to the homicide, he had allegedly confided his intent to kill the young woman to his psychologist at the University of California (*Tarasoff*, 1976, p. 339). The victim's parents filed suit on a variety of legal theories, including the alleged failure on the part of the psychologist to warn them that the patient posed a risk of harm to their daughter. The court concluded that the psychologist owed a legal duty not only to his patient but also to any "would-be victim" (p. 346). The court reasoned that

> once a therapist does in fact determine, or under applicable professional standards reasonably should have determined, that a patient poses a serious danger of violence to others, he bears a duty to exercise reasonable care to protect the foreseeable victim of that danger. While the discharge of this duty of due care will necessarily vary with the facts of each case, in each instance the adequacy of the therapist's conduct must be measured against the traditional negligence standard of the rendition of reasonable care under the circumstances. (p. 345)

The decision in *Tarasoff* has had substantial impacts elsewhere. Indeed, most states that have addressed the issue have tended to accept the *Tarasoff* analysis, although a few states have rejected the approach (Reisner & Slobogin, 1990). In addition, the legislatures in several states have enacted statutes placing limits on the potential liability of psychiatrists and psychologists to third parties (Reisner & Slobogin, 1990). Moreover, even those court decisions in other jurisdictions that have embraced the *Tarasoff* rule have not been unanimous in determining when the "duty to warn" should apply. For example, in *Peck v. Counseling Service of Addison County* (1985), a Vermont court broadly construed the *Tarasoff* rule to apply to all mental health professionals—not just psychiatrists or psychologists—in a case in which an outpatient burned down his parents' barn. The Vermont Supreme Court determined that the local mental health center that was providing the outpatient's care owed a duty to warn the parents about the patient's threats to burn down their barn. Thus *Peck* represents an extension of the reach of *Tarasoff*. On the other hand, a number of other courts have tended to limit the reach of *Tarasoff* (Perlin, 1994). For example, in *Brady v. Hopper* (1983), a federal court took the view that no duty to warn arises unless a patient's threats have been directed at a specific and identified victim. The *Brady* case involved a suit by three individuals wounded by John W. Hinckley, Jr., in his attempt to assassinate President Reagan. The suit was brought against Hinckley's psychiatrist for failure to warn. Significantly, the *Brady* court relied on a California case that had arisen after *Tarasoff* in which the California court appeared to retreat from some of its language in *Tarasoff*. In *Thompson v. County of Alameda* (1980), the California Supreme Court had declined to apply *Tarasoff* to a situation in which a patient had made generalized threats regarding an intent to kill but had not made any specific threats concerning any specific individual. Although the patient indeed killed a young boy after being released, the court did not impose liability for failure to warn because of the lack of threats to any specific victim.

What is the impact of *Tarasoff* and its progeny on treatment? Some of the impact could be adverse. Perlin (1992) has discussed concerns that hospitals may be used simply to detain potentially dangerous persons out of the fear of potential liability, not to treat persons with serious mental illness. On the other hand, the requirement to warn a potential third-party victim might be a matter that could be discussed with the patient in a beneficial manner—in the event a specific threat has been made. For example, Perlin (1992) has collected studies demonstrating that warnings that were discussed with patients have had positive results, but warnings not discussed with patients have tended to be therapeutically harmful. Moreover, a warning to a third person in the event of a specific threat about a specific victim could be the only plausible way to avoid grave danger. Clearly, these issues cannot be successfully resolved in this short space. Without doubt, however, *Tarasoff* and related cases have generated substantial controversy, study, and analysis. There has also been a great deal of confusion about the extent of the doctrine given the various approaches taken by different states across the country. Certainly, this line of cases has provided a real impact on mental health professionals with respect to important considerations in the evaluation and treatment of patients who make specific negative threats, and will no doubt continue to do so.

Court Decisions Involving Persons With Mental Illness and the Criminal Law

The Problem

A recent survey of the nation's 3,000-plus jails by the National Alliance for the Mentally Ill and Public Citizen's Health Research Group revealed that 7.2% of the inmates in the 1,391 jails that responded to the survey suffer from serious mental illness (Torrey et al., 1992). This suggests that many individuals who are suffering from serious mental illness have treatment needs within jail or prison. One analysis has suggested that although "prisons and jails were not created to be mental hospitals . . . , because of the failure of public psychiatric services, prisons and jails have become *de facto* shelters of last resort for psychiatrically ill individuals" (Torrey, Erdman, Wolfe, & Flynn, 1990, p. 6). The Texas Criminal Justice Policy Council (1993) has theorized as follows:

> A deinstitutionalization of state psychiatric hospitals and hospitals for the mentally ill and mentally retarded occurred in Texas in the 1980s. However, community resources did not keep pace with the needs of the deinstitutionalized population, leaving a significant population of mentally impaired clients with unmet residential and service needs. Many of these clients ended up in the criminal justice system because of these unmet needs. (p. 1)

Are these individuals being caught up in the criminal justice system solely because of culpable conduct? The authors of the recent survey of the nation's jails conclude that the vast majority of crimes committed by persons with serious mental illness *"are trivial misdemeanors that are often just manifestations of mental illness*" (Torrey et al., 1992, p. iv). The survey also reveals that even in cases involving far more serious offenses, often the perpetrators' mental illness has not been treated (Torrey et al., 1992). These authors also observe that although the vast majority of seriously mentally ill persons in jail are not dangerous, "it is also clear . . . that a *small number* of seriously mentally ill persons, *if not treated for their illness,* do become dangerous, may commit serious crimes, and usually end up in jail" (p. 85). Thus treatment initiatives should be pursued not only as a response to medical needs but also to avoid the potential for danger to the community.

Competence to Stand Trial

Under our legal system, a criminal defendant must be able to understand the proceedings that are being conducted against him or her, or may not undergo trial. The U.S. Supreme Court has determined that a person is incompetent to stand trial for the charged offense if he or she either (a) cannot communicate with his or her lawyer with a reasonable degree of rational understanding, or (b) does not have a rational and factual understanding of the ongoing proceedings at that time (*Drope v. Missouri,* 1975).

A finding that a person is incompetent to stand trial is not a defense to the crime charged. Instead, such a finding generally permits the state to provide treatment to the defendant, with the goal of restoring the individual's competence to stand trial. The Supreme Court has condemned indefinite criminal commitments but has authorized commitments for reasonable periods to ascertain whether affected defendants can attain the necessary competence (*Jackson v. Indiana,* 1972). Many jurisdictions, however, still authorize virtually indefinite commitments upon findings of continuing incompetence to stand trial (Perlin, 1994).

A criminal conviction should not stand if indeed the defendant was truly incompetent to stand trial at the time the trial proceeded (*Morales v. State,* 1979). Most criminal convictions are the result of guilty pleas, but if a defendant is incompetent to stand trial, that defendant is also incompetent to plead guilty to an offense (*Ex parte Lewis,* 1979). It would be inconsistent to suggest that a defendant can understand the ramifications of a guilty plea if that defendant is truly incompetent and, accordingly, unable to understand the proceedings against him or her. Although the Supreme Court has recently held that the general competence standard for pleading guilty is no higher than the competence required for standing trial, the Court acknowledged that a defendant must knowingly and voluntarily enter any guilty plea (*Godinez v. Moran,* 1993, pp. 2687-2688). Finally, even if a defendant is truly incompetent, due process of law may require that he or she be permitted to proceed to trial on the underlying offense if necessary as part of the defendant's efforts to prove the insanity defense (*Riggins v. Nevada,* 1992). A defendant (and his or her counsel) may desire to have the jury observe the defendant while not stabilized on psychotropic medication to better enable the jury to consider the defendant's likely mental state at the time of the offense (which is the requisite time frame for consideration of the standards for the insanity defense).

The Insanity Defense

The insanity defense is the second major aspect of criminal law that an offender with mental illness may encounter. Unlike a determination of incompetence, successful proof of a plea of insanity is a defense to the crime charged. Contrary to popular myth, in most jurisdictions the insanity defense is quite narrow in scope and seldom successfully invoked (Perlin, 1994). There was much public outcry after a jury found John Hinckley not guilty by reason of insanity of the attempted assassination of President Reagan. Thereafter, most jurisdictions narrowed their insanity defense. For example, in Texas the defendant has the burden of demonstrating that "as a result of severe mental disease or defect, [the defendant] did not know that his [or her] conduct was wrong" (Texas Penal Code Ann. § 8.01[a], 1994). This right/wrong test is very limited.

Another common misconception is that a finding of not guilty by reason of insanity results in the automatic freeing of the defendant. Instead, most jurisdictions impose some type of commitment requirement on such a defendant. Treatment rights have traditionally been limited in such situations (Perlin, 1994). The U.S. Supreme Court, however, has held that the state may not continue to keep an insanity acquittee who is not mentally ill in a forensic treatment facility (*Foucha v. Louisiana,* 1992). Presumably, then, there are limits to continued commitment of an insanity acquittee once the individual no longer meets the general criteria for an inpatient commitment.

Because of the narrow scope of the insanity defense, many persons who suffer from serious mental illness are convicted of crimes and sent to jail or prison. Treatment issues then become a part of the province of the corrections system. Some courts have mandated that mental health treatment be afforded to prisoners who suffer from serious mental illness (Perlin, 1994).

Diversion of Offenders

Some jurisdictions are also considering methods to divert persons with serious mental illness into more appropriate treatment settings. For example, legislation was enacted in Texas in 1993 in an attempt to divert persons with mental illness charged with nonviolent offenses out of the jail setting and into treatment facilities pending further criminal proceedings (Shannon & Benson, 1994). The legislation also permits a judge to impose a mental health treatment condition as part of the probating of a mentally ill offender's sentence. The official analysis that accompanied the bill declared that there is

> grave injustice that is visited on those who are mentally ill . . . and who are in need of medical care. Regardless of guilt or innocence, these citizens should be provided appropriate care. The system of justice may proceed with the procedure that is called for; but, the health care issue is to be addressed if we are to act as a civilized society. (House Committee on Criminal Jurisprudence, 1993)

This diversion legislation should afford a better means of providing treatment than under former law.

Court Decisions Affecting Insurance for
Persons With Mental Illness

The Problem

Because of a lack of health insurance or inadequate insurance, millions of Americans do not have coverage against serious mental illnesses. These persons generally must obtain mental health services through the public sector. The relative availability of resources can have an impact on the services received. Some persons suffering from serious mental illness are insured, however. Several court decisions in the past few years have raised issues concerning the scope and breadth of the coverage afforded by these policies. Although the 1994 efforts of the Clinton administration concerning health care reform included various provisions for mental health coverage, the failure of the various proposals resulted in the maintenance of the status quo. Thus an examination of these judicial opinions is still highly relevant.

Discrimination by Insurers

As described by William Wilson in Chapter 6 of this volume, recent neuroscientific research has revealed that serious mental illnesses such as schizophrenia, bipolar affective disorder, and depressive illness are neurobiological diseases of the brain. Despite the overwhelming findings in the medical community that serious mental illnesses are in fact organic diseases of the brain, health insurance policies tend to treat these illnesses differently from other physical ailments. In contrast to much more extensive coverage for most medical disorders, insurance policies generally restrict coverage for mental illnesses "to a limited number of days of hospitalization and a dollar ceiling on outpatient treatment" (Appelbaum, 1989, p. 993). These restrictions on coverage for mental illnesses include such measures as

> capping benefits at arbitrary, and often very low levels, on a per-treatment basis, an annual basis or through lifetime limits; requiring insureds to pay a high deductible, i.e., to make a major out-of-pocket investment before services are reimbursed; [and] requiring high co-payments by policyholders, e.g., limiting reimbursement to 50% of actual costs. (O'Keefe, 1991, pp. 13-14)

What accounts for this disparity in coverage? Stigma certainly represents part of the problem. Many members of the public and the insurance industry still view individuals with mental illness as being the cause of their own mental problems—that they should be able to overcome mental illness simply by trying to do so. As one medical commentator has observed, "Stigma is reflected in the attitudes of payers who view mentally ill individuals as bringing on their own anxiety states . . . [or] depressions" (Sharfstein, 1991, p. 453). Another writer has commented that "it probably will still take years before people with mental illnesses are treated with the same degree of compassion—and insurance protection—as are victims of . . . heart disease or cancer" (Findlay, 1991, p. 49).

Another basis for the current limits on coverage for mental illness relates to the nature of what is being covered. A typical policy may provide benefits for "mental health" coverage or for "mental/nervous disorders" without further definition of what is intended to be covered by the clause. Rubin (1991) has noted that these vague, undefined terms lend themselves to ambiguity about what conditions or treatments are covered by such limitations. These types of clauses can (and do) cover a broad spectrum of problems. Insurers have generated confusion by including serious mental illnesses that are neurobiological disorders along with all other mental, emotional, and behavioral problems under policy limitations that employ broad rubrics such as "mental health" or "mental/nervous disorders."

Judicial Challenges to Insurance Limits on Coverage for Mental Illness

In recent years several courts have considered challenges to insurance policies that discriminate against serious mental illnesses. The challenges have met with mixed results, however. In several cases challengers to insurance limitations for mental health coverage have succeeded in persuading the courts to focus on the causes of the illnesses or conditions involved. In other cases, the courts have instead accepted insurers' arguments that the manifestations or symptoms of the illnesses involved are more critical than the origins of the problems for determining insurance coverage.

Advocates for persons suffering from serious mental illness achieved a significant judicial victory in *Arkansas Blue Cross & Blue Shield, Inc. v. Doe* (1987). In *Doe,* the insured's daughter suffered from bipolar affective disorder, and she underwent hospitalization and other treatment. The Blue Cross policy provided only limited benefits for "mental, psychiatric, or nervous conditions." After Blue Cross paid only for these limited benefits upon describing the bipolar disorder as a mental condition, the insured sued for recovery of the full benefits set forth in the policy for illnesses of a physical nature. The Arkansas Court of Appeals upheld the trial court's finding that the patient's illness was actually a physical condition under the policy. At the trial, one of the insured's experts had testified that the medical research identifying bipolar affective disorder as a physical illness is overwhelming. *Doe* represents the first judicial recognition that bipolar affective disorder, one of the serious mental illnesses, is actually a physical illness of the brain. A subsequent decision by a Florida court is in accord with *Doe* and determined that "reasonable persons could find that Bipolar Affective Disorder is a physical illness which manifests itself through mental symptoms, such that the medical expenses incurred . . . are not limited by the limitations clause of the policy" (*Rosenthal v. Mutual Life Insurance Co.,* 1990, pp. 110-111).

Similar challenges have also been successful with respect to a few other illnesses. In *Kunin v. Benefit Trust Life Insurance Co.* (1990), an insured sued for reimbursement for the treatment of his son's autism. The insurer paid only the $10,000 policy limit for "mental illness or nervous disorders." The insured offered expert testimony from psychiatrists that the term *mental illness* refers to "a behavioral disturbance with no demonstrable organic or physical basis" (*Kunin,* 1990, p. 536) and that autism falls outside that definition of mental illness. The court determined that the term *mental illness* as used in the policy was ambiguous and construed the ambiguity against the insurance company. Accordingly, the court upheld the decision that the insurer had to pay in full for the treatment for autism—accepting the construction that autism is not a mental illness for purposes of the policy in question. Another court set forth a similar analysis in finding that a policy providing for lower benefits for "mental illness" did not apply to the treatment of organic brain syndrome, a disease classified by the American Psychiatric Association as a mental disorder (*Phillips v. Lincoln National Life Insurance Co.,* 1991).

Cases such as those described above reflect judicial receptivity to arguments about the physical origins or causes of the diseases in question. Upon finding the various illnesses at issue in those cases to be physical in origin, those courts have refused to find applicable the insurance policies' limits for mental health coverage. On the other hand, other recent court challenges of insurance policy limits for mental illness have proven to be unsuccessful. For example, in *Equitable Life Assurance Society v. Berry* (1989), the insured became totally disabled from his occupation as a result of bipolar affective disorder. Although Berry's employer provided both medical insurance and long-term disability coverage, both policies were limited with respect to coverage for mental illness. Similar to the insured in *Doe,* Berry asserted that he had a physical illness, not a mental disorder, and that the coverage limitations for "mental/nervous" disorders in his policies should not apply to him. The California court declined to follow the lead of *Doe* and rejected focusing on the cause of a person's illness to determine whether the illness falls within an insurance policy's exclusion or limitation for mental illness coverage. Instead, the court opined that "manifestation, not cause, is the yardstick" (*Berry,* 1989, p. 824) for determining whether a person's disorder is to be considered as a mental illness for purposes of an insurance policy. Because Berry's symptoms included delusions and hallucinations, the court concluded that "every reasonable layman would view a person manifesting such derangement as suffering from a mental disease" (p. 824) excluded from coverage. Accordingly, the court reasoned that the policy excluded any mental disease, regardless of the cause.

Similarly, a federal court has rejected arguments that affective mood disorder, another biologically based mental illness, should not be subject to an insurance policy's limits for mental disorders. Like the California court in *Berry,* in *Brewer v. Lincoln National Life Insurance Co.* (1990), the court focused on the symptoms of the mental illness, rather than its causes. The court reasoned that it should construe the terms of an insurance contract according to ordinary laypersons' understandings and rejected the approach taken in *Kunin.* Accordingly, the *Brewer* court postulated that because laypersons are inclined to focus on the symptoms of an illness, an illness whose primary symptoms include "depression, mood swings and unusual behavior" would be "commonly characterized as mental illnesses [by laypersons] regardless of their cause" (*Brewer*, 1990, p. 154). One problem with this "layperson's understanding of symptoms" approach is that the average layperson's understanding should be constantly changing with advances in medical research. As the public learns more and more about the actual causes of and treatments for mental illness, it follows that the average layperson's understanding about the meaning of the term *mental illness* will change as well.

Despite the few successes that challengers to limitations of coverage for mental illness have enjoyed in the courts, judicial victories may result in only short-term benefits for persons suffering from serious mental illnesses. In Arkansas, for example, when the time came for renewal of policies following the decision in *Doe*, Arkansas Blue Cross & Blue Shield simply revised its exclusionary language to limit coverage for psychiatric illnesses "whether organic or non-organic, whether of biological, non-biological, chemical or non-chemical origin, and irrespective of cause, basis or inducement" (Appelbaum, 1989, p. 994). Thus insurers may simply react to adverse judicial decrees by amending their policies to ensure continued discrimination against persons suffering from serious mental illnesses.

A Need for Legislation?

As I have argued elsewhere, to avoid the problem of insurers' simply amending their policies, there is likely a need for legislative limitations on this form of discrimination. Certain states, such as California, Maine, and Texas, have made progress in that direction (Shannon, 1993). The U.S. Supreme Court has upheld the states' right to impose mandates for mental illness coverage on insurers (*Metropolitan Life Insurance Co. v. Massachusetts*, 1985). On the other hand, the Supreme Court has indicated that the Employee Retirement Income Security Act of 1974 preempts the ability of the states to impose similar mandates on fully self-insured employee benefit plans. Accordingly, state coverage mandates will likely not reach a number of employees because their employers have chosen to self-insure. Whether the same conditions will be covered by the fully self-insured plans will be up to those plans themselves. Moreover, the number of self-insured firms is growing, and one factor for this growth has been an attempt to escape minimum benefit laws (Frank, 1989). Accordingly, additional federal legislation may be required to eliminate this discrimination.

Conclusion

This chapter has focused on certain significant legal decisions and their impacts on mental health policy and services with regard to the civil commitment process, individuals' rights regarding treatment and the refusal of treatment, the potential for liability by a mental health professional in the rendering of services, the interplay between the criminal justice process and offenders with mental illnesses, and the extent to which private insurance has limited coverage for serious mental illnesses. My intent in this chapter has been to introduce the reader to some of these difficult, and often controversial, legal topics. This is by no means an exhaustive study of these issues.

Medical science has made great advances in the past decade in discovering many of the mysteries of the brain, including the identification of organic bases for a variety of serious mental illnesses. Indeed, the medical world generally recognizes illnesses such as schizophrenia, bipolar disorder, and severe depressive illness as biologically based diseases of the brain. The law, however, is largely retrospective in its analysis of issues. Courts often make decisions based on earlier judicial precedents and legal and medical scholarship that may be quite dated. Accordingly, judicial decisions of today may be premised on medical learning that is years or decades old. For example, Isaac and Armat (1990, pp. 19-64) have postulated that largely abandoned and discredited ideas about mental illness pursued by so-called antipsychiatrists such as Thomas Szasz and R. D. Laing in the 1960s have influenced today's legal concepts about mental illness. Modern psychiatry has certainly rejected such theories. As greater knowledge is acquired about the diagnosis and treatment of serious mental illness, the courts and judicial system will eventually catch up. Unfortunately, however, there is often a time lag between medical learning and judicial acceptance of new developments. As old stigmas and inaccurate assessments of serious mental illnesses as somehow not being real diseases fade away, the courts and advocates will likely become more attuned to appropriate treatment needs.

References

Addington v. Texas, 441 U.S. 418 (1979).

Appelbaum, P. S. (1989). Litigating insurance coverage for mental disorders. *Hospital and Community Psychiatry, 40,* 993-994.

Arkansas Blue Cross & Blue Shield, Inc. v. Doe, 733 S.W.2d 429 (Ark. App. 1987) (en banc).

Arnold v. Department of Health Services, 775 P.2d 521 (Ariz. 1989).

Brady v. Hopper, 570 F. Supp. 1333 (D. Col. 1983), *aff'd,* 751 F.2d 329 (10th Cir. 1984).

Brewer v. Lincoln National Life Insurance Co., 921 F.2d 150 (8th Cir. 1990), *cert. denied,* 111 S. Ct. 2872 (1991).

Brooks, A. (1989). Notes on defining the "dangerousness" of the mentally ill. In R. L. Spring, R. B. LaCoursiere, & G. Weissenberger (Eds.), *Patients, psychiatrists and lawyers: Law and the mental health system* (pp. 248-257). Cincinnati: Anderson.

Davis v. Watkins, 384 F. Supp. 1196 (N.D. Ohio 1974).

Drope v. Missouri, 420 U.S. 162 (1975).

Employee Retirement Income Security Act of 1974, 29 U.S.C. §§ 1001-1461 (1988).

Equitable Life Assurance Society v. Berry, 260 Cal. Rptr. 819 (Cal. Ct. App. 1989).

Ex parte Lewis, 587 S.W.2d 697 (Tex. Crim. App. [Panel Op.] 1979).

Findlay, S. (1991, August 5). The revolution in psychiatric care. *U.S. News & World Report,* p. 49.

Foucha v. Louisiana, 112 S. Ct. 1780 (1992).

Frank, R. G. (1989). Regulatory responses to information deficiencies in the market for mental health services. In C. A. Taube, D. Mechanic, & A. A. Hohmann (Eds.), *The future of mental health services research* (DHHS Publication No. ADM 89-1600, pp. 113-137). Rockville, MD: U.S. Department of Health and Human Services, Public Health Service.

Godinez v. Moran, 113 S. Ct. 2680 (1993).

House Committee on Criminal Jurisprudence, Bill Analysis, Tex. H.B. 1605, 73rd Leg., Reg. Sess. (1993).

In re Oakes, 8 Law Rep. 123 (1845-1846).

In re Richard Roe III, 421 N.E.2d 40 (Mass. 1981).

Isaac, R. J., & Armat, V. C. (1990). *Madness in the streets: How psychiatry and the law abandoned the mentally ill.* New York: Macmillan.

Isaac, R. J., & Brakel, S. J. (1992). Subverting good intentions: A brief history of mental health law "reform." *Cornell Journal of Law and Public Policy, 2,* 89-119.

Jackson v. Indiana, 406 U.S. 715 (1972).

Kunin v. Benefit Trust Life Insurance Co., 910 F.2d 534 (9th Cir.), *cert. denied,* 111 S. Ct. 581 (1990).

Lessard v. Schmidt, 349 F. Supp. 1078 (E.D. Wis. 1972), *vacated and remanded,* 414 U.S. 473 (1974), *on remand,* 379 F. Supp. 1376 (E.D. Wis. 1974), *vacated and remanded,* 421 U.S. 957 (1975), *reinstated,* 413 F. Supp. 1318 (E.D. Wis. 1976).

Lynch v. Baxley, 386 F. Supp. 378 (M.D. Ala. 1974).

Metropolitan Life Insurance Co. v. Massachusetts, 471 U.S. 724 (1985).

Mills v. Rogers, 457 U.S. 291 (1982).

Morales v. State, 587 S.W.2d 418 (Tex. Crim. App. [Panel Op.] 1979).

O'Connor v. Donaldson, 422 U.S. 563 (1975).

O'Keefe, A. M. (1991). *Advocating for insurance reform.* Washington, DC: National Alliance for the Mentally Ill.

Peck v. Counseling Service of Addison County, 499 A.2d 422 (Vt. 1985).

Perlin, M. L. (1992). Tarasoff and the dilemma of the dangerous patient: New directions for the 1990's. *Law and Psychology Review, 16,* 14-63.

Perlin, M. L. (1994). *Law and mental disability.* Charlottesville, VA: Michie.

Phillips v. Lincoln National Life Insurance Co., 774 F. Supp. 495 (N.D. Ill. 1991), *aff'd,* 978 F.2d 302 (7th Cir. 1992).

R.A.J. v. Miller, 590 F. Supp. 1310 (N.D. Tex. 1984).

Reisner, R., & Slobogin, C. (Eds.). (1990). *Law and the mental health system: Civil and criminal aspects* (2nd ed.). St. Paul, MN: West.

Rennie v. Klein, 462 F. Supp. 1131 (D.N.J. 1978), *suppl.,* 476 F. Supp. 1294 (D.N.J. 1979), *modified,* 653 F.2d 836 (3d Cir. 1981), *vacated and remanded,* 458 U.S. 1119 (1982), *on remand,* 720 F.2d 266 (3d Cir. 1983).

Riggins v. Nevada, 112 S. Ct. 1810 (1992).

Rogers v. Okin, 478 F. Supp. 1342 (D. Mass. 1979), *modified,* 634 F.2d 650 (1st Cir. 1980), *vacated sub nom.,* Mills v. Rogers, 457 U.S. 291 (1982), *on remand,* 738 F.2d 1 (1st Cir. 1984).

Rosenthal v. Mutual Life Insurance Co., 732 F. Supp. 108 (S.D. Fla. 1990).

Rubin, J. (1991). Financing mental health care. *Houston Law Review, 28,* 143-173.

Shannon, B. D. (1993). The brain gets sick, too: The case for equal insurance coverage for serious mental illness. *St. Mary's Law Journal, 24,* 365-398.

Shannon, B. D., & Benson, D. H. (1994). *Texas criminal procedure and the offender with mental illness.* Austin: Texas Alliance for the Mentally Ill.

Sharfstein, S. S. (1991). Articulating the case for equitable mental health coverage. *Hospital and Community Psychiatry, 42,* 453.

Spring, R. L., LaCoursiere, R. B., & Weissenberger, G. (Eds.). (1989). *Patients, psychiatrists and lawyers: Law and the mental health system.* Cincinnati: Anderson.

Spring, R. L., LaCoursiere, R. B., & Weissenberger, G. (Eds.). (1994). *Patients, psychiatrists and lawyers: Law and the mental health system 1994/95 supplement.* Cincinnati: Anderson.

State ex rel Hawks v. Lazaro, 202 S.E.2d 109 (W. Va. 1974).

Stone, A. A. (1987, June 3). Civil rights for mentally ill must be redefined. *Wall Street Journal,* p. 30.

Tarasoff v. Regents of University of California, 551 P.2d 334 (Cal. 1976).

Texas Criminal Justice Policy Council. (1993). *Mentally retarded and mentally ill criminal offenders: Effectiveness of community intervention programs.* Austin: Author.

Texas Department of Mental Health and Mental Retardation v. Petty, 848 S.W.2d 680 (Tex. 1992).

Texas Penal Code Ann. § 8.01(a) (Vernon Supp. 1994).

Thompson v. County of Alameda, 614 P.2d 728 (Cal. 1980).

Torrey, E. F. (1988a). *Nowhere to go: The tragic odyssey of the homeless mentally ill*. New York: Harper & Row.

Torrey, E. F. (1988b). *Surviving schizophrenia: A family manual* (Rev. ed.). New York: Harper & Row.

Torrey, E. F., Erdman, K., Wolfe, S. M., & Flynn, L. M. (1990). *Care of the seriously mentally ill: A rating of state programs* (3rd ed.). Washington, DC: Public Citizen's Health Research Group and National Alliance for the Mentally Ill.

Torrey, E. F., Steiber, J., Ezekiel, J., Wolfe, S. M., Sharfstein, J., Noble, J. H., & Flynn, L. M. (1992). *Criminalizing the seriously mentally ill*. Washington, DC: National Alliance for the Mentally Ill and Public Citizen's Health Research Group.

Wyatt v. Stickney, 325 F. Supp. 781 (M.D. Ala. 1971), 334 F. Supp. 1341 (M.D. Ala. 1972), 344 F. Supp. 373 (M.D. Ala. 1972), 344 F. Supp. 387 (M.D. Ala. 1972), *aff'd sub nom.,* Wyatt v. Aderholt, 503 F.2d 1305 (5th Cir. 1974).

Youngberg v. Romeo, 457 U.S. 307 (1982).

CHAPTER 5

Personnel

The Professionals and Their Preparation

James W. Callicutt

David H. Price

This chapter focuses on the traditionally recognized core mental health professions: psychiatry, nursing, psychology, and social work. Other important patient care professions involved in the provision of mental health services have been clearly acknowledged. For example, *Mental Health, United States, 1992* contains a section on developing areas of practice that includes discussions of marriage and family therapy, clinical mental health counseling, and psychosocial rehabilitation (Dial et al., 1992). In this chapter, we will discuss staffing in mental health organizations (emphasizing the core professions), followed by overviews of social work, mental health nursing, psychiatry, and psychology.

Staffing

As shown in Table 5.1, among the core mental health professions, registered nurses are most numerous (77,635), followed by social workers (53,375), psychologists (22,825), and psychiatrists (18,181). Each of these professional groups showed numerical increases over the times reported in the table—that is, 1972, 1978, 1986, 1988, and 1990. Whereas all staff positions increased by 50% from 1972 to 1990, professional patient care staff expanded by 170%.

Table 5.1 Number and Percentage Distribution of Full-Time Equivalent Staff in All Mental Health Organizations, by Staff Discipline: United States, Selected Years, 1972–1990

Staff Discipline	1972	1978[a]	1986[b]	1988	1990
Number of FTE Staff					
All staff	375,984	430,051	494,515	531,072	563,619
Patient care staff	241,265	292,699	346,630	381,216	415,719
Professional patient care staff	100,886	153,598	232,481	248,430	273,374
Psychiatrists	12,938	14,492	17,874	18,132	18,181
Other physicians	3,991	3,034	3,868	3,959	3,865
Psychologists[c]	9,443	16,501	20,210	23,131	22,825
Social workers	17,687	28,125	40,951	46,218	53,375
Registered nurses	31,110	42,399	66,180	73,387	77,635
Other mental health professionals (B.A. and above)	17,514	39,363	56,245	71,148	84,071
Physical health professionals and assistants	8,203	9,684	27,153	12,455	12,785
Other mental health workers (less than B.A.)	140,379	139,101	114,149	132,786	142,345
Administrative, clerical, and maintenance staff	134,719	137,352	147,885	149,856	147,900
Percentage Distribution of FTE Staff					
All staff	100.0	100.0	100.0	100.0	100.0
Patient care staff	64.2	68.1	70.1	71.8	73.8
Professional patient care staff	26.9	35.8	47.0	46.8	48.5
Psychiatrists	3.4	3.4	3.5	3.4	3.3
Other physicians	1.1	0.7	0.8	0.8	0.7
Psychologists[c]	2.5	3.8	4.1	4.4	4.0
Social workers	4.7	6.5	8.3	8.7	9.5
Registered nurses	8.3	9.9	13.4	13.8	13.8
Other mental health professionals (B.A. and above)	4.7	9.2	11.4	13.4	14.9
Physical health professionals and assistants	2.2	2.3	5.5	2.3	2.3
Other mental health workers (less than B.A.)	37.3	32.3	23.1	25.0	25.3

SOURCE: Reprinted from Redick et al. (1994, p. 107). Published and unpublished inventory data from the Survey and Analysis Branch, Division of State and Community Systems Development, Center for Mental Health Services.
NOTE: The computation of full-time equivalent staff is based on a 40-hour workweek.
a. Includes data for CMHCs in 1978. In 1986, 1988, and 1990, these staff are subsumed under other organization types. Data for CMHCs are not shown separately.
b. For 1986, some organizations had been reclassified as a result of changes in reporting procedures and definitions.
c. For 1972–1978, this category included all psychologists with B.A. degrees and above; for 1986–1990, it included only psychologists with M.A. degrees and above.

Thus the increase in professional patient care staff accounted for nearly 92% of the increase in all full-time equivalent (FTE) staff for the 18-year period.

Although it is important to consider the overall picture, it is revealing to look at the disaggregated data in terms of the four professional groups in staffing specific categories of mental health organizations, as reported by Redick, Witkin, Atay, and Manderscheid (1994). Relative to state and county mental hospitals, full-time equivalent staff showed consistent decreases from 223,886 in 1972 to 175,566 in 1990. Similarly, all patient care staff declined from 138,307 to 114,198. However, counter to these trends, the number of *professional* patient care staff rose from 38,516 in 1972 to 50,035 in 1990. Psychiatrists decreased from 4,389 to 3,849, psychologists increased from 2,484 to 3,324, registered nurses expanded from 13,353 to 20,848, and social workers increased from 5,324 to 7,013. Registered nurses are the largest professional patient care staff category for both all mental health organizations and state and county hospital settings, followed in order by social workers, psychologists, and psychiatrists. Generally, this order applies to staffing arrangements in most of the mental health organizations providing inpatient and residential programs. However, there are some types of mental health organizations in which staffing by the four professions diverges markedly from the general pattern.

In nonfederal general hospitals, psychiatrists outnumber psychologists 6,500 to 3,951; in addition, there are 7,241 social workers and 28,473 registered nurses in these settings (Redick et al., 1994). In Department of Veterans Affairs medical centers there are more psychiatrists (2,103) than social workers (1,855) or psychologists (1,476), but not registered nurses (5,888) (Redick et al., 1994). Yet a different professional staffing arrangement is seen in residential treatment centers for emotionally disturbed children, freestanding outpatient psychiatric clinics, and freestanding partial care and multiservice mental health organizations. In each of these three types of organizations, social workers are the dominant professionals, numerically followed by psychologists. Psychiatrists are third in number in freestanding outpatient psychiatric clinics, followed by registered nurses. Social workers (22,978) and psychologists (8,692) were followed by registered nurses (6,053) and then psychiatrists (3,600) in freestanding partial care and multiservice mental health organizations in 1990 (Redick et al., 1994). This last type of mental health organization includes community mental health centers (CMHCs) unless they are part of either a private psychiatric hospital or a general hospital.

Next we turn to presenting an overview of the professions of social work, mental health nursing, psychiatry, and psychology. The overview of each of these professions presents information regarding professional degrees, accreditation of degree programs, curriculum content areas, characteristics of students, attention to specialization in the mental health arena, and delineation of roles and professional functions.

Social Work

Social work education includes degree programs at the baccalaureate, master's, and doctoral levels. In 1993, there were 356 accredited baccalaureate programs with 32 in candidacy and 111 accredited master's degree programs with 8 in candidacy (Lennon, 1994); there were 53 doctoral programs.

Baccalaureate and master's programs are accredited by the Council on Social Work Education (CSWE), the national organization concerned with ensuring the quality of social work education. Doctoral programs are not accredited by the CSWE, but rather as part of the college or university's accreditation by a regional accrediting body. Bachelor's and master's programs may be accredited for a maximum period of 8 years, after which programs are reviewed for reaffirmation of accreditation.

Most of the graduate and joint (undergraduate and graduate) programs are located in institutions having enrollments of 10,000 or more students and are under public auspices (Lennon, 1994). The eastern half of the United States accounts for nearly 69% of the programs, with states in the Midwest having the highest concentration of social work education programs and faculty (Lennon, 1994).

Degree Program Emphasis and Curriculum Content Areas

Baccalaureate social work education prepares the student for beginning generalist social work practice, master's programs prepare the student for advanced social work practice, and doctoral programs emphasize preparation for academic and research careers, although some focus on clinical or administrative and community practice.

The master's curriculum provides a professional foundation in the first year of the traditional two academic years of full-time study. The second-year curriculum may provide a concentration organized around fields of practice, populations at risk, problem areas, and intervention methods or roles (Council on Social Work Education, 1994). Table 5.2 displays the number of master's degree students enrolled on November 1, 1993, by primary field of practice or social problem concentration. The mental health or community mental health concentration accounted for 4,133 (12.9%) of the total of 32,020 students enrolled.

Table 5.3 shows master's degree students enrolled on November 1, 1993, as classified by primary field of practice in field instruction. As the table indicates, 16.6% of the students chose mental health or community mental health internship settings. It is reasonable to assume that for the 35.2% not yet assigned to field instruction or not in field instruction for the 1993-1994 academic year, mental health settings would be the most frequently chosen, followed by health, family service, and child welfare. It is clear that the mental health arena is a prominent area of practice concentration for students enrolled in master's degree programs in social work.

Both bachelor's and master's degree programs provide for study in the content areas of social welfare policy and services, social work methods, human behavior and the social environment, research, and field instruction involving a supervised internship. Master's programs include further emphasis on advanced practice, which may include a focus on health, child welfare, mental health, or corrections/criminal justice, among other areas.

Through curriculum design, organization, and implementation, the content areas identified above are structured to provide students with an education incorporating a synthesis of knowledge, values, and skills requisite for professional practice. These content areas may be briefly described as follows (see CSWE, 1994, the major source of these summaries):

Table 5.2 Master's Degree Students Enrolled on November 1, 1993, by Primary
Field of Practice or Social Problem Concentration

Type of Concentration	Number	Percentage
Aging/gerontological social work	670	2.1
Alcohol, drug, or substance abuse	517	1.6
Child welfare	2,172	6.8
Community planning	325	1.0
Corrections/criminal justice	183	0.6
Family services	2,600	8.1
Group services	181	0.6
Health	2,243	7.0
Occupational/industrial social work	184	0.6
Mental health or community mental health	4,133	12.9
Mental retardation	151	0.5
Public assistance/public welfare	208	0.6
Rehabilitation	94	0.3
School social work	696	2.2
Other	1,165	3.6
Combinations	331	1.0
Not yet determined	6,762	21.1
None (methods concentration only)	9,405	29.4
Total	32,020	100.0

SOURCE: Lennon (1994, p. 35). This table is from an article first published by the Council on Social Work
Education and is reprinted here with the permission of the Council on Social Work Education.
NOTE: Column totals may not correspond among tables within this report due to variance in response rates.

- *Social welfare policy and services:* This area includes a historical perspective on social work and social welfare, including the philosophy and mission of social work. It covers perspectives on minorities, women, and at-risk populations; knowledge of analytic models and development of skills in analyzing policies; and political and organizational factors involved in the process of policy formulation.

- *Social work practice:* This area encompasses learning involving knowledge, values, and skills assessment that focuses on client strengths. Emphasis is placed on choosing and applying the appropriate intervention approaches with clients from differing social, cultural, racial, and other backgrounds, and with systems of all sizes, aimed at enhancing individuals' well-being.

- *Human behavior in the social environment:* This covers theories and knowledge about human development from a biopsychosocial perspective, examining the range of social systems in the human environment (e.g., families, groups, organizations, communities, and institutions). It includes content about ethical issues and values relating to theoretical approaches as well as the skills needed to evaluate theory and apply it to client situations.

- *Research:* This area of the curriculum provides an understanding and appreciation of the scientific approach to knowledge building for practice and for evaluating all aspects of service delivery. This includes quantitative and qualitative research methodologies, with attention given to ethical standards of scientific inquiry.

- *Field practicum:* The practicum engages the student in supervised practice, emphasizing educational goals and structured learning opportunities in the process of applying classroom learning in the field setting. The focus is the integration of

Table 5.3 Master's Degree Students Enrolled on November 1, 1993, by Primary
Field of Practice in Field Instruction

Type of Concentration	Number	Percentage
Aging/gerontological social work	894	2.8
Alcohol, drug, or substance abuse	790	2.5
Child welfare	2,696	8.5
Community planning	584	1.8
Corrections/criminal justice	408	1.3
Family services	2,901	9.1
Group services	354	1.1
Health	3,125	9.9
Occupational/industrial social work	314	1.0
Mental health or community mental health	5,272	16.6
Mental retardation	288	0.9
Public assistance/public welfare	370	1.2
Rehabilitation	218	0.7
School social work	1,508	4.8
Other	812	2.6
Combinations	331	1.0
Not yet assigned field instruction	4,637	14.6
Not to be in field instruction this academic year	6,547	20.6
Total	31,718	100.0

SOURCE: Lennon (1994, p. 36). This table is from an article first published by the Council on Social Work
Education and is reprinted here with the permission of the Council on Social Work Education.
NOTE: Column totals may not correspond among tables within this report due to variance in response rates.

the knowledge, values, and skills necessary for professional social work practice.
The field practicum, a major component of social work education, requires the
completion of 900 clock hours for the master's degree.

In 1993, baccalaureate programs awarded 10,288 baccalaureate degrees.
Approximately 76% of the students receiving these degrees were white; 14%
were African American (Lennon, 1994). In 1993, there were 21,063 full-time
and 11,132 part-time students enrolled in master's programs and 1,085
full-time and 949 part-time students enrolled in doctoral programs (Lennon,
1994). During the academic year 1992–1993, programs reported that 12,583
students were awarded master's degrees and 229 were awarded doctoral
degrees (Lennon, 1994).

Faculty

According to Lennon (1994), 92.6% of all social work faculty hold the
master's degree in social work. The typical full professor on faculty at a school
of social work holds a doctorate, and a majority of full professors, associate
professors, and assistant professors who teach in graduate programs hold
doctorates. More than half the baccalaureate faculty hold the master's degree
in social work as the highest degree earned.

Women faculty members are less likely than men to hold doctoral degrees and, as a group, the women tend to be younger. Baccalaureate faculty are 2.1 years younger than their graduate faculty colleagues. African Americans have the greatest representation of all minority faculty, making up 63% of minority graduate faculty and nearly 69% of minority baccalaureate faculty.

Men are more likely to be deans and directors of programs than are women, though women hold more administrative positions. Women far outnumber men in fieldwork (80.8% at the graduate level and 72.2% at the baccalaureate level). Further, more female than male faculty members are primarily classroom teachers at all levels of social work education. Male full professors hold tenured positions at twice the rate for similarly qualified females in graduate programs. However, women's tenure posture is improving at levels below that of full professor in both graduate and baccalaureate programs.

Students

Historically, the field of social work has been predominantly composed of women (Dial et al., 1992). In 1993, more than 82% of enrolled master's students were female, and more than 83% of the master's degrees awarded were earned by females in 1992–1993 (Lennon, 1994). Almost 70% of the doctoral students enrolled in 1993 were female, with nearly 66% of doctoral degrees awarded to females in academic year 1992–1993 (Lennon, 1994).

Students enrolling in master's programs tend to come from two major sources. Many are returning for graduate study after some work experience in social work or related fields, whereas others are continuing their education directly after receiving the bachelor's degree in social work (Dial et al., 1992). Social work students bring rich, diverse backgrounds of experience, interests, and expectations.

Licensure and Certification

Social work practice is regulated in all 50 states, the District of Columbia, the Virgin Islands, and Puerto Rico (Biggerstaff, 1995). With the exception of Michigan, Hawaii, and Puerto Rico, written examinations are required for legal regulation. These tests are designed with respect to the social worker's level of education, experience, and practice setting (Biggerstaff, 1995).

In addition to legal regulation, the National Association of Social Workers (NASW) provides for five voluntary credentialing programs to "identify those social workers who demonstrate knowledge and experience beyond the entry level regulated in state laws and who meet national standards for professional practice" (Biggerstaff, 1995, p. 1618). These programs are the Academy of Certified Baccalaureate Social Workers, Diplomate in Social Work, Academy of Certified Social Workers (ACSW), Qualified Clinical Social Worker, and School Social Work Specialist.

Professional Roles and Functions

The roles and functions of social workers practicing in the mental health arena have been discussed in the context of social work methods, including direct practice with individuals (Watkins, 1983) and with families and groups (Bardill & Saunders, 1983) and community practice emphasizing administration (Kane, 1983), planning (DeMoll, 1983), and community organization (Tarail, 1983).

In the administrative area, social workers have held top appointed positions as commissioners or directors in state mental health agencies, including those for the states of Texas, Massachusetts, and South Carolina. In addition, social workers have held prominent administrative and management positions in state agencies, as executives in community mental health centers, and as superintendents at state hospitals. They often occupy important supervisory positions. Social workers also function as planners, community organizers, counselors, department heads, and case managers, and in a wide array of other roles that call on their professional knowledge, values, and skills. In addition, they may head advocacy organizations, including mental health associations. Currently, the president and chief executive officer of the National Mental Health Association is a social worker.

Nursing

Degree Program Emphasis and
Curriculum Content Areas

Nursing education includes programs conferring a diploma, associate degree, baccalaureate degree, master's degree, and doctorate. Enrollments in basic nursing education programs (diploma, associate, and baccalaureate degrees) reached a record high in 1993 for the second consecutive year, with a total of 270,228 (National League for Nursing [NLN], 1995a). However, the increases were not consistent across program categories, and there was a decline in enrollments in diploma programs as well as in the number of such programs, reflecting nursing's movement toward a degree as the minimum requirement for entry into practice (NLN, 1995a).

The number of baccalaureate nursing programs increased from 427 to 507 between 1984 and 1993. In 1993, the South region had 175, the Midwest region had 161, the North Atlantic region had 113, and the West region had 58. Among the 507 programs, 260 were public programs and 247 were private (NLN, 1995a). There were 41,290 admissions to these programs in 1993 and 110,693 students enrolled in them. Also, in 1993, there were 88,149 graduations, the highest number recorded from basic R.N. programs. Baccalaureate programs accounted for 24,442 of them.

Doctoral programs in nursing emphasize preparation for research and teaching careers. From 1991 to 1993, the number of doctoral programs held steady at 54. There were 2,754 students enrolled in them in 1993, and 381 graduations from them (NLN, 1995a).

Specialty training in psychiatric/mental health nursing takes place at the graduate level (Dial et al., 1992). In 1993 there were 252 master's programs in nursing, with the North Atlantic region taking the lead for the first time with 76 programs (NLN, 1995a). The South was second with 74. Total enrollments of 30,385 were reported, with significant increases in part-time enrollment occurring over the past 10 years (NLN, 1995a). There were 7,926 graduations from these programs (NLN, 1995a). The National League for Nursing (1995b) reports that 116 programs offer master's degrees in psychiatric/mental health nursing: 12 are offered through nurse practitioner programs, 74 through clinical nurse specialists programs, and 30 through teaching/nursing education programs.

Psychiatric nursing education at the master's level "focuses on knowledge about mental disorders and the development of advanced practice skills, such as psychotherapy, psychoeducation, and psychosocial rehabilitation" (Dial et al., 1992, p. 147). Content areas judged as important include psychopharmacology, psychopathology, neuropathology, and individual, family, and group therapy (Fox & Chamberlain, 1988; cited in Dial et al., 1992).

The nursing content area specialization of psychiatric/mental health produced 64 graduations from nurse practitioner programs, 404 graduations from advanced clinical practice programs, and 54 from teaching programs at the master's level in 1993, for a total of 522, representing almost 6.6% of the number of graduations from master's programs (NLN, 1995a). The nursing content area of adult health/medical-surgical claims the largest numbers of graduations from advanced clinical practice and teaching programs, and the content area of family (not a category listed in the other two program types) has the highest numbers from nurse practitioner programs (NLN, 1995a).

Among the estimated 7,926 master's graduates in 1993, 6,776 were white, 440 black, 158 Hispanic, 262 Asian, 40 American Indian, and 250 unknown, a total of 900 identified minorities, or 11.4% (NLN, 1995a). Reports provided by 194 master's programs (excluding American Samoa, Guam, Puerto Rico, and the Virgin Islands) show there were 6,798 total graduations, with 346 of the graduates male (5.1%) (NLN, 1995a).

Faculty

According to the *Nursing Data Review, 1994* (NLN, 1994), nurse educators are highly credentialed in terms of academic degrees. The majority of nurse faculty hold master's degrees, but it is noteworthy that the number of doctorates is growing. Approximately half (47.9%) of all nursing education administrators held doctorates in 1994, and 51.8% held master's degrees as their highest educational attainment.

Most nurse educators are in instructor positions (32.5%) or hold the title of assistant professor (31.2%). Instructors tend to work in associate degree and diploma programs, and assistant professors are more likely to work in baccalaureate and higher degree programs.

Only 10% of nurse faculty hold the doctorate, although increasing numbers are being educated to the doctoral level. The numbers are still not sufficient to fill the potential academic positions that will be available in the future. Resolving the incongruence between the supply of and demand for R.N.s with advanced degrees is a challenge for the nursing profession.

Licensure and Certification

Individual states provide licensure as a registered nurse to a person who has completed an approved educational program for registered nurses and passed a written examination. A registered nurse may work in psychiatric nursing, a specialty area. Two levels of credentialing are available through national certification by the American Nurses Association. The first level is that of generalist psychiatric nurse. These nurses are identified as possessing practice expertise in mental health and psychiatric nursing as well as understanding "theories concerning personality development and the behavior patterns involved in the treatment and case management of mental illness" and having "knowledge of the expected effects of treatment upon client behavior and of the relationship this has to nursing care" (American Nurses Credentialing Center, 1996, p. 10).

Specialists in psychiatric/mental health nursing must obtain advanced credentials, achieved through graduate education in this area of nursing. The licensure laws of each state determine how the specialty practice of nursing is affected (Dial et al., 1992). Further, the American Nurses Association certifies clinical specialists in child/adolescent and adult psychiatric nursing. Certification requirements include master's level education, clinical supervision/consultation of past master's experience, and a passing score on a nationally administered written examination (American Nurses Credentialing Center, 1996). These specialists must demonstrate proficiency in therapeutic and interpersonal skills. Their roles and functions include advancing nursing theory and therapy as well as research, teaching, consultation, management, and coordination of patient care (American Nurses Credentialing Center, 1996).

Psychology

Education for psychologists includes the baccalaureate, master's, and doctoral levels. Most states now require an individual to attain the doctoral degree to practice psychology independently. The American Psychological Association (APA) has been the major accrediting body for doctoral training programs and predoctoral internships since 1947.

Formal training for the practice of psychology focuses on three specialties: school psychology, counseling psychology, and clinical psychology. The degree awarded may be one of three. The doctor of philosophy (Ph.D.) degree is normally awarded in programs that train for research, teaching, and clinical practice. The doctor of psychology (Psy.D.) is awarded by programs that emphasize direct delivery, evaluation, and improvement of professional services (Fox, Kovacs, & Graham, 1985; Korman, 1976). The doctor of education (Ed.D.) degree is awarded when it is the degree authorized by the institution. The degree awarded does not always strictly correlate with a specific training model, because host institutions have considerable leeway in deciding which degrees to offer.

In 1992, there were 42 APA-accredited doctoral training programs in school psychology, 60 in counseling psychology, and 170 in clinical psychology. Four programs offered combined professional-scientific training tracks. In addition, there were 144 APA-accredited predoctoral internship sites. Participation in an APA-accredited internship is frequently seen as a factor favorable to employment and subsequent advancement (Dial et al., 1992). According to APA (1989) guidelines, a doctoral student must undergo a minimum of three years of academic study, at least two of which must be at the institution that grants the degree—one of those two years must be in full-time residence. In addition, the student must satisfactorily complete a predoctoral internship and accomplish a scholarly dissertation. Before the degreed individual can begin professional practice, he or she must satisfy the specific licensing and/or certification requirements of the state. Most states license and/or certify in accordance with three criteria: (a) a doctoral degree from a regionally accredited institution; (b) two years of supervised clinical practice, at least one performed after receiving the degree; and (c) successful completion of an examination administered by the state (Dial et al., 1992).

Program Emphasis and Curriculum Content Areas

The APA (1989) requires every accredited program to include in its curriculum a minimum of three academic years of full-time resident graduate study. Every doctoral program must include the following:

> Instruction in scientific and professional ethics and standards, research design and methodology, statistics, psychological measurement, and history and the systems of psychology . . . [and] require each student to demonstrate competence in each of the following substantive content areas: (1) biological bases of behavior (e.g., physiological psychology, comparative psychology, neuropsychology, sensation, psychopharmacology), (2) cognitive-affective bases of behavior (e.g., learning, memory, perception, cognition, thinking, motivation, emotion), (3) social bases of behavior (e.g., social psychology, cultural, ethnic, and group processes; sex roles; organizational and systems theory), and (4) individual behavior (e.g., personality theory, human development, individual differences, abnormal psychology). (pp. 6-7)

The APA (1989) stresses the importance of both practicum and internship as field experience necessary to the educational experience at the doctoral level.

Both provide "systematic intensive training in the application of psychological principles and skills to human problems," are offered sequentially, and are "generally graded in intensity and responsibility" (p. 16).

Practicum precedes internship and may take place either on or off campus. Practicum training seeks to develop in students the following capacities:

1. The ability to conceptualize human problems
2. An understanding of the range of human variability
3. An awareness of their own biases and personalities and their impacts upon others in professional interactions
4. Improved skills in interpersonal interactions, such as interviewing, psychological testing, behavioral observation, psychotherapy, counseling, and consultation
5. The ability to contribute to current knowledge and practice
6. The ability to understand and commit to constructs of social and professional responsibility as defined by the professional code of ethics and applicable statutes

Internships follow the completion of practicum and other academic work and precede the granting of the doctoral degree. The internship is a crucial component in the training of a professional psychologist. It offers the student experience in carrying out major professional functions with appropriate supervision and provides exposure to professional role models and relevant administrative structures. The internship builds upon the skills, knowledge, and sensitivities that were the focus of the practicum.

Clinical internships require full-time participation for one calendar year or two years of half-time experience. Internships for school and counseling psychology are only slightly briefer. All three specialties allow an experience in more than one agency unless specified otherwise.

In 1986, the median time required to earn the psychology doctorate was 7.5 years, up from 5.9 years in 1967 (Tuckman, Coyle, & Bae, 1990). This is consistent with similar increases in other scientific fields. In psychology, this may be caused in part by a 28% reduction in federal training support from 1981 to 1989 (National Science Foundation, 1990). Clinical training support, in particular, has been especially hard hit. NIMH-sponsored traineeships fell from 1,553 in 1979 to only 168 in 1986 (Wohlford, 1990). During the 1990-1991 academic year, approximately 60% of all full-time doctoral students in psychology received some financial support, compared with 13% of part-time doctoral students. The overall trend is a shift from federal or institutional financial aid to reliance on personal resources—the student's own or resources provided by family or spouse (Wicherski & Kohout, 1992).

Faculty

In U.S. graduate departments of psychology in 1991, 48% of all full-time faculty were full professors, and 70% were tenured. More than 25% were associate professors, and approximately 20% were assistant professors; 98% held doctorates.

Women represented 27% of all full-time graduate psychology faculty in 1991 and accounted for 26% of the full professorships. Women were twice as likely as men to be assistant professors. Women's representation among tenured faculty was 20% (up from 14% in 1981), and women made up 45% of faculty on tenure track (up from 35% in 1981).

In 1992, 6% of full-time faculty in U.S. departments of psychology were members of ethnic minority groups, the largest subgroup being African Americans. Native Americans were the smallest subgroup represented, less than 1%. Among women faculty, 8% were ethnic minorities, whereas less than 5% of male faculty were in that category. Ethnic minorities made up 8% of lecturers and instructors, 11% of assistant professors, 7% of associate professors, and 3% of full professors (Wicherski & Kohout, 1992).

Students

The majority of practicing psychologists in 1990 had been undergraduate psychology majors. The remainder came from education and other professional fields. Those who wish to pursue a doctorate in clinical, counseling, or school psychology may apply directly for admission to a doctoral program, bypassing the master's level. Some wait—in 1986, the mean time between receipt of the baccalaureate and entrance to graduate school was 1.5 years (Tuckman et al., 1990). Acceptance is competitive. In 1989, the acceptance rate was 10% (Kohout, Wicherski, & Cooney, 1991). The numbers of doctoral students have increased steadily, growing 19% from 1985 to 1990. Of all doctoral students in 1990, 48% were enrolled in programs emphasizing the practitioner training models (Pion, 1992).

Women made up 62% of all full-time psychology graduate students in 1990, an increase of 4% from 1985 levels. This general trend is consistent with the growing participation of women in employment and graduate education (Howard et al., 1986).

In 1990, 88.4% of all psychology students were white, 4% were black, 4% Hispanic, and 2% Asian, with participation by Native Americans remaining extremely low. During the period from 1985 to 1990, the proportion of black full-time students declined and the participation of Hispanics and Asians increased.

Most student enrollments in 1990 were in the Middle Atlantic, South Atlantic, East North Central, and Pacific regions of the United States, areas that have large population centers and several academic institutions offering doctoral programs in psychology. Graduates do not necessarily stay in the regions where they train, however. The highest rates of practitioners per 100,000 population are in the New England (30.4), Middle Atlantic (23.7), Pacific (20.2), and Mountain regions (17.3) (Dial et al., 1992).

Psychiatry

Training in Residence

Training to become a professional psychiatrist begins at the undergraduate level. Because psychiatry is a medical specialty, future psychiatrists must complete requirements for admission to medical school, completing course work in biology, physics, mathematics, and chemistry.

In matriculation at a school of medicine, course work includes the subjects of pharmacology, human physiology, anatomy, microbiology, genetics, endocrinology, biochemistry, and the behavioral sciences. The medical specialties of surgery, pediatrics, internal medicine, obstetrics and gynecology, neurology, and psychiatry are also introduced in medical school.

Would-be psychiatrists are required to complete a residency period of at least four years, during which all aspects of mental illness are covered in detail. All residency programs emphasize clinical care of patients. Programs vary, but a typical residency might include 4 to 6 months' experience in internal medicine, pediatrics, or family medicine; at least 2 months in neurology; and some months in emergency care. The remaining 36 months focus on psychiatry. Child psychiatry residency normally requires an additional year beyond that required for general psychiatry. The computerized National Residency Matching Program matches senior medical students to available residency positions based on the preferences of both program directors and graduates.

Subspecialty training is also available in fields other than child psychiatry. Training for subspecialties may involve brief electives or full- or part-time year-long programs.

Psychiatric Residents

Psychiatric residents are concentrated around large metropolitan areas that have medical schools with affiliated residency training sites. They are found mainly in the Middle Atlantic, South Atlantic, East North Central, and Pacific regions. Five states—Alaska and four states in the Rocky Mountain West region—have no psychiatric training sites at all.

The number of new psychiatric residents grew by 40% in the 1980s, and then the upward trend flattened and even dropped somewhat in 1989-1990. There are no indications that the growth experienced in the 1980s will recur in the next few years.

The growth in new residents in the 1980s was affected by the numbers of women entering psychiatric residency programs. For example, research by De Titta, Robinowitz, and More (1991) on the phenomenon they label "the feminization of psychiatry" (p. 855) reveals that the proportion of women increased from 32% of all psychiatric residents in 1979 to 41% in 1988, and that 35% of all psychiatrists under 35 years of age in 1988 were women. The American Medical Association reports that 9,028 women were in the psychiatric specialty in 1992, up from 4,361 in 1980 (Roback, Randolph, & Seidman, 1993). Women have long been more heavily represented in psychiatry than in the other medical specialties. The implications of the growth of the numbers of women in the specialty include necessary adjustments to training program structure and curriculum content (Reider, 1988).

The growth in numbers of women in psychiatry also has implications for practice. Female psychiatrists are less often board certified than are men, their earnings are lower, they tend to work in institutional settings, and they generally work fewer hours per week than do men (Goldstein, Bromet, & Hanusa, 1981). Referring to findings by Fenton, Robinowitz, and Leaf (1987), De Titta et al. (1991) note that "female psychiatrists spend a greater proportion of their time in organized settings and are less involved in academia or private practice, that they tend to see a greater number of female patients, and that they see their patients more frequently, a finding that also holds for female practitioners in family practice and internal medicine" (p. 857).

Maheux, Dufort, and Beland (1990) have found certain attitudinal differences in female physicians, compared with male physicians, that can be generalized to female psychiatrists. Generally, women are more likely to counsel their patients about health matters, are more likely to use education as a means to prevent health problems, and tend to value psychosocial factors in caring for their patients. Women's contributions to the quality of health care are real, but there are institutional challenges for female physicians to overcome.

Licensing and Certification

Licensing of psychiatrists is administered by state medical boards. The process takes place after the individual's graduation from medical school and results in a license to practice as a medical doctor rather than as a psychiatrist per se.

Certification, although not required to practice psychiatry, may be a prerequisite of certain positions. After completion of an accredited psychiatric residency program, a psychiatrist may take oral and written examinations for certification in general psychiatry, child psychiatry, or geriatric psychiatry as an additional qualification. The American Psychiatric Association is responsible for the process of certification in administrative psychiatry.

Conclusion

As is briefly discussed in Chapter 9 of this volume, Greenwood (1981) identifies three components of professionalism: the cognitive or intellectual component, the collectivity orientation and the normative or service component, and the monopolistic component. As Hughes (1963) has noted, "A profession delivers esoteric services—advice or action or both—to individuals, organizations, or government; to whole classes or groups of people or to the public at large" (p. 655). In this context, and based on convention in the mental health arena, in this chapter we have discussed the staffing of mental health services by the four core mental health professions: social work, mental health nursing, psychology, and psychiatry.

Confronted by continued expansion of the knowledge base by social and neuroscientific research, the impetus of consumerism, and increased accountability demands linked, in part, to controlling mental health program and service costs, curricula of the professional schools as well as professional roles and services will further evolve. Although we face challenging and unsettled times, enthusiasm and optimism are voiced by (some) chief executive officers of mental health agencies regarding a current environment favorable for improvement in client services and concurrently for professional stimulation and opportunities for satisfying professional practice and careers (T. B. Mulloy & L. Evans, personal communication, March 5, 1996). We share this sense of excitement and optimism.

References

American Nurses Credentialing Center. (1996). *1996 certification catalog.* Washington, DC: Author.

American Psychological Association (APA). (1989). *Criteria for accreditation of doctoral training programs and internships in professional psychology.* Washington, DC: Author.

Bardill, D. R., & Saunders, B. E. (1983). Services to families and groups. In J. W. Callicutt & P. J. Lecca (Eds.), *Social work and mental health* (pp. 69-93). New York: Free Press.

Biggerstaff, M. A. (1995). Licensing, regulation, and certification. In R. L. Edwards (Ed.), *Encyclopedia of social work* (19th ed., pp. 1616-1624). Washington, DC: NASW Press.

Council on Social Work Education. (1994). *Handbook of accreditation standards and procedures.* Alexandria, VA: Author.

DeMoll, L. E. (1983). Planning. In J. W. Callicutt & P. J. Lecca (Eds.), *Social work and mental health* (pp. 128-148). New York: Free Press.

De Titta, M., Robinowitz, C. B., & More, W. W. (1991). The future of psychiatry: Psychiatrists of the future. *American Journal of Psychiatry, 148,* 853-858.

Dial, T. H., Pion, G. M., Cooney, B., Kohout, J., Kaplan, K. O., Ginsberg, L., Merwin, E. I., Fox, J. C., Ginsberg, M., Staton, J., Cawlson, T. W., Windermuth, V. A., Blankertz, L., & Hughes, R. (1992). Training of mental health providers. In R. W. Manderscheid & M. A. Sonnenschein (Eds.), *Mental health, United States, 1992* (CDHHS Publication No. SMA-92-1942, pp. 142-162). Washington, DC: Government Printing Office.

Fenton, W. S., Robinowitz, C. B., & Leaf, P. J. (1987). Male and female psychiatrists and their patients. *American Journal of Psychiatry, 144,* 358-361.

Fox, J. C., & Chamberlain, J. (1988). Preparing nurses to work with the chronically mentally ill. *Community Mental Health Journal, 24*(4).

Fox, R., Kovacs, A., & Graham, S. (1985). Proposals for a revolution in the preparation and regulation of professional psychologists. *American Psychologist, 40,* 1042-1050.

Goldstein, M. Z., Bromet, E. J., & Hanusa, B. H. (1981). Psychiatrists' life and work patterns: A statewide comparison of women and men. *American Journal of Psychiatry, 138,* 919-924.

Greenwood, E. (1981). Attributes of a profession revisited. In N. Gilbert & H. Specht (Eds.), *The emergence of social welfare and social work* (2nd ed., pp. 255-276). Itasca, IL: F. E. Peacock.

Howard, A., Pion, G. M., Gottfredson, G. D., Flattau, P. E., Oskamp, S., Pfafflin, S. M., Bray, D. W., & Burstein, A. G. (1986). The changing face of American psychology: A report from the Committee on Employment and Human Resources. *American Psychologist, 41,* 1311-1327.

Hughes, E. C. (1963). Professions. *Daedalus, 92,* 655-668.

Kane, T. J. (1983). Administration. In J. W. Callicutt & P. J. Lecca (Eds.), *Social work and mental health* (pp. 97-127). New York: Free Press.

Kohout, J., Wicherski, M., & Cooney, B. (1991). *Characteristics of graduate departments of psychology: 1989-1990*. Washington, DC: American Psychological Association.

Korman, M. (Ed.). (1976). *Levels and patterns of professional training in psychology*. Washington, DC: American Psychological Association.

Lennon, T. M. (1994). *Statistics on social work education: 1993*. Alexandria, VA: Council on Social Work Education.

Maheux, B., Dufort, F., & Beland, F. (1990). Female medical practitioners: More preventive and patient oriented? *Medical Care, 28,* 87-92.

National League for Nursing (NLN). (1994). *Nursing data review 1994*. New York: Author.

National League for Nursing (NLN). (1995a). *Nursing data review 1995*. New York: Author.

National League for Nursing (NLN). (1995b). [Master's degree programs in psychiatric, mental health nursing]. Unpublished raw data.

National Science Foundation. (1990). *Academic science and engineering: Graduate enrollment and support, fall 1989* (NSF Publication No. 90-324). Washington, DC: Author.

Pion, G. M. (1992, March). *Clinical counseling and school psychology: The changing balance among research and practice*. Paper presented at the American Psychological Association Accreditation Summit, Chicago.

Redick, R. W., Witkin, M. J., Atay, J. E., & Manderscheid, R. W. (1994). Highlights of organized mental health services in 1990 and major national and state trends. In R. W. Manderscheid & M. A. Sonnenschein (Eds.), *Mental health, United States, 1994* (CDHHS Publication No. SMA 94-3000, pp. 99-125). Washington, DC: Government Printing Office.

Reider, R. (Ed.). (1988). Roundtable dialogue: The impact of increasing numbers of female psychiatric residents. *AADRT Newsletter, 16*(3), 1-6.

Roback, G., Randolph, L., & Seidman, B. (1993). *Physician characteristics and distribution in the U.S.* Chicago: American Medical Association.

Tarail, M. (1983). Community organization. In J. W. Callicutt & P. J. Lecca (Eds.), *Social work and mental health* (pp. 149-171). New York: Free Press.

Tuckman, H., Coyle, S., & Bae, Y. (1990). *On time to the doctorate: A study of the increased time to complete doctorates in science and engineering*. Washington, DC: National Academy Press.

Watkins, T. R. (1983). Services to individuals. In J. W. Callicutt & P. J. Lecca (Eds.), *Social work and mental health* (pp. 45-68). New York: Free Press.

Wicherski, M., & Kohout, J. (1992). *Characteristics of graduate departments of psychology: 1990-1991*. Washington, DC: American Psychological Association.

Wohlford, P. (1990). National responsibilities to improve training for psychological services for children, youth, and families in the 1990s. In P. R. Magrab & P. Wohlford (Eds.), *Improving psychological services for children and adolescents with severe mental disorders: Clinical training in psychology*. Washington, DC: American Psychological Association.

PART II

The Expanding Base of Knowledge in Mental Health

Progress in the mental health field relies on knowledge from many sources. In recent years the major thrust of research into the etiology and treatment of mental illness has been in biochemistry. In Chapter 6, William Wilson presents a summary of the neuroscientific research findings that have led to significant, perhaps revolutionary, advances in treatment of severe mental illnesses. The strength of the chapter is not only its economical presentation of a large body of research findings but also its comprehensibility for the scientifically unsophisticated reader.

Balancing and supplementing the neuroscientific perspective, David Millard presents in Chapter 7 a unique integration of several decades of research on social factors in mental illness and its treatment. Much of the research he reports comes from studies done outside the immediate influence of American scientific research priorities. Consequently, this review will expand the awareness of American readers, particularly, concerning the ongoing lines of research into psychosocial factors.

Psychoeducation has emerged as one of the most promising approaches for helping to integrate and maintain persons with severe mental illness in the community. As Cassandra Simon points out in Chapter 8, psychoeducation has developed in the context of continuous empirical investigation. The range of settings for its application is expanding dramatically, leading to the conclusion that it will soon be an integral part of every comprehensive treatment facility. Psychoeducation entails the presentation and explanation of information from neuroscientific and social research to persons with mental illness and their families, so that facilitative accommodations to the individual's needs can be made in the home and family environment. Simon presents several empirically validated models of psychoeducational intervention.

Ted Watkins and James Callicutt, in Chapter 9, report on the qualitative impacts of self-help and advocacy groups on mental health policies and services. Long ignored or discounted, these groups, made up of individuals who are the closest to the day-to-day problems related to mental illness, have gained power, credibility, and legitimacy in the field. Their expertise is experiential, and their "research" contribution comes from their cumulative experience as consumers of services provided by mental health professionals. Watkins and Callicutt explain the origins, functions, and impacts of these groups on the field and note ways in which their unique contributions can add significantly to the relevance and effectiveness of services to persons with mental illness and their families.

CHAPTER 6

Neuroscientific Research in Mental Health

WILLIAM H. WILSON

Modern neuroscientific research provides an essential perspective on mental illness and its treatment. The human brain is a uniquely complex organ that generates mood, thought, behavior, and consciousness. Like any other organ in the body, the brain may not develop normally or may not function normally. When problems in brain function occur, they may be expressed through problems in mood, thought, and behavior—that is, as "mental illness." As the human organism's center for sensory integration, planning, and behavioral response, the brain maintains a constant interplay with the organism's physical and psychosocial environment. From the point of view of brain neuroscience, there are no rigid distinctions between mind and body, inside and outside, neurological and psychological. Rather, these dichotomies represent points of view from which one might describe a single living, evolving, responding system. From a practical standpoint, one must consider both neuroscientific and psychosocial perspectives if one is to understand "mental illness" and to plan effective treatment. In this chapter I focus on brains and molecules, but my aim is humanistic: to enhance the lives of persons who suffer, or who are disabled, due to disordered mood, thought, or behavior. To increase readability, I use references sparingly. I have relied heavily upon the books and review articles that I cite here, and these works are themselves richly referenced.

The chapter begins with a review of brain structure and function (Brodal, 1992; Cooper, Bloom, & Roth, 1991; Hall, 1992). This is followed by a discussion of the high-technology approaches that allow the study of living, functioning brains (Daniel, Aigun, & Weinberger, 1992; Prichard, 1995). After brief discussion of psychiatric classification (American Psychiatric Association, 1994), the chapter turns to the neuroscientific underpinnings of three categories of mental disorder (Schatzberg & Nemeroff, 1995). Schizophrenia, a major public health problem, was once thought to be caused by abnormal parenting, but it is now clearly established as a brain disorder, with strong genetic determinants (Andreasen, 1994; Benes, 1995; Keefe & Harvey, 1994). Mood disorders are associated with the altered function of basic brain control systems. Post-traumatic stress disorder provides a robust example of the interplay of psychosocial and neurological perspectives: Social events lead to neurological conditions that are expressed as continued psychosocial distress. The chapter concludes with an overview of psychopharmacology (Bernstein, 1995).

Functional Anatomy of the Brain

Basic Brain Structure

The human brain is intricately organized from specialized body cells called *neurons.* These cells differ from other body cells in that they are adapted to send, receive, and process neurochemical signals to and from other nerve cells. These cells are supported by specialized connective cells called *gila* and are richly supplied with energy and nutrition by an abundant network of blood vessels. The lower portions of the brain, termed the *brain stem* and *midbrain,* are located just above the spinal cord and have the simplest patterns of cells. The cell pattern, or cytoarchitecture, of this region is similar to what is found in the entire brains of relatively simple vertebrate animals, such as reptiles. These areas are concerned with basic "housekeeping" tasks of the organism, such as temperature and blood pressure regulation, as well as with basic behavioral states, such as relative alertness or disengagement from the environment. The cerebellum, a brain division concerned mostly with coordination of bodily movement, is also in this area. Moving forward in the brain, one finds areas that are somewhat more complex in their cellular architecture, similar to the organization found in large mammals, such as the horse. These *limbic* areas and *basal ganglia* serve as "switchboards" for information coming from the body and the special sense organs and for information from higher levels in the brain. The basal ganglia are concerned with gait, posture, muscle tone, and other aspects of bodily movement that are usually outside of conscious awareness. The limbic area is critical to basic emotional states (contentment, rage, and so on) and basic emotional desires (to love, to mate, to defend oneself and one's family, and so on).

The cerebral cortex forms the highest levels of the brain. These areas are the last to develop in the fetus and have cellular patterns found in no other animals except the great apes, with humans showing the most extensive development. These areas process information from the sense organs to create vision, hearing, and the other sensations, and coordinate conscious movement of the body. Language, much of memory, and symbolic processing are cortical functions. The frontal lobes, which are the most uniquely human parts of the brain, are especially concerned with complex decisions regarding motivation, interest, and judgment. Consciousness itself appears to arise from the inter-working of the brain areas, rather than being localized in one particular area.

Neurons and Neurotransmission

Neurons are composed of three principal areas: cell body, dendrites, and axon. The cell body contains the nucleus with the cell's genetic material (DNA) and most of its metabolic machinery. The cell body has projections termed *dendrites* that are specialized to receive messages from other neurons. Signals to other cells are sent through a projection termed the *axon*. The number and frequency of chemical messages received from other neurons determine when and how often the cell "fires," sending an electrochemical signal (action potential) down the axon. At the end of the axon is the specialized site, termed the *synapse,* where the message is passed on to another nerve cell through the process of *neurotransmission*. The term *synapse* comes from the Greek word meaning "junction." Synapses allow information transmission in one direction only. The cell that is sending the message is termed the *presynaptic neuron,* and the cell receiving the message is the *postsynaptic neuron.*

Messages are passed between nerve cells in the form of small molecules called *neurotransmitters*. The brain uses 2,000 or more different molecules as neuro-transmitters, but a few predominate in the study of mental illness: dopamine, norepinephrine, serotonin, acetylcholine, and gamma-aminobutyric acid. The presynaptic neuron manufactures neurotransmitter molecules and stores them in balloonlike structures (*vesicles*) near the synapse. When an action potential arrives at the synapse, these vesicles join with the cell membrane and release neurotransmitter molecules into the space between the pre- and postsynaptic neurons (the *synaptic cleft*). Neurotransmitter molecules diffuse across the cleft to the postsynaptic neuron, where they attach to large, complex molecules termed *receptors*. Because of the specific fit between the neurotransmitter and the receptor, the neurotransmitter may be thought of as a key and the receptor may be thought of as the lock that receives the key.

When the neurotransmitter is bound to the receptor, the receptor changes in shape (*conformation*) in a particular way. Receptors are divided into two main categories, depending upon what happens when they change conforma-tion in response to binding a neurotransmitter. Receptors from the first class open or close a pore in the cell membrane, which allows an electrically charged atom to enter or exit the cell (*ion channel receptors*). The second class of receptors are connected to specialized proteins within the postsynaptic cells termed *G proteins*. When a neurotransmitter binds to a *G protein-coupled receptor,* the receptor changes in shape. This in turn causes changes in the G proteins. Changes in the G proteins activate a cascade of chemical changes in the postsynaptic neuron. These changes have immediate effects but also cause neurochemical readjustments that take days or weeks to accomplish. Most receptors that are affected by psychiatric medications are of the G protein-coupled variety. Several distinctly different receptors may be activated by the same neurotransmitter molecule. For example, there are 5 known different receptors for the neurotransmitter dopamine and 18 known receptors for serotonin.

Neurotransmitters do not stay attached permanently to receptors. Rather, they release from the receptors and diffuse back into the fluid within the synaptic cleft. Neurotransmitters are cleared from the cleft by two mechanisms, so that the synapse is readied to receive the next message. In the first mechanism, the neurotransmitter diffuses out of the synapse and is broken down to simpler compounds that are eliminated as wastes in the bloodstream. In the second mechanism, neurotransmitters are recycled, saving the energy that would be required to synthesize them again. The presynaptic neuron contains molecular pumps to transport neurotransmitter molecules from the synaptic cleft back into the presynaptic neuron. There are separate pumps for the various neurotransmitters. Once neurotransmitter molecules have been pumped back into the cell, they are repackaged into storage vesicles. Excess neurotransmitter in the presynaptic neuron is broken down to simpler components by enzymes. The most important enzyme involved in neurotransmitter degradation within the cell is called *monoamine oxidase* or MAO. MAO promotes an oxidative reaction that degrades a variety of neurotransmitter molecules that have a single amine group, including norepinephrine, serotonin, and dopamine.

Neurotransmitter System Anatomy

Some of the neurotransmitters are not found in all parts of the brain. Rather, they are found in particular groups of neurons. Dopamine, serotonin, and norepinephrine, which are neurotransmitters of particular importance to psychopharmacology, are found in tracts of neurons that originate in midbrain structures and then branch widely into the higher levels of the brain. This organization suggests that these neurons modulate a wide range of activities in the brain, rather than being involved with more specific activities. Change in function of these neurons would be expected to affect many brain systems in a variety of ways, which is what is seen in mental illnesses such as depression and schizophrenia. For example, symptoms of depression include disruption of sleep patterns, changes in appetite, decreased energy, poor concentration, and decreased mood. All of these functions are in some way modulated by norepinephrine- and serotonin-producing neurons.

The Technology of Neuroscience

Up until the past few years, the study of mental illnesses as brain disorders was hindered by the lack of methods available for the study of living brains. That situation has changed and continues to change rapidly with the development of noninvasive brain imaging techniques that allow accurate depiction of the structures and workings of the brain. Two techniques are now routinely employed to obtain high-quality images of living human brains, without causing damage to the persons involved. The first of these, computerized axial tomography (CT scan, or CAT scan), produces an image by obtaining X-ray views of the head at a number of angles. These views are integrated by computer to produce pictures, which look like brain X rays, at particular angles or depths of the brain. A newer technique, magnetic resonance imaging (MRI), produces even better-quality images without the use of X rays. MRI involves placing the subject within a strong magnetic field and variable radio frequency electromagnetic fields. Atoms within the brain then emit radio frequency waves that are detected by special sensors and integrated by computer into high-quality brain images. Both CT and MRI scans are routinely available for clinical use in all areas of the United States. CT and MRI technologies have led to the discovery that individuals with schizophrenia have larger ventricles (fluid-filled spaces) within their brains than do normal subjects (further discussion on this topic is offered later in this chapter).

Enhanced computing power is used within research settings to display MRI data as detailed, accurate, three-dimensional images. Such reconstructions lead to the virtual dissection of a living brain without any damage to the individual. For research purposes, brain reconstructions from many individuals can be averaged to find differences among populations. This technique was recently used by Andreasen and her colleagues at the University of Iowa to study the brain structure in schizophrenia. Averaged, composite images of normal brains were compared with those of people with schizophrenia. A particular part of the brain, the thalamus, was found to be smaller in the brains of people with schizophrenia. The thalamus is a structure deep within the brain that integrates sensory and emotional material. Although the implications of this finding are not yet clear, the finding itself demonstrates the power of these technologies. Without MRI and the application of massive computer power, these data could not have been obtained. Brains from autopsy would not have been representative of normal populations or of living individuals with schizophrenia. Even if brain material were available, the study would have been impossible because of the astronomical numbers of person-hours that would have been required for the dissection and data analysis.

Even more exciting are techniques that allow direct visualization of the working of living human brains. The brightly colored "brain maps" obtained from these techniques now appear frequently in popular newsmagazines. Positron emission tomography (PET), its close cousin single-photon emission computed tomography (SPECT), and its more distant relative ^{131}Xe rCBF (xenon regional cerebral blood flow monitoring) now allow visualization of chemical processes in the brain. In PET scanning, the subject receives a small amount of a particular sort of radioactive material by injection. The subject lies within a scanning device, and emissions from the radioactive material are detected. A computer generates images or maps of the radioactive material within the brain. PET is particularly useful because of the types of atoms that can be used as radioactive tracers. Oxygen, phosphorus, and other small atoms that form the molecules in normal cells may be used as tracers. The radioactive atoms behave exactly like nonradioactive atoms in chemical reactions. Thus researchers can study the routine functioning of the brain without altering brain function in the process.

One common PET application allows investigators to observe energy use in the brain, which directly reflects activity of the brain. The primary source of brain energy is glucose. In this technique, glucose molecules are slightly altered to produce molecules that will stay put in the cells where they are first used for energy production. The altered glucose molecules (2-deoxyglucose) are labeled with radioactive oxygen. A subject is given the radioactive tracer both at rest and when engaged in the particular activity in question. For example, the subject may be scanned while resting in a quiet room and again while listening to music. Comparison of these scans shows increased glucose utilization in the areas of the brain involved with listening to music.

Molecules other than glucose can be labeled for PET scanning. For example, medication molecules can be labeled. The location and quantity of binding of these molecules may then be studied. Before such scans, estimates of drug binding in the living brain were based on extrapolations from test-tube binding studies. Now such effects are measured directly.

PET and SPECT are research techniques and are not likely ever to be used in routine clinical practice. The techniques are too cumbersome and expensive for routine use. The radioactive agents are very short-lived, such that they must be prepared at a cyclotron in the same location as the scanner and immediately synthesized into pharmaceutical tracers. The amount of radiation to which a subject is exposed is quite small, and the resulting risk to health is negligible, but any radioactive exposure must also be seen as a limitation of the technique.

Fortunately, the limitations of PET techniques are being overcome through refinement of MRI technology. Functional MRI (fMRI) uses the same principles as those described above but is able to provide images based on measures of particular organic molecules as well as the more general structural information. As development of fMRI continues, it may become a routine clinical practice as well as provide the next generation of scientific data.

Psychiatric Classification

A first step in finding the causes of disorders of thought and emotion is to separate these disorders into smaller categories that share similar characteristics. These smaller categories may be broken down into ever more homogeneous categories. It is more likely that the mechanisms and causes can be discovered for a specific type of illness than for a more general category of illness, or for mental illness as a whole. When a cause is known for a disorder, the illness is categorized according to the cause. For example, when an individual has a psychosis that is due to a low level of thyroid hormone, the disorder is termed *psychotic disorder due to hypothyroidism*. When the causes are unknown, disorders are defined solely on the basis of symptoms. For example, the cause of schizophrenia is unknown. The illness known as schizophrenia is defined by the presence of certain types of symptoms (delusions, hallucinations, thought disorder) occurring over a sufficient period of time (6 months or longer), without the presence of other factors that could lead to psychosis (such as hypothyroidism). With this approach, the term *schizophrenia* has a fairly specific meaning in research and clinical practice. This approach to illness classification is the same as that used in other branches of scientific medicine. Continuing development of precise psychiatric diagnosis is essential to research regarding the causes and treatment of illness. For an individual, accurate diagnosis is a crucial step in treatment planning. The current official consensus regarding psychiatric diagnosis is contained in the American Psychiatric Association's (1994) *Diagnostic and Statistical Manual of Mental Disorders,* fourth edition (*DSM-IV*). Accurate diagnosis using *DSM-IV* criteria allows research and treatment to be standardized across individuals, treatment centers, and national boundaries. However, the work of psychiatric classification is far from complete. *DSM-IV* should be regarded as a working document, rather than as a final product. Research regarding the classification of psychiatric disorders will continue in tandem with neuroscientific research into these disorders.

Neurobiological Basis of Selected Psychiatric Syndromes

Schizophrenia

Schizophrenia is a common, devastating illness that has its basis in a disorder of brain structure and function. Approximately 2 million Americans are affected, with an annual cost to the U.S. economy of $40 to $60 billion. The history of schizophrenia over the past century illustrates the progress that has been made in the neuroscientific understanding of mental illness.

In 1899, Emil Kraeplin, an eminent German psychiatrist, described two types of chronic psychotic disorder. One of these had cyclic mood features, which we now term bipolar affective disorder. The other disorder, which he termed *dementia praecox,* was, in essence, what *DSM-IV* calls schizophrenia. The key features of the second disorder, according to Kraeplin, were delusions, hallucinations, thought disorder, and chronicity. Kraeplin regarded dementia praecox as an organic brain syndrome. In 1911, Eugen Bleuler, a Swiss psychiatrist, coined the term *schizophrenia* to emphasize the fragmentation of thought and emotion in dementia praecox. The search for the organic cause of schizophrenia bore little fruit. With the neuroscientific tools of the day, principally the light microscope, no clear-cut findings could be obtained. In the same period, Sigmund Freud developed psychologically based ideas regarding emotional disturbance. These notions were applied to schizophrenia without scientific validation but nonetheless were accepted as its cause by many psychiatrists, especially in the United States. The term *schizophrenia* was applied to an increasingly wider group of individuals and lost much of its initial meaning. In the 1960s, additional untested psychological explanations were given for schizophrenia, based on supposed communication styles in the families of schizophrenics. Treatments based on psychoanalytic or family communication styles were largely ineffective in treating the illness. However, these treatment programs succeeded in blaming the devastating illness on the schizophrenic individual's parents, especially the mother.

Starting in the 1950s, neuroscientific evidence had accumulated to the point that schizophrenia was clearly established as a brain disorder. First, specific medications were found to be effective against specific symptoms. This indicated that symptoms were associated with particular chemical processes in the brain. Next, the familial pattern of schizophrenia was investigated through epidemiological studies that used the precise records of Scandinavian countries. The babies of mothers who had schizophrenia where found to be at higher-than-usual risk for schizophrenia. These babies had increased rates of schizophrenia even when they were adopted away from their mothers at birth and reared by nonschizophrenic parents. Some babies whose biological mothers did not have schizophrenia were adopted by women who then developed schizophrenia; these babies did not develop schizophrenia with any greater frequency than that found in the general population. The studies demonstrated the genetic component of schizophrenia and argued against parenting as a cause. Further studies have shown that an individual's risk of developing schizophrenia is determined by how closely related he or she is to an individual with schizophrenia. The likelihood of developing schizophrenia is 10 times greater for first-degree relatives (parents and siblings) of an individual with schizophrenia than it is for the population as a whole. Clearly, there is a strong genetic component, yet something else is involved in the genesis of schizophrenia. Identical twins have the same genetic material, but if one twin has schizophrenia, there is only a 40-60% likelihood that the other twin will also have the disorder.

Individuals with schizophrenia have more "neurological soft signs" than do members of the general public. Soft signs are mild incoordination, clumsiness, and the like, indicative of minor neurological impairments. Neuropsychological testing shows that individuals with schizophrenia have impairments of concentration, problem solving, and memory. These findings are also consistent with brain dysfunction.

Studies of CAT and MRI scans have consistently demonstrated that, as a group, individuals with schizophrenia have larger cerebral ventricles than do normal controls. The ventricles are spaces within the brain that are filled with cerebral spinal fluid. Enlargement indicates the relative absence of brain tissue, which would otherwise fill the space. Studies of identical twins show that for twin pairs in which one individual has schizophrenia and one does not, the affected twin has larger ventricles. The large ventricles seem to be stable in size over adulthood, and there is no evidence of scarring. This finding suggests that the larger ventricles result from maldevelopment of the brain rather than from later damage.

PET scanning and other new technologies (such as ^{131}Xe blood flow monitoring) have demonstrated defects in brain function in schizophrenia that were not previously evident. In studies using these technologies, a subject's brain is scanned while the subject performs a fairly simple standardized task that requires a degree of judgment. The scans of control subjects show a marked increase in brain activity in the frontal lobes, whereas individuals with schizophrenia show little activation of the frontal lobes. Although the lobes may appear normal structurally, these brain areas are simply not working. This finding is one of the most consistent in the neuroscientific study of schizophrenia. There are other indications that schizophrenia is a brain disorder, but those I have noted here suffice to make the point.

The dopamine neurotransmitter system functions abnormally in schizophrenia. Postmortem studies show that the brains of individuals with schizophrenia contain increased numbers of dopamine D2 receptors, compared with brains from people who do not have the illness. PET studies of living, never-medicated individuals with schizophrenia confirm that dopamine D2 receptor levels are indeed increased as a feature of the illness, independent of medication treatment. The overproduction of D2 receptors may be one of the key features underlying the disorder, or it may represent the brain's adaptive response to another brain abnormality.

The exact cause and nature of schizophrenia remain elusive. One of the most compelling current theories is that schizophrenia is a neurodevelopmental disorder. According to this theory, genetically susceptible individuals are exposed to some unknown event during the first few months of uterine life. This event triggers abnormal brain development that results in schizophrenia. The trigger may be a virus, a toxin, or something else entirely. The abnormalities produce relatively little dysfunction until late adolescence, when they impair normal maturational processes and result in the expression of psychotic symptoms.

Neuroscience is well on its way to understanding schizophrenia. With continuing research and continuing development of neuroscientific technology, it is reasonable to expect further understanding, better treatment, and, perhaps, an eventual cure. Affected individuals and their families should be reassured that they did not cause the illness and do not need to take the blame for it.

Mood Disorders

Sadness, elation, irritability, and other mood states are aspects of normal life. Moods are considered to be abnormal only when they are extreme, out of proportion to external circumstances, and the cause of disability or suffering. *DSM-IV* differentiates a number of distinct patterns of mood abnormalities that differ somewhat in their neurobiology. It is beyond the scope of this chapter to detail each of these disorders; rather, I will focus on neuroscientific findings regarding mood and its regulation.

As with schizophrenia, genetics plays a major role in determining whether an individual is susceptible to a mood disorder. And, as with schizophrenia, the genetic influences are not simple, but rather seem to depend upon more than one gene. The more closely related an individual is to a person with affective disorder, the greater the risk. For example, the identical twin of an individual with bipolar illness has a 70% risk of having the disorder, whereas a nonidentical twin has only an 11% chance. Genetic factors also influence the type of affective disorder an individual may develop. The relatives of persons with bipolar affective disorder (depressions and manic episodes) are at higher risk of bipolar illness than are the relatives of individuals who have unipolar depression (depressions only).

The actual expression of abnormal mood states depends not only on genetic background but also on a variety of other factors, including early parental loss, the quality of early life experiences with parental figures, history of traumatic events, and current levels of psychosocial support and stress. Clinical mood disorders consist of both subjective symptoms—primarily the experience of an abnormal mood state—and signs of altered physical functioning, such as disrupted sleep, changes in appetite, and decreased or increased energy. These feelings and bodily functions are related to neurochemical and hormonal balances within the brain. Evidence for this proposition comes from a number of directions. For example, the antihypertensive medication reserpine reduces blood pressure by depleting the body's stores of norepinephrine, serotonin, and dopamine. As well as lowering blood pressure, reserpine may cause profound depression and suicidal behavior. Fortunately, there are now safer medications for the treatment of hypertension. Decreased serotonin levels have been associated with violence and suicidal behavior in depression, whereas increasing levels of serotonin with medication may normalize depressed moods. Antidepressant medications normalize mood over a period of a few weeks by increasing levels of the neurotransmitters norepinephrine and serotonin (these are discussed below, in the section on psychopharmacology).

Abnormally low levels of thyroid hormone lead to profound depression. Abnormally high levels of the same hormone can induce irritability and elation, or, at times, may also cause depression. Clinical depression is often accompanied by an activation of the hormonal system known as the hypophyseal-pituitary-adrenal axis (HPA). The HPA coordinates the body's reaction to stress, both physical and emotional. In the presence of stress, a part of the brain called the hypothalamus sends hormonal signals to the pituitary gland, which in turn releases hormonal signals to the adrenal gland. In response to these signals, the adrenal gland secretes cortisol into the blood. Cortisol alerts cells throughout the body to respond to stress. The HPA system, under normal conditions, shows predictable variation in activity over the course of 24 hours. In depression, much of this diurnal variation is lost, with the system in a more constant state of activation. It is as if the body is under unremitting stress. Research has focused on HPA activation as a response to the stress of depression. More recent work focuses on the possibility that abnormalities of the HPA are, in fact, the cause of depression.

Post-Traumatic Stress Disorder

The brain disorder associated with post-traumatic stress disorder (PTSD) is particularly intriguing because its cause is clearly experiential. PTSD is a pattern of neurobiological dysfunction that follows severe psychological stress. First recognized in combat veterans, the syndrome may be induced by almost any overwhelmingly stressful situation. Common precipitants in civilian life include rape and other criminal victimization, automobile and industrial accidents, and severe burns. PTSD symptoms include vivid flashback experiences triggered by environmental cues. For example, a young man was severely injured in an automobile wreck. A year later, while quietly sitting in a college classroom, he heard the sounds of a passing helicopter, much like the one that had transported him to the hospital from the scene of the accident. He instantly felt himself to be back in the wreck, virtually reliving the pain and horror of the incident. Nightmares, depressed mood, impaired interpersonal relationships, and general withdrawal from the world are among the other symptoms of PTSD.

Combat veterans with PTSD have been shown to have elevated pulse rates and blood pressure, even when they are not exposed to reminders of combat. Individuals with PTSD startle with abnormal intensity to unexpected noises. These and related findings demonstrate that PTSD is associated with a long-lasting abnormal reactivity of the autonomic nervous system. The autonomic system is a coordinated group of neural structures both within the brain and in the peripheral nervous system. In dangerous situations, the autonomic system coordinates reactions to danger through the "fight or flight" response. In PTSD, the autonomic system is tuned to an excessive sensitivity, such that an individual's body responds as if danger were present even in innocuous situations.

A recent neuroimaging study using MRI found that the volume of the brain region known as the hippocampus was decreased in men with combat-related PTSD. The investigators hypothesized that hippocampal damage was caused by sudden and intense combat stress. Damage to the hippocampus results in memory defect, which may be a part of PTSD. This finding must be replicated through further research, but it shows the interactions among experience, brain structure, and brain function that are at the heart of modern neuroscience.

Psychopharmacology

Medication plays an essential role in the treatment of mental and emotional disorders. Psychopharmacology is the scientific study of medications that treat disorders of thinking and feeling. When used in the context of accurate diagnosis and concurrent psychosocial care, medications substantially decrease the disability and suffering that accompany mental disorders. There is no justification for an "either/or" approach to psychosocial and psychopharmacological treatment. Rather, medication is one of the modalities—along with psychotherapy, social planning, case management, vocational therapy, and so on. Treatment of a mental disorder requires an integration of one or more modalities that meet the needs of the individual. Medication treatment clearly does not interfere with psychosocial treatment of psychosis, depression, or anxiety disorders. Rather, combined approaches tend to be more effective than either approach used in isolation.

For thousands of years, people have used natural products to affect their thoughts and emotions. However, scientific psychopharmacology is only about 50 years old. The field began in earnest in the 1950s with the observation that individuals with schizophrenia had fewer delusions and hallucinations after receiving the medication chlorpromazine (Thorazine). Chlorpromazine blocks the effects of a number of neurotransmitters in the synapse, but its antipsychotic activity was found to be due to blockade of the postsynaptic dopamine receptor (now known to be the D2 variety). Knowledge about neurotransmitters, receptors, and mental disorders has progressed to the point that mental disorders are treated with "designer molecules." Medications are crafted to perform particular activities at the synapse. Medications that have highly specific receptor-blocking properties, and that do little else, may be highly effective without having bothersome side effects.

Below, I briefly review the major categories of psychiatric medications. These medications are classified according to their primary therapeutic activities, although they may have other uses as well. Medications tend to be useful for particular symptoms rather than for particular disorders. For example, antipsychotic medications are useful for treating auditory hallucinations that occur as a part of schizophrenia and also as a part of bipolar affective disorder. The medications are further classified based on their general molecular structure. Each medication has a particular chemical (generic) name and may also have a brand name used by a particular manufacturer. For example, the antipsychotic medication haloperidol (generic name), a butyrophenone (general chemical class), is marketed in the United States by McNeil Pharmaceuticals as Haldol.

Antipsychotic Medications

The antipsychotic medications are the core treatment of schizophrenia. The newer "atypical" agents, clozapine and risperidone, are substantial improvements over the older "typical" antipsychotic medications. The typical antipsychotic medications were introduced in the 1950s and 1960s, beginning with chlorpromazine. These medications were effective in reducing the hallucinations and delusions of schizophrenia and other psychotic disorders. Once it was determined that the therapeutic activity of chlorpromazine was due to its dopamine-blocking properties, other dopamine blockers were developed. This resulted in a number of medications with similar therapeutic effects, but with somewhat different side effects. Today we localize this dopamine receptor blockade to the D2-type dopamine receptor in the limbic and cortical tracts.

Although the benefits were dramatic, the shortcomings of these medications were soon evident. These agents block D2 receptors with equal efficiency in basal ganglia, causing motor system side effects, such as muscle cramps, rigidity, tremor, and a generalized decrease in all motor activity. In most cases these side effects are fairly mild, but they are clearly undesirable. In occasional cases the side effects are of such intensity that patients may report "feeling like zombies." Long-term use of these medications may result in permanent muscle tics, known as tardive dyskinesia, which can be disfiguring and disabling. Clinicians have become increasingly sophisticated in reducing symptoms while avoiding motor system effects. The problem of motor side effects remains a serious drawback to these medications. Antipsychotic response is also limited. Approximately one-third of patients with schizophrenia have good symptomatic relief with the typical antipsychotics, one-third have more partial response, and one-third derive marginal benefit from these medications. Further, these medications have little therapeutic effect on what are termed the negative symptoms of schizophrenia—social withdrawal, lack of interest in the world, lack of motivation, and little emotional response to their interpersonal environment.

A major treatment advance occurred in 1990, when the atypical antipsychotic clozapine (Clozaril) was introduced for clinical use in the United States. Clozapine has a receptor-blocking profile that is distinct from the typical agents. Dopamine D2 blocking occurs, but there is relatively little binding in the basal ganglia. Dopamine D4 blockade is enhanced, and there is very strong blockade of certain serotonin receptors. Clozapine is often a highly effective treatment for psychotic symptoms that do not respond to conventional antipsychotics. Clozapine is also often effective in treating negative symptoms. There are few to no motor system side effects, and there is apparently no risk of tardive dyskinesia. However, clozapine has its own set of side effects. In approximately 1% of treated individuals, clozapine causes a marked decrease in the production of white blood cells by the bone marrow. Without sufficient white blood cells to fight bacteria, the individual is at risk of life-threatening infection. For this reason, the federal Food and Drug Administration requires that all patients have weekly blood tests for as long as they receive clozapine.

Risperidone (Risperdal) was the next antipsychotic to be introduced. It is as effective as usual agents and may be more useful in the treatment of negative symptoms. At usual doses, there are fewer motor system side effects than with typical antipsychotics. Risperidone is not associated with bone marrow dysfunction and does not require blood testing. Like clozapine, it is a somewhat selective dopamine receptor blocker and a potent serotonin receptor blocker. Although there is little solid scientific proof, it seems that some individuals respond to clozapine who do not respond to risperidone, and perhaps vice versa.

At the time of this writing, four new atypical antipsychotic agents are nearing the final stages of development by pharmaceutical companies. These are all agents that have been designed specifically to mimic certain neurochemical actions of clozapine without causing bone marrow depression, motor system effects, seizures, or other serious side effects. These medications have an intermediate level of blocking activity at the D2-type dopamine receptor, a high level of blockade at the serotonin type 2 receptor, and relatively little binding to other receptors.

Antidepressant Medications

Depression, whether it comes "out of the blue" or follows a psychosocial loss, often responds to antidepressant medication. The psychosocial context of the depression does not predict whether or not symptoms will respond to medications. However, response is predicted by the presence of physical symptoms. Individuals who have disturbances of sleep, appetite, and physical energy are more likely to respond to antidepressants than are individuals who have decreased mood without physical symptoms. Severity of depression does not predict response. It is well known that medications are effective for acute, severe depression. Low-level chronic depression (dysthymia) is often responsive to medications as well.

The mechanisms of action of the antidepressant medications are similar in that they all increase the levels of norepinephrine and/or serotonin within the synapse. These increases occur promptly when the medication is taken. Antidepressant response, however, occurs slowly over a period of 3 to 6 weeks. This time course suggests that antidepressant activity is due to complex adjustments within the brain that occur in response to the higher neurotransmitter levels. Physical signs usually improve first, with an individual's mood improving somewhat later.

The tricyclic antidepressants (TCAs, sometimes called heterocyclic) are a group of effective medications that have been in use for about 30 years. Imipramine (Tofranil) and amitriptyline (Elavil) are common examples, but there are others. These agents block the action of the presynaptic neurotransmitter reuptake pumps. Because less neurotransmitter is being removed from the synapse for recycling, the amount of neurotransmitter in the synapse is increased. These medications have a number of unpleasant side effects that limit their use, such as dry mouth, sedation, dizziness on standing, and constipation. They are highly toxic in overdose. A week's worth of medication may well be a lethal dose, especially in combination with alcohol. Although these are highly effective agents for many people, the toxicity in overdose and the side effects at therapeutic doses limit their utility.

Selective serotonin uptake inhibitor antidepressants (SSRIs) were developed to counter the problems associated with the TCA antidepressants. Examples include fluoxetine (Prozac) and sertraline (Zoloft). These molecules were specifically designed to block only the reuptake of serotonin. They are effective antidepressants that cause relatively few side effects. The SSRIs are not toxic in overdose, even when combined with alcohol. With few side effects and little danger from overdose, these medications have achieved far wider use than the previous antidepressants. Many individuals with chronic milder depressions find treatment with SSRIs to be beneficial, whereas they would have found the side effects of TCA treatment to be intolerable. SSRIs do have side effects of their own. Headache and jitteriness often occur during the early weeks of treatment. Sexual side effects occur in both men and women, including decrease in sexual desire, difficulty with penile erection and orgasm in men, and orgasmic difficulties in women. Such side effects are relatively minor for individuals who suffer from life-threatening major depression, but for individuals with milder depression, decreased sexual ability may interfere significantly with self-esteem and interpersonal relationships.

Several atypical antidepressants capitalize on the success of the SSRIs with, at times, less potential for sexual dysfunction. Serzone (nafazodone), Wellbutrin (bupropion), and Effexor (venlafaxine) were developed or are promoted for this purpose. Their mechanisms are somewhat variable, but they rely on increasing neurotransmitter levels by decreasing the uptake for recycling.

The last major class of antidepressants comprises the monoamine oxidase inhibitors (MAOI). These medications increase synaptic levels of epinephrine and serotonin by inhibiting the function of MAO, the enzyme that breaks down these neurotransmitters. Because of their numerous side effects, MAOIs are usually reserved for depression that does not respond to other medications. Individuals who take MAOIs must follow a diet that scrupulously avoids such foods as ripe cheeses, sausage, and Italian broad beans. These foods contain tyramine, a substance that causes increases in blood pressure and that is usually broken down in the body by MAO. Although the clinical use of MAOIs is limited, they seem to be especially effective in treating a form of depression that is characterized by increased sleep, increased appetite, and intense emotional reactions to interpersonal rejection.

Aside from medications, two other somatic treatments are used for depression: bright light and electroconvulsive therapy (ECT). Exposure to bright light on a scheduled daily basis benefits individuals with seasonal affective disorder. These individuals become depressed each autumn, when the days become shorter, and their mood returns to normal as the daylight period lengthens in the spring. This mood disorder is thought to be caused by an abnormality in regulation of the body's internal timing of daily hormonal rhythms. Dysregulation of melatonin production, a hormone produced by the brain during periods of darkness, is a key element. Treatment with bright light helps to normalize these hormonal irregularities.

Electroconvulsive therapy is a highly effective treatment for serious depression—more effective, in fact, than antidepressant medication. ECT, as it is administered today, is a safe treatment that causes little discomfort. However, many depressed individuals are reluctant to receive ECT because of their impressions based on its use in a bygone era, when ECT was overused, poorly administered, and accompanied by a full epileptic-type seizure. Today, ECT is reserved for the few situations in which it is known to be effective. It is usually administered in an operating room, or in the recovery area outside of an operating room, in a general hospital. The patient is fully anesthetized, and so does not consciously experience the procedure. The patient's muscles are fully relaxed with medication, so that there is no shaking, cramping, or other muscle response to the treatment. A small, controlled electrical signal is passed through the brain that causes the brain to have the type of brain wave activity that occurs during epileptic seizures. This *seizure activity,* which is limited to the brain, lasts for about a minute. The individual awakens from anesthesia a few minutes later and is able to resume usual activities within a few hours. Treatments are given every 2 to 3 days, for a total of 6 to 10 treatments. The exact mechanisms of action are unknown, but increases in the levels of neurotransmitters follow the brain seizure activity. With current procedures, the principal risk of ECT comes from the anesthesia, not the procedure itself. Individuals may experience mild subjective long-term memory difficulties, but these are quite minor. Nonetheless, ECT is best reserved for cases of extreme depression in which quick response may be lifesaving, for cases of less severe depression that have not responded to vigorous treatment with medication, and for individuals who express a clear preference for it.

Mood-Stabilizing Medications

Individuals with bipolar affective disorder have periods of abnormally elevated, irritable, or expansive mood in addition to periods of depression. The mood stabilizers decrease these manic-type symptoms and prevent their emergence during treatment with antidepressant medications. These agents also provide protection against the recurrence of severe depression or mania. Lithium is the most common agent. Lithium is given as a salt that completely dissociates in the gastrointestinal system to yield the lithium ion. Lithium treatment has effects on the serotonin, norepinephrine, and acetylcholine neurotransmission systems in the brain. It also affects the passage of sodium and other electrically charged particles across nerve cell membranes. The exact mechanisms by which lithium exerts its beneficial action are unknown.

Valproic acid, a medication that was developed originally to control epileptic seizures, is also an effective mood stabilizer. It is more effective than lithium when symptoms of mania and depression occur simultaneously. To avoid gastrointestinal upset, valproate is usually given as a related molecule, divalproex (DepakoteO), which the body converts to valproic acid.

Antianxiety Medications

The benzodiazepines (e.g., diazepam [Valium] and alprazolam [Xanax]) remain the most-used medications for generalized incapacitating anxiety. Benzodiazepines bind to a complex receptor for the neurotransmitter GABA (gamma-aminobutyric acid), leading to increased GABA activity. They reliably decrease anxiety and are of considerable benefit when used with proper supervision in properly selected patients. There are several substantial drawbacks to their use. For individuals who are prone to alcohol or prescription drug abuse, benzodiazepines may become abused drugs. Their sedative effects are additive to those of alcohol, such that mixing the two in overdose is often fatal. Abrupt discontinuation of benzodiazepine use may lead to a withdrawal syndrome with flulike symptoms and epileptic-type seizures. The medications in this class are similar to each other. They differ primarily in the length of time they remain active in the body and the dosage required to achieve the same effects.

Buspirone (Buspar) is a newer antianxiety medication that does not have abuse potential and is not dangerous in overdose. For many individuals it is an effective alternative to benzodiazepines. The mechanism of action is unknown. In contrast to the benzodiazepines, the antianxiety properties of buspirone do not occur the first day an individual takes the medication. Rather, anxiety remits gradually over a few weeks' time, much like the effects of the antidepressant medications. Because of this, individuals who want quick relief from symptoms may not be satisfied with buspirone treatment. Benzodiazepines are often used in addition to buspirone in the first few weeks of treatment and then discontinued when the anxiety is reduced by the buspirone.

When anxiety occurs in the context of obsessive compulsive disorder, post-traumatic stress disorder, or panic disorder, alternative medication strategies are more effective. Anxiety associated with these disorders often responds to antidepressants, particularly the SSRIs.

Summary

Neuroscience now provides an essential perspective regarding the causes and treatments of mental disorders. In the coming years, it is likely that we will increasingly regard mental illnesses as common, unfortunate physical ailments, much as we now regard diabetes or rheumatoid arthritis. The neurological sequelae of unfortunate experiences will be better understood, as is occurring now with PTSD. Distinctions among body, brain, mind, and experience will further meld as we better conceptualize the effects that experiences have on brain function and the ways in which brain function determines experience. Effective, humanistic treatments for mental illness will be heavily influenced by neuroscientific research.

References

American Psychiatric Association. (1994). *Diagnostic and statistical manual of mental disorders* (4th ed.). Washington, DC: Author.

Andreasen, N. C. (1994). *Schizophrenia from mind to molecule*. Washington, DC: American Psychiatric Press.

Benes, F. (1995). Is there a neuroanatomic basis for schizophrenia? An old question revisited. *Neuroscientist, 1*(2), 104-115.

Bernstein, J. G. (1995). *Handbook of drug therapy in psychiatry* (3rd ed.). St. Louis: C. V. Mosby.

Brodal, P. (1992). *The central nervous system*. New York: Oxford University Press.

Cooper, J. R., Bloom, F. E., & Roth, R. H. (1991). *The biochemical basis of neuropharmacology* (6th ed.). New York: Oxford University Press.

Daniel, G., Aigun, J. R., & Weinberger, D. R. (1992). Brain imaging in neuropsychiatry. In S. C. Yudofsky & R. E. Hales (Eds.), *Textbook of neuropsychiatry* (2nd ed., pp. 165-186). Washington, DC: American Psychiatric Press.

Hall, Z. W. (Ed.). (1992). *An introduction to molecular neurobiology*. Sunderland, MA: Sinauer.

Keefe, R. S. E., & Harvey, P. D. (1994). *Understanding schizophrenia: A guide to the new research on causes and treatment*. New York: Free Press.

Prichard, J. W. (1995). The nuclear magnetic resonance revolution in basic and clinical neuroscience. *Neuroscientist, 1*(2), 84-94.

Schatzberg, A. F., & Nemeroff, C. B. (1995). *The American Psychiatric Press textbook of psychopharmacology*. Washington, DC: American Psychiatric Press.

CHAPTER 7

Research Into Social Factors in Mental Illness

David W. Millard

Only the sketchiest outline of the contemporary field of social research was apparent before World War II. This review covers recent research from the United States, Britain, and Australia. In a short time, a great deal has been accomplished, making comprehensive coverage impossible in the space available here. Readers may find further information in Henderson's *An Introduction to Social Psychiatry* (1988) and in *Common Mental Disorders: A Bio-Social Model* (1992), by the British authors David Goldberg and Peter Huxley, professors of psychiatry and social work, respectively. In this chapter I will generally refer to this area of interest as *social psychiatry,* a term that obviously relates to social psychology and to aspects of sociology and social policy. The major findings of social research in relation to mental illness may be grouped under three broad headings: social causation, social treatment, and social policy.

Social Research and Social Theory

Fundamental to investigating social causation is the process of counting the number of occurrences of a particular phenomenon in a particular population. This is epidemiological research. However, as soon as we begin to contemplate that apparently straightforward task, a number of problems arise. For example, in the question of the influence of a social factor such as unemployment on the causation of a mental disorder such as depression, one of the first problems is to decide precisely what we will take as a "case of mental illness" and, further, and even more taxing, what we actually mean by *mental illness*. Within such an inquiry there are a number of assumptions that are questionable.

A crucial issue concerns the nature of the reality that we ascribe to social events. Broadly, there are two approaches. The first is associated with theoretical positions such as positivism, empiricism, and realism. They have in common the feature that social events are thought of as analogous with physical events. There is a real world "out there" that forms and influences us, similar to the operation of physical mechanisms. Just as molecules become "excited" and vibrate more rapidly as heat is applied, so persons in a crowd become excited and react more vigorously when roused by popular music or political oratory or when attacked by an oppressive police force. We can record and analyze such happenings independent of anyone's interpretation of them: The facts speak for themselves; social events have objectivity.

The other approach, associated with positions such as idealism and social constructionism, denies that people are simply the passive recipients of external social forces. In this view, the social world is created by people's thoughts and actions. How we are and how we act are not matters of cause and effect analogous with heated molecules; there is a place for choice, or perhaps "free will." We may *feel* that our behavior is externally and absolutely constrained by, say, the laws of the state, yet there also exists the political doctrine that people are ultimately governed only with their own consent. Clearly, our social world is to a considerable degree orderly; that is, there are many social regularities upon which we all rely. Yet these are not the consequences of social laws like the laws of physics, but, according to this view, are a reflection of the operation of *social rules*. Social life is rule forming, rule guided, and rule breaking, and this fact has considerable implications for social research and imposes significant limitations on the extent to which we can predict human behavior.

> People are constantly engaged in the process of interpretation and it is this we should seek to understand. In other words researchers should concentrate upon how people produce social life. Social life cannot simply be observed (empiricism), it can be and understood only as a result of examining people's selection and interpretation of events and actions. Understanding these processes and the rules which make them possible is the aim of research for schools of thought within this tradition. . . . The ideal of an internal social "reality" has now been abandoned because the meanings which we attach to the world are not static nor universal, but always multiple and variable and constantly subject to modification and change. (May, 1993, pp. 8-9)

A number of scholars have attempted to reconcile these two approaches. For example, Giddens (1976, 1984) emphasizes both social construction of reality and its social transmission. Thus society may be largely a human construct, meaningful and subject to varied interpretation. But in the process of its replication or transmission to us, this same society structures our experience and constrains our actions. The family, then, is seen as an institution that is a place not only of biological reproduction but also of the *social reproduction* in successive generations of the social constructs of the past.

Thus we may accept that in a vital way, it has been a matter of human choice or decision that a specific pattern of behavior should be called a mental disorder. Nevertheless, we experience these decisions as "given." So it is possible to have a notion of schizophrenia or depression that successive generations of practitioners or researchers, operating in different localities, are able to use with reasonable confidence. The existence of well-known systems of classification such as the mental disorders section of the World Health Organization's (1992) *International Classification of Disease* (now in its tenth revision and thus referred to as *ICD-10*) and the American Psychiatric Association's (1994) *Diagnostic and Statistical Manual of Mental Disorders* (now in its fourth edition, thus *DSM-IV*) attests to the possibility of agreed-upon and settled concepts of mental illness—a rule-governed matter. On the other hand, the fact that these systems have undergone laborious, occasionally contentious, process revisions (which will doubtless continue) reflects the element of continuous reinterpretation in what is essentially a social process. An essentially *negotiated* ordering of social constructs has acquired an apparent *objectivity*.

Foundations for Research in Social Psychiatry

Due to the problems discussed above, the information we have in social psychiatry comprises generalizations that are inevitably approximate. However, if such generalizations are to be useful in practice, it is plainly important that they should be as accurate as possible. Much effort has gone into devising methods of counting instances of mental disorder that rank high in terms of both reliability (that is, if something is measured once, the result will be the same when it is measured again) and validity (that is, what is actually measured corresponds to what should have been measured). While accepting the fact that what we are attempting to capture is to some extent defined by individual interpretations of rule-governed definitions, these methods nevertheless maximize agreement among those using the definitions by using standard forms of data collection. Much effort has gone into establishing their validity and reliability. What have emerged are a number of research instruments now in international use, which fall into two categories: questionnaires and standardized interviews.

Questionnaires

Among questionnaires, probably the best known is the General Health Questionnaire, developed by Goldberg and colleagues (Goldberg, 1972; Goldberg & Williams, 1988). It is a self-report questionnaire existing in several

Table 7.1 Goldberg and Huxley's Five Levels on the Pathway to Psychiatric Care

Level 1	Overall prevalence in the community	265-315/1,000/year
	(First filter: "illness behavior" [Mechanic, 1978], including consulting a primary care physician)	
Level 2	Total mental morbidity among attenders at primary care	230/1,000/year
	(Second filter: doctors' ability to detect such mental disorder correctly)	
Level 3	"conspicuous psychiatric morbidity"; that is, mental disorder detected by the doctor	101.5/1,000/year
	(Third filter: referral to specialist mental health services)	
Level 4	Total morbidity in the mental health services	23.5/1,000/year
	(Fourth filter: admission to psychiatric beds)	
Level 5	Psychiatric inpatients	5.71/1,000/year

SOURCE: Based on Goldberg and Huxley (1992, p. 4).

forms (60, 30, 28, and 12 items) and was originally a screening instrument to detect persons likely to have psychiatric disorders in the general population or when seen by primary care physicians (general or family practitioners). Its use by different researchers in investigations involving different populations has produced findings that suggest that it taps similar constructs of mental disorder and affirms that there is widespread consensus that certain phenomena should, and others should not, count as instances of mental disorder.

Goldberg and Huxley (1992) have surveyed the world research literature dealing with the matter of prevalence in various settings. They conceive this in terms of five "levels," separated by four "filters," on what they have called the "pathway to psychiatric care." Their estimates of annual prevalence (the total number of cases occurring per 1,000 population in the course of a year) are shown in Table 7.1.

It must suffice here to make two comments. First, the figures shown at each level in Table 7.1 are based on repeated studies in many parts of the world and in both rural and urban environments. Second, they point to the well-recognized fact that only a very small minority of sufferers find their way into specialist psychiatric services, and still fewer into residential treatment. This is only partly a matter of severity; it concerns also the type of mental disorder. The vast majority of those identified at the level of community surveys will have mild or moderate degrees of anxiety or depression. They include a few with psychosis or organically based mental disorder, and such persons will pass the filters selectively so that they appear disproportionately frequently at Levels 4 and 5. In comparison to the bulk of "Level 1-type" disorders, these tend to be long-lasting and frequently do not resolve spontaneously. Such persons often need substantial, specialized, and expensive resources for treatment and care, and they use them heavily.

It should be noted, however, that the practice of mental health professionals is largely based on this highly atypical and select group. This has given rise to a radical critique along the lines that definitions derived from such experience cannot be applied appropriately to community-level disorders. On the other hand, it may be argued that research and planning throughout the mental health field require the expertise of specialists. Whatever position one takes in that debate, the fact is that the standardized interview—the second category of widely used methods—is precisely a standardization of parts of the conventional diagnostic interview. Two examples may be cited.

Standardized Interviews

Probably the most widely used standardized diagnostic interview is the Present State Examination (PSE), first developed in Britain by Wing (1972) and others. There are two versions—a shorter version for population studies, which nonmedical and lay interviewers can be trained to use reliably, and the full version for use in clinical settings. As its name suggests, the PSE allows ratings to be made of the respondent's current mental state, but it can also be used to assess the respondent's state over the preceding 4 weeks. The PSE is associated with a computerized Index of Definition, which provides eight levels of likelihood that sufficient symptoms are present to make a classification according to the *ICD*. Over Level 5, the program provides a tentative *ICD* diagnosis.

The second example of a standardized interview is the Diagnostic Interview Schedule (DIS). This was developed for use in a particular research program in the United States, the Epidemiological Catchment Area Studies (Robbins, Helzer, Croughan, & Ratcliff, 1981). The DIS aims to capture lifetime prevalence as well as the respondent's current state, and it is longer than the PSE. However, it too is used in conjunction with an associated computer program that covers a wider range of possible diagnoses as defined by *DSM-III*.

Armed with instruments like these, social psychiatrists have begun the lengthy and painstaking task of researching social factors in mental disorder. In the first place, this results in a variety of descriptions, but it also makes possible certain explanatory statements, some of which have therapeutic implications.

Both Henderson (1988) and Goldberg and Huxley (1992) have useful summaries of some of the main descriptive findings of social psychiatry research. They show, for example, the extent of the well-known excess in general population surveys of cases among females. For instance, in London one study using the PSE gives a total monthly prevalence of 109/1,000, with the rate for males of 61/1,000 and for females of 149/1,000 (Bebbington, Hurry, Tennant, Sturt, & Wing, 1981). On the other hand, in the Epidemiological Catchment Area Studies in five cities in the United States, the figures for males and females are almost equal (males = 140/1,000; females

Table 7.2 Prevalence Rates per 1,000 per Month

	Anxiety States	Depression	Schizophrenia/ Paranoid States	Bipolar Affective Disorder	Total
Bebbington et al., 1981	29	70	6	8	109
Reiger & Burke, 1988	18[a] (+62)	22	7	4[b]	112

a. Panic disorder plus obsessive compulsive; the additional 62/1,000 are phobias.
b. Mania only; other figure in this column includes psychotic depression.

= 166/1,000; total = 154/1,000) because the survey, using the DIS, included cases of cognitive impairment and (especially) of substance abuse and antisocial conduct disorder—both much more common among males (Reiger & Burke, 1988). If these diagnostic groups are excluded, the rates in this study change to males, 7/1,000; females, 145/1,000; and total, 112/1,000—that is, very close indeed to the figures in Bebbington et al.'s (1981) study, which also excluded those groups. Of course, as indicated above, it is a matter of equally legitimate social definition either to include or to exclude such categories from one's notion of what constitutes the concept of "mental disorder."

From the same two studies, the distribution in the general community of some of the common diagnostic categories can be illustrated as shown in Table 7.2. Obviously, such overall figures do not disclose other significant differences. These would include such matters as variation with age (in general, rates show a peak in the middle years of life, especially for affective disorders, but drug dependency is most common in the younger age group and the dementias among the elderly) and social class (where the effects are mixed, but the general tendency, especially for psychotic disorders, is toward a clustering in the lower social classes).

Social Causation

Theoretical Considerations

We first need to isolate those factors that can fairly be described as social. In practice, most professionals in the mental health field, whatever orientation they claim for themselves, probably work with a general model something like that shown in Figure 7.1. This is an *explanatory* model, and the explanations it offers are essentially *causal*. The model suggests that the causal factors for any piece of human behavior, including those underlying an event of mental disorder, come from three broad categories.

1. They may be *genetic*—fixed at the moment of conception and delivered to the individual as she or he is at the present time (i.e., often after a considerable delay)

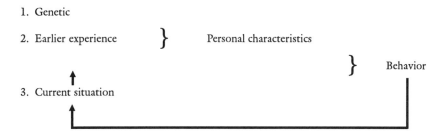

Figure 7.1. Interactional Model of Causation

through biological mechanisms, especially in the brain. However unclear we may be about the precise mechanisms involved, the fact of a strong genetic contribution to the causation of the major psychoses—schizophrenia and manic depressive disorder—is well established, and in certain organic disorders, such as Huntington's chorea, it is paramount. Social psychiatry must take cognizance of such factors, but they are not the primary business of this chapter.

2. They may be derived from *earlier life experience* and somehow "saved up" in the individual—partly as memory and presumably, therefore, again involving some biological change in the brain but also importantly social and psychological—and active in the individual's current life. Not all of the most important of these earlier experiences are social (they include, for example, illnesses), but very many are—and where they have been researched by social scientists they tend to be described as *predisposing* or *vulnerability* factors. These are discussed further below.

A great deal is implied by the relationship between past and present in category 2: Our experiences are not stored mechanistically (like photographs, for example); rather, they are "worked on" and modified through time. This is the territory of psychology. Indeed, much of the psychology of perception, memory, and information processing, and the whole of the great systems of psychological explanation—Freudian, Jungian, social learning, and other theories—are essentially about how past events are carried down to be active in the present. Now, our technical literature frequently uses the term *psychosocial,* but is clear that two conceptual worlds, the world of mental events (the subject matter of psychology) and the world of social events, must be considered separately.[1] For instance, within social psychiatry the distinction is often made between social events per se and the subjective experience a person has of them. I offer several illustrations of this point later in the chapter.

To return to Figure 7.1, as most people nowadays regard the 19th-century *nature versus nurture* debate to have been wrongly posed, and adopt instead an interactionist position, the first bracket is placed in the figure to indicate that factors drawn from these two categories somehow interact with one another. This interaction between genetic and environmental factors results in a person's having the particular characteristics that he or she possesses. The suggestion of the model is that the individual having these characteristics finds him- or herself in

3. a *particular situation* having specifiable characteristics. Human behavior in general is strongly influenced by situational variables, a point of importance in studies of normal functioning. In the more specific context of mental disorder, we would refer to precipitating or destabilizing factors.

The interaction between the individual and the situation, represented by the second bracket in Figure 7.1, issues in the *behavior* we wish to account for (which appears on the right-hand side of the figure).

Thus one example of a behavior might be the achievement of a particular score on an IQ test. A 19th- or even early-20th-century view might well have been that an IQ score reflects only a person's genetic endowment with respect to intelligence—that is, that category 1 factors feed through directly to *behavior*. But it was soon realized that environmental factors could influence intelligence—certainly in the direction that adverse factors would depress it, but possibly also that favorable factors might enhance it—so for some time, IQ tests were widely thought to reflect the *personal characteristics* element in the model. However, in recent decades it has been realized that factors in the actual testing situation—for instance, whether the tester and testee are of the same or different sex, race, or whatever—also influence the score. Thus factors from category 3 also need to be taken into consideration in accounting for behaviors of this kind.

Another example of the interplay among genetic factors, early experience, and current situation would be an instance of breakdown in a person with a schizophrenic disorder. The research is reasonably conclusive that an individual does not have schizophrenia unless he or she carries a significant genetic predisposition to the condition (category 1), but this genetic loading is not sufficient to account entirely for the appearance of the disorder, and there is very sound evidence that adverse life events often precipitate breakdowns in vulnerable individuals (category 3). Careful examination of the statistical evidence suggests, however, that factors derived from these two categories together do not exhaustively account for instances of schizophrenia, and there is room for admitting the influence of factors about which we are much less clear but that seem to be drawn from earlier life experience (category 3).

Obviously, accounting for disorders such as anxiety states or other neuroses is likely to involve drawing most heavily on factors from category 2, although genetic predisposition and contemporary situational factors are also significant; accounting for states of affairs such as bereavement reactions or post-traumatic stress disorder requires drawing heavily on category 3; Huntington's chorea is almost exclusively accounted for by category 1; and so on. But in virtually every case, an accurate account compels us to draw to a greater or lesser extent on factors from each of these classes: Multidimensional accounts are mandatory.

One addition must be made to complete the model in Figure 7.1. Because humans have a unique capacity for self-reflection, our own behavior is in fact part of the social situation that we can ourselves observe, and the situation may be influenced by it. Thus the model requires the feedback loop represented by the arrow in Figure 7.1. Moreover, because today's *current situation* is tomorrow's *earlier experience,* we must protract the feedback loop from the third to the second category of explanatory factors, whence it can of course feed into *personal characteristics.* This represents diagrammatically one kind of "learning from one's own experience": In principle, personal characteristics may change as a result of the individual's own participation in social situations—a fact that obviously provides scope within the model for personal development, response to therapy, and so on.

A Methodological Note

In considering the effects of social factors in more detail, we must first recall the important truth that simply because a statistical correlation may be shown between a particular social event and a frequent occurrence of a mental disorder, we are not thereby entitled to infer a causal relationship. The correlation may arise fortuitously, or because both social event and mental disorder are the consequences of some third and independent influence. However, this is not to say that genuinely causal relationships can never be demonstrated. Generally, that process involves an element of theorizing. Researchers would typically develop an explanatory model for the specific problem before them, then collect data to try to substantiate—or, more properly, to attempt to disprove—this explanation. Different factors may act independently, additively, or in more complex interactions. One sort of interaction is that between predisposing and precipitating factors.

Predisposing Factors

A considerable body of research has been directed toward tracing the associations between particular social factors and specific disorders such as anxiety, depression, and substance abuse. A representative list of such factors, based on the account given by Goldberg and Huxley (1992, pp. 84-101), would include those shown in Table 7.3. Obviously, the significance of such factors varies from one situation to another; the factors may occur in combination, and all are mediated by the individual's subjective responses to them, but each of the factors listed is statistically supported in well-conducted research.

Precipitating Factors

The commonsense notion that stress causes mental disorder has been considerably modified by research but retains a certain broad validity. An obvious basis for research in this area was the compilation of lists of social situations thought to be stressful. An early and well-known example of such a list comes from Holmes and Rahe (1967). In their Social Readjustment Rating Scale, 43 situations are placed in rank order, with an accompanying index of stressfulness. Table 7.4 gives some illustrative examples from this scale. Note

Table 7.3 Predisposing Factors

Family factors	Parental loss; lack of parental care	Parental death, separation; parental discord; mental or physical illness; alcohol abuse/ criminality/affectionless control/ institutional upbringing; physical/sexual/ emotional violence
Social relationships	Marital discord	(especially chronic difficulties)
	Weak social support	Impoverished social network; lack of close confiding relationship
Social adversity ("structural vulnerability")	Poor housing	High-rise apartments; raised walkways; overcrowding
	Unemployment	Poverty; low self-esteem

Table 7.4 Extracts From Social Readjustment Rating Scale

Rank	Life Event	Mean Value
1	Death of spouse	100
2	Divorce	73
3	Marital separation	65
4	Jail term	63
9	Marital reconciliation	45
17	Death of close friend	37
25	Outstanding personal achievement	28
30	Trouble with boss	23
37	Mortgage or loan of less than $10,000	17
41	Vacation	13
43	Minor violations of the law	11

that these events relate to a wide array of areas of life experience and that they include not only losses but gains.

More recent research designs, however, have put greater emphasis on respondents' being free to define their own life stresses, in which case different arrangements have to be made for attributing some agreed-upon standard of severity to the events they report. One famous piece of British research that adopted this technique was conducted by a team led by Professor George Brown, a medical sociologist, and published as *Social Origins of Depression: A Study of Psychiatric Disorder in Women* (Brown & Harris, 1978). This study is notable for its careful methodology and as an example of the construction of a convincing theoretical model to bring together the various factors.

The study population was 114 psychiatric in- and outpatients living in South London suburb and carefully randomized control groups totaling 458 women living in the same community. The researchers took particular care to demonstrate the comparability of the study and control groups in terms of background factors such as social class, and to exclude psychiatric cases from the latter; to define precisely the "onsets" of the episodes of depression; to collect comprehensive accounts of both chronic social difficulties and specific life events occurring in the preceding 12 months among the study and control groups, and to be precise about the timing of such events in relation to the onsets; and to rate the severity of the life events on a 6-point scale for which typical examples are published. The significance of this last point is that (a) it allows the events to be selected by the respondents themselves—that is, not from a "forced-choice" list—but, on the other hand, (b) a public judgment is possible of the extent to which we might agree with the investigator's attributions of severity to specific events, along the lines of a social constructionist approach to social reality (as discussed in the first section of this chapter). In other words, the rule-governed aspect of this procedure is open to public inspection.

The Brown and Harris (1978) report is important not only for its methodological sophistication but also for its detailed results, which have contributed substantially to knowledge in the area of social psychiatry. The following risks were associated with mental illness among working-class women:

- Vulnerability factors
  - o Loss of mother before age 11
  - o Not working outside the home
  - o Lack of a confiding relationship with husband or boyfriend
  - o Having three or more children under 15 years at home

- Precipitating factors
  - o Loss or threat of loss, especially of high severity and where the loss carried long-term implications and did not involve purely health difficulties

- Symptom formation factors
  - o An association between past loss through death and the "psychotic" type of depression
  - o An association between loss through separation with the "neurotic" type of depression

Social Factors in Prevention and Treatment

During the middle decades of the 20th century, there was some bias toward viewing social psychiatry as mainly concerned with etiology—the branch of medicine concerned with causation. More recently, this emphasis has been redressed and there now exists an established place for research and practice in social therapy. This section briefly considers four approaches: (a) research into protective factors of a social nature—more or less equivalent to social prevention, (b) social support operating at the level of the individual, (c) intervention into the social relationships of the family, and (d) residential or day care institutions as a mode of social therapy.

Protective Factors

Among the earliest contributors to research concerning protective factors was Gerald Caplan, whose volume *The Principles of Preventive Psychiatry* (1964) was groundbreaking. Caplan proposed in his conceptual model "that in order not to become mentally disordered, a person needs continual 'supplies' commensurate with his current stage of growth and development. These supplies can be specified and roughly classified into three groups: physical, psychosocial and socio-cultural" (p. 31). Physical supplies obviously include life support and protection against bodily disease: food, shelter, sensory stimulation, exercise, and so on. Psychosocial supplies include the stimulation of cognitive and emotional development through personal interaction in the family and in wider society—school, work, and so on. Sociocultural influences are those exerted upon the individual by the customs of the encompassing society and culture: the language, values, norms, and social structural phenomena that influence the socialization of individuals. Caplan (1964) notes: "Just as in physical nutrition, disorder can occur if there are qualitative or quantitative shortages of these supplies . . . [or, it may be added, the threat of such shortfalls] . . . and sometimes if there is an overprovision which 'poisons' the organism" (p. 31).

This wide-ranging conceptual analysis was certainly influential in its time. However, it was not at that stage backed by empirical research. Characteristically, later developments have moved from the "broad-brush" approach toward a consideration of more specifically definable matters. Also, they have gone hand in hand with the investigation of vulnerability factors, although it must be emphasized that protective factors are not necessarily in any simple sense the obverse of those contributing to vulnerability.

A distinguished British child psychiatrist, Michael Rutter (1985), points out that a protective factor is not synonymous with a positive or beneficial experience: It may be quite negative (e.g., in the case of a sociopath, who may be much less permeable than others to certain stressful experiences), it may not be an experience at all (e.g., where a person's sex or developmental stage influences his or her vulnerability), or it may be that the protective effect comes into operation only when an additional stressor is experienced (e.g., although programs to prepare children and their families for hospitalization are known to be effective, in the absence of admission of the child to the hospital they may have no discernible effects; Wolkind & Rutter, 1985). Rutter refers to a large body of empirical research, and his conclusions are worth summarizing:

1. A person's response to a stressor will be influenced by his or her appraisal of the situation and capacity to process the experience, attach meaning to it, and incorporate it into a more general system of belief.
2. How people deal with adversity, in particular a positive capacity to act, rather than react, appears to be important.

3. This capacity to act is related to self-esteem and a feeling of self-efficacy as much as to the individual's range of problem-solving skills.

4. Such a cognitive set reflects secure, stable affectional relationships—particularly those obtaining in the family situation in childhood and in adult (marital) partnerships, both of which can be shown to have measurable effects both on the actual incidence of adverse life events and on their impacts on the individual.

5. Such personal, psychological characteristics operate largely in interaction with and in responses from other people—that is, they are socially mediated.

6. Coping successfully with stress can be strengthening throughout life. Success lies not in the avoidance of stress but in increasing social competence and mastery.

Rutter (1985) concludes:

> All the evidence points to developmental links. Prevention does not primarily lie in the buffering effect of some supportive factor operating at one point in time or even over a prolonged time. Rather the quality of resilience resides in how people deal with their life changes and what they do about their situations. That quality is influenced by early life experiences, by happenings during later childhood and adolescence, and by circumstances in adult life.
>
> None of these is in itself determinative of later outcomes, but in combination they may serve to create a chain of indirect linkages that foster escape from adversity. (p. 608)

Probably the types of protective factors best empirically established are those relating to (a) a background of good parenting and (b) close, confiding relationships in the present situation (generally, as in Brown & Harris's 1978 study discussed above, partner or marital relationships).

Social Support

Social support has recently attracted a good deal of research interest, both on the side of causation (the effects of a lack of social support) and on the side of treatment (the efficacy of providing it). There is no necessary connection between these. On one hand, we may not be able to remedy the effects of deficient social support simply by providing it, even in superabundance. On the other hand, there is no a priori reason the provision of social support should not be therapeutically useful, even where other interventions are concurrently in use and there may be no specific evidence in its favor beyond ordinary clinical experience.

A notable contributor to the research literature in this field is Henderson (1988), who points to three broad hypotheses about social support:

> [a] that it has a direct and independent effect in its own right on mental and/or physical health whether or not adversity is also present; [b] that it provides a buffer or cushioning effect against stress, but has no independent effect in its absence; or [c] that in persons who have developed affective or neurotic symptoms, it has a therapeutic effect, shortening the effect and reducing the symptoms. (p. 98)

The second hypothesis is broadly confirmed by research such as that reported by Brown and Harris (1978), but it is the third that is our concern here. Unfortunately, of the three, this area has attracted the least empirical investigation, though what exists provides some experimental justification (e.g., Parker & Barnett, 1987). Part of the problem is that the notion of social support fades off on one side into concepts of counseling or psychotherapy by professionals that (as in the example of, say, post-traumatic stress disorder) is certainly held to be valuable, and on the other side into social network theory and the consideration of wider societal issues. Here the therapeutic recommendations effectively become matters of social policy. One good example of this is the notion that, rather than recruiting formally trained "supporters," the preferred approach would be through self-help groups involving fellow sufferers and perhaps their careers—that is, manifestations of the relevant social network. Of course, professionals such as social workers or community psychiatric nurses may have a role in facilitating access to such services.

Family Interventions

Sociologists of the family have traditionally suggested that one of its major functions is to mediate for individual members the pressures and opportunities arising in wider society (Goode, 1964). Therefore, family processes have attracted much attention in modern mental health practice. Two examples from a wide range of research into family interventions are selected here.

The first is a study of *brief focal family therapy* in treating disturbed children, conducted by Kingston and Bentovim (1978). This is a treatment technique involving the formulation of minimum psychodynamic hypotheses to account for the child's disturbances based on a careful initial assessment. Family therapy is then conducted, focusing on these hypotheses. Criteria are established at the outset for what will count as improvement at the completion of treatment or at short-term (3- to 6-month) follow-up. The short-term outcomes for the 22 out of 29 intake cases who successfully engaged in therapy in Kingston and Bentovim's study were as shown in Table 7.5. This study represents an early example of a rigorous attempt to assess the efficacy of this form of social therapy.

Evaluation research in family therapy has continued vigorously over the years. Very broad questions—such as, Does family therapy work?—are of very limited value, but in recent years meta-analysis has been employed to address some of them. Studies of this nature involve aggregating the results of several published investigations in the given field that meet some minimal criteria for reliability, in order to obtain larger sample sizes and more convincing conclusions. One such study in family therapy leads to the general conclusion that the average patient participating in family therapy is better off than 76% of patients undergoing alternative treatment, minimal treatment, or no treatment (Marcus, Lenge, & Pettigrew, 1990). This beneficial effect appears to increase in the first year after therapy but may diminish steeply in the subsequent months.

Table 7.5 Results From Kingston and Bentovim (1978)

Improvement	Index Patient		Family as a Whole	
Nil (or worse)	3	(14%)	11	(50%)
Some	12	(55%)	7	(32%)
Much	7	(32%)	4	(18%)

The second example is a well-known series of investigations into *expressed emotion,* "steadily developed over three decades to become one of the more notable successes in psychiatric care" (Henderson, 1988, p. 148). As discussed in relation to the multifactorial model of causation presented above, in schizophrenic disorders genetic influences are a powerful and necessary component, but not the *only* component. Different causal factors may influence different aspects of a phenomenon. Brown and Harris (1978), whose work on the causation of depression is noted above, have also been interested in social determinants among the schizophrenic disorders. This team was responsible for clearly establishing a role for stressful life events in precipitating relapse into overt illness among persons predisposed (presumably genetically) to such disorder. Among such social stresses, particular attention has focused on high levels of expressed emotion (EE) in the families of schizophrenic patients. The research has involved the use of standardized forms of observation and family interviewing using tape recordings for subsequent analysis. In its early phases, the research was directed toward understanding causation. Later, it became the basis for studies of the effectiveness of family intervention (Leff, Kuipers, Berkowitz, Ebedien-Vries, & Sturgeon, 1982). High-EE relatives are characterized by a greater tendency toward criticism, hostility, or overinvolvement, as measured by both the content of communications and their style. More specifically, high-EE relatives display the following (Henderson, 1988, p. 151):

- Intrusiveness, often in the form of fussing and persistently offering unsolicited help
- More dramatic responses to the patient's illness
- Less inclination to believe the patient is ill
- Lower tolerance of the patient's behavior and diminished performance

Based on this understanding, the researchers studied a sample of 24 schizophrenic patients selected for contact with high-EE families, half of whom were assigned to routine outpatient care and half of whom received a package of social interventions, including a program of education about schizophrenia and a relatives' group and family sessions for relatives and patients. In the control group, 50% relapsed within 9 months, compared with 9% in the experimental group. The methodology applied in this study crucially included measures to ensure that the therapeutic interventions were in fact what they were supposed to be, and that results were not contaminated because the trial, although controlled, could not be "blind" in the sense of the investigators' being kept unaware of which patients were in which group. Subsequently, this work has been developed through the production of literature for relatives and guidance for professionals involved in this kind of work.

Two final findings of research in this area should be noted. First, there is a clear interactive effect of high EE with other factors, for example, the duration of daily exposure to relevant family members and the influence of concomitant medication. Second, it has been shown that high EE is also associated with relapse in other conditions—depression and neurotic disorders—and that there is some association with other life events.

Social Therapy in Institutions

Work in residential or day care settings plays an indispensable part in the care and treatment of mental illness, yet the literature in this field, which includes an extensive research component, rarely receives much notice in the textbooks of social psychiatry. Perhaps this relative neglect reflects the bias of many researchers toward focusing on individuals rather than groups or organizations, and also the relatively low professional status of residential care.

Although it is true that during the middle decades of the 19th century, publications appeared in both the United States and Britain discussing the so-called moral treatment of the insane in the mental hospitals, this had faded by the turn of the century, and the earliest stage of a recognizably continuous process of research into residential or day care as therapy for mental disorders belongs to the period between the world wars. Very broadly, this process falls into three overlapping phases: first, a phase of narrative descriptions of life in residential settings; second, the introduction of serious attempts to become explicit about the theoretical underpinning of such practice; and third, the collection and analysis of systematic data (often numerical) more or less grounded in such theory.

The earliest examples from the phase of descriptions are mainly of residential institutions for psychologically disturbed children and adolescents. They include, from the United States, the experimental Junior Republics—a movement out of which Homer Lane (a controversial figure) crossed the Atlantic to establish in Britain an institution known as the Little Commonwealth, which in turn was the inspiration for other pioneering places of this kind. Typically, these institutions were founded by charismatic individuals who held the view that maladjusted or delinquent children and young people were best helped by regimes providing a large measure of self-government together with a good deal of support to encourage them to make use of, and learn from, such opportunities. David Wills is a British example, but there were other isolated examples—earlier in the period, Makarenko in Russia and Bruno Bettelheim, who joined the Chicago Orthogenic School in 1944. But the overwhelming majority of child-care institutions remained, in contrast, dependence inducing and essentially repressive, though, to a variable extent, benign, and always included what would later be called institutionalism. The same characteristics were virtually universal in provisions for mentally disordered adults.

The importance of narrative accounts of this work was as a source of hypotheses, and World War II marks the turning point toward the second phase, when definable theory began to play a part. Two major sources may be described: psychoanalysis and systems theory as applied to organizations. Much of the earlier work on residential therapy for disturbed young people was rethought as part of the growing influence of psychoanalytic ideas on child psychiatry and the child guidance movement. A parallel, though more sporadic, movement was taking place in adult mental health. A classic U.S. study of this period is that conducted by Stanton and Schwartz (1954)—a psychiatrist and a sociologist—in a small psychiatric hospital operating along psychoanalytic lines. The research consisted of a good deal of participant observation with some attempt at systematic data collection, and Stanton and Schwartz's book is a good early example of the "narrative with numbers" school of research reporting characteristic of this field. An influential finding was the strong tendency among psychotic patients for periods of exceptionally disturbed behavior to result from covert staff disagreement about the patients' management. This has acquired the status of a generalization widely applied in the world of residential therapy. It is the *hiddenness,* not the *fact,* of the disagreement that matters, and this suggests, entirely in line with the earlier work with maladjusted children, that openness of communication is a vital factor in residential therapy.

A British example that also belongs to the second methodological phase, but draws more on organizational theory, is research conducted by Revans (1976) and coworkers over several years in a variety of hospital settings. Again, the method was one of observation with systematic data collection. These studies provide strong empirical understanding of the interactions among four variables: anxiety, communication, morale, and efficiency. Thus is reached what might be thought of as virtually an axiom of residential care: Poor patterns of internal *communication* within the staff group (as measured by interview techniques and participant observation) are associated with high levels of *anxiety* (same methods, plus rating scales) and with poor staff *morale* (sickness rates and premature dropout of trainees) and lower levels of *institutional efficiency* (longer periods of inpatient stay)—and conversely.

The damaging effects of large-scale psychiatric hospitals led to many changes, including the wholesale shift to community care (see the section below on social policy) and attempts to make healthier places of the institutions themselves. One example of the latter that occurred strongly in Britain and the United States, but also elsewhere, was a range of developments associated with the concept of the *therapeutic community*. Although numerically small, this work has attracted a more coherent and sustained body of thought and empirical research than perhaps any other field of institutional therapy. Readers are referred to *The Therapeutic Community Movement: Charisma and Routinization* (Manning, 1988) for a discussion of the history outlined above, something of the theory of the therapeutic community, a substantial review of the research literature, and an example of a particular investigation belonging to the third phase.

Manning (1988) conducted a painstaking study in Australia of six hostels (halfway houses) for psychiatric patients operated by a voluntary organization, the Richmond Fellowship. His report opens with an extended discussion of the methodological problems of institutional research. This refers to the distinction between studies of outcome ("spot the winner" research) and studies of process, tracing carefully the arguments that both are necessary, and underlines the necessity of comparing institutions. Manning then presents a good deal of numerical data to describe aspects of the functioning of the houses and proceeds to relate these to measures of outcome. The results are subject to a sophisticated statistical analysis (path analysis), which generates the results illustrated here in Figure 7.2. Multiple observations and measurements are condensed into seven variables, as shown in Table 7.6.

The statistical analysis may be presented diagrammatically as in Figure 7.3. Briefly, the factors are grouped according to whether they belong to the pretreatment phase, the treatment program itself, or the outcome. The arrows display the directions of the influences of factors upon one another, and the boxed figures indicate the strength of each separate association (1.00 is the theoretical maximum).

Research of this degree of sophistication begins to record something of the complexity of the relationships among factors that approximates real life. It is notable in this instance that the largest single influence on outcome is that of the treatment experience. Manning (1988) comments:

> The relevance of this finding is in the criticism often made of therapeutic communities (and psychotherapy in general) that its effectiveness lies in a combination of spontaneous remission and a careful pre-selection of "suitable" patients. The data from this study are clearly quite incompatible with such a model. (p. 176)

Social Policy

There are many topics that might legitimately be considered here, but I choose to discuss briefly one that is of overriding concern throughout the Western world: the shift from hospital to community as the principal locus for the care of the mentally ill. For purposes of this discussion, *community care* is defined as care provided outside the walls of hospitals.

Unease about the effects of large-scale psychiatric hospitals on patients had gathered strength throughout much of the 20th century, but World War II certainly gave that process considerable impetus. The experiences of military doctors working under field conditions convinced many of them that the hospitals from which they had been drafted were probably doing their patients a good deal of harm. Two policies resulted: One was to modify hospital regimes to make them less institutionalizing (including developments such as the therapeutic community), and the second was to keep people out of hospitals as much as possible (leading to community care). The history of the process that Andrew T. Scull called *decarceration* has been written several times (see

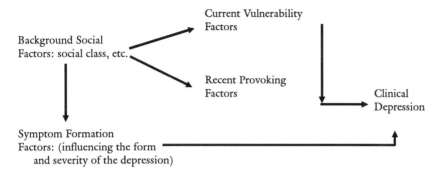

Figure 7.2. Brown and Harris's Causal Model
SOURCE: Based on Brown and Harris (1978).

Table 7.6 Manning's Seven Variables

Factor	Measured By
Resident's social background	Variables recorded in social background questionnaire
Resident's level of functioning at intake	Ratings by staff and self-ratings by resident
Particular house occupied by resident	Self-evident
The resources of that house	Multiphasic Environmental Assessment Procedure (Moos, 1980), omitting Atmosphere Scale items
Resident's perception of the house	House Atmosphere Scale (Moos, 1980)
Resident's "treatment experience"	Rank ordering of group experiences as "helpful"; staff and resident's ratings of impact of regimen on outcome; length of stay; weekly time spent in formal groups
Outcome for the resident	Ratings by staff and self-ratings by resident

SOURCE: Based on Manning (1988).

Jones, 1972). The process started in a general atmosphere of uncritical enthusiasm. It was thought to lead to greater well-being among the patients; to financial savings attractive to economists, politicians, and the public; and to greater professionalization among occupational groups such as nurses and social workers—indeed, to a multiplicity of desirable outcomes.

This uncritical attitude has now been severely modified. The increased visibility of homeless mentally ill people, the rising incidence of violent acts directed at innocent victims or of suicide or bizarre behavior and public-order disturbances, expressions of resentment by caregivers, and the recognition by community agencies that resources are inadequate have all contributed to this

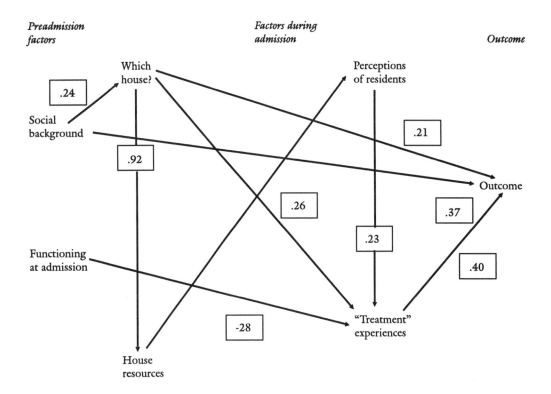

Figure 7.3. Manning's Results
SOURCE: Based on Manning (1988, p. 176).

change of attitude. In such circumstances there is a serious need for accurate research to provide the foundations for policy formation. It is difficult to conduct such research, however. In the first place, the social contexts in which it occurs are difficult to define and apt to change continuously under various pressures—some largely indefinable, others the result of economic constraints or the passing whims of powerful political forces. As Ruggeri and Tansella (1995) point out in a recent review, where research does occur, it should be able to focus on the multiple components of care and to take into account the heterogeneity of patients, families, and professional staff; it should employ measures of both objective and subjective change; and it is essential that it use longitudinal designs. Such studies are time-consuming, expensive, and require sophisticated statistical analysis, and their results are difficult to apply to practice.

One recent British example of a controlled comparison between hospital and community management (replicating studies in Wisconsin and Sydney) was conducted by Marks et al. (1994). Patients assessed for emergency admission with serious mental illness were randomly allocated either to a home-based care program (*n* = 92) for 20 months or to standard inpatient plus outpatient care (*n* = 97). There were small but significant advantages in the first 20 months for the home care Daily Living Program patients compared with the standard management group in level of symptoms, social adjustment (these two variables, incidentally, are frequently found to be independent), and ratings of both patient and caregiver satisfaction. In this clinical group, levels of pathology nevertheless remained quite high, and several deaths from self-harm and one homicide occurred. Also during this time, there were significant financial savings (19%) in the community care group over the 20-month period. Such economic advantages are by no means always found (Knapp et al., 1994). But in the second phase of the study, which involved the withdrawal of the community care program compared with its continuation, most of the gains were lost, except on measures of clients' and relatives' satisfaction (which were independent of clinical status). The significance of these findings is that they offer further verification that high-quality community care is complex to organize and sustain, and there is growing evidence to suggest that it loses its effectiveness over time. The issues are entangled, and much research will be needed to place social policy for the mentally ill on a sound foundation.

Concluding Comment

This chapter has illustrated the variety of social research in the field of mental illness. Clearly, the research has substantial achievements to its credit; equally clearly, much is left to do. My own view is that social psychiatry has an unending task. If social life—including the very definition of mental disorder as well as the manifold kinds of social relationship that influence its causation, its phenomenology, and its management at the levels of both social policy and individual treatment—is a matter of constant construction and reconstruction, the conclusions of social research will always be provisional, and the work will always need to be reviewed. However, this by no means renders it worthless. Its conclusions are as reliable within the limits of its applicability as those of any other behavioral science, and it is to be hoped that their practical importance for the care of the mentally ill is now beyond question.

Note

1. I know that there exists disagreement among philosophers on this point, but this is the position I adopt (see, e.g., Ruben, 1985).

References

American Psychiatric Association. (1994). *Diagnostic and statistical manual of mental disorders* (4th ed.). Washington, DC: Author.

Bebbington, P. E., Hurry, J., Tennant, C., Sturt, E., & Wing, J. K. (1981). Epidemiology of mental disorders in Camberwell. *Psychological Medicine, 11,* 1-19.

Brown, G. W., & Harris, T. (1978). *Social origins of depression: A study of psychiatric disorder in women.* London: Tavistock.

Caplan, G. (1964). *The principles of preventive psychiatry.* New York: Basic Books.

Giddens, A. (1976). *New rules of sociological method.* London: Hutchinson.

Giddens, A. (1984). *The constitution of society: Outline of the theory of structuration.* Cambridge, MA: Polity.

Goldberg, D. (1972). *The detection of psychiatric illness by questionnaire* (Maudlsey Monographs No. 21). New York: Oxford University Press.

Goldberg, D., & Huxley, P. (1992). *Common mental disorders: A bio-social model.* London: Tavistock/Routledge.

Goldberg, D., & Williams, P. (1988). *A user's guide to the General Health Questionnaire.* Windsor: NFER/Nelson.

Goode, W. J. (1964). *The family.* Englewood Cliffs, NJ: Prentice Hall.

Henderson, A. S. (1988). *An introduction to social psychiatry.* Oxford: Oxford University Press.

Holmes, T., & Rahe, R. H. (1967). The Social Readjustment Rating Scale. *Journal of Psychosomatic Research, 11,* 213-218.

Jones, K. (1972). *A history of the mental health services.* London: Routledge & Kegan Paul.

Kingston, W., & Bentovim, A. (1978). Brief focal family therapy when the child is the referred patient, II: Methodology and results. *Journal of Child Psychology and Psychiatry, 19,* 119-144.

Knapp, M., Beecham, J., Koustogeorgopolou, V., Hallam, A., Fenyo, A., Marks, I. M., Connolly, J., Audini, B., & Muijen, M. (1994). Service use and costs of home-based versus hospital-based care for people with serious mental illness. *British Journal of Psychiatry, 165,* 195-203.

Leff, J., Kuipers, L., Berkowitz, R., Ebedien-Vries, R., & Sturgeon, D. (1982). A controlled trial of social intervention in the families of schizophrenic patients. *British Journal of Psychiatry, 141,* 121-134.

Manning, N. P. (1988). *The therapeutic community movement: Charisma and routinization.* London: Routledge.

Marcus, E., Lenge, A., & Pettigrew, T. F. (1990). Effectiveness in family therapy: A meta-analysis. *Journal of Family Therapy, 12,* 205-221.

Marks, I. M., Connolly, J., Muijen, M., Audini, B., McNamee, G., & Lawrence, R. E. (1994). Home-based versus hospital-based care for people with serious mental illness. *British Journal of Psychiatry, 165,* 179-194.

May, T. (1993). *Social research: Issues, methods and process.* Milton Keynes: Open University Press.

Moos, R. H. (1980). Evaluating the environments of residential care settings. *International Journal of Therapeutic Communities, 1,* 211-225.

Parker, G., & Barnett, B. (1987). A test of the social support hypothesis. *British Journal of Psychiatry, 150,* 72-77.

Reiger, D., & Burke, J. D. (1988). Population surveys: Their relevance to mental healthcare. In A. S. Henderson & G. D. Burrows (Eds.), *Handbook of social psychiatry.* Amsterdam: Elsevier.

Revans, R. W. (1976). *Action learning in hospitals: Diagnosis and therapy.* London: McGraw-Hill.

Robbins, L. N., Helzer, J. E., Croughan, J., & Ratcliff, K. S. (1981). National Institute of Mental Health Diagnostic Interview Schedule: Its history, characteristics and validity. *Archives of General Psychiatry, 38,* 381-388.

Ruben, D. H. (1985). *The metaphysics of the social world.* London: Routledge & Kegan Paul.

Ruggeri, M., & Tansella, M. (1995). Evaluating outcome in mental health care. *Current Opinion in Psychiatry, 8,* 116-121.

Rutter, M. (1985). Resilience in the face of adversity: Protective factors and resilience in psychiatric disorder. *British Journal of Psychiatry, 147,* 598-611.

Stanton, A. H., & Schwartz, M. S. (1954). *The mental hospital.* New York: Basic Books.

Wing, J. K. (1972). The social context of evaluation. In J. K. Wing & A. M. Hailey (Eds.), *Evaluating a community psychiatric service: The chamber register* (pp. 11-39). Oxford, UK: Oxford University Press.

Wolkind, S., & Rutter, M. (1985). Separation, loss and family relationships. In M. Rutter & S. Hersow (Eds.), *Child and adolescent psychiatry: Modern approaches.* Oxford: Blackwell Scientific Publications.

World Health Organization. (1992). *The ICD-10: Classification of mental and behavioural disorders—clinical descriptions and diagnostic guidelines.* Geneva: Author.

CHAPTER 8

Psychoeducation: A Contemporary Approach

CASSANDRA SIMON

Psychoeducation is the name applied to a group of approaches used in working with persons with mental illness and their families. Despite the proven utility of psychoeducation, there are still many areas associated with it that remain unclear and controversial. In this chapter, I discuss the meaning, purposes, and various models of psychoeducation, and then examine the issues surrounding psychoeducation as applied to persons with mental illness and their families. Among these issues are psychoeducation's strengths, limitations, and unexplored areas. I conclude the chapter with a brief discussion of projections for the future of psychoeducation and their implications.

Psychoeducation: The Beginnings

The development of psychoeducation as applied to persons with mental disorders and their families occurred as a result of numerous contemporary and historical factors. One of the major contributors to the eventual development of psychoeducation was the passage of the Community Mental Health Centers Act of 1963. The purpose of the act was to ensure community-based care for persons with mental illness as they were released from psychiatric institutional facilities (Lecca, 1983). It was assumed that persons with mental illness could be provided the opportunity for more "normal" life through improved treatment and comprehensive care while remaining with their families (Iodice & Wodarski, 1987).

Deinstitutionalization seemed to be in the best interest of persons with mental illness, who historically had been denied their rights and sometimes mistreated by those persons charged with their care and treatment. However, the high expectations of deinstitutionalization were not realized, and frequently the problems of persons with mental illness and their families were compounded (Goldman, 1982; Lamb, 1981; Messina & Davis, 1981). Deinstitutionalization did result in the massive release of persons with mental illnesses from psychiatric facilities, but they were released to a community-based care system unequipped to provide adequate services. As related to psychoeducation, the failure of deinstitutionalization has had two major results. First, this failure resulted in well over a quarter of a million persons with mental illness living in the community, receiving inadequate care and supervision (Fentress & Friend, 1981). Second, the primary responsibility of care for persons with mental illness was shifted to their families. Goldman (1982) estimates that as many as 65% of persons released from psychiatric facilities return to their families, and almost 25% are diagnosed as chronically mentally ill; other researchers estimate even higher percentages (Torrey, 1988). In any case, the fact remains that far too many families are left to provide primary care for their mentally ill family members without being provided adequate skills, information, and resources.

The Family and Psychoeducation's Development

Another factor directly linked to the development of psychoeducation has been the shift in thinking about families and their role in the etiology, assessment, and treatment of and recovery from mental illness. Whereas early theories, often termed *family-blaming* or *interactional* theories, viewed families as causative agents in the development and perpetuation of mental disorders, mental health professionals eventually accepted the fact that these theories lacked any empirical base. As a result of the family-blaming theories, families were often ignored or mistreated by mental health professionals, adding to the difficulties they were already dealing with. Families were emotionally and/or physically separated from their mentally ill family members, ineffectually utilized, and made to feel guilty, responsible, ashamed, and confused regarding their family members' illness (Appleton, 1974; Bernheim & Lehman, 1985; McGill & Lee, 1986). As families began to gain power by joining together in such organizations as the Alliance for the Mentally Ill, the theories that blamed some form of family interaction for the development of mental illness lost favor. With the reduction of support for these theories and recognition of the needs of the families of persons with mental illness, a paradigmatic shift in thinking occurred. Four major factors have been identified as leading to this change in the status of families: (a) evidence that refuted family-blaming theories, (b) increased empirical support for alternative explanations (in contrast to family-blaming theories) in the etiology of mental disorders, (c) pharmacological control of the symptoms of mental disorders, and (d) the failure of deinstitutionalization (Simon, McNeil, Franklin, & Cooperman, 1991). These factors, taken collectively, have been attributed with leading to a reexamination of the dynamics of families with mentally ill family members and family-focused interventions. Also, it has been recognized that those familial characteristics that once were viewed as causing mental disorders are possibly actually *effects* of the presence in the family of a person with a mental disorder (Anderson, 1983; Appleton, 1974; Torrey, 1988).

As families of the mentally ill became recognized not only as a population in need of services but also as useful resources in intervention with persons with mental illness, there was an increase in family-focused programs. Professionals from a variety of theoretical orientations and disciplines began to develop family-oriented strategies and initiatives (Atkinson, 1986; Falloon, 1985; Hudson, 1975; Kanter & Lin, 1980). Out of the development of these family-focused programs, psychoeducation emerged as the most encouraging.

Psychoeducation: A Definition

The development of psychoeducational approaches to working with persons with mental illness and their families is unique in that these approaches were developed "within the context of controlled outcome research" (Simon et al., 1991, p. 329). Initial research on psychoeducation was based on work that focused on the degree of emotional bonding in families. This familial interaction component, termed *expressed emotion* (EE), comprises three components: critical comments, hostility, and overinvolvement (Brown, Birley, & Wing, 1972). It has been postulated that EE is directly related to the mentally ill family member's relapse rate, symptomatology, and hospitalization rate. Families with high EE are more critical of mentally ill family members and less tolerant of their behavior. Conversely, families with low EE view mentally ill family members as more "normal" than do their high-EE counterparts (Berkowitz, Eberlein-Fries, Kuipers, & Leff, 1984; Brown et al., 1972; Vaughn, 1977; Vaughn & Leff, 1976). Other studies document improved prognosis and behavior control for persons with a mental illness when EE and affective responsiveness are reduced in families (Atkinson, 1986; Hogarty et al., 1986; Vaughn, Snyder, Jones, Freeman, & Falloon, 1984).

As research began to support the relationship between the environment and the course of mental disorders, studies began to focus on altering the environmental conditions in which persons with mental illnesses live. With a large proportion of persons with mental illness returning to their families, a natural progression included concentration on the familial environment. Thus emerged psychoeducation interventions designed to alter the familial environment. Although most psychoeducational approaches to working with families of the mentally ill are based on the diathesis-stress model of mental illness, which views the mentally ill person as being biologically vulnerable to environmental stressors, they lack precise definition and theoretical orientation (Hatfield, 1990; Johnson, 1986). The term *psychoeducation* refers to a variety of models that differ in specific techniques and emphasis, yet share common components and purposes. Based on the identified needs of families of the mentally ill, the need for knowledge, the need for skills, and the need for support, psychoeducation programs contain what I have referred to in earlier work as "common areas of inclusion" (Simon, 1992, p. 14). Two of the most commonly included areas are communication and problem solving.

The focus on communication in psychoeducation is a direct outgrowth of the research on expressed emotion. Attention is given to providing skills and education aimed at improving communication within the family. The focus is often on decreasing critical comments and increasing direct statements. A critical comment is defined as "a statement which, by the manner in which it is expressed, constitutes an unfavorable comment upon the behavior or personality of the person to whom it refers" (Leff & Vaughn, 1985, p. 38). A direct statement, identified as a healthy component of communication, is defined as an "I-stance statement" and is recognized as a statement made to or about the diagnosed family member that explicitly states what is expected, not expected, desired, felt, or accepted (Frampton, 1987; Simon, 1992).

Problems of various magnitudes often arise in families with mentally ill family members. If familial stress is to be reduced, family members must be equipped with skills and knowledge that allow them to handle problems effectively. The ability to handle problems and crises that occur has a major impact on family functioning and intrafamilial stress.

Additional components often found in psychoeducation programs include information on mental illness itself as well as on stress reduction, emotionality, medication maintenance, how to handle bizarre behavior, community resources, and support and advocacy (Barter, 1984; Iodice & Wodarski, 1987; McGill & Lee, 1986). This information is provided to families in easy-to-understand, nontechnical language. The major ways in which psychoeducation programs differ from one another are in the areas of the location of therapy (home or office), patient involvement, number of sessions, family members to be involved, and emphasis on the various components (Simon, 1992). In the following section, I review various models of psychoeducation.

Models of Psychoeducation

Several different prototypical psychoeducation models have been developed and implemented with persons with mental illness and their families. In earlier work, my colleagues and I presented five major psychoeducation models (Simon et al., 1991); these as well as others are presented below, with discussion surrounding their empirical support and evaluation.

Bernheim

The particular approach taken by Bernheim and colleagues could more appropriately be referred to as a framework rather than as a specific program. From this framework, specific programs can be developed. Characterized as supportive family counseling, this approach has some identified fundamental elements (Bernheim, 1982; Bernheim & Lehman, 1985):

- *Therapeutic relationship:* A "therapeutic alliance" relationship should be encouraged between the family and the therapist. Two outcomes of such successful incorporation are reduced feelings of helplessness and attainment of the family's cooperation and support. In this approach, the establishment of a therapeutic alliance with the family is of primary importance.
- *Family acceptance:* Always of clinical importance, family acceptance from the therapist is especially emphasized in this approach. Family concerns also are of paramount importance, and services are provided within a supportive environment. Ideally, mastery of this element is manifested by unconditional acceptance of the family by the therapist.
- *Stylistic issues:* There is an eclectic environment within this framework, as therapists are encouraged to develop and use different styles of working. The styles selected should be those that best meet the needs of the families being served.

In addition to these three elements, Bernheim's (1982) framework has three components:

- *Family strength:* The framework includes the therapist's and the family's utilization of the strengths of the family in learning to deal effectively with the negative emotions often found in families with mentally ill members (e.g., guilt, anger, and despondency).
- *Family education:* A component common to most psychoeducation programs is family education; that is, families are helped to understand their members' mental illness. This education includes description of the illness, treatment options, familial expectations, and the development of monitoring skills.
- *Daily living strategies:* Bernheim's framework includes teaching families with mentally ill members the skills that will assist them in daily living. The entire well-being of the family is concentrated on in a proactive environment. Problem solving and decision making also are addressed.

Anderson and Associates

The psychoeducation model developed by Anderson and colleagues is directly linked to the diathesis-stress model of mental illness. The model includes the mentally ill family member and attempts to reduce her or his vulnerability to stress, with an emphasis on medication maintenance (Anderson, 1983; Anderson, Hogarty, & Reiss, 1980). Through education, skills, and support, this model attempts to decrease familial stress, anxiety, and instability. Four different phases of this program have been identified:

- *Initial phase:* This phase begins soon after the mentally ill family member is hospitalized and involves a series of meetings between the family and the clinician. Major goals of this phase are to engage the family in the therapeutic process, to encourage and demonstrate clinician acceptance of the family, and to assess family reactions. An outcome of this phase is the establishment of a treatment contract.

- *All-day survival skills workshop:* Early in treatment, family members participate in a day-long workshop with other families who have mentally ill members. A focus of this phase is to educate families about mental illness and its course. As multiple families are involved in this phase, the opportunity for peer support is provided.

- *Family sessions:* This phase of the psychoeducation model involves family sessions that include the mentally ill family member. Initiation of this phase occurs when the mentally ill family member is functional enough to participate. Family sessions are held every 2-3 weeks for 6 months to a year. A goal of this phase is to make families aware of and comfortable with community and therapeutic resources.

- *Continued family therapy:* The final phase of this psychoeducation model allows families a choice in ceasing or continuing family sessions. All families are given the option of returning for family therapy in the future when needed.

Goldstein and Associates

The model of psychoeducation developed by Goldstein and colleagues involves a 6-week crisis-oriented program implemented immediately after the mentally ill family member is released from the hospital. The program initially focuses on three areas of concern: (a) addressing unrealistic beliefs, (b) recognizing the family's experience with mental illness and its impact on the family, and (c) making the mentally ill family member and the family amenable to stress management. There are four specific treatment objectives sought by this model. These objectives are the focus of concentration following successful resolution of the three identified areas of concern (Goldstein & Kopeikin, 1981; Kopeikin, Marshall, & Goldstein, 1983):

- *Objective 1: Identify stressors.* This is achieved by having the family identify, discuss, and explore stressors for the mentally ill family member.

- *Objective 2: Develop stress prevention and coping strategies.* Problem-solving and prevention strategies and coping strategies are the focus of this part of the model.

- *Objective 3: Implement the problem-solving and problem prevention strategies.* Families are instructed in evaluating the success of the implemented strategies.

- *Objective 4: Engage in anticipatory planning.* This phase is focused on planning and implementation strategies for use in handling future potential stressors.

Leff and Associates

The model of psychoeducation developed by Leff and colleagues has three basic components that are reflected in their corresponding segments. Each segment of this approach has a specific purpose that corresponds with the basic components: education, family therapy, and peer support (Berkowitz et al., 1984).

- *Family education:* The first segment focuses on educating families about mental illness—its etiology, course, and management. This segment is held before the mentally ill person is discharged from the hospital.
- *Family therapy:* The second segment consists of family therapy that includes the family member with mental illness. The focus is on conflict resolution and management. The entire family is offered the opportunity to identify potential areas of conflict and to develop problem-solving strategies.
- *Peer support:* The last segment addresses the area of peer support. The family participates in a multifamily group, without the mentally ill family member. Here family members are allowed to share information, conflicts, resources, and emotions with one another in a supportive, nonstigmatizing environment.

Falloon and Associates

The intervention model developed by Falloon and colleagues is strongly influenced by behavior theory and utilizes many techniques (e.g., token economy and contingency contracting) associated with behavior therapy (Falloon et al., 1985; Falloon & Liberman, 1983; McGill, Falloon, Boyd, & Wood-Siverio, 1983). There are five basic components in this model: family assessment, education, communication training, problem solving, and behavior management strategies (McGill & Lee, 1986). The entire program is provided using sequential family therapy. In three separate family therapy sequences, the five major components are addressed. The first sequence of family therapy sessions lasts for approximately 3 months and involves weekly sessions. In the second sequence of family therapy, sessions are held every 2 weeks for approximately 6 months. The last and final sequence involves monthly family therapy sessions. These sessions can last anywhere from 9 months to a year and sometimes include multifamily sessions.

The five models described above have been given the most attention in the literature. Newer models have been developed that have both provided answers and raised further questions regarding the utility of psychoeducation. The four models briefly described below make innovative and unique contributions to the development of psychoeducational intervention.

Shenoy and Associates

The psychoeducation model developed by Shenoy, Shires, and White (1981) involves ongoing multifamily groups for family members of the mentally ill. Termed Schiz-Anon, this model is tailored after Al-Anon, a group for the families of alcoholics. The goals and objectives of Al-Anon are adapted to this multifamily group. Families are provided education on the etiology of schizophrenia and on medications, side effects, and problem management. Other multifamily group sessions focus on peer support and exchange of information.

Carpenter and Heinrichs

Similar to the Goldstein model, Carpenter and Heinrichs's (1983) psychoeducation model reserves medication use for those instances in which there is clear deterioration in functioning. The family is acknowledged as being more knowledgeable than the therapist about the behavior of the mentally ill family member. This approach is time limited and consists of six sessions. It has been used successfully with families of mentally ill persons participating in neuroleptic treatment programs.

Mills and Associates

The model developed by Mills, Hansen, and Malakie (1986) emphasizes education and skills acquisition. Psychoeducation is delivered in multifamily group sessions of 2 hours each, held over 10 weeks, that include the mentally ill family members. Major topics include family interactional types, positive statements, emotional responsiveness, conflict resolution, active listening, nonverbal behavior, medication, and community resources.

Simon

My own intervention model is based on a time-limited approach consisting of six weekly sessions lasting 2½ to 3½ hours each. Education and skills acquisition are the focus. The reduction of intrafamilial stress is emphasized through education and improvement of problem-solving skills. The emphasis is on assisting the family. The family member with mental illness is seen as another source of information to assist the therapist in better understanding the family. Sessions do not include the diagnosed family member. Areas covered include etiology, symptoms, medication, communication, community resources, problem solving, skills acquisition, and support (Simon, 1992).

The above review of different psychoeducation models, although not all-inclusive, demonstrates the variable characteristics of psychoeducational approaches to working with persons with mental illness and their families. Psychoeducation, unlike many other approaches to working with persons with mental illness and their families, has been developed and conducted "in the context of controlled outcome research" (Simon et al., 1991, p. 329). One result is the rich body of research available in the area of psychoeducation.

Research and Psychoeducation

Psychoeducational approaches show a great deal of promise, as evaluation of their efficacy provides continued support for their use (Simon, 1992). Having come out of research related to communication and expressed emotion, psychoeducation has developed within an empirically grounded environment. Just as approaches to psychoeducation are characterized by variation, so are the approaches to its empirical investigation. A majority of the research to date has utilized relatively traditional group comparison evaluation designs that concentrate on aggregate effects. There has, however, been increasing focus on evaluation using more idiographic methods of investigation (Bentley, 1990; Mills et al., 1986; Simon, 1992). Additionally, whereas many of the outcome data are focused on such variables as hospitalization, relapse rates, and symptomatology of the mentally ill family member, other studies have focused more on familial outcomes. A presentation of the evaluation procedures used for some of the psychoeducation approaches presented will best illustrate the variation present in the empirical investigation of psychoeducation.

Group Approaches to Investigation

Based on comparative group studies, Anderson (1983) examined the effectiveness of one psychoeducation approach. Using 33 clients and their families, Anderson studied the effects of family therapy alone (control group) in contrast to family therapy with social skills training (experimental group). Results indicated that both groups benefited from family therapy, with the most noticeable improvement among the group receiving both family therapy and social skills training. The relapse rate for both groups combined was only 16%. The experimental group (family therapy and socialization skills) accounted for only a small proportion of the relapse group, with no relapses 3 years following program participation.

In evaluating the effectiveness of a psychoeducation program based on their model, Goldstein and associates also used a comparative group study format (Kopeikin et al., 1983). Using a sample of 104 persons with schizophrenia and their families, the researchers compared four different treatment groups. The treatment conditions were medication levels (low versus moderate) and family therapy (crisis-oriented family therapy versus no family therapy). Using symptomatology and relapse rates as their outcome measures, the researchers found that both medication and family therapy applied independently had positive effects. The most beneficial results, however, occurred in the group receiving both.

Leff and associates evaluated their model's effectiveness by comparing outcomes of 30 persons with mental illness and their families (Berkowitz et al., 1984). Families were randomly assigned to one of two groups: the experimental group, which received psychoeducational services, or the control group, which received "routine" services, characterized by less inclusion of the family. Results indicated that psychoeducation was more effective in reducing relapse rates of the diagnosed family members. The experimental group had a 9% relapse rate, compared with a 50% relapse rate for the control group.

Another comparative model was used to assess the effectiveness of a psychoeducation approach to intervention based on the model of Falloon et al. (1985). A sample of 36 persons with schizophrenia and their families were assigned to one of two treatment conditions: in-home family therapy or individual-based clinical services. Results indicated that the in-home family therapy was more effective in reducing symptomatology and hospitalization rates. Other benefits of the in-home family therapy approach included improved family management, reduction in mental and physical health problems, improved communication, reduced emotional environment, and fewer feelings of disruption and burden (Doane, Goldstein, Milkowitz, & Falloon, 1986; Falloon & Pederson, 1985; McGill et al., 1983).

These group methods in the investigation of psychoeducation have added greatly to the continued use of psychoeducation approaches to working with persons with mental illness and their families. Although these group comparison methods have been invaluable in establishing psychoeducation as an empirically based, effective intervention method, it has also been recognized that there are questions that can be best addressed using alternate methods of investigation. Group comparison methods have been criticized for their use of global outcome indicators and for providing little information on individual effects and the therapeutic process (Mills et al., 1986; Zipple & Spaniol, 1987). Recognizing the utility of other forms of investigation, other researchers have been examining the efficacy of psychoeducation using more idiographic methods.

Idiographic Approaches

Investigation into the efficacy of psychoeducation using idiographic procedures has not been as widely acknowledged as have more traditional methods. With the clinical utility of traditional models being questioned, there has been an increase in the number of evaluation studies focusing on the client and clinical outcomes (Mills et al., 1986).

Mills et al. (1986) investigated the effects of a psychoeducation model using what they term *descriptive assessment*. Rather than using group data, the researchers evaluated families individually on cohesion, organization, conflict resolution, and communication. Mills et al.'s study sample consisted of four families. Their results indicate that three of the four families benefited from the program, especially in the areas of conflict resolution, cohesion, and communication.

Bentley (1990) used a multiple-baseline across-subjects design to evaluate a 10-week psychoeducation program. Using repeated, pre-, post-, and follow-up measures, Bentley assessed four families along different dimensions of family functioning. Although differential outcomes were present with the families in this study, there was overall support for the efficacy of psychoeducation. The study further provides support for the continued use of idiographic, clinically oriented, empirical investigation of the effects and efficacy of psychoeducation.

In an effort to investigate the utility of a more clinically oriented evaluation method, I also, like Bentley (1990), used a single-system design (Simon, 1992). Specifically, through the use of an A-B design, I investigated the effects of a 6-week psychoeducation program. Although limited, in that the sample consisted of only two families, each of which included a family member with schizophrenia, the study also provides support for the use of psychoeducation. It represents an early endeavor to provide a feasible clinical evaluation tool for those working with persons with mental illness and their families. Additionally, the study serves as a prototype for empirically grounded work focusing on individual as opposed to aggregate change.

With a strong empirical base, a good environment exists for continued investigation into psychoeducation using both nomothetic and idiographic methods. Group comparisons, using experimental designs, should be in place to provide essential information regarding efficacy and aggregate effects. Through their application, valuable information, direction, and insight can be provided based on more scientifically sanctioned methods of investigation. Despite the power of group comparison methods, their clinical value has been questioned as therapists and clinicians recognize their inability to provide meaningful information on individual families in the clinical setting. Idiographic methods of investigation are clinically useful and lend themselves to implementation with relative ease by therapists working with persons with mental illness and their families.

Issues in Psychoeducation

Despite the vast amount of support provided for psychoeducation programs, there are areas around which ambiguity and controversies exist. As may be expected in an area with such unclear theoretical definition, there are concerns and criticisms. In addition to unanswered questions regarding effective components and more thorough definition, several areas of concern deserve attention.

One area of concern surrounds the duality present in the focus of the intervention. The development of psychoeducation occurred out of a desire to alter the familial environment of the mentally ill family member, the goal being the reduction of stressors for the identified client. Traditionally, benefits for the family have been viewed as secondary. Hatfield (1987b) raises the problematic nature of this stance for the family. Principal attention is given to the well-being of the client, but in reality, family members must be concerned with the positive functioning of individual family members and the family as a unit. The potential exists for family members who might not be able to devote the required attention to the family member with mental illness to experience conflict and guilt.

Simultaneously, secondary benefits should not be underestimated. Does the secondary nature of family outcomes substantially reduce the positive benefits of psychoeducation for the family? Much power seems to lie with the therapist in alleviating the experiential reality of these conditions. With the growth of psychoeducation, investigation into new areas continues to develop. A new emphasis on the family has emerged. An increased focus on the effects of psychoeducation on the family is evidence of this shift. Family outcome measures are increasing at the core of measurement in psychoeducation research (Bentley, 1990; Mills et al., 1986; Simon, 1992). Families are also beginning to be viewed as the primary beneficiaries of psychoeducation. Although this secondary view of the family could most definitely have an impact on delivery and quality of services, the benefits that families receive should not automatically be reduced.

Another concern is the potential for family blame that is present in psychoeducation. As an outgrowth of work that has developed concentrating on negative characteristics of families, many have posited that psychoeducation only lessens family blame. Rather than being blamed in the etiological sense, however, the family is viewed as having the power to perpetuate the disorder (Simon et al., 1991). The causal implications are clear, as high-EE families are associated with increased relapse rates and low-EE families with decreased relapse rates (Hatfield, 1987a). The meaning of the relationships among EE levels, parental characteristics, family dynamics, and client functioning has been questioned by Anderson, Hogarty, Bayer, and Needleman (1984), who present an alternative explanation. They purport that high EE and parental overinvolvement can have some positive influences. High-EE parents might be more socially oriented, rather than highly oriented to the family member with a mental illness. Anderson et al. go on to raise questions regarding relapse rates and parenting styles. They suggest that relapse might be more related to client vulnerability than to a mismatch of parental style that is not conducive to optimal functioning for that individual. The recognition that other factors contribute to the environment in which the person with a mental illness must function supports the view that family impact is not equatable with causality. Psychoeducation, like most other forms of family therapy, operates within a person-in-environment framework. Other approaches to working with families often have a systemic frame of reference, yet their utility is not scrutinized as forcefully as psychoeducation's. Many helping professions, especially social work, have at the core of their helping approaches improving the social functioning of the identified client by working with the systems in the person's environment that might detract from his or her ability to function optimally. Yet the preponderance of blame, whether concerning cause or perpetuation, is not a central issue in these situations. Perhaps the issue is paid more attention in the case of psychoeducation because of the family's historical roots connecting it to blame in relation to mental illness.

Culture and Psychoeducation

The efficacy of psychoeducation has been demonstrated repeatedly. Most of the research has, however, been conducted without examination of its utility with diverse ethnic minority groups. There is a need for the development of culturally sensitive approaches to working with persons with mental illness and their families. Examination of the literature demonstrates that there is a dearth of knowledge in this area.

In investigating culturally sensitive approaches to mental health service delivery for Hispanic populations, Rogler, Malgady, Costantino, and Blumenthal (1987) discuss three different types of programs: (a) those improving accessibility of traditional treatments to Hispanic populations, (b) those selecting treatment approaches that are congruent with perceived cultural traits of Hispanic populations, and (c) those modifying traditional treatment approaches by integrating Hispanic cultural elements. Although identified through the examination of culturally sensitive mental health services to Hispanic populations, these kinds of program adaptations can be expanded to other groups and treatment approaches. A comprehensive approach to effective delivery of psychoeducation to ethnically diverse groups should examine each of these elements.

Although limited, documentation does exist of some of the differences among groups that might be of relevance in the development and implementation of psychoeducation for traditional ethnic minorities. Black families, for example, seem to experience feelings of shame less often and to have fewer problems related to self-esteem than do their dominant-culture counterparts (Pickett, Vranick, Cook, & Cohler, 1993). Thus members of black families may be more willing to share experiences and engage in supportive networks once they have established a trusting relationship with a helping professional. Extended family networks and flexibility in relationships are additional characteristics with implications for psychoeducation. For some groups, it might be wise to include in family psychoeducation persons who are related to the identified client by other than traditional blood ties. Additionally, the historical and contemporary experience of black people in America has caused a basic distrust of the "system" and of therapists of European descent on the part of many African Americans. This can affect not only therapists' ability to engage African Americans in psychoeducation programs but also the potential effectiveness of such programs. Consequently, a useful added component for a psychoeducation program might be an attempt to address racism both within and outside the mental health system.

The diverse groups who make up the category often referred to as Hispanic also have characteristics that indicate the need for investigation into culture-specific psychoeducation. These characteristics include an emphasis on family, a propensity to seek the assistance of community healers and leaders (Rogler et al., 1987), spirituality (Kreisman, 1975), and language. For many Hispanic persons, English is a second language. Implications of this for culturally sensitive psychoeducation include the accuracy of the content of information presented and received by the participants, the accuracy of the assessment of emotionality in the family, and the selection of appropriate interpreters, when necessary. Pitta, Ruiz, and Alvarez (1978) address the issue of emotionality and posit that when an individual speaks in a language other than his or her native tongue, defensiveness and control often take precedence over free emotional expression. This issue of language as a barrier should also be recognized as it concerns other ethnic groups. In addressing the use of interpreters with Mexican Americans, Ho (1987) recommends not asking children from the families involved in therapy to act as interpreters, as this may cause conflict in these families, which often are hierarchical in nature.

For many families of Asian ancestry, relevant issues for culturally sensitive psychoeducation may be related to the sense of shame that accompanies publicizing family business, a reluctance in sharing emotion, and emphasis on authority. These may all be obstacles to getting families of Asian ancestry involved in group psychoeducation programs. Vandiver, Jordan, Keopraseuth, and Yu (1994) report on the successful use of multifamily psychoeducation with Laotian families, but for many Asian American families it might be more fruitful to use a more idiographic approach to psychoeducation (see, e.g., Simon, 1992). In this way, family members are not forced to publicize what many view as "family business." The reluctance to share emotions openly can affect both how Asian American families are perceived and how they are evaluated in family interaction areas. Such families might be evaluated errone-ously as detached, aloof, and unconcerned. The traditional Asian emphasis on authority can be used by the therapist involved in psychoeducation to promote compliance within the treatment milieu and in the development of family problem-solving strategies.

Although the therapist must consider the individuality of any client system, it is important that he or she recognize the manner in which cultural similarities might manifest themselves. Jordan, Lewellen, and Vandiver's (1994) prelimi-nary work addressing culture and psychoeducation represents an attempt to develop recommendations for professionals working with Laotian, African American, and Mexican American families. Jordan et al. discuss individual versus group approaches, length of treatment, program membership, the content to emphasize, group leadership, and other considerations. Although the culturally sensitive model presented by these investigators represents some important preliminary work in this area, empirical support and corroboration are needed before such a model is widely accepted and integrated into psy-choeducation. Despite professional recognition of the importance of examin-ing cultural issues in psychoeducation (Hatfield, 1990), there is still much work to be done.

Conclusion: Projections and Implications

Psychoeducation is unique in that it has been developed within a strong empirical environment. Despite extensive empirical support for psychoeduca-tion, however, many underdeveloped and unexamined issues remain. Psy-choeducation will remain a central focus of mental health professionals and researchers; in this chapter, I have provided an overview of psychoeducation, discussed its development, and touched on some major issues concerning its use.

Future research will focus on identifying the theoretical foundations of psychoeducation. Because there is so much variety among psychoeducation programs, attention also will be directed toward identification of the specific effective components of psychoeducation programs. Future research should also concentrate on the impact of client diversity, ethnic and otherwise, on psychoeducation programs. Questions should be raised and answers sought regarding how specific factors should be considered and integrated in psychoeducation's development and implementation.

The major criticisms aimed at psychoeducation do not seem to detract substantially from the benefits of the approach. Most of the criticisms surround (a) who should be the focus of the intervention, (b) indicators used in the measurement of program effectiveness, (c) the potential for putting families in a double-bind situation by disproportionately focusing on the well-being of one family member (the member with the mental illness), and (d) the potential that remains for blaming the family. Still, there is much support for the continued use and efficacy of psychoeducation. Addressing these issues effectively could lead to the strengthening of psychoeducation.

The future of psychoeducation will be an exciting one. As families of the mentally ill gain more political power, attention paid to these families will continue to increase. Explanations of differential outcomes for families will be a focus of investigation. As idiographic processes gain prominence, clinicians and researchers will provide the information needed to answer these and other questions.

References

Anderson, C. M. (1983). A psychoeducation program for families of clients with schizophrenia. In W. R. McFarlane (Ed.), *Family therapy in schizophrenia* (pp. 99-115). New York: Guilford.

Anderson, C. M., Hogarty, G., Bayer, T., & Needleman, R. (1984). Expressed emotion and social networks of parents of schizophrenic clients. *British Journal of Psychiatry, 144,* 247-255.

Anderson, C. M., Hogarty, G. E., & Reiss, D. J. (1980). Family treatment of adult schizophrenic patients: A psychoeducational approach. *Schizophrenia Bulletin, 6,* 490-505.

Appleton, W. S. (1974). Mistreatment of clients' families by psychiatrists. *American Journal of Psychiatry, 131,* 655-657.

Atkinson, J. M. (1986). *Schizophrenia: A guide to helping the family.* New York: New York University Press.

Barter, J. T. (1984). Psychoeducation. In J. A. Talbott (Ed.), *The chronic mental patient: Five years later* (pp. 83-191). Orlando, FL: Grune & Stratton.

Bentley, K. F. (1990). An evaluation of family based intervention with schizophrenia using single-system research. *British Journal of Social Work, 20,* 101-116.

Berkowitz, R., Eberlein-Fries, R., Kuipers, L., & Leff, J. P. (1984). Educating relatives about schizophrenia. *Schizophrenia Bulletin, 10,* 418-429.

Bernheim, K. F. (1982). Supportive family counseling. *Schizophrenia Bulletin, 8,* 630-638.

Bernheim, K. F., & Lehman, A. F. (1985). *Working with families of the mentally ill.* New York: W. W. Norton.

Brown, G. W., Birley, J. L., & Wing, J. K. (1972). Influence of family life on the course of schizophrenic disorders: A replication study. *British Journal of Psychiatry, 121,* 241-258.

Carpenter, W. T., & Heinrichs, D. W. (1983). Early intervention, time-limited, targeted pharmacotherapy of schizophrenia. *Schizophrenia Bulletin, 9,* 533-542.

Doane, J. A., Goldstein, M. J., Milkowitz, D. J., & Falloon, I. R. H.. (1986). The impact of individual and family treatment on the affective climate of families of schizophrenics. *British Journal of Psychiatry, 148,* 279-287.

Falloon, I. R. H. (1985). Behavioral family therapy: A problem solving approach to family coping. In J. P. Leff & C. E. Vaughn (Eds.), *Expressed emotion in families* (pp. 150-171). New York: Guilford.

Falloon, I. R. H., Boyd, J. L., McGill, C. W., Razani, J., Moss, H. B., Gilderman, A. M., & Simpson, G. M. (1985). Family management in the prevention of morbidity of schizophrenia. *Archives of General Psychiatry, 42,* 887-896.

Falloon, I. R. H., & Liberman, R. P. (1983). Behavioral family interventions in the management of chronic schizophrenia. In W. R. McFarlane (Ed.), *Family therapy in schizophrenia* (pp. 117-137). New York: Guilford.

Falloon, I. R. H., & Pederson, J. (1985). Family management in the prevention of morbidity of schizophrenia: The adjustment of the family unit. *British Journal of Psychiatry, 147,* 156-163.

Fentress, C., & Friend, D. M. (1981, May). Emptying the madhouse. *Life,* pp. 56-63, 66, 68, 70.

Frampton, J. (1987). *Schizophrenia: Family education.* Unpublished manuscript.

Goldman, H. (1982). Mental illness and family burden: A public health perspective. *Hospital and Community Psychiatry, 33,* 557-560.

Goldstein, M. J., & Kopeikin, H. S. (1981). Short- and long-term effects of combining drug and family therapy. In M. J. Goldstein (Ed.), *New developments in interventions with families of schizophrenics* (pp. 5-26). San Francisco: Jossey-Bass.

Hatfield, A. B. (1987a). Coping and adaptation: A conceptual framework for understanding families. In A. B. Hatfield & H. P. Lefley (Eds.), *Families of the mentally ill* (pp. 60-84). New York: Guilford.

Hatfield, A. B. (1987b). Families as caregivers: A historical perspective. In A. B. Hatfield & H. P. Lefley (Eds.), *Families of the mentally ill* (pp. 3-29). New York: Guilford.

Hatfield, A. B. (1990). *Family education in mental illness.* New York: Guilford.

Ho, M. K. (1987). *Family therapy with ethnic minorities.* Newbury Park, CA: Sage.

Hogarty, G. E., Anderson, C. M., Reiss, D. J., Kornbeth, S. J., Greenwald, D. P., Javna, C. D., & Madonia, M. J. (1986). Family psychoeducation, social skill training, and maintenance chemotherapy in the aftercare treatment of schizophrenia. *Archives of General Psychiatry, 43,* 633-641.

Hudson, B. J. (1975). A behavior modification project with chronic schizophrenics in the community. *Behavior Research and Therapy, 13,* 239-341.

Iodice, J. D., & Wodarski, J. S. (1987). Aftercare treatment for schizophrenics living at home. *Social Work, 38,* 122-128.

Johnson, H. C. (1986). Emerging concerns in family therapy. *Social Work, 32,* 299-305.

Jordan, C., Lewellen, A., & Vandiver, V. (1994). *A social work perspective of psychosocial rehabilitation: Psychoeducational models for minority families.* Manuscript submitted for publication.

Kanter, J. S., & Lin, A. (1980). Facilitating a therapeutic milieu in families of schizophrenics. *Psychiatry, 43,* 106-119.

Kopeikin, H. S., Marshall, V., & Goldstein, M. J. (1983). Stages and impact of crisis-oriented family therapy in aftercare of acute schizophrenia. In W. R. McFarlane (Ed.), *Family therapy in schizophrenia* (pp. 69-97). New York: Guilford.

Kreisman, J. (1975). The curandero's experience: A therapeutic integration of folk and medicinal healing. *American Journal of Psychiatry, 132,* 81-83.

Lamb, H. (1981). What did we really expect from deinstitutionalization? *Hospital and Community Psychiatry, 32,* 105-109.

Lecca, P. J. (1983). Current trends in mental health services and legislation. In J. W. Callicutt & P. J. Lecca (Eds.), *Social work and mental health* (pp. 11-29). New York: Free Press.

Leff, J. P., & Vaughn, C. E. (Eds.). (1985). *Expressed emotion in families.* New York: Guilford.

McGill, C. W., Falloon, I. R. H., Boyd, J. L., & Wood-Siverio, C. (1983). Family educational intervention in the treatment of schizophrenia. *Hospital and Community Psychiatry, 34,* 934-938.

McGill, C. W., & Lee, E. (1986). Family psychoeducation intervention in the treatment of schizophrenia. *Bulletin of the Menninger Clinic, 50,* 269-286.

Messina, J. J., & Davis, J. W. (1981). Deinstitutionalization: Myth or reality? *Journal of Rehabilitation, 47,* 30-36.

Mills, P. D., Hansen, J. C., & Malakie, B. B. (1986). Psychoeducational treatment for young adult chronically disturbed clients. *Family Therapy, 13,* 275-285.

Pickett, S. A., Vranick, D. A., Cook, J. A., & Cohler, B. J. (1993). Strength in adversity: Blacks bear burden better than whites. *Professional Psychology: Research in Practice, 24,* 460-467.

Pitta, P., Ruiz, R., & Alvarez, R. (1978). Language switching as a treatment strategy with bilingual patients. *American Journal of Psychoanalysis, 38,* 255-258.

Rogler, L. H., Malgady, R. G., Costantino, G., & Blumenthal, R. (1987). What do culturally sensitive services mean? The case of Hispanics. *American Psychologist, 42,* 565-570.

Shenoy, R. S., Shires, B., & White, M. S. (1981). Using a Schiz-Anon group in the treatment of chronic ambulatory schizophrenics. *Hospital and Community Psychiatry, 32,* 421-422.

Simon, C. (1992). *Single systems evaluation of a psychoeducation program for families with a schizophrenic family member: Implications for practice.* Unpublished doctoral dissertation, University of Texas, Arlington.

Simon, C., McNeil, J., Franklin, C., & Cooperman, A. (1991). The family and schizophrenia: Toward a psychoeducational approach. *Families in Society, 72,* 323-333.

Torrey, E. F. (1988). *Surviving schizophrenia: A family manual* (Rev. ed.). New York: Harper & Row.

Vandiver, V., Jordan, C., Keopraseuth, K., & Yu, M. (1994). *Family empowerment and service satisfaction: An exploratory study of Laotian families who care for a mentally ill family member.* Manuscript submitted for publication.

Vaughn, C. E. (1977). Patterns of interaction in families of psychiatric clients. *British Journal of Social Work and Clinical Psychology, 15,* 157-165.

Vaughn, C. E., & Leff, J. P. (1976). The influence of family social factors on the course of psychiatric illness: A comparison of schizophrenic and depressed neurotic clients. *British Journal of Psychiatry, 129,* 125-137.

Vaughn, C. E., Snyder, K. S., Jones, S., Freeman, W. B., & Falloon, I. R. H. (1984). Family factors in schizophrenic relapse. *Archives of General Psychiatry, 41,* 1169-1177.

Zipple, A. M., & Spaniol, L. (1987). Current educational and supportive models of family intervention. In A. B. Hatfield & H. P. Lefley (Eds.), *Families of the mentally ill* (pp. 261-277). New York: Guilford.

CHAPTER 9

Self-Help and Advocacy Groups in Mental Health

Ted R. Watkins

James W. Callicutt

Definitions and History

The emergence of self-help and advocacy groups into positions of prominence is one of the major changes that have taken place in the mental health field over the past three decades, along with deinstitutionalization, neuroscientific breakthroughs, and an increase in community-based services. It has been estimated that 750,000 self-help groups are active in the United States and that these groups have between 10 and 15 million members (Poole, 1995). These groups comprise laypersons such as clients, members of clients' families, and other nonprofessional advocates who represent clients.

Both group support and advocacy are deeply rooted in American culture, as families, friends, and neighbors have traditionally gotten together to share mutual problems and to organize coordinated efforts to change attitudes or policies disadvantageous to these groups. The formalization of such activities, however, is relatively recent, and now extends far beyond the local community, even to national and international organizations with permanent staffs that have impacts on national priorities and legislation. The National Association for Mental Health is an example of an advocacy group that has grown to encompass national-, state-, and local-level groups coordinated to change community attitudes, promote services, and influence public policy. Most self-help and advocacy groups begin as small, local organizations, but their eventual affiliation on a national or international level enables them to address both specific parochial concerns and larger policy issues. The national offices serve to provide stability, structure, and communication channels, as well as publicity, training, and recruitment functions. These systemic supports are often crucial to the successful functioning of local organizations (Leventhal, Maton, & Madara, 1988).

Self-help and advocacy groups related to mental health have emerged as a result of many factors within and external to the mental health field. The deinstitutionalization movement shifted the responsibility for the care of the mentally ill from the institution back to the family and community. The 1978 report of the President's Commission on Mental Health encouraged the self-help movement by stressing the need for more services in the community. Families of the mentally ill have often felt that they have received insufficient resources—emotional support, information, and respect—from the mental health establishment, and this dissatisfaction created motivation for the development of advocacy groups and a self-help system. External to the mental health field was the massive societal consumer movement that began in the 1960s, with its emphasis on empowering consumers and demanding greater accountability of all social institutions and services, from marriages to consumer products to government agencies. The concept of empowerment has included a cognitive change from passivity to competence, the development of self-help methods, and social action. It has been suggested that "the perception of having some power over the forces that control one's self [is] essential to one's mental health" (Cox, 1991, p. 79). Other writers attribute the rise of the self-help movement to such macrosystem factors as industrialization, the breakdown of family systems, and the decline of community (Kurtz, 1990).

As in many dimensions of the mental health field, there is confusion about boundaries regarding self-help and advocacy groups—that is, when is a group a mental health group? For example, the Widow to Widow program obviously supports the mental health of persons adjusting to the loss of a spouse, but it does not present itself as a "treatment" program. Also, when is a group a self-help group? How about those that are established by professionals or under the auspices of professional agencies? (These have been called "hybrid organizations"; Powell, 1987.) Also, although there is much overlap between self-help and patient advocacy groups, some discussion of them as separate types is warranted.

Self-Help Groups

Self-help is discussed in the literature as a form of treatment, as ideology, as a social institution, and as empowerment (Schilling, Schinkke, & Weatherly, 1988). For the purposes of this chapter, we borrow Kurtz and Powell's (1987) definition of self-help groups as "groups of peers who use experientially-oriented techniques to achieve control of their problematic behaviors or to reduce the stress associated with their conditions or circumstances" (p. 70), specifically relating this definition to the aim of improving one's mental health or adjustment to a condition of mental disorder. Some literature uses the term *mutual help* to reflect the fact that it is the interaction among group members that brings the members relief/improvement. "In a self-help group, members make new relationships, and through these ties learn that many other, clearly respectable individuals struggle with the same problems" (Kurtz & Powell, 1987, p. 70). These groups are distinguished from "support" groups, which are led by professionals and have a more limited expectation of empathic support only. Powell (1987) comments, "The category *self-help organization* is heterogeneous, and most generalizations are subject to numerous exceptions, given the great diversity among these organizations" (p. 11). In some cases the self-help group's purpose may be limited to emotional support and the sharing of information about resources; an example of such a group is Widow to Widow. But in some groups, change is achieved through a structured process of "recovery," such as Recovery, Inc., Alcoholics Anonymous, and Rational Recovery, which contain elements of instruction, reinforcement, and modeling (Kurtz & Powell, 1987). In either case, the purpose of the group can be characterized as primarily expressive rather than instrumental.

Self-help groups represent an alternative way of coping with both normal and unusual crises in life. They offer unique comfort and enlightenment because of the mutuality, reciprocity, intimacy, and nonjudgmental acceptance inherent in sharing with others who have experienced or are experiencing the same type of problem as oneself. Silverman (1980) draws a family analogy: Self-help groups are like sibling relationships, whereas professional counseling is more like a parent-child relationship. The sharing of experience is the distinguishing concept of self-help groups. Personal narratives are often used to promote identification among members and to facilitate growth and learning (Kurtz & Chambon, 1987).

Professional credentials are irrelevant in self-help groups, and often leadership by persons with professional credentials is actively discouraged (Kurtz & Chambon, 1987). According to Steinman and Traunstein (1976), the majority of members of self-help groups believe that experiencing a problem is prerequisite to an individual's ability to comprehend it adequately. Thus self-help group members have needs that they believe "can be appreciated only by someone who has had the same problems and overcome them successfully" (Silverman, 1980, p. 10). Members are both providers and recipients of services, and the "helper" benefits from the process as well as does the "helpee" (Lemberg, 1984). "Through helping another person, the helper learns to perceive or think about him- or herself differently. This change in the self-concept simultaneously fosters the growth of new skills and relationships" (Kurtz & Powell, 1987, p. 71). In the mutual help group the volunteers control resources and make decisions on the basis of their own experiences with their common problem (Silverman, 1980).

Self-help groups appear to help the members in them in a number of ways. The literature on this subject universally recognizes the role of group support in helping persons to deal with personal stressors. Additionally, group participants pick up new vocabularies and perspectives from which to view their situations, giving them new tools with which to frame their experiences cognitively. And, through offering assistance to others with similar problems, participants gain a new sense of strength and competence. "Self-help groups have been observed to offer feedback, confrontation, insight, interpretation, opportunities for goal setting, and identification with veterans who have made a successful transformation" (Kurtz, 1990, p. 107).

Advocacy Groups

We use the term *advocacy group* to identify the type of group whose purpose is to change factors outside the group on behalf of the members or their constituents. Advocacy groups are clearly goal oriented and therefore more instrumental than expressive, though both elements may be present. Some of them are essentially special interest groups, focused on a single issue such as services to the chronically mentally ill. Advocacy groups concerned with mental health issues may have targets for change that are external to the mental health system per se. The National Association for Mental Health, for example, has historically made the enlightenment of the general public about mental health issues a major focus. The target for change may be all or some component of the mental health service delivery system, however. For example, the National Alliance for the Mentally Ill has pushed the mental health service delivery system for greater internal allocation of resources to services for the chronically mentally ill. Some advocacy groups have "radical anti-establishment agendas antagonistic to professional treatments; others advocate a partnership with professionals and share beliefs consistent with professional understanding about the problem and its treatment" (Kurtz, 1990, p. 107). In some cases the major function of an advocacy program may be the monitoring of the quality and appropriateness of clinical care. Appelbaum (1986) asserts that "the only hope for protecting the rights of the mentally ill and affording them adequate treatment lies in establishing a monitoring system independent of the agency through which their care is provided" (p. 10). Advocacy groups have taken on the role of that monitoring system.

In general, advocacy groups develop through several identifiable stages (Cnaan & Adar, 1987), beginning with an awareness among potential members that their situation is not as they would like it to be. Families of the chronically mentally ill, for example, may perceive that public mental health treatment resources are disproportionately used for nonchronic patients, and dissatisfaction may then arise among several affected families, who gravitate toward each other to form a group. The group becomes formalized and begins to plan action. Specific actions are taken, with identified targets and alliances. This is followed by assessment of the results and decisions regarding whether to continue with further steps or to disband. Each stage involves an ideological-value dimension, an organizational-administrative dimension, an active-professional dimension, and an interpersonal-social dimension, each of which includes specific activities. These stages and activities, although theoretically identifiable, occur spontaneously, growing out of the situation at hand among the group participants. The result is the magnification of individual discontent into group action, which may be very powerful in bringing about change in policies or conditions.

Although the overt purpose of advocacy groups is to bring change, the tangible gains for individual participants are often minimal in comparison with the effort exerted; nevertheless, advocacy groups provide their members with a sense of belonging and other expressive satisfactions (Back & Taylor, 1976).

The Relationship Between Self-Help and Advocacy Groups and Mental Health Professionals

The relationship between mental health professionals and families of persons with mental illness has a history of mutual distrust, which is illustrated specifically with regard to schizophrenia in the following excerpt:

> For many years research on [schizophrenia] focused far less on biological factors than on the profound psychosocial impairments associated with the disease. . . . In the absence of an identifiable patho-physiology, theories about the origin of the disease placed heavy emphasis on its occurrence as a reaction to psychological or environmental stressors—including events within the family. The net effect was to drive a wedge between researchers and clinicians on the one hand, and potential advocates for research and treatment programs on the other. Family members, described by some in the clinical and research communities of those days as a potential "cause" of the disorder, often were alienated. . . . In effect, early theories of family processes in the etiology of schizophrenia served to create a sense of guilt and shame among parents . . . which inhibited their becoming vocal advocates of the victims they were said to "produce." As an outgrowth of this sense of self-blame, those close to victims tended to practice denial and thus felt little zest for joining a constituency support system. (National Institute of Mental Health, 1988, p. 58)

In view of this history, the surge in involvement of patients' families and other laypersons in the mental health field has not always been welcomed by professionals, who traditionally have administered service delivery systems under their own rules and according to their unique perspectives. Mental health professionals have traditionally assumed that their professionalism should protect them from intrusion by others, including the families of clients and advocates for the mentally ill. Greenwood (1981) conceptualizes three attributes of professionalism: (a) the cognitive or intellectual component, (b) the collectivity orientation and the normative or service component, and (c) the monopolistic component. The rise to prominence of lay groups such as client advocate and self-help organizations has challenged some of these components by offering an alternative knowledge base growing out of day-to-day living with mentally ill family members and loved ones as well as a different kind of peer-oriented service model. It is important to look at how the interests, and hence the perspectives, of professionals and lay participants in the mental health field differ.

Perspective of the Professionals

The following two statements illustrate one extreme view of professionals' perspective on lay involvement in mental health service decisions:

Mental health professionals . . . have always held that (1) their primary duty is to treat the patient, and (2) no one is more qualified than they to know what treatment the patient needs. Any attempt to do other than what the [mental health professional] thinks necessary has been strongly objected to as interfering with the treatment plan. (Willetts, 1980, p. 372)

Historically, many problems have arisen because of the professional's limited understanding of the unique qualities of the mutual help experience, his or her overestimation of the value of professional help, and fear that an "untrained" person might be at best a useless and at worst a dangerous helper. (Silverman, 1980, pp. 20-21)

Professionals sometimes believe that self-help groups foster negative identities (Powell, 1987), or that they "frequently foster dependence . . . promote an authoritarian belief system or orthodoxy[,] . . . have a strong antiprofessional stance . . . [and have] problems related to succession of leadership, sharing of responsibilities and group work, overemphasis on procedural matters at the expense of substantive issues, and a tendency toward factionalism" (Lemberg, 1984, p. 648). Some of the problems of self-help groups are obvious: "the desultory and eccentric activities; the leadership struggles; and the lack of resources that, in varying degrees, beset such organization. Under these circumstances, the fair-minded observer will conclude that self-help services are not always superior to professional services" (Powell, 1987, p. 9). The common problem that brings the self-help group together may not always generate sufficient cohesion to maintain the group but may tend to drain the members' energy so that they are not able to invest fully in the self-help process (Lemberg, 1984).

Professionals are often leery of the intense personal involvement of mutual aid helpers because professionals stress objectivity and the ability to remain uninvolved. And yet Powell (1987) has reported on research suggesting that the informal, social contact that self-help group members have between formal meetings may be a potent variable in effectiveness. Professionals imply that effective help must involve a restructuring of personality (Silverman, 1980), but as Cox (1991) points out, empowerment, such as occurs in self-help, is a way of bringing about intrapsychic change.

Silverman (1980) warns that professionals who romanticize lay involvement in self-help to the extent of demeaning their own abilities are abdicating professional responsibility: "This response is as inappropriate as is a haughty contempt for the efforts of laypersons" (p. 22). A minority of professionals may have negative attitudes about self-help groups, but most simply do not know enough about them to make appropriate referrals to them. Mental health professionals are more likely to refer clients to Alcoholics Anonymous than to mental health self-help groups (Kurtz & Chambon, 1987).

Patient advocacy groups have met with a variety of defensive reactions from professionals, ranging from mental health workers' discounting the advocates as mentally ill themselves to staff attempts to co-opt or defuse groups by "legitimating" them via agency sponsorship and placing them under the supervision of professional staff. Advocacy groups that operate outside professional auspices, or in opposition to professionals, tend to have more instrumental value (Back & Taylor, 1976). That is, they are more likely to be action oriented than are those that are supported by professionals, which are likely to be limited to expression of frustration only.

Perspective of Clients and Families

Lieberman (1990) provides a functionalist explanation for the self-help movement: that new institutions arise in a society when there are significant needs that are not being met by existing institutions. Tracy and Gussow (1976) assert that self-help groups developed in the mental health field because persons in distress, either from their own mental illnesses or the mental illnesses of loved ones, had needs that were not being met to their satisfaction by the "mental health system," which has been either inaccessible or insufficient in some way to meet the needs of a segment of the population at need.

As Williams, Williams, Sommer, and Sommer (1986) note:

> Families represent an expanding constituency within the mental health field whose views and interests are not identical to those of professional organizations or of patients' rights representatives. They are a distinct entity with a personal and legitimate stake in the quality and effectiveness of mental health care and treatment. (p. 253)

Families of the chronically mentally ill face problems on a daily basis that professionals most likely have not experienced. Professional understanding of some problems is not always supported by the experiences of those who have had them. Whereas professional knowledge is theoretical and scientific, developed over years of specialized education, and therefore limited to a select few, "the parents of chronic mentally ill patients have become 'experts by experience'" (Castaneda & Sommer, 1985, p. 1239). That expertise may be partialized and fragmented, but it is their "truth," and any minimizing of that experiential expertise by professionals is viewed by the affected families as discounting, and leads to further frustration with and hostility toward professionals. Self-help group members value their own expertise and are likely to see themselves and professionals as "co-learners," not "higher" and "lower" elements in a status hierarchy (Steinman & Traunstein, 1976). One complaint of many advocacy groups is that professionals have a deficit in their knowledge of the problems they are charged with ameliorating; they lack experiential knowledge relating to living with those problems (Borkman, 1976). As we have noted above, the majority of self-help group participants believe that experiencing a problem is prerequisite to the ability to comprehend it adequately.

A major complaint of family advocates is that professionals do not communicate adequately with clients and their families. Some have suggested that the lifestyles of clients' families may inhibit communication. Affluent families are likely to be assertive and, therefore, ill prepared for the passive and submissive role that mental health professionals traditionally have expected them to play in relation to the service delivery system. On the other hand, unsophisticated families may have trouble deciphering the jargon professionals use when talking with them and may find it difficult to link their understanding, perceptions, attitudes, and skills with those necessary for them to follow the professionals' prescribed programs successfully (Tyler, 1976).

Some proponents of self-help groups believe that there have been deliberate efforts to marginalize such groups by withholding recognition and legitimacy (Powell, 1993). Yet supporters of self-help point out several advantages of self-help services. Self-help groups tend to foster a sense of health and competence rather than the "deficit" model often applied by mental health professionals. Thus they are likely to take into account the influence of social factors rather than just individual pathology in the development of problems (Powell, 1987). Another major advantage is their accessibility: They do not charge fees, and they are available on an ongoing rather than time-limited basis (Kurtz & Chambon, 1987). Far from replacing professional services, as many professionals have feared, participation in self-help groups actually increases the likelihood that a person will hear about and use professional services (Powell, 1987). Silverman (1980) has reported on a survey of Alcoholics Anonymous members that revealed that 26% were referred to the organization by mental health or rehabilitation professionals. Furthermore, a considerable body of research demonstrates that self-help groups do work in many mental health-related cases (Kurtz & Powell, 1987; Lieberman, 1990), as evidenced by shorter hospital stays and reduced rates of rehospitalization (Kurtz & Chambon, 1987).

There are a variety of ways in which self-help groups are related to mental health professionals. Some groups, such as Alcoholics Anonymous, clearly limit the involvement of outsiders. On the other hand, the national office of Parents Anonymous "suggests that every chapter have a professional consultant to advise the president and to facilitate group discussion, but requires that the consultant be a volunteer who is performing this function outside his or her regular agency duties" (Silverman, 1980, p. 23). An intermediate position is taken by organizations that include professionals on advisory committees in order to benefit from their professional expertise, while giving them little authority or control over the activities of the group. In general, groups that operate outside professional auspices or in opposition to professionals tend to be more action oriented, whereas those that include professionals in leadership roles are more likely to be limited to expressive functions (Back & Taylor, 1976). In view of this, Tyler (1976) cautions professionals to allow such organizations to maintain their own unique identities and enthusiasm: Co-opting them would be self-defeating.

If self-help and professional services sometimes perceive that they are in competition with each other, it may be because of differences in their values and ideologies related to the definitions of the problems with which they are concerned and, consequently, the determination of appropriate means of resolving those problems. These differences make self-help and professional services simultaneously diverse and complementary (Silverman, 1980).

Recent Developments

The historical trend of mutual distrust between mental health professionals and patient families and other advocates has fortunately been reversed. Treatment paradigms have changed in recent years, so that mental health professionals place less emphasis on clients' "working through" every problem and now focus more on adapting to or controlling symptoms. This means that self-help groups are viewed as less "deficient" than they were in the past. Scientific developments that clearly support physiological (as opposed to sociofamilial) factors in the etiology of severe mental illness, and the emergence in the late 1970s of a new national focus from the National Alliance for the Mentally Ill, the National Mental Health Association, and the National Mental Health Consumers Association, fixed the attention of the research and clinical communities on the specific challenges posed by schizophrenia and encouraged increased public and legislative attention to the needs of the severely mentally ill. Advocacy groups are applying their activism on behalf of mental health services and research. Although each advocacy group has its own priorities, these groups are especially effective when they coalesce into a "critical mass," pooling their efforts in a particular area. For example, the National Alliance for Research in Schizophrenia and Depression was formed through a coalition representing the National Alliance for the Mentally Ill, the National Mental Health Association, the Schizophrenia Research Foundation, and the National Depression and Manic-Depressive Association. Their unified efforts effectively focused on research needs regarding the etiology and treatment of schizophrenia. The alliance of advocacy groups with the research community holds promise of significant rewards (National Institute of Mental Health, 1988).

The National Institute of Mental Health has begun to support the establishment of self-help groups (Bond & De Graaf-Kaser, 1990). Recently, health community professionals have acknowledged that self-help groups tend to promote lifestyle changes that reduce the incidence of chronic disease and disability, and consequently curb the growth of medical costs (Poole, 1995). We still lack specific knowledge about who benefits from what kinds of self-help and how they benefit, but the evidence to date is consistent with an assumption that participants do benefit (Powell, 1993).

Self-help groups and professionals can work together, and they are doing so increasingly. Silverman (1980) points out that "human service professionals can interact fruitfully with mutual help groups in at least four ways: (1) by making referrals; (2) by serving on professional advisory boards; (3) by serving as consultants to existing groups; and (4) by initiating or helping to develop new mutual help groups" (p. 23). Poole (1995) suggests that mental health professionals can find a role in the self-help movement by assisting these groups as consultants, facilitators, educators, resource developers, and advocates.

The Florida Mental Health Institute recently experimented with the development of self-help groups for former mental patients, focusing on social and recreational activities. Some former patients were paid to lead peers. Random assignment of subjects to either a self-help group or a control group was part of the experimental design. After 10 months, it was found that the experimental group participants had been rehospitalized at only half the rate of those in the control group, and then only for one-third as long. Self-help group members depended less on the official mental health system for service. According to Powell (1987), "This finding was more than the simple shift in service patterns that characterizes so much deinstitutionalization; in this case, the absolute amount of service was reduced" (p. 31).

The literature on social movements, such as McLaughlin's *Studies in Social Movements* (1969), suggests that advocacy activities have taken on some of the characteristics of a social movement. Social movements start with agitation when needs are not met by the agents of society who have the responsibility for meeting those needs. An esprit de corps develops among the members of the disillusioned group, and group members' morale is enhanced through their making a virtue out of the stigmatizing condition for which they are seeking help. To this point, the characteristics of mental health advocacy groups resemble those of social movements. Additionally, however, social movements develop firm ideologies and eventually become political movements. Mental health advocacy groups have not yet moved this far. Although these groups have taken part in political activity, specifically lobbying, with mixed levels of success, their current direction seems to be toward input through the established systems of service delivery rather than full-scale rebellion. Representatives of such groups as the National Alliance for the Mentally Ill serving on various boards of directors and advisory committees give voice to the concerns of the groups concerning resource allocation and other areas of policy decision making.

Patient advocacy groups have essentially become a monitoring system. In the mid-1980s, this monitoring role was formalized at Northampton State Hospital in Massachusetts, where the administration of the state Department of Mental Health supported the Western Massachusetts Alliance for Mentally Ill Citizens in observing conditions in the hospital and giving feedback to administrative staff regarding their concerns. This advocacy function changed the focus of the families involved from one of constant sorrow to one of collaboration with professionals. As Reiter and Plotkin (1985) note in their report on this case, "The department believes that the relationship will strengthen mutual efforts to improve the services and the quality of care provided in the state system" (p. 393).

Projections and Recommendations

Service

Self-help groups continue to be misunderstood and underutilized by professionals (Lyon & Moore, 1990). It is essential that mental health professionals accept self-help and advocacy groups as legitimate partners in the mental health arena—not as competition, but as members of an expanded team of complex services to persons with mental illness and their families. They are, in fact, important supplements to professional services (Bland, 1987; Kurtz, 1988; Lyon & Moore, 1990; Silverman, 1980). They seem to do some things better than professionals can, such as providing members with a sense of belonging and acceptance, empathic support, and a greater sense of ownership of their own recovery and coping capacity. Participation in self-help groups has been found to increase compliance with medication orders and presumably other professional guidance (Kurtz, 1988). Better acceptance and use of self-help services will mean greater effectiveness of the overall service delivery system. As a beginning toward that end, professionals need to become more aware of extant self-help groups and their goals, methods, and outcomes, so that they can refer clients appropriately to those groups. Until professionals become more knowledgeable about self-help programs, their clients and patients will be denied maximum benefit from them (Powell, 1993). Kurtz (1990) reports that only 3% of social workers surveyed learned about self-help groups in their professional education and that mental health professionals are more involved with Alcoholics Anonymous than with self-help groups that are specifically related to the mental health field. She also found that self-help group members recognized that professionals were not antagonistic to them, but uninformed.

It is important that professionals make referrals to self-help groups differentially; that is, the professional must take into account the needs of the specific client as well as the characteristics of the group. Only recently have research findings become available that are relevant to this need for matching, so "practice wisdom" will have to be the professional's guide in some cases. Kurtz and Powell (1987) offer helpful suggestions concerning which kinds of clients may benefit most from self-help participation:

> For clients whose social networks are too small, or who are unable to reach needed help, the self-help group can be an important asset. The group can be used to develop new relationships in [an] accepting environment. . . . For clients who are excessively dependent on either the service provider or on other significant persons, the self-help group can be a useful resource. From the beginning, the

client's dependency will be spread over a number of people in the group. Moreover, as the client begins helping others, his or her relationships will take on an increasingly mutual, interdependent character. . . . For clients who need, as most do, a structured action program or an explicit set of behavioral instructions, the self-help group can provide a set of action tools. . . . For clients with compulsions, impulse control difficulties, or poorly developed social skills, such groups offer opportunities to acquire and practice new skills. . . . Professionals have found that the reticence of clients can sometimes be overcome by introducing potential members to the groups while they are still part of the original treatment setting. However, this must be done in a way that preserves the integrity of the self-help group and of the treatment program as independent units. . . . For clients with negative self-perceptions or a tendency to dwell on the negative aspects of their environment, the self-help group can provide a corrective cognitive lens. (pp. 77-78)

For a referral to be most effective, the professional must be informed and positive, but realistic, about the self-help group to which the client is being referred. Powell (1993) recommends that the professional use part or all of several sessions with the client to give information about the group and to deal with any difficulties experienced by the prospective member in his or her early contacts with the group.

Mental health professionals can also support and add credibility to the self-help movement in ways other than referrals of clients. Involvement of mental health professionals with self-help groups may consist of consultation, speaking to membership, sponsorship of groups, or attending meetings as observer or member. A professional may be a valuable source of technical advice for such groups (Kurtz, 1990). If there is a local need for a particular kind of self-help group, professionals and clients may request a kit to start up a local chapter of an existing organization from that group's national headquarters, rather than attempt to start, develop, and maintain an entirely new and unaffiliated group. If an entirely new group is being started, professionals assisting clients should draw on the experience of earlier initiatives and utilize the psychosocial processes that have worked with other groups (Kurtz & Powell, 1987).

Self-help organizations have poor records with members of minority groups. For the most part, their programs reflect the symbols and practices of the majority culture (Powell, 1987). Professionals should encourage the establishment of homogeneous chapters to serve various populations. Professionals involved in starting new self-help groups or chapters of existing organizations should consider the importance of evolving group ideologies that explain and offer coping tools for clients' problems: "Such ideologies provide a vocabulary for understanding between members and a means by which members can take action to reduce feelings of anxiety and helplessness over their condition" (Kurtz & Powell, 1987, p. 78).

"Overinvolvement" of a professional in a self-help organization endangers the basic nature of self-help by transforming the group into a bureaucratic human service organization. A professional serving as group facilitator may easily become overinvolved (Kurtz, 1990). Professional leadership tends to result in less expression, independent action, self-revelation, and sense of ownership than is found in groups led by indigenous members. On the other hand, consultation of lay leaders with professionals results in greater group stability than is found in groups whose leaders do not consult with professionals (Kurtz, 1990).

Advocacy

Advocacy organizations can become partners with professionals, too. Because patient advocates are outside the service delivery system, they are able to make contributions that mental health professionals often cannot. Advocates can, for example, be extremely effective in applying political pressure to increase funding levels for mental health services and research, whereas professionals may be prohibited by their employing agencies from taking part in such "political" activity.

Advocacy is no substitute for adequate funding. Advocacy that does not result in more funding leads only to win-lose situations in which resources are shifted from one program or patient population to another. Only through greater resource allocation to the entire system can a win-win situation occur. Because mental health professionals often are either directly forbidden to participate in lobbying efforts or too busy trying to cope with service delivery challenges to become activists themselves, advocates can be extremely helpful in carrying out this needed function. In order for the partnership to work, communication between the two systems is necessary, so that the advocates have a clear picture of the limitations of current resources, the needs of patient populations other than their own, and the fact that a major frustrating factor is inadequate, rather than poorly distributed, funding.

Tyler (1976) advises that advocacy organizations should maintain their own unique identities and enthusiasm, noting that for the service delivery system to co-opt them is self-defeating. O'Connell (1978), endorsing empowerment of advocates, suggests that we make "full use of the truly exciting multiplication of people and groups who care and who are prepared to do something about their caring" (p. 197).

Policy

Powell (1993) notes: "It would be inappropriate for self-help to substitute for professional care. Self-help should not be thought of as a 'poor person's psychotherapy' or, perhaps more aptly, as 'uninsured person's psychotherapy.' Nonetheless, it is quite appropriate to discourage costly, excessive professional care by providing access to more appropriate self-help programs" (p. 162). Lieberman (1990) also expresses concern that society's interest in professional services may be diverted by the apparent appeal of self-help groups.

Sometimes the existence of self-help groups is used to justify the view that problems are caused by the victims rather than by social conditions, thereby excusing government or other social institutions from responsibility for providing needed services. *Self-help* is sometimes used by politicians as code for the dismantling of social welfare programs (Powell, 1987). Although self-help is not generally a substitute for professional care, it is appropriate to discourage professional care in instances when self-help is equally or more appropriate, as in cases of persons coping with long-term conditions who need to implement or maintain lifestyle changes for more effective management of their conditions (Powell, 1993).

Mental health advocacy coalitions could be more effective if their various components were less divided. It has been difficult for such groups to arrive at consensus regarding treatment methods and service priorities. Divisions within the mental health community sometimes result in self-defeating behavior that undermines the influence and effectiveness of mental health advocates. Ross (1992) suggests that coalitions should be able to facilitate the answers to such questions as, What do we want? and How do we get there?

Research

Although self-help groups are recognized by researchers as settings that promote individual, interpersonal, and social change (Luke, Roberts, & Rappaport, 1993), there has been little research into the broad areas of self-help and advocacy group activities, dynamics, and effectiveness. Bond and De Graaf-Kaser (1990) go so far as to say that "research on the efficacy of mental health self-help groups is virtually nonexistent" (pp. 29-30). This may be due to the general separation of these predominantly lay efforts from the trappings of professionalism, which research is seen to represent. Also, the methods by which persons choose to join self-help groups make the usual research design elements of random assignment, alternating treatments, and delayed treatment controls logistically difficult (Lieberman, 1990). An additional factor is the relative lack of emphasis on bureaucratic record keeping in self-help organizations, which makes the tracking of progress with specific clients or particular activities difficult. As Powell (1993) notes: "Formal enrollment procedures are rare . . . , and new people are accepted as members if they so regard themselves. Attendance at meetings is likely on an irregular, as-needed basis with the definition of need controlled by the user rather than the provider" (p. 159). The very nature of the phenomenon will require different-from-usual outcome research (Lieberman, 1990). Also, federal agency supports for such research have been "too little and too few" (Powell, 1993, p. 158).

Research is needed regarding what factors result in participation by whom, in what kinds of self-help groups, and with what results. Beginning, small-scale research with specific regard to persons with histories of serious mental illness indicates that ongoing participation in self-help groups is dependent on the impression the client has of the group at the first meeting. Therefore, attention needs to be given to adequate preparation of the newcomer regarding what to expect, so that disappointment is minimal. Initial confusion and disappointment are lessened if all are clear about who the group is for. Luke et al. (1993), researching group attendance, found that longer-term attenders were older, unmarried, educated, and low functioning. First-timers were less likely to return if the group was predominantly female. Persons whose marital status or whose psychiatric hospitalization histories differed from those of the majority of the group were less likely to continue to attend. Research is needed regarding who is not joining such groups and their reasons for choosing not to participate; with such information, strategies can be developed to make groups more attractive to targeted populations (Luke et al., 1993). More specifically, research is lacking regarding explanations for the disproportionately low representation of racial minority group members in self-help groups. It would seem that the empowering effect of self-help group participation would be particularly helpful to such oppressed groups. It is not known whether minority group members are referred less often, are culturally disinclined to participate, experience discomfort in groups whose members are primarily members of the majority culture, or do not find participation helpful.

Borkman (1991) points out that the emphasis on self-help groups' roles as human service organizations that provide "therapeutic" services has ignored their roles as alternative kin networks or as new forms of communities of interest that are uniquely structured to suit mobile urban middle-class lifestyles. In those roles, these groups can serve powerful preventive functions in mental health. These roles open new avenues for research.

Although there has been little research on self-help and advocacy groups, these groups have given significant support to research efforts in other aspects of the mental health field:

> The National Depressive and Manic-Depressive Association and the National Alliance for the Mentally Ill have formulated ambitious and sophisticated neuroscience research agendas. Less attention, however, has been paid to the development of a psychosocial research agenda. Such an agenda would address the day-to-day issues their members face in terms of stigma, jobs, education, housing, and their satisfaction with mental health services. (Powell, 1993, p. 160)

It can be anticipated that lay groups focusing on self-help and advocacy activities will eventually shape and support research efforts with as great an impact as they have had in areas of service delivery and resource allocation. If this occurs, the resulting research is likely to be marked by its relevance to the day-to-day lives of the mentally ill and their families. It is likely that such groups' insistence that the findings be intelligible to consumers will also make findings more understandable to professionals who are not themselves sophisticated in research methods, reinforcing the view of professionals and nonprofessionals as co-learners in the mental health field.

References

Appelbaum, O. (1986). The rising tide of patients' rights advocacy. *Hospital and Community Psychiatry, 37,* 9-10.

Back, K., & Taylor, R. (1976). Self-help groups: Tool or symbol? *Journal of Applied Behavioral Science, 12,* 295-309.

Bland, R. (1987). Social work with the family of the schizophrenic patient. *Australian Social Work, 40,* 25-30.

Bond, G. R., & De Graaf-Kaser, R. (1990). Group approaches for persons with severe mental illness: A typology. *Social Work With Groups, 13,* 21-36.

Borkman, R. (1976). Experiential knowledge: A new concept for the analysis of self-help groups. *Social Service Review, 50,* 445-456.

Borkman, T. (1991). Introduction to the special issue. *American Journal of Community Psychology, 19,* 643-650.

Castaneda, D., & Sommer, R. (1985). Patient housing options as viewed by parents of the mentally ill. *Hospital and Community Psychiatry, 37,* 1239-1242.

Cnaan, R. A., & Adar, H. (1987). An integrative model for group work in community organization practice. *Social Work With Groups, 10,* 5-24.

Cox, E. O. (1991). The critical role of social action in empowerment oriented groups. *Social Work With Groups, 14,* 77-90.

Greenwood, E. (1981). Attributes of a profession revisited. In N. Gilbert & H. Specht (Eds.), *The emergence of social welfare and social work* (2nd ed., pp. 255-276). Itasca, IL: F. E. Peacock.

Kurtz, L. F. (1988). Mutual aid for affective disorders: The manic depressive and depressive association. *American Journal of Orthopsychiatry, 58,* 152-155.

Kurtz, L. F. (1990). The self-help movement: Review of the past decade of research. *Social Work With Groups, 13,* 101-115.

Kurtz, L. F., & Chambon, A. (1987). Comparison of self-help groups for mental health. *Health and Social Work, 12,* 275-283.

Kurtz, L. F., & Powell, T. J. (1987). Three approaches to understanding self-help groups. *Social Work With Groups, 10,* 69-80.

Lemberg, R. (1984). Ten ways for a self-help group to fail. *American Journal of Orthopsychiatry, 54,* 648-650.

Leventhal, G. S., Maton, K. I., & Madara, E. J. (1988). Systemic organizational support for self-help groups. *American Journal of Orthopsychiatry, 58,* 592-603.

Lieberman, M. A. (1990). A group therapist perspective on self-help groups. *International Journal of Group Psychotherapy, 40,* 251-278.

Luke, D., Roberts, L., & Rappaport, J. (1993). Individual, group context, and individual-group fit predictors of self-help group attendance. *Journal of Applied Behavioral Science, 29,* 2216-2238.

Lyon, E., & Moore, N. (1990). Social workers and self-help groups for transitional crises: An agency experience. *Social Work With Groups, 13,* 85-100.

McLaughlin, B. (1969). *Studies in social movements: A social psychological perspective.* New York: Free Press.

National Institute of Mental Health. (1988). *A national plan for schizophrenia research: Report of the National Advisory Mental Health Council* (DHHS Publication No. ADM 88-1571). Washington, DC: Government Printing Office.

O'Connell, B. (1978). From service to advocacy to empowerment. *Social Casework, 59,* 195-202.

Poole, D. L. (1995). Shaking the kaleidoscope. *Health and Social Work, 20,* 163-166.

Powell, T. J. (1987). *Self-help organizations and professional practice.* Silver Spring, MD: National Association of Social Workers.

Powell, T. J. (1993). Self-help research and policy issues. *Journal of Applied Behavioral Science, 29,* 151-165.

President's Commission on Mental Health. (1978). *Report to the president* (Vol. 3). Washington, DC: Government Printing Office.

Reiter, M., & Plotkin, A. (1985). Family members as monitors in a state mental hospital. *Hospital and Community Psychiatry, 36,* 393-395.

Ross, C. (1992). Success and failure of advocacy groups: A legislative perspective. *Administration and Policy in Mental Health, 20,* 57-66.

Schilling, R., Schinkke, L., & Weatherly, R. (1988). Service trends in a conservative era: Social workers rediscover the past. *Social Work, 33,* 5-8.

Silverman, P. R. (1980). *Mutual help groups: Organization and development.* Beverly Hills, CA: Sage.

Steinman, R., & Traunstein, D. (1976). Redefining deviance: The self-help challenge to the human services. *Journal of Applied Behavioral Science, 12,* 347-361.

Tracy, G., & Gussow, Z. (1976). Self-help health groups: A grassroots response to a need for services. *Journal of Applied Behavioral Science, 12,* 381-396.

Tyler, R. (1976). Social policy and self-help groups. *Journal of Applied Behavioral Science, 12,* 444-448.

Willetts, R. (1980). Advocacy and the mentally ill. *Social Work, 25,* 372-377.

Williams, P., Williams, W., Sommer, R., & Sommer, B. (1986). A survey of the California Alliance for the Mentally Ill. *Hospital and Community Psychiatry, 37,* 253-256.

PART III

Mental Health Services to Special Populations

It could be cynically stated that current mental health policies and treatment techniques were developed by middle-class Euro-American males for the benefit of the same. There are many subcultural groups who do not fit the "model" for which services and policies were devised, and who, therefore, have special needs in the mental health area. Their "differentness" may be in their ethnicity or race (as with refugees, immigrants, and minorities of color), gender, social position (e.g., the homeless, veterans), stage in the life cycle (children, adolescents, the elderly), or the nature of their problems (the severely and persistently mentally ill, criminal offenders, and substance abusers). Whatever the nature of their deviation from the white male model, their special needs must be addressed by the mental health system.

We have enlisted contributors for Part III of this volume who have expertise in these areas to describe the major special populations, their needs, and the current status of mental health services to them. These chapters illustrate the extreme diversity of cultures and needs in U.S. society and challenge us to expand the boundaries of extant service delivery systems to meet those needs more flexibly and effectively.

CHAPTER 10

Mental Health Services to Immigrants and Refugees

MURIEL YU

Voluntary and involuntary migration of populations has taken place since the beginning of human history. Being uprooted from a familiar environment and having to adjust to unknown territory poses hardships for people under the best of circumstances. Given the additional stresses of war, natural disasters, and political persecution, immigrants and refugees are among the most traumatized and vulnerable groups of people.

The psychiatric disorders of immigrants and refugees may include aggravated symptoms due to decompensation or agitation. Frequent diagnoses include depression, post-traumatic stress disorder, and posttraumatic psychosis (Ganesan, Fine, & Lin, 1989; Kinzie & Boehnlein, 1989). Other immigrants and refugees suffer from reduced social and economic status caused by lack of transferable job skills and/or English-language proficiency. During times of economic recession, when job competition becomes severe, newly settled immigrants and refugees are more likely to encounter greater racial/ethnic discrimination and hostility. These added psychosocial stressors often exacerbate their sense of threat and isolation, further reducing their already diminished coping resources. The result may be tragic individual or family disintegration. Family violence, marriage dissolution, and acting-out behavior among the young are but a few examples of the known social costs (Kim, 1985). Mental health service providers, human service professionals, and school personnel are increasingly confronted with the various needs of members of immigrant and refugee populations. These professionals need specific skills and knowledge to work effectively with such clients.

Uprooted and Displaced People:
Who Are They and Where Do They Come From?

The United States is known for its diverse and varied people. However, until the early 20th century, most of the U.S. population consisted of people of European decent. Since that time, more immigrants have come from Africa, Asia, and South America in search of a better life for themselves and their children. Although refugees may come from any war-torn or natural-disaster-stricken region or country, the greatest proportion of refugees in the United States come from Southeast Asia, because of the Vietnam War. Between 1975 and 1991, more than 1,214,000 refugees settled in the United States; of that total number, Southeast Asian refugees represent the single largest group at 920,000 (U.S. Department of Health and Human Services, 1993). Other notable groups include Jews from the former Soviet Union, Ethiopians, Cubans, and, most recently, Bosnians and Haitians.

Immigrants and refugees have much in common with all newcomers to the United States. They have left their homeland and emerged in a new country, where they must learn new customs and a new language and adapt to a new culture. Non-European newcomers who are also people of color may face discrimination and racism. The differences between immigrants and refugees are important, however. Immigrants are, generally, voluntary entrants to a new country. Immigrants to the United States may be motivated by political and/or socioeconomic conditions, but they are also often joining family or friends. Immigration is usually planned, and many immigrants are sponsored by U.S. residents. Though immigrants may not suffer severe economic hardship or trauma in the process of their move, many have waited years to immigrate. Uncertainty about their destiny and the adjustments they need to make to a new environment once they arrive in this country are equally stressful.

Refugees, on the other hand, are people who have left their homelands due to a "well-founded fear of being persecuted for reasons of race, religion, nationality, membership in a particular social group or political opinion" (Nernez, 1991, p. 630). Many governments also recognize as refugees people who are not targets of persecution, but who are victims of war, violence, or other social and political disasters. The U.S. Immigration and Naturalization Act of 1980 defines a refugees as follows:

> Any person who is outside any country of such person's nationality or, in the case of a person having no nationality, is outside any country in which such person last habitually resided, and who is unable or unwilling to return to, and is unable or unwilling to avail himself or herself of the protection of that country because of persecution on race, religion, nationality, membership in a particular social group, or political opinion. (p. 12)

Therefore, depending on the global situation at large, the refugee population in the United States varies over time.

Psychiatric Symptoms and Categories

Studies on the mental health status of people who have experienced the traumas of war, Nazi concentration camps, and natural disasters have found that traumatic social and natural events are related to various forms of psychological problems (Roberts et al., 1982; Van der Kolk, 1984). The majority of epidemiological surveys among refugees and displaced populations have found increased rates of serious psychopathology among them (Garcia-Peltoniemi, 1991; Weisaeth & Bickman, 1991). In a comprehensive analysis of the relationship between traumatic events in particular disasters, and psychiatric symptoms, Rubonis and Bickman (1991) found that between 7% and 40% of all subjects surveyed showed some psychiatric symptoms. General anxiety (40%), phobia (32%), somatization (36%), alcohol abuse (36%), and depression (26%) were among the most frequently cited categories. A more recent review of refugee samples shows the prevalence of psychiatric disorders ranging from a low of 3.5% to a high of 88%, with a median value of 50% (de Girolamo, 1994).

Dube (1968) was the first to support the relationship between the refugee experience and increased rates of disorder. In comparing Punjabi refugees exposed to high rates of stress with Sindhi migrants not exposed to stress, he found that the Punjabis had higher rates of psychiatric disorder. Krupinski, Stoller, and Wallace (1973) report similar findings among migrants to Australia after World War II—those who had undergone stressful events such as imprisonment and torture had higher subsequent rates of psychiatric hospitalization.

Because of the large number of Southeast Asian refugees in the United States and the severe trauma most of them underwent prior to their resettlement, researchers in recent years have conducted a number of studies on this group of people. Among the psychological complaints, depression and posttraumatic stress disorder seem to have been the most frequent diagnoses (Ganesan et al., 1989; Lin, Carter, & Kleinman, 1985; Mollica, Wyshak, & Lavell, 1987). Other frequent complaints include somatic illnesses and acting-out behavior (McQuaide, 1989). Most of the symptoms of these disorders do not surface immediately upon a refugee's arrival in this country. Earlier reports by clinicians indicate that symptoms can surface as soon as 2 to 6 months after arrival (Tyhurst, 1977) or as late as 36 months after resettlement (Nguyen, 1982).

Post-Traumatic Stress Disorder

Post-traumatic stress disorder (PTSD) is a relatively recent entry into diagnostic categories, even though its symptoms have long been observed in war veterans and political prisoners. The fourth edition of the *Diagnostic and Statistical Manual of Mental Disorders* states that the essential features of PTSD include the development of characteristic symptoms following exposure to an extreme traumatic stressor involving direct personal experience of an event that involves actual or threatened death or serious injury, or other threat to one's physical integrity; or witnessing an event that involves death, injury, or threat to the physical integrity of another person; or learning about unexpected or violent death, serious harm, or threat of death or injury experienced by a family member or other close associate. (American Psychiatric Association, 1994, p. 424)

Thus PTSD is seen as arising out of a delayed or protracted response to a stressful event or situation of an exceptionally threatening or catastrophic nature, which is likely to cause pervasive distress in individuals.

Considering the high rate of violent life events many Southeast Asian refugees experienced before leaving their home countries, it is understandable that a large percentage of these individuals are diagnosed with PTSD in psychiatric settings. For example, Mollica et al. (1987) report that 50% of their sample of Southeast Asian refugees in a Boston mental health clinic suffered from PTSD. Other studies show the extremely high rate of 70% PTSD among patients at an Oregon psychiatric clinic (Kinzie & Boehnlein, 1989) and a low rate of 14% PTSD among the refugees who attended a mental health clinic in Minneapolis. All of the researchers cited above relate the psychiatric disorders found to the refugee experience and demonstrate that there is a higher incidence of psychiatric symptomatology among both men and women who report traumatic experiences compared with those who do not. Kinzie and Boehnlein (1989) also note the chronicity of PTSD, with the trauma usually having occurred 10 to 15 years before and the symptomatology strength increasing with stressors that occurred in the United States.

Depression and Adjustment Disorders

In addition to PTSD, depression and adjustment disorders are frequently diagnosed among refugees. Tran (1993) investigated the relationships among premigration stresses, acculturation stresses, personal efficacy, and depression in a sample of 147 adult Vietnamese Americans. Results of the study show that 60% of the variance in depression was explained by premigration stresses, acculturation stresses, personal efficacy, and gender. People who experienced more problems with their adjustment to the new country tended to lose their sense of personal efficacy, and men had more personal efficacy than did women. Other findings regarding the high prevalence of depression among refugee populations have been noted above.

Adjustment disorders are states of subjective distress and emotional disturbance arising in the periods of adaptation to significant life changes or the consequences of stressful life events. Individual predisposition or vulnerability may contribute to the occurrence of an adjustment disorder, but it is assumed that the disorder would not have arisen without the stressor (Orley, 1994). Refugees in general are subjected to exceptionally stressful life events, such as violence, serious losses, and prolonged deprivation of physical and emotional needs in their premigration stage. Once they arrive in the new country, different social and cultural norms, along with environmentally or self-imposed self-sufficiency and independence, can be overly stressful. Downward social movement, economic loss, and role changes within the family unit and resultant conflicts among family members compound the emotional distress for many immigrants and refugees.

Serious psychological and behavioral disturbances have also been observed among war-affected children. These children, whose experiences included family loss and separation, were further affected by other traumas and deprivations, including the witnessing of murder (of their own parents or relatives sometimes), homelessness, hunger, persecution, and direct involvement in violent activities (UNESCO, 1952). As a result, such children do not have confidence in others or in themselves and are distrustful of adults. Some internalize their problems because of their cultural orientation to stoicism, obedience, and respect for authority. Teachers have observed acting-out behavior and emotional withdrawal among Southeast Asian adolescents (McQuaide, 1989).

Unique Psychosocial Factors Contributing to Refugee At-Risk Status

Privation and Trauma in Homeland

Many refugees have personally suffered or have witnessed torture, rape, brutality, and deprivation prior to fleeing their homelands. The constant prolonged state of heightened vigilance against danger and threat, coupled with a sense of total powerlessness and lack of control over their fate, often causes long-lasting emotional symptoms. Additionally, victims of war or natural disaster have suffered significant multiple losses: death of or separation from family members and close friends/comrades; loss of body parts or functions; loss of personal possessions, homes, and wealth; loss of personal identity; and loss of a sense of belonging, purpose, and meaning in life. Moreover, some refugees develop a serious sense of guilt because they survived and their loved ones did not, or they feel that they were somehow responsible for loved ones' tragic deaths. All such losses and related negative affect may interfere with their ability to begin new lives for themselves.

Escape, Travel, and Refugee Camp Experience

During political upheavals or active civil wars, escape to a safe haven can involve a great deal of danger and anxiety. The tragic fate of Bosnians in the former Yugoslavia demonstrates the tremendous human suffering of refugees in that region. Others, such as Laotians and Salvadorans, often have to travel through several hostile countries before reaching a safe harbor. Horrifying stories of "boat people" emerged at the end of the Vietnam War, stories of many refugees who paid high fares for tickets to a safe port, only to be drowned because of unsafe boat conditions. Women were raped and some were killed or severely traumatized by pirates at sea. Some of theses human tragedies, unfortunately, were repeated more recently by Cubans and Haitians.

In the process of migrating to a new host country, many refugees are detained in temporary receiving camps or shelters for processing. These facilities have cramped living quarters, food shortages or restrictions, limited water supplies, and substandard hygiene facilities. Some refugees are forced to live in such deplorable conditions for as long as 4 years (Lee & Oberst, 1989). Such lengthy existence in subsistence conditions, along with anxiety over an uncertain future, causes extreme stress. Among refugees who make it directly to the United States, such as El Salvadorans, many must seek refuge in sanctuaries, where they must wait until the federal government decides whether or not they can stay. If their refugee status is not approved, they are deported and again face an unknown future.

Adjustment to the United States

Bereavement

Once in the United States, refugees and immigrants must deal with loss associated with leaving their homelands. I have already noted above the dramatic losses that refugees suffer. Voluntary migrants also go through stages of loss and grief as they leave behind family members, community support, valued professional or social positions, and familiar cultural norms and environments. Subsequent normative losses often trigger intense reactions resulting in serious psychiatric symptoms. Henry and Stephens (1977), in their psychophysiological model of stress, refer to bereavement as a stressor associated with a neurohormonal reaction of the hypophysioadrenal axis. They posit that distress such as that caused by bereavement, helplessness, and loss of control is associated with the production of the adrenocorticotropic hormone and is conducive to mental and physical illness. Clinical observations can support such a model, as the following case example demonstrates.

A recent female immigrant from Asia sought mental health services a year after arriving in the United States. This 33-year-old woman was severely depressed because her mother, who lived in Asia, had died. The family, which consisted of the woman, her husband, their son and daughter, and the woman's mother-in-law, had to struggle financially to begin a new life in this country. She had limited education and limited English-speaking skills, so she worked at home as a labor contractor. The mother-in-law, who had not lived with the family prior to migration, harbored a great deal of hatred toward the young woman. Because of the teachings of the traditional culture, the young woman suffered in silence. Upon learning of her mother's death, she became severely depressed and hallucinatory. She was subsequently treated for psychosis (Yu, 1994). Given that this woman did not have any known prior psychiatric illness, it is reasonable to assume that the onset of her episode was closely related to the stresses of grief over her mother's death and the losses she suffered as an immigrant as well as to her position as persecuted victim of her mother-in-law. These elements could very well have had negative impacts on her emotional health to the extent that she became unable to function.

Acculturation

When the differences between an immigrant's culture and the majority culture of the new country are great, the newcomer will experience more intense stress and strain in adaptation (Hopkins-Kavanagh & Sanankone, 1981). The difference between new immigrants to the United States (mostly Asian) and old immigrants (mostly European) is as great as that between East and West. Differences are found in family structures and values, language (specifically alphabets), religion, philosophy (including beliefs about mind, spirit, and body), and medicine and healing. Add to these differences the fast-paced urban settings in which most immigrants find themselves and consequent information overload, and the "culture shock" of most new arrivals to the United States is clear. Yet, despite the overwhelming demands of acculturation, the new immigrant is required to adapt immediately to survive. The problems are exacerbated by the fact that many new arrivals come from rural areas and have been transplanted to urban centers without any transferable job skills.

Existing Mental Health Services and Their Limitations

Public mental health facilities have always been limited in resources, even for native-born U.S. citizens. Given language and cultural differences, providing adequate and effective services for immigrants and refugees can truly be a challenge for mental health professionals with the best resources and intentions. Existing mental health systems, although willing to provide needed services, often become frustrated due to lack of adequately trained personnel and inadequate funding. A broader mental health issue lies with traditional practice based on the assumption that existing psychological theories of mental health are valid across cultures and situations; services are assumed to be effective with diverse groups of clients (Sue & Morishima, 1982). Inappropriately administered mental health services to the culturally different patient can have disastrous results, as the following incident, related in the April 11, 1979, edition of the *Seattle Times,* testifies.

The Illinois Department of Mental Health reportedly kept a Chinese-speaking patient, identified as David T., in custody for 27 years. The man, who was an immigrant, was at first a patient in the Oak Forest Tuberculosis Hospital; he was later transferred to a state mental hospital. The physicians there, while admitting that they could not give David T. a mental exam because he spoke little English, diagnosed him as psychotic. The reason they gave for this diagnosis was that the patient had answered questions in an "incoherent and unintelligible manner." Additionally, although he was quiet and caused little trouble in the hospital, David T. was placed in restraints sometimes to prevent him from wandering to a nearby ward where the only other Chinese-speaking patient could be found. In subsequent legal action against the Illinois mental health authorities, the public guardian charged that the Illinois Department of Mental Health never treated David T. for any mental disorders and only found a Chinese-speaking psychologist to speak to him after keeping him in custody for 25 years.

Obstacles and Barriers to Service Utilization

As much as immigrants and refugees are at risk for poor mental health, the obstacles and barriers to service for them are the same as for other minorities of color. Underutilization and premature termination of mental health services among minority populations have long been documented (Wu & Windle, 1980). Furthermore, people of color have much higher rates of admission to state and county hospitals than do whites. Factors that may contribute to this state of affairs include (a) inadequate public outpatient facilities for minority populations, (b) lack of preventive health behaviors on the part of minorities, (c) lack of adequate resources among minorities to seek the least restrictive mental health care, and (d) minorities' lack of access to outpatient facilities due to transportation or service hours (Isaacs & Benjamin, 1991).

Too often, members of ethnic minority groups are blamed for not properly utilizing mental health services when, in fact, more creative, culturally relevant programming and service delivery models should be developed. Adding to the above-mentioned factors are the specific obstacles and barriers discussed below.

Cultural Barriers

Individuals' perceptions of health and illness are greatly affected by social and cultural influences. The scientific medical model common in the United States is not adequate for understanding the perception of illness and the help-seeking behaviors of immigrants and refugees whose cultures and life experiences are different from those of mainstream Americans. The model of mental health treatment commonly accepted by professionals in the United States may be inappropriate to many newcomers, as people develop culture-based or life experience-based explanatory models to understand their illnesses and what their symptoms mean. The following case example demonstrates this fact.

RJA, a 53-year old widow with two adult sons, emigrated from Kiev to a large midwestern city in the United States. Her husband had died suddenly following a "heart attack" four years prior to her emigration. She was an English teacher, had a good job and friends, and did not want to leave Kiev, but did so because she "would have lost her sons" when they decided to emigrate to the United States. She was here only two weeks, when she was hospitalized because of stomach pains. She described the onset of "liver pains" when she was twenty-five years old and the addition of "pancreas pain," which began after her husband died. The pain then moved to the left intercostal region below the heart. Now in the United States, the pains "explode all of a sudden like a bomb," including pain, nausea, and, sometimes, vomiting and diarrhea. (Wenger, 1993, p. 28)

Even though this immigrant woman was of Western heritage, her life experiences influenced her way of looking at health and illness and her interpretation of her symptoms and perceived needs. The metaphor of pain exploding like a bomb is important; her pains had historical significance, because she grew up during World War II in Russia, where bombs and explosions were very real. Although she appreciated the American physicians and nurses and the technology that was used to diagnose and treat her symptoms, this woman said that the U.S. health care system was not prepared to understand and treat her symptoms because Americans did not experience the war as she did and do not have the "nervousness" brought on by being a Jew in a hostile political environment. She said that although surgeons and surgery are excellent in the United States, they do not know about treating "stomach pains" caused by war and "nervousness" related to political vulnerability. Furthermore, she disputed the lack of diagnosis of her symptoms by saying, "I am a sick woman. . . . inside where you cannot see, I am sick" (quoted in Wenger, 1993, p. 29).

In some cultures, diseases are often attributed to supernatural causes. For instance, immigrants from Jamaica and Haiti may be especially influenced by the health beliefs and practices of their native countries. Their beliefs about the causes of illness, treatment, and prevention differ markedly from those of American health care practitioners (Wilks, 1985-1986). Health professionals do not elicit, or sometimes reject, such clients' explanatory models, attending only to the biomedical or their own professional explanations for the symptoms. Worse still, they see it as their professional responsibility to convince the client of the rightness of the dominant view.

Many Hispanics approach mental health clinics with physical complaints such as *dolor de cabeza,* literally "pain in the head." Traditionally, many Hispanics classify illness as either natural or unnatural. They have a holistic approach toward health care—the mind and body are seen as one, and they are likely to express emotional reactions in somatic terms (Congress, 1990). In Asian cultures, mental illness is often stigmatized, so among Asians emotional problems are often expressed somatically, which is more acceptable. For example, when Chinese are depressed or under stress, they describe symptoms such as dizziness, headaches, lethargy, and appetite and sleep disturbances. In China, a majority of patients with psychological manifestations of depression are diagnosed as neurasthenic (Chrisman & Kleinman, 1983; Tseng & McDermott, 1981).

Studies have shown that newcomers tend to have beliefs directly related to their homelands' medical traditions, whereas those who have lived in the United States for some time have become socialized in the medical model of this country (Angel & Clery, 1984; Angel & Thoits, 1987). Additionally, socioeconomic status is a significant factor in diverse cultural beliefs concerning health and treatment. Also, older, recently arrived immigrants are more likely to adhere to the health beliefs and practices of their original cultures than are younger immigrants.

Geographic Location of Facility and Language Barriers

Most mental health service facilities are located in neighborhoods where mainstream Americans work or live. This often poses a hardship for newly arrived migrants, as social and economic constraints limit their residential choices. Many migrants may be greeted by hostile resistance from the host population, so they elect to reside in communities where earlier migrants live, which affords them a sense of security. Other newly arrived migrants are known to stay with and depend on relatives or friends (who were migrants themselves) to support them; thus, they maintain their residences in the same ethnic neighborhoods. As neighborhoods become more racially diverse, whites tend to move out and property values decrease, enabling more low-income migrants to move in. Enclaves with labels like Little Cuba, Chinatown, and Little Saigon are the results of such phenomena. These communities of migrants already transplanted into the host community can be a stable receiving mechanism for newcomers. Socially visible immigrants (for instance, those whose behavior and accents, as well as physiognomy, color, and clothing, make them obviously different from the majority) with limited job skills and limited English fluency are more likely to find employment and support in the ethnic enclave. These ethnic communities are often stigmatized with the label of ghetto (Brody, 1994), however, and therefore are not likely to be selected as the centers of practice by service providers. Given the lack of public transportation in many cities and migrants' low economic status, access to mental health facilities poses a serious obstacle for this population.

For those extraordinary migrants who are able to overcome geographic barriers and come to a mental health facility, the inability to communicate with staff often poses an additional barrier. Due to lack of resources or sensitivity, service providers are known to disregard clients' lack of communication skills when working with non-English-speaking clients. A case in point is the story of the negligence and mistreatment of the Chinese immigrant by the Illinois Department of Mental Health cited earlier. Other similar tragic incidents have been reported (Sue & Morishima, 1982). In dealing with mental health issues such as confusion, depression, delusions, and hallucinations, even patients who are proficient in the English language have difficulty precisely describing their symptoms. Clearly, for immigrants and refugees whose cultural and social meanings of mental illness are drastically different from those of Americans, language becomes far more complicated than what is usually expected in ordinary communication. Metaphors, semantic networks, gestural codes, and taxonomies are some of the linguistic and semantic forms that can add much confusion between migrants and mental health workers in communicating with each other. Bilingual clinicians are a scarce commodity in most parts of the United States. The language barrier is a serious obstacle to mental health services for immigrants and refugees.

Financial Costs and Lack of Insurance Coverage

Although not uniquely applicable to immigrants and refugees, the high cost of mental health care and lack of health insurance coverage do present significant obstacles to these individuals' access to mental health care. Poverty is widespread among this population, due to unemployment and underemployment. Immigrants from primarily rural and developing countries lack transferable job skills or the necessary English proficiency to compete with natives for jobs in the urban areas where they reside. Professionals—such as physicians and engineers from the former Soviet Union, the Philippines, and Vietnam—often find themselves working at minimum-wage jobs (Kelly, 1986). Jones and Strand (1986) report that among the Southeast Asian refugee population in the San Diego area, 55% have monthly income of less than $1,000. A more recent survey of Southeast Asian refugees in the Dallas/Fort Worth metropolitan area revealed similar findings. For example, 54% of the surveyed households, with an average of five persons per household, had annual income of less than $15,000 (Yu, 1990). Along with unemployment and underemployment, members of this population generally lack any health insurance coverage.

Critical Elements in Program Development and Service Delivery

Because of the unique characteristics identified above as prevalent among immigrants and refugees, mental health professionals need to be aware of critical elements in program development and service delivery when addressing the needs of this population. Factors such as geographic location of services, hours of operation, and community perception of facilities' functions should be important considerations for increasing access to and use of mental health services by ethnic minority groups. Understanding these groups' communication and information acquisition mechanisms can also promote increased access and use. For example, Hispanics have been found to rely on radio and television for their primary news about their communities. Therefore, printed materials or written announcements regarding the availability of mental health services are of little benefit to members of this population. Similarly, although some aspects of psychological theories and intervention techniques have universal applicability, cultural biases and ethnocentric practices often render well-intended services ineffective. As Gerber (1994), a psychoanalyst who has worked with Southeast Asian refugees, notes, "The literature on Eastern healing is helpful in revealing how ethnocentric our Western conception of treatment, healing, and psychotherapy are" (p. 282). The following subsections are devoted to some recommendations for addressing the cultural biases inherent in the present-day U.S. mental health delivery system and to some suggestions for overcoming known barriers so that immigrants and refugees may be more effectively served.

Culturally Competent Intervention

Because people develop culturally based explanatory models to understand their illnesses and what their symptoms mean, clinicians must respect patients' perceptions of their illnesses. Culturally competent intervention goes beyond culturally sensitive practice, as sensitivity alone is not sufficient to address the complexity of mental health issues. Isaacs and Benjamin (1991) define cultural competence as "a set of congruent behaviors, attitudes and policies that come together in system, agency, or amongst professionals and enables that system, agency or those professionals to work effectively in Cross-Cultural situations" (p. 16). Thus culturally competent mental health intervention requires sensitivity, knowledge, skills, and appreciation of contributions made by cultures and societies other than the practitioner's own. Because the clinician and the patient also have different life experiences and worldviews, those differences need to be taken into account in the context of mental health intervention as well.

Wenger (1993) recommends that practitioners search for cultural meaning when working with patients who are from dissimilar cultural backgrounds. To understand the patient's symptoms and provide competent care, Wenger suggests, the health professional should elicit cultural meaning from the client's/patient's perspective and restructure that knowledge with the scientific and humanistic knowledge of his or her own culture to create a fit. This involves a translation process that is bidirectional and requires negotiation whereby the health professional learns the terminology the client/patient uses for symptoms and the meanings attributed to specific symptoms. At the same time, the health professional assumes the responsibility of translating the scientific meaning generally attributed to physiology and psychological data and therapeutic intervention. This process goes beyond so-called culturally sensitive practice, for it requires far more rigorous discipline on the part of the professional and the client. Through negotiation and analysis, the cultural meanings of the symptoms may be reconstructed in a manner that is congruent with the professional's scientific disciplines. The end result can be the product of a "culture-congruent care modality" (Wenger, 1993, p. 27) sensitive to the client's cultural difference yet adhering to proven treatment efficacy.

Wenger's model can be applied to the case of a 26-year-old refugee from Vietnam named Huu Tien. Huu Tien was admitted by police to a psychiatric inpatient unit for a psychiatric evaluation. According to her aunt and a younger sister, Huu Tien had exhibited extremely bizarre behavior, had been fired from her job, and had threatened to kill her sister, her only surviving immediate family member. She had been in the United States for 2 years, living with her aunt and uncle. Her young sister, who had immigrated several years earlier, also lived with the aunt. Huu Tien had been hospitalized for psychiatric treatment at age 17 in Vietnam, shortly after her younger brother was killed accidentally in the war-torn streets of Saigon. Her father, to whom she had been very close, had also been killed under similar unexpected circumstances a few months prior to her brother's death. Huu Tien felt especially responsible for her brother's death because she was present when he died. Being the oldest child and without any male figure left in the family, Huu Tien had to assume the caretaking role for her mother and sister. She also resented her mother's painful comments about "losing all that was precious" to her—meaning her husband and son. In their subsequent escape from Vietnam, Huu Tien and her mother suffered further trauma and witnessed acts of brutality, including murders and rapes, during the sea passage. Shortly after their arrival at a refugee camp in Thailand, Huu Tien's mother died of an infectious disease that could have been prevented had there not been a shortage of medicine at camp. Huu Tien felt not only devalued by her mother all of her life because she was a woman, which is the Asian tradition, but now abandoned by her mother. Out of anger, she did not clothe her mother's body in a precious beloved purple dress, as had been her mother's dying request. Instead, she laid the dress on the top of the corpse. Huu Tien had to wait for another 3 years at the refugee camp before she was finally granted legal status to enter the United States to reunite with her aunt and sister. One of her bizarre behaviors during the outbreak leading to her hospitalization was her attempt to destroy everything purple in sight—she proclaimed all purple objects to be dangerous and fatal (Lee & Oberst, 1989).

To evaluate this case accurately, the mental health professionals at the psychiatric hospital had to be able to understand the cultural meaning of Huu Tien's symptoms in the context of her experiences as an Asian and a victim of the atrocities of war, long residency in a refugee camp, and entry into a totally strange new country where her own sister had become a stranger to her. But just knowing about this background information is not enough to make meaningful intervention. The treating clinician also needed to interpret to Huu Tien the unnecessary guilt she carried over the deaths of her father and her brother and over her disobedience concerning her mother's dying wish. Preference for males is a long-standing tradition in Asian societies. As much as Huu Tien was angry at her mother for devaluing her because she was female, she needed to be told that her mother was reacting from her own cultural upbringing. Through support and culturally competent intervention, Huu Tien was discharged from the hospital after 2 months. The final comment about the patient reads:

> The patient was discharged today. She will go back with her sister to live at their aunt and uncle's home. She agreed to continue her medication and see an outpatient therapist once a week. She has also enrolled at City College to improve her English. There are still problems to be worked on, but given time and ongoing therapy, she should do well. As a refugee, she has demonstrated a great deal of

courage to endure the scar of war and the pain of mental illness. It is hoped that now will begin the time of joy for her. (Lee & Oberst, 1989, p. 115)

Just as immigrants and refugees have different perceptions and interpretations of psychiatric symptoms, they also have had exposure to different methods of treating the mentally ill. Many non-Western and other societies outside the United States are known to rely primarily on informal health healers (Grossman, 1979). *Curanderos,* or spiritualist folk healers, are known to be the healers of choice for some Hispanics. This is consistent with many Latinos' holistic view of mind and body as one (Congress & Lyons, 1992). The taking of herbal treatments before or concurrently with attending a health care facility is common practice among some Hispanics (Delgado, 1979). Their perception is that particular herbs can have positive effects in the treatment of both natural and unnatural illness. Shamans, Buddhist monks, and acupuncturists are relied upon by some Asian refugees for emotional ill health. The young Asian woman whose story I related above, who became depressed after her mother's death, went first to an acupuncturist for help, but the acupuncturist told the woman's husband that her condition was too severe for treatment with acupuncture.

Another application of Wenger's (1993) model involves mental health professionals' working collaboratively with natural/folk healers. Hagman (1994) relates the case of a middle-aged Chinese man who had severe depression. He had seen a variety of healers in his city's Chinatown and finally accepted mental health treatment, including medication, that relieved his symptoms. He never conceded that his illness was as described by his psychiatrist, nor did he stop pursuing folk remedies. Isaacs and Benjamin (1991) note in a report on the South Cove Community Health Center in Boston, where the clientele consists exclusively of Asian immigrants and refugees, the necessity of therapists' indulging in "benign participation" with natural healers. It is also interesting to note that the natural healers know that their clients attend mental health sessions and that the clients often incorporate both methods in their solutions to problems.

Staffing

Because of the multiple needs of immigrants and refugees and the language and cultural barriers in mental health service delivery, special attention needs to be given to management strategies. The best way to ensure a basic level of communication between service providers and immigrant or refugee clients is for staff to be bilingual. Where this is not possible, English-speaking direct service staff may be supplemented by indigenous bilingual staff, or bilingual individuals may be hired to serve as interpreters. Additionally, creative staffing may include utilization of volunteers from ethnic/refugee communities to serve as interpreters. Most major metropolitan cities have established ethnic civic clubs and service organizations whose members may view aiding fellow newcomers in extenuating circumstances as obligatory or as an act of kindness.

Organizations such as mutual assistance associations (which provide mutual social support for refugees by refugees), churches, synagogues, and temples can also be sources of volunteer interpreters. Informal ethnic community leaders may also be willing to provide such services.

When the services of voluntary or contracting interpreters are used, issues of confidentiality, cultural constraints concerning such matters as gender and age, and the desirable characteristics required of interpreters should be important considerations for mental health services managers. Interpreters should undergo a period of training that includes information on the mission and goals of the facility, specific functions of the staff, and the purposes of various interviews to be conducted. Given the nature and complexity of treatment issues in mental health service delivery, terminology, symptom descriptions, and attitudes toward illness and health may all affect transactions between providers and clients. Therefore, English proficiency may not be the only viable requirement for interpreters' service. In many ways, providers must rely on interpreters to be cultural brokers whose task is to interpret cultural meanings beyond simple translation.

Finally, many studies have indicated that the higher the number of staff from a minority group in a mental health service facility, the higher the rate of utilization of services by members of that minority group (Snowden, Storey, & Clancy, 1989; Wu & Windle, 1980). Although ideally staffing should reflect the cultural makeup and diversity of the client population, this is difficult to achieve. One of the obstacles is the scarcity of ethnic minority mental health professionals. All three of the largest mental health professional groups—the National Association of Social Workers, the American Psychological Association, and the American Psychiatric Association—have extremely low ethnic representation. Membership statistics do not precisely reflect the ethnic makeup of these organizations, as some members elect not to respond to questions regarding ethnic background, but they provide a crude estimate. In all, the National Association of Social Workers (1994) reports that 1.3% of its members are ethnic minorities; corresponding figures reported by the American Psychological Association (1989) and the American Psychiatric Association (1991) are 3% and 8%, respectively. In addition to utilizing paraprofessionals, mental health systems have to be creative in identifying, recruiting, and retaining minority professionals. The mental health profession as a whole should also consider encouraging members of minority groups to obtain professional training and education to increase the professional pool.

Conclusion

Although the mental health needs of immigrants and refugees can be clearly delineated and anticipated, aid to refugee populations has been limited mainly to direct cash assistance, health screening, housing, transportation, and training in English as a second language for a period of 8 months (Le-Doux &

Stephens, 1992). The logic behind this standard is the expectation that all refugees should become self-sufficient within 12 weeks of arrival, or at least no later than 8 months after settlement. Not only is this expectation unrealistic insofar as the physical well-being of this population is concerned, but the lack of mental health service provision to aid in immigrants' and refugees' adjustment and adaptation and prevention of psychological deterioration amounts to serious neglect. Further, upon arrival in the United States many refugees hold overly optimistic views of their futures and are full of anticipation. Their enthusiasm fades quickly when they are confronted with the harsh realities of life as a refugee. For some, the expectation is that they should feel grateful for having survived the cruel destiny of war or disaster, as many of their family members and compatriots did not. The guilt alone can propel them to withhold any complaints, either physical or emotional. Many immigrants and refugees may have delayed reactions to their stressful situation, and symptoms may not surface for years after their arrival in this country. Although individual dispositions and other variables may account for the wide range of reactions, the common factor seems to be a period of "incubation" that exists prior to the eruption of symptoms (Ganesan et al., 1989). Policy makers and service providers should be aware of this phenomenon and should allocate funds for preventive mental health services, which could prove to be cost-effective as well as humanitarian.

The high prevalence of psychological disorders among displaced persons has been well documented. The war-torn and politically and economically unstable regions of the world have made the United States a haven for many of these victims of circumstance. Their mental health needs require special consideration and creative programming. Culture-specific competent service delivery models are needed if we are to serve the diverse cultural backgrounds this population represents. Although their immediate needs in health and other related services may be greater than those of other groups of people, history has shown the contributions that have been made by so-called newcomers to this country. The United States represents the world's best example of an amalgamated society. The diversity of this nation's people is one of its great strengths. Mental health professionals are in a position to enhance the well-being of all Americans by being committed to responding to the needs of the new brothers and sisters who have come here to seek a safe harbor.

References

American Psychiatric Association. (1991). *Directory*. Washington, DC: Author.

American Psychiatric Association. (1994). *Diagnostic and statistical manual of mental disorders* (4th ed.). Washington, DC: Author.

American Psychological Association. (1989). *Directory*. Washington, DC: Author.

Angel, R., & Clery, P. D. (1984). The effects of social structure and culture on reported health. *Social Science Quarterly, 65,* 814-828.

Angel, R., & Thoits, P. (1987). The impact of culture on the cognitive structure of illness. *Culture, Medicine, and Psychiatry, 11,* 465-494.

Brody, E. (1994). The mental health and well-being of refugees: Issues and directions. In A. Marsella, J. Bornemann, S. Ekblad, & J. Orley (Eds.), *Amidst peril and pain: The mental health and well-being of the world's refugees.* Washington, DC: American Psychological Association.

Chrisman, N. J., & Kleinman, A. (1983). Popular health care, social networks, and cultural meanings: The orientation of medical anthropology. In D. Mechanic (Ed.), *Handbook of health, health care, and the health professions.* Berkeley: University of California Press.

Congress, E. (1990). Crisis intervention with Hispanic clients in an urban mental health clinic. In A. Roberts (Ed.), *Crisis intervention handbook: Assessment, treatment, and research.* Belmont, CA: Wadsworth.

Congress, E., & Lyons, B. (1992). Cultural differences in health beliefs: Implications for social work practice in health care settings. *Social Work in Health Care, 17*(3), 81-96.

de Girolamo, G. (1994). Epidemiology of posttraumatic stress disorder. In A. Marsella & M. H. Fridman (Eds.), *Ethnocultural aspects of posttraumatic stress and related stress disorders.* Washington, DC: American Psychological Association.

Delgado, M. (1979). Herbal medicine in the Puerto Rican community. *Health and Social Work, 4*(2), 25-40.

Dube, K. C. (1968). Mental disorder in Agra. *Social Psychiatry, 3,* 139-143.

Ganesan, S., Fine, S., & Lin, T. Y. (1989). Psychiatric symptoms in refugee families from Southeast Asia: Therapeutic challenges. *American Journal of Psychotherapy, 43,* 168-173.

Garcia-Peltoniemi, R. (1991). Epidemiological perspectives. In J. Westermeyer, C. L. Williams, & A. N. Nguyen (Eds.), *Mental health services for refugees* (DHHS Publication No. ADM 91-1824). Washington, DC: Government Printing Office.

Gerber, L. (1994). Psychotherapy with Southeast Asian refugees: Implications for treatment of Western patients. *American Journal of Psychotherapy, 48,* 280-293.

Grossman, L. (1979). The pattern of organized health care: Non-response to differing health beliefs and behavior. In E. Watkins & A. Johnson (Eds.), *Removing cultural and ethnic barriers to health care: Proceedings from a national conference* (pp. 29-48). Chapel Hill: University of North Carolina Press.

Hagman, G. (1994, October 20). *Multicultural issues in work with the severely and persistently mentally ill.* Paper presented at the annual meeting of the National Association of Social Workers, Nashville, TN.

Henry, J., & Stephens, P. (1977). *Stress, health, and the social environment: A sociobiological approach to medicine.* New York: Springer.

Hopkins-Kavanagh, K., & Sanankone, P. (1981, Spring). Migration, mental health and the Laotian refugee. *Migration News,* pp. 15-23.

Immigration and Naturalization Act of 1980, USC 1158. (1980).

Isaacs, M. R., & Benjamin, M. P. (1991). *Towards a culturally competent system of care* (Vol. 2). Washington, DC: CASSP Technical Assistance Center.

Jones, W., Jr., & Strand, P. (1986). Adaptation and adjustment problems among Indochinese refugees. *Sociology and Social Research, 71,* 42-46.

Kelly, G. (1986). Coping with America: Refugees from Vietnam, Cambodia, and Laos in the 1970s and 1980s. *Annals of the American Academy of Political and Social Science, 487,* 138-149.

Kim, S. (1985). Family therapy for Asian Americans: A strategic-structural framework. *Psychotherapy, 22,* 342-348.

Kinzie, J. D., & Boehnlein, J. K. (1989). Post-traumatic psychosis among Cambodian refugees. *Journal of Traumatic Stress, 2,* 185-198.

Krupinski, J., Stoller, A., & Wallace, L. (1973). Psychiatric disorders in East European refugees now in Australia. *Social Science and Medicine, 7,* 31-49.

Le-Doux, C., & Stephens, K. S. (1992). Refugee and immigrant social service delivery: Critical management issues. In A. S. Ryan (Ed.), *Social work with immigrants and refugees.* New York: Haworth.

Lee, E., & Oberst, G. (1989). My mother's purple dress. In E. Lee & G. Oberst (Eds.), *Asian Women United of California: Making waves.* Boston: Beacon.

Lin, E., Carter, W., & Kleinman, A. (1985). An exploration of somatization among Asian refugees and immigrants in primary care. *American Journal of Public Health, 75,* 1080-1084.

McQuaide, S. (1989). Working with southeast Asian refugees. *Clinical Social Work, 15*(4), 165-177.

Mollica, R., Wyshak, G., & Lavell, J. (1987). The psychosocial impact of war trauma and torture on Southeast Asian refugees. *American Journal of Psychiatry, 144,* 1567-1572.

National Association of Social Workers. (1994). *Active membership file.* Washington, DC: Author.

Nernez, G. (1991). Current refugee situations and international public policy. *American Psychologist, 46,* 630-672.

Nguyen, D. S. (1982). The psychosocial adjustment and the mental health needs of Southeast Asian refugees. *Psychiatric Journal of the University of Ottawa, 144,* 1567-1572.

Orley, J. (1994). Psychological disorders among refugees: Some clinical and epidemiological considerations. In A. Marsella, J. Bornemann, S. Ekblad, & J. Orley (Eds.), *Amidst peril and pain: The mental health and well-being of the world's refugees.* Washington, DC: American Psychological Association.

Roberts, W. R., Penk, W. E., Gearing, M. L., Robinowitz, R., Dolan, M. P., & Patterson, E. T. (1982). Interpersonal problems of Vietnam combat veterans with symptoms of posttraumatic stress disorder. *Journal of Abnormal Psychology, 91,* 444-450.

Rubonis, A., & Bickman, L. (1991). Psychological impairment in the wake of disaster: The disaster-psychopathology relationship. *Psychological Bulletin, 109,* 384-399.

Snowden, L., Storey, C., & Clancy, T. (1989). Low income blacks and continuation in treatment in a black community mental health center. *Journal of Community Psychiatry, 17,* 111-118.

Sue, S., & Morishima, J. K. (1982). *The mental health of Asian Americans.* San Francisco: Jossey-Bass.

Tran, T. V. (1993). Psychological traumas and depression in a sample of Vietnamese people in the United States. *Social Work, 18*(3), 184-194.

Tseng, W. S., & McDermott, J. F. (1981). *Culture, mind and therapy: An introduction to cultural psychiatry.* New York: Brunner/Mazel.

Tyhurst, L. (1977). Psychosocial first aid for refugees. *Mental Health and Society, 4,* 319-343.

UNESCO. (1952). *The psychological and social adjustment of refugee and displaced children in Europe.* Geneva: Author.

U.S. Department of Health and Human Services. (1993). *Report to Congress: Refugee resettlement program.* Washington, DC: Author.

Van der Kolk, B. A. (1984). *Post-traumatic stress disorder.* Washington, DC: American Psychiatric Press.

Weisaeth, L., & Bickman, L. (1991). Posttraumatic stress phenomena: Common themes across wars, disasters, and traumatic events. In J. Wilson & B. Raphael (Eds.), *International handbook of traumatic stress syndromes* (pp. 69-78). New York: Plenum.

Wenger, A. F. Z. (1993). Cultural meaning of symptoms. *Holistic Nurse Practice, 7*(2), 22-35.

Wilks, R. (1985-1986). The Haitian refugees: An analysis of patients' presenting complaints. *American Sociological Review, 5,* 141-155.

Wu, I., & Windle, C. (1980). Ethnic specificity in the relative minority use and staffing of community mental health centers. *Community Mental Health Journal, 16,* 156-168.

Yu, M. (1990). *Southeast Asian refugees needs assessment: A survey among the refugees in the Dallas/Fort Worth metropolitan area.* Unpublished survey.

Yu, M. (1994). [Clinical record]. Unpublished.

CHAPTER 11

Current Perspectives on the Homeless Mentally Ill

R. Duane Hopson

Ted R. Watkins

Homelessness

The homeless are a segment of society that many have chosen to ignore or to deal with by handing out change from their driver's-side windows at red lights. Currently comprising close to a million individuals in the United States, the homeless population can no longer be ignored, even though it is made up of people who spend most of their lives outside the realm of the experiences of typical Americans. Our goals in this chapter are (a) to provide a description of homelessness as it exists in the United States, and specifically in one local community (Dallas, Texas); (b) to describe the needs of the homeless and their particular characteristics requiring special attention; and (c) to present a description of a unique treatment approach developed within the Dallas area.

Before one can talk about the homeless, one must understand the essence of homelessness itself. As Bachrach, Santiago, and Berren (1990) have noted, "The boundaries of the population have never been precisely identified" (p. 419), but most observers of the homeless population agree that homelessness is a state of disaffiliation from others and from the things that are valued by persons in the mainstream of society. Many people have questioned whether a cardboard box or an abandoned hut might be considered to constitute a house, and whether an individual living within such a makeshift dwelling is homeless. In Great Britain, observers have introduced the concept of "house-lessness" in contradistinction to homelessness (Baily, 1987). The distinction is important, in that it allows the recognition of the difference between the lack of a physical residence and homelessness, which is a more generalized and more serious state of loss and deprivation. Most researchers agree that for an individual to be homeless, he or she must lack a physical residence, as well as live in a state of social isolation and disaffiliation from others. Homeless individuals lack many of the relationships that tie mainstream Americans to communities, families, and friends, and this disconnectedness contributes to their psychological fragility and the difficulty of providing them with psychosocial services (Slagg, Lyons, Cook, Wasmer, & Ruth, 1994). So the condition of homelessness represents a lack of both physical (house) ties and social (interpersonal) ties. The isolation of homelessness is worsened by mental illness. As Dumont (1994) writes, "To be mentally ill is to feel one's membership in society is up for question" (p. 62).

Numbers

Determining the number of homeless persons poses a difficulty for investigators owing to the mobility of this population and its members' ability to "blend in" and thereby become inconspicuous within their environment. Who suspects that the lady walking down the sidewalk with a large shopping bag is homeless? Who suspects that the man walking the streets without a briefcase or other semblance of "business attire" is homeless?

Aside from visiting various shelters that provide services to the homeless mentally ill in several counties in California, the first author's experience with the homeless has been confined to Dallas County, specifically the downtown area of Dallas proper. Within this geographic area there are several shelters available for the homeless population, and according to the most recent estimates, Dallas has approximately 4,500 homeless individuals staying within shelters at any given time.

There are several obstacles to assessing the proportion of the homeless population made up of mentally ill persons—the lack of a standard definition of homelessness, difficulties in determining the presence of mental illness among the homeless, the overlap of homeless and other mentally ill groups, the wide diversity within this population, and where and when one is counting (Bachrach, 1992). The usual estimates found in the literature indicate that anywhere from 30% to 50% of the homeless population suffer from some form of mental illness, many with illnesses that are chronic in nature (Torrey, 1988). In 1983, the U.S. Department of Health and Human Services estimated that there were 2 million people on the streets in the United States, with up to 50% of them suffering from alcoholism, drug abuse, or mental illness. These figures were refuted, however, by a 1984 study that estimated there were only 350,000 homeless individuals in the United States. That report, however, has come under great attack, and the general belief is that the latter survey was taken from nonrepresentative communities with homeless populations smaller than the national norm (Lamb, 1990).

Another problem in counting the homeless population is its overlap with other groups on the streets, who have been referred to as *urban nomads, revolving-door patients, chronic crisis patients,* and *young adult chronic patients,* and even individuals released from jails and correctional facilities. Many of these persons flood the streets and make the identification and counting of homeless people very difficult. In their study in the Los Angeles area, Lamb and Grant (1982) found that 36% of males and 42% of females in jails had been living on the streets at some point prior to their arrest.

The "geographic migration" of the homeless population likewise contributes to the difficulty of obtaining an accurate count. The reasons for this migration are several. First, individuals living on the streets frequently move about—from one city to another, from one coast to the other—in search of better living situations. Frequently jobs are migratory in nature, and some members of this population move in search of employment. Many may find jobs and settle for months to a year at a time and then pick up and move again. The distance of migration and movement may be as great as from the East Coast to the West Coast or as short as the length of a subway ride from lower Manhattan to the end of the line in Queens, which is estimated at less than 2 hours in duration.

Mental Illness Among the Homeless

In any discussion of homelessness, the question of the impact of deinstitutionalization always arises. From colonial times until very recently, the mentally ill have been set apart from the rest of society, and isolation from the community environment was for many years the mainstay of treatment. Large mental hospitals did provide some degree of safety, shelter, food, clothing, such treatment as was available at the time, and facilities needed for cleanliness (Bachrach et al., 1990; Martin, 1990). Deinstitutionalization was attempted to allow the chronically mentally ill to live within communities, where they would receive a continuum of treatment and not be forced to live out their lives within the confines of hospitals (Leukefeld, 1991).

The problems with deinstitutionalization have been debated for many years. As Rochefort (1993) points out, "The great discrepancy between the idealism of the national community mental health program and so many of its outcomes was both analytically puzzling and morally troubling" (p. xiii). Basically, providers of care within the community quickly realized that they were being asked to provide more services than it was possible to provide to the population that was "given to them." Many individuals in this population, having been housed for so many years within the relative safety and support of institutions, were unable to provide for themselves, seek out appropriate medical and psychiatric care, or follow up with scheduled appointments made for this care.

They also had difficulty locating and accessing the various social service agencies that were available to provide support and assistance.

Belcher and Toomey (1988) followed persons discharged from a state psychiatric hospital and found that 36% were homeless within 6 months of discharge. Deinstitutionalization itself is, of course, not responsible for homelessness; it merely provides one contribution to the homeless population, that being an influx of the chronically mentally ill. Over time, the number of chronic mentally ill individuals has continued to rise as a result of the difficulties these persons have in accessing services within their communities. Currently community mental health centers exist in every region of the United States, but the homeless have more difficulty accessing these services, compared with other populations, and are more likely to refuse treatment even when it is accessible (Caton, 1995). Unfortunately, due to the large number of clients these centers serve, it is often difficult for them to address the very special needs of the homeless.

An increasingly vocal group within the psychiatric community is made up of persons who believe that mental illness does not cause homelessness, but that recent socioeconomic and political shifts have caused homelessness among the citizenry as a whole, including individuals who are mentally ill (Cohen & Thompson, 1992). "To many observers the homeless mentally ill are vivid testimony to governmental indifference to the plight of poor citizens; they represent our nation's failure to respond compassionately to its people's needs for shelter, sustenance, and effective medical care" (Mossman & Perlin, 1992, p. 951). Homeless mentally ill persons challenge mental health professionals in two ways: to identify causes and effective treatment and "to acknowledge the cultural, economic, legal, and political context of homelessness as it affects judgments about medical issues" (Mossman & Perlin, 1992, p. 952). Frequently, mental health centers have been criticized for inaccessibility due to rigid admission policies. There now exist walk-in services in mental health centers located in larger cities, as well as mobile crisis teams that are called to assess and triage homeless individuals in crisis. Smaller communities are becoming aware of the growing numbers of homeless mentally ill individuals and are developing systems whereby they can assess these individuals and make appropriate referrals to treatment or housing facilities.

Difficulties in the Treatment of Mentally Ill Homeless

When considering treatment of the homeless mentally ill, one is immediately faced with multiple problems, ranging from physical health issues to social barriers and ultimately, with housing, to a growing concern for those involved in treating this population. The first author's experience in working with the homeless mentally ill of greater Dallas for the past 10 years has led him to appreciate the fact that this is a very diverse population whose members frequently avoid and even reject help. Others have also reported on the anger, resentment, alienation (Chafetz, 1990), confusion, fear, despair, and "diminished capacities to trust" that characterize many of the homeless mentally ill (Sheridan, Gowen, & Halpin, 1993). "Often they simply don't fit into the bureaucratic framework" (Heyding, 1990, p. 373). Chafetz (1990) has noted that some psychiatric caregivers, overwhelmed with this client group's problems, withdraw from them. The first author's goal has been to develop a treatment program aimed at establishing rapport and trusting relationships with members of a frequently paranoid and mistrustful population. Services that are offered in a supportive environment that recognizes homeless individuals as deserving clients and treatment delivered within a flexible framework represent mental health professionals' best chance of being successful in working with homeless persons. Providing such services and treatment is, of course, an overwhelming task. The members of this population have multiple needs, and one agency alone is unable to meet them all. Due to the fragmentation of services, as Bush, Langford, Rosen, and Gott (1990) have noted, extensive liaison with agencies such as physical medicine clinics, mental health clinics, social services, emergency housing authorities, and food and clothing banks is vital in providing the care that these individuals need. These agencies must be able to communicate and develop an effective treatment plan for each individual so that specific needs are met and the client does not become involved in redundant care or overlapping goals. Additionally, access to facilities that most individuals take for granted—such as toilets, laundry services, telephones, mailboxes, showers, and social service agencies—are frequently overlooked. Within downtown Dallas, a day shelter was established to bring together various social service agencies, where the homeless population could interface, on a daily basis if necessary, and have access to telephones, laundry, toilets, and so on. It is in facilities such as this that relationships with members of this population are most easily developed and a rapport aimed at treatment is defined.

Frequently the word *flexibility* comes to mind in relation to the treatment of homeless persons. The homeless population is ever changing and fluid due to its geographic mobility, therefore the treatment approach itself must be flexible. Cohen's (1990) book *Psychiatry Takes to the Streets* outlines a variety of atypical approaches that are frequently useful in dealing with this population. Nontraditional forms of treatment may often prove the most successful.

Grunberg and Eagle (1990) write of "shelterization," which is the "process of acculturation endemic to shelter living characterized by a decrease in interpersonal responsiveness, a neglect of personal hygiene, increasing passivity, and increased dependency on others" (p. 521). Shelter life has its own culture, its own rules and mores. Some homeless persons may spend one night in a shelter and move on. Others may stay in shelters for many years. During the first author's work over the past several years, he has become well acquainted with shelters in Dallas, including those that provide overnight housing. Many individuals have remained in these shelters for as long as 8 years and have, in the course of that time, adapted to shelter life as their world. Many fear leaving the shelter and taking on the responsibility of life outside, with its risk of failure. Life in the shelter can be very structured. Support and assistance from various agencies may be readily available within the shelter. The shelter may become a site for dependence and passivity. Therefore, life in the shelter itself may be one aspect of the continuum of "treatment" that years ago might have been provided in a state-supported institution, but is now being provided in the shelter. Clearly, there are individuals who remain in shelters for a number of years who gradually gain the capacity to interface with society, learn to trust people, and become self-sufficient. Others are unable to effect this transition and continue their daily struggle with homelessness.

After developing a site for assessing and treating the homeless population, one must still be prepared to deal with the multitudes of problems homeless persons present, which include mental and physical illness, alcohol and drug abuse, and sociopathy (Schutt & Garrett, 1992). The physical health needs of this group are staggering. Numerous cardiovascular problems, including hypertension, peripheral vascular disease, and chronic heart conditions, have been found. Additionally, there is ever-increasing incidence of pulmonary problems—tuberculosis and pneumonia. Pneumocystis secondary to AIDS is prevalent on the streets. Health care workers who serve the homeless are frequently faced with ulcerations and secondary infections of the feet and extremities as well as cellulitis, lice, scabies, and even fire ant bites. Although not treated directly within the context of a psychiatric clinic, these physical disorders pose a challenge and often are the entry point for the development of a working relationship with this population. That is, if one can help a paranoid schizophrenic with the treatment of sores on his feet secondary to shoes with holes in them, one might then begin to develop a relationship with the ultimate goal—whether days, weeks, or months away—of the administration of a psychotropic medication.

Those who work with the homeless are also faced with the comorbidity of substance abuse and alcoholism on the streets, which some estimate to be as high as 50-60%. Substance abuse has been identified as the most problematic impediment to functioning for many homeless mentally ill persons (Mowbray, Bybee, & Cohen, 1993). Some treatment settings establish rigid rules that exclude anyone actively using illicit drugs. Inpatient care for substance abuse among the homeless is all but nonexistent. Residential treatment, frequently considered a gold standard for this type of care, is highly underdeveloped. The first author's approach has been to consider substance abuse as yet another of the treatment challenges of this population and not allow it to act as a restriction to service. Drug abuse simply becomes another of the items on the list of problems that need to be assessed and addressed. Access to treatment or services should not be denied on the grounds of drug or alcohol abuse alone.

Sexually transmitted diseases also are prevalent on the streets. An increasing number of HIV-positive individuals are presenting themselves for evaluation and treatment, and this provides yet another challenge. Professionals must assist them in finding appropriate care for their very special health needs. Poor nutrition also frequently poses a complication, especially for individuals with special health needs, such as diabetics or those who might require low salt intake. Children also have special dietary needs, and this is an increasing problem considering the growing number of children on the streets. The mental health professional must be cognizant of all of these variables that require assessment in order to be aware of the special needs of the members of this population and to treat them effectively.

A 1983 citywide study of residents in Dallas shelters over a 2-night period indicated that 20% of them were "traditional street people"—that is, individuals who have chosen that lifestyle. History has always provided evidence of this component of society in writings about "hoboes" and "vagabonds." Another 20% of the shelter residents sampled were identified as the "new poor," individuals who had lost their homes and the support systems necessary to maintain their lives off the streets. More often than not, these individuals had some underlying mental illness responsible for their loss of fortune or business that ultimately led to their homelessness. Of the rest of the subjects in this study, 30% were identified as deinstitutionalized chronic mentally ill individuals and 25% were transients; 5% of the population were identified as "troublemakers," and the proportion in this category continues to grow at an alarming rate.

One of the concerns of shelter providers within greater Dallas is that as this "troublemaking" population grows it also becomes younger and more aggressive, and it tends to push more chronic, paranoid, frightened, and incapacitated mentally ill individuals away from the inner parts of Dallas, where the shelters, agencies, and services are available. The growth of this part of the population is of concern also because it adds an ingredient of danger not only for individuals on the streets but also for persons providing care and treatment to the homeless.

Subjects of the Dallas survey were predominantly male (88%). By ethnicity, they were Anglo-American (53%), African American (37%), Native American (7%), and Hispanic (3%). Their levels of education varied, with the largest proportion (54%) having dropped out of high school; 16% had dropped out of school before reaching high school. College graduates accounted for 3% of the sample, 13% had attended college without graduating, and 29% had high school graduation as their highest educational attainment. The average age of individuals in shelters during the study was 36 (with a range of 4-74 years); 44% of the subjects were married, 40% were divorced or separated, and 4% were widowed. Subjects originally from urban areas accounted for 42% of the sample; 58% were originally from rural areas. The proportion who admitted they had been released from prison in the past year was 15%; another 13% admitted they had been released from state hospitals.

Care providers in greater Dallas are concerned about the growing numbers of young families and women with children on the streets. Many of these families fall into the category of the new poor, having sustained some catastrophic event responsible for their homelessness. Many of the young women with children are there as a result of having left abusive relationships. These women often find safety and solitude within battered women's shelters and face a multitude of barriers as they attempt to rebuild their lives and obtain services for themselves and their children.

The growing number of adolescents and children on the streets is alarming to care providers. This population is highly vulnerable and poses special treatment dilemmas. Many of the young children alone on the streets are thought to be runaways. The availability of drugs and the potential for violence among this population is great. Children of intact families or children on the streets with a single parent are also at high risk. Clearly, these individuals could benefit from evaluation and treatment for the trauma they have sustained as children living on the streets or in shelters.

As the homeless population grows and changes, chronic mentally ill individuals are increasingly pushed away from the central parts of the city, where services are available. This enables the persons with mental illness to avoid interaction with people as well as to escape the violence and potential for being harmed. Furthermore, it increases the need for outreach, and this translates into increased need for dollars and personnel. Research in other cities has clearly demonstrated that more frequent outreach and monitoring activities bring greater stability to this population (Rife, First, Greenlee, Miller, & Feichter, 1991). However, the cost of coordinated community treatment has been estimated at $8,000 or more per person per year (Satel, 1994). Agencies dealing with this population are already overburdened by the numbers of individuals they assess and treat. There are fewer and fewer dollars to spread around, and many agencies are forced to cut corners due to lower levels of funding. This crisis in resources is neither just local (Dumont, 1994) nor limited to the United States (Coid, 1994). Although federal legislative initiatives have increased funding for housing for the poor, funding for treatment of the homeless mentally ill has not been increased (Satel, 1994).

Dallas Response

The treatment of homeless mentally ill persons has been approached by different communities in a variety of ways, as is appropriate, given that "mental health is not just in the community but of the community" (Dumont, 1994, p. 62). Aggressive case finding and hospitalization—often involuntary (Katz, Nardacci, & Sabatini, 1993; Lamb, 1990; Lamb, Bachrach, & Kass, 1992; Marcos, Cohen, Nardacci, & Brittain, 1990)—neighborhood clinics (Dumont, 1994), intense case management (Rife et al., 1991; Satel, 1994; Sheridan et al., 1993), advocacy toward meeting client-identified goals (Freddolino & Moxley, 1992; Susser, Goldfinger, & White, 1990), and even jail-centered treatment (Leukefeld, 1991) are approaches that have been tried and documented.

The development of a progressive treatment approach to the homeless mentally ill in Dallas began in the early 1980s with the interest of several concerned citizens who met and talked about the growing problem of homelessness in Dallas, in particular the growing percentage of homeless mentally ill individuals in the shelters of Dallas at that time. This group grew and began to meet with shelter care providers as well as philanthropic individuals and organizations interested in providing funding. The city of Dallas and Dallas County Mental Health Mental Retardation became involved, and the development of the Community Outreach Coalition was under way. The initial treatment team consisted of one psychiatrist with two caseworkers and one psychiatric registered nurse provided by the city. The plan was to provide services to the homeless mentally ill within the shelters themselves. It was understood from the outset that this population tends to avoid services due to previous bad experiences or fear of being hospitalized involuntarily. Also, "because homeless people are often shy, withdrawn, and frightened, it may take months just to approach some of them, let alone question them" (Bachrach, 1992, p. 454). Early in the development of the organization, care providers presented themselves as simply being available in the shelters. They functioned as quasi-volunteers, passing out food, bandaging sore feet, and treating fevers and headaches. This approach was consistent with the findings of other programs that homeless clients are initially more interested in meeting immediate survival needs, such as food, clothing, and shelter, than in the mental health needs identified by mental health professionals (Sheridan et al., 1993).

The goal of the whole approach was for the care providers to become part of the "community of the shelter" and become accepted by the client population as a part of their environment. It was also necessary to develop trust prior to the actual initiation of psychiatric care. During these early times, staff members were allowed to mingle with those residing in the shelter at night and thereby, with the assistance of the shelter staff, identify individuals who might need psychiatric services. Simultaneously, when not actively involved in a clinic, staff were providing outreach services. Targeted areas included spaces under bridges, abandoned warehouses, buildings, and alleyways, where the caseworkers and nurse established rapport with individuals residing outside the shelter. These persons frequently were in more acute need of psychiatric services, due to severe paranoia. Many were gradually introduced to and grew to accept residence within a shelter.

Over time, trust was established with those who were receiving outreach services both inside and outside the shelter, and gradually it was discussed that some medication might help them feel better or alleviate some of their discomfort. It was at this point that the psychiatrist made contact and began discussing with them their lives on the streets and some of their history. Very slowly, this worked into more formal and structured psychiatric examinations. Often medications were not mentioned in the initial stages of working with particular individuals so as to avoid frightening them off, and then as time went on various medications were mentioned, discussed, and prescribed as appropriate.

Over the years, the Community Outreach Coalition has continued to approach individuals in this manner. It has grown from its original size to now providing services at five different clinics in four different shelter settings with the help of three full-time caseworkers, a psychiatric registered nurse, and two part-time psychiatrists. As the treatment team has matured and become more knowledgeable, its members have refined their timing regarding when to bring up with clients the subjects of medication, housing, or need for various kinds of medical care.

The consistency of the staff is a vital part of the Community Outreach Coalition and is likely responsible in large measure for the success of the program. There has been little staff turnover in the treatment team itself, and the policy has been for staff to work very closely, using a team approach, with all clients being part of every team member's caseload. Thus a client can walk into the clinic at any time and know that all the caseworkers are acquainted with his or her particular needs and situation. The development of the treatment alliance with the population is extremely important, and often assistance will be provided for housing and other needs long before actual psychiatric care is administered.

Achievable expectations are an integral part of the treatment plan for each client. Fear of failure is omnipresent in the homeless population, and therefore only easily achievable expectations are placed on these clients. The primary expectation is that clients will feel open and willing to come to the clinic and free to discuss their situations with their caseworkers or their psychiatrists and be honest with the team. If patients are not taking their medications, they are encouraged to be open and honest about that and to talk with the staff about why they have stopped the medication. Staff do not approach clients in a critical or punitive manner.

The flexibility of the treatment team is extremely important. The population is mobile, moving about from state to state or city to city. It is not uncommon for an individual to be seen regularly for a period of months and then disappear for 3 to 6 months or maybe even a year before returning to Dallas and to the clinic. Appointment cards with the phone number of the clinic are given to each client; however, all clients are well acquainted with the fact that they can come to the clinic at any time if they are having problems. Also, if a client misses a clinic appointment, he or she can come at the next available clinic and essentially "walk in" and be seen. This easy access to caseworker, nurse, or physician has proven highly successful, as demonstrated by the consistency with which individuals make their appointments and return to the clinic. Initially, an individual may be seen in clinic weekly as rapport is established. It is not uncommon for the initial medication prescribed to be in very low doses, simply to avoid any side effects that might pull the patient out of treatment or frighten him or her away. As the client's trust in the treatment team increases, medication management can be more aggressive, with improved compliance and a higher level of trust on the client's part. One survey completed by the clinic staff indicated an 86% show rate at the scheduled time of reappointment, which is amazingly high for this population.

Clearly, clients appreciate the easy access the program provides, but also over time they have developed relationships with the treatment team that promote this remarkable clinic attendance rate. Medication compliance is of course encouraged and is accompanied by warnings about potential side effects and the client's informed consent. Medication compliance is, however, not required for an individual to continue to receive services through the Community Outreach Coalition.

Case management is provided by the caseworkers as a team effort and involves referral to appropriate social service agencies. Recently the development of an ongoing women's group has brought together a number of women who have experienced incest or other forms of abuse. They meet regularly to talk about problems they are currently experiencing. They have become mutually supportive, and as the group has grown and its members have reached various degrees of stability with their illnesses and housing situations, they have been encouraged to participate in social outings as a group, as part of an effort to reintegrate them gradually and supportively back into society.

Researchers have investigated the prevalence of specific *DSM* diagnoses in numerous homeless populations and shelters across the United States. Clearly, more than 50% of the members of the homeless population with mental illness have dual diagnoses involving some form of substance abuse, and it has frequently been reported that alcoholism is twice as prevalent among homeless men as among homeless women. Most studies also conclude that the prevalence of the more severe mental illnesses—including schizophrenia, dementia, and severe antisocial personality disorders—is exceedingly high in the homeless population. The Community Outreach Coalition has observed that the greatest percentage of patients are diagnosed with schizophrenia, followed by bipolar and major affective disorders, and then by antisocial personality disorder. Again, these diagnoses are complicated due to their comorbidity with various substance abuse disorders.

Community Outreach Coalition clinics see almost a 50/50 split between men and women, with women reporting higher incidence of major affective disturbance, particularly if they are elderly or if they are young and have children. Children are not actively treated at the Community Outreach Coalition clinics, but their situations are assessed and, if psychiatric care or other services are required, the appropriate agency is notified and the parent is encouraged to seek services through that clinic or facility. The current number of patients actively treated by the Community Outreach Coalition clinics is 500, with an average of 400 patients evaluated, treated, or making some contact with a caseworker or nurse during the course of a month. These numbers are growing as the population continues to expand. The needs of the patients change as the conditions they face on the street change. The current locations of the clinics range from overnight sleeping shelters to daytime walk-in shelters where a mix of social service agencies are available under one roof, to a stew pot where lunch is provided on a daily basis. The most recently developed clinic is housed within a church. Each of the clinics is purposefully located in an area where outreach by caseworkers has indicated a need for services. Access to public transportation is very important to assist those individuals residing in boardinghouses and single-room occupancy apartments in getting to their appointments. Snacks are available at all clinics, and traditionally a Christmas party is provided for all shelter clients and patients of the Community Outreach Coalition. Companies and other organizations donate food, and a local hotel donates a banquet room. For many of the clients this may be their only opportunity to socialize as they once did or perhaps have always dreamed of doing. It is clear that the establishment of relationships with members of the homeless population is vital to the success of treatment, and this has remained part of the mission of the Community Outreach Coalition.

Homelessness is much more complex than it may at first appear. The homeless person is much more than just the hobo or beggar on the corner. The homeless population encompasses a large segment of society with wants and needs not too different from those of mainstream Americans. Mentally ill individuals among the homeless are the most vulnerable and represent a particular challenge to those involved in their care. A systemwide approach is needed (Bachrach et al., 1990; Martin, 1990) because the homeless need a range of supervised and supportive housing settings, comprehensive case management, accessible crisis intervention in the community and in hospital settings, less restriction on involuntary treatment, and long-term treatment and rehabilitation services (Lamb, 1990). Adequate services can be made available only if those providing the services appreciate the human aspects and idiosyncrasies of this population. Chafetz (1990) points out that delivering specialized services to the homeless mentally ill may be seen as accepting the conditions that create their dilemma. However, through the development of services for this population, we are discovering approaches that will enable us to serve other mentally ill persons more successfully (Cohen, 1992); therefore, we all reap benefits from serving this vulnerable population.

References

Bachrach, L. L. (1992). What we know about homelessness among mentally ill persons: An analytical review and commentary. *Hospital and Community Psychiatry, 43,* 453-459.

Bachrach, L. L., Santiago, J., & Berren, M. (1990). Homeless mentally ill patients in the community: Results of a general hospital emergency room study. *Community Mental Health Journal, 26,* 415-423.

Baily, R. (1987). *The homeless and empty houses.* Middlesex, England: Penguin.

Belcher, J., & Toomey, B. (1988). Relationship between the deinstitutionalization model, psychiatric disability, and homelessness. *Health and Social Work, 13,* 145-153.

Bush, C., Langford, W., Rosen, P., & Gott, W. (1990). Operation outreach: Intensive case management for severely psychiatrically disabled adults. *Hospital and Community Psychiatry, 41,* 647-649.

Caton, C. (1995). Mental health service use among homeless and never-homeless men with schizophrenia. *Psychiatric Services, 46,* 1139-1143.

Chafetz, L. (1990). Withdrawal from the homeless mentally ill. *Community Mental Health Journal, 26,* 449-461.

Cohen, C., & Thompson, K. (1992). Homeless mentally ill or mentally ill homeless? *American Journal of Psychiatry, 149,* 816-822.

Cohen, N. L. (Ed.). (1990). *Psychiatry takes to the streets: Outreach and crisis intervention for the mentally ill.* New York: Guilford.

Cohen, N. L. (1992). What we must learn from the homeless mentally ill. *Hospital and Community Psychiatry, 43,* 101.

Coid, J. (1994). Failure in community care: Psychiatry's dilemma. *British Medical Journal, 308,* 805-806.

Dumont, M. (1994, March-April). Deep in the heart of Chelsea. *Mother Jones, 19,* 60-64.

Freddolino, P., & Moxley, D. (1992). Refining an advocacy model for homeless people coping with psychiatric disabilities. *Community Mental Health Journal, 28,* 337-351.

Grunberg, J., & Eagle, P. F. (1990). Shelterization: How the homeless adapt to shelter living. *Hospital and Community Psychiatry, 41,* 521-525.

Heyding, R. (1990). Providing medical care to mentally ill women in the community. *Community Mental Health Journal, 26,* 373-378.

Katz, S., Nardacci, D., & Sabatini, A. (Eds.). (1993). *Intensive treatment of the homeless mentally ill.* Washington, DC: American Psychiatric Press.

Lamb, H. R. (1990). Will we save the homeless mentally ill? *American Journal of Psychiatry, 147,* 649-651.

Lamb, H. R., Bachrach, L. L., & Kass, F. (Eds.). (1992). *Treating the homeless mentally ill.* Washington, DC: American Psychiatric Press.

Lamb, H. R., & Grant, R. W. (1982). The mentally ill in an urban county jail. *Archives of General Psychiatry, 39,* 17-22.

Leukefeld, C. (1991). Chronic mental illness. *Health and Social Work, 16,* 7-10.

Marcos, L., Cohen, N., Nardacci, D., & Brittain, J. (1990). Psychiatry takes to the streets: The New York City initiative for the homeless mentally ill. *American Journal of Psychiatry, 147,* 1557-1561.

Martin, M. (1990). The homeless mentally ill and community-based care: Changing a mindset. *Community Mental Health Journal, 26,* 435-447.

Mossman, D., & Perlin, M. (1992). Psychiatry and the homeless mentally ill: A reply to Dr. Lamb. *American Journal of Psychiatry, 149,* 951-956.

Mowbray, C., Bybee, D., & Cohen, E. (1993). Describing the homeless mentally ill: Cluster analysis results. *American Journal of Community Psychology, 21,* 67-93.

Rife, J., First, R., Greenlee, R., Miller, L., & Feichter, M. (1991). Case management with homeless mentally ill people. *Health and Social Work, 16,* 58-67.

Rochefort, D. (1993). *From poorhouses to homelessness: Policy analysis and mental health care.* Westport, CT: Auburn House.

Satel, S. (1994, October 3). Out in the cold. *New Republic, 211,* 13-14.

Schutt, R., & Garrett, G. (1992). *Responding to the homeless: Policy and practice.* New York: Plenum.

Sheridan, M., Gowen, N., & Halpin, S. (1993). Developing a practice model for the homeless mentally ill. *Families in Society, 74,* 410-421.

Slagg, N. B., Lyons, J., Cook, J., Wasmer, D., & Ruth, A. (1994). A profile of clients served by a mobile outreach program for homeless mentally ill persons. *Hospital and Community Psychiatry, 45,* 1139-1141.

Susser, E., Goldfinger, S., & White, A. (1990). Some clinical approaches to the homeless mentally ill. *Community Mental Health Journal, 26,* 463-480.

Torrey, E. F. (1988). *Nowhere to go: The tragic odyssey of the homeless mentally ill.* New York: Harper & Row.

CHAPTER 12

Services to the Severely and Persistently Mentally Ill

Vikki L. Vandiver

People with severe and persistent mental illness pose a considerable challenge to the mental health system. In part, this is because of the complexity and the degree of need resulting from such illness. The population of individuals with severe and persistent mental illness represents a range of psychiatric diagnoses that includes schizophrenia, mood disorders, delusional disorders, and other psychotic disorders (Menninger, 1989). However, my purpose in this chapter is not to compare or contrast one diagnostic group with another, but to discuss the common issues (e.g., health, agency barriers, and stigma) that tie many people together who share the experience of severe and persistent mental illness. These issues are influenced by individual, community, and societal factors that must be understood from a multilevel systems framework, such as the biopsychosocial model. Further discussion is devoted here to historical and epidemiological trends and interventions related to the severely and persistently mentally ill.

Overview of Mental Illness

Historical Perspectives

Mental illness is as old as the history of humankind. As early as the fourth century B.C.E., the Greek physician Hippocrates described it as a disease with specific characteristics and a distinct natural cause. However, throughout most of history, the more popular concept has been that madness or insanity is due to supernatural forces—victims are either possessed by demons or visited by divine beings. As a result, people with mental illness have been stigmatized and maltreated for hundreds of years (Szasz, 1970).

Until late in the 18th century, insanity was generally considered to be an unnatural condition brought on by external causes. Patients were, in effect, controlled or punished, rather than treated. This view changed when Phillipe Pinel, a French physician, advanced the view that patients were afflicted with natural internal passions beyond their control. He literally took patients out of their chains and out of the dungeons in which they had been confined (Algera, 1981). Consequently, Pinel reintroduced Hippocrates' ancient concept of insanity as illness and began to care for and treat patients accordingly.

The late 19th century embraced the thoughts of Sigmund Freud and his explanation that mental illness results from unconscious conflicts that develop primarily out of anxiety and early childhood experience. Treatment focused on the interplay of these unconscious forces, attempting at least to alleviate the illness by bringing unconscious thoughts and feelings into the patient's conscious awareness (Shore, 1989). Although, on one hand, this treatment approach revolutionized mental health care at the turn of the century, on the other hand it did little to deal with the more disabling forms of mental illness that were present in institutions. Despite its popularity and dominance with middle-class individuals with neurotic complaints, it offered little relief to those troubled by the more severe and disabling symptoms of mental illness. Despite the narrow audience of patients who benefit from a psychoanalytic approach to the treatment of mental illness, it is still widely used today, with modifications.

More recent research indicates that disturbances in body chemistry affect mental and emotional functioning. This research grew out of the discovery in the 1950s that certain drugs (e.g., chlorpromazine) have significant therapeutic effects in the treatment of severe depressions and psychotic disorders. Since that time, the systematic study of potent medications in the treatment of mental illness has come to be known as *psychopharmacology*. Despite extensive research over the past 25 years, there is still no definitive biological explanation for any of the psychiatric disorders. Research has demonstrated that psychopharmacological medications have clinical efficacy for at least some patients with a wide variety of disorders. However, despite the dramatic effects of medications in reducing or preventing psychopathology, medications still leave untouched some core aspects of the disorders, which must be treated with other modalities, such as case management, psychosocial interventions, and clinical therapy (Gitlin, 1990).

Epidemiology

Although the terms *chronic* and *persistent mental illness* have traditionally been associated with older patients who have long histories of psychiatric hospitalization, more recently these terms have come to include younger adults who may never have been hospitalized. Whether occurring in young or old persons, mental illness is known to exist in all human societies. Epidemiology is one way of examining mental illness across populations in any society.

Epidemiology is the study of the distribution, incidence, prevalence, and duration of disease. When used to evaluate mental illness, psychiatric epidemiological methods contribute to an understanding of the causes, treatment, and prevention of mental illness, as well as help in the planning and evaluation of mental health programs at international, national, and regional levels. For example, international epidemiological studies reveal that at any given time, at least 2% of the world's population suffer from severe psychiatric disorders (Sugar, Kleinman, & Eisenberg, 1992). In both developing and industrialized countries, severe mental illness presents a substantial health burden (e.g., along with such illnesses as epilepsy and tuberculosis).

National epidemiological surveys reveal that about one-third of all Americans have had or will have psychiatric disorders at some time in their lives. The most common mental disorder is anxiety, followed by depression and alcohol and other substance abuse. In the United States, the disabilities associated with severe and persistent mental illness are known to afflict more than 3 million people. Severe and persistent mental illness is extremely costly in terms of lost work potential and compromised health conditions, and it creates pain for affected individuals, their families, and society (Okin & Borus, 1989).

One major research study that sought to assess psychopathology using a national sample was the National Institute of Mental Health Epidemiologic Catchment Area (NIMH-ECA) Project. The major goal of the NIMH-ECA study was to determine specifically the prevalence of mental disorders in a noninstitutionalized population. Some findings from this study reveal that rates of depression are twice as high for females as for males, males are more likely than females to have problems of alcoholism, and drug use is more common in persons under age 30 than in older persons (Kaplan & Sadock, 1991).

Epidemiological studies also use sociodemographic variables (e.g., age, gender, race, and socioeconomic status) to assess the mental health of a population. For example, higher rates of almost every emotional disorder are found in persons under age 45. Women report higher rates of depression and anxiety than do men, whereas men have higher rates of substance use disorder and antisocial personality disorder than do women. Schizophrenia, which affects about 1% of the population, has similar rates among women and men until approximately middle age; women tend to show more symptoms after age 45. Although gender alone has reflected an overrepresentation of women in some diagnostic groups, differences in rates and patterns for those groups emerge when race or ethnicity is included as a moderating variable (Greene, 1994). For example, Russo and Olmedo (1983) found that whereas depression is the leading diagnosis for all women, African American women in their sample reported higher rates of depression (42%) and use of drug therapy (56%) compared with European American women. Depression has also been found to be more common in alcoholic women than in alcoholic men. Studies reveal that in some alcoholic men a history of panic disorder precedes development of alcohol abuse (Kaplan & Sadock, 1991).

Epidemiological studies have examined how mental illness can overlap with other specific populations, including criminals, homeless persons, substance abusers, the elderly, children, and AIDS patients. Teplin (1990) found that after controlling for demographic differences, the prevalence of serious mental illness was two to three times higher within the incarcerated sample than among the general population. Tessler and Dennis (1989), who reviewed 10 studies, estimate that approximately 30% of homeless people are suffering from mental illness. Ross, Glaser, and Germanson (1988) found that among a population in treatment for substance abuse, two-thirds had current diagnoses of psychopathology, including 20% with major depression and 4% with a schizophrenic disorder. Dworkin (1992) suggests that people with mental illness may have comorbid substance abuse problems because of the organic changes to the brain induced by prolonged use of one or more psychoactive substances. Felton (1982) found that mental illness varied between 10% and 20% for the elderly living in the community. Specifically, prevalence rates of psychoses ranged between 4% and 8%, with dementia estimated as high as 5%. These rates increased for elderly adults who were institutionalized or living in nursing homes.

Studies of childhood and adolescent mental illness are limited. However, the NIMH-ECA study identified four major adult disorders that commonly begin in adolescence: anxiety disorders, major depression, drug abuse or dependence, and alcohol abuse or dependence (Christie et al., 1988).

Finally, Cournos, McKinnon, Meyer-Bahlburg, Guido, and Meyer (1993) report HIV seroprevalence rates between 5.5% and 8.9% among hospitalized psychiatric patients in New York City.

As the studies cited above illustrate, people with severe and persistent mental illness constitute a complex, heterogeneous group. Although epidemiological studies can begin to provide a picture of how mental illness is distributed in a community, they are limited in their ability to describe the finer characterizations of the people who make up these populations.

Characteristics

Mental illness still lacks a solid definition that satisfies most mental health professionals and consumers. Definitions have changed frequently throughout medical history and continue to do so as people strive to find terms and concepts that explain and define mental conditions. Terms such as *patient* and *client* are steadily being replaced with *psychiatric survivor, consumer, member,* or *customer* to describe participants in the mental health system. These changes arise, in part, from the fact that the cause or causes of mental illness are still largely theoretical and multifaceted.

Not every individual who has a mental illness is severely or persistently mentally ill. Most clinic caseloads are made up of individuals with diagnoses of anxiety disorder or depression. However, those people who do have mental illnesses that are considered severe and persistent (e.g., schizophrenia) are often the most frequent users and most active consumers of mental health services, despite the fact that they may constitute a relatively small portion of the clinician's caseload.

Who are the severe and persistently mentally ill? They are people who happen to be experiencing an illness that is confusing, painful, and frightening, but not hopeless. They are also people who may have children, who live with families, who are employed, who do volunteer work and also participate, in varying levels, in the activities of their community. Although the full range of possible *DSM-IV*-related diagnostic categories totals more than 200, people who are classified as "severe and persistent" are typically those who have diagnoses of schizophrenia and/or bipolar disorder. Likewise, they seem to share a biological vulnerability to stress and disordered neurochemical processing that is sometimes ameliorated by external support systems, medication, and changes in troubling personal situations. It is generally recognized that no single symptom is pathognomonic of schizophrenia or bipolar disorder; rather, the illness involves a constellation of signs and symptoms associated with impaired thinking and occupational and social functioning (American Psychiatric Association, 1994). Unfortunately, most diagnostic procedures rely on categorical methods of assessment, which tend to narrow a set of symptoms, signs, and adaptive capacity to a single diagnosis or two.

People with severe and persistent mental illness frequently display emotional, cognitive, and relational disturbances that interfere with their functional capacities in relation to primary aspects of daily life, such as self-care, interpersonal relationships, and work and school (Menninger, 1989). Additionally, these individuals often experience distress within their social and community environments that can result in feelings of isolation and confusion as well as in conditions of homelessness, incarceration, and physical injury. These emotional and situational disturbances often necessitate continuous and supportive health and mental health care services. Overall, people with severe and persistent mental illness represent a heterogeneous group whose individual members' profiles are distinct portraits of resilient survivors (Menninger, 1989).

Models for Practice:
Theory, Issues, and Interventions

Theories

The assessment of individuals with severe mental illness requires a comprehensive view of persons within their life situations and environments. Currently, there is no single theory that is acceptable as a sufficient explanation for the etiology of the many disorders encompassed by the term *mental illness*.

Although most clinicians and researchers tend to hang their hats on one theory/model or another, most mental health practitioners recognize diverse contributing factors in mental illness. There are four models for understanding the etiology of mental illness: the stress-diathesis model, social causation theory, social selection theory, and the biopsychosocial model. The *stress-diathesis model* postulates that a person may have a specific vulnerability (diathesis) that, when acted upon by some stressful environmental influence, allows the symptoms of mental illness to emerge. In other words, the diathesis or the stress can be biological (e.g., an infection), environmental (e.g., homelessness), or both (Kaplan & Sadock, 1991). *Social causation theory* holds that an individual's being a member of a low socioeconomic group is etiologically significant in influencing the development of mental illness. *Social selection theory* suggests that mental illness is caused by genetic or psychological factors that, in turn, lead persons in a downward drift to a lower socioeconomic group. The *biopsychosocial assessment model* of mental health care examines the interplay among the environmental, physical, behavioral, psychological, and social factors of a person's life. The biological system emphasizes the anatomical, structural, and molecular substrate of disease and its impact on the patient's biological functioning; the psychological system emphasizes the impact of psychological factors, such as motivation and personality, on the experience of illness; and the social system emphasizes cultural, environmental, and familial influences on the expression and experience of illness (Kaplan & Sadock, 1991).

Research has not yet shown conclusively that any one of these models is more predictive than others for capturing the full expression of mental illness. A common criticism of these models is that they exclude social and structural factors. Armstrong (1987) argues that the biopsychosocial model, in particular, is still inherently biomedical in its causal ordering (e.g., bio → psycho → social). He points out that biochemical abnormalities, rather than being causes, can have effects on an individual's social environment. However, all of these models are interrelated—and because of the complexity of this interrelationship for each individual, this web will continue to be complex.

In general, practicing clinicians are likely to view mental illness as being "caused" by a combination of interrelated factors. These "causes" or factors are most often attributed or linked to biological, psychological, and sociocultural factors. These contributing factors may increase a person's vulnerability to mental illness. The word *predispose* literally means "to place at risk due to some influence or stimulus" (Kaplan & Sadock, 1991). Just as prolonged and heavy cigarette smoking may predispose a person to, or put a person at risk for, a variety of lung and heart diseases, biopsychosocial factors may predispose a person to, or place him or her at risk for, a variety of mental disorders.

In this sense, the biopsychosocial model can be a suitable framework in which to understand the experience of mental illness. This model is rooted in general systems theory, which holds that all levels of organization are linked to each other in a hierarchical relationship, such that a change in one part produces a change in others (Kaplan & Sadock, 1991).

The *bio* aspect points to the effects of comorbid health conditions that compromise the overall health and mental health of people with severe and persistent mental illness. This aspect of the model suggests that biochemical or biological factors—such as genetic preconditions or activities at the nerve synapse—contribute to mental health. In assessing this aspect of the biopsychosocial model, Algera (1981) suggests that there are three different types of biochemical factors that contribute to mental illness: neuroendocrine, biogenic amines (i.e., neurotransmitters known as norepinephrine, dopamine, and serotonin), and genetic. Neuroendocrine theories seek to determine the relationship between the nerve response to internal or external stimuli and its role in abnormal endocrine gland release. Biogenic amines have been implicated in a variety of theories that postulate that a deficiency or imbalance in the means or rate of transmission of impulses across the nerve synapses in the brain may be a significant contributing factor in certain mental illnesses. For example, dopamine and serotonin imbalances have frequently been associated with schizophrenia (Marder & Meibach, 1994). Genetic factors or familial tendencies have been associated with certain illnesses, most notably schizophrenia and some types of depressive illnesses. Numerous studies of twins and adoptees have demonstrated that familial tendencies appear fairly independent of environmental influences. For example, when the female child of a depressed mother is raised by a foster mother in an entirely different environment, that child is more likely to develop a depressive illness than is the child of a mother who has not experienced depression. In general, people with severe and persistent mental illness show increased vulnerability to the physical complications of tuberculosis, HIV and AIDS, substance abuse, traumatic head injury, and medical and medication noncompliance.

The *psycho* aspect of the biopsychosocial model points to the areas of psychological functioning. It implies that both psychological conflicts and learned behavior patterns contribute to mental illness. In the assessment of psychological factors, there are three areas that can contribute or predispose an individual to mental illness: response to stress, response to loss, and degree of involvement in meaningful social activities. These are often expressed in patients with depression. The way a person responds to stress may give clinicians a clue as to his or her ability to adapt to the environment, level of mental health, and susceptibility to mental illness. For example, a person with a susceptibility to a depressive illness often responds to stress with a great deal of anxiety, tension, and irritability, but tends not to express anger appropriately.

The *social* aspect of the biopsychosocial model refers to both the immediate social/community environment and the larger cultural setting. There are numerous sociocultural experiences that are related to mental health or illness. Although environmental factors (e.g., social and cultural) may not directly cause mental illness, it is clear that they are important influences in the way people function in their day-to-day lives. Every individual is affected by a variety of social environments, including family, community, and work environments. For example, a person with a depressive illness may be less able to cope with a loss (e.g., divorce or death) than is a person who is not depressed.

The degree of relatedness or involvement with others that an individual has may prove to be a contributing factor in mental health or illness. Moreover, a network of meaningful social activities can serve as a buffer to the impact of stress—individuals with caring and rewarding networks are simply more tolerant of stress than are those without such networks. Finally, the family typically exerts the most influence, and whether that influence is largely beneficial or detrimental to a person's growth and well-being, the imprint remains throughout the individual's life.

Issues and Interventions

People with severe mental illness face a multitude of individual, community, and societal issues daily. For example, at the individual level, the severely mentally ill often experience multiple problems associated with physical, mental, and family health care. At the community level, people with mental illness experience difficulties with community integration. At the societal level, stigma plays a large role in how policy makers and service agencies plan for the care of people with severe and persistent mental illness. In conjunction with the biopsychosocial model, which stresses a multisystem perspective, I provide in this section a systemic examination of several mental health issues and the interventions and limitations associated with these issues.

Individual Issues

Clinicians are seeing an increase in clients with multiple problems who are high-cost service users (e.g., users of inpatient and emergency room care). Buckley and Bigelow (1992) suggest that this changing profile reflects the complexity of issues relating to comorbid health conditions (e.g., HIV, substance abuse, and tuberculosis) and sketchy family relationships (e.g., familial estrangement and parenting strains). Similar to the general population, people with severe and persistent mental illness will be at risk for deteriorating physical health, participate in risk-taking behaviors, have babies and become parents, and experience isolation from biological and extended family networks. For many, contact with the formal mental health system is sporadic and irregular.

Of increasing concern to mental health and other health workers is the risk of HIV and AIDS-related illnesses for people with mental illness. A recent study of patients from a day treatment program, an acute inpatient unit, and a state hospital revealed that unprotected heterosexual intercourse is the most frequent current HIV risk activity among patients with chronic mental illness (Cournos et al., 1993). Consequently, community mental health centers need to begin to assume greater responsibility for health education in the areas of medication, AIDS prevention, and family planning and counseling.

One intervention that is emerging in response to the needs of the multi-problem client is health promotion through education (Labonte, 1994), which emphasizes individual responsibility for behavioral change. This is an approach that requires the individual to assume responsibility for his or her own health through demonstrated changes in lifestyle choices and individual behavior (Israel, Checkoway, Schulz, & Zimmerman, 1994). Wallerstein and Bernstein (1994) assert that the role of the professional is to educate the client for the purpose of empowerment. They suggest that professionals should serve as a resource to help create favorable conditions for people to share in personal growth and awareness, to reconnect with estranged support networks (e.g., family and/or friends), and to contribute to opportunities for community dialogue. The role of the professional, according to Wallerstein and Bernstein, is to engage in the empowerment process in partnership with clients, clients' families, and other professionals. Promoters of this strategy appear to believe that through educative intervention, professionals can help individuals to alter the behaviors that are causing their health and social problems.

There are limitations to this type of intervention, however. In general, the health promotion model fails to consider the interrelationship between willful choice and physical and environmental vulnerabilities. It also overlooks issues of inequitable access. Blaming mentally ill people or holding them responsible for their inability to obtain prenatal care or to pay for expensive medications (e.g., AZT) does not correct the problem of economic disparities. Finally, although mental health educators committed to improving mental health and well-being might want to teach individuals how to find alternative solutions to their problems, this approach has the danger of both blaming the victim and doing little to correct the sources of the problems (Israel et al., 1994).

Community Issues

People with severe and persistent mental illness face numerous issues in relation to community integration: Clients and their families may be ill prepared to coordinate the care needed for community integration; they may face barriers that make it difficult or impossible for them to access services; and some may have unrealistic employment expectations.

Many discharged patients have inadequate support systems and limited links to community programs, which leaves them isolated and ill prepared to manage in the community. Consequently, their families and other caregivers often find themselves in the position of trying to manage the care of the discharged persons, without the community resources or knowledge to do so. Research has suggested that more than half of adult psychiatric patients live with their families before and after hospitalization, and that family members tend to become the primary caretakers for a large proportion of adults with severe and persistent mental illness (Straznickas, McNeil, & Binder, 1993).

Two forms of intervention that have demonstrated effectiveness in addressing family/caregiver needs have been the use of psychoeducational approaches (see Simon, Chapter 8, this volume) and professionally guided self-help groups (see Watkins & Callicutt, Chapter 9, this volume). Both of these are based on an educational model, the goal of which is to provide the families and other caregivers of persons with mental illness with concrete information about such illness and methods they may use to advocate for better systems of care (Anderson, Reiss, & Hogarty, 1986). The limitation of these programs is that they do little to correct the problems of inadequate support systems and fragmented linkage to care systems. Rather than forcing the provider system to correct these problems, they still place the burden of making the situation better or more manageable on the individuals involved. Consumer advocates frequently report that the reason mental health consumers do not receive services is that there are numerous structural barriers (e.g., inaccessible clinic locations, restrictive eligibility criteria, and bureaucratic obstacles) interfering with consumers' abilities to engage or participate in available services. Consequently, staff may be inclined to regard the "no-show" consumer as "treatment noncompliant" or "resistant." Carrion, Swann, Kellert-Cecil, and Barber (1993) found that of patients with schizophrenia who attended an outpatient clinic, the main reasons reported for not coming to follow-up appointments were transportation difficulties and forgetting. Additionally, these researchers' findings suggest that once consumers are attached to a mental health facility, they are more likely to keep their appointments.

Interventions for dealing with barriers to services require a model that reflects an open communication network. This network involves a seamless system of care in which catchment areas no longer define service boundaries. Currently, community mental health centers are moving beyond region-restricted care and are locating satellite offices in numerous spots throughout a city. Once geographic barriers are removed, programs can enhance client contact (whether at home or in the clinic) by sending personal letters, using telephone prompts, and increasing staff awareness of clients' problems, such as transportation and finances (Carrion et al., 1993).

Finally, many persons with serious mental illness have unrealistic expectations concerning employment. Although psychosocial rehabilitation programs include prevocational and vocational training, they often use settings that are a part of the agency system. Interventions that can assist in the effort toward providing persons with serious mental illness meaningful employment opportunities begin with philosophical changes. Vocational rehabilitation programs must counter the notion that all mentally ill people can and must engage in competitive work activities (Bachrach, 1991). Economic policies will no doubt influence communities' abilities to deliver the quality of services that people with severe and persistent mental illness actually need. Vocational rehabilitation centers need to be sensitive to economic conditions and economic recession, both of which have profound effects on the job market for people with mental illness (Bachrach, 1991).

There are limitations to each of the interventions mentioned above. Conceptually, many mental health systems are still driven by a medical model that tends to view consumers' lives in terms of symptoms and deficits. Financially, many community-based programs still remain tied to fiscal service models, in which reimbursement is associated with aspects of what professionals *do* rather than with supporting successful efforts of clients, families, natural support systems, and community organizations. Structurally, many programs lack specificity for differing client needs and thus provide service systems that are inflexible and mechanistic.

Societal Issues

Stigma remains one of the most pervasive problems faced by people with severe and persistent mental illness. Goffman (1963) defines stigma as an attribute that is socially "deeply discrediting" and marks the person in a way that discredits him or her in the eyes of others. Being marked as a person with mental illness transforms a person's beliefs about the devaluation and discrimination of mental patients into a personal expectation of rejection (Link, Cullen, Mirotznik, & Struening, 1992). It affects every aspect of an individual's life and is the harbinger of problems in areas ranging from insurance, housing, and jobs to every aspect of daily living. Stigma may even stop people from getting treatment (Dubin & Fink, 1992). People with severe mental illness still continue to be viewed as constitutionally weak, dangerous, and responsible for their own plight.

Part of this belief is rooted in myth and misunderstanding about the nature of persistent mental illness. Society's willingness to let people remain medically and psychiatrically untreated because of fear of infringing on their civil rights, to let people go without food because they have no vouchers, or to let people lie in the streets because that is where it is assumed they want to be is testimony of a general unwillingness to accept and provide for the members of this most vulnerable population. Much of this has to do with lack of public awareness, as well as bureaucratic obstacles. This is best illustrated by the recent public health movement in which health and mental health issues are categorized as health conditions that are preventable through changes in collective and individual lifestyles.

Pepper (1987) recommends that stigma be countered by a coalition of mental health professionals, government agencies, and families of the mentally ill, coming together in a broad, integrated campaign to educate the public and secure the resources necessary for adequate and comprehensive care of persons with mental illness. Through this approach, stigma can be reduced and prevention programs can be aimed at subduing the psychosocial and vocational disability associated with mental illness. The limitation of this plan, however, lies in the fact that mental health policies do not fully support prevention models. Knowing what we do about the benefits of an integrated model of services (e.g., housing, medical care, and support services that emphasize day programs and family/peer support groups), policy planners still do not create systems that are physically and financially accessible to low-income mentally ill people. However, we know that when supportive mental health structures are in place, illness and relapse rates decline, quality of life increases, and society at large benefits from a dignified response to its more vulnerable members.

Implications and Discussion

As the above discussion illustrates, there are common issues for people with severe and persistent mental illness that transcend traditional diagnostic categories (e.g., schizophrenia or bipolar disorder) and group labels (e.g., patient or consumer). The issues of basic health standards, community and family integration, and stigma represent fundamental concerns that need to be addressed through three levels of analysis: individual, community, and societal. The biopsychosocial model of assessment is one method of analysis that can be useful in understanding the broader issues surrounding the experiences of people with mental illness.

Mental health professionals, consumers, and families face many challenges. As a group, they need to engage in the empowerment process as partners, plunging themselves equally into the listening and learning process. As mental health professionals, we must ensure that we value and honor individual contributions and expressions of need (e.g., as voiced by consumer and advocacy groups) while at the same time working at the community and societal levels to change underlying conditions that promote stigma and feelings of powerlessness for people with mental illness. For empowerment strategies to work, clinicians must be willing to change their practice to one of partnership with consumers, families, and communities (Wallerstein & Bernstein, 1994).

Increasingly, mental health professionals are seeing the importance of integrating family members into service delivery systems. One lesson to be gained comes not from the latest technology or research efforts, but from epidemiological studies in developing countries. While we struggle to learn new ways to integrate medical and mental health services, non-Western countries have long incorporated the model of family and community involvement. Reports from international studies have shown that persons with major psychiatric disorders have a more benign course of illness in developing nations than in the technologically advanced societies of the West (Day et al., 1987). It is presumed that strong familial and community ties deflect some of the more socially disabling aspects of the illness. The training of a new generation of clinicians is beginning to focus on working in a collaborative model with families of the mentally ill instead of perpetuating the use of ineffective insight-oriented psychotherapy.

As health care systems move into evaluating service outcomes, consumers can benefit from the information provided, in that it may help them choose treatment methods. This has the potential to replace the mechanistic and inflexible service systems that are prominent today. Outcome assessments will move away from the medical model, which emphasizes symptom presentation and deficit thinking, into a broader role for assessment. Some areas that will be assessed will include the consumer's social functioning, emotional health, cognitive functioning, and life satisfaction. Even the way we refer to people with mental illness is poised for change, yet again; another term that is being advocated to replace the term *mental illness* is *neurobiological disorder* (Francell, 1994). It has been proposed that, just as in the medical field people who have hypertension are referred to as having a cardiovascular disorder, people with schizophrenia or bipolar disorder should be referred to as having a neurobiological disorder.

Conclusion

Many people with severe and persistent mental illness are unaware of the special strengths, skills, and resilience they possess. Helping them to become aware of their assets, to use them consciously, and to access available resources is an important part of clinical and community mental health work (Greene, 1994).

The biopsychosocial model of mental illness combines the best of current knowledge with theory. It incorporates the individual's biology, psychological functioning, and adaptation to the environment. This model, by including community and societal factors, also has the potential to force clinicians, consumers, consumers' families, and policy makers to consider the greater social issues of stigma, oppression, and inadequate funding. Only through such multiple-level evaluation—including the individual, community, and society—will the conditions of people with severe and persistent mental illness change sufficiently to allow them equal participation in their treatment. Ultimately, when the (mental) health of an individual is enhanced, the health of the community is enhanced.

References

Algera, G. (1981). *Overview of mental illness.* Summit, NJ: CIBA Pharmaceutical.

American Psychiatric Association. (1994). *Diagnostic and statistical manual of mental disorders* (4th ed.). Washington, DC: Author.

Anderson, C. M., Reiss, D. J., & Hogarty, G. (1986). *Schizophrenia and the family.* New York: Guilford.

Armstrong, D. (1987). Theoretical tensions in biopsychosocial medicine. *Social Science and Medicine, 25,* 1213-1218.

Bachrach, L. (1991). The chronic patient: Perspectives on work and rehabilitation. *Hospital and Community Psychiatry, 42,* 890-891.

Buckley, R., & Bigelow, D. A. (1992). The multiservice network: Reaching the unserved multi-problem individual. *Community Mental Health Journal, 28,* 43-50.

Carrion, P. G., Swann, A., Kellert-Cecil, H., & Barber, M. (1993). Compliance with clinic attendance by outpatients with schizophrenia. *Hospital and Community Psychiatry, 44,* 764-767.

Christie, K. A., Burke, J. D., Jr., Regier, D. A., Raie, D. S., Boyd, J. H., & Locke, B. Z. (1988). Epidemiologic evidence for early onset of mental disorders and higher risk of drug abuse in young adults. *American Journal of Psychiatry, 145,* 971-975.

Cournos, F., McKinnon, K., Meyer-Bahlburg, H., Guido, J., & Meyer, I. (1993). HIV risk activity among persons with severe mental illness: Preliminary findings. *Hospital and Community Psychiatry, 44,* 1104-1106.

Day, R., Neilson, J. A., Korten, A., Ernberg, G., Dube, K. C., Gebhart, J., Jablensky, A., Leon, C., Marsela, A., Olatawura, M., Sartorius, N., Stromgren, E., Takahashi, R., Wig, N., & Wynne, L. C. (1987). Stressful life events preceding the acute onset of schizophrenia: A cross-national study from the World Health Organization. *Culture, Medicine, and Psychiatry, 11,* 123-205.

Dubin, W. R., & Fink, P. J. (1992). Effects of stigma on psychiatric treatment. In P. J. Fink & A. Tasman (Eds.), *Stigma and mental illness* (pp. 1-10). Washington, DC: American Psychiatric Press.

Dworkin, R. J. (1992). *Researching persons with mental illness.* Newbury Park, CA: Sage.

Felton, B. J. (1982). The aged: Settings, services, and needs. In L. R. Snowden (Ed.), *Reaching the underserved* (pp. 23-42). Beverly Hills, CA: Sage.

Francell, E. G. (1994). What mental illness needs: Public education and a new name. *Hospital and Community Psychiatry, 45,* 409.

Gitlin, M. J. (1990). *The psychotherapist's guide to psychopharmacology.* New York: Free Press.

Goffman, E. (1963). *Stigma: Notes on the management of spoiled identity.* Englewood Cliffs, NJ: Prentice Hall.

Greene, B. (1994). Diversity and difference: Race and feminist psychotherapy. In M. P. Mirkin (Ed.), *Women in context: Toward a feminist reconstruction of psychotherapy* (pp. 333-351). New York: Guilford.

Israel, B. A., Checkoway, B., Schulz, A., & Zimmerman, M. (1994). Health education and community empowerment: Conceptualizing and measuring perceptions of individual, organizational, and community control. *Health Education Quarterly, 21,* 149-170.

Kaplan, H. I., & Sadock, B. J. (1991). *Synopsis of psychiatry* (6th ed.). Baltimore: Williams & Wilkins.

Labonte, R. (1994). Health promotion and empowerment: Reflections on professional practice. *Health Education Quarterly, 21,* 253-268.

Link, B. G., Cullen, F. T., Mirotznik, J., & Struening, E. (1992). The consequences of stigma for persons with mental illness: Evidence from the social sciences. In P. J. Fink & A. Tasman (Eds.), *Stigma and mental illness* (pp. 87-96). Washington, DC: American Psychiatric Press.

Marder, S. R., & Meibach, R. C. (1994). Resperidone in the treatment of schizophrenia. *American Journal of Psychiatry, 151,* 825-835.

Menninger, W. W. (1989). The chronically mentally ill. In H. I. Kaplan & B. J. Sadock (Eds.), *Comprehensive textbook of psychiatry* (5th ed., Vol. 2, pp. 2090-2098). Baltimore: Williams & Wilkins.

Okin, R. L., & Borus, J. F. (1989). Primary, secondary, and tertiary prevention of mental disorders. In H. I. Kaplan & B. J. Sadock (Eds.), *Comprehensive textbook of psychiatry* (5th ed., Vol. 2, pp. 2067-2071). Baltimore: Williams & Wilkins.

Pepper, B. (1987). A public policy for the long-term mentally ill: A positive alternative to reinstitutionalization. *American Journal of Orthopsychiatry, 57,* 452-457.

Ross, A. O., Glaser, F. B., & Germanson, T. (1988). The prevalence of psychiatric disorders in patients with alcohol and other drug problems. *Archives of General Psychiatry, 45,* 1023-1031.

Russo, N. F., & Olmedo, E. L. (1983). Women's utilization of outpatient psychiatric services: Some emerging priorities for rehabilitation psychologists. *Rehabilitation Psychology, 28,* 142-155.

Shore, J. H. (1989). Community psychiatry. In H. I. Kaplan & B. J. Sadock (Eds.), *Comprehensive textbook of psychiatry* (5th ed., Vol. 2, pp. 2063-2066). Baltimore: Williams & Wilkins.

Straznickas, K. A., McNeil, D. E., & Binder, R. L. (1993). Violence toward family caregivers by mentally ill relatives. *Hospital and Community Psychiatry, 44,* 385-387.

Sugar, J. A., Kleinman, A., & Eisenberg, L. (1992). Psychiatric morbidity in developing countries and American psychiatry's role in international health. *Hospital and Community Psychiatry, 43,* 355-360.

Szasz, T. S. (1970). *The manufacture of madness: A comparative study of the Inquisition and the mental health movement.* New York: Harper & Row.

Teplin, L. A. (1990). The prevalence of severe mental disorder among male urban jail detainees: Comparison with the Epidemiologic Catchment Area Program. *American Journal of Public Health, 80,* 663-669.

Tessler, R. C., & Dennis, D. L. (1989). *A synthesis of NIMH-funded research concerning persons who are homeless and mentally ill.* Rockville, MD: National Institutes of Mental Health.

Wallerstein, N., & Bernstein, E. (1994). Introduction to community empowerment, participatory education, and health. *Health Education Quarterly, 21,* 141-148.

CHAPTER 13

Mental Health Services to America's Veterans

DAVID H. PRICE

That in case necessity require to send forces abroad, and there be not volunteers sufficient offered for this service, then it be lawful for the Governor and [his] assistants to presse [men] into service in his Majesties name . . . provided that any that shall goe return mamed and hurt, he shall be mayntayned completely by the Colony duringe his life.

Plymouth Colony, 1636; quoted in U.S. Congress,
Medical Care of Veterans (1967, p. 21)

The unique contribution of soldiers throughout the history of the United States has been broadly recognized and publicly accepted from the early colonial period. The special treatment of veterans has provided valuable precedent for later extension of social welfare policies to minorities and other disadvantaged groups (Axinn & Levin, 1992).

Beginning with the Revolutionary War, more than 41 million men and women have served in the armed forces of the United States during wartime. As of July 1, 1993, approximately 26.8 million veterans were living in the United States and Puerto Rico. Vietnam veterans represent 31% of the total veteran population, followed closely by the veterans of World War II, who make up 30%. Almost 1.2 million women (4.4%) are included in the total veteran population. Of all civilian male citizens in the United States, 29% are veterans (U.S. Department of Veterans Affairs, 1994).

It is important to recognize the sheer magnitude of this unique group, whose members share the common background of service in the armed forces. Often the psychological wounds absorbed as a result of wartime service demand treatment and services from mental health service providers (Kelly, 1985). Also, it is significant that the largest single category of illness treated in Department of Veterans Affairs (VA) hospitals is mental illness (U.S. Department of Veterans Affairs, 1994).

This chapter begins with a review of the evolution of the current system providing mental health services to the veteran population. First, I will examine briefly the nature of combat and its psychological effects on participants. My intent is to examine the war-related neuroses that have affected U.S. veterans over the years and the mental health community's responses thereto.

This chapter is not about military medicine as practiced in the active-duty armed forces, except where that directly affects or provides information on the veteran population. For purposes of this chapter, *veterans* are defined as people who have served in the armed forces and are no longer on active duty.

The major institutional response to the needs of veterans in the United States is the Department of Veterans Affairs. Here I trace the history of that federal agency and define its current status and role, with an emphasis on how it provides mental health services.

The scope of the challenge facing mental health professionals dealing with the veteran population is presented demographically. Because a large number of psychologically troubled veterans are treated and served by the Department of Veterans Affairs, I focus here on levels of participation and types of problems encountered in veterans' mental health programs. Much of this information may be generalizable to other situations where veterans seek and receive mental health treatment and services.

The relatively recent recognition of post-traumatic stress disorder (PTSD) as the major psychological debility of combat veterans has thrust it to center stage among mental health professionals dealing with affected veterans and their families. Because of the attention given PTSD in the wake of the Vietnam War, I give this subject prominent attention here. I consider current assessment and intervention strategies in light of the diagnostic information in the *Diagnostic and Statistical Manual of Mental Disorders* (*DSM-III-R;* American Psychiatric Association, 1987) and recent research.

Background

> *They may write home to their parents and sweethearts that they are unchanged, and they may even be convinced of it. But the soldier who has yielded himself to the fortunes of war, has sought to kill and escape being killed, or has even lived long enough in the disordered landscape of battle, is no longer what he was.*
>
> Glenn J. Gray, *The Warriors* (1970, p. 27)

Throughout recorded history, human combat has negatively affected the lives of the people who experience it. Not only have limbs been shattered and organs maimed by weaponry wielded by human beings, but war is a traumatic life experience that wounds the minds of its participants. In his book *Achilles in*

Vietnam, Jonathan Shay (1994) sketches compelling parallels between the experiences of Achilles and his cohorts in the Trojan Wars and the combat trials of the American soldier in Vietnam some 3,000 years later.

American experience with the traumatic effects of war began in the earliest of the colonial and Indian wars. After the American Revolution, returning heroes experienced severe psychological and economic readjustments. Captain Daniel Shays, who some years later led a violent rebellion in Massachusetts, brought home from the war a sword awarded to him for his heroic service against the British. He was so poor and demoralized after the war that he had to sell the sword to feed his family. Desertion among demoralized soldiers was rampant during the Revolution, and continued through the Civil War. Many soldiers simply left the field of battle and went home (Friedel, 1990). We do not have data to show why these soldiers quit the fight, but we do know that many soldiers returned home with chronic psychological problems after the Civil War. In 1871, Dr. Jacob DeCosta labeled the phenomenon "irritable heart" (Mason, 1990). Hendin and Haas (1984) discuss the tragic cases of Union volunteer Ambrose Bierce and Confederate soldier Lewis Paine. Bierce's nightmares, emotional numbing, heavy drinking, and insistence on having a weapon constantly close by cost him his marriage and the prospect of a normal life. After the war, Paine tried to kill Secretary of State Seward as part of a plot that resulted in Lincoln's assassination. His lawyer pleaded that he had homicidal mania due to his 4 years as a combat soldier.

World War I's psychological casualties were labeled "shell-shocked" because of the intensity of the artillery barrages characteristic of that war. A few years later it became apparent that this phenomenon was not limited to the battlefield. By 1922, 50,000 British men were receiving pensions for mental problems. By 1929, the number had risen to 65,000 (Mason, 1990). In a landmark argument in 1919, Sigmund Freud held that war neurosis was psychological in origin and advocated psychotherapy as its treatment (see Scott, 1990).

In World War II, despite efforts to screen out marginally adjusted inductees, about 102 of every 1,000 U.S. casualties in Europe were psychiatric, suffering from what was commonly called "combat fatigue" (Scott, 1990). Perhaps because the military had recognized by this time that men could be psychologically "broken" by combat and had taken actions to provide treatment, the incidence of lifelong psychological injuries from World War II was reduced (Shay, 1994). That, of course, is speculation. What is not speculation is that in 1993, 22,273 veterans aged 65-79 (placing them squarely in the World War II era) spent 2,005,404 days in VA hospitals as a result of psychiatric illnesses. The average length of stay for this group was 90 days (U.S. Department of Veterans Affairs, 1994).

In 1952, during the Korean War, the first *Diagnostic and Statistical Manual of Mental Disorders* (*DSM*) was published to help guide psychiatrists' diagnoses (American Psychiatric Association, 1952). It contained a category called "gross stress reaction," which covered reactions to trauma, including war. However, in 1968, the period of the Tet Offensive and the battles around Khe Sahn that made it the bloody watershed year in America's Vietnam experience, *DSM-II* was published without the gross stress reaction category (American Psychiatric Association, 1968). Instead, "transient situational disturbance" took its place. In short, if the condition lasted longer than 6 months, which it frequently did, psychiatrists should diagnose it as a preexisting condition and therefore present before the combat experience. That tragic interpretation effectively allowed the VA to deny afflicted veterans' claims for disability compensation, because it could not have been exposure to battle service that caused the condition (Mason, 1990).

Many psychiatrists considered the old *DSM* gross stress reaction category diagnostically valid and useful (Scott, 1990). However, "most American psychiatrists . . . based their encounters with Viet Nam veterans on the official view that no such thing as PTSD existed," and the veterans' behaviors were seen as "dysfunctional and bizarre" (Blank, 1985, pp. 73-74).

There is no way to know the costs in human suffering paid by America's veterans and their families over the years. Before the Vietnam War forced the mental health community to recognize postcombat trauma, "troubled" veterans languished at home, making the lives of those with whom they lived as miserable and dysfunctional as their own (Mason, 1990; Matsakis, 1988). Thousands wandered from their homes, from job to job, and finally into homelessness. Those with serious enough readjustment problems may have been diagnosed with some supposedly preexisting condition, such as schizophrenia or bipolar disorder and hospitalized or heavily medicated to numb their symptoms.

As mentioned previously, the U.S. government's institutional response to veterans' needs is the VA. In 1977, the National Research Council of the National Academy of Sciences reported to the U.S. Congress on an evaluation of the care of 50,971 psychiatric patients in VA health care facilities. The evaluation concluded that intervention and treatment were dismal. The report went on to cite underqualification of VA psychiatric staff and understaffing in VA facilities throughout the system. In the VA psychiatric hospitals, patients were being overprescribed antipsychotic drugs while receiving very little psychotherapy, as little as 2.9 average planned treatment hours per patient per week. At that time, veterans were receiving inadequate care. An examination of the Department of Veterans Affairs is appropriate at this point.

The Department of Veterans Affairs

To care for him who shall have borne the battle and . . . his widow, and his orphan.

Abraham Lincoln, Second Inaugural Address (1864)

Veterans' programs in the United States have evolved through three distinct phases. The first lasted from the Revolutionary War period to the years between the Spanish-American War and World War I. During this period, compensation for service-connected disability and death, mustering-out pay, grants of free land, and pensions evolved and became institutionalized over time. Beneficiaries included the widows and orphans of soldiers who perished in war. Domiciliary and incidental medical care, begun in the National Home for Disabled Volunteer Soldiers, was established throughout the country. Veterans were given preference in federal civilian employment. These separate and diverse program beginnings had no central administration, however, and efficiency suffered.

The years between World War I and World War II saw genuine attempts to revamp the old apparatus to make it more efficient. The War Risk Insurance Act of 1917, enacted early after U.S. entry into World War I, added a new program—life insurance. The concept of vocational rehabilitation was born. Management of the diverse veterans' service and entitlement programs rested with three separate federal agencies. In 1921, the Veterans Bureau was formed to consolidate and coordinate government activities affecting war veterans. The Bureau became the Veterans Administration (VA) in 1930. At that time, 54 federally operated veterans' hospitals were in use throughout the country.

World War II dramatically increased the requirements to provide for soldiers and their families. More than 16 million citizens answered the call to military duty. The need for readjustment services for soldiers returning to civilian life resulted in the Servicemen's Readjustment Act of 1944. This legislation, which proved to be of profound importance to the World War II generation, "was based on the philosophy that veterans whose lives had been interrupted by military service, or had been handicapped by virtue of military service, were to be provided assistance for a limited time, to aid them in becoming self-supporting and useful members of society" (President's Commission on Veterans' Pensions, 1956, p. 47).

In 1973, the VA was charged with the additional responsibility of operating the National Cemetery System. On March 18, 1989, the Department of Veterans Affairs was created, giving full cabinet-level status to the administration of veterans' programs. Meanwhile, in the years since World War II, the VA health care system has grown to include "171 medical centers; more than 350 outpatient, community, and outreach clinics; 126 nursing home care units; and 35 domiciliaries" (U.S. Department of Veterans Affairs, 1994, p. xv). The distribution of these facilities is shown in Table 13.1.

The VA and Mental Health

The VA is a national system. It is, by far, the largest centrally controlled mental health care system in the United States. It reaches, in one form or another, into all states and territories. In 1993, according to the U.S. Department of Veterans Affairs (1994), of 920,311 patients treated in its hospital facilities, 188,816 were treated in its psychiatric bed sections. The average cost per psychiatric patient treated was $8,487, or $312.20 per patient day.

Table 13.1 Veterans Administration Health Care Summary: 1980 to 1992 (for years ending September 30)

Item	Unit	1980	1990	1992
Facilities operating				
Hospitals	number	172	172	171
Domiciliaries	number	16	32	35
Outpatient clinics	number	226	339	362
Nursing home units	number	92	126	128
Employment[a]	1,000	194	199	204
Obligations[b]	millions of $	6,215	11,827	14,011
Prescriptions dispensed	millions	36.7	58.6	58.5
Laboratory	millions	215	188	NA
Radiology examinations	millions	5.7	5.5	6.2
Inpatients treated[c]	thousands	1,359	1,113	1,085
Average daily	thousands	105	88	84
Outpatient visits	millions	18.0	22.6	24.2

SOURCE: Reprinted from U.S. Department of Commerce (1993, sec. 11, Table 576). The data are from U.S. Department of Veterans Affairs, *Annual Report of the Secretary of Veterans Affairs; Directory of VA Facilities,* biennial; and unpublished data.
NOTE: NA = not available.
a. Not full-time equivalent.
b. In 1980, cost basis; thereafter, obligation basis.
c. Based on the number of discharges and deaths during the fiscal year plus the number on the rolls (bed occupants and patients on authorized leave of absence) at the end of the fiscal year. Excludes interhospital transfers.

Table 13.2 shows pertinent representative data on the psychiatric inpatient population at the end of fiscal year 1993. Of the 40,924 patients, 78.6% stayed in residence at the hospital for fewer than 100 days. Note the relative incidence of substance abuse and other psychotic mental disorders (which include PTSD). Dual diagnosis is common among veterans in treatment.

Table 13.3 displays data on the age groupings of the veteran psychiatric patient population. The World War II generation is within the 65-74 age category and may include a group who served in the Korean conflict and Vietnam as well. The Vietnam-period population falls generally within the 35-54 range. The number of Vietnam-period veterans exceeds that of World War II-period veterans by roughly 1,000. This difference will increase as both groups age and die.

The total number of patients discharged for mental disorders during fiscal year 1993 can be seen in Table 13.4. Of the 601,140 patients discharged, it should be noted that, with the exception of schizophrenic disorders, the average age of those treated and discharged is solidly within the age group representing Vietnam-period veterans.

The National Research Council's report to the Congress in 1977 was highly critical of mental health services as provided by the Veterans Administration. Some of these problems remain, and some have been addressed. In an attempt to complement national health care reform, the VA revised its mental health and behavioral sciences procedures manual in 1993, "to set policy for state-of-the-art, integrated continuum of care for mental health services. Also, new standards for psychiatric inpatient programs were published" (U.S. Depart-

Table 13.2 VA Medical Centers—Hospital Care Component: Patients Remaining, Percentage by Attained Stay, and Diagnostic Group, September 30, 1993

| | | | | *Percentage in Each Diagnostic Category for Specified Length of Stay* | | | | |
| | | | | | *More Than (Years)* | | | |
Diagnostic Composition of Patients	*Total*	*90 Days or Fewer*	*100 Days or More*	*1*	*2*	*5*	*10*	*20*
All patients	40,924	78.6	21.4	11.3	7.8	3.7	1.6	.4
Psychotic patients	10,642	49.9	50.1	31.9	22.9	11.2	5.0	1.4
Alcohol psychoses (291)	415	42.4	57.6	37.6	29.4	11.6	3.1	—
Drug psychoses (292)	43	88.4	11.6	4.7	2.3	—	—	—
Other psychoses (290, 293-299)	10,184	50.1	49.9	31.8	22.8	11.3	5.1	1.5
Other psychiatric patients	7,459	92.7	7.3	2.5	1.6	0.9	0.5	—
Alcohol dependence and abuse (303, 305.0)	3,541	97.6	2.4	0.2	0.1	0.1	0.1	—
Drug dependence and abuse (304, 305.1-305.9)	1,416	95.2	4.8	—	—	—	—	—
Other nonpsychotic mental disorders (300-302, 306-319)	2,502	84.3	15.7	7.1	4.6	2.6	1.5	0.1

SOURCE: Excerpted from U.S. Department of Veterans Affairs (1994, p. 37). The data are based on the Annual Patient Census and may vary from AMIS counts.
NOTE: The diagnostic categories and selected diagnoses included in this table are based on U.S. Department of Health and Human Services (1980). The numbers following the diagnoses are the identifying code numbers of these diagnostic classifications.

ment of Veterans Affairs, 1994, p. 13). It is too early to evaluate the effects of those changes, particularly in light of ongoing attempts to make substantive changes to the nation's health care system.

According to remarks made by its chief medical director in addressing Congress, the VA remains "committed to ongoing excellence in treating the psychological as well as the physical trauma of war" (U.S. Senate Committee on Veterans Affairs, cited in Grady, 1990, p. 287). The VA offers a variety of outpatient and inpatient treatment options, one of the most innovative and effective of which has been the Vet Centers.

Readjustment Counseling Service (Vet Centers)

In the years following the Vietnam War, it became apparent that "(1) a substantial number of Vietnam veterans continued to experience problems of readjustment, and (2) many Vietnam veterans could not or would not avail themselves of services within the traditional VA system" (Kulka et al., 1990, p. 5). Estimates of the numbers of veterans so affected varied from as few as 250,000 to as many as 2 million. In response to this growing concern, the

Table 13.3 VA Medical Centers—Hospital Care Component: Patients Remaining, Age, and Diagnostic Group, September 30, 1993

Diagnostic Composition of Patients	Total	Age Group						
		Under 35	35–44	45–54	55–64	65–74	75–84	85 and Over
All patients	40,924	2,107	6,902	6,290	7,681	12,077	5,131	736
Psychotic patients	10,642	604	2,225	1,809	1,839	2,809	1,196	160
Alcohol psychoses (291)	415	4	26	51	97	178	57	2
Drug psychoses (292)	43	8	16	10	4	4	1	—
Other psychoses (290, 293-299)	10,184	592	2,183	1,748	1,738	2,627	1,138	158
Other psychiatric patients	7,459	984	3,051	2,110	707	457	127	23
Alcohol dependence and abuse (303, 305.0)	3,541	477	1,415	990	426	201	30	2
Drug dependence and abuse (304, 305.1-305.9)	1,416	363	785	225	37	6	—	—
Other nonpsychotic mental disorders (300-302, 306-319)	2,502	144	851	895	244	250	97	21

SOURCE: Excerpted from U.S. Department of Veterans Affairs (1994, p. 38). The data are based on the Annual Patient Census and may vary from AMIS counts.
NOTE: The diagnostic categories and selected diagnoses included in this table are based on U.S. Department of Health and Human Services (1980). The numbers following the diagnoses are the identifying code numbers of these diagnostic classifications.

Congress directed the Department of Veterans Affairs to set up a readjustment counseling program, which quickly became known as the Vet Center program. Although it was supposed to be a temporary measure, to be discontinued when no longer needed, the program has grown to meet the demands not only of Vietnam veterans but also of returnees from other conflicts such as those in Lebanon, Grenada, and Panama, and the Persian Gulf War (U.S. Department of Veterans Affairs, 1993).

The mission of the Vet Centers is to provide outreach and counseling "to help veterans resolve war-related psychological difficulties and to help them achieve a successful post-war readjustment to civilian life" (U.S. Department of Veterans Affairs, 1993, p. 56). Vet Centers are normally located in "storefronts" in downtown or suburban areas. They are seldom, if ever, colocated with Department of Veterans Affairs medical facilities because of the aversion many veterans have to the VA.

Vet Centers offer several treatment modalities, including individual, group, and family counseling and psychotherapy. Each center has at least one mental health professional on staff. Trained counselors, 60% of whom are themselves veterans, assist veterans in finding services from the VA or other sources if needed. Counselors help veterans to conduct employment searches as well as making them aware of the benefits and entitlements authorized for veterans by federal and state governments. As of 1990, 194 Vet Centers were in operation throughout the United States (Grady, 1990).

Table 13.4 VA Medical Centers—Hospital Care Component: Patients Discharged, Average
Age, and Diagnostic Group, Fiscal Year 1993

Diagnostic Group[a]	Total Diagnoses	Principal Diagnosis[b]	Associated Diagnoses[c]	Average Age (Principal Diagnosis)[d]
Mental disorders	601,140	209,748	391,392	47.2
Alcohol psychosis (291)	26,747	4,869	21,878	53.7
Drug psychosis (292)	6,085	1,104	4,981	46.0
Organic psychotic conditions, excluding alcohol drug psychosis (290, 293-294)	24,246	8,716	15,530	67.9
Schizophrenic disorders (295)	54,640	35,958	18,682	46.0
Other psychoses (296-299)	54,706	26,530	28,176	51.0
Neurotic disorders (300)	37,602	5,983	31,619	49.6
Personality disorders (301)	37,541	1,816	35,725	41.8
Alcohol dependence or abuse (303, 305.0)	165,718	75,836	89,882	46.2
Drug dependence or abuse (304, 305.1-305.9)	119,644	23,427	96,217	39.5
Other nonpsychotic mental disorders (302, 306-319)	74,211	25,509	48,702	46.8

SOURCE: Excerpted from U.S. Department of Veterans Affairs (1994, p. 40). The data are based on the Patient Treatment File (PTF) and may differ from tables based on AMIS data. Any difference is due to corrections made to AMIS data subsequent to the closing of input to AMIS and to incomplete PTF records. In addition, the PTF counts transfers between medical facilities as discharges, whereas AMIS totals exclude transfers from the total discharges.
a. The diagnostic categories and selected diagnoses included in this table are based on U.S. Department of Health and Human Services (1980). The numbers following the diagnoses are the identifying code numbers of these diagnostic classifications. Category XV, "Certain Conditions Originating in the Perinatal Period," in which no cases occurred, is not included in this table.
b. Principal diagnosis is that diagnosis designated by the discharge physician as responsible for the major portion of the patient's length of stay.
c. Associated diagnoses are established diagnoses, other than the principal diagnosis, for which treatment was given.
d. Average age was not calculated for totals of fewer than 100 cases.

Utilization of VA Mental Health Services

Mental health services offered by the VA have been heavily used by Vietnam veterans. War-zone veterans are much more likely to seek help than are their noncombat (same-era) veteran counterparts. Male combat veterans have sought help at a rate four times that of those who have not seen combat. Among women, war-zone veterans are 20 times more likely to seek help than their same-era peers. Treatment assistance has been sought from across the full continuum of services offered, from inpatient care to Vet Centers (Kulka et al., 1990, pp. 232-235). This demand has not diminished with time, as other armed conflicts have created more psychological casualties and have been responsible for the continued growth of VA mental health services.

The Veteran Population

The VA estimates that as of 1993, 26.8 million veterans were living in the United States and Puerto Rico.[1] Vietnam veterans made up 31% of the overall total, followed closely by World War II veterans at 30%.

Table 13.5 Estimated Number of Veterans Living in the United States, by Age and Period of Service, July 1, 1993 (in thousands)

Age Group (in years)	Total Veterans	Wartime Veterans								Peacetime Veterans			
		Total[a]	Persian Gulf War		Vietnam Era		Korean Conflict		World War II[f]	Total	Post-Vietnam Era[g]	Service Between Korean Conflict and Vietnam Era Only	Other Peacetime[h]
			Total[b,c]	No Prior Wartime Service	Total[b,c,d,e]	No Prior Wartime Service	Total[c,d,f]	No Prior Wartime Service					
All veterans													
All ages	26,655	20,576	1,021	858	8,252	7,705	4,656	3,862	8,125	6,079	3,038	2,869	172
Under 20	3	3	3	3	—	—	—	—	—	—	—	—	—
20-24	363	280	280	280	—	—	—	—	—	82	82	—	—
25-29	963	302	302	302	—	—	—	—	—	661	661	—	—
30-34	1,360	182	155	155	—	—	—	—	—	1,178	1,178	—	—
35-39	1,636	786	88	65	721	721	—	—	—	850	850	—	—
40-44	2,491	2,310	103	23	2,287	2,287	—	—	—	181	178	3	—
45-49	3,416	3,198	60	17	3,182	3,182	—	—	—	218	48	168	1
50-54	2,452	1,222	21	8	1,198	1,197	18	18	—	1,230	24	1,202	3
55-59	2,540	1,225	6	4	347	235	986	986	—	1,315	13	1,285	16
60-64	3,085	2,834	2	1	251	41	2,585	2,495	297	251	3	182	66
65-69	3,403	3,361	—	—	129	10	684	329	3,022	42	—	16	25
70-74	2,908	2,892	—	—	76	5	251	22	2,865	16	—	5	11
75-79	1,375	1,353	—	—	26	—	97	8	1,345	21	—	3	18
80-84	474	456	—	—	5	—	27	4	451	18	—	2	16
85 and over	188	171	—	—	1	—	8	1	144	17	—	1	15
Median age[i]	56.3	61.4	28.4	27.0	46.4	46.1	62.4	61.7	71.2	48.4	33.4	55.2	65.1
Female veterans													
All ages	1,176	723	123	117	229	221	98	83	301	453	366	74	13
Under 20	1	1	1	1	—	—	—	—	—	—	—	—	—
20-24	42	31	31	31	—	—	—	—	—	11	11	—	—
25-29	113	40	40	40	—	—	—	—	—	73	73	—	—
30-34	166	27	25	25	2	2	—	—	—	139	139	—	—
35-39	163	61	14	12	49	49	—	—	—	102	102	—	—
40-44	113	85	9	5	80	80	—	—	—	28	28	—	—
45-49	77	62	3	2	60	60	—	—	—	15	8	7	—
50-54	58	21	1	1	20	20	1	1	—	37	3	33	—
55-59	56	29	—	—	7	6	23	23	—	27	2	24	1
60-64	58	51	—	—	4	3	42	41	7	8	—	5	2
65-69	82	78	—	—	3	1	16	13	63	4	—	2	3
70-74	146	143	—	—	3	1	8	3	140	3	—	1	2
75-79	60	57	—	—	1	—	4	1	56	3	—	1	2
80-84	27	24	—	—	—	—	2	1	24	2	—	1	2
85 and over	16	13	—	—	—	—	1	—	11	2	—	—	1
Median age[i]	43.5	59.5	27.7	27.2	42.9	42.7	61.6	60.8	71.4	34.1	32.6	53.4	70.9

SOURCE: Reprinted from U.S. Department of Veterans Affairs (1994, p. 5).
NOTE: Excluded are veterans whose only active-duty military service occurred since September 8, 1980, and who failed to satisfy the minimum service requirement. Also excluded are a small indeterminate number of National Guard personnel or reservists who incurred service-connected disabilities while on an initial tour of active duty for training only. Details may not add to totals shown due to rounding.
a. Veterans who served in more than one wartime period are counted only once. Total wartime equals the sum of Persian Gulf War (no prior wartime service), Vietnam era (no prior wartime service), Korean conflict (no prior wartime service), World War II, and World War I. Also includes an indeterminate number of Mexican border period veterans, of whom 45 were receiving VA benefits, and 25,000 veterans (1,000 female) of World War I, all of whom were over 90 years old.
b. Includes 163,000 (6,764 female) who served in both the Persian Gulf War and the Vietnam era.
c. Includes 189 who served in the Persian Gulf War, the Vietnam era, and the Korean conflict.
d. Includes 313,000 (4,017 female) who served in both the Korean conflict and the Vietnam era.
e. Includes 233,000 (3,790 female) who served in the Vietnam era, in the Korean conflict, and World War II.
f. Includes 560,000 (11,103 female) who served in both World War II and the Korean conflict.
g. Service only between May 7, 1975, and August 2, 1990.
h. Includes those who served only between World War II and the Korean conflict, those who served only between World War I and World War II, and those who served prior to World War I only.
i. Computed from data by single year of age.

Almost 1.2 million American women (4.4%) are veterans. The increasing levels of participation by women in the armed forces will increase their representation in the overall veteran population accordingly in the future. It is important to note that nearly 42% of all women veterans served in the years following the Vietnam era. Therefore, the numbers of women actually involved in hostilities has, up to now, been comparatively small. In accord with these recent trends, the median age for women veterans (44.5) is declining, in contrast to that of men (56.7), which is rising. As more and more women become veterans, it will be necessary to identify and respond to their unique needs.

Contrary to the negative image often associated with Vietnam-period veterans, overall veterans' achievement levels in education and employment compare favorably with the rest of the U.S. population. For example, the educational attainment levels of male veterans and male nonveterans reflect a higher rate of high school completion for veterans (37.5%) than for their nonveteran counterparts (33.3%). More veterans enter college than do nonveterans, but their completion rate for the full 4 years is lower (21.2%) than that for nonveterans (24%). For both groups, the median years of school completed is 12.9. Also, veterans' participation in the labor force is higher than that of the nonveteran population. The unemployment rate for veterans in 1993 was 5.9%, compared with 6.4% for nonveterans.

Figure 13.1 depicts the current veteran population by age groupings, clearly showing the dramatic increases brought about by the wartime demands for manpower during World War II, the Korean War, and the Vietnam War. Table 13.5 further expands on the veteran population by detailing their service during the wars of the 20th century and their relative numbers within the overall group. The veteran population is declining slightly as mortality has increased among World War II veterans. Vietnam-period veterans now constitute the largest single grouping, having surpassed World War II veterans in 1993.

The data presented above clearly show the utilization of VA mental health services, but what the data do not reflect is the degree to which the VA is meeting the needs of today's veteran population. For that information, we turn to the findings of the National Vietnam Veterans Readjustment Study (NVVRS), mandated in 1983 by the U.S. Congress as Section 102 of Public Law 98-160. The NVVRS was to establish "the prevalence and incidence of posttraumatic stress disorder (PTSD) and other psychological problems in readjusting to civilian life" among Vietnam veterans (Kulka et al., 1990, p. xxiii).

Senator Allen Cranston, chairman of the U.S. Senate Committee on Veterans Affairs, authored the legislation that commissioned the study. He reported alarming findings:

The study . . . reveals, 829,000 of the 3.14 million—over one-fourth—of the veterans who served in Vietnam are *currently* suffering from some degree of PTSD. . . . 15.2 percent of the male Vietnam theater veterans (479,000) and 8.5 percent of the female theater veterans (610) are currently suffering from full-

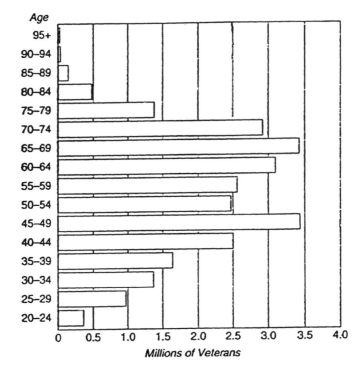

Figure 13.1. Estimated Veteran Population, by Age, as of July 1, 1993
SOURCE: Reprinted from U.S. Department of Veterans Affairs (1994, p. 2).

blown cases of PTSD. . . . Another 350,000 theater veterans suffer from PTSD symptoms that adversely affect their lives but are not of the intensity or breadth required for a diagnosis of PTSD. These data indicate that, over 20 years later, psychological problems associated with service in our most divisive war since the Civil War continue to take a terrible toll on the lives of those who served in Vietnam. (quoted in Kulka et al., 1990, pp. v-vi)

Against this backdrop of today's veteran population, we move now to a discussion of the major mental health challenge facing veterans, a problem recognized in 1980 with its own diagnostic category.

Post-Traumatic Stress Disorder

Background

The official Vietnam era lasted from August 5, 1964, to May 7, 1975. During that period, approximately 8,300,000 Americans served in the armed forces. Approximately 38% of that number served in the Vietnam theater of operations, the war zone. Of those, 3,143,645 were men and 7,166 were women.

The NVVRS, upon which much of the information presented here is based, found that more than 960,000 men (30.6%) and more than 1,900 (26.9%) women Vietnam veterans had full-blown PTSD sometime in their lives before 1990, and that one-half of the men and one-third of the women still had it in 1990. Members of ethnic minority groups have experienced more mental health and readjustment problems than have those in the Anglo majority. In 1990, the prevalence of PTSD among Hispanic veterans was 27.9%; for blacks, it was 20.6%; and among Anglos and others, it was 13.7%. PTSD is a chronic disorder among the members of the Vietnam veteran population who suffer from it.

The problem is more widespread than the above figures indicate. Many Vietnam veterans cannot or will not use the services available to them through the Department of Veterans Affairs to help them cope with their problem (Kulka et al., 1990). The tragedy has revealed itself in other ways: In 1986, a leading journal reported that Vietnam veterans were 65% more likely to commit suicide and 49% more likely to die in motor vehicle accidents than their nonveteran age-group peers (Hearst, Newman, & Hulley, 1986). Mason (1990) highlights a 1971 report from the National Council of Churches that revealed that 49,000 Vietnam veterans had died, many of them violently, since returning from the war. The war was still going strong in Vietnam at that time.

Diagnosis

PTSD was first recognized with a specific diagnosis in *DSM-III* in 1980 (American Psychiatric Association, 1980). The criteria were continued in *DSM-III-R* (American Psychiatric Association, 1987).[2] Selley (1991, p. 636) provides a useful summary of that diagnostic information:

- Markedly distressing event outside of normal human experience
- Traumatic event reexperienced, i.e.:
  - Distressing intrusive recollections
  - Recurrent dreams
  - Feeling or acting as if the event is recurring
  - Intense distress at exposure to symbolic events
- Avoidance or reduced responsiveness to stimuli associated with trauma, i.e.:
  - Avoidance of thoughts and feelings associated with the event
  - Lack of recall of the events
  - Loss of interest
  - Detachment or estrangement from others
  - Limited feelings
  - Sense of foreshortened future
- Increased arousal, i.e.:
  - Difficulty falling asleep or staying asleep
  - Irritability or outbursts of anger

         o   Poor concentration

         o   Increased vigilance

         o   Exaggerated startle response

         o   Adverse physiological response to symbolic events

    •   Duration of above symptoms for at least one month

Symptom Recognition

Veterans suffering from PTSD may be recognized by any number of an array of behaviors that characterize this population. They may have difficulty with interpersonal relationships, including intimacy and sociability, which causes problems with friends and family (Barry, 1994; Kulka et al., 1990; Mason, 1990; Matsakis, 1988; Nezu & Carnevale, 1987). They may appear cold and detached, without emotion, even on the death of a parent or other family member (Sherwood, 1991). A large segment of this population attempts to numb and repress painful memories with drugs and/or alcohol. One study of a group of PTSD-diagnosed veterans found that 91% had lifetime diagnoses of substance abuse (Boudewyns, Woods, Hyer, & Albrecht, 1991).

Anxiety, panic attacks, and hypervigilance cause some veterans with PTSD to avoid crowded areas or to insist on sitting where they can keep their backs to a wall. They have been conditioned to survive through awareness of their surroundings. Emotions ranging from extreme rage to deep depression often invade their thoughts. Many are subject to intense disturbing nightmares and other sleep disorders. During their waking hours, they may be subject to unwanted intrusive thoughts or flashbacks of the horrors they experienced decades ago in combat (Lantz & Greenlee, 1990).

Hendin and Haas (1991) found Vietnam veterans with PTSD to be at risk of attempting suicide and further found that combat-related guilt was the most significant explanation for that finding. Yehuda, Southwick, and Giller (1992) believe that type of combat trauma has an affect on the amount and severity of PTSD symptoms. Their studies have shown that veterans who witnessed or participated in atrocities are prone to extreme guilt feelings resulting in depression. Other research supports the notion that those veterans who experienced combat up close, as in the infantry, are more at risk for experience of PTSD than are those who had relatively safe, rear-area jobs (Kulka et al., 1990).

The NVVRS found that veterans who saw combat in Vietnam were more prone to hostility and actual violence later in life, and of those with a PTSD diagnosis a full 25% had committed at least 13 violent acts in the past year (Kulka et al., 1990). Combat veterans often experience symptoms of rage, and other evidence suggests that they are at significant risk for suicide (Hendin & Haas, 1991) and other violent-death scenarios such as automobile accidents (Hearst et al., 1986). However, Calvert and Hutchinson (1990) suggest that such assertions are based in myth. Their research revealed no relationship between levels of combat and violent tendencies in later life. In light of the more conclusive NVVRS study, however, there is reason to question the validity of Calvert and Hutchinson's findings.

Encountering Veterans With PTSD

Mental health professionals can expect to encounter Vietnam veterans and their families in any practice setting. Practitioners in government agencies work with members of this population in the delivery of basic human services and assistance. Although the numbers vary, virtually all sources agree that of the nation's homeless males, a large proportion are Vietnam veterans, probably with diagnosed or undiagnosed PTSD. Because of their documented propensity for hostile, violent acts, veterans suffering with PTSD often end up in jail. Of the Vietnam veterans with PTSD surveyed by the NVVRS, 35% had been homeless at one time or another, and 45.7% had been arrested or jailed more than once (Kulka et al., 1990).

Many health care professionals will meet veterans with PTSD as they present themselves for treatment of physiological pathologies. In 1990, Blake et al. published findings of research that revealed that in a sample of 161 combat veterans and former prisoners of war hospitalized for nonpsychiatric illness, 24% had PTSD. Many of these veterans had repressed their psychological symptoms, being reluctant to admit their existence. As a result, they may have developed psychosomatic illnesses later.

Mental health settings provide obvious opportunities for interaction with Vietnam veterans with PTSD. Besides being venues for PTSD treatment itself, mental health clinics and hospitals also address other psychiatric disorders. It has been shown that PTSD may lead to other autonomous psychiatric disorders (Mellman, Randolph, Brawman-Mintzer, Flores, & Milanes, 1992). Professionals working in substance abuse programs can expect to interact with veterans who also have PTSD, given the frequency of dual diagnosis (Boudewyns et al., 1991).

Mental health professionals in corporate settings will encounter veterans with PTSD. Resentment of authority and distrust of leadership, common attitudes among many Vietnam veterans, may result in conflicts with supervisors on the job. Professionals in independent practice will find veterans coming to them for help with family or other problems. Some who have the financial means will seek such private help because of the individual attention they can expect to get in comparison with the services offered by the VA, an agency of government that veterans have learned to distrust anyway (Sherwood, 1991).

As noted above, veterans with combat stress are to be found in significant numbers among the homeless. Rosenheck, Leda, and Gallup (1992) found that in their sample of 627 homeless Vietnam veterans, 43% showed evidence of combat stress. As in the NVVRS a few years before, these researchers found that those with evidence of combat stress also experienced more substance abuse, severe psychiatric problems, and social and vocational dysfunction than did those without such evidence. The authors conclude that "homeless mentally ill Vietnam veterans appear to be significantly underserved and in need of specialized services directed at both their combat-related psychiatric problems and their severe housing, financial, and social difficulties" (p. 149).

The VA is attempting to respond to the challenge presented by homeless veterans. In 1993, it provided active residential rehabilitation services in 30 Domiciliary Care for Homeless Veterans sites. In addition, the VA served 18,674 homeless veterans at 45 Homeless Chronically Mentally Ill program sites during the same period, providing comprehensive medical, psychological, and rehabilitation treatment programs through community-based residential care and case management.

Other VA initiatives in collaboration with other government agencies involve assistance in the acquisition of housing for homeless veterans and provision of outreach services to more than 20,000 homeless veterans in 1993. A major success has been the VA initiative "stand-down," a 2- or 3-day event during which homeless veterans receive food, shelter, health care, and assistance in accessing VA and other government or community services to which they may be entitled. In 1993, 27 stand-downs accommodated approximately 10,000 homeless veterans (U.S. Department of Veterans Affairs, 1994).

Assessment

Accurate assessment of the veteran client is essential to effective treatment intervention. Identifying the presence and probability of PTSD in the client is usually not easy, nor is developing a therapeutic relationship. Rapport and trust must be earned. Shay (1991) asserts:

> One cannot approach a Veteran of prolonged, heavy combat from the position of *knowing* anything, other than one's own mortality and finitude. Every claim of authority external to the personal trust between Veteran and caregivers is doomed, although other veterans vouching for the caregivers is often an essential step to letting them come close enough to discover they are worthy of trust. (p. 577)

Sherwood (1991) suggests a direct questioning approach in the assessment interview, including fact-oriented questions, both open- and closed-ended, that deal directly with the type of experience the veteran had in the military and in Vietnam. The client's responses about that experience are then carefully evaluated, both what the client says and how he or she says it. Above all, the caregiver must communicate a genuine desire to know about the client. Many veterans have talked little about their painful combat episodes. Also, it is important for the professional to try to discern what the client's pre-Vietnam experience was like, in comparison with the behaviors and attitudes being presented currently, in order to assess whether or not the problem is a lifelong matter or something that has its causation in combat trauma.

A comprehensive interview guide for use with Vietnam veterans, such as that used by the VA's Readjustment Counseling Service (Vet Centers), is presented by Scurfield and Blank (1985). It is quite long and detailed and is intended to be used over a number of assessment interviews. The section containing cautions for clinicians is particularly useful for practitioners and others attempting to work with a veteran population with which they may not be familiar.

It is important to note the age at which the client served in combat. The average age during combat for the Vietnam veteran was 19, in comparison to 26 for veterans of World War II. It is during this period in human development when "normal" life skills, problem-solving skills, and social skills are developed. For many Vietnam veterans, the critical separation-individuation phase, occurring around age 18, was interrupted by induction into military service. When this happens, particularly in the midst of a war, entrance into the military "is a major psychosocial intervention which frequently leads to devastating results" (Tanay, 1985, p. 31). In effect, these young men were robbed of their adolescence and early adulthood. Many learned to survive in the totally irrational environment of combat, a setting that has very little to do with managing everyday life (Lantz & Greenlee, 1990). Educating veterans to be aware of the effects of combat at such a crucial developmental stage in their lives is important to gaining their willingness to cooperate with appropriate interventions (Harmless, 1990).

PTSD: A Family Disorder

Before moving from assessment to intervention, it is essential to point out that PTSD is a family disorder. The NVVRS found that "there are more problems in the families of Vietnam veterans with PTSD than in the families of Vietnam veterans without PTSD" (Kulka et al., 1990, p. 256). Unfortunately, the veteran is often treated alone as the identified patient, although his or her family is also impaired and in need of treatment. Dealing with the dysfunctional behaviors of PTSD sufferers causes great strain on the rest of the family (Williams & Williams, 1985). Matsakis (1988), Mason (1990), and Figley (1993) have made major contributions to the literature in this vital area.

Intervention

For the diagnosed PTSD client, two general therapeutic goals are appropriate. The first is the successful integration of traumatic experiences so that they no longer impede social functioning and growth. The second goal is successful interaction with others—an end to the veteran's isolation and alienation (Sherwood, 1991). These goals are broad and require refinement into relevant, meaningful, achievable, and measurable individually identified objectives, the accomplishment of which results in goal attainment.

The VA's National Center for Posttraumatic Stress Disorder provides each patient with a clear set of client-centered goals upon admittance to the PTSD treatment program (U.S. Department of Veterans Affairs, 1990):

1. Understand the relationship between your war experience and current life problems.

2. Learn skills to manage stress and replace destructive behaviors such as fighting, substance abuse, and isolating.
3. Relearn how to have satisfying relationships with people.
4. Place war-zone experiences in a new perspective.
5. Gain self-acceptance and recognize the value of yourself as a member of our society.

Clear goals are vital, but interventions vary with each individual case. Therefore, accurate assessment is important. Practitioners who are not capable of working with veterans or who are not qualified to handle particular cases should refer veterans to those who are. The VA's broad continuum of mental health service options, from medical centers to Vet Centers, should be among the first considerations, if available. The medical centers and Vet Centers have trained staff prepared to diagnose and treat all veterans suffering from PTSD. They provide individual and group treatment techniques and strive to include the veterans' families in therapy (Kulka et al., 1990).

Chiaramonte (1992), a clinical practitioner at a major VA medical center, recommends a four-phase treatment regimen developed by Figley in 1985. It "incorporates phase-oriented treatment, systemic desensitization, and rational emotive therapy" (p. 469). The first phase, catastrophe assessment, consists of the patient and clinician recalling and identifying as many traumatic experiences as possible and arranging them in a priority order. The second phase, traumatic induction recapitulation, involves recalling the relevant experiences leading up to the event. The third phase, trauma neutralization, involves the clinician's helping the patient to reconceptualize the episodes. In the final phase, trauma resolution, the clinician helps the patient to understand rational explanations for seemingly irrational acts. This is an attempt to get beyond the trauma, and the clinician suggests ways to deal with intrusive thoughts differently. Patient self-esteem and self-worth are reinforced, and new life goals and aspirations are suggested.

Lantz and Greenlee (1990) suggest an existential model for working with Vietnam veterans and their families. They believe veterans are searching for the meaning of their combat experience. Coming home from war to a thankless, often hostile reception after surviving hellish experiences in combat caused many to wonder what their experiences meant. The goal is to help the veterans find their personal meanings for what they have been through. The intervention consists of three parts. The first part consists of existential reflection that seeks to help the client identify opportunities and potentials for meaning. The second part, network intervention, is intended to increase the veteran's social contact with others. Finally, the practitioner takes the role of teacher, imparting communication, social, and coping skills so that the veteran can make maximum use of his or her improved environment.

In his recent work, Charles Figley, an authority on combat-related trauma, has been involved with Persian Gulf War veterans and their families. Figley (1993) makes six fundamental points that the practitioner would be wise to consider:

(1) the psychosocial impact of the war on families as well as on the troops has already been quite profound . . . ; (2) by the time troopers are reunited with their families . . . the families may have endured more profound stress than the troopers have; (3) homecoming—for both the troops and the families—may be more stressful than the departure; (4) to effectively help these service people and their families recover quickly from the war we must understand the sources of stress, methods of coping, and potential mental health consequences; (5) the characteristics of all helping—no matter if the help comes from professionals or volunteers or from the military or civilian sector—must include four fundamental elements: respect, information, support, and empowerment (RISE); and (6) military family specialists can play a vital role in promoting postwar recovery. (pp. 188-189)

Figley developed his RISE intervention model from the four fundamental elements identified above. He suggests it as an appropriate model for practitioners working with war-traumatized veterans and their families.

Viola and McCarthy (1994), mental health professionals at Tripler Army Medical Center, have developed a layered model of treatment, based on group therapy, to be conducted in an intensive 30-day inpatient setting. Each layer of treatment is addressed before advancing to the next. The first layer is education, to acquaint the patient with PTSD, why he or she has it, and how it can be managed. Accomplishing this initial layer prepares the veteran for the next layer, cognitive-behavioral therapy and gestalt therapy.

The third layer, described as the critical thinking phase, features marathon group therapy, during which the veterans are encouraged not only to express feelings but also to reframe and develop new ways of thinking about themselves and their environments. Discharge planning occurs in the fourth phase; the veteran is encouraged to connect with programs such as Vet Centers to help with readjustment after leaving the hospital.

The debriefing phase is the final layer. This voluntary phase may be conducted in either an inpatient or an outpatient setting. Depending on the desires of the veteran, this phase may include "soul work" (revealing of secrets and the like). Eye movement desensitization and reintegration (EMDR) therapy may also be a part of this phase. EMDR is a relatively new treatment strategy that has been shown to be effective in reducing anxiety, sleep disturbances, flashbacks, and intrusive thoughts. One of the shortcomings of Viola and McCarthy's description of their layered intervention model is that they provide no evaluation of its effectiveness.

Women Veterans

More than 7,000 military women served in and around Vietnam. Thousands more (their numbers have not been established) served in the area with the Red Cross, as U.S. government employees, and in other civilian occupations. They constitute a population that only recently has begun to be recognized. The Vietnam Women's Memorial was dedicated in Washington, D.C., on

November 11, 1993, to that end. Although several women have published memoirs and other personal accounts in recent years, the plight of women veterans has not been studied thoroughly.

The NVVRS provides the most recent data available on female Vietnam veterans. Most military women who served in Vietnam were nurses, and therefore subject to high levels of war-zone stress in attending to large numbers of horrible casualties under grueling conditions. They were not immune to attack themselves and often were targets of mortar and rocket assaults on the base areas in which they worked. They tended to be older and better educated than their male counterparts at the time they served.

The incidence of PTSD among women veterans is directly related to the level of war-zone stress they encountered, a factor consistent with findings among male veterans. Women veterans who are divorced or separated are more likely to have PTSD than are their married counterparts. Some 37% of women who served in Vietnam reported having at least one serious postwar readjustment problem. Almost one-third of that number said that this problem has not been resolved. Like their male peers, those who saw the war "up close and personal" were more likely to experience readjustment problems than were those not so exposed to traumatic events. Both women and men with readjustment problems also tend to have substance abuse problems and military service-connected physical disabilities (Kulka et al., 1990).

Ott (1985) found that, like male Vietnam veterans, the women tend to deny their pain and have difficulty in requesting help. When they do request help, they do so for the same reasons as men:

> Women will often seek help initially because of depression, nightmares, insomnia, or flashbacks precipitated by sounds (helicopters, fireworks) or smells. Once in group or individual therapy, they tend to focus on their anger toward the military, the Veterans Administration, the Vietnamese, and those in society who "don't understand": they complain bitterly about these institutions and individuals. (p. 315)

Wolfe, Brown, and Bucsela (1992) studied women Vietnam veterans' responses to the Persian Gulf War in 1991. These women veterans were not participants in the conflict. Some of the respondents had PTSD symptoms and some did not. Wolfe et al.'s findings indicate that, "while most of the women war veterans experienced some intensification of stress-related symptoms during Operation Desert Storm, those who had previously reported high levels of PTSD were significantly more susceptible to greater distress" (p. 676).

Interventions for women veterans closely resemble those for men. The goal is the establishment of a trusting relationship between client and therapist, and between client and other group members if group therapy is used. Groups made up exclusively of women seem to be ideal, and positive outcomes for such groups have been reported (VanDevanter, 1985). However, because the number of women veterans is relatively small, it is also appropriate to include them in groups with men, with the caution that they must not be allowed to become nurturers or caretakers of these groups. The introduction of women clients to books and memoirs by other women veterans may be useful in group therapy to establish a common ground for discussion. The sharing of personal photographs and memorabilia may be encouraged as a way to help women tell their stories. As with men, the painful reexperiencing of trauma, with all its attendant shame and absence of meaning, when expressed in an empathic group or individual therapy setting, is essential to these women's self-acceptance and self-forgiveness (Ott, 1985). Much more attention and research needs to be directed toward the issues faced by female war veterans. There is some evidence that this has begun to take place; for example, in 1992 the first separate women's PTSD treatment unit was opened at the VA medical facility at Menlo Park, California.

Challenges for Practitioners

Practitioners may face several personal challenges when working with veterans, especially Vietnam veterans. It is safe to assume that many practicing mental health professionals harbored strong feelings for or against the war in the 1960s that may even persist to this day. These internal conflicts must be resolved, or they may interfere with the treatment process. Some Vietnam veterans can be expected to distrust nonveteran practitioners. Listening to veterans relating their war experiences is traumatic in itself—it can be horrible, gruesome, and grotesque, the dark side of life. The listening clinician may find his or her professional functioning inhibited. Practitioners who work with Vietnam veterans have encountered hostility from their colleagues for doing so, although this seems to be declining as more is becoming known about the Vietnam veteran with PTSD.

Only since 1980, with the diagnosis of PTSD in *DSM-III,* has the mental health field provided much in the way of emphasis on specialized training for dealing with war-traumatized veterans. Vietnam veterans participated in a national tragedy of historic proportion. This factor cannot be overlooked in treatment. Most will require participation in some sort of survivor mission, in which the veteran tries to make right what was for him or her so wrong. Some veterans may undertake work to establish memorials or find other ways to be involved in helping other veterans. Some have even gone back to Vietnam to help the Vietnamese people in humanitarian endeavors. The clinician must understand this drive and take it into account in a balanced treatment program (Blank, 1985).

The PTSD-suffering veteran and his or her family present unique challenges for mental health practitioners. In many ways such veterans form an oppressed population—stigmatized for their connection with what many consider to have been a bad war. PTSD affects the lives of American veterans of both genders and all ethnic groups. The readjustment problems of Vietnam veterans drove the mental health community to recognize PTSD for what it is, and to apply that recognition, along with diagnosis and treatment modalities, to other trauma victims in our society. That may be the Vietnam veterans' special contribution to mental health in this country.

Discussion

The nature of the veteran population in the United States continues to evolve, as it has throughout the country's history. Certain trends are readily apparent. For one, racial and ethnic minority groups are heavily represented in the U.S. armed forces today, as they have been for some time. Members of these groups can be expected to continue to serve, and cross-cultural skills will remain a necessity for the mental health professional. More and more military jobs are being opened to women, and many of the new jobs available will bring them closer to the dangers of the battlefield. Women will have the opportunity to observe and experience the full range of possible outcomes from such exposure, including the taking of a human life and the risk of one's own death, wounding, or capture. This happened on a limited scale during the Persian Gulf War and can be expected to recur in future conflicts. Practitioners need to be prepared to respond to the particular treatment needs of women veterans.

The large military force established for World War II and used throughout the Cold War as both a deterrent and combatant force is rapidly being disassembled in the wake of the collapse of the Soviet Union. In the interest of economy, more and more reliance is being placed on the National Guard and reserves—our citizen-soldiers. Thousands of reservists were called upon to serve in the Persian Gulf War. Several became casualties alongside their active-duty counterparts. These reserve component forces are made up primarily of civilians who train one weekend a month and for two weeks in the summer. Nevertheless, reserve forces are much cheaper to train and maintain than are active military organizations. Lawmakers searching for ways to redirect scarce funds are attracted to reserves in the absence of a World War III scenario.

Many citizen-soldiers are now veterans, and all will become veterans in the future. Because they live and work in communities throughout the nation, they can be expected to provide challenges for mental health professionals in civilian communities, perhaps far away from expert advice or help that might be found at VA medical facilities, Vet Centers, or active military installations.

Adjustment from military to civilian life is another area in which practitioners need to be competent. Most veterans achieve such status simply by serving a few years on active duty with one of the armed forces branches. Most do not encounter the dangers of combat, although all train regularly for its possibility. However, the period spent on active duty is very different from the civilian lifestyle. Service members are subjected to an authoritarian environment while serving. It is an environment that extends to off-duty time as well as the time spent actively working at the job. They swear an oath to their country demanded nowhere else in American society. They lose many of their civil rights and become subject to a separate and specific military code of laws called the Uniform Code of Military Justice. They are affected by the experience, and they may need help to reenter and readjust to civilian life. Generally, the longer an individual serves, the more profound and lasting the impact of the military lifestyle. The active-duty military offers counseling and advice primarily in the employment arena prior to discharging a service member. The area of social readjustment is generally not adequately addressed by active-duty counselors.

Practitioners must carefully consider the nature of the military experience of the veteran and his or her family and not underestimate the effects of military service on their ability to function in civilian life. This is an area recently brought to my attention by a Vet Center counselor, who has noticed an increase in requests for such assistance from young former service members recently made eligible for Vet Center programs as a result of service during the low-intensity conflicts up to and including the Persian Gulf War (H. McKay, Fort Worth, Texas, Vet Center, personal communication, August 3, 1994).

At the time of this writing, it seems apparent that the national systems for all health care delivery are bound to undergo some degree of reform. This situation raises several questions concerning the mental health needs of the veteran population. Will the VA medical system survive the changes, or will it wither away as Canada's veterans' system did when Canada's health care system was nationalized? Will military retirees and their families continue to be able to use military medical facilities? Will the reforms bring about greater availability and better quality of care than are currently the norm for veterans and their families? Will the historical preferential treatment offered to veterans and their families since before the founding of the Republic be lost? Is it time to scrap the VA and place everyone in the same category of health care recipient? There are no answers at this time, and intelligent speculation seems impossible for now.

Conclusion

Veterans and their families have unique requirements for mental health services, based on the special nature of their contribution to the nation. Historically, the U.S. government has recognized that need and has responded by putting in place a mental health delivery system especially suited to those needs under the auspices of the VA. Generally, the system has worked, but not always efficiently or effectively.

During the years since the Vietnam War, the American Psychiatric Association has recognized the effects of post-traumatic stress on combat participants. Post-traumatic Stress Disorder has been a specific diagnostic category in *DSM* since 1980. This is real progress. PTSD is the major mental health challenge for practitioners working with veterans. The abundance of studies on PTSD has resulted in much recent literature. However, the treatment interventions I have described in this chapter are all reactive in nature. Is it possible to "normalize" combat and therefore make its effects more understandable and preventable? How have other cultures dealt with their warriors? Is it possible to prevent or at least minimize combat stress? More research needs to be directed toward such questions.

In my view, the United States should retain for our veterans mental health care services appropriate to their specific needs. As a nation, we owe them that much.

Notes

1. Data in this section are based on U.S. Department of Veterans Affairs (1994).

2. *DSM-IV* (American Psychiatric Association, 1994) contains the latest diagnostic criteria for PTSD; they differ little from those in *DSM-III-R*.

References

American Psychiatric Association. (1952). *Diagnostic and statistical manual of mental disorders.* Washington, DC: Author.

American Psychiatric Association. (1968). *Diagnostic and statistical manual of mental disorders* (2nd ed.). Washington, DC: Author.

American Psychiatric Association. (1980). *Diagnostic and statistical manual of mental disorders* (3rd ed.). Washington, DC: Author.

American Psychiatric Association. (1987). *Diagnostic and statistical manual of mental disorders* (3rd ed., rev.). Washington, DC: Author.

American Psychiatric Association. (1994). *Diagnostic and statistical manual of mental disorders* (4th ed.). Washington, DC: Author.

Axinn, J., & Levin, H. (1992). *Social welfare: A history of the American response to need* (3rd ed.). New York: Longman.

Barry, P. D. (1994). *Mental health and mental illness* (5th ed.). Philadelphia: J. B. Lippincott.

Blank, A. S., Jr. (1985). Irrational reactions to post-traumatic stress disorder in Vietnam veterans. In S. M. Sonnenberg, A. S. Blank, Jr., & J. A. Talbott (Eds.), *The trauma of war: Stress and recovery in Viet Nam veterans* (pp. 69-98). Washington, DC: American Psychiatric Press.

Boudewyns, P. A., Woods, M. G., Hyer, L., & Albrecht, J. W. (1991). Chronic combat-related PTSD and concurrent substance abuse: Implications for treatment of this frequent "dual diagnosis." *Journal of Traumatic Stress, 4,* 549-559.

Calvert, W. E., & Hutchinson, R. L. (1990). Vietnam veteran levels of combat: related to later violence. *Journal of Traumatic Stress, 3,* 103-113.

Chiaramonte, J. A. (1992). And the war goes on. *Social Work, 37,* 469-470.

Figley, C. R. (1993). Weathering the war at home: War-related family stress and coping. In F. W. Kaslow (Ed.), *The military family in peace and war* (pp. 173-190). New York: Springer.

Friedel, F. (1990). Foreword. In C. R. Figley & S. Leventman (Eds.), *Strangers at home: Vietnam veterans since the war* (pp. xiii-xvi). New York: Brunner/Mazel.

Grady, D. A. (1990). Epilogue: A self-guide for Vietnam veterans. In R. A. Kulka, J. A. Schlenger, R. L. Fairbank, R. L. Hough, B. K. Jordan, C. R. Marmar, & D. S. Weiss, *Trauma and the Vietnam War generation: Report of findings from the National Vietnam Veterans Readjustment Study* (pp. 276-308). New York: Brunner/Mazel.

Gray, G. J. (1970). *The warriors: Reflections on men in battle.* New York: Harper & Row/Torchbook.

Harmless, A. (1990). Developmental impact of combat exposure: A comparison of adolescent and adult Vietnam veterans. *Smith College Studies in Social Work, 60,* 185-195.

Hearst, N., Newman, T. B., & Hulley, S. B. (1986). Delayed effects of the military draft on mortality. *New England Journal of Medicine, 314,* 620-624.

Hendin, H., & Haas, A. P. (1984). *The wounds of war.* New York: Basic Books.

Hendin, H., & Haas, A. P. (1991). Suicide and guilt as manifestations of PTSD in Vietnam veterans. *American Journal of Psychiatry, 148,* 586-591.

Kelly, W. E. (Ed.). (1985). *Post-traumatic stress disorder and the war veteran patient.* New York: Brunner/Mazel.

Kulka, R. A., Schlenger, J. A., Fairbank, R. L., Hough, R. L., Jordan, B. K., Marmar, C. R., & Weiss, D. S. (1990). *Trauma and the Vietnam War generation: Report of findings from the National Vietnam Veterans Readjustment Study.* New York: Brunner/Mazel.

Lantz, J., & Greenlee, R. (1990). Existential social work with Vietnam veterans. *Journal of Independent Social Work, 5*(1), 39-52.

Mason, P. H. (1990). *Recovering from the war: A woman's guide to helping your Vietnam vet, your family, and yourself.* New York: Penguin.

Matsakis, A. (1988). *Vietnam wives: Women and children suffering with veterans suffering from post-traumatic stress disorder.* Washington, DC: Woodbine House.

Mellman, T. A., Randolph, C. A., Brawman-Mintzer, O., Flores, L. P., & Milanes, F. J. (1992). Phenomenology and course of psychiatric disorders associated with combat-related posttraumatic stress disorder. *American Journal of Psychiatry, 149,* 1578-1574.

National Research Council of the National Academy of Sciences. (1977). *Health care for American veterans* (Report submitted to the Committee on Veterans Affairs, U.S. Senate, 95th Cong., 1st Sess., June 7, 1977). Washington, DC: Government Printing Office.

Nezu, A. M., & Carnevale, G. J. (1987). Interpersonal problem solving and coping reactions of Vietnam veterans with post-traumatic stress disorder. *Journal of Abnormal Psychology, 96,* 155-157.

Ott, J. (1985). Women Viet Nam veterans. In S. M. Sonnenberg, A. S. Blank, Jr., & J. A. Talbott (Eds.), *The trauma of war: Stress and recovery in Viet Nam veterans* (pp. 309-320). Washington, DC: American Psychiatric Press.

President's Commission on Veterans' Pensions. (1956). *The historical development of veterans' benefits in the United States* (Report to the 84th Cong., 2nd Sess., May 9, 1956; House Committee Print No. 244). Washington, DC: Government Printing Office.

Rosenheck, R., Leda, C., & Gallup, P. (1992). Combat stress, psychological adjustment, and service use among homeless Vietnam veterans. *Hospital and Community Psychiatry, 43,* 145-149.

Scott, W. J. (1990). PTSD in DSM-III: A case in the politics of diagnosis and disease. *Social Problems, 37,* 294-310.

Scurfield, R. M., & Blank, A. S. (1985). A guide to obtaining a military history from Viet Nam veterans. In S. M. Sonnenberg, A. S. Blank, Jr., & J. A. Talbott (Eds.), *The trauma of war: Stress and recovery in Viet Nam veterans* (pp. 263-292). Washington, DC: American Psychiatric Press.

Selley, C. (1991). Post-traumatic stress disorder. *Practitioner, 235,* 635-641.

Shay, J. (1991). Learning about combat stress from Homer's *Iliad. Journal of Traumatic Stress, 4,* 561-579.

Shay, J. (1994). *Achilles in Vietnam.* New York: Atheneum.

Sherwood, R. J. (1991). Vietnam veterans: A hidden population in social work practice. *Journal of Independent Social Work, 5*(2), 7-17.

Tanay, E. (1985). The Vietnam veteran: Victim of war. In W. E. Kelly (Ed.), *Post-traumatic stress disorder and the war veteran patient* (pp. 29-42). Washington, DC: American Psychiatric Press.

U.S. Congress. (1967). *Medical care of veterans* (Report for use of the Committee on Veterans Affairs, 90th Cong., 1st Sess., April 17, 1967; House Committee Print No. 4). Washington, DC: Government Printing Office.

U.S. Department of Commerce, Bureau of the Census. (1993). *Statistical abstract of the United States* (113th ed.). Washington, DC: Government Printing Office.

U.S. Department of Health and Human Services. (1980). *International classification of diseases* (9th ed., DHHS Publication No. 80-1260). Washington, DC: Government Printing Office.

U.S. Department of Veterans Affairs, National Center for Posttraumatic Stress Disorder. (1990). *Program guide.* Unpublished manuscript.

U.S. Department of Veterans Affairs. (1993). *Federal benefits for veterans and dependents.* Washington, DC: Government Printing Office.

U.S. Department of Veterans Affairs. (1994). *Annual report of the secretary of veterans affairs: Fiscal Year 1993*. Washington, DC: Government Printing Office.

VanDevanter, L. M. (1985). The unknown warriors: Experiences of women in Vietnam. In W. E. Kelly (Ed.), *Post-traumatic stress disorder and the war veteran patient* (pp. 148-169). Washington, DC: American Psychiatric Press.

Viola, J., & McCarthy, D. (1994). An eclectic inpatient treatment model for Vietnam and Desert Storm veterans suffering from post-traumatic stress disorder. *Military Medicine, 159,* 217-220.

Williams, C. M., & Williams, T. (1985). Family therapy for Viet Nam veterans. In S. M. Sonnenberg, A. S. Blank, Jr., & J. A. Talbott (Eds.), *The trauma of war: Stress and recovery in Viet Nam veterans* (pp. 193-210). Washington, DC: American Psychiatric Press.

Wolfe, J., Brown, P. J., & Bucsela, M. L. (1992). Symptom responses of female Vietnam veterans to Operation Desert Storm. *American Journal of Psychiatry, 145,* 676-679.

Yehuda, R., Southwick, S. M., & Giller, E. L., Jr. (1992). Exposure to atrocities and severity of chronic post-traumatic stress disorder in Vietnam combat veterans. *American Journal of Psychiatry, 149,* 333-336.

CHAPTER 14

Mental Health Services to Minority Groups of Color

JOHN S. MCNEIL

ROBIN KENNEDY

In this chapter, the term *minority groups of color* is used to refer to four groups in the United States: Asian Americans, African Americans, Hispanics, and Native Americans. We begin discussion of each group with a brief historical paragraph or two, followed by a section examining selected areas of mental health risk, and conclude with a review of utilization of mental health services that includes issues of diagnosis and treatment. Each of these groups has its own unique experiences, yet considerable commonality can be seen in the oppression and racism to which all have been subjected. Each has developed ways to combat or cope with these stressors. Depending upon one's perception, relative degrees of success or failure may be seen, but there is no denying that all have been affected by the treatment they have received from society. The accumulation of these stressors adds to the burden of mental health risk and adversely affects the inclination to utilize formal mental health services.

Increased attention to cultural diversity over the past two or three decades has forced some reevaluation of the manner in which the mental health professions have traditionally dealt with members of minority groups. Perhaps most marked is the shift from an intrapsychic stance to greater appreciation of the importance of ecological-systems influences. The "melting pot" ideology as the sine qua non of acculturation is being replaced by more acceptance of a pluralistic, multicultural society. Unfortunately, the Euro-American belief system continues to dominate our thinking, and more often than not it has negative impacts on the members of minority groups of color. In this chapter we seek to illuminate some of the many ways this occurs.

Asian Americans

Defining who is an Asian American is a formidable task, in that there are at least 29 distinct subgroups that differ in language, religion, and values (Sue & Sue, 1990). Asian Americans constitute a rapidly growing group that increased from 0.5% of the U.S. population in 1960 to 2.9% in 1990. This segment of the population had a 107% growth rate between 1980 and 1990. It is projected that by the year 2050 Asian Americans will constitute 9.3% of the U.S. population. Some groups within this category have grown more dramatically than others, with varying percentages being foreign-born.

Based on 1990 U.S. Census estimates, Chinese Americans are the largest group of Asian Americans, at just over 1.5 million. They are followed closely by Filipinos, who number just under 1.5 million. Japanese, Korean, and Indian American populations are about equal, at 800,000. The Vietnamese American population is a little more than 600,000, and Cambodian Americans number 400,000. The rest of the diverse Asian population in the United States—about half a million—is made up of Hawaiians, Laotians, Thais, and others. Southeast Asians are the most likely population to be foreign-born, with more than 80% of Vietnamese and Cambodian Americans born outside the United States. Korean Americans (71%) and Filipino Americans (64%) are slightly behind Southeast Asian Americans in the proportion of foreign-born. They are followed by Indian Americans and Chinese Americans, with more than 50% of the current populations having been born outside the United States. The proportion of Japanese Americans who are foreign-born is much smaller than that of any other Asian group: 33% (Uba, 1994, p. 3).

The first Asian immigrants to come to the United States in great numbers were Chinese who arrived on the West Coast during the 1840s. Japanese began arriving in large numbers during the last decade of the 1800s. Both groups were welcomed initially as farm and/or construction laborers, but as economic downturns occurred they were subjected to severe legal and community-sanctioned discriminatory practices. Over the next century, each subsequently arriving group received its share of oppression, thereby increasing its vulnerability to mental health risk (Lum, 1986). Southeast Asians, the most recent immigrant/refugee group, have encountered the same type of treatment—welcomed at first, they later became the recipients of oppressive behaviors.

The reasons various Asian groups have come to the United States have differed: Chinese and Japanese came seeking employment opportunities, whereas Southeast Asians came as refugees. Many of these later experienced extreme hardship throughout their ordeal of leaving their native countries and journeying to the United States. U.S. relocation policy has been to disperse

Southeast Asians throughout the nation; therefore, many have been essentially isolated, adding to their readjustment problems.

Language has been a significant problem that has complicated the acculturation process. Many foreign-born Asian Americans speak only their native language. Members of the mainstream American culture are usually monolingual and tend to be impatient with individuals who do not speak English, concluding that non-English-speaking persons are "inferior, lack awareness, or lack conceptual thinking powers" (Sue & Sue, 1990, p. 47). This erroneous interpretation proceeds to invade every aspect of mainstream Americans' contact with, and evaluation of, such persons' behaviors. Nonverbal components of communication interactions are treated similarly. Inextricably intertwined with language are cultural values.

Historically, Asian American values have evolved out of Buddhism, Taoism, and Confucianism, philosophies that emphasize the maintenance of harmony in relationships. Values subsumed under this cardinal value are those that maintain interpersonal harmony. Ho (1983) itemizes eight values that he believes should be considered in work with Asian Americans: filial piety, dominance and deference in parent-child interaction, self-control, shame as a behavioral influence, middle position virtue, awareness of the social milieu, fatalism, and inconspicuousness. It is apparent that some of these values are not consistent with those espoused in mainstream U.S. culture.

Stressors and Stereotypes That Contribute to Mental Health Risk

Three factors seem to be especially pertinent in the assessment of mental health vulnerability among Asian Americans: racism, cultural conflicts, and the "model minority" myth.

Racism

Amazingly, a majority of Americans do not believe that Asian Americans are discriminated against in the United States. Some believe that Asian Americans receive too many special advantages (U.S. Commission on Civil Rights, 1992). This belief persists in spite of the existence of widespread discrimination, prejudice, and barriers to equal employment opportunity. Racism today is relatively subtle compared with the blatant behavior of the past, and this may create a real quandary for the victims of racism. They may doubt the accuracy of their perceptions and attempt to deny their "gut feelings." The resultant cognitive dissonance, if prolonged, is fertile ground for the development of anxiety, depression, or somatic distress.

Cultural Conflicts

Cultural conflicts can pose problems for any immigrant or refugee group. Among Asian Americans, whose very foundations of values are built upon harmonious relationships, the potential for conflicts is magnified within the Eurocentric American culture. American values honor harmony, but great emphasis is also placed upon independence, assertiveness, and self-determination. Harmony is to be desired, but when it impedes the achievement of an individual's aspirations it may become necessary to "let the chips fall where they may." An Asian American individual's struggles for acculturation and success (American style) may create stress as well as generate conflictual relationships within the family (Carlin & Sokoloff, 1985).

The Model Minority Myth

Asian Americans have long been depicted as the "model minority" in the United States. The general perception is that through hard work Asian Americans have become successful economically, educationally, and occupationally. Unspoken is the question, If Asian Americans can overcome their minority status, why do other minorities not do likewise? Continuing with this logic, then, there is no need for civil rights initiatives to improve opportunities for equality. Closer inspection reveals, however, that the *model minority* sobriquet is primarily based in myth. One example used to support this myth is that the family incomes of Asian Americans are among the highest in the country. Although this may be true, it should be noted that Asian Americans tend to live in areas where both the cost of living and incomes are high, such as California, New York, Hawaii, and Washington. Also, more members of Asian American families tend to be in the workforce than is the case in non-Asian families. When these variables are held constant, the income differential disappears. Although some select groups of Asian Americans have worked hard and have succeeded in advancing, their efforts have not produced results commensurate with the incomes of white males with comparable credentials (Woo, 1989). Many Asian Americans live below the poverty line and encounter on a daily basis all of the stressors facing persons with inadequate resources.

Needs for and Utilization of Mental Health Services

Needs for Services

Determining the prevalence rates of mental or emotional disorders among Asian Americans is problematic for a number of reasons, including the fact that assessment criteria often are not sufficiently sensitive to distinguish between cultural manifestations and true psychopathology. Agreement levels among clinicians leave much to be desired, even when sociocultural factors are relatively homogeneous. A great likelihood exists, therefore, that Asian Americans may be misdiagnosed or inaccurately labeled as having mental disorders when no disorders are present.

Considering all Asian American groups collectively, Uba (1994) concludes that the rate of psychopathology is equal to or higher than it is for Anglo-Americans. Some minor disagreement with this belief is evidenced in a recent book edited by Gaw (1993) in which different writers examine the psychiatric care of five subgroups: Chinese Americans, Indochinese Americans, Japanese Americans, Korean Americans, and Filipino Americans. Each group is discussed with the caution that reliable data regarding epidemiological accuracy are lacking. Furthermore, some of these studies were done on populations living in their native countries and then generalized to reflect psychopathology rates of persons living in the United States. Keeping in mind these types of qualifiers, it can be said that mental disorder rates are not significantly higher for Asian Americans than they are for other groups. There may be some relationship between level of acculturation and incidence of psychopathology—the higher the level of acculturation, the lower the prevalence rate for mental disorder. Assuming the accuracy of this hypothesis, one would expect relatively high rates among the Indochinese, and this appears to be the case (Kinzie & Leung, 1993). Many of the data regarding prevalence are based upon utilization rates of mental health services, which is a flawed measure; use of services is influenced by myriad factors.

Utilization of Services

Numerous studies spanning a period of approximately two decades appear to agree that Asian Americans underutilize mental health services (Uba, 1994). Consistently, the rate of usage is 50% or more below what would be expected on the basis of representation in the population. This holds whether inpatient or outpatient services are being considered. Illustrative of this underutilization are the results of a California survey concerning Southeast Asians: approximately 14% needed inpatient care and more than 50% needed outpatient services, yet only 3% and 12%, respectively, sought help (Gong-Guy, 1987).

Among the reasons services are not sought, stigmatization in a major one. Seeking mental health services places a stigma not only upon the individual, but upon the family as well. Psychological problems are often manifested through physical symptoms, so help may be sought from a physician, acupuncturist, spiritualist, or some other nontraditional provider. Intrapsychic causes are unlikely to be explored as an explanation. When help is sought there is a decided hierarchy: First the family, then the ethnic community, and as a last resort non-Asian professionals may be contacted (Uba, 1994). Even when professional help is sought, psychotherapy or psychopharmacology may be unacceptable choices. Additionally, individuals may not even know about the existence of services.

Among all minority groups, help-seeking behavior is impeded or facilitated by "the four A's": availability, accessibility, acceptability, and affordability. Mental health services designed especially for Asian American populations are unlikely to be available due to their proportionally small representation in the community. Location of services may also pose a problem if emphasis is placed upon reaching the largest number of potential clients possible. Access is thus likely to be a problem for many potential clients. Acceptability is a barrier to utilization if there is a lack of culturally relevant symbolism in the agency.

Included here would be such things as the presence of Asian American professional or clerical staff who speak the potential clients' language. Finally, the cost of the service may be beyond the limit potential clients are willing and/or able to pay.

Summary

Asian Americans have had a varied historical experience in the United States. Large numbers arrived during the 19th century, and then there was a hiatus due to racism, which was expressed partially through restrictive legislation. Within the past two decades, Asian Americans who have entered the country as immigrants or refugees have again increased the numbers significantly. Most of these latter entrants have been Southeast Asians. All have experienced some degree of oppression. Asian Americans, however, have been saddled with another layer of burden in view of being labeled the model minority. Vulnerability to mental disorder is an ever-present danger for members of this minority group.

African Americans

African Americans differ from other minorities of color in that they were brought to America involuntarily, as slaves. Other groups entered seeking economic betterment and/or as refugees attempting to escape tyranny and oppression. The institution of slavery necessitated dehumanization and devaluation as means of control, and negative attitudes regarding the quality and worth of African Americans have persisted to the present. Evidence of the existence of these pejorative beliefs can be found in every aspect of U.S. society. Their impacts on African Americans are reflected in the succession of preferred names for this group among its own members as part of a search for self-esteem over the past two or three decades: Afro-American, Black, African American.

Demographics

As of the 1990 U.S. Census, African Americans accounted for slightly more than 12% of the U.S. population, or approximately 30 million persons. This represents a 13.2% increase since the 1980 census, when the corresponding figures were 11.7% and approximately 26.5 million. By the year 2050, African Americans are predicted to constitute 15.1% of the U.S. population (U.S. Department of Commerce, 1993).

The highest concentrations of African Americans are found in the southern states. Large numbers are also found in such northern cities as New York, Chicago, and Detroit, and in western areas such as Los Angeles and San Francisco (Ruiz, 1990). Almost one-third of African Americans live below the poverty line, and the proportion is increasing: In 1975, the proportion was 31.3%, and in 1990, it had risen to 32.7%. In contrast, 9.7% of Anglos lived below the poverty line in 1975; in 1990, the proportion among Anglos was 11.3%.

Among African Americans, males outnumber females at birth, but due to the loss of adolescent and young adult males to homicide, suicide, and substance abuse, women begin to outnumber men after the age of 15, and this pattern persists through the remainder of the life cycle (Griffith & Baker, 1993). Another survival statistic is that of life expectancy, which differs markedly between African Americans and whites. Currently, the life expectancy for African American males is 65.6 years; for African American females, average life expectancy is 74.3 years. In contrast, white American males have a life expectancy of 73.0 years, and white females 79.7 years (Tidwell, 1993).

African Americans are disadvantaged compared with whites in other ways as well. Approximately two-thirds are high school graduates, compared with seven-eighths of whites. College graduation rates also lag; 11.5% for African Americans versus 25.2% for whites. Unemployment rates for African Americans are typically much higher (12.4% versus 6.0% for whites) and these figures increase even more when individuals are included who have given up on looking for work (23.1% versus 11.5% for whites) (Tidwell, 1993).

Multiple factors impinge upon the well-being of African Americans, and this is expressed in myriad emotional stressors and diminished mental health. A cherished value system, however, serves to mitigate some of these negative influences.

Values

Centuries of oppression have required African Americans to develop survival strategies that are reflected in a value system that undergirds everyday functioning. Robert Hill (1971), in a seminal volume, refers to the strengths of black families. He explicates the importance of family, religion, and work. Family is seen as an entity that goes beyond the nuclear family to include the extended family as well as non-blood-related "fictive" kin. Each member of such an extended family group can depend upon the others for nurture and support. Flexibility of family roles encourages the willingness of all members to take on the roles of others, regardless of gender. A strong religious orientation provides the spiritual substance individuals need to travel the hazardous road of life. In spite of persistent stereotypes of African Americans as lazy and incompetent, work and achievement are important values. Each of these values is part of a historical helping tradition among African Americans that provides some protection from negative societal influences.

Stressors and Stereotypes That Contribute to Mental Health Risk

Racism and Oppression

In U.S. society, members of minority groups are valued to the extent that they disassociate from their own cultural heritages and embrace Euro-

American values. African Americans, like other minorities of color, are therefore pulled in two directions, experiencing stress that may not be consciously perceived by the affected individuals. Although racism and oppression are not the only societal factors that affect mental health, they are important influences. Racism, in fact, has been described as "an infection of the belief system, a mental illness with the following symptoms: 1) perceptual distortion, 2) denial of reality, 3) delusions of grandeur, 4) projections of blame (to the victim), 5) phobic reactions to differences" (Hilliard, 1978; quoted in Landrum-Brown, 1990). Oppression and racism affect the individual in several ways. The degree to which an individual internalizes racially oppressive messages has an influence on the individual's view of him- or herself. Further, the degree to which the individual's worldview is defined, proposed, and limited by Euro-American ideology influences who he or she becomes. In addition, the individual must develop the necessary internal and external resources to survive oppression and racism (Landrum-Brown, 1990). Poussaint (1990) has concluded that African Americans are at high risk for maladaptation, behavioral disorders, and mental illness throughout the life cycle.

Family Structure

A persistent belief has been that the African American family is pathological, and that this is related in part to its matriarchal structure; that is, the mother is seen as the central figure in the family, with the father or other male figure relegated to a subordinate role. This structure conflicts with the Euro-American model, and therefore is seen as inherently inferior. Several researchers have convincingly rejected this thesis, however (Coner-Edwards & Spurlock, 1988; Mullins, 1985; Pinderhughes, 1982). Fluidity of roles is another perspective from which to evaluate families' interactional patterns, and this characteristic of African American families can be viewed as a strength. Individuals within the African American family are willing to undertake any role that facilitates the survival of the family.

Concern has to be registered regarding the increasing numbers of single-parent, predominantly female-headed, families. During the 1960s, 78% of all African American families included a married couple (Logan, 1990), but currently female-headed households account for approximately half of all African American families. Numerous explanatory hypotheses have been proposed, ranging from individual and/or family systemic pathology to ecological-systems causes. Although no single causative factor can be delineated, this family form has to be reflective of mental health risk.

Utilization of Mental Health Services

As we have noted above, the four A's—availability, accessibility, acceptability, and affordability—are directly related to the utilization of mental health services. Subsumed under these variables are a multitude of factors, such as diagnosis and treatment issues. Additionally, there appears to be considerable disagreement over the accuracy of prevalence rates of mental disorders among minorities of color.

Many problems have been identified regarding the accuracy of prevalence rates (Neighbors, 1984; Vega & Rumbaut, 1991). Estimates of rates often have been extrapolated from case records of individuals who sought treatment, thereby beginning with a skewed population. Field surveys have relied upon symptom checklists; these instruments have questionable validity when it comes to the assessment of diagnosable mental conditions. Furthermore, these symptom checklists tend not to have been normed for minority groups. Some improvement in protocol emerged with the use of the Diagnostic Interview Schedule, which was used to conduct the large regional field surveys known as the Epidemiological Catchment Area Program (Reiger, Myers, Kramer, & Robins, 1984). Problems persist, however.

Diagnosis and Treatment

There has been a lengthy documented history of African Americans' receiving the most severe psychopathological labels. In 1851, Dr. S. A. Cartwright diagnosed slaves who ran away seeking freedom as suffering from "drapatomania" (Poussaint, 1990). To this day, the word *draptomania,* defined as an uncontrollable impulse to wander, remains in some psychiatric dictionaries.

African Americans, for example, tend to be diagnosed as having schizophrenia more frequently than do Anglo-Americans. Additionally, when this diagnosis is given at the point of entry into treatment, it remains as a discharge diagnosis, which differs from the situation with the majority group. Worthington (1992) has supported this finding, as have Mathura and Baer (1990). Affective disorders, in contrast, are underdiagnosed among African Americans. Any diagnosis of psychiatric disorder can be stigmatizing, but the label of schizophrenia is likely to be much more damaging to the individual than the diagnosis of an affective disorder.

Misdiagnosis directly affects treatment decisions, in that diagnosis guides treatment. The African American patient is more likely than the Anglo patient to be treated with psychotropic medications, and there is also a greater likelihood of an African American's being treated by a paraprofessional. Many therapists who lack sufficient cultural knowledge and sensitivity may believe that African American patients are unable to benefit from psychotherapy. Perceiving such a negative evaluation, an African American patient may be more likely to reject treatment. Client-therapist racial identity preferences have been the subject of considerable controversy, but to date no definitive answers have evolved. Even if the therapist's racial identity is found to be an important variable, there are not enough professionally trained minority therapists to pair all clients and therapists by race.

There is no perfect or one best therapy for the African American client; however, successful intervention is much more likely if the therapist is aware of his or her biases and relates to the client in an interested, empathic, genuine, and understanding manner. Many published sources of help are available to therapists working with minority clients, as reflected in the limited reference list at the end of this chapter.

Summary

African Americans have faced centuries of oppression that have forced them to develop survival skills that some observers see as running counter to mainstream white American values. Negative perceptions that date from stereotypes and myths devised during slavery persist to the present. African Americans are disproportionally denied equal access to opportunities afforded members of the white majority population. Stressors and stress are ever present, creating fertile ground for high rates of mental disorder. In spite of their apparent need for mental health services, African Americans are under-represented in the service delivery system.

Hispanics

The Hispanic population has increased dramatically over the past decade. The 1990 U.S. Census puts growth in this population since the 1980 census at 53%; however, it is widely accepted that census counts underrepresent the true number of Hispanics. With increasing numbers of immigrants from Mexico and Cuba, Hispanics are expected to form the nation's largest ethnic minority group by the year 2000 (Marcias, 1977). The states with the highest concentrations of Hispanics are California, Arizona, New Mexico, Texas, Florida, and New York. Research on the migratory habits of Mexican American families is unclear. Migration to follow employment is relatively high within certain areas of the United States, but many families tend to settle in one community and remain there. There is some evidence that Mexican Americans are more geographically stable than are Anglos (Carillo, 1982).

The term *Hispanic* applies to persons in the United States of various Latino origins, the largest group being Mexican Americans, at 60%; the next largest is Puerto Ricans, at 12%; Cuban Americans make up 5% of the Hispanic population, and individuals whose origins are in Central and South America constitute 13%. The remaining 10% are of various other Latin/Spanish origins (U.S. Department of Commerce, 1993). Although the Hispanic population as a whole shares many common traits, there is a great deal of diversity within this group. For example, Mexican Americans living in southwestern states can return to their original homeland almost at will, whereas visits home by Puerto Ricans and Central and South Americans are limited by distance. Cubans are not permitted to return to their homeland at all. In addition, however, there are a number of similarities among Hispanic populations that have particular bearing on mental health care. The majority have come from poor rural areas and migrated to overly congested urban environments. The majority are also undereducated, with high levels of illiteracy. Dropout rates are estimated to be as high as 44% (U.S. Department of Commerce, 1993). They have come to the United States seeking employment and a better life, but in doing so, they have often separated and disrupted their families.

Stressors and Stereotypes That Contribute to Mental Health Risks

Padilla and Ruiz (1973) point out that Hispanics suffer some unique high-stress indicators: (a) poor communication skills in English (more than 20% report difficulty with the English language; see President's Commission on Mental Health, 1978), (b) limited education, (c) higher unemployment rates and lower incomes than those in the majority population (19% live below poverty level; U.S. Department of Commerce, 1993), (d) low social status, (e) substandard housing (Hispanics live in crowded conditions three times more frequently than do Anglos; U.S. Department of Commerce, 1993), (f) survival in an oppressive and prejudiced society, and (g) minimal political influence.[1] At least in part as a result of these stressors, Hispanics experience higher rates of alcoholism, drug abuse, and suicide than do members of the majority population (Carillo, 1982).

Needs for and Utilization of Mental Health Services

Despite apparent needs among Hispanics for community mental health services, it has been repeatedly documented that members of this population often underutilize such services (Carillo, 1982; Sue, Allen, & Conaway, 1978; Torrey, 1973; Weaver, 1973; Wells, Hough, Golding, Burnam, & Karno, 1987). The most frequent explanations cited for underutilization include (a) high use of non-mental health services, such as physicians, family and friends, *curanderos,* and priests; (b) lack of knowledge about available mental health services; (c) negative attitudes toward psychiatric professionals and services; (d) inaccessible facilities (physical as well as economic barriers); (e) language barriers; (f) cultural unresponsiveness; and (g) inappropriate treatment models.

High Use of Non-Mental Health Services

It is often assumed that increased use of formal mental health services decreases the use of informal services, and that, in turn, increased use of informal mental health services decreases the use of formal services. Research has shown that this is not the case, however. Mexican Americans who acknowledge the use of *curanderos* and physicians for the purposes of mental health counseling often utilize the services of community mental health clinics at the same time. *Curanderos* and physicians frequently make referrals to local mental health centers (Keefe, 1979; Weclew, 1975).

There is evidence that Hispanics with traditional extended families are more likely to seek advice from friends or family members than to see professional caregivers (Carillo, 1982; Martinez, 1993). Family values dictate that personal problems be taken care of within the family unit; to do otherwise might be taken as an insult to the family. Research, however, reflects some change in this attitude: The more acculturation has taken place within individuals and families, the more professional help is sought (Wells et al., 1987).

Knowledge and Attitudes Toward Mental Health

Karno and Edgerton (1969), who surveyed 200 Euro-American subjects and 400 Mexican American subjects, have commented: "Our initial analysis indicated that there are remarkably few statistically significant differences between the interview responses of Mexican Americans and Anglos involving perceptions and definitions of mental illness" (p. 237). Further studies have shown that Chicano utilizers and nonutilizers of mental services, overall, hold positive attitudes toward mental health services (Keefe, 1979).

Inaccessibility and Unresponsiveness

In the past three decades, important strides have been made in eliminating obstacles to mental health service delivery to Hispanics. The most serious of these obstacles has been language. Hispanic and Spanish/English bilingual personnel are underrepresented in nearly all professions, mental health being no exception. This has a direct impact on Hispanics' usage of mental health services. Minority recruitment efforts have increased the number of Hispanic mental health professionals; however, the need still far exceeds the available personnel. As a San Francisco mental health worker has observed: "It has been my experience that when one makes it known that one is Spanish-speaking and that one is motivated to work with Latinos, the frequency of referrals increases rapidly. Sometimes the response is overwhelming, even in a setting where formerly Latinos came only rarely" (Munoz, 1982, p. 366).

The Hispanic mental health professional needs to overcome not only language barriers but cultural barriers as well. Culturally astute mental health professionals who acknowledge the unique cultural aspects of Hispanic life and the importance of culture in the client's problem, without making assumptions based on stereotypes, are perceived as more competent than are those who ignore culture (Atkins, Casas, & Abreu, 1992). Numerous studies have shown that increased use of multicultural staffs and bilingual professionals has a favorable impact on Hispanics' use of mental health services (e.g., Bloom, 1975; Flores, 1978; Sue, Fujino, Hu, Takeuchi, & Zane, 1991). In a study of 220 federally funded mental health clinics throughout the United States, Wu and Windle (1980) found that the clinics that served the greatest number of Hispanics were also the clinics that employed the greatest number of Hispanic staff members.

There is a great deal of variability within Hispanic populations—ethnic origins, socioeconomic levels, regional identification, and education are just some of the areas in which clients may differ. Thus it is imperative for mental health professionals working with Hispanics to be culturally sensitive as well as to view each person as an individual. Cultural ignorance compounded by reliance on stereotypes can lead to inaccurate assessment, misdiagnosis, and inappropriate treatment plans.

Utilization of Services

Munoz (1982) identifies three stages involved in a Hispanic individual's becoming a mental health center user:

1. *The individual identifies the mental health system as an appropriate source of help for the problem he or she is facing.* Factors influencing this identification include past experiences with mental health services, referral sources (formal or informal), and availability and visibility of Spanish-speaking personnel.
2. *The individual initiates contact with the mental health center in person or by phone.* This is often the greatest obstacle to the Hispanic consumer; it is essential that the receptionist be bilingual. A quick complete explanation (both written and verbal) of services should be available to the client in both Spanish and English.
3. *The individual comes to the intake appointment and continues with the prescribed treatment.* In a study published in 1976, Miranda, Andijo, Caballero, Guerrero, and Ramos found that 60% of Mexican Americans dropped out of mental health treatment following the initial interview, compared with 35% for non-Mexican Americans. Sue et al. (1991), in contrast, found no significant differences in Mexican American dropout rates compared with those in the Anglo population. Although differences in sample populations should be considered in the interpretation of these findings, increased cultural sensitivity may be a factor in the improved statistics. In addition, Mexican Americans who continued with follow-up visits have been judged to be more acculturated than those who had early dropout rates (Miranda et al., 1976; Wells et al., 1987).

Service Delivery

Assessment and diagnosis. The social history is one of the most important assessment tools the mental health professional has when dealing with an individual from another culture. He or she can directly acquire a description of norms in an individual's culture and family on marital customs, schooling, employment, and problem solving (Munoz, 1982).

It is important to note that professionals working with Hispanics and members of other minority groups should use assessment and diagnostic instruments with caution. The validity and reliability of these instruments have often been established only with middle-class white populations. Different populations vary greatly in terms of customs, language, and vocabulary (even regionally).

Inpatient services. Most Hispanic families will attempt to take care of family members at home and will use inpatient services as a last resort (Martinez, 1993). This factor may account for the low number of Spanish-speaking individuals generally found on psychiatric inpatient units (Padilla, Ruiz, & Alvarez, 1975). It is imperative that such units have 24-hour Spanish-speaking staff, preferably professional staff, to communicate with psychotic or suicidal patients. Programs utilizing specialized Hispanic inpatient treatment groups have shown great improvement on outcome measures under termination (Dolgin, Salazar, & Kort 1980).

Emergency services. In areas where significant proportions of the population speak only Spanish, bilingual staff need to be available 24 hours a day. Staff members need to have the ability to make quick and accurate evaluations of individuals' potential for hurting themselves or others, as well as to determine individuals' capacity to obtain food, shelter, and clothing (Munoz, 1982). The use of translators can result in misinterpretation and inappropriate treatment; in crisis situations, the results can be devastating.

Aftercare and rehabilitation. Hispanic foster homes and halfway houses are in short supply; however, they are vital to successful aftercare. Returning to a comfortable, familiar environment contributes to an individual's successful rehabilitation (Munoz, 1982). For individuals in their homes, Spanish-speaking fieldworkers can assist clients as well as families in stabilization and the prevention of mental health crises.

The need for educational and vocational programs for Hispanic mental health clients is exacerbated by the population's generally low economic and education levels. Effective programs include those that offer job training and placement, classes in English as a second language, educational opportunities, and case management services.

Summary

Hispanics face a number of obstacles in obtaining mental health services; however, there have been numerous successes for Hispanic mental health services delivery in the past three decades. Since the passage of the Community Mental Health Centers Act of 1963, utilization has increased, due in part to the opening of mental health centers in local communities, increased numbers of bilingual staff members, the availability of low-cost services, and increased public information regarding mental health services. Recent referenda and proposed legislation threaten to erode seriously the successes of the past three decades. In 1994, Proposition 187 passed in California; this initiative proposes to eliminate mental health services (as well as a number of other services) to all undocumented persons. As this publication goes to press, the constitutionality of Proposition 187, as well as similar proposed legislation in other states, is still in question.

Native Americans

The diversity among Native Americans is enormous. Tribes that were geographically separated shared little in common, and tribes that were geographically close often had their own unique languages, cultures, and traditions. Although most states have sizable Native American populations, the majority of Native Americans live in California, Oklahoma, Arizona, New Mexico, Alaska, and Washington (U.S. Department of Commerce, 1993).

Demographics

Native Americans have been referred to as the most severely disadvantaged population within the United States (Yates, 1987). By young adulthood, Native Americans show higher rates of suicide (McIntosh & Santos, 1981), alcoholism (Beiser & Attneave, 1982), drug abuse (Goldstein, Oetting, & Edwards, 1974), delinquency (Forslund & Meyers, 1974), and out-of-home placement (Byler, 1977) than do their counterparts in many other groups. Disability among Native Americans is four to six times higher than the national average (Association on American Indian Affairs, as cited in Swinomish Tribal Mental Health Project, 1991); the rate of infant mortality among Native Americans is the highest of any ethnic group in the United States (Kemberling, 1973). Native American teen pregnancy and child neglect rates are twice the national rates (Nagi, 1977). Nationwide, Native Americans have the lowest educational level of all minority groups; only 15% of Native American adults have a high school diploma or GED (Office of Minority Mental Health, 1988). The overall Native American unemployment rate is 40%; on some reservations, it is as high as 90% (U.S. Department of Commerce, 1993). Some 49% of Native Americans live in poverty (U.S. Department of Commerce, 1993). The overall rate of alcoholism among Native Americans is two to three times the national average, although the rate varies widely among tribes (Jensen, Stauss, & Harris, 1977).

Stressors and Stereotypes That
Contribute to Mental Health Risk

The years between 1500 and 1900 have been called the Indian holocaust (Thompson, Walker, & Silk-Walker, 1993). Europeans brought infectious diseases for which the Indians were immunologically unprepared (Dobyns, 1983). It has been estimated that as much as five-sixths of some Indian tribes perished these early epidemics. Chiefs and elders died, leaving the communities without leadership. Disease-infested blankets were presented as "gifts" to the Indians, in an early version of germ warfare (Stiffarm & Lane, 1992).

The four critical historical stressors of Indian life most often cited as having negative impacts on tribal mental health are Indian child welfare practices, religious persecution, destructive educational practices, and the introduction of alcohol.

Child Welfare

Disrespect for the Indians' way of life and lack of understanding of Native American religious customs and family systems led to destructive practices by state workers and non-Indian court systems. Children were removed from their homes and parents were intimidated into placing their children in foster care or relinquishing them permanently for adoption. In fact, some religious organizations made it a policy to try to remove and "save" as many Native American children as possible. As a rule, most of these children who were placed in non-Native American homes did not adjust well. In fact, in contrast to "saving" Native American children, non-Indian foster and adopted homes created confusion and a sense of frustration that left the children with a sense of belonging to neither the Native American nor the non-Indian culture. In some cases children grew up unaware not only of their tribal affiliations but also of anything about their Native American heritage (Green, 1983). (The enactment of the Child Welfare Act of 1978 drastically reduced such abuses of Native American children.) It is this history of the treatment of the children that established fear of and hostility toward caseworkers among many Native Americans (Swinomish Tribal Mental Health Project, 1991).

Suppression of Native American Religion

The early settlers rarely took the time to understand Native Americans' religious beliefs and customs. In the late 1800s, Native Americans' practice of traditional religions, spiritual dances, and healing practices was outlawed (Swinomish Tribal Mental Health Project, 1991). As a consequence of this law, Native Americans began to carry out their traditional spiritual practices and ceremonies in hiding. Native American children who grew up during this time were justifiably confused about religion and were unable to grasp the real meaning of the traditional rituals. Legal prosecutions for breaking the law prohibiting these practices decreased after 1935, but the ban was not officially repealed until the passage of the Indian Freedom of Religion Act in 1978.

Forced Acculturation Through Education

Treaty rights guaranteed Native Americans an education for their children. These so-called rights gave the U.S. government permission to remove children from their homes on the reservations and require them to attend faraway boarding schools. Native American boarding schools have been compared to prisons; they were overcrowded and understaffed (Swinomish Tribal Mental Health Project, 1991).

Students who adjusted to the boarding school environment were often miserable when they returned home to their tribal environment. If they did not accept acculturation, they were miserable in the school setting. Native American parents often resisted sending their children to boarding schools; some went so far as to hide their children. The Bureau of Indian Affairs responded by denying food rations and sometimes kidnapped the children to take them away to school (Swinomish Tribal Mental Health Project, 1991). By the 1960s, most authorities had realized that removing young children from their families was a terrible mistake, and they instituted reservation-based schools.

Effects of Alcoholism

In considering alcoholism within the Native American community, it is vital to view it within the context of history. Generally, Native Americans were unfamiliar with alcoholic beverages and their effects prior to contact with white traders. Traders often gave them alcohol in the hope of taking advantage of their intoxication in making deals. Current high rates of alcoholism among Native Americans now have led researchers to look into the possibility of a genetic reason for their high vulnerability. Although there is no conclusive evidence, it is clear that early Native American culture's lack of social norms for drinking behavior combined with historical and modern-day stressors to place Native American people at high risk for alcohol-related problems (Weber, 1982).

Needs for and Utilization of Mental Health Services

Most authorities agree that among Native Americans the problems of substance abuse, depression, and violent behavior are connected, and each influences and contributes to the others, forming a "triad of disturbance" (Swinomish Tribal Mental Health Project, 1991).

Depression

Drinking, suicide, and violent acting out are considered to be symptoms of underlying depression. Authorities agree that historical stressors have greatly contributed to high rates of depression among Native Americans (Manson, Shore, & Bloom, 1985). Therefore, it is the responsibility of tribal-based mental health services to instill and nurture positive cultural self-concepts to counteract a history of tragedy and loss.

Alcohol Abuse

Alcoholism rates among Native Americans vary; they are abnormally high in certain areas, and in other areas they are equivalent to alcohol rates in the general U.S. population (Stratton, Zeiner, & Paredes, 1978). Native Americans appear to have developed an idiosyncratic drinking pattern. Many abstain from alcohol; surprisingly few are moderate or social drinkers. Drinking at all usually means problem drinking, often to the point of losing consciousness (Cohen, 1982). Where alcohol abuse is pervasive, the effects on the individual and family as well as on tribal self-image can be devastating. Native American communities are beginning to view alcohol abuse not just as a problem of individuals but as a community problem.

Acting Out and Violent Behavior

Violent behavior is often viewed as a response to an accumulation of life stresses. Violent behaviors common to Native Americans include suicide attempts, domestic violence, rape, reckless driving, and fighting. These behaviors are thought to be outlets for tension and stress. Violence against self and others is a major mental health concern in Native American communities. Although drinking increases the risk of these behaviors, they are not necessarily entirely alcohol related (Swinomish Tribal Mental Health Project, 1991).

Barriers to Service Delivery

Sharing one's innermost thoughts with a stranger is difficult enough, but in the case of Native Americans this is compounded by the stranger's being perceived as part of an entity that has traditionally brought betrayal and shame, the federal government. In addition, Native Americans are confused by Western medicine's exclusion of and resistance to traditional folk treatments. In fact, some Native Americans believe that mainstream mental health services are detrimental to their spiritual well-being (Swinomish Tribal Mental Health Project, 1991).

The use of standardized diagnostic instruments with Native Americans can be problematic: Standardization for one tribe does not guarantee standardization for another (Thompson et al., 1993). Little research has been conducted in this area, no doubt at least in part because of the cost and time such research involves.

Utilization

Because of the diverse record-keeping methods of different tribal mental health services, it is difficult to determine rates of Native American utilization of services. Unfortunately, most records do not differentiate between initial visits and follow-up visits; determining the overall dropout rate is thus problematic. In one Seattle mental health clinic, the dropout rate among Native Americans was found to be 55%, compared with 30% among all other ethnic populations (Sue, 1977).

There is evidence that Native Americans rely heavily on informal support networks consisting of extended family, tribal elders, and traditional healers (Red Horse, Lewis, Feit, & Decker, 1978). Traditional healers combine the responsibilities of doctor, counselor, priest, and historian (Greenberg & Greenberg, 1984).

Service Delivery

The Indian Health Service (IHS), established in 1955, has primary responsibility for the health care of Native Americans. In addition to IHS, there are a number of other sources of mental health care services: state and local mental health services, university counseling centers, and veterans' health care facilities. Because of the large number of sources, it is unclear how responsibility for mental health services to Native Americans should be distributed among federal, state, tribal, and charitable agencies. Assumptions that other agencies are responsible or obligated have tended to contribute to underutilization.

Existing tribal mental health programs are underfunded and understaffed, and the available staff are poorly trained (Indian Health Service, 1989); 40% of the total staff and 62% of the Native American staff are considered to be paraprofessionals. Thompson et al. (1993) estimate that overall Native American mental health services are only 43% staffed. A conservative estimate would be that there is roughly one direct service worker for every 2,000 Native Americans (Swinomish Tribal Mental Health Project, 1991).

The IHS operates two short-term inpatient units. Most inpatient services are contracted with local public or private psychiatric hospitals. IHS has no programs for partial hospitalization, transitional living, or children's residential treatment, except for contracts with non-Indian treatment facilities. Alcohol abuse programs are, for the most part, run by the individual tribes using IHS funds.

Staffing and funding constraints have severely limited the mental health services available to Native Americans. The IHS system has failed to meet urgent needs for direct mental health care in both quantity of services and cultural sensitivity. This seems to be true for three reasons:

1. The federal bureaucracy inhibits adequate local tribal control over the development of services unique to individual tribal customs.
2. Inadequate funding and severe staffing shortages limit the services available.
3. Western medicine has been ineffective in dealing with Native American mental health, substance abuse, and social problems (Swinomish Tribal Mental Health Project, 1991).

Summary

Native Americans share a unique set of circumstances. Historical stressors, traditional religious beliefs, distrust of the government, extreme poverty, and high rates of unemployment and alcoholism all present challenges to mental health professionals. Unique interventions are critical not only for the mental health of individual Native Americans but for the well-being of their families and tribes as well.

U.S. society has generally assumed that the breakdown of Native American culture is desirable and that the acculturation of Indian people into white society is inevitable. The feeling that Indian people should be educated, civilized, and assimilated is often evident in official and unofficial attempts to abolish the Indian race. In 1980, more than 50% of all married Native Americans had non-Indian spouses (Red Horse, 1988). Native Americans were not granted U.S. citizenship until 1924.

Conclusion

Minorities of color have faced many barriers in their quest for equality in American society. Community-sanctioned discrimination, which has often been enforced through rules, regulations, and laws, has perpetuated a pattern of racism and oppression. This has had long-term impacts on the emotional well-being and mental health of minority group members. Demographic statistics reflect these adverse impacts: Poverty and unemployment rates are higher and income levels are lower for minority members, compared with those in the white majority, as are educational levels. Language is a problem for many. Life expectancy is shorter. Cultural conflicts abound. These stressors pose decided risks for mental health. Although epidemiological studies may be flawed, there is sufficient evidence to indicate that minority groups tend to have higher prevalence rates of mental disorder in several diagnostic categories than does the white majority population. In spite of this apparent need for mental health services, minorities of color are underrepresented as recipients of service. Reasons for this underutilization are essentially similar for all groups.

As we have pointed out, minorities of color are not likely to utilize mental health services unless the delivery system satisfactorily meets the needs of the population in regard to the four A's: availability, accessibility, acceptability, and affordability. Services simply may not be available in many areas that are accessible to low-income minorities. Even when services are available, the setting may not express the cultural ambiance that welcomes the potential client. No one may be present who speaks the language of the individual, and securing an interpreter may prove problematic. There is a serious shortage of professionally trained minority mental health practitioners. Similarly, there is a shortage of skilled minority researchers. As a result, research findings may not accurately reflect the phenomena upon which practice theory is built. Stereotypes and myths continue to pervade the mental health arena, thereby increasing the probability that false conclusions may be drawn regarding the mental status of clients. Assessment instruments, for the most part, have been developed and normed using white middle-class populations. In using such instruments with minority populations, the margin for error is immense. If publicly funded mental health services are not available, the individual may not be able to afford the needed treatment. Because of past experiences with formal systems and oppressive treatment, minority members may be loath to seek help outside of informal networks.

Although these observations are by no means new revelations, unfortunately the conditions we have described persist as barriers to help seeking. Minorities of color are in fact "brothers under the skin" and collectively share the negative impacts of such conditions. However, recent trends toward greater cultural sensitivity in mental health practice lead us to believe that the future can be viewed with cautious optimism.

Note

1. Although Padilla and Ruiz's work is more than 20 years old, the stressors have, unfortunately, remained constant over the decades.

References

Atkins, D. R., Casas, A., & Abreu, J. (1992). Mexican American acculturation, counselor ethnicity and cultural sensitivity, and perceived counselor competence. *Journal of Counseling Psychology, 39,* 515-520.

Beiser, M., & Attneave, C. L. (1982). Mental disorders among Native American children: Rates and risk periods for entering treatment. *American Journal of Psychiatry, 139,* 193-198.

Bloom, B. L. (1975). *Changing patterns of psychiatric care.* New York: Human Sciences.

Byler, W. (1977). The destruction of American Indian families. In S. Unger (Ed.), *The destruction of the American Indian family.* New York: Association on American Indian Affairs.

Carillo, C. (1982). Changing norms of Hispanic families: Implications for treatment. In E. Jones & S. Korchin (Eds.), *Minority mental health.* New York: Holt, Rinehart & Winston.

Carlin, J., & Sokoloff, N. (1985). Mental health treatment issues for Southeast Asian refugee children. In T. Owan (Ed.), *Southeast Asian mental health: Treatment, prevention, services, training and research.* Washington, DC: U.S. Department of Health and Human Services.

Cohen, S. (1982, May). Alcohol and the Indian. *Drug Abuse and Alcoholism Newsletter.*

Coner-Edwards, A. F., & Spurlock, J. (1988). *Black families in crisis: The middle class.* New York: Brunner/Mazel.

Dobyns, H. F. (1983). *Their number become thinned.* Knoxville: University of Tennessee Press.

Dolgin, D. L., Salazar, A. A., & Kort, G. A. (1980). A culturally-relevant treatment program for the Hispanic inpatient. *Borderlands, 4*(1), 131-142.

Flores, J. L. (1978). The utilization of a community mental health service by Mexican Americans. *International Journal of Social Psychiatry, 24,* 271-275.

Forslund, M. A., & Meyers, R. E. (1974). Delinquency among Wild River Indian Reservation youth. *Criminology, 12,* 97-106.

Gaw, A. C. (Ed.). (1993). *Culture, ethnicity, and mental illness.* Washington, DC: American Psychiatric Press.

Goldstein, G. S., Oetting, E. R., & Edwards, R. (1974). Drug use among Native American young adults. *International Journal on Addiction, 14,* 855-860.

Gong-Guy, E. (1987). *California Southeast Asian mental health needs assessment.* Oakland, CA: Asian Community Mental Health Services.

Green, H. J. (1983). Risks and attitudes associated with extra-cultural placement of American Indian children: A critical review. *Journal of the American Academy of Child Psychiatry, 22,* 63-67.

Greenberg, H., & Greenberg, G. (1984). *Carl Gorman's world.* Albuquerque: University of New Mexico Press.

Griffith, E., & Baker, F. M. (1993). Psychiatric care of African Americans. In A. C. Gaw (Ed.), *Culture, ethnicity, and mental illness.* Washington, DC: American Psychiatric Press.

Hill, R. B. (1971). *The strengths of Black families.* New York: Emerson-Hall.

Hilliard, A. (1978). *Return to the source: African origins of Western civilization*. Unpublished resource bibliography.

Ho, M. K. (1983). Social casework with Asian Americans. In F. Turner (Ed.), *Differential diagnosis and treatment in social work*. New York: Free Press.

Indian Health Service. (1989). *National plan for the Native American mental health services*. Rockville, MD: U.S. Department of Health and Human Services.

Jensen, G. F., Stauss, J. H., & Harris, V. W. (1977). Crime, delinquency and the American Indian. *Human Organization, 36*, 252-257.

Karno, M., & Edgerton, R. B. (1969). Perception of mental illness in a Mexican American community. *Archives of General Psychiatry, 20*, 233-238.

Keefe, S. E. (1979). Mexican Americans' underutilization of mental health clinics: An evaluation of suggested explanations. *Hispanic Journal of Behavioral Sciences, 1*(2), 93-115.

Kemberling, S. R. (1973). The Indian Health Service: Commentary on a commentary. *Pediatrics, 51*, 6-9.

Kinzie, J. D., & Leung, P. K. (1993). Psychiatric care of Indochinese Americans. In A. C. Gaw (Ed.), *Culture, ethnicity, and mental illness*. Washington, DC: American Psychiatric Press.

Landrum-Brown, J. (1990). Black mental health and racial oppression. In D. S. Ruiz (Ed.), *Handbook of mental health and mental disorder among Black Americans*. Westport, CT: Greenwood.

Logan, S. (1990). Diversity among black families: Assessing structure and function. In S. Logan, E. Freeman, & R. McRoy (Eds.), *Social work practice with Black families*. New York: Longman.

Lum, D. (1986). *Social work practice and people of color*. Monterey, CA: Brooks/Cole.

Manson, S. M., Shore, J. H., & Bloom, J. D. (1985). The depressive experience in American Indian communities: A challenge for psychiatric theory and diagnosis. In A. Kleinman & B. Good (Eds.), *Culture and depression*. Berkeley: University of California Press.

Marcias, R. F. (1977). U.S. Hispanics in 2000 AD: Projecting the number. *Agenda, 7*, 16-20.

Martinez, C. (1993). Psychiatric care of Mexican Americans. In A. C. Gaw (Ed.), *Culture, ethnicity, and mental illness* (pp. 431-466). Washington, DC: American Psychiatric Press.

Mathura, C. B., & Baer, M. A. (1990). Social factors in diagnosis and treatment. In D. S. Ruiz (Ed.), *Handbook of mental health and mental disorder among Black Americans* (pp. 167-178). Westport, CT: Greenwood.

McIntosh, J. L., & Santos, J. L. (1981). Suicide among Native Americans: A compilation of findings. *Omega, 11*, 303-316.

Miranda, M. R., Andijo, E., Caballero, I. L., Guerrero, C. C., & Ramos, R. A. (1976). Mexican American dropouts in psychotherapy as related to level of acculturation. In M. R. Miranda (Ed.), *Psychotherapy with the Spanish speaking: Issues in research and service delivery* (Monograph No. 3). Los Angeles: University of California, Spanish Speaking Mental Health Research Center.

Mullins, L. (1985). Anthropological perspective of the Afro-American family. In M. T. Fulliove (Ed.), *The Black family: Mental health perspectives*. San Francisco: Rosenberg Foundation.

Munoz, R. F. (1982). The Spanish speaking consumer and the community mental health center. In E. Jones & S. Korchin (Eds.), *Minority mental health*. New York: Holt, Rinehart & Winston.

Nagi, S. Z. (1977). *Child maltreatment in the United States*. New York: Columbia University Press.

Neighbors, H. W. (1984). The distribution of psychiatric morbidity: A review and suggestions for research. *Community Mental Health Journal, 20*, 5-18.

Office of Minority Mental Health. (1988, July 7). [Testimony given before the U.S. Senate Select Committee on Indian Affairs].

Padilla, A. M., & Ruiz, R. A. (1973). *Latino mental health: A review of the literature* (DHEW Publication No. HSM 73-9143). Washington, DC: Government Printing Office.

Padilla, A. M., Ruiz, R. A., & Alvarez, R. (1975). Community mental health services for the Spanish speaking/surnamed population. *American Psychologist, 30*, 892-895.

Pinderhughes, E. (1982). Afro-American families and the victim system. In M. McGoldrick, J. K. Pearce, & J. Giordano (Eds.), *Ethnicity and family therapy* (pp. 188-222). New York: Guilford.

Poussaint, A. F. (1990). The mental health status of black Americans, 1983. In D. S. Ruiz (Ed.), *Handbook of mental health and mental disorder among black Americans*. Westport, CT: Greenwood.

President's Commission on Mental Health. (1978). *Report to the president* (Vol. 3.). Washington, DC: Government Printing Office.

Red Horse, J. G. (1988). Cultural evolution of American Indian families. In C. Jacobs & D. D. Bowles (Eds.), *Ethnicity and race: Critical examples in social work*. Silver Spring, MD: National Association of Social Workers.

Red Horse, J. G., Lewis, R. L., Feit, M., & Decker, J. (1978). Family behavior of urban American Indians. *Social Casework, 59*, 67-72.

Reiger, D. A., Myers, J. K., Kramer, M., & Robins, L. N. (1984). The NIMH Epidemiological Catchment Area Program: Historical context, major objectives and population characteristics. *Archives of General Psychiatric Nursing, 6*, 195-204.

Ruiz, D. S. (Ed.). (1990). *Handbook of mental health and mental disorder among black Americans*. Westport, CT: Greenwood.

Stiffarm, L. A., & Lane, J. (1992). The demography of native North America: A question of American Indian survival. In M. A. Jaimes (Ed.), *The state of Native America: Genocide, colonization, and resistance*. Boston: South End.

Stratton, R., Zeiner, A., & Paredes, A. (1978). Tribal affiliation and prevalence of alcohol problems. *Journal of Studies on Alcohol, 39*, 1166-1177.

Sue, D. W., & Sue, D. (1990). *Counseling the culturally different: Theory and practice* (2nd ed.). New York: John Wiley.

Sue, S. (1977). Community mental health services to minority groups: Some optimism, some pessimism. *American Psychologist, 32*, 616-624.

Sue, S., Allen, D. B., & Conaway, L. (1978). The responsiveness and equality of mental health care to Chicanos and Native Americans. *American Journal of Community Psychology, 6*, 137-146.

Sue, S., Fujino, D. C., Hu, L., Takeuchi, D. T., & Zane, N. (1991). Community mental health services for ethnic minority groups: A test of the cultural responsiveness hypothesis. *Journal of Consulting and Clinical Psychology, 59*, 533-540.

Swinomish Tribal Mental Health Project. (1991). *A gathering of wisdom*. LaConner, WA: Swinomish Tribal Community.

Thompson, J. W., Walker, R. D., & Silk-Walker, P. (1993). Psychiatric care of American Indians and Alaska Natives. In A. C. Gaw (Ed.), *Culture, ethnicity, and mental illness* (pp. 189-241). Washington, DC: American Psychiatric Press.

Tidwell, B. J. (1993). *The state of Black America*. New York: National Urban League.

Torrey, E. F. (1973). *The mind game: Witchdoctors and psychiatrists*. New York: Bantam.

Uba, L. (1994). *Asian Americans: Personality patterns, identity, and mental health*. New York: Guilford.

U.S. Commission on Civil Rights. (1992). *Civil rights issues facing Asian Americans in the 1990's*. Washington, DC: Author.

U.S. Department of Commerce, Bureau of the Census. (1993). *Statistical abstract of the United States* (113th ed.). Washington, DC: Government Printing Office.

Vega, W. A., & Rumbaut, R. G. (1991). Ethnic minorities and mental health. *Annual Review of Sociology, 17*, 351-383.

Weaver, J. L. (1973). Mexican American health care behavior: A critical review of the literature. *Social Science Quarterly, 54*, 85-102.

Weber, R. (1982). Alcoholism in the Indian community. In Seattle Indian Health Board (Ed.), *Indian and Alaska Native mental health seminars*. Seattle, WA: Seattle Indian Health Board.

Weclew, R. V. (1975). The nature, prevalence and level of awareness of "curanderismo" and some of its implications for community mental health. *Community Mental Health Journal, 11*, 145-154.

Wells, K. B., Hough, R. L., Golding, J. M., Burnam, M. A., & Karno, M. (1987). Which Mexican Americans underutilize health services? *American Journal of Psychiatry, 144*, 918-922.

Woo, D. (1989). The gap between striving and achieving: The case of Asian American women. In Asian Women United of California (Ed.), *Making waves: An anthology of writings by and about Asian American women* (pp. 185-194). Boston: Beacon.

Worthington, C. (1992). An examination of factors influencing the diagnosis and treatment of black patients in the mental health system. *Archives of Psychiatric Nursing, 4*, 195-204.

Wu, I., & Windle, C. (1980). Ethnic specificity in the relationship of minority use and staffing of community mental health centers. *Community Mental Health Journal, 16*, 156-168.

Yates, A. (1987). Current status and future directions of research on the American Indian child. *American Journal of Psychiatry, 144*, 1135-1142.

CHAPTER 15

Women as Mental Health Service Recipients and Providers

Theresa Bruno Mulloy

In his presidential address to the 1991 annual meeting of the American Psychological Association, held in San Francisco, Stanley R. Graham (1992) said of the male/female dilemma:

> We are currently in the midst of a great revolution, and the half of the human race called *female* has, after countless centuries of oppression and exploitation, stood up and cried "Nonsense!" The good that will accrue to all of us is immeasurable. The lies and distortions relative to the nature of women have diminished the entire human race. The sooner they are lost in antiquity, the better. (p. 841)

In this chapter I address select issues in the field of mental health as they relate to women and the male/female dilemma. In the first section, I take a look at women as receivers of services and why many women may not successfully access the mental health system. This section is intended to introduce a limited number of the issues related to women as recipients of mental health services. The matters discussed include the definition or rejection of a psychology of women, women in the homeless population, sexual harassment and the mentally ill, and issues of litigation as related to false memories of sexual abuse.

The second section is a threefold look at women as mental health service providers. The discussion includes a brief overview of women's role in mental health history, an account of women's role in mental health services today, and finally a look at trends that appear to be shaping the future of women as providers of mental health services.

One lesson to be learned from the study of the gender dilemma is that women are not the opposite of men, nor do women form a homogeneous group. Maybe the real lesson is that males do not constitute a homogeneous group either. This knowledge may help service providers to be aware that they should address all clients as individuals rather than as members of subgroups based on gender. One may predict that all human services will be more effective when they start from a position that is free of gender bias.

Women as Service Recipients

In the United States, male and female social roles have changed over the past two decades. Traditional roles have been altered as changes have taken place in the demands of society. As women have entered the workplace in increasing numbers, men have been forced to accept more active roles in family and household work. The stressors identified with gender are being challenged. Even a mental health issue such as "empty nest syndrome," previously considered a woman's problem, has begun to surface with males who have been involved in rearing children. Such changes in the social environment will require major changes in mental health counseling with families in the future (Dickstein et al., 1991).

The Development of a Psychology of Women

Feminists, along with others, challenge a basic principle of Freudian psychoanalytic tradition, the Oedipal theory, as a cover-up for actual sexual abuse of female children. Freudian theory places blame on the victim, avoiding confirmation of the situation and substituting an explanation that the woman's unfulfilled fantasies are now resulting in neurotic behavior. A primary goal of feminist theory is to validate the reality of the situation and take control of maladaptive behaviors (Courtois, 1991).

Attempts to compare the psychologies of males and females have uncovered several findings. First, the universal standard of normal behavior that has been developed in the present literature may need to be reevaluated for accuracy concerning male populations other than white, middle-class, young, mentally capable individuals, as well as concerning females. The traditional approach to understanding the behavior of any group has been to make a comparison to a control group, or "norm." In the study of human behavior, the norm has predominantly been based on white middle-class men. In fact, the norm has often been further described as based on college sophomores, a highly accessible population for academic research. This group has been the basis of the universal standard, and all behavior that differs from this group's behavior has been considered deficient. Clearly, research is needed to check the accuracy of past "truths" of human behavior.

There is a pressing need to consider the many similarities, as well as differences, between male and female humans. These similarities and differences include elements of human behavior that apply to the study of mental health and mental illness. Recently, psychology has addressed the differences between men and women, prescribing techniques to bridge the variance. The social sciences have clearly addressed teaching males to be more sensitive while teaching females to be more assertive. Such teachings are designed to negate the differences between males and females and to create social settings where gender is of little importance in behavior management.

As noted above, women do not form a single homogeneous group. To understand the behavior of an individual, one must know that person's race and social class as well as gender (Yoder & Kaha, 1993). A psychology of women must address women's differences from the male norm and the differences among women. The assumption that females constitute a homogeneous class grossly ignores the differences among women of varying racial, ethnic, and social classes (Spelman, 1988). The psychological study of women is a product of the field of individual differences. Therefore, to gain a gender-free study, one must foster an appreciation of differences in and between any subgroup being researched or discussed (Riger, 1992).

Gender-Biased Research Into Human Behavior

Movement from a philosophical approach to a more scientific approach to the explanation of human behavior has long been a goal of psychology and sociology. However, attempting to define the truth creates complex questions. Some critics of the scientific method say that the political and cultural values of scientists cannot be separated from their findings. Others claim there are no laws of science, and that science is not defining laws of human behavior but only describing how people act at a time in history under a certain set of conditions. These two approaches should not be confused with the importance of gaining a clearer view of the nature and/or behavior of both males and females.

It is obvious that past "truths" concerning human behavior have been studied by male researchers, and most often have been examined using male subjects. Numerous critics have addressed the subject of gender bias as an element present in the social science literature. Studies on subjects relevant to women, such as rape and housework, are rarely found in serious research, whereas subjects that reflect traditional male roles, such as power and leadership, have been studied in great detail (Epstein, 1988). Women who present themselves and their families for mental health services deserve to be served by caregivers who are well informed about symptoms and illnesses that are serious, real, and medically significant, rather than by professionals who address women's illnesses as gynecological symptoms not based on scientific knowledge.

Women as Primary Clients of the
Private and Public Sectors

Today women are the primary customers of mental health service systems in the United States. Women select services for themselves and also for another increasing population of mental health service recipients, children and adolescents. Children and adolescents represent the fastest-growing segment of state-supported mental health service systems, in both numbers of clients and overall costs (Realmuto, Bernstein, Maglothin, & Pandey, 1992).

American children are likely to live with their mothers and to have varying degrees of involvement with their fathers. Approximately 50% of marriages in the United States currently end in divorce, and 85-90% of the children of divorce are placed in the custody of their mothers (Bray & Hetherington, 1993). Children of divorced parents are often subject to multiple changes, including conflict between their parents, the divorce itself, and their parents' remarriages, resulting in blended families. Such transitional lifestyles place these families at increased risk for problems with achievement, poor social relations, mental illness, and aggression (Bray & Hetherington, 1993). Therefore, these children and their mothers have an increased likelihood of seeking the assistance of specialty services. As her family's conservator, the divorced mother becomes the selector of products and services for her children. These youths are most often accompanied to mental health services by their mothers or by female social service providers acting on behalf of the parents.

This trend appears to place women squarely in the role of selectors of future services for a growing market segment. With the emphasis on freedom of choice of public and private providers, women make up the dominant market to be considered as programs are planned, developed, and maintained. The mental health services provided must be attractive and accessible to women, offered in settings and according to schedules that accommodate female users of services.

Issues Related to Women as Service Recipients

Women as Victims in an Age of Emphasis on Victimizers

In the late 1980s, the feminist movement was instrumental in identifying many forms of gender-based victimization (Courtois, 1991). Victimization has become the social and legal cry of the 1990s. It is common to hear the defense, "I did it, but I'm not responsible." This lack of responsibility may be attributed to the individual's helplessness under control by another or to the individual's fear of harm, real or imagined, resulting from previous abuse.

One kind of victimization is sexual harassment, which has become a battle cry of workers and the legal sector. As early as 1988, surveys indicated that 42% of all working women had experienced some unwanted and uninvited sexual attention that they considered to be sexual harassment. One only has to browse through a few newspapers or newsmagazines to realize that sexual harassment is a major occupational hazard in the workplace today.

A woman who is new to the workforce enters with the hopes of being successful, but often finds herself in an unfamiliar environment. As sexual harassment begins, she may believe that this is a normal workplace situation. Although she may see herself as a victim of male actions, she may believe this sort of male behavior is commonplace and is to be tolerated, a belief that accounts for the low numbers of women who challenge such behavior on a timely basis and the higher numbers who change jobs due to sexual harassment.

Sexual harassment lowers the victim's self-esteem. If a woman has a history of low self-esteem or mental illness, her ability to take action against harassment is reduced. She is likely to be angry, frustrated, depressed, and anxious. As her symptoms increase, she may lose her job or quit as a secondary result of the harassment. Unfortunately, she may leave the workplace with the idea that sexual harassment is a "fact of life" and may enter another abusive situation (Riger, 1991).

To break this cycle, women must know how to stop sexual harassment and how to prevent themselves and others from becoming subject to it. Such education must entail more than we have seen in the general mass-media efforts that have brought sexual harassment to the headlines. Education programs must address the attitudes learned early in life that can create an environment in which sexual harassment can occur. This is not to place blame on women for past harassment situations, but to teach women how to act so as to send the clear message that they will not be the victims of abusive behavior.

In combating sexual harassment, a cognitive-behavioral small group approach is useful; success is enhanced if the group is homogeneous in gender. Neither large group therapy settings nor psychodynamic approaches promote the open environment necessary to address effectively the personal nature of sexual harassment. A small group educational setting allows women to learn the skills they need to prevent sexual harassment and to practice these newly learned skills (Bray & Hetherington, 1993; Comer, 1992).

Women and the False Memory Controversy

Female victims of abuse constitute a growing mental health clientele. The courts are becoming a common place for families to recall the painful secrets of bygone years. The American criminal justice system is the appropriate place for victims to tell their stories and seek restitution for wrongs. In cases of sexual abuse memories, approximately 87-93% of survivors are women (Gold, Hughes, & Hohnecker, 1994).

When a decades-old case of alleged incest is brought to court, one must question whether restitution for the victim is the driving force of the litigation. Do such cases represent real attempts to get justice for real victims, or are they the products of creative therapists who have planted and/or cultivated "false memories" in women clients? It is certain that memories are not blueprints of the past, but rather stories of what the person believes happened after the passage of time. All memories are characterized by some distortions (Begley & Brant, 1994). The very fact that an individual remembers a given situation in great detail can be questioned. On a daily basis, American women are filing litigation against parents, other family members, and past caregivers, alleging sexual abuse. Often the abuse is not current and evidence is not present—the lawsuits are being filed based solely on the women's memories. In some cases the period between the alleged abuse and the filing of suit is 30 years or more.

Sexual abuse of children is never acceptable. Every victim should be allowed and encouraged to report such crimes; however, not every memory about the past is valid. Some reports of child abuse have been based not on memories but on false memories. False memories are all too often the result of powerful or even subtle suggestions introduced through questionable therapeutic techniques (Byrd, 1994).

Elizabeth Loftus (1993) considers the responsibility of the therapist to incest and other sexual abuse clients to be a moral one. She points out the importance of collecting empirical evidence relating to what appear to be abuse memories. To reduce the likelihood of therapists' contributing to the development of false memories, she recommends that they, first and foremost, listen objectively and not inject their biases or theories into clients' stories. The therapist must remember that the client is often a person in need of identity who, if she can support the theories of the therapist, will equate this with building comradeship.

The therapist must be very careful in developing therapeutic memory pictures for the client of the client's abusive situation. Through discussions of old environments and looking at pictures of her old neighborhood, combined with the biases of the therapist, the client may develop false memories that appear real to her. In fact, often these false memories are clearer and more detailed than other memories of the same period.

Loftus recommends not only that the therapist not identify with the client as related to the therapist's biases but that the therapist also avoid placing the client in group therapy or bibliotherapeutic situations. The development of false memories can be an unintentional product of women's desires to identify with other members of a group of abused women.

The phenomenon of the implantation of false memories has become so common that the term *retractor* has been coined to refer to women who have come to believe that they were sexually abused and have later realized they were subject to false memories (Loftus, 1994). Litigation has now turned from accused abusers toward the therapists considered responsible for the implanting of false memories and the pain and suffering caused by those therapists (Loftus, 1994).

Mentally Ill Women as a Subset of the Homeless Population

As the number of homeless persons increases, the percentage of women in that population increases disproportionally. The image of the homeless person has historically been male. Programs that were originally developed to assist the homeless were designed to help a male population. Today we find that the number of women and children joining the ranks of the homeless has become significant. To prevent the continuation of homelessness, social scientists must address the characteristics of homeless women.

The one thing that appears certain is that homeless women, like women in general, do not constitute a homogeneous group. However, there are some characteristics that may help identify women who are at risk of becoming homeless in the near future, as well as characteristics that appear to intensify the stresses that increase the duration of homelessness.

One major difference between homeless and domiciled women is the poorer health of the homeless. Homeless women have less access to appropriate health care than do other women. They are also subject to more serious illnesses and injuries than are homeless men. This higher incidence of health problems among homeless women is reflected in their greater likelihood, compared with other women, of having mental disorders or substance abuse problems (Levine & Rog, 1990). Although reports show a higher rate of serious mental illness in the homeless compared with the general population, actual counts are difficult to obtain. Research on the health of the homeless has been limited, and the literature refers most often to two homeless groups: men and families.

Mental illness can be the forerunner or the cause of many of the life stressors that result in an individual's becoming and remaining homeless. Women who are mentally ill have a difficult time acquiring and maintaining employment. A major difference between homeless men and women in the area of employment is that homeless women are more likely to have poor to no work history. Often they began families when very young. With the responsibility of child care, homeless women are generally unable to find employment (Milburn & D'Ercole, 1991).

When homeless women are able to get work, they are at high risk of such difficulties such as sexual harassment, demotion, layoff, and termination. The inability to gain and maintain employment becomes a factor in prolonged homelessness.

Homeless women's lives are characterized by hopelessness, with lack of housing compounded by unemployment, severely limited medical and mental health care, poverty, and responsibility for dependent children. Aside from the daily dangers they face, homeless women find themselves the victims of complex, interrelated problems. Many homeless women speak of having been subjected to physical abuse, both as adults and as children. In fact, the reason many give for having left a domicile is abuse by a family member. The history of mental health problems among these women also appears to be a precursor to homelessness. In mental health settings, homeless women often present as depressed individuals with histories of victimization by family, employers, and even the systems that are set up to assist the needy.

It is difficult for the social service system to define homeless women's needs and provide appropriate services because homeless women represent a complex problem. They are in urgent need of shelter, but shelter is only a beginning; for many homeless women, shelter may be a very low priority. Service providers must remember that these women have been told directly and indirectly by society that they are on the lowest rung of the social structure. They have been victimized by those who appear to be caregivers. They may often contact parents, other relatives, and friends, but they have no secure belief that these contacts will assist them in their plight (Shinn, Knickman, & Weitzman, 1991). Likely sick, both physically and mentally, homeless women often find the challenge of change too great a task for today and often are noncompliant with social service workers who try to aid them. Therefore, progress in assisting homeless women is often slow. Social service professionals must address a multitude of factors in relating to homeless women, while taking a simplified approach to the women themselves. Trying to address too many problems at once can reinforce homeless women's sense of helplessness and contribute negatively to the complexities of their physical and mental conditions (Milburn & D'Ercole, 1991).

Women as Service Providers

History of Women in the Field of Mental Health

Many readers may be tempted to avoid this section, thinking that this is the 1990s and things have changed. Although a review of women's place in the field of mental health may have been worthwhile a few years ago, they believe, things have changed and women are equal now—why belabor this subject one more time? Although it is true that the women's movement and equal opportunity laws have brought about many positive changes, problems still remain, and new voices advocate the slowing of progress.

The growing enforcement of laws designed to ensure equal opportunity has left in its wake people who believe they lost opportunities for advancement as women accelerated. These people are hurt, angry, and resentful of both equal opportunity legislation and the women who have shared in its benefits. One need only look at the extremes gone to by some all-male military prep schools to know there remains a powerful population of influential persons who do not believe in equality—especially in programs that have a long, proud history of male domination.

The field of mental health is one that has had a long, proud history of male domination. The image of the competent, progressive practitioner remains that of a bearded, pipe-smoking gentleman. Women have a rich history in the fields of social work and nursing; however, even in those fields the most influential jobs, with the highest salaries and final authority, have generally gone to men.

Throughout history, women have played a dominant role in the direct care of the sick, suffering, and afflicted. The field of mental health is no exception; however, as mental health services began to develop into a science, professional women were quietly refused entry into its higher levels. Historians have noted that the rise of modern science in Europe during the 17th and 18th centuries began the pattern of excluding women from scientific study, development of scientific colleagues, and receipt of the credentials needed to progress in science (Furumoto, 1992).

One example of this exclusion of women from the science of psychology is found in the life of psychologist Christine Ladd-Franklin (1847-1930), the American woman who developed the scientific theory of color vision. One cannot review Ladd-Franklin's educational experiences without concluding that she lived in a time when gender ruled who would receive both opportunities and recognition. Women's sphere was considered to be that of home and family responsibilities, whereas men were identified with the public realm and the responsibilities of fiscal support of the family.

Ladd-Franklin was the product of an era of change in the family and the professionalized sphere of science. Prior to the death of her mother, Augusta Ladd, when Christine was only 12 years old, she was reared in a home where women's rights and women's need for higher education were foremost. In a recent study of the lives of women scientists, Abir-Am and Outram (cited in Furumoto, 1992) found that a common factor among these women was a strong father-daughter relationship, in which the father demonstrated a zealous interest in his daughter's education and professional development. A second common thread among successful women scientists appears to be change in social stability during the women's developmental period. For Ladd-Franklin, this change in stability took the form of her mother's death, coupled with the beginning of the Civil War.

After graduating from Vassar, Ladd-Franklin taught in high school for nearly 10 years. In the fall of 1878, she gained entrance to the Johns Hopkins University. Though newly opened, Johns Hopkins followed the established standard of excluding or limiting the educational opportunities of women. The authorities feared that women on campus would become emotionally entangled with male students. And, just as they feared, Christine became involved with and married a fellow student, Fabian Franklin. In later life, she often attributed her success in science to the interest and encouragement of her husband (Furumoto, 1992).

Upon successful completion of 4 years of graduate work at Johns Hopkins, Ladd-Franklin was not allowed to receive any degree because of her gender. Such restrictions did not deter her, however. She continued her study of science and began to enter into cooperative relationships with European scientists. In spite of her society's prescribed role for women, Ladd-Franklin persisted with her scientific work and produced her theory of color vision. Her lifelong dedication to scientific psychology led her to confront openly such psychologists as John B. Watson, who supported Freudianism. She asserted that the renowned G. Stanley Hall had done grave damage to the field of psychology by supporting the concepts of Freud. Though she entered into many debates about the psychology of women, she was not allowed to pursue the field of psychology formally.

Even with her recognized scientific achievements, it was not until 1914 that Ladd-Franklin was offered an appointment to the faculty of Columbia University. The university was thought to be a progressive institution because it appointed a woman to teach, but it should be noted that Ladd-Franklin was not awarded any salary. Because she needed to affiliate with a university to gain status in her field, Ladd-Franklin lectured in a male-dominated world for no pay. Unfortunately, even with her Columbia University affiliation, Ladd-Franklin was not admitted to the elite ranks of experimental psychology because of her gender. Not until the Johns Hopkins University celebrated its 50th anniversary in 1926 did Ladd-Franklin receive her Ph.D., which she had actually earned in 1882.

More a product of her times than Ladd-Franklin, Elizabeth Ricord also made significant achievements in the field of psychology that went unnoticed. While administering the Geneva Female Seminary, she was the first woman to write a comprehensive textbook of psychology. She intended her writings to provide a unique opportunity for women to study psychology as presented by a woman. Throughout her textbook, she gave examples of misconceptions of female genius and classical scholarship. She described the differences of gender in such areas as scholarship to be akin to opportunity and the circumstances of women's lives. Ricord described young girls as being seen as the "tenderest objects of human affection" and thereby taught to seek what served to meet their own gratification.

Ricord strongly believed that women are as capable of intellectual work as men. Such beliefs caused her to find few supporters for her theories and writings. Though she is not well remembered in the history of psychology, it should be noted that Ricord wrote a text and taught women the value of their intellect, free from the consideration of gender, as early as 1840. History shows that Ricord was encouraged only to administer an all-girl school, and her text was never introduced to male-dominated academic institutions (Scarborough, 1992).

These are but two examples of women who dedicated their lives to the promotion of women in the human sciences. Certainly history has failed to record even the names of many early female scientists. Shut out of entry and promotion, women were to make little difference to the global scientific base of knowledge and services. Until the introduction and passage of federal legislation addressing the value and rights of people without regard to gender, women's contributions to science were severely limited.

Equal Opportunity Legislation and Its Effects
on the Professional Employment of Women

The Civil Rights Acts removed many of the barriers that had prevented the advancement of women in professional circles. For the first time, legislation stated that applicants must be considered for admission to educational institutions without regard to gender. The addition of women to these institutions served to introduce a wider perspective on human behavior.

The inclusion of women brought about marked changes in the field of psychology. For the first time, women spoke out individually and in groups regarding the misconceptions of the psychology of women and women as providers of mental health services. The teachings of Freud came under serious question. Even the concept that a competent professional therapist could be an individual, male or female, who did not meet the stereotype was being scrutinized.

Issues Related to Women as Service Providers

Women's Underrepresentation in Mental Health Administration

With the rise of awareness of gender bias in professional circles, behavioral scientists began to consider whether gender bias was playing a part in the paucity of females in the professional ranks of mental health services. Questions surfaced about the domination of the profession by white males. Teghtoonian (cited in Gannon, Luchetta, Rhodes, Pardie, & Segrist, 1992) found that women encountered discriminatory practices in graduate training, in hiring, and in the publication of their research.

Although a philosophy supporting equality of gender is now in place, practice remains in favor of males. The groups in control of hiring, selection of research subjects, and review of research to be published continue to be predominantly male. Therefore, the proliferation of male-oriented research and literature remains unchecked. Many male decision makers tend to be unaware of the gender bias and sexist language present in many reports of research found in the professional literature (Gannon et al., 1992).

The elimination of sexism is not a political issue, but rather a scientific goal. To deliver the most appropriate services, mental health professionals must be free of bias. Also, professionals providing care must have adequate understanding of their clientele. Gender-fair research reported in a gender-fair manner provides professionals with the basic information they need to make sound professional, clinical decisions (Gannon et al., 1992).

Women Who Enter the Field Late and Refuse to Pay Dues

As executives review résumés in hopes of acquiring the best and the brightest additions to their administrative ranks, they employ several criteria. The first is usually the individual's work history. Has the person had a full-time, continuous work history? Does the individual have a clear track of sequential positions that relate to his or her career development? Has the individual been in a position of responsibility in a similar population in a similar industry?

Such criteria often leave women's résumés sorted out of the favorable candidates for administrative positions. Women's work histories often reflect a tendency to accept jobs that do not meet their expectations in favor of such benefits as proximity to home, flexible hours, and little or no competition from peers. Even in the 1990s, it is rare for men to change careers to be closer to their families or because their wives have changed employers. On the other hand, many women applying for administrative positions will mention a family move related to a husband's job as the reason for seeking a new position. As family caregivers, women are also expected to tend to ill or aging family members, which also may cause them to relocate and seek new employment.

A second common cause of a break in women's employment is marriage and child rearing. Many professional women will relate that they made conscious decisions either to take the well-traveled road leading to marriage and family coupled with a lower-level job or to venture out on the path to development of a successful administrative career. Such decisions are usually less dramatic than realistic. The young executive is expected to be well educated prior to entering the job market. The first job is where dues are to be paid; the administrative hopeful must put work first and family second. The neophyte must be willing to work as many hours as the job demands and be able and willing to travel out of town on short notice. Such demands are restrictive, and they have slowed the career development of many women who are married and/or have children.

The business world has formally and informally announced that any woman who reaches the administrative level must be first and foremost a "business-person." In the 1970s, she was even told that to be successful in an administrative position she should wear business suits fashioned after menswear. She was never to speak of family or children in the business setting, although her male counterparts were encouraged to speak of their families and to adorn their desks with cozy family portraits.

Women who were determined to succeed in business often had to live two lives. The businesswoman had to put in long office hours and take on weekend projects, while the wife and mother tried to pick up the family chores by shifting daily duties to nighttime hours. Grocery stores and other retailers rapidly saw the changes in women's available shopping hours and began staying open later.

During the 1970s and 1980s, the trade literature was full of articles advising women on how to "do it all." The feminist movement encouraged women to "go for it all." The concept was that, with the right management skills, a woman could get an education, rear children, be a good community citizen, and be a successful businesswoman. Women tried, but all too often they found no fiscal and emotional support for the new "do it all" philosophy. Women began to become disenchanted.

Today, women are speaking of choices and are involving other family members in the responsibilities of home and family. However, primary responsibility for the family remains with the wife and mother. Interestingly, women do not tend to assist other women with chores. Except in rare cases, professional women do not share cooking, cleaning, shopping, or caring for children with other women in an effort to promote them as professionals.

As professional women have chosen to have family responsibilities, they have chosen to close the door to administrative roles. In the field of mental health this has been acceptable, because there are other professional roles for women who choose not to pay the price that goes with being in an administrative position. As a nurse, social worker, caseworker, case manager, classroom teacher, or midlevel supervisor, a woman can enter and vacate positions with few or no negative consequences, except that she marks herself with a work history that will restrict upward mobility in the future.

A woman who chooses to develop a job history that will be viewed positively by search committees learns that to be an executive, she is expected to be a man at work and a woman at home. She is advised to restrict her business social life, thereby demonstrating that she has rightfully earned her position and has not used sexual favors to promote her career. The catch is that these women have no opportunity to play golf or work out in the gym with the decision makers.

The work-related social life of the female mental health administrator remains difficult today. Female administrators generally do not have entrée into the informal social circles of their male counterparts. In offering informal invitations to lunch or after-hours activities, men tend to choose other men of similar age, race, and position. When questioned about why they avoid including women in these groups, men often respond that they assume the women would choose not to go. Trying to become "one of the boys" so as to be included usually just compounds the problem for female administrators. One strategy women may use to avoid being left out is to take the lead in setting up social occasions. This allows them to select places and activities that fit both males and females and that promote professional relations.

To make certain that she is given every opportunity to develop a positive career path, a woman must be willing to say with confidence that she wants a career and that she is willing to confront the problems she will inevitably encounter in trying to balance career and family. She must take control of her life and plan her future—she cannot trust her career to chance.

The costs and rewards of a management career can be sizable. Women who desire administrative roles must early on see themselves as professionals who will have long work lives. They must realize that every interruption in their careers may be evaluated as a negative when their work histories are compared with those of other candidates who have not had interruptions.

The system of opportunity in the field of mental health services is not free of gender bias; rather, it reflects the gender biases of the society at large. Only as the general society comes to see the value of a diverse workforce will women be allowed equal opportunities to take their position in the more responsible ranks of mental health services. The administration of mental health services reflects the society those services are designed to assist.

Professional Women's Failure to Mentor Other Women

If one observes the participants at a general mental health professional conference, one notes that the female participants outnumber the male. However, on closer inspection, it is clear that the women tend to be in the lower range of the profession, in both titles and salaries. The fact of this situation is not debatable; why it continues, however, is a pressing issue.

Changes in the laws in the 1970s established a foundation for real improvement in the fate of professional women. One issue that is relevant to the gender differences that remain is that professional women tend not to assist other women along the path to professionalism. Only when women attain positions of authority allowing them to make decisions regarding research and the publication of professional literature will they be able to facilitate meaningfully the professional growth of other women.

The advice given to anyone desiring to rise in an organization is to find a mentor. This can be very difficult for women. If a woman attempts to choose a male mentor, the many hours she must spend with that mentor can lead to social and personal conflicts or gossip. Female mentors, on the other hand, are often difficult to find. Women tend to have very poor track records in mentoring other women, for various reasons. Unfortunately, women administrators often must work so hard to achieve and retain their positions that they do not have the luxury of time and energy to assist other women. Further, when men promote women, they often select women who have not been victims of gender bias. If a woman in authority has not been subject to gender bias herself, she may have a difficult time identifying with those in the larger female group who have failed to achieve in part because of institutional sexism in our society. Such a woman may not realize the importance of helping other women to reach higher levels of professional success.

Women's Intuition: The Key to Rapid Diagnosis and Brief Therapy Issues

Psychotherapy is no longer a multisession, ongoing experience. The managed care movement of the 1990s has refocused therapy on rapid diagnosis with a minimum of corrective therapy, addressing only the most pressing problem. In this atmosphere, women's communication skills tend to place them in an advantageous position, both as therapists and as clients. Women tend to achieve intimate communication with other women much more rapidly than do men. Women tend to have communication skills that allow them to develop trusting relationships quickly, whereas men tend to be slower to develop relationships that involve either asking intimate questions or giving intimate information (Graham, 1992).

Women have what might be called a sixth sense, or women's intuition, a sense that men have educated themselves out of—this is the sense of first impressions. Women are taught early to be observant about details, including details about the people around them. Women tend to be detail oriented and therefore make excellent gatherers of information for diagnostic work. A "give me the details" attitude pays off in complex cases. It is not surprising that attorneys have begun incorporating the assistance of women social scientists in the jury selection stage of litigation. These social scientists examine the gestalt of the candidates, taking into account body language, tone of voice, speed of speech, dress, eye contact, body build, and other factors that may be so subtle they are hard even to describe verbally, whereas men tend to listen only to potential jurors' answers to direct questions.

Women are very good at interpreting their first impressions. This talent has increased value for female mental health professionals as brief therapy is replacing long-term therapy. No longer do mental health practitioners have the luxury of lengthy assessment and diagnosis after several sessions with a client. Rather, practitioners must be able to gather information quickly, make rapid decisions, and begin treatment. Quick achievement of client-therapist rapport is very important.

Conclusion

The issues discussed in this chapter are not exhaustive. Women are faced with many other issues in the area of mental health services that require further study and review. One of the implications that is becoming clear is that mental health professionals have a responsibility to be aware of the effects of gender on the mental health and social adjustment of individuals.

Mental health professionals must give special attention to how clients are similar and different based on gender. In recent years, changes in gender roles have been pronounced in the United States. It is the responsibility of professionals to be aware that these changes are real and that society is not characterized by stability. Therefore, today's changes are just that—they apply only to the present. Professionals must continue to be cognizant of the changes constantly taking place and must alter their services to the mentally ill to address those changes.

References

Begley, S., & Brant, M. (1994, September 26). You must remember this: How the brain forms "false memories." *Newsweek, 124,* 68-69.

Bray, J. H., & Hetherington, E. M. (1993). Families in transition: Introduction and overview. *Journal of Family Psychology, 7,* 3-8.

Byrd, K. R. (1994). The narrative reconstructions of incest survivors. *American Psychologist, 49,* 439-440.

Comer, D. R. (1992). Exploring gender-based differences to combat sexual harassment. *American Psychologist, 47,* 819.

Courtois, C. A. (1991). Theory, sequencing, and strategy in treating adult survivors. *New Directions for Mental Health Services, 51,* 47-60.

Dickstein, L. J., Stein, T. S., Pleck, J. H., Myers, M. F., Lewis, R. A., Duncan, S. F., & Brod, H. (1991). Men's changing social roles in the 1990s: Emerging issues in the psychiatric treatment of men. *Hospital and Community Psychiatry, 42,* 701-705.

Epstein, C. F. (1988). *Deceptive distinctions: Sex, gender and the social order.* New Haven, CT: Yale University Press.

Furumoto, L. (1992). Joining separate spheres: Christine Ladd-Franklin, woman-scientist (1847-1930). *American Psychologist, 47,* 175-181.

Gannon, L., Luchetta, T., Rhodes, K., Pardie, L., & Segrist, D. (1992). Sex bias in psychological research, progress or complacency? *American Psychologist, 47,* 389-396.

Gold, S. N., Hughes, D., & Hohnecker, L. (1994). Degrees of repression of sexual abuse memories. *American Psychologist, 49,* 441-442.

Graham, S. R. (1992). What does a man want? *American Psychologist, 47,* 837-841.

Levine, I. S., & Rog, D. (1990). Mental health services for homeless mentally ill persons: Federal initiatives and current service trends. *American Psychologist, 45,* 963-968.

Loftus, E. F. (1993). The reality of repressed memories. *American Psychologist, 48,* 518-537.

Loftus, E. F. (1994). The repressed memory controversy. *American Psychologist, 49,* 443-445.

Milburn, N., & D'Ercole, A. (1991). Homeless women. *American Psychologist, 46,* 1161-1169.

Realmuto, G. M., Bernstein, G. A., Maglothin, M. A., & Pandey, R. S. (1992). Patterns of utilization of outpatient mental health services by children and adolescents. *Hospital and Community Psychiatry, 43,* 1218-1223.

Riger, S. (1991). Gender dilemmas in sexual harassment policies and procedures. *American Psychologist, 46,* 497-505.

Riger, S. (1992). Epistemological debates, feminist voices. *American Psychologist, 47,* 730-740.

Scarborough, E. (1992). Mrs. Ricord and psychology for women, circa 1840. *American Psychologist, 47,* 274-280.

Shinn, M., Knickman, J. R., & Weitzman, B. C. (1991). Social relationships and vulnerability to becoming homeless among poor families. *American Psychologist, 46,* 1180-1187.

Spelman, E. V. (1988). *Inessential women: Problems of exclusion in feminist thought.* Boston: Beacon.

Yoder, J. D., & Kaha, A. S. (1993). Working toward an inclusive psychology of women. *American Psychologist, 48,* 846-850.

CHAPTER 16

Treatment of Children and Adolescents

Inpatient and Outpatient Mental Health Issues

CHRISTIAN E. MOLIDOR

The use of psychiatric hospitalization with children and adolescents has evolved dramatically over the past two decades. There has been steady movement from inpatient state hospitalization of children toward de-institutionalization, privatization, and the use of outpatient mental health services. Because of this rapid evolution and the lack of research literature, most clinicians lack clarity as to what is the most appropriate setting for the child or adolescent who needs immediate attention due to mental illness, out-of-control behavior, and/or substance abuse problems. In this chapter, I review the history of psychiatric hospitalization of children and adolescents; describe some aspects of inpatient care, such as the unique milieu and various treatment approaches; and finally examine some of the effects of privatization and the use of outpatient mental health services.

History

The practices of the modern private psychiatric hospital began to develop in the latter part of the 18th century, as Pinel introduced the notion of moral treatment. William Webb (1988) describes the time prior to moral treatment:

> The mentally ill were regarded as beasts and, therefore, insensitive to their surroundings. They were subject to a variety of abusive treatments designed to drive out the toxic influences thought to be responsible for the animal-like behavior. . . . Moral treatment took an entirely different approach, operating from a humanistic and religious position. The treatment emphasized kindness and the conception that the mentally ill continued to have internal resources that, if encouraged, would restore them to mental health. (p. 3)

One pioneer of child and adolescent psychiatric hospitalization was Dr. William Healy, who, while working for the Illinois Juvenile Court in the early 1900s, began an exploratory study of adolescent juvenile offenders. Historically, the hospitalization of children and adolescents evolved more as a mechanism to detain juvenile delinquents than as a treatment approach to emotional disorders. Applying some of the contemporary thought of the growing psychiatric research, Healy began to individualize the treatment of juvenile offenders rather than simply "holding" them in detention. By 1917, Healy's state-supported Institute for Juvenile Research expanded the project to include a broader range of children and adolescents, such as emotionally disturbed children, whether they were delinquent or not (Kadushin, 1974).

The domain of child psychiatry was largely influenced by the psychoanalytic school of thought. For the first time, the strong effects of childhood experiences on adolescent and adult mental health were becoming a major focus. During the early 1920s, Melanie Klein, who greatly influenced the development of child psychiatry, pioneered the use of play therapy with children in a way that was similar to the use of free association with adults. She saw the child's play as a symbolic representation of unconscious content and interpreted it as such directly to the child (McCausland, 1985).

Psychoanalysis, however, was not the only influence on the development of child psychiatry. Jean Piaget, a Swiss psychologist, studied the development of the child's perceptual and sensorimotor systems, whereas the behaviorists Pavlov, Watson, and Skinner contributed the ideas of stimulus-response, which have been used to modify troubled behavior in children and adolescents (McCausland, 1985). An extensive strategy developed to individualize and treat children with mental health problems. This new comprehensive approach focused on four specific areas: (a) a medical examination to inspect the child's physical assets and abilities, (b) psychological tests, (c) psychiatric interviews to determine the child's attitudes and the character of his or her mental life, and (d) a study of the child's developmental history and social situation (Ackerman, 1966). Thus an ecological approach grew, and is used still today, that examines not only the physical and psychological components of development but also the vital interaction between family members and the child. Finally, assessments have been expanded to include social and environmental components as causative factors in children's agitated and out-of-control behavior.

Elements of Treatment Approaches

Whereas the average length of stay of a child in a psychiatric hospital in 1980 was 90 to 120 days, it is rare today to have a child hospitalized for more than 10 days to 2 weeks. The movement toward shorter stays has affected every area in the treatment of hospitalized children and adolescents. In the psychiatric treatment of children and adolescents, the emphasis should be on helping patients learn the life skills essential for successful functioning in their homes, schools, and communities. The rules, behavior expectancies, and discipline of the hospital must be consistent with those of a reasonable and fair home environment as well as the school system from which the patient comes in order to achieve a transfer of learning from the intense preparation of the hospital to the outside world. The hospital setting uses a multidisciplinary approach to treatment. In the following pages, I present an examination of the most common treatment modalities employed within the psychiatric hospital setting.

Milieu Therapy

The major role in the progress and improvement of mental health of the child or adolescent in the psychiatric hospital is played by the unique 24-hour milieu of the unit. The milieu model views the hospital environment as a therapeutic tool in its own right. Extensive research evidence confirms the significant impacts, both positive and negative, of milieu therapy upon the patient's recovery. In his groundbreaking study of the therapeutic power of the milieu on patients, Jones (1953) notes that patients are much more likely to adapt and heal when they begin taking active responsibility not only for their own individual treatment but also for that of others. With this concept, Jones developed the community meeting, which is a therapeutic tool used today in almost every psychiatric hospital setting. Here patients begin to take owner-ship of their treatment by working in a democratic collaboration, as equals, with each other in arriving at decisions that affect the patients on the unit.

In a major work addressing what actually transpires in the therapeutic milieu, Adler (1988) outlines several specific functions of milieu therapy: safety and control, structure, social reintegration, support, confrontation, problem solving, and education.

Safety and Control

It is crucial that the milieu provide a safe and controlled environment for child and adolescent patients. Developmentally, the healthy adolescent is already coping with the normal apprehensions surrounding physical changes, social changes, and changes in family roles (Lewis, 1989). The hospitalized child or adolescent is experiencing an acute state of excitement and fear. The stigma of being treated in a psychiatric hospital remains even today, and newly hospitalized children often feel that they have just entered the "loony bin," the "crazy house," or the "psych ward."

The connotation is such that patients often expect to experience violence, aggression, and craziness. These patients will begin to discuss their painful issues only after they feel safe, both physically and emotionally. To allow patients to achieve those feelings of safety and comfort, the hospital must set up specific rules and clear expectations that must be followed on the unit. Explicit and meaningful sanctions against violence or threats of violence must be enforced immediately when adverse situations occur so that the patients know from the beginning that the staff are in control of the environment and are not afraid to address extreme issues.

Structure

Most often the child or adolescent will arrive at the hospital immediately after a crisis; however, the child's out-of-control behavior has usually developed gradually and is not the result of any single incident. This behavior, no matter how it is physically displayed, indicates an internal disorganization. Although adolescents often show signs of extreme confidence and bravado upon entering the unit, they will later admit that when they first arrived, they were feeling lost, confused, and scared. These patients frequently have been reared in chaotic environments where they have not known what to expect from one moment to the next.

Setting up the milieu so that it has a consistent and effective structure allows the children and adolescents to focus on the specific nature of their problems rather than on the generalized anxiety they feel when they experience internal disorganization. Time must be structured, routines developed, activities organized, and rules of behavior identified and backed up by consequences, with rewards given for good behavior and penalties imposed for inappropriate, rule-breaking behavior. The patient's time is thoroughly and consistently scheduled. Participation in activities should be mandatory, and therapeutic activities should be scheduled well in advance so that the patient knows exactly what to expect on a consistent basis.

Social Reintegration

A major role of the treatment milieu is the reintegration of the child or adolescent into family, school, and community settings. Quite often, the patient has damaged or shattered his or her relationships to one or more of those systems and does not have the cognitive or emotional ability to repair those relationships. Here the staff and patients can work to help the adolescent reconnect and rebuild new and stronger relationships with support systems on the outside.

Support

An influential tool in increasing each child's sense of well-being and self-esteem is the therapeutic use of support. Children and adolescents will flourish when given praise and admiration. Before esteem can develop internally, the child or adolescent has to experience it externally. By consistently experiencing positive responses for positive behaviors, patients begin to internalize that feedback and ultimately experience feelings of confidence and self-worth.

Confrontation

It is a matter of some controversy whether the milieu should be the locus for confrontation of patient issues. Some clinicians feel that this process should be saved for individual or group therapy. They fear that confrontation will only make patients feel worse about themselves and hinder their progress; however, the milieu often affords unique opportunities for the use of therapeutic confrontation.

There are two levels of confrontation that go on continuously and simultaneously in a therapeutic milieu: that of the individual and that of the group. The former focuses upon the individual's ability or inability to confront, challenge, and explore painful issues or unhealthy coping behaviors. The latter deals with the child's or adolescent's need to learn the skill of confrontation, to be able to confront and resist negative behaviors with his or her peer group or family. Although this skill can be extremely difficult and often frightening to learn, it is critical that the child or adolescent master it. Understanding and mastering the ability to confront negative peers or unhealthy behaviors indicates that the child or adolescent has developed an inner confidence that will then assist him or her in difficult situations.

Problem Solving

Most child and adolescent patients have lost or never developed confidence in their ability to solve problems, particularly their own. One of the most important tasks of the milieu is to restore patients' faith in their own ability to overcome difficulties through striving to find solutions. By allowing the children and adolescents to have some ownership of their treatment through community meetings and interactions with the staff, the milieu consistently encourages patients to develop healthy social skills and problem-solving skills—skills they can learn while in the hospital and will use after their discharge.

Education

A common theme among hospitalized children and adolescents is their experience of the school system. Most child and adolescent patients are well behind in their schoolwork, are several grade levels behind their age group, or have simply dropped out of school. The experience of getting further and further behind sets up a hopeless scenario for students. Most of them have been labeled troublemakers, and their experiences in school often include being isolated, made fun of, beaten, ignored, or kicked out. The core experience is one of failure.

Each hospital program has its own school program. The individual attention and consistent structure of the hospital school setting helps children and adolescents in many ways. For the first time, many of them experience school as a place where they can learn and succeed. The work is set up at their level of learning and, because of the individual attention, progress is often accelerated, so that the patients have caught up to their peer group upon discharge. The connection between the hospital and the home school can be a powerful tool toward reintegration. The children are given a chance to begin anew with their schools on schedule with their peers, with hope.

Short-Term Intervention

With the move toward a short-term crisis intervention model of child and adolescent hospitalization, milieu therapy loses much of its strength in the contribution to treatment of children and adolescents. The positive effects of milieu therapy are not immediate; they come only with time. It is unrealistic to expect that an out-of-control child or adolescent will immediately begin to trust and open up to adults. A consistent environment of support, structure, therapeutic confrontation, and care must be in place for the child or adolescent to develop a trusting relationship with doctors, social workers, clinical specialists, and peers. Fortunately, many of the techniques of milieu therapy that have been developed in hospital settings have been successfully adapted to other treatment settings, such as partial hospitalization, residential settings, and psychosocial day programs (Adler, 1988).

Insight-Oriented Therapies

Within the hospital setting, various forms of insight-oriented therapy occur on a daily basis. Individual psychodynamic therapy, group therapy, and family therapy all become a normal part of the child's or adolescent's treatment. The attending psychiatrist most often employs a psychodynamic approach in dealing with patients. The results of psychodynamic therapy come only after a great deal of time and work, as the repressed and unconscious material gradually integrates with the total structure of the personality. The more immediately beneficial treatment results (e.g., improved social skills, increased communication of feelings, less negative acting out) often are seen by the treatment staff who run the groups and the social workers who conduct family therapy.

The insight-oriented group therapy approach can provide a very rewarding and enriching experience to the troubled child or adolescent. Behavior is viewed as a symptom, and the insight-oriented group presumes some deeper conflict. The significance of the underlying issues or conflicts the children or adolescents are experiencing becomes the focus of the group, rather than the specific behaviors. By examining the core conflicts, the patients begin to realize that they are not the only ones having these extreme feelings of failure, worthlessness, and hopelessness. After skillful group development by the therapist, a peer culture of support, therapeutic confrontation, and sharing becomes the norm, and the role of the therapist becomes much less authoritative as the group begins to run itself.

One of the many vital tasks of the mental health professional in the hospital is to conduct family therapy groups. This is very difficult in the beginning because of the extreme conflict occurring between the child and his or her parents upon the child's hospitalization. The scope of issues the professional has to work with, and be adept at, is exceedingly complex and diverse. Issues ranging from child physical and sexual abuse, drug and alcohol use, severe depression, attempted suicide, expulsion from school, and gang violence to legal matters will be covered. To make some sense out of all these diverse issues, the mental health professional must first accept the proposition that a close interrelationship exists between the psychosocial functioning of the family as a group and the emotional adaptation of each of its separate members.

One major approach taken by family therapists in examining the relationship between the family and its social context has been the use of the ecological model (Longres, 1990). Many professionals currently use an ecological approach, which locates family problems in the stresses caused by the interaction between the family and connecting systems (i.e., groups, organizations, and institutions that make up the family's environment). By using this approach, the professional can help the parents and child identify specific problem areas and begin intervention in these areas. The mental health professional will be able to resolve or reduce the conflict and distress within the pattern of interpersonal relationships, identify and teach family members how to increase the fulfillment of one another's emotional needs, promote more appropriate role relations, and strengthen the potential of the individual and family as a whole to deal with detrimental issues from within the family and from the surrounding environment.

Privatization

The trend toward for-profit ownership of hospitals, with its emphasis on the business aspects of health care, has had a tremendous influence on the development of psychiatric hospital services. This privatization of psychiatric care has greatly affected issues ranging from treatment modality, staffing patterns, and length of stay to the increased involvement of insurance payers in the treatment/discharge planning of the patient. The privatization of psychiatric hospitalization has also been the single most forceful explanation for the dramatic increase in numbers of hospitalized children and adolescents. Private psychiatric hospitals have aggressively marketed their inpatient services for children and adolescents as they have discovered the availability of reimbursements by third-party health care providers (Mason & Gibbs, 1992). This aggressive competition among hospitals has fostered, in several areas, unethical behavior on the part of mental health professionals (Brock, 1992; Mason & Gibbs, 1992). Some of these unethical practices include extended lengths of stay (Schroeder, 1992), deliberate misdiagnosis (Kirk & Kutchins, 1988), and signing off, a practice in which a psychiatrist or psychologist signs an insurance claim even though the services were provided by a social worker, in order to maximize reimbursement (Karger & Stoesz, 1994). Signing off has become prevalent because many insurance policies cover only services provided by psychiatrists or psychologists, or will reimburse at higher rates when the services are rendered by psychiatrists or psychologists than when they are provided by social workers.

During the 1970s and 1980s, clinical social workers, family counselors, psychologists, and other mental health care professionals became more active in the rapidly growing movement toward hospitalization of children and adolescents with diagnosed mental disorders and/or problems with substance abuse. Inpatient psychiatric admissions for children under 18 years old increased more than 450% between 1980 and 1984 (Brock, 1992). These figures, however, actually depict two contrasting trends in the hospitalization of youths under the age of 18: the rapid growth of private, for-profit hospital admissions and the steady decrease in hospitalization of children and adolescents in state and county mental hospitals.

The number of private, or nongovernmentally funded, psychiatric hospitals in the United States increased dramatically between 1970 and 1988, from 947 to 1,928. The number of available beds in these hospitals expanded from 36,689 in 1970 to 76,201 in 1988 (Manderscheid & Sonnenschein, 1992). Total revenues reported by private nonfederal psychiatric hospitals in 1986 alone were more than $5 billion. Children and adolescents accounted for a high percentage of total admissions to private psychiatric hospitals and were significantly more likely to be hospitalized in private for-profit hospitals than in state-run programs. In 1986, children and adolescents accounted for more than 36% of total admissions in private psychiatric hospitals, compared with only 16% in government-funded state hospitals. Children under the age of 18 were the second most frequently admitted group in private psychiatric hospitals. In addition, children and adolescents had longer stays than any other age group, with a median stay of 41 days in private psychiatric hospitals, compared with 21 days for other age groups (Manderscheid & Sonnenschein, 1992).

Although the 1970s and 1980s saw rapid growth in the business of for-profit psychiatric hospitalization of children and adolescents, state and county mental hospitals declined in number, from 310 in 1970 to 285 in 1988. The number of beds available in public hospitals dramatically decreased, from 413,006 in 1970 to 119,066 in 1988. The reduction is attributed to the reduced size of hospitals, rather than to their closing. The number of inpatients admitted to state mental hospitals fell steadily between 1969 and 1988. This number has decreased every year since 1955, the year that marks the beginning of the deinstitutionalization movement in the United States (Manderscheid & Sonnenschein, 1992).

Recent exposure of unethical behavior on the part of private hospital clinicians and administrators across the nation has fueled the long-running debate over the need for hospitalization of children and adolescents. Patricia Schroeder (1992), chairwoman of the Senate Committee on Children, Youth, and Families, opened a recent report with these remarks:

> What we're talking about today is the disturbing practice in mental health care that is taking place from coast to coast. Our investigative team found that thousands of adolescents and children have been hospitalized for psychiatric care that they really didn't need. They found hospitals that hired bounty hunters to almost kidnap patients who were then kept against their will until their benefits ran out. Often psychiatrists are pressured by hospitals to alter diagnoses to increase their profit. Hospitals would go into schools and initiate kickbacks to counselors who could find students that had mental health insurance and would then be put into that hospital. Bonuses were even paid to employees if they could keep the beds filled. (p. 1)

In addition to concerns of unethical behavior, insurance payers challenge the medical necessity of each patient's hospitalization, as a result of rapidly escalating health care costs, and review continued hospital need on a daily basis. These payers cite the well-documented negative consequences of lengthy psychiatric hospitalizations, which include difficulty in reentry to community roles, institutional dependence, atrophy of skills, and internalization of the patient role (Gove & Lubach, 1969; Hoffmann & Mastrianni, 1992; Rosenhan, 1973). However, this documentation refers to difficulties of extended hospitalization with adult patients. There have been no studies focused on the effects of long-term hospital stays on children or adolescents. Brock (1992) recently outlined several of the major problems with hospitalization of adolescents as shared by third-party payers:

- Psychiatric costs continue to rise, but care is frequently of inferior quality and is not cost-effective. Yet inpatient admissions for children under the age of 18 increased approximately 450% between 1980 and 1984.
- Age-appropriate school functioning, with an emphasis on necessary remediation and adaptive school skills, is frequently underemphasized.

- Psychiatric diagnosis and treatment are often characterized by vagueness, inconsistency among providers, lack of definitive effectiveness, and multiple treatment options and levels of treatment.
- The readmission rate for adolescents hospitalized for psychiatric treatment is very high. According to national statistics, there is a 55% likelihood that a second psychiatric admission will occur within 12 months of a first.
- There are problems in the availability and accountability of adequate aftercare programs for adolescents discharged from the hospital.
- Psychiatric care continues to be constrained by the stigma associated with mental illness, especially for children and adolescents.

Hospital clinicians argue that, because of lack of funding, they are having to discharge patients who are at a delicate crossroads in their illnesses, the results of which will be high societal, monetary, and human costs later. The out-of-control behavior of hospitalized children and adolescents, they stress, stems from complex internal struggles that took a great deal of time to develop and, therefore, will take time to change and improve. This is best accomplished in a highly structured environment where these patients are compelled to examine their lives, both internally and externally.

The major treatment implication surrounding the issue of for-profit versus not-for-profit hospitalization is length of stay. The movement toward short stays (3-14 days) has shifted the treatment modality from a long-term psychodynamic model toward short-term crisis intervention hospitalization. After the immediate crisis has been dealt with, the patient is released to the care of community mental health centers, which were launched, in large part, to reduce the damaging effects of hospitalization by providing mental health support services in a more normal environment (Hoffmann & Mastrianni, 1992).

The issues of relationship building, trust, safety, control, family relationships, and social relationships are all anticipated to be worked on during outpatient therapy rather than in the structured environment of the hospital. The multiple roles of the milieu staff and social workers change most drastically as they attempt to keep their priority of a safe environment through the "revolving-door model." Mental health professionals become overwhelmed at the task of completing comprehensive individual and family assessments and searching for appropriate placements for the many children and adolescents who are unable to return home due to the severity of their problems. The primary work of the family therapist becomes less possible when the social worker sees the family only two or three times.

The atmosphere of an adolescent mental health care unit in a short-term hospital is completely different from that for a long-term stay. During a long-term stay, the adolescent usually spends the first 10 to 14 days working on issues of anger and feelings of resentment stemming from his or her placement in a hospital. Development of a positive peer culture is one of the most beneficial qualities of a long-term stay in the hospital setting in getting adolescent clients to begin examining their issues. The relationships and trust that are built in peer groups are often stronger than those developed with the staff. However, if patients are coming and going on a 1- to 2-week basis, the peer culture of the unit is more often negative and angry, and the work of helping the patients falls completely to the staff.

Conclusion

The history of child and adolescent hospitalization reflects an evolution that continues today with the struggle of long-term programs to adapt and change into more short-term crisis intervention programs. This change has many implications for the treatment of the child or adolescent while hospitalized. Minimal qualitative or quantitative research has been conducted on the optimal length of stay for the hospitalized adolescent. Rather, policies are being developed by third-party payers in reaction to the spiraling costs of hospitalization and the recent exposure of unethical practices by hospitals across the nation. Financial and economic considerations may encourage for-profit practitioners to employ unethical or controversial practices. "Other practitioners are obliged to report allegations of violations to the state licensing board or the professional association. Ultimately, it is in the interest of the professional community, as well as the client, to address questionable practices of practitioners" (Karger & Stoesz, 1994, p. 172). Unfortunately, this situation is perplexing for families, because they do not know which psychiatric facilities (the vast majority) are ethical, caring treatment centers and which are not.

Both long- and short-term hospital stays should be available, and decisions should be made between them based on which is most appropriate for a particular client's situation. Many children and adolescents need only crisis intervention to help them become reconnected to their families, schools, and communities. Other children and teenagers, however, need the longer-term care of a nurturing, structured, therapeutically confrontational, and supportive environment. Unfortunately, the unethical behavior of some is now being paid for in the suffering of children and adolescents who need longer-term stays.

All children and adolescents, on long- or short-term units, will need some form of care after they have been discharged from the hospital unit. Deliberate reintegration of the patient into family, school, and community is a critical component of any hospitalization plan. Careful awareness of termination issues with the child or adolescent upon discharge will help to make reintegration into the family or residential setting more successful.

References

Ackerman, N. (1966). *Treating the troubled family*. New York: Basic Books.
Adler, W. N. (1988). Milieu therapy. In J. R. Lion, W. N. Adler, & W. L. Webb (Eds.), *Modern hospital psychiatry* (pp. 109-128). New York: W. W. Norton.

Brock, T. F. (1992). A model adolescent hospital-based program. In G. W. Lawson & A. W. Lawson (Eds.), *Adolescent substance abuse: Etiology, treatment, and prevention* (pp. 105-119). Gaithersburg, MD: Aspen.

Gove, W., & Lubach, J. (1969). An intensive treatment program for psychiatric patients. *Journal of Health and Social Behavior, 10,* 225-235.

Hoffmann, F. L., & Mastrianni, X. (1992). The hospitalized young adult: New directions for psychiatric treatment. *American Journal of Orthopsychiatry, 62,* 297-302.

Jones, M. (1953). *The therapeutic community.* New York: Basic Books.

Kadushin, A. (1974). *Child welfare services.* New York: Macmillan.

Karger, H. J., & Stoesz, D. (1994). *American social welfare policy: A pluralist approach.* New York: Longman.

Kirk, S. A., & Kutchins, H. (1988). Deliberate misdiagnosis in mental health practice. *Social Service Review, 62,* 225-237.

Lewis, M. (1989). Historical, developmental, and societal perspectives on adolescence. In L. K. G. Hsu & M. Hersen (Eds.), *Recent developments in adolescent psychiatry* (pp. 3-12). New York: John Wiley.

Longres, J. F. (1990). *Human behavior in the social environment.* Itasca, IL: F. E. Peacock.

Manderscheid, R. W., & Sonnenschein, M. A. (Eds.). (1992). *Mental health, United States, 1992* (CDHHS Publication No. SMA-92-1942). Washington, DC: Government Printing Office.

Mason, M. A., & Gibbs, J. T. (1992). Patterns of adolescent psychiatric hospitalization: Implications for social policy. *American Journal of Orthopsychiatry, 62,* 447-457.

McCausland, M. P. (1985). Child and adolescent disorders. In A. Burges (Ed.), *Psychiatric nursing in the hospital and the community* (pp. 497-520). Englewood Cliffs, NJ: Prentice Hall.

Rosenhan, B. S. (1973). On being sane in insane places. *Science, 179,* 250-258.

Schroeder, P. (1992). *The profits of misery: How inpatient psychiatric treatment bilks the system and betrays our trust* (Report presented at a hearing before the Select Committee on Children, Youth, and Families, U.S. House of Representatives, 102nd Cong., 2nd Sess.). Washington, DC: Government Printing Office.

Webb, W. L. (1988). The private psychiatric hospital. In J. R. Lion, W. N. Adler, & W. L. Webb (Eds.), *Modern hospital psychiatry* (pp. 3-21). New York: W. W. Norton.

CHAPTER 17

Mental Health Services to Older Adults

JOHN S. MCNEIL

ROBERT L. CANON

In 1900, life expectancy at birth in the United States was age 47; in 1990, life expectancy at birth for males exceeded age 70, and for females it was almost 80 years (U.S. Department of Commerce, 1993). The fastest-growing segment of the U.S. population is made up of individuals 65 years of age and older. Growth in this age group was quite moderate during the first half of the 20th century, averaging less than a 0.5% increase until World War II. The growth in the proportion of the U.S. population over age 65 is now expected to exceed 1% in each decade preceding 2050 except one. Significant increases are also evident relative to larger cohorts within age categories as the elderly population grows older. People are living longer, as reflected by the greater numbers of persons 75 to 84 years of age and the numbers 85 years of age and older. In fact, the fastest-growing segment of older persons is those aged 85 and over. By the year 2000, almost 5 million Americans will be 85 and older. They will account for 1.8% of the population, a proportion projected to increase to 5.2% by the year 2050 (see Table 17.1). In 1985, approximately 25,000 persons in the United States were 100 years of age or older; by the year 2000, there will be more than 100,000 centenarians.

Increased longevity is a desirable social goal, but it does bring to the fore a number of issues with which society must wrestle. For example, if society is roughly proportioned into three groups—dependent children, working adults, and retired older adults—it appears that the members of one group (the

Table 17.1 Actual and Projected Growth of the Older U.S. Population, 1900–2050 (in thousands)

Year	Total Population, All Ages	55 to 64 Years No.	55 to 64 Years %	65 to 74 Years No.	65 to 74 Years %	75 to 84 Years No.	75 to 84 Years %	85 Years and Older No.	85 Years and Older %	65 Years and Older No.	65 Years and Older %
1900–1909	76,303	4,009	5.3	2,189	2.9	772	1.0	123	0.2	3,084	4.0
1910–1919	91,972	5,054	5.5	2,793	3.0	989	1.1	167	0.2	3,950	4.3
1920–1929	105,711	6,532	6.2	3,464	3.3	1,259	1.2	210	0.2	4,933	4.7
1930–1939	122,775	8,397	6.8	4,721	3.8	1,641	1.3	272	0.2	6,634	5.4
1940–1949	131,669	10,572	8.0	6,375	4.8	2,278	1.7	365	0.3	9,019	6.8
1950–1959	150,967	13,295	8.8	8,415	5.6	3,278	2.2	577	0.4	12,270	8.1
1960–1969	179,323	15,572	8.7	10,997	6.1	4,633	2.6	929	0.5	16,560	9.2
1970–1979	203,302	18,608	9.2	12,447	6.1	6,124	3.0	1,409	0.7	19,980	9.8
1980–1989	226,505	21,700	9.6	15,578	6.9	7,727	3.4	2,240	1.0	25,544	11.3
1990–1999	249,657	21,051	8.4	18,035	7.2	10,349	4.1	3,313	1.3	31,697	12.7
2000–2009	267,955	23,767	8.9	17,677	6.6	12,318	4.6	4,926	1.8	34,921	13.0
2010–2019	283,238	34,848	12.3	20,318	7.2	12,326	4.4	6,551	2.3	39,195	13.8
2020–2029	296,597	40,298	13.6	29,855	10.1	14,486	4.9	7,081	2.4	51,422	17.3
2030–2039	304,807	34,025	11.2	34,535	11.3	21,434	7.0	8,612	2.8	64,581	21.2
2040–2049	308,559	34,717	11.3	29,272	9.5	24,882	8.1	12,834	4.2	66,988	21.7
2050–2059	309,488	37,327	12.1	30,114	9.7	21,263	6.9	16,034	5.2	67,411	21.8

SOURCE: From Schick, F. L. (Ed.). (n.d.). *Statistical Handbook on Aging Americans*. Phoenix, AZ: Oryx Press. Reproduced with permission.

working) are the source of support for those in the other two. The two dependent groups must then compete for the limited resources produced by the working group. This struggle has already begun.

As people age, they are afflicted by more chronic degenerative disorders, such as arteriosclerosis, cerebrovascular accidents, and arthritis. These conditions are expensive to treat, and they also take a toll on the emotional well-being of the affected individuals and their significant others. Depression, paranoia, and dementias are mental health conditions that have high prevalence rates among the elderly. In this chapter we address these conditions as well as some of the other issues that affect mental health policy as it relates to older adults.

Depression

Depression is the most frequently diagnosed mental disorder in the older adult population. Prevalence rates vary from about 15% to 25%, with women tending to report depression symptoms more often than men. Blazer, Hughes, and George (1987) surveyed 1,300 community-dwelling older adults, aged 60 and over, who resided in both urban and rural areas and found that 27% presented depressive symptoms. The largest group (19%), however, reported experiencing only mild symptoms of dysphoria. In contrast, data from an epidemiological survey of five communities reported a significantly lower prevalence rate of 2.8% in a sample of 1,351 community-dwelling persons 60 years of age and over. Much of the discrepancy in findings can be explained by the more stringent definition of depression that was used in the latter study. This difference in findings illustrates the necessity of distinguishing between major depression and minor depression. More severely depressed individuals are more at risk for suicide, and the symptomatology may complicate accurate assessment of other medical conditions commonly found in older populations.

The rate of suicide among elderly people (i.e., persons 65 and older) is higher than for any other age cohort. Stillon, McDowell, and May (1989, p. 165) make four observations regarding the incidence of suicide in the older adult population:

1. The elderly are overrepresented among those persons who commit suicide. They constitute about 11% of the population, but they account for 17% of the suicides.

2. The suicide attempt/completion ratio is higher for the elderly than for other groups. Among the general population, the attempt/completion ratio is estimated to be between 8:1 and 15:1, whereas for persons 65 and over it is 4:1.

3. The ratio of male to female suicides is greater in the elderly population—5:1 versus 3:1 in the total population.

4. The suicide rate among elderly persons is more underreported than in the general population.

White males are more likely to commit suicide than are members of any other group, and there is a positive correlation between age and suicide rate among white males. The suicide rate for the general population is estimated to be 12.8 per 100,000 persons (McIntosh, 1991), whereas for white males at age 60 it is approximately 25 per 100,000; at age 70 the rate is about 32 per 100,000; at age 80 this increases to approximately 44 per 100,000 (Blazer, 1989).

The fact that males are more likely to commit suicide means that there are greater numbers of grieving and/or depressed elderly widows than there are depressed males. Women are affected in another manner, in that caregivers are predominantly female. Typically, persons over age 65 have one or more chronic health conditions that may cause minimal or major degrees of impairment. When these impairments are coupled with depression, the stress on caregivers is magnified and they themselves are at risk for succumbing to caregiver burden.

Depression, therefore, is not a condition isolated to the elderly sufferer; rather, it affects the individual, his or her significant others, and society. Although a reversible disorder, depression is often overlooked during the assessment process, for a variety of reasons. The clinician may not be knowledgeable about the indicators of depression in the elderly person. Some clinicians may believe that depression in the elderly is "normal." Even when they recognize depression, some clinicians may not be sufficiently aware of the positive results that can be derived from appropriate treatment. Positive responses have been found with the use of antidepressive medication and cognitive-behavioral psychotherapy. Electroconvulsive therapy has also proven to be effective with elderly patients who have not responded to other therapies.

Paranoid Disorders and Schizophrenia

Paranoid disorders are relatively rare among older adults, with estimates ranging between 1% and 3% among community-dwelling samples (Post, 1980). Among older persons seeking professional psychiatric help, suspiciousness, persecutory ideation, and paranoid delusions are frequently presented symptoms (Christison, Christison, & Blazer, 1989). Paranoid disorders account for approximately 10% of all psychiatric impatient admissions of the elderly (Edinberg, 1985). Older adults with paranoid symptoms are rarely seen in mental health facilities because they may be too paranoid to believe there is anything wrong with them. A morbid fear of many older persons is that they will be considered "crazy," so they avoid mental health professionals.

Schizophrenia and paranoid disorders are often spoken of in concert, as if they are identical conditions. Persons with schizophrenia may present with paranoid ideation, but paranoid persons may not have the disintegration of personality seen in persons with schizophrenia. Late-life schizophrenia is discussed in the literature; however, *DSM-IV* stipulates that for any diagnosis of schizophrenia, onset must occur before the age of 46 (American Psychiatric Association, 1994).

Some writers have made efforts to eliminate this confusion by delineating types of paranoid reactions in the elderly. Post (1980) suggests three categories: simple paranoid psychosis, schizophrenia-like illness, and paranoid schizophrenia states. Simple paranoid psychosis is characterized by a few delusional beliefs, experiences, and hallucinations. Persons with this psychosis seldom come to the attention of medical or mental health professionals because their behavior is usually not of sufficient intensity and duration to exhaust the tolerance levels of significant others. Their delusions tend to focus on molestation by others in the immediate environment. Schizophrenia-like illness presents with greater disturbance in mental functioning and more evidence of illusions, hallucinations, and loose associations. The individual may become so distressed that he or she may demand help from family, police, or others he or she perceives to be persons of power. Paranoid schizophrenia states are characterized by either narrowly defined delusional beliefs or more expansive psychotic ideas. Other symptoms, such as distress over perceptions of persecution, depressed affect, and indistinct speech, may be present, as well as evidence of impairment in reality testing. Antipsychotic medication has proven to be effective in the treatment of late-onset schizophrenia-like symptoms.

Dementia

Dementia is primarily a disorder of old age (Cummings, 1995). The prevalence of dementia increases with age, particularly after age 75 (American Psychiatric Association, 1994). Community-based studies estimate that 20% of the elderly experience some form of mental disorder, and 60% of those suffer from dementia (Koh, 1994). Alzheimer's disease (AD) is the "most common irreversible dementia in late life, accounting for 50 to 70 percent of all dementias," with multi-infarct dementia being the second most common, accounting for 15-20% of nonreversible dementias (Hooyman & Kiyak, 1996, p. 258). All other forms of dementia are much less common (American Psychiatric Association, 1994).

The United States will see an increase in dementias as the numbers of older Americans increase (Volicer, Fabiszewski, Rheaume, & Lasch, 1988). Projections suggest that by the year 2050, the number of Americans 85 years and older will grow to 15 million (Hooyman & Kiyak, 1996). As Haulotte (1991) notes, these estimates are particularly "sobering when [we take] into account that Alzheimer's disease is the fourth leading cause of death for people over 75 years old" (p. 1) and that "one in four individuals over the age of 80 [is] affected by the disease" (p. 1).

Elderly people with various types of dementia exhibit the following common symptoms: (a) memory impairment, including impaired ability to learn new material, inability to recall previously learned information, and general forgetfulness; (b) aphasia, or deterioration of language skills; (c) apraxia, or impaired ability to perform motor activities despite intact motor and sensory function; and (d) disturbance of executive functioning, such as the ability to think abstractly and to engage successfully in complex behaviors (American Psychiatric Association, 1994).

Alzheimer's Disease

DSM-IV nomenclature for Alzheimer's disease is "dementia of the Alzheimer type," with subtypes of early onset and late onset (American Psychiatric Association, 1994, p. 139). AD is a progressive neurological disorder that causes confusion and changes in affect (Haulotte, 1991; Leng, 1990; Turner, 1992). It is characterized by memory impairment and disturbances in one or more of the following cognitive areas: use of language, motor activities, object recognition, and executive functioning (American Psychiatric Association, 1994). "The intellectual impairment progresses gradually from forgetfulness to total disability" (Mace & Rabins, 1991, p. 6), "until patients become incontinent and require constant nursing care" (Leng, 1990, p. 65). The risk of developing Alzheimer's disease increases from about 1-2 out of 100 cases of people age 65 and older to about 8 in 100 cases if a close relative has the disease (Mace & Rabins, 1991, p. 300). Down's syndrome "is a clear risk factor in the development of the condition" (Volicer et al., 1988, p. 6). Previous head injury has been found to increase the risk of developing AD 3 times, whereas a history of thyroid dysfunction increases the risk 1.5 times (Kociol & Schiff, cited in Turner, 1992). Metabolism of the metals zinc ("Zinc Metabolism," 1993) and aluminum (Kociol & Schiff, cited in Turner, 1992) has been associated with Alzheimer's disease in some studies, although "researchers continue to debate whether an elevated level of aluminum in the brains of Alzheimer's patients is a cause or an effect of the disease" (Turner, 1992). Gender and race have been identified as "questionable" risk factors. Prevalence rates of AD are higher for blacks than for whites (Volicer et al., 1988, p. 6). Recent genetic studies have identified specific genes that, if present in the right combination, increase the risk of developing Alzheimer's 34 times (Butler, 1994).

Multi-Infarct Dementia

Multi-infarct dementia results from multiple cerebral infarcts that are secondary to vascular diseases of the heart and extracranial arteries. Diagnosis is largely based on an ischemia score, although that tool has several limitations in cases with mixed etiology. (*Ischemia* refers to a decrease in blood supply caused by constriction or obstruction of blood vessels.)

An almost staggering array of other conditions and agents are capable of causing dementia in the elderly. These include other vascular conditions, brain disorders, movement disorders, depression, and any systemic condition that impairs cerebral blood circulation and oxygenation of the brain.

Diagnosis and Intervention

Differential diagnosis of dementia is based on etiology, as are treatment and intervention. Although the most common forms of dementia—Alzheimer's and multi-infarct—are at present irreversible, some conditions that cause dementia are easily treatable. The first step in treatment is to rule out infection and toxic or metabolic problems. If identified, these problems are amenable to established therapies that usually reverse the dementia. Once these conditions are ruled out, the most likely cause of dementia is Alzheimer's disease or multi-infarct (Jutagir, 1994).

Although the presenting symptoms are similar and the conditions may coexist, with some cases resulting from a combination of vascular and degenerative causes, sufficient differences generally exist to allow differential diagnosis. The key differences are that multi-infarct dementia is characterized by stepwise deterioration temporally related to a vascular event, with focal neurological symptoms including gait abnormalities and weakness of an extremity, and hypertension. AD, on the other hand, displays a slowly progressive course in the absence of any diagnostic criteria specific to another form of dementia.

Because "no specific test exists for Alzheimer's disease" (Volicer et al., 1988, p. 1), definitive diagnosis in living patients remains difficult. Diagnosis in living patients is a process of "exclusion" (Haulotte, 1991, p. 5), or the ruling out of other causes through extensive testing. Postmortem examination of brain tissue has been called "the gold standard for diagnosis of AD" (Connolly & Williams, 1993, p. 134). A postmortem diagnosis, although helpful in corroborating and establishing success rates of diagnoses based on other criteria, is of very little use for informing clinical intervention.

Research on a variety of methods of early diagnosis has been reported in the literature. Promise has been shown by medical-technological methods; neuropsychological, psychophysical, and cognitive measures; functional assessments; demographic characteristics; and retrospective accounts of dementia symptoms provided by caregivers.

Because of AD's uncertain etiology, no definitive preventive measures exist. Estrogen therapy, the development of neural connections through intellectual pursuits, and a varied repertoire of mechanisms or strategies for coping with loss have all been theorized to be effective in forestalling the behavioral and cognitive manifestations of AD. There is no cure for the disease at this time (Haulotte, 1991); however, in the early 1990s the U.S. Food and Drug Administration approved the first drug for the treatment of Alzheimer's disease, tacrine hydrochloride, sold under the brand name Cognex. "In two controlled trials, Cognex provided a small but clinically meaningful benefit for some patients with mild to moderate Alzheimer's disease" ("First Alzheimer's Drug Approved," 1993, p. 2).

Prophylactic measures for vascular dementias are the same as those for general vascular disease; these include diet, exercise, not smoking cigarettes, and the treatment of hypertension. Vascular dementia patients may be treated with aspirin to lessen the risk of additional strokes, and anticoagulants may be considered in some instances (Cummings, 1995).

Anxiety

There is disagreement regarding the extent to which anxiety is a problem of sufficient prevalence among the elderly to be considered a significant public heath concern. The primary symptom of anxiety is fear, and to be classified as a diagnosable condition the level of anxiety must interfere considerably with everyday functioning. Some early studies of the epidemiology of anxiety in community-dwelling older adults reported relatively high prevalence rates, hovering around 20%. A positive correlation was found between age and level of anxiety; that is, persons over the age of 65 were several times more likely to report anxiety than were persons younger than 65 (Sheikh, 1992, pp. 411-413). Findings from the Epidemiological Catchment Area Studies of the mid-1980s contradict the earlier studies, however, reporting markedly lower rates of anxiety and a negative correlation between age and anxiety symptoms (Brickman & Eisendorfer, 1989, pp. 416-422).

Much of the conflict on this topic can be attributed to the paucity of research dealing with anxiety in the elderly. Some may also be attributed to expectations that older persons should have anxiety because of all the adaptations that are required in the natural course of aging. In any event, anxiety is a treatable condition that is found in the elderly population; depending upon the diagnostic criteria used, rates may be as low as 2% to 3% or as high as 20% (Sheikh, 1992).

Substance Abuse

Reliable prevalence rates of alcoholism among older adults are elusive. Estimates vary from 2% to 15% of elderly community-dwelling adults (Hooyman & Kiyak, 1996). Alcoholics are less likely to be found in the age group of 60 and above because of their higher death rates at younger ages. Older men are four times more likely to be problem drinkers than are older women. Although many elderly alcoholics have long patterns of heavy intake, a significant number begin drinking at a problematic level in response to age-related stressful incidents and isolation.

Drug abuse among elderly persons usually centers on prescription and over-the-counter medications. In fact, older adults purchase approximately 30% of all prescription drugs sold, although they make up only 12% of the population. The elderly individual is quite likely to be taking two or more medications and often may abuse them (Hooyman & Kiyak, 1996, p. 264). *Polypharmacy* is a term often used to describe the medication intake of older adults.

Service Delivery and Utilization

For more than two decades, the literature dealing with mental health and aging has repeatedly documented the fact that older persons are grossly underserved by the mental health system (Edinberg, 1985, p. 258; Lebowitz & Niederehe, 1992, p. 17). As of 1985, elderly clients accounted for only approximately 2% of patients in psychiatric clinics and about 6% of those in community mental health centers (Edinberg, 1985). Even though these latter figures are dated, more recent data do not seem to indicate that utilization rates are significantly better at the present time. Consistent with this pattern, a disproportionally small percentage of patients seen by private psychiatrists are older persons.

There are many reasons for this underutilization pattern, including myths and stereotypes about aging, the small number of trained gerontological professionals, and myriad problems found in mental health service delivery systems. Entrenched stereotypes equating aging and senility discourage the elderly from seeking needed psychiatric help for fear of being labeled mentally ill. These same stereotypes, as well as ignorance about the normal processes of aging, also influence students in the mental health field, who may thus have no impetus to take on gerontological studies as a career choice.

The "four A's" of availability, accessibility, acceptability, and affordability describe other possible barriers to service utilization. *Availability* pertains to whether needed services in fact actually exist. *Accessibility* refers to the extent to which available services can be accessed by the older adult. Included here are agency-based services and services that are provided in the home. *Acceptability* of the service delivery system is influenced by its sensitivity to the self-respect and dignity of the older adult as well as to other cultural dimensions deemed important by the service recipient. *Affordability* refers to the expense of the needed services and whether these are within potential clients' price range.

Obviously, many factors influence elderly persons' underutilization of mental health services. This suggests the need for a focused and coherent social policy aimed at addressing those factors.

Public Policy

There is a clear need for a comprehensive long-term policy to deal with the mental health needs of the elderly in the United States. In another quarter of a century, approximately one-fifth of the U.S. population will be age 65 or older. A significant number of persons in this age group will have one or more chronic impairments. Although most such impairments do not seriously affect everyday functioning in the young-old group (65–74), by the age of 75 or older many are affected with severe limitations to their activities of daily living. Because of these limitations, they require assistance from various caregiving sources, whether in the community or in institutional settings.

For the past several decades there has been a movement toward government responsibility in providing assistance in the care of the frail elderly. Within the past few years, however, a decidedly conservative political trend has begun, the proponents of which argue for less government involvement in activities that some see as falling within the domain of individual/family/private responsibility. This conservative trend is growing, although relatively few families are able to afford needed community-based services. Institutional care, such as in a nursing home, is literally out of the financial range of most families, making Medicaid support a necessity for a large portion of the population who may require institutional care.

One group of individuals reflecting the shortsightedness of public policy is that of deinstitutionalized chronic schizophrenics. Many of the older cohort of chronic schizophrenics currently living in the community are those individuals who were deinstitutionalized during the massive push of the 1960s to empty the state mental hospitals following the passage of the Community Mental Health Services Act (Hooyman & Kiyak, 1996, p. 265). That many older chronically mentally ill persons are homeless indicates a lack of national policy anticipating negative long-term outcomes associated with deinstitutionalization. This group accounts for approximately one-third of the homeless and has shifted the burden from the mental health system to the legal system. Concurrently, local communities have been forced to pick up the slack, and local charities have been stretched to the maximum to provide services.

This failure to develop policy that adequately addresses the needs of the elderly chronically mentally ill is echoed in the current lack of public policy concerning dementia. "Beginning at age 60, the frequency of dementia in the population doubles every 5 years: it affects 1% of 60- to 64-year-olds but 30% to 40% of those over age 85" (Cummings, 1995, p. 1481). More than half of the residents of long-term health care facilities are persons with dementing illnesses (see Sloane & Mathew, 1991, p. xiii). "As the number of persons aged 65 and older increases, so too does the number of those suffering from Alzheimer's disease; hence the ever-increasing need for available long-term health care policy" (Jarvik & Winograd, 1988, p. 147).

During a joint hearing before the Select Committee on Aging, Chairman Edward R. Roybal described Alzheimer's disease as a "time bomb" in our health care system (U.S. Senate, 1992, p. 1). He went on to say that "Americans currently spend about $100 billion a year or one in every seven health care dollars in the care and treatment of Alzheimer's disease" and that, despite this increase in costs, the government is "decreasing monies that are being used for this purpose" (p. 2). Alzheimer's disease research receives around $350 million per year; AIDS research, in contrast, receives almost $2 billion (p. 2).

Mental health and dementia in elderly populations are major public health and policy issues not just in the United States but internationally. As the segment of the population over 65 in the United States is expected to increase by 105% from 1985 to 2025, with a concomitant rise in the need for mental health and dementia services, other countries will also experience increases in their elderly populations. In the United Kingdom this segment of the population is expected to increase 23% in the same period; in Canada, it is estimated to increase 135% (Cummings, 1995). The situation is even more critical in developing countries, where recent advances in public health have drastically extended longevity. India will experience a 264% increase in people over the age of 65 from 1985 to 2025, and Mexico and Guatemala will experience 324% and 357% increases, respectively (Cummings, 1995).

A search of an academic periodical index at a major university using the term *mental health policy* found 56 items. When the terms *geriatric, aging,* and *older* were each added to the search criteria, the number of items found was reduced to 1. This in itself highlights the need for more definitive policy regarding mental health and the elderly.

In a thorough exploration of mental health policy for older Americans, Fogel, Furino, and Gottlieb (1990) conclude their edited volume by offering three ideas to guide future policy development: (a) Improve identification and recognition of neuropsychiatric problems, (b) generalize the idea of case management, and (c) develop new programs on a regional basis through public/private/academic collaboration. Clearly, improved identification and recognition of mental health problems is essential before effective interventions can be provided. This continuum begins with the perception of need on the part of the prospective patient and moves through accessibility of services, problem recognition by the service provider, and finally treatment.

Case management is typically utilized with clients who require a complex mix of services best coordinated by an experienced guide. Clients whose cognition and judgment are impaired owing to late-life neuropsychiatric disorders, who may also be faced with possible limitations on physician mental health knowledge and time, can be greatly assisted by individuals with the specialized knowledge and skills of experienced case managers (Fogel et al., 1990).

In the prevailing political climate of reduced federal responsibility for social services, it appears unlikely that the federal government will take the lead in establishing innovative mental health programs for the elderly. This situation, in conjunction with significant regional differences in age distribution, health care infrastructure, and financial resources, makes regional development of mental health policies and programs for the elderly appropriate. State and local agencies, private industries, and academic institutions can all contribute unique resources to the creation of a more responsive and effective system of care (Fogel et al., 1990).

As mental health professionals engage in the process of developing mental health policy and providing services for the elderly, they should avoid the tendency to seek simple, unidimensional solutions for complex, multifaceted problems. The diversity in etiology and progression of mental health problems experienced by the elderly, combined with quickly evolving available interventions, requires an awareness of this complexity.

References

American Psychiatric Association. (1994). *Diagnostic and statistical manual of mental disorders* (4th ed.). Washington, DC: Author.

Blazer, D. G. (1989). The epidemiology of psychiatric disorders in late life. In E. W. Busse & D. G. Blazer (Eds.), *Geriatric psychiatry* (pp. 249-252). Washington, DC: American Psychiatric Press.

Blazer, D. G., Hughes, D. C. & George, L. K. (1987). The epidemiology of depression in an elderly community population. *Gerontologist, 27,* 281-287.

Brickman, A. L., & Eisendorfer, C. (1989). Anxiety in the elderly. In E. W. Busse & D. G. Blazer (Eds.), *Geriatric psychiatry* (pp. 415-428). Washington, DC: American Psychiatric Press.

Butler, R. N. (1994). ApoE: New risk factor in Alzheimer's; potential is real of abuse of genetic testing for susceptibility to dementia. *Geriatrics, 49*(8), 10-11.

Christison, C., Christison, G., & Blazer, D. G. (1989). Late life schizophrenia and paranoid disorders. In E. W. Busse & D. G. Blazer (Eds.), *Geriatric psychiatry* (pp. 403-414). Washington, DC: American Psychiatric Press.

Connolly, N. K., & Williams, M. E. (1993). Plaques and tangles in approaching dementia. *Gerontologist, 33,* 133-135.

Cummings, J. L. (1995). Dementia: The failing brain. *Lancet, 345,* 1481-1484.

Edinberg, M. A. (1985). *Mental health practice with the elderly.* Englewood Cliffs, NJ: Prentice Hall.

First Alzheimer's drug approved. (1993). *FDA Consumer, 27*(9), 2.

Fogel, B. S., Furino, A., & Gottlieb, G. L. (Eds.). (1990). *Mental health policy for older Americans: Protecting minds at risk.* Washington, DC: American Psychiatric Press.

Haulotte, S. M. (1991). *The valley of shadows.* Unpublished manuscript.

Hooyman, N. R., & Kiyak, H. A. (1996). *Social gerontology* (4th ed.). Boston: Allyn & Bacon.

Jarvik, L. F., & Winograd, C. H. (Eds.). (1988). *Treatments for the Alzheimer's patient.* New York: Springer.

Jutagir, R. (1994). Psychological aspects of aging: When does memory loss signal dementia? *Geriatrics, 49*(3), 45-49.

Koh, K. (1994). Dementia in elderly patients: Can the 3R Mental Stimulation Program improve mental status? *Age and Aging, 23*(3), 195-199.

Lebowitz, B. D., & Niederehe, G. (1992). Concepts and issues in mental health and aging. In J. E. Birren, R. B. Sloan, & G. D. Cohen (Eds.), *Handbook of mental health and aging* (pp. 3-26). New York: Academic Press.

Leng, N. R. C. (1990). *Psychological care in old age.* New York: Hemisphere.

Mace, N. L., & Rabins, P. V. (Eds.). (1991). *The 36 hour day.* Baltimore: Johns Hopkins University Press.

McIntosh, J. L. (1991). Epidemiology of suicide in the U.S. In A. A. Leenarks (Ed.), *Life span perspectives on suicide* (pp. 55-70). New York: Plenum.

Post, F. (1980). Paranoid and schizophrenic disorders among the aging. In L. L. Cartensen & B. A. Edelstein (Eds.), *Handbook of clinical gerontology* (pp. 43-56). Elmsford, NY: Pergamon.

Schick, F. L. (Ed.). (n.d.). *Statistical handbook on aging Americans.* Phoenix, AZ: Oryx.

Sheikh, J. I. (1992). Anxiety and its disorders in old age. In J. E. Birren, R. B. Stone, & G. D. Cohen (Eds.), *Handbook of mental health and aging* (pp. 410-432). New York: Academic Press.

Sloane, P. D., & Mathew, L. J. (Eds.). (1991). *Dementia units in long-term care.* Baltimore: Johns Hopkins University Press.

Stillon, J. M., McDowell, E. E., & May, J. H. (1989). *Suicide across the life span: Premature exits.* New York: Hemisphere.

Turner, F. J. (1992). *Mental health and the elderly: A social work perspective.* New York: Free Press.

U.S. Department of Commerce, Bureau of the Census. (1993). Population projections of the U.S. by age, sex, race, and Hispanic origin: 1993-2050. In *Current population reports* (Series P-25, No. 1104). Washington, DC: Government Printing Office.

U.S. Senate. (1992). *Alzheimer's disease: The time bomb in our health care system* (Committee Publication No. 102-861). Washington, DC: Government Printing Office.

Volicer, L., Fabiszewski, K. J., Rheaume, Y. L., & Lasch, K. E. (Eds.). (1988). *Clinical management of Alzheimer's disease.* Gaithersburg, MD: Aspen.

Zinc metabolism affects Alzheimer's. (1993, November 1). *USA Today,* p. 120.

CHAPTER 18

The State of Mental Health Services to Criminal Offenders

CHARLES TURNBO

DONALD W. MURRAY, JR.

In 1993, the number of inmates in U.S. state and federal prisons climbed to nearly 1 million—almost triple the 1980 figure. Some reasons for exploding inmate populations include stiffer sentences brought on by the war on drugs, mandatory minimum sentences, and more restrictive, if not repealed, parole policies. Nationwide, drug offenders made up 30% of newly sentenced inmates, compared with 7% in 1980. In the federal prison system, almost two-thirds of new inmates were drug offenders.

Perhaps not receiving the attention it deserves is an equally incredible level of growth in the probation and parole population in the United States. This group makes up 75% of the population under criminal justice supervision, whereas those confined make up the remaining 25%. The total number under formal criminal justice supervision today is well over 3 million. With such large numbers, state and federal criminal justice budgets have grown dramatically over the past decade.

Because of the deinstitutionalization of the mentally ill, the criminal justice system now increasingly has become the destination of mentally ill and developmentally disabled individuals. In a 1993 report, the National Coalition on the Mentally Ill in the Criminal Justice System estimated that the mentally ill represent 15-30% of the nation's prison population, and that between 5% and 10% of criminal offenders are developmentally impaired.

The increase in criminal offenders and the growing numbers of mental health issues concerning them have presented new demands on the criminal justice system. Today's criminal population is a highly diverse group. It represents a microcosm of the total population, except that its members have been arrested and have become the responsibility of the criminal justice system. The criminal population today includes sophisticated "white-collar" inmates, violent gang-affiliated inmates, truly mentally ill inmates, chemically dependent inmates (estimated at 40% in the federal prison system), and classic psychopaths, pedophiles, and paraphiliacs.

The inmates presenting mental health issues may range from passive-dependent neurotics to severely psychopathic individuals. Their offenses often do not typify their personality characteristics, and many may have been committed while the individuals were under the influence of alcohol or drugs, particularly in the case of violent acts. A frequent concern with criminal offenders is the potential for suicide, particularly early in the course of their entry into the system.

Recent History

Two trends of the past several decades have had dramatic impacts on the criminal justice system. First, the move to deinstitutionalize mental health clients, in favor of community mental health treatment, has shifted many from this group into the criminal justice area. The second trend has been the increasing use of prison sanctions for offenders. Considered together, as mentioned earlier, these trends have resulted in a current prison population of more than 1 million inmates, of whom a significant number are in need of mental health interventions.

In the federal prison system there has been a substantial increase in the number of mental health service providers employed in institutions. These individuals include psychiatric nurses, psychologists, psychiatrists, and social workers. They have been utilized to screen initial commitments for mental health issues, to provide care during inmates' stays, and to influence the prison environment through training and services to prison staff.

The diversity of the federal prison inmate population is a source of great professional interest and continuous challenge. One-third of this population is made up of foreign nationals, who are generally deported upon sentence completion. Subpopulations of the alien population have necessitated special programs, such as the long-term Cuban Units established to house the so-called Mariel Cubans awaiting repatriation to their native country. Mental health staff have created new delivery systems that accommodate cultural, language, and belief system differences.

As a result of the federal war on drugs, the inmate population is increasingly younger, more aggressive, and substance dependent. New strategies have been developed to deal with drug abuse through a 500-hour intensive drug treatment program. This initiative has been developed and is largely being administered by Federal Bureau of Prisons (BOP) psychologists.

Today's prison population is more violent than that of the past, and there have been significant violent disruptions in federal prisons in recent years that have caused the BOP to create new initiatives to deal with individual and group violence. Mental health providers are now being asked to conduct training and programs for both staff and inmates on conflict resolution, confrontation avoidance, and alternative dispute resolution.

The prison mental health population continues to present challenges for cost-effective service delivery. Special units for both male and female inmates serve the special needs of this population. When an inmate is discharged from a mental health unit, special transitional programs may be used, if possible, to provide follow-up—in the general institutions as well as in the community.

Inmate Programs and Services

Mentally Ill Inmates

Like the larger society in which it operates, the prison system contains numerous individuals who are mentally ill. Offenders who are severely mentally ill, suffering from a variety of psychoses, including the schizophrenias, are managed based upon the symptoms that are readily apparent. All BOP staff are trained in the recognition and management of mental health problems upon initial hire and in subsequent annual refresher training. Usually, severely mentally ill inmates are managed locally with psychopharmacological treatments and mainstreamed into the general population with close monitoring.

In some acute care situations, and in more chronic and intractable cases, individuals may be sent directly to one of five modern, staff-intensive BOP medical centers that specialize in the treatment of chronic mental illness. Regardless of location, the goal is the same—to reintegrate the mentally ill individual, once stabilized and fully functioning, into a general population unit. Often transitional care units are used to provide closer monitoring of a mentally ill offender before a judgment is made to return him or her to a regular prison facility. Typically speaking, less than 2% of offenders in any general population are prescribed any form of psychotropic intervention, with less than 1% on any form of major antipsychotic medication. This is true despite the incredibly stressful experience that incarceration can be for many offenders. These data point to the success of treatment approaches employing skills-building strategies to enhance self-efficacy and self-management.

Substance Abuse Programs

Although the BOP has historically perceived substance abuse treatment programs as part of the overall mission of the agency, nothing in BOP history compares with the dramatic increase in drug program activities since 1989. Driven in large measure by the increase in the number of offenders entering the system with substance abuse problems, the BOP developed a comprehensive substance abuse strategy (Murray, 1991, 1992) that ensures the availability of both drug education and outpatient treatment services at virtually every BOP facility. Of even greater significance, however, is the development of more than 33 new residential treatment programs. These programs are intensive, 500-treatment-hour efforts based throughout the system. These residential programs involve comprehensive assessment and both group and individual treatment.

These intensive programs are based on a biopsychosocial model of addiction (Marlatt & George, 1984; Marlatt & Gordon, 1985). Strong relapse prevention and skills-building efforts, in both psychoeducational and process formats, are uniformly delivered through BOP staff-designed and -developed modules. Core modules include "Interpersonal Skills/Problems Solving," "Relapse Prevention," "Criminal Thinking Confrontation," "RET/RBT Cognitive Skills Development," "Wellness Lifestyle Training," "Transitional Care Planning," and other standardized interventions. In addition to the structured group interventions, individualized treatment is also integrated into the programs. This provides an opportunity for practitioners to deal with each individual's unique situation.

It is encouraging to note that even prior to the passage of the 1994 Crime Bill, which provided nonviolent offenders with substance abuse/dependence histories the possibility of a 1-year sentence reduction if they successfully complete a comprehensive residential treatment program, the BOP programs nationwide were operating at above 100% of their rated capacity. Currently more than 2,040 offenders are on waiting lists for treatment in these programs. Outcome data are available in the report of a recent research study supported by the National Institute on Drug Abuse (Pelissier & McCarthy, 1992).

Transitional Care Programs

It is recognized that treatment gains made in prison may be lost upon release if there is no significant aftercare period. Individuals released from residential treatment are confronted with a world that is filled with opportunities for relapse. An aftercare period of 6-18 months is generally recommended as a period of continued community-based treatment and follow-up for offenders discharged from their sentences (Murray, 1991, 1992). BOP programs provide for up to 6 months of transitional care in a community corrections center, with treatment services contracted with local community providers. Often, for purposes of continuity of care, these providers are the same contractors utilized by the BOP within the prisons. Upon discharge of the sentence, the offender is usually placed on supervised release status with the Administrative Office of the U.S. Court, Probation Division, which also contracts with local providers for up to a year for additional aftercare and follow-up services. Mental health aftercare is frequently contracted in the same manner.

Just as relapses for noncriminal individuals can lead to many family- and work-related problems following treatment, the same is true for criminal offenders. Unfortunately, substance-abusing offenders may often find themselves involved in other criminal activities if they do not find meaningful work, avoid substance-abusing peers, establish positive group or family support where available, maintain effective coping skills in dealing with negative emotions, and develop a wellness-oriented lifestyle. The importance of an effective, community-based transitional care program cannot be overemphasized in the monitoring of these high-risk relapse categories, which constitute up to 75% of the reasons that individuals relapse following treatment (Marlatt & Gordon, 1985).

Hospice Programs

Hospice programs are also operated at virtually every BOP medical center. Many inmates are afflicted with chronic and terminal illnesses, including AIDS and cancer, that result in their deaths prior to the expiration of their sentences. Although compassionate release is encouraged in many cases, the majority of offenders with terminal illnesses continue to expire in BOP custody. Hospice staff are specially trained to manage this population through both group and individual programs involving both spiritual and psychological interventions.

Suicide Prevention Programs

For many individuals, imprisonment is the most traumatic experience of their lives. The pervasive guilt and sense of personal failure, as well as feelings of hopelessness, helplessness, inadequacy, and inefficacy, are at times overwhelming. As a result, it is not uncommon for many to consider suicide as a means of permanently silencing these chronically pervasive themes. The mental health professional's task is to educate, identify, evaluate, and monitor individuals with suicide risk potential. Prevention is key—interventions must be timely and effective.

Since 1982, when the BOP issued its first formal policy on the topic of suicide prevention and implemented the Suicide Prevention Program throughout all facilities, the number of suicides occurring within the system has been below that of the national average for the general male population (White & Schimmel, 1993): The suicide rate in the BOP for 1988-1992, the most recent period for which figures are available, was slightly lower than 16/100,000, whereas the rate among the general nonincarcerated male population is approximately 18/100,000 (White & Schimmel, 1993). This is particularly important given the fact that the federal prison system comprises approximately 93% male offenders. Any individual's death by suicide is tragic, and the BOP's goal is to prevent any and all suicides. Comparable data from

Schmidt (1978) and Gaes (1981) indicate a suicide rate of approximately 35/100,000 for the period 1970-1981. Hence, following the implementation of the Suicide Prevention Program, a dramatic decrease in the rates of suicide has been noted since 1982.

Forensic Programs

Psychologists and psychiatrists conduct a variety of evaluations for the federal courts. Specifically, Title 18, U.S. Code, Chapter 313, Sections 4241-4247, outlines federal laws for managing "offenders with mental disease or defect." Typically, the court poses questions regarding the offender's mental competence to stand trial (4241), determination of the existence of insanity at the time of the offense (4242), hospitalization of a person found not guilty only by reason of insanity (4243), hospitalization of a convicted person suffering from a mental disease or defect (4244), hospitalization of an imprisoned person suffering from mental disease or defect (4245), and hospitalization of a person due for release but suffering from mental disease or defect (4246). Section 4247 of the statute provides general provisions for the chapter, definitions, and qualifications of examiners pursuant to federal law.

Although the laws are specific that the critical opinion is that of the psychiatrist or psychologist conducting the evaluation, observations of all staff working with these offenders are important to the quality and accuracy of the evaluation process. A team approach is of paramount importance. A number of interesting and high-profile cases are evaluated by forensic mental health professionals and medical center staff every year. In the recent past, a few such cases committed under federal study and observation statutes, and thus on which information is publicly available, include failed presidential assassin John Hinckley, television evangelist Jim Bakker, Manson family members and presidential threateners Lynette "Squeaky" Fromm and Sara Jane Moore, and *Hustler* magazine publisher Larry Flynt.

Sex Offender Treatment Programs

A residential sex offender treatment program was developed at the Federal Correctional Institution (FCI) in Butner, North Carolina, in October 1990. This 24-bed intensive program was designed to handle volunteers with a history of sexual deviance (Norris, 1993); today there are plans to expand the program to 70 beds.

Participants in the program are carefully screened by a clinical psychologist prior to admission. Each inmate must have at most 24 months remaining on his sentence and must be willing to participate in a comprehensive 12-month full-time program and follow-up. State-of-the-art treatment modalities are employed, including psychological and physiological assessment of deviance through the use of the penile plethysmograph.

Group therapies include a core group of 12 peers, all of whom disclose their autobiographies to each other. Further, self-development groups invite participants to discuss any history of physical, emotional, or sexual abuse in the offenders' families of origin. Studies suggest that 60% to 70% of all sex offenders have been victims themselves of one of these types of abuse or neglect. Additionally, participants are required to participate in victim empathy groups, behavior therapy, anger management, cognitive distortions groups, social skills groups, sex education, substance abuse groups (for those with histories of such abuse), and relapse prevention training. Finally, all offenders are required to undergo individual psychotherapy on a weekly basis throughout the period of the program.

Although it is clearly too early to tell about long-term outcomes in this extremely recalcitrant treatment population, the newer treatment technologies upon which this program is based appear promising. To date, 54 individuals have completed the program at FCI, Butner, and have been released to the street. Of those 54, one of whom has been out of prison for 3½ years, there has not been a single rearrest of any type. Again, long-term outcome studies are needed in this area if we are to better understand and prevent these horrific crimes. Outcome studies will further enable us to determine more efficiently which sex offenders respond best to treatment, as well as which should be selectively incapacitated.

Prosocial Values Development Programs

In a new initiative started in 1992, a program designed to stimulate the development of positive social values was piloted at several BOP locations. The Living Free Program, as it is currently known, became operational in virtually all BOP facilities by the end of 1995. This standardized 20-hour program requires inmates to examine themselves from the perspective of what it takes to become an honest, contributing member of society. Values that the larger society holds as important, and that the participants can agree would be of benefit to them as individuals, family members, workers, and so on, are emphasized. Using a group format and both psychoeducational and group process dynamics, the values clarification and development exercises are implemented.

HIV/AIDS Counseling Programs

Mental health staff provide services to offenders who have tested positive for the human immunodeficiency virus (HIV). In addition to the medical interventions indicated, mental health staff work to provide counseling and helpful information to HIV-infected offenders. Often, a mental health professional is in the office with the diagnosing physician at the time the inmate is given the information regarding his or her HIV-positive status. This enables the mental health professional to make judgments immediately as to how the individual will likely manage the crisis that such a diagnosis can bring about.

Further, it provides the professional with an opportunity to develop a trusting relationship with the inmate, to plan subsequent individual follow-up and monitoring, and to offer additional information on HIV and how best to manage it.

Unfortunately, there are some offenders whose HIV status does not preclude them from further sexual acting out. Such indiscriminate sexual behavior in the facility may pose a serious danger to the welfare of others. Psychologists and other mental health professionals are sometimes asked to evaluate the potential for this type of acting out on the part of the inmate. Specific policies govern the management of HIV-infected inmates who are found to be threats to others due to their sexual conduct in the prison, including individual detention and segregation. Mental health reviews are conducted routinely for individuals found to be a danger to others as a result of their conduct.

It would be wrong to suggest that this behavior is a high-frequency problem within the prison setting. In fact, the second author can recall being directly involved in only one such case between 1982 and 1989. Most HIV-positive offenders handle their status discreetly and according to the professional advice given to them. Only about 1% of the BOP's general inmate population tests HIV positive, based upon the rate discerned for those tested prior to release.

Self-Help Groups

Staff also serve to coordinate many community volunteers who offer support services to offenders who wish to make changes in their lives. These volunteers contribute tens of thousands of hours annually through spiritual support groups, Alcoholics Anonymous, Narcotics Anonymous, Gamblers Anonymous, Veterans Groups, posttrauma groups, groups devoted to parenting skills development, and so on. Services of community volunteers are a tremendous asset to the BOP in a variety of ways. For many offenders who have lost hope and given up on themselves or their perceived ability to make positive changes, volunteers can and do make a world of difference. Many offenders who later discharge successfully to the community have talked retrospectively about how community volunteers gave them something to believe in and a reason to change.

Women Offenders and Special Needs Populations

Mental health professionals have identified several groups of offenders who may benefit from specialized services due to the nature of their disabilities. In addition to the mentally ill previously discussed, there are mentally retarded, physically disabled, chronically/terminally ill, and geriatric offenders. Women offenders are also considered a special needs population because of the unique needs and situations of many women offenders.

Generally speaking, many accommodations are made for special needs groups due to the handicaps they demonstrate, including specialty units in many major medical centers. These facilities often house many mentally ill and mentally retarded offenders. Again, these offenders constitute a very small proportion of the general prison population. The BOP continues to mainstream as many inmates as possible into regular facilities, making the special accommodations only when mainstreaming is not feasible. All facilities should, to the extent possible, manage offenders with diverse needs, including the physically challenged and the geriatric population of offenders. Many design changes have been made to allow wheelchair access, and workdays have been modified to accommodate those who are able to work only part-time due to advanced age, disease, or illness. Medical, psychological, and wellness programs geared to these specialty populations are offered. These include patient education in a variety of chronic illnesses and diseases (e.g., diabetes, cancer, HIV, and hypertension).

Women offenders make up approximately 7% of the total federal prison population. Unfortunately, according to a 1990 admissions cohort study of women offenders entering the system, women offenders have a higher substance abuse problem rate than do their male counterparts (Murray, 1992). Despite some methodological limitations of this admissions cohort study (an unrepeated, single-point-in-time sample) and questions by many professionals experienced in substance abuse treatment regarding the diagnostic utility of some of the pathognomonic indicators for substance abuse or dependence contained in the *DSM-III-R,* the study points out a specialty population with many problem areas.

Specialty substance abuse treatment units for women have been developed at a number of facilities. In these units women offenders have an opportunity to address many emotional issues related to their own development and many self-concept, self-efficacy issues that have influenced their decision making as adults. Group and individual treatment addressing such core issues as incest, rape trauma, and domestic violence that many have experienced is an ongoing part of treatment in virtually every women's program. Experienced clinicians working with women offenders have told us that between 65% and 75% of all women offenders have experienced physical or sexual abuse prior to their incarceration.

In one very dramatic case, a young female offender serving time for a drug offense, a divorced mother of two children, worked through her own tragic experiences as an incest victim in individual treatment, even though it was her drug problems that brought her to the attention of staff. By coming to prison and "cleaning up," as she articulated it, she was facing the core reasons she had begun to use drugs—to cope with the pain of her abusive past. Treatment helped her to become aware that this same fate could be experienced by her own children, who were in her parents' care. Believing strongly that the uncle who had abused her when she was a child would continue to perform those acts on the children of other unsuspecting family members, with the support of the warden and the psychologist involved she contacted local authorities and Child Protective Services with this information. An investigation revealed that there were other children currently being abused, as she had feared. With this intervention, the abuse was halted, the perpetrator arrested, and assistance generated for other family members who were victims. The young woman's self-esteem, sense of personal control over her life, and belief in her own abilities to effect positive change in the lives of others were substantially enhanced by her actions to end this case of transgenerational sexual abuse.

In addition, women offenders with children and pregnant women offenders who are incarcerated are provided specialty medical services and other programs, such as parent education classes. (Men are also able to participate in parenting groups within male facilities.) The goal of such programs is to help offenders who return to their children upon release to be better equipped to serve as parents than they were when they came to prison. Parents do not stop being parents even if incarcerated. Their children may be raised by others, but the advice, counsel, and support that children receive from incarcerated parents continue to have impacts on the children's development. Parenting programs help offenders to help their own children with positive parenting techniques. They may also help offenders to encourage their children to avoid the kinds of potential errors in judgment to which they fell victim that resulted in conflicts with the authorities and imprisonment.

Mental health staff may also help offenders who have children with serious problems, including drugs or alcohol abuse, gang membership, or other behavioral or emotional problems, to seek help from appropriate community-based providers. Sometimes they assist in direct referrals of these individuals in conjunction with the parent, depending on the seriousness of the problem and their legal/ethical responsibilities. Offenders' children who have been suicidal have been referred by BOP mental health professionals who were made aware of these crisis in the offenders' families.

Staff Services

Mental health professionals also provide services to BOP staff members. They are active in employee assistance programs and on family and employee assistance teams, during hostage situations, and in general training and human resource management situations.

Employee Assistance Programs

The BOP offers confidential services to employees and their families who are experiencing emotional difficulties. For staff who are experiencing family, marital, work-related, legal, substance abuse, physical, financial, or other emotional difficulties, mental health staff provide free assessment and referrals to local community resources. The goal is to assist staff in managing difficulties that may result in work performance problems or, if so identified, to provide resources to help staff members better manage their problem situations. Within the BOP, the employee assistance program is confidential, voluntary, and professionally operated. Early intervention with staff members helps to keep the workplace safe and productive.

Family and Employee Assistance Teams

Crises in law enforcement settings are often dramatic. They can range from natural disasters such as tornadoes, floods, hurricanes, and fires to human-made problems such as hostage situations, riots, and other disturbances. The BOP recognizes that preparedness to respond and intervene in these situations is essential. There is an entire office within the agency dedicated to emergency preparedness. Mental health staff are a critical part of that preparedness and of actual interventions.

In hostage situations, mental health professionals serve a variety of roles. They advise the executive staff, or "brain trust," and members of the "command center" on numerous issues. They may look at the cultural and personality characteristics of perpetrators and other individuals involved and make predictions about behavior. They may serve directly as negotiators. They may serve to monitor group dynamics and the dynamics of leadership change among the hostage takers. They also frequently consult with other agencies and mental health experts. The questions posed to mental health professionals in such situations are often as unique as the situations themselves—and as challenging to manage effectively as any the professionals will ever face.

Mental health professionals serve in similar ways in riot situations and during smaller group disturbances—in some cases intervening directly to de-escalate threats of harm to self or others made by inmates through the use of confrontation avoidance strategies. Negotiation, confrontation avoidance, and conflict resolution strategies are always paramount in any such crisis, regardless of the scale of occurrence. The use of force is always the last resort, despite the omnipresent and immediate preparedness of tactical staff to do so in life-threatening situations.

Although working with family members of loved ones who may be held hostage is also an expected role for today's practitioners, this was not always the case. In fact, it was not until after November 1987, when one of the nation's most protracted hostage situations ever took place at the Federal Detention Center in Oakdale, Louisiana, that a Victim Assistance Program became part of Bureau of Prisons formal policy. The first author was the on-site coordinator of the tremendous effort undertaken during the Oakdale hostage incident, which involved a team of dozens of psychologists, chaplains, and others. Working closely with other well-trained staff, the team sought to help manage the pain and fear of the family members (including children) of staff held hostage for more than 10 days before a negotiated settlement to this crisis was finally achieved. Afterwards, formal and informal debriefing sessions were held for all involved as an important part of the overall healing intervention. Mental health providers worked closely with the Religious Services Department of the facility and staff and mental health professionals from many BOP facilities and outside agencies. Highly specialized, detailed policies derived from professionals' experiences in this and other challenging situations now govern roles in comparable circumstances. From our perspective, there may well be no greater test of a professional's skills and stamina than incidents involving hostage and victim assistance interventions.

To this end, mental health staff can and do play key roles through continuous efforts at prevention: the diffusion of potentially volatile and violent situations before they emerge. They train staff in appropriate management techniques with differing types and personalities of offenders, and they train and work with BOP tactical squads, or Special Operations Response Teams, in many facets of their various operations. In fact, many Special Operations practice scenarios are conducted each year at facilities throughout the BOP in preparation for the management of such incidents. Colleagues in the Federal Bureau of Investigation, U.S. Marshal's Service, and numerous local and state law enforcement agencies also participate in these exercises.

Despite efforts toward prevention on a daily basis, the frequency of such incidents appears not to be decreasing, but increasing. This is perhaps due to the large numbers of offenders entering the system and the fact that the prison population is an international one. World events and opinions entering the facilities through television, radio, and print media have dramatic effects on the inmate population. Decisions made and actions taken in parts of the world with whom most people in the United states are largely unfamiliar may be enough to trigger great concern among some members of the international inmate population. Within our own borders, even policy decisions made by other agencies and departments can sometimes create concern and unrest, particularly with regard to policies in the areas of immigration and deportation. Regardless, if and when critical situations arise in prisons in the future, mental health staff will be there, playing significant roles to resolve these situations as expediently and safely as possible, and to do whatever follow-up is necessary for all involved.

Employee Development/Human Resources Management

Mental health professionals have valuable training that is of great potential benefit to prison systems. As such, their specialized knowledge of human behavior is often used by senior managers to provide training in all of the previously described areas. Psychologists assist in the interviewing process, facilitating the selection of qualified applicants—applicants who are capable of performing well under the stress of a law enforcement setting.

Mental health staff also train supervisors in the management of employee-supervisor conflicts. Training to refer staff to the employee assistance program and to make supervisors aware of this very powerful means of helping employees improve job performance is a part of every BOP facility. Finally, training of other staff, including correctional counselors as well as line officers, in specialized knowledge areas greatly expands the role, acceptance, and effectiveness of the mental health professional in today's correctional settings.

Beyond 2000: New Roles for Providers

Correctional settings provide fertile ground for contemporary mental health practitioners. The roles and opportunities discussed above are among the most captivating and challenging for mental health staff anywhere. The past two and a half decades have demonstrated the effectiveness of the mental health professional as a systems-oriented, integrated consultant/practitioner. This is in stark contrast to the pure medical model—a doctor-patient, direct-services-only role—often depicted in traditional practice settings. Mental health professionals are now seen as integral to the prison system, not as expensive add-ons that can be done without in periods of fiscal austerity. There have been times in the past when this was clearly not the case. Of course, it would be unfair to leave the reader with the impression that all correctional systems and agencies across the nation have embraced and refined the roles of mental health professionals working within them to the extent that the federal system has. Many, however, clearly have.

From our perspective, today's mental health practitioners in prison settings owe an enormous and unrepayable debt to mental health professionals over the past 25 years who were torchbearers in the system, whose job performance and contributions to corrections and the BOP made it possible for us to succeed them. This was accomplished in systems that had not had opportunities to interact substantially with mental health providers or to know of their potential contributions beyond a direct services capacity. This includes new roles in administration and management of local prisons. It also includes regional BOP leadership, as in the case of the first author, and even leadership of entire agencies, as is the case with the Federal Bureau of Prisons. Dr. Kathleen M. Hawk, the sixth director in the history of the BOP and the first woman director, began her career as a psychologist at the Federal Correctional Institution in Morgantown, West Virginia, in 1977. A number of members of the current Executive Staff of the BOP, as well as retired members, have backgrounds and professional degrees in the helping professions.

It is instructive to point out that the mental health professions have also evolved as a result of experiences within the correctional system. Those mental health professionals who have been most willing to tackle the challenges posed by the complexities of the correctional environment—and there are many— have had great success and will likely continue to do so. Those who have not made concerted efforts to accept different roles, to serve the system within all reaches of their professional capacity, to pursue such challenges vigorously and willingly, have not—and likely will not.

In any event, the potential for contributions by mental health professionals in correctional settings nationwide is far greater today than it has been at any point in the past. And our prisons are safer, more humane social institutions, as are our local communities, as a result of these professionals' often-seen but seldom-heralded efforts.

References

Gaes, G. (1981). [Unpublished internal report]. Federal Bureau of Prisons, Washington, DC.

Marlatt, G. A., & George, W. H. (1984). Relapse prevention: Introduction and overview of the model. *Journal of Addictive Behavior, 79,* 261-273.

Marlatt, G. A., & Gordon, J. R. (Eds.). (1985). *Relapse prevention: Maintenance strategies in addictive behavior change.* New York: Guilford.

Murray, D. W. (1991, June). New initiatives in drug treatment in the Federal Bureau of Prisons. *Federal Probation,* pp. 35-41.

Murray, D. W. (1992). Drug abuse treatment programs in the Federal Bureau of Prisons: Initiatives for the 90's. In C. G. Leukefeld & F. M. Tims (Eds.), *Drug abuse treatment in prisons and jails* (NIDA Research Monograph 118, DHHS Publication No. ADM 92-1884, pp. 62-83). Rockville, MD: National Institute on Drug Abuse.

Norris, C. (1993). *Criteria for admission and program description: Sex offender treatment program at FCI Butner.* Unpublished manuscript, Federal Correctional Institution, Butner, NC.

Pelissier, B., & McCarthy, D. (1992). Evaluation of the Federal Bureau of Prisons' drug treatment programs. In C. G. Leukefeld & F. M. Tims (Eds.), *Drug abuse treatment in prisons and jails* (NIDA Research Monograph 118, DHHS Publication No. ADM 92-1884, pp. 261-278). Rockville, MD: National Institute on Drug Abuse.

Schmidt, A. (1978). [Unpublished internal report]. Federal Bureau of Prisons, Washington, DC.

White, T. W., & Schimmel, D. J. (1993). *Suicide prevention in federal prisons: A successful five step program.* Unpublished manuscript.

CHAPTER 19

Mental Health Services to Substance Abusers

TED R. WATKINS

Substance abuse is the most frequently coexisting disorder among seriously mentally ill persons (Drake, Alterman, & Rosenberg, 1993). The coexistence of substance abuse and mental illness presents serious questions and is perceived to be a pressing service delivery problem in the mental health field.

Controversies exist over the issues of defining the nature of the two diagnostic groups (i.e., the mentally ill and substance abusers), determining which should be the primary diagnosis when both are present, and deciding what kinds of treatment should be provided in what order, in what kind of facilities, and with what sort of treatment staff. There is little consensus in this area of practice. The substance abuse may be viewed as one of the causes of the mental disorder or as a result of the mental disorder (Jung, 1994). Persons who have both mental illnesses and substance abuse problems present a new constellation of needs and therefore challenge the mental health community to make adaptations in both treatment planning and system design.

> The implications for community mental health agencies of this ever-spreading use and abuse of drugs are profound. Instead of working with distinct populations of "mentally ill" *or* substance-abusing people, each with a well-established protocol for treatment, we are trying to address ourselves to a mixed population with various symptom profiles and with multiple causative factors. In their interplay, these factors complicate assessment and treatment to a point where we have no recourse but change and adaptation in our treatment systems. (Ryglewicz & Pepper, 1992, p. 276)

Definition

Even the terminology used in referring to persons with coexisting problems of mental illness and substance abuse varies from author to author. The term most frequently used to refer to such a combination is *dual diagnosis*. "A 'dual diagnosis' person is an individual with both a substance abuse or dependency problem and a coexisting psychiatric disorder" (Evans & Sullivan, 1990, p. xi). Schmidt (1991) points out that *dual diagnosis* also refers to the fact that the problems crosscut two distinct and specialized treatment systems. Read, Penick, and Nickel (1993) suggest the term *multiple diagnosis*. Other terms include *mental disorders with chemical dependency* (Alterman, 1985) and *mentally ill chemical abuser* (Cohen & Levy, 1992).

For the purposes of this chapter, I prefer the terminology of Ryglewicz and Pepper (1992), who note: "We use the term *dual-disorder* rather than *dually diagnosed*, *MICA* (Mentally Ill Chemical Abuser), *SAMI* (Substance Abusing Mentally Ill), and so on, and the term substance *use* or *use/abuse,* in order to stress a broad conception of this client population" (p. 276).

Both mental illness and substance abuse disorders vary over a spectrum from mild to severe, and overlap with normal behavior. When both are present, the clinician must determine whether the person's problems are caused mainly by the substance abuse or by the psychiatric disorder, or by the interaction of the two.

Subtypes of Dual Disorder

Ryglewicz and Pepper identify four subgroups within the dual-disorder population. First are "people with *major mental illness* involving intermittent psychotic episodes even without the use of alcohol and drugs, and more frequent and severe episodes when these substances are used. For this group, even minimal *use* further jeopardizes their mental/emotional stability" (p. 277). This group would qualify for an Axis I diagnosis of mental illness, applying *DSM-IV,* but would be unlikely to have a diagnosis specifying alcohol or drug abuse.

Second are "people with *other psychiatric disorders such as severe personality disorder,* who suffer psychotic episodes *only* under the influence of alcohol and drug use. For this group, too, substance *use* at any level is a hazard, and there is a high potential for misdiagnosis" (p. 277). These individuals might be given an Axis I diagnosis when, without alcohol or drug influence, an Axis II diagnosis would be more appropriate. Gorski (1994) describes the difference: "Axis I mental disorders refer to episodes of dysfunction or acute crisis that present themselves and then subside. Axis II personality disorders refer to long-standing problems resulting from how a person habitually perceives the world and deals with thoughts, feelings and actions" (p. 51). Both of these first two subgroups described by Ryglewicz and Pepper are most likely to be found in psychiatric treatment programs.

Ryglewicz and Pepper's (1992) third subtype comprises "people whose persistent alcohol and/or drug use/abuse/dependence/addiction (and sometimes other factors) may lead to and reinforce persistent *personality immaturity and dysfunction*. For this group it is important to explore the relationship between the substance use and other patterns and skill deficits, as well as the level of the use or abuse itself" (p. 277).

Fourth are "people whose most obvious problem is alcohol and/or other substance use, but the use or withdrawal from use uncovers problematic symptoms and behavior. For this group, too, it is important to explore the circumstances, function, and consequences of the use and whether the person is substance-dependent or potentially able to exercise controls" (p. 277). Misdiagnosis in these cases is likely to involve lack of recognition of the mental illness, which is disguised by the chemical abuse.

Persons in the third and fourth groups are likely to be found in substance abuse treatment programs, where they may or may not benefit from treatment; however, they may also seek service, perhaps unrecognized, at mental health outpatient clinics.

Authorities in the fields of both mental health and substance abuse agree that the combination of the two disorders is more serious than either disorder alone, because the two exacerbate each other. For mentally ill individuals, any use of nonprescribed psychoactive drugs, including alcohol, may result in problems in functioning (DiNitto & Webb, 1994; O'Hare, 1992). As Ryglewicz and Pepper (1992) point out, "Alcohol and drug use places an additional and often overwhelming stress on an already shaky and stress-vulnerable system" (p. 278).

Biopsychosocial Aspects of Dual Disorder

Chemical dependency and mental illness both are currently seen as biopsychosocial conditions, although "no theoretical system exists currently that was specifically designed to address the development of dual diagnosis subtypes" (Read et al., 1993, p. 143). The *bio* (biological) dimension refers to the brain chemistry problems that underlie both disorders. Many persons with mental disorders have such fragile brain chemistry that even "social" use of alcohol or drugs can destabilize them and cause psychotic episodes, perhaps resulting in unnecessary hospitalization (Cutler, 1993; DiNitto & Webb, 1994; Ryglewicz & Pepper, 1992). Additionally, even casual use of alcohol and street drugs may bring on transient psychiatric problems in drug abusers, especially while they are actively using drugs or just after stopping use (National Institute on Drug Abuse [NIDA], 1991).

Psycho refers to the habitual patterns of perceiving, thinking, feeling, and acting that are related to the disorders (Gorski, 1994). "A person with a mental/emotional/personality disorder has, by definition, some impairment of ego functions involving one or more of the capacities for judgment, reality testing, impulse control, affect modulation, memory, mastery, competence, and so forth" (Ryglewicz & Pepper, 1992, pp. 279-280). Psychoactive drugs are, by definition, those that affect these ego functions.

Social refers to problems that develop in work, social, and intimate relationships as a result of the disorders (Gorski, 1994). Persons with mental/emotional disorders are vulnerable socially, their relationships and life situations often only tenuously maintained. Their social relationships tend to be nonreciprocal; that is, they involve much receiving and little giving (Westermeyer, 1985). Their families, friends, and lovers already have lived through many crises related to the disorders and may not be willing to endure more. People who have used up too much of their "social margin" through episodes of their psychiatric illness may pay an extra-heavy price for getting into trouble with alcohol and drugs (Ryglewicz & Pepper, 1992).

Incidence of Dual Disorders

There is an obvious overlap between the portion of the population made up of substance abusers and that made up of those who experience serious and chronic psychiatric problems. Psychoactive drugs such as crack cocaine, heroin, and amphetamines have become readily available and affordable in recent years, and their usage has increased among the mentally ill as well as in the general population. Most mentally ill individuals have used psychotropic drugs at some point in their lives.

Estimates of the incidence of dual disorders vary widely, but persons with mental illnesses appear to be at greater risk for substance abuse disorders than are members of the general population (Evans & Sullivan, 1990; Nuckols & Repotosky, 1994; O'Hare, 1992; Ryglewicz & Pepper, 1992). For example, Drake et al. (1993) report that persons with schizophrenia have a 10.1 times greater rate of alcohol use disorders than nonschizophrenic people. Different research studies suggest that from 7% to 60% of all psychiatric patients also have substance abuse problems (Cohen & Levy, 1992). The estimates are even higher when only young adult mentally ill are considered, and in some settings the majority of young adult psychiatric clients have problems with substance use (Cutler, 1993; DiNitto & Webb, 1994; Ryglewicz & Pepper, 1992). Gorski (1994) reports that studies of relapse-prone chemical dependency patients show that more than 85% have coexisting personality or mental disorders.

Much of the variance in estimates of the incidence of the coexistence of mental illness and substance abuse is related to the specific diagnostic category of the mental illness reported. Several authorities have observed that the specific mental disorder of the individual drug abuser seems to be related to the type of substance chosen for abuse, and some have suggested that this fact supports a theory of drug abuse as a form of self-medication (DiNitto & Webb, 1994; NIDA, 1991). Additional factors that may be associated with differences in the proportions of psychiatric diagnoses seen among substance abusers are gender, primary drug of abuse, and socioeconomic status. The lack of standardization of diagnostic procedures and the different mixes of gender and socioeconomic levels make it impossible to draw conclusions regarding the relative frequencies of different diagnoses among the various substance abuse samples (NIDA, 1991).

A major impediment to the gathering of valid figures concerning the prevalence of coexisting substance abuse and mental problems is found in the biases of treatment personnel. Substance abuse professionals tend to interpret symptoms of mental illness as byproducts of the drug use (Jung, 1994; Lewis, Dana, & Blevins, 1994), and mental health professionals often overlook substance abuse. In reality, it is often impossible to determine whether the primary cause of aberrant behavior is mental illness, substance abuse, or the interaction of the two.

In spite of the factors discussed above, it is nevertheless clear that substance abuse research samples generally have higher proportions in every mental disorder category than do general community samples. The one diagnostic category that is most dramatically overrepresented among substance abusers, regardless of gender and socioeconomic status, is antisocial personality disorder (NIDA, 1991).

The dual-disordered population currently appears to be increasing. It is uncertain, however, whether this is a genuine increase related to heavier drug use, beginning at earlier ages and accompanied by family and socioeconomic problems; a perceived increase based in heightened awareness and better detection procedures; or both. Younger individuals may be at greater risk for developing multiple disorders than are individuals born at an earlier time (Read et al., 1993). Certainly the combination of deinstitutionalization and the increasing acceptance of drug use have resulted in more persons with mental illness, particularly young persons, being "at large" in the society, where street drugs and alcohol are readily available. Cutler (1993) states that current methods of treating the severely mental ill strip them of "the relative comfort" of their hallucinations and delusions, then thrust them into the stark reality of life outside the hospital with minimal social support. "It isn't surprising that many of them turn to . . . substances that are readily available" (p. 194). Large numbers of homeless, a lack of community services, decreased funding for mental health and drug abuse treatment, the refusal of many specialized programs for the treatment of mental illness or substance abuse to admit dual-disordered patients, and generally poor coordination of services all contribute to an accumulation of the untreated in the community (Cohen & Levy, 1992).

Persons having dual disorders are expensive patients to treat, in financial as well as human terms. They make disproportionate use of medical, legal, and social services (often under emergency conditions) and require substantial administrative and treatment staff time. In addition to the time and resources required for their treatment, they are frustrating to treatment staff in traditional mental health or substance abuse programs (Fitsimones, 1994), having poor prognosis (Schmidt, 1991) and extremely high rates of recidivism (Gorski, 1994; NIDA, 1991), creating more problems of acting-out behavior and poorer medication compliance than patients having only one disorder (O'Hare, 1992), and having more than the usual ability to disrupt staff relations. Standard procedures that are effective with most other clients do not work well with those in this group.

Controversies Regarding the Dually Disordered

Historically, there has been considerable challenge to the categorization of substance abuse disorders as diseases separate from mental illnesses. It is often difficult to determine whether an individual's symptoms represent substance abuse or mental illness. Symptoms of a primary depressive disorder, for example, may look like symptoms that are secondary to long-term substance abuse. Or an intoxicated individual who claims to hear voices may be assumed to be in need of detoxification, but if once sober he or she continues to demonstrate psychotic behavior, this indicates that the problems are more complicated. On the other hand, overdiagnosis can occur when treatment staff mistake the withdrawal symptoms of early recovery from substance abuse for the symptoms of a mental illness. Substance abusers who are in early recovery may be diagnosed as having dysthymia or a major depressive illness, when in fact their depression is a normal part of the withdrawal process and will spontaneously go into remission with continuing abstinence.

The issue of whether substance abuse and mental illness are separate entities is related to assumptions regarding the causes of the disorders. Many mental health professionals view alcoholism and addiction as symptoms of underlying psychiatric disorders rather than as illnesses in their own right. Therefore, these professionals focus treatment on the "underlying" psychiatric problem, assuming that the substance abuse behavior will disappear as the "real" problem is resolved.

Conversely, some authorities suggest that chronic drug use causes mental illness by producing biological changes in the individual (DiNitto & Webb, 1994; Schmidt, 1991). Others maintain that substance use/abuse is an effort by the individual to "self-medicate" for mental illness (Schmidt, 1991), as demonstrated by the observation that "depressed individuals are drawn to barbiturate, benzodiazepine, and sedative-hypnotic use because these drugs help alleviate distressful symptoms (although over the long run, they may exacerbate depression)" (DiNitto & Webb, 1994, p. 316). However, the self-medication explanation does not fit the case of paranoid schizophrenics' use of hallucinogens and amphetamines, which exacerbate hallucinations, confusion, and suspiciousness.

Yet another perspective regarding the origins of dual disorders is that both the substance abuse and psychiatric disorders may be results of a third factor, which may be biological, familial, or social in nature (Read et al., 1993).

Despite the often similar appearances of substance abuse and mental illness, programs for treatment of mental illness and those for treating substance abuse are usually separate (Drake, Osher, & Wallach, 1991). Evans and Sullivan (1990) note that "governments continue to have separate departments for mental health and for alcohol and drug matters. . . . Separate training programs are the norm. Funding sources provide different benefit levels for the two sets of disorders, and funding for nontraditional programs is in short supply" (p. 6).

Achieving a valid diagnostic assessment and developing an appropriate treatment plan is difficult with dual-disordered clients. The clinician must determine whether the client will benefit more from services from a mental health facility, a substance abuse program, or a special program for dual-disordered clients. Often the diagnosis and treatment are determined by the bias of the professional seeing the client, rather than the client's needs (Cohen & Levy, 1992). The client may also be barred from treatment because he or she does not fit into the diagnostic categories of specialized programs. "Typically, this client is the dual-problem victim of a single-problem program and receives appropriate attention to one but not both of his or her problems—the psychiatric disorder *or* the substance abuse" (Ryglewicz & Pepper, 1992, p. 278). Mental health staff typically have been inattentive to problems of substance use and abuse (Gorski, 1994; Orlin & Davis, 1993), and "some mental health professionals refuse to treat alcoholics and addicts, even those with a coexisting psychiatric disorder, seeing them as resistant to traditional mental health approaches or as unlikely to benefit from treatment as long as they continue to use substances" (Evans & Sullivan, 1990, p. 6).

Several factors have been suggested as contributors to the lack of appropriate response of mental health professionals to the dual-disordered client. Training for the mental health professions usually does not include significant content on the use of or dependency on alcohol or drugs, or the assessment or treatment of substance abuse. Mental health treatment personnel often do not subscribe to the goal of abstinence, which may be needed by clients whose illness is easily exacerbated by even minor amounts of substance use. Mental health treatment programs seldom have formal assessment procedures for substance abuse, and substance use, when recognized, may be benignly viewed as merely "self-medicating" and essentially ignored while the psychiatric problems are addressed. Treatment philosophy is likely to be "supportive" rather than confrontive (Schmidt, 1991). When a serious substance abuse problem is recognized, it is likely to result in a referral to a substance abuse treatment program without psychiatric treatment. If the client is not referred, sequential treatment of one disorder, then the other, is more likely to be used than concurrent, coordinated treatment. Such sequential treatment is likely to be ineffective because of the interactive nature of the two disorders (Ryglewicz & Pepper, 1992). Sometimes improvement of one of the disorders through treatment is even associated with the worsening of the other diagnosed problem.

On the other hand, some substance abuse counselors either do not recognize psychiatric disorders in their clients or underestimate the need to treat the psychiatric disorder in dual-disordered clients. Education for the treatment of substance abuse does not include extensive training in psychopathology. Symptoms of mental illness are often misinterpreted as "resistance" to treatment or "denial" of a substance abuse problem. Substance abuse treatment facilities seldom include psychiatric evaluations and differential diagnoses, except, perhaps, after the client has already been labeled as "treatment resistant" or a "treatment failure." Symptoms of severe anxiety or depression are sometimes interpreted as by-products of the substance abuse or abstinence from it. When the client's mental illness causes atypical response to substance abuse treatment, the staff are more likely to refer to a psychiatric program than to modify their substance abuse treatment protocol to accommodate the dual-disordered client. Additionally, substance abuse treatment programs are seldom attuned to the need for outreach: in fact, they may rely heavily on the client's persistence in finding service as a sign of the client's "readiness" for treatment. The dual-disordered client often requires outreach, individualized treatment, and adaptations of the usual protocols for sustained and successful treatment. The typical program's emphasis on abstinence may cause the personnel to reject the mentally ill client who cannot maintain abstinence because of erratic motivation, difficulty with reality testing, and poor judgment and goal-directed effort (Ryglewicz & Pepper, 1992). This is especially troublesome when the client requires psychotropic medication, which many substance abuse counselors view as mood altering and therefore undermining to a person's recovery (Evans & Sullivan, 1990; Schmidt, 1991; Wich, 1994).

In view of the above, it is apparent that the separation of programs for the treatment of psychiatric disorders and substance abuse, and the lack of cross-trained staff, results in clients' emerging from either source of treatment with unmet needs and the experience of "failure."

> It is also a "system failure" that reinforces the lack of a perceived connection between substance use or abuse and the persistence or worsening of psychiatric symptoms. . . . Failure of the treatment system to respond adequately to the needs of dual-disorder clients has three aspects: (a) limitations within the mental health system, (b) limitations within the substance abuse system, and (c) lack of integration between the two systems. (Ryglewicz & Pepper, 1992, p. 280)

Recent Developments

Treatment

The significant economic, social service, and health care delivery problems presented by the population having both mental illness and substance abuse problems have resulted in a dramatic increase in the amount and types of clinical treatment offered them. Orlin and Davis (1993) have developed the Dual Diagnosis Assessment Form, which is an innovative way to clarify the relatedness of the client's psychiatric and substance use disorders. One type of treatment structure has been treatment in psychiatric programs utilizing substance abuse professionals to provide educational or treatment groups as "add-ons" to the mental health treatment. This has also led to the addition of urine monitoring and breath tests to track the progress of clients with substance abuse problems. Some "therapeutic community" treatment programs for drug abusers have opened up their programs to mentally ill abusers. This has necessitated a softening of confrontational techniques and a shift away from the hard-line resistance to the use of psychotropic medicines in many drug treatment programs.

Newer models attempting simultaneous treatment of both disorders are being tried in some settings, based on the similarities of the two disorders: extremes in behavior and impairment of functioning in numerous areas, chronicity and relapse, denial, multifactorial etiology, social isolation, inattention to physical health, negative impact on the family, loss of control, and sense of helplessness. Another impetus for simultaneous treatment of both disorders is their cyclical nature as well as the interplay of the disorders: Each problem exacerbates the other, so that progress in the treatment of one disorder is unlikely to be long-lasting unless the other illness is also brought under control (DiNitto & Webb, 1994; Orlin & Davis, 1993). In the past decade, large numbers of both public and private hospitals have opened specialty units for the treatment of mentally ill substance abusers. Elements in the treatment may be drawn from both psychiatric and substance abuse programs, combining individual, group, and family therapy; educational groups for clients and families; and introduction to self-help groups (DiNitto & Webb, 1994).

Psychoeducation is a new approach that has been gaining momentum with dual-disordered populations. Its nonjudgmental, didactic format provides patients with information that they can use to understand and protect themselves. Its work through the cognitive dimension of the client's functional ability complements psychotherapy's use of the emotional and evokes little resistance (Orlin & Davis, 1993). Orlin and Davis (1993) suggest the following topics for psychoeducational groups: defining mental illness and addiction in terms that the clients can understand and accept, theories of etiology, triggers for relapses, symptoms of mental illness and addiction, progression and patterns, family roles and involvement, good drugs and bad drugs, social and political issues in mental illness and addiction, and treatment planning. DiNitto and Webb (1994) recommend that psychoeducation stress the serious life problems that result from substance use, so that clients can see the ways in which their use exacerbates their psychiatric symptoms. This insight enables clients to recognize when symptomatic behaviors are beginning to occur so that they can seek assistance before complications become too serious.

DiNitto and Webb (1994) report on a psychoeducational group therapy program called Good Chemistry, which teaches clients to make more appropriate use of self-help groups, permits discussion of both mental and substance abuse illnesses, and reinforces the benefits of maintaining mental stability, including following medical recommendations regarding psychotropic medications and staying sober and clean. Additionally, some settings are sponsoring groups of Dual Recovery Anonymous, a 12-step organization specifically modified to meet the needs of persons with dual disorders.

Research

The increased clinical attention to the population of dual-disordered persons is matched by an increase in the number and diversity of research efforts: There were twice as many articles in professional journals about this diagnostic group in the 1980s as in all the years prior to 1980 (NIDA, 1991). Systematic research has been facilitated by improvements in diagnostic criteria and by the development of structured diagnostic interviews such as the Diagnostic Interview Schedule, the Psychiatric Diagnostic Interview—Revised, the Schedule for Affective Disorders and Schizophrenia, and the Alcohol Research Center Intake Interview (Read et al., 1993). The Addiction Severity Inventory Index has been used to identify substance-abusing psychiatric patients and has been considered the single best predictor of treatment outcome for substance-abusing populations. Generally, patients with the highest levels of psychiatric problems have the poorest outcomes, whereas those with the least severe problems are most likely to improve regardless of the type of treatment they receive (NIDA, 1991).

Further research has explored the effects of the duration of treatment, comparing the effectiveness of therapeutic community and methadone maintenance programs for substance abusers with various levels of severity of mental illness and other variables. Results seem to indicate that greater length of time in treatment increases the likelihood of positive change in all levels of clients and in both therapeutic communities and methadone maintenance programs, with one notable exception: Severely mentally ill clients worsened over time when treated in therapeutic community programs. This negative outcome is thought to be related to some of the characteristics of the therapeutic community model: sanction against the use of psychotropic medications, use of paraprofessionals and former addicts as counselors, and punitive and/or embarrassing confrontational group encounters. Although these techniques have proved effective with opiate abusers without serious mental illnesses, today's high-severity patient is often younger, uses more nonopiate drugs, and has few social and personal supports, and is therefore more psychologically fragile (NIDA, 1991; Schmidt, 1991).

The current research efforts will enable clinical personnel to make increasingly sound differential treatment decisions. However, there is still considerable measurement and criterion variability, and this remains a focus of ongoing research and reviews by professional standards committees. One major problem remaining is a definitional one, concerning whether or not symptoms that emerge following the onset of substance abuse should qualify as an additional psychiatric diagnosis. For example, many behaviors associated with antisocial personality (such as frequent job changes, criminal activity, and the use of illicit substances) are also associated directly with a protracted period of substance abuse. It may be argued that the consideration of these behaviors in the diagnosis of antisocial personality has resulted in an overestimate of this disorder among substance abuse populations (NIDA, 1991).

There is still much to be done in researching dual disorders and their treatment. Read et al. (1993) have observed that scientifically validated knowledge about dually disordered individuals is still skimpy: "This paucity is particularly true about the natural long-term course of these disorders and which kinds of treatments are more effective for which diagnosed conditions" (p. 123). Both basic research and outcome studies can contribute greatly to this field.

> Program evaluation and outcome research are always complicated endeavors, and perhaps especially so when the presenting problems are multifaceted. Participating staff believe in what they do and frequently hear informal accounts of their former clients' successes. However, observation, anecdotes, and intuition are not adequate substitutes for organized empirical studies, and systematic collection of history, intake, and follow-up data has now begun. . . . Relevant criteria of success include frequency and duration of psychiatric hospitalizations and chemical-dependency treatments; quality and length of abstinence; general medical care utilization; occupational functioning; financial independence; legal conflicts; satisfaction in interpersonal relationships; self-esteem; and personal and social responsibility. (Harrison, Martin, Tuason, & Hoffmann, 1985, p. 389)

Other Developments

The combination of the growth of awareness of the dual-disordered population and the continuing difficulty in finding appropriate and effective services for its members has resulted in the development of advocacy groups such as Addiction Intervention With the Disabled and the Institute on Alcohol, Drugs and Disabilities. These groups are pressing for substance abuse treatment adapted or designed specifically for multidisabled clients (DiNitto & Webb, 1994).

Treatment Recommendations

As Read et al. (1993) note, "Surprisingly little is known about how most effectively to treat individuals and their families with a dual diagnosis" (p. 144). The professional literature clearly shows that the population having coexisting and interdependent problems with substance abuse and mental illness is a diverse one. Often this diversity is not recognized by those making programming decisions or those referring specific clients for treatment. It is impossible to develop a single uniform model appropriate for all dual-disordered clients. As Gorski (1994) notes:

> What is needed . . . is a systematic analysis that will help clinicians to complete a differential assessment, determine the appropriate level of care, design a general

holistic treatment plan that will support the management of common or overlapping symptoms, and develop a disorder-specific treatment plan that will address the unique symptoms of each disorder. (p. 51)

Some subclassifications (based on several factors) are needed to guide programming and treatment decisions. Of primary importance are the nature and extent of the client's mental illness. Clearly, a client with chronic distortions of thought, such as hallucinations and delusions, requires a very different treatment protocol from one whose thinking is lucid but whose major psychiatric symptom is a chronic disregard for the rights of others. Broadly speaking, the mental status of the client needs to be classified as (a) an Axis I major mental disorder (such as schizophrenia or bipolar disorder), (b) an Axis II personality disorder, or (c) a disorder that is secondary to the substance abuse.

A second crucial factor consists of the nature and extent of the client's substance abuse. This includes the level of addiction (dependence) and the characteristics of the substance(s) being used. As Donovan and Marlatt (1988) point out:

It is important to avoid a "uniformity myth" that all addictions are equivalent. There are special characteristics of various addictions that make them distinguishable from one another. . . . Thus, it is important to consider both the commonalities involved in the addictive process and the unique features associated with specific objects of addiction when attempting to understand, assess, and treat an individual with an addictive behavior problem. (p. 22)

The third factor that must be taken into account in treatment planning is the client's current psychosocial situation. A treatment program for dual-disordered clients must look beyond traditional methods and conceptions of such programs' mission (Ryglewicz & Pepper, 1992). Such factors as homelessness, whether the individual's social network will support treatment or undermine it, and the financial resources available will heavily influence decisions concerning whether treatment can be handled on an outpatient basis or a period of inpatient treatment is required, how lengthy treatment may be, and what follow-up care options can be considered.

Prochaska and DiClemente (1986) have developed a transtheoretical model of treatment that first applies behavioral techniques to achieve a cessation of drug use, followed by cognitive techniques to identify the maladaptive thought patterns and feeling states that may trigger the substance use, family or network therapy to address relationship problems that may be a source of pain for the substance abuser, skills training for dealing with chronic problems the client has with the social environment, and, if needed, psychodynamic techniques for resolving intrapsychic problems. This comprehensive model is particularly relevant and helpful in the case of the client who has a mental disorder in addition to a substance abuse problem.

When circumstances prevent the use of such an extensive repertoire of techniques, behavioral and cognitive interventions will be sufficient in many cases. Evans and Sullivan (1990) report that they "place particular emphasis on the integration of cognitive-behavioral and the disease process and Twelve Step Recovery models as the most effective way we have found to work with these clients" (p. xiii).

Much of the literature gives a perhaps negatively biased view of treatment of dual-disordered persons, but Cohen and Levy (1992) put a positive spin on the process: "Dealing with mentally ill chemical abusers is always a story about human renewal. It is also about pluck, innovation, counterculture, outrageousness, and belief in the human spirit" (p. 11). What more can a therapist want?

Harrison et al. (1985) have noted:

> For many of the dual patients, "recovery" must be defined with cautious realism in view of their limitations. Some cannot be expected to achieve optimum recovery goals: permanent abstinence from alcohol and other drugs, a future free of psychiatric hospitalization, a return to the work force, and stable interpersonal relationships. Rather, recovery for some patients must be measured in terms of less frequent and less destructive encounters with chemicals, increased intervals of abstinence and satisfying sobriety, compliance with medication maintenance and fewer hospitalizations, less injurious behavior, and increased social responsibility and self-esteem. (p. 372)

Policy Recommendations

Several policy issues need to be resolved if mental health services to substance abusers are to be effective. First, the artificial boundary between "mental health" and "substance abuse" services must be breached or eliminated entirely. The connection between substance abuse and mental status is apparent to all who work in the field; only bureaucrats and some administrators seem to conceptualize the two as separate. Policies against "crossover" services (e.g., policies that require mental health agencies to refuse services to substance abusers, or funding channels to withhold funds for such services) are unethical and should be challenged legally. As Evans and Sullivan (1990) state, "Stricken by the disease of chemical dependency and suffering from a psychiatric disorder, the dually diagnosed individual is not well armed to deal with the system's conflicts" (p. 10). Some beginnings are being made in bringing the two kinds of services together. Some state mental health agencies are now employing persons with expertise in substance abuse treatment to help them serve the dual-disordered population more effectively.

Unfortunately, the current crisis over managed care and problems with high costs to insurance companies create a climate in which there seems to be some clamoring to cut costs by excluding groups of persons who need services. This leaves the dual-disordered client vulnerable to exclusion, although rationally, the client with mental illness and substance abuse problems should be eligible for both services rather than neither.

In the best of worlds, special expertise, and perhaps some special services and facilities, would be available specifically for dual-disordered clients. These services would be staffed by persons with "dual" training—that is, who have expertise in both mental health and substance abuse treatment. Such training would break down much of the distrust (and even contempt) that some professionals in the two fields hold for each other. This has implications for professional training programs, because at present there is little cross-training among any of the helping professions. Special facilities must not be discriminated against in licensing or third-party payments (O'Hare, 1992; Schmidt, 1991).

In the case of aggressive persons with personality disorders, such as those with antisocial personality disorder, treatment should be incorporated into any prison or probation sentence, so that the changes presumably sought as part of the sentencing can actually occur. A legal climate that fosters mandatory treatment for self-destructive mentally ill substance abusers would facilitate recovery for many persons now disabled by their dual disorders.

Prevention and early detection of dual disorders would reduce the casualties of these disorders. Blankertz, Cnaan, and Freedman (1993) note that "about one-fourth of [homeless dually diagnosed clients] had parents with a dually diagnosed profile. . . . We may be witnessing an intergenerational transmission of comorbidity" (p. 593). At present, there are few programs available to the children of dual-disordered clients. Further, child protection workers do not have the authority to require a dual-disordered client to seek help until there is a clear and present danger to a child. It has been frequently reported that intervention during adolescent or young adult years offers the best results in the treatment of character-disordered substance abusers. These youths often come to the attention of the police, school officials, and other authority figures in the community. Concerted efforts should be directed toward utilizing all these sources so that prevention and early intervention can succeed.

Clearly, as O'Hare (1992) puts it, "a framework for continued research and program development is needed" (p. 185). Research funding should be a high priority. The present time is one of extensive experimentation with different models of service to persons with coexisting mental illness and substance abuse problems. A national research agenda that can set a framework for state, local, and private efforts could go far in correcting and clarifying the mass of contradictory, and for the most part pessimistic, perspectives on this needy population. As Evans and Sullivan (1990) have observed: "Debate still exists about the best approach for counseling the chemically abusing or dependent individual and, in some cases, persons with certain psychiatric disorders. Dual diagnosis individuals can intensify this debate. . . . The available literature and research, although beginning to grow, are still limited" (p. xii).

References

Alterman, A. I. (Ed.). (1985). *Substance abuse and psychopathology.* New York: Plenum.

Blankertz, L. E., Cnaan, R. A., & Freedman, E. (1993). Childhood risk factors in dually diagnosed homeless adults. *Social Work, 38,* 587-596.

Cohen, J., & Levy, S. J. (1992). *The mentally ill chemical abuser: Whose client?* Lexington, MA: Lexington Books.

Cutler, D. L. (1993). Substance abuse in severely mentally ill patients: Why is there a problem? *Community Mental Health Journal, 29,* 193-194.

DiNitto, D. M., & Webb, D. K. (1994). Compounding the problem: Substance abuse and other disabilities. In C. A. McNeece & D. M. DiNitto (Eds.), *Chemical dependency: A systems approach* (pp. 312-348). Englewood Cliffs, NJ: Prentice Hall.

Donovan, D. M., & Marlatt, G. A. (Eds.). (1988). *Assessment of addictive behaviors.* New York: Guilford.

Drake, R. E., Alterman, A. I., & Rosenberg, S. R. (1993). Detection of substance use disorders in severely mentally ill patients. *Community Mental Health Journal, 29,* 175-192.

Drake, R. E., Osher, F. C., & Wallach, M. A. (1991). Homelessness and dual diagnosis. *American Psychologist, 46,* 1149-1158.

Evans, K., & Sullivan, J. M. (1990). *Dual diagnosis: Counseling the mentally ill substance abuser.* New York: Guilford.

Fitsimones, T. (1994). Dual diagnosis at Glenbeigh. *Behavioral Health Management, 14,* 40-41.

Gorski, T. T. (1994). A suggestion for conceptualizing dual diagnosis: A systematic analysis to help cut through the confusion and mismanagement. *Behavioral Health Management, 14,* 50-53.

Harrison, P. A., Martin, J. A., Tuason, V. B., & Hoffmann, N. (1985). Conjoint treatment of dual disorders. In A. I. Alterman (Ed.), *Substance abuse and psychopathology* (pp. 366-390). New York: Plenum.

Jung, J. (1994). *Under the influence: Alcohol and human behavior.* Pacific Grove, CA: Brooks/Cole.

Lewis, J. A., Dana, R. Q., & Blevins, G. A. (1994). *Substance abuse counseling: An individualized approach* (2nd ed.). Pacific Grove, CA: Brooks/Cole.

National Institute on Drug Abuse (NIDA). (1991). *Drug abuse and drug abuse research: The third triennial report to Congress from the secretary, Department of Health and Human Services.* Rockville, MD: Author.

Nuckols, C. C., & Repotosky, J. (1994). Clinical observations on the dually diagnosed. *Behavioral Health Management, 14,* 36-37.

O'Hare, T. (1992). The substance-abusing chronically mentally ill client: Prevalence, assessment, treatment, and policy concerns. *Social Work, 37,* 185-187.

Orlin, L., & Davis, J. (1993). Assessment and intervention with drug and alcohol abusers in psychiatric settings. In S. L. A. Straussner (Ed.), *Clinical work with substance-abusing clients* (pp. 50-68). New York: Guilford.

Prochaska, J. O., & DiClemente, C. C. (1986). Toward a comprehensive model of change. In W. R. Miller & N. Heather (Eds.), *Treating addictive behaviors: Processes of change* (pp. 3-27). New York: Plenum.

Read, M. R., Penick, E. C., & Nickel, E. J. (1993). Treatment for dually diagnosed clients. In E. M. Freeman (Ed.), *Substance abuse treatment: A family systems perspective* (pp. 123-156). Newbury Park, CA: Sage.

Ryglewicz, H., & Pepper, B. (1992). The dual-disorder client: Mental disorder and substance use. In S. Cooper & T. H. Lentner (Eds.), *Innovations in community mental health* (pp. 270-290). Sarasota, FL: Professional Resource Press.

Schmidt, L. (1991). Specialization in alcoholism and mental health residential treatment: The "dual diagnosis" problem. *Journal of Drug Issues, 21,* 859-874.

Westermeyer, J. (1985). Substance abuse and psychopathology: Sociocultural factors. In A. I. Alterman (Ed.), *Substance abuse and psychopathology* (pp. 45-68). New York: Plenum.

Wich, M. J. (1994). Pioneering dual diagnosis care at St. Anthony's Medical Center. *Behavioral Health Management, 14,* 38-39.

PART IV

*Implications for the
21st Century*

There is always uncertainty involved in contemplating the future. Some trends in mental health policy and practice from the past and present may reasonably be projected into the next century. Certainly the "information age" will continue to influence mental health policies and services as it does many other facets of our lives. In Chapter 20, Albert Farrell describes the impact of technology on mental health services up to the present time and anticipates technology's influence well into the future.

In Chapter 21, E. Clarke Ross and Colette Croze provide an up-to-the-minute report on managed care, looking at the historical means of paying for services and several options now being promoted as cost-control measures. As these authors explain, the future of funding for mental health services is likely to follow one or more of the models now being tried.

Finally, we end this volume with a brief discussion of the issues that we believe will weigh heavily in decision making concerning the future of mental health services and policy.

CHAPTER 20

The Influence of Technology on Mental Health Services

ALBERT D. FARRELL

Scientists, futurists, political leaders, and members of the media have suggested that computers represent a revolutionary technological development as significant as written language and the printing press (Elwork & Gutkin, 1985). There can be little doubt that advances in computer technology during the past 20 years have had profound impacts on our everyday lives. Application of this technology to a wide array of problems has changed the way we go about such mundane tasks as scheduling airline reservations (computerized booking systems), paying for merchandise (optical scanners), writing letters (word processors), sending letters (e-mail, fax machines), and shopping for cars (computerized databases). Computer chips can be found in automobiles, heating and cooling systems, musical instruments, children's toys, and hearing aids. In the coming years we can expect to see increasing reliance on computer technology as systems become increasingly powerful and less expensive.

The potential offered by computer technology has not gone unnoticed by those working in the mental health field. Indeed, there has been a long history of efforts to develop computer applications to facilitate and improve mental health services. These efforts have yielded some promising applications that could result in dramatic changes in mental health practice. In this chapter I present an overview of some of the types of applications that have been developed, discuss the current status of computer utilization by mental health service providers, and describe some of the barriers to more widespread use of computer applications in the mental health field.

By the end of the 1970s there was already a considerable literature discussing the application of computer technology to mental health services. Enthusiastic descriptions of the potential of computers for facilitating and improving services were backed up by examples of creative applications of computer technology (see, e.g., Angle, Ellinwood, Hay, Johnsen, & Hay, 1977; Greist, Klein, & Van Cura, 1973; Schoech & Arangio, 1979). By 1981, Hedlund et al. were able to identify nearly 1,400 articles on computer applications in mental health published between 1966 and early 1980. In their state-of-the-art review they discuss applications of computer technology to a wide range of tasks, including interviewing clients; keeping treatment notes; administering, scoring, and interpreting psychological tests; assigning psychiatric diagnoses; making treatment suggestions; and conducting interventions with clients.

These early efforts are particularly impressive considering the hardware available at the time. Early computer applications were developed for centrally located mainframe computers or minicomputers such as the PDP-11. The development of applications for these systems required a high degree of technical sophistication; this was many years before the concept of "user-friendliness" was in vogue. Because of these limitations, the applications that were developed were often slow, cumbersome, and difficult to access. Applications such as mental health information systems were often run in batch mode, which required keypunching data onto cards that were read into a mainframe computer, which then generated printed output (Hedlund, 1987). The development of microcomputers in the late 1970s dramatically improved this situation, although the early microcomputers did not have many features we currently take for granted. For example, a typical system purchased in 1979 came with 48 kilobytes of memory, monochrome monitor, a single floppy disk drive, and thermal printer, did not offer such features as lowercase letters, and cost nearly $3,000. Nonetheless, microcomputers provided increased access to computer technology and encouraged greater numbers of mental health professionals to develop applications.

Developers of computer applications in the mental health field during the early stages enthusiastically embraced whatever technology was available and creatively applied it to a variety of problem areas. These early pioneers had a broad vision of what computers could do and of the positive impacts computers could have on the profession. Although few of the systems they developed remain in use today, their work demonstrated the variety of problems that could be addressed by computer technology and set the stage for more sophisticated applications that followed. At another level, these efforts forced professionals to consider what it was appropriate for computers to do. The field as a whole has yet to reach consensus regarding the appropriateness of using computers for tasks such as implementing interventions and guiding treatment decisions. I will return to this issue after giving an overview of the wealth of applications that have been developed in the mental health field.

The Potential: An Overview of Computer Applications in Mental Health Services

Over the past decade, the number and variety of computer applications within the mental health field have increased dramatically. Butcher (1987), for example, listed 170 test-scoring and interpretation packages. A sourcebook of "psychware" by Krug (1988) listed several hundred applications. In 1987, the American Psychological Association published a directory listing more than 150 computer applications for use in clinical practice (Stoloff & Couch, 1987). In this section I provide an overview of some of the types of computer applications that have been developed within the mental health field and describe a few representative applications. This discussion is not intended to serve as a review of everything computers have been used for; rather, my intent is to examine some promising applications that show what is possible. Readers interested in more extended discussion of these applications should consult the works listed in the reference section by Butcher (1987), Krug (1988), and Stoloff and Couch (1987); the review by Hedlund, Vieweg, and Cho (1987); and the recent text by Schlosser and Moreland (1993).

Computer-Based Assessment Applications

A wide variety of computer applications have been developed to facilitate the collection and recording of information directly from clients. These include computer-based versions of self-report inventories, computerized interviews, and computer systems designed to record behavioral and physiological variables.

Computer versions of a variety of psychological tests are available (Hudson, Nurius, & Reisman, 1988; Moreland, 1985). In contrast to the paper-and-pencil forms of these tests, the computer versions present clients with test items on the computer screen; clients enter their responses directly into the computer, using the keyboard or other input device. Computerized tests can save clerical time and improve accuracy by eliminating the need for hand scoring. Objective personality tests have been particularly easy to adapt to the computer (Butcher, Keller, & Bacon, 1985). This has been facilitated by questionnaire drivers, authoring systems that enable users to construct computer versions of tests by simply entering the test questions into the computer. Computers are also capable of more sophisticated applications. One particularly promising development is computerized adaptive testing, in which items are tailored to the individual based on his or her responses to earlier items. It has been suggested that this approach could reduce the length of some psychological tests by as much as 50%, without compromising measurement quality (Weiss & Vale, 1987).

Computers have also been used to conduct clinical interviews. As with computerized test administration, clients enter their responses directly into the computer. Computer-based interviews differ from computerized tests in that they cover the same content as do clinical interviews. Just as a human interviewer asks follow-up questions, computer-based interviews use branching to determine which questions to ask based on responses to earlier questions. In this manner, computer interviews provide more flexibility than paper-and-pencil tests. Computer-based interviews also offer advantages over human interviewing. Erdman, Klein, and Greist (1985) note that computer interviews are (a) reliable in that they always ask the questions they are supposed to, (b) have the potential for being less uncomfortable or embarrassing to the client because they do not respond to the client's answers to sensitive questions, and (c) provide a complete record of responses to every question. Computer-based interviews have been developed to collect general information about psychiatric and social history and to address specific areas such as suicide risk, alcohol and drug use, sexual dysfunction, and mental status (Erdman et al., 1985). Although practitioners have been skeptical about clients' reactions to computer-based interviews, there is now considerable evidence indicating both that clients are capable of completing computer interviews and that they typically respond positively to them (Farrell, Camplair, & McCullough, 1987). Indeed, several studies have shown that some clients prefer answering questions on the computer rather than to a human, and that under certain conditions their responses on the computer may be more candid (Erdman et al., 1985).

The Computerized Assessment System for Psychotherapy Evaluation and Research (CASPER; McCullough, Farrell, & Longabaugh, 1986) is an example of a computer interview. CASPER was designed to identify clients' presenting problems, track them during treatment, and evaluate treatment outcomes. This system includes a comprehensive intake interview that assesses clients' presenting problems. When a client's responses suggest the presence of a particular problem, the client is asked additional questions about that problem (e.g., Is it a major problem? How long has it been a problem? How severe is it? What is its priority for treatment?). Upon completion of the interview, CASPER prints a report that includes the responses to all items and a problem list. This information is also entered into a client database. During subsequent interviews, the computer accesses the client's problem lists and asks the client to rate the severity of each major problem. To determine the effectiveness of treatment, CASPER provides individualized client and therapist outcome measures that include measures of global therapy outcome as well as ratings of the severity, change, and focus during treatment for each of the client's major problem areas. These data can be aggregated and used to conduct group analyses for treatment outcome studies or program evaluation. Studies examining the validity of CASPER have been encouraging, and clients have responded well to using the system (Farrell et al., 1987).

Computers have also been used to facilitate the collection of behavioral assessment data. Behavioral assessment differs from traditional assessment in that it focuses directly on behavior and the situations within which particular behavior occurs, rather than on underlying traits (Goldfried & Kent, 1972). In my own work, I have reviewed computer applications developed for behavioral assessment, including systems developed to conduct behavioral interviews, to collect self-monitoring and observational data, and to record physiological variables (Farrell, 1991). An excellent example of how computers can be used to collect behavioral assessment data is provided by Agras, Taylor, Feldman, Losch, and Burnett (1990), who developed a system for treating obesity that enables the client to monitor his or her own behavior using a small, hand-held computer. The client enters in the computer his or her daily goals for caloric intake and exercise and records caloric information for all meals and snacks. During the day, the client can check his or her total caloric and exercise values. The computer also includes a meal planner, a trainer to promote slow eating, random messages to motivate the client and remind him or her of "distorted cognition" regarding eating, reinforcing messages contingent on progress, and graphs of the client's daily caloric intake, exercise, and weight. Evaluations of this system have found it to be as effective as therapist-conducted weight-loss programs.

Decision Support Systems

Computer applications have also been developed to improve clinical decision making. Mental health practitioners are called upon to make numerous decisions about any given case, such as assigning a diagnosis, determining a community placement, selecting a referral agency, designing a treatment plan, and determining when to terminate treatment. These are complex decisions that require the professional to have information about the individual case and procedural knowledge about how to use this information to arrive at the best decision. A variety of computer applications have been developed to assist practitioners in this decision-making process. Examples include information services, computer-based test interpretation programs, and expert systems.

Information services are designed to provide practitioners with up-to-date access to the scientific literature. These services can provide information about the relative effectiveness of different intervention strategies for a particular type of client, the availability of new assessment instruments, and risk factors for specific problem areas (e.g., suicide, sexual abuse). The Lithium Information Center described by Carroll et al. (1986) is an example of such a service. The center was established in 1975 to disseminate information about the medical uses of lithium to mental health professionals, physicians, patients, and patients' friends and families. In addition to housing more than 12,000 articles pertaining to lithium, the center allows individuals to use their computers to gain remote access to the Lithium Library, a bibliographic retrieval system; the Lithium Index, a set of literature summaries that also includes clinical recommendations; and the Lithium Consultation, an interactive interview that provides clinical information relevant to individual cases. During its first 10 years of existence, the Lithium Information Center responded to more than 5,000 requests for information. This center is an excellent example of how computers can provide human service professionals with detailed, clinically relevant information to inform their treatment decisions.

Computer-based test interpretation programs are another example of how computers can be used to facilitate clinical decision making. As Roid (1985) notes, correct test interpretation requires familiarity with a massive body of research literature and clinical lore associated with each assessment instrument. Practitioners may have considerable difficulty personally storing and retrieving this information for every instrument they use. In contrast, computer-based test interpretation programs can apply complex decision rules with greater accuracy and consistency than can humans, process a greater number and variety of variables more rapidly, and provide considerable savings in time and effort (Roid, 1985). These systems are based on rules that relate specific patterns of test scores to interpretive statements. These rules may be based on empirically derived sets of rules or designed to simulate an expert's test interpretations.

Another approach to using computers to support decision making involves the construction of expert systems. Expert systems represent an application of developments in the area of artificial intelligence. These systems attempt to simulate the decision-making strategies of experts (Gingerich, 1990b; Schoech, Jennings, Schkade, & Hooper-Russell, 1985). In contrast to statistical models, which use quantitative data and algorithms to make decisions, expert systems use inference or reasoning to draw conclusions. Some expert systems are even able to examine their own reasoning and explain it to the user. These features enable expert systems to address problems where complete information may not be available (Gingerich, 1990b). As Gingerich (1990b) notes, the development of human expertise requires years of training and experience, and it is often in short supply. In contrast, computer-based expert systems may be easily and inexpensively reproduced and permanently stored, and they may perform more consistently than humans. Such systems can also be updated on a periodic basis. The construction of expert systems requires a multidisciplinary effort involving a partnership between a domain expert and a knowledge engineer (Gingerich, 1990a). This process can be difficult, because experts are rarely sufficiently conscious of their expertise to explain it to others (Schoech et al., 1985). One of the benefits of undertaking this task is that the process of building such a system may provide a wealth of information about the procedural knowledge within a given area (Nurius & Nicoll, 1992).

The Mental Retardation Expert (MRE), developed by Hile and his colleagues (see Hile & Desrochers, 1994), provides an excellent example of a decision support system that incorporates features of an expert system. MRE was designed to provide state-of-the-art consultation to practitioners treating aggressive, self-injurious, and destructive behaviors displayed by individuals with mental retardation or developmental disabilities. The expert system component of MRE is based on knowledge obtained from multiple sources, including the research literature and experts. The user responds to a series of questions about the client's behaviors, the situation, and past interventions, and is provided with functional hypotheses and treatment recommendations. Throughout this process, MRE allows the user to refine initial responses and, when prompted, can explain the reasoning behind each question it asks. Hile and Desrochers (1994) note that the emphasis of MRE is on improving clinical decision making, not replacing it. MRE makes specific treatment recommendations but requires the clinician to integrate them into the treatment plan. MRE also includes reviews and detailed summaries of the current scientific literature on specific behaviors, examples of standard treatment plans for specific behaviors, and a glossary of 356 relevant behavioral terms and procedures. MRE has been found to provide suggestions that agree substantially with those of human experts, to influence treatment decisions significantly, and to have a high degree of acceptance among clinicians (Hile, Campbell, & Ghobary, in press).

Computer-Based Interventions

Computer applications have also been developed to implement interventions directly with clients. This type of application has been extremely controversial, particularly when computers have been used to simulate traditional, face-to-face, verbally interactive, conversational-mode psychotherapy (Lawrence, 1986). Concerns have been based not only on the technical limitations of current computer programs, which cannot successfully process natural language, but on whether it is even appropriate to use computers to conduct psychotherapy (Bloom, 1992; Lawrence, 1986). More progress has been made in developing interventions based on behavioral principles. In particular, computers have been used as an adjunct to therapy (e.g., biofeedback, self-monitoring) and to train clients in specific behavioral and cognitive skills (Bloom, 1992; Lawrence, 1986).

Most computer-based interventions have focused on training clients in specific skills. Computer-based education programs have been developed to prevent alcohol and drug use, increase responsible sexual behavior, prevent delinquent behavior, enhance self-esteem, modify self-destructive lifestyles, and reduce disruptive classroom behavior (Bloom, 1992). The majority of these programs have been based on computer-assisted instruction, or the use of computers to present didactic material to clients. Computer-assisted instruction offers a number of advantages: (a) Users are active participants in the learning process; (b) users can proceed at their own pace; (c) the computer is patient, impartial, and objective; (d) the computer provides immediate feedback; (e) instruction can be modified based on previous responses; (f) the computer can control audiovisual media; (g) the computer can simulate real-life situations; and (h) the computer provides improved reinforcement of learning (Flynn & Kuczeruk, 1984; Sampson, 1986).

Although early systems used text to present most material, the development of computer-interactive video has made possible simulations that include video presentations. Olevitch and Hagan (1989) developed a computer-interactive videodisc simulation for training chronic psychiatric inpatients to use community resources to reduce the likelihood of rehospitalization. This video shows the main character being released from a psychiatric hospital. At various points, the video action is frozen and the user is asked to make decisions about what the main character should do in response to different problem situations. The user selects from choices presented on a touch-sensitive screen, and the video continues based on the responses selected. At the end of the simulation, the user is given feedback based on the consequences of the decisions he or she made. This simulation provides a safe way for patients to learn about the consequences of various behaviors by vicariously experiencing problems that might arise from not taking prescribed medications and from making poor use of community resources.

Another approach to designing computer-based interventions has been taken by Servan-Schreiber and Binik (1989), who developed a system based on intelligent tutoring. Their program, Sexpert, was developed to assess and treat sexual dysfunction. Sexpert includes a diagnostic module that attempts to identify problems based on responses to a series of questions asked of each partner. The order in which questions are asked is designed to simulate a therapeutic dialogue by following dialogue plans that determine what questions to ask based on the user's responses to previous questions. Once a problem has been diagnosed, the system is capable of designing and implementing specific treatment plans, which include homework. Sexpert can also monitor treatment progress and infer reasons a couple may succeed or fail at an exercise.

One of the potential benefits of computer-based interventions is that they may ultimately increase access to services. Schneider, Walter, and O'Donnell (1990), for example, offered an interactive smoking cessation program through a national computer network with about 360,000 subscribers. Computer networks have become increasingly popular among home computer users, who access the networks through computer modems connected to telephone lines. These networks provide numerous services, such as banking, airline reservations, computer games, home shopping, weather reports, news wire service reports, and stock information. As Schneider et al. note, only a small percentage of smokers who could benefit ever enroll in face-to-face smoking cessation programs. They posited that offering such a service through a computer network might be a way to involve smokers who might not otherwise seek treatment. Their program included a variety of behavioral techniques users could use to stop smoking and prevent relapse. Instructions were tailored to individual users, who were able to access the program 24 hours a day, as often as they wished. A total of 1,158 smokers enrolled in the program during the 3-month period it was offered. Results of a comparison study indicate that there was a trend for smokers who received a full version of the program to show the highest abstinence rates. As this experiment illustrates, advances in technology such as computer networks and interactive public access television (Ruberg, 1989) may further increase the availability of services, particularly in remote areas.

The Reality: Issues Affecting the Use of
Computers in Mental Health Practice

Although a wealth of clinical computer applications have been developed, little progress has been made toward routine use of these applications in mental health settings (Greist, Klein, Erdman, & Jefferson, 1983; Hedlund, 1987; Mathison, 1987). This is particularly true for such clinical applications as computerized interviews, decision support systems, and interventions. For example, one study found that although more than half of a sample of practicing psychologists reported using computers in their practices, less than 10% reported routine or frequent use of their computers for anything other than clerical applications (Farrell, 1989a). Similarly, Monnickendam and Cnaan (1990) found that information technology has had little significant impact on the daily activities of frontline social workers. In this section I discuss some of the factors that appear to have impeded the routine use of clinical computer applications and suggest how some of these barriers may be overcome.

Practitioner Issues

The most frequently cited obstacle to the routine use of clinical computer applications is resistance among practitioners (Greist et al., 1983; Hedlund, 1987). Practitioners' reluctance to incorporate computers into their clinical work has been attributed to a variety of concerns. Hammer and Hile (1985) conducted an extensive review of this literature and identified nine process variables related to practitioners' acceptance of computer applications: (a) discrepancies between clinicians' preferred methods for gathering information and making decisions and those required by computers; (b) concerns that clients will respond negatively to interacting with the computer; (c) beliefs that computers are not yet sufficiently advanced to be useful in mental health settings; (d) value conflicts, or concern over whether computers should be used in mental health settings; (e) goal conflicts between different user constituencies; (f) concerns that computers will decrease clinicians' power and status; (g) fears related to evaluation; (h) concern over legal issues; and (i) concern over potential ethical issues.

Although Hammer and Hile's summary of the literature reflects a range of concerns about computer applications that have been attributed to mental health professionals, the current importance of these factors is not clear. As these authors point out, much of the literature in this area consists of anecdotal reports based on unsuccessful attempts to implement specific applications. Few systematic, empirical studies of practitioners' attitudes have been conducted. Moreover, practitioners' attitudes may have changed since much of this research was conducted. Most of this research was based on practitioners' experiences with early mental health information systems, which were difficult to use and of little benefit to practitioners (Hedlund et al., 1987). It is unclear whether practitioners would react the same way to more sophisticated, user-oriented applications. Other dramatic changes in the mental health field in recent years may have further influenced some of these factors. The managed care movement and increasing paperwork demands by third-party payers may have led practitioners to accept evaluation and documentation of services as an inevitable part of their work. Computer applications that facilitate this process may now be viewed as useful tools rather than agents of regulation. The experiences of those who have employed computer applications with clients, such as computerized interviews, have shown that most clients are able to complete the applications and generally react positively to them (Erdman et al., 1985). Increasing familiarity with computers may also have influenced practitioners' general attitudes toward clinical computer applications. As members of an increasingly computer-dependent society, mental health professionals have had to accept a greater role for computers in other aspects of their lives. This situation will no doubt continue to change with the emergence of a new generation of professionals who grew up with computers (Greist et al., 1983).

My own work provides support for the notion that practitioners' attitudes toward computer applications may have changed (Farrell, 1989a). Participants in a survey were asked to rate their attitudes toward the use of computers for specific applications. Although practitioners were somewhat negative toward using computers for decision making (e.g., generating a diagnosis) and direct interventions (e.g., conducting psychotherapy with clients), they were positive toward using computers for test administration and scoring, and for instructing clients in various areas (e.g., health promotion, vocational counseling). Practitioners who were not using computer applications in their practices were also asked to rank order the factors responsible for this decision. Factors that received the highest rankings from nonusers were mostly related to practical issues, such as lack of time to learn how to use applications and lack of adequate training or experience, rather than to factors associated with negative attitudes toward computer applications.

Results of this survey suggest that many practitioners may be interested in using computers but lack information about how to get started. Although most professionals have some familiarity with using computers for tasks such as word processing, few have the skills needed to implement clinical computer applications. Practitioners interested in using computers for more than clerical tasks face a variety of ominous tasks, including (a) determining the tasks for which the computer will be used; (b) identifying, purchasing, and installing the hardware best suited to these applications; (c) identifying applications that meet accepted professional standards; (d) learning how to use these applications appropriately; (e) evaluating how well these applications meet their needs; and (f) monitoring the ongoing use of these applications in their practice (Farrell, 1989a). Successful completion of this process requires access to a considerable body of information, much of which is not readily accessible. Although lists of software are available (e.g., Krug, 1988; Stoloff & Couch, 1987), these sources provide little evaluative information about individual applications. Software displays at conventions provide opportunities to examine applications and to obtain information about their use. However, obtaining information from vendors regarding the extent to which their software meets accepted standards can be very difficult (Farrell, 1989b).

As Hammer and Hile (1985) state at the outset of their review, some resistance to computer applications may be appropriate. Simply increasing practitioners' use of computers is not a desirable goal in and of itself. Whether a given computer application is beneficial or not is an empirical question that needs to be addressed as such (Erdman at al., 1985). Practitioners bear the responsibility for the appropriate use of computers and cannot be expected to use clinical computer applications unless there are carefully developed, thoroughly evaluated applications available for them to use. Ensuring that computers are used in a responsible manner will require a major effort not only on the part of practitioners but also among developers of computer applications and the field as a whole.

Developer Issues

Developers of clinical computer applications must share responsibility for the slow dissemination of computer applications in mental health. Although many applications have been developed and described in the literature, most have been demonstration projects. Relatively few off-the-shelf clinical applications are currently available, and few of those that are available have been adequately evaluated. I discuss below some of the difficulties associated with developing, evaluating, and disseminating clinical computer applications, and consider some of the issues that need to be addressed in this area.

One weakness of many clinical computer applications is that their developers have lacked needed expertise. Developers of applications need more than the technical expertise required to ensure that their applications run correctly; they must have other types of specialized expertise. For example, the development of an expert system requires expertise in both artificial intelligence and decision theory (Gingerich, 1990a). Developers of clinical applications need thorough knowledge of the content areas addressed by their applications. For example, the development of a computer-based test interpretation package requires expertise in test construction and assessment, as well as a thorough understanding of the factors that influence the interpretation of the specific test. Regrettably, the needed expertise has not always been in place. Moreland (1985) notes that many computer-based test interpretation systems have been developed by individuals with no special qualifications who develop systems that stray far from the empirical data. Such systems produce impressive-looking reports of questionable validity. The quality of clinical computer applications could clearly be improved through the encouragement of collaborative efforts between individuals with technical expertise and those with a thorough grasp of the targeted substantive area (Flynn, 1990; Reinoehl & Hanna, 1990).

Attempts to integrate clinical computer applications into routine use have also been hindered by developers' failure to pay sufficient attention to process variables. Hammer and Hile (1985) identify several factors that have caused difficulties in the implementation of computer applications. One crucial factor is the involvement of clinicians and other users throughout the development process. Involving users in the early stages of development ensures that the program will meet their needs and adds to their sense of personal power and investment in the application. Applications are also more likely to be accepted if they save time. Hammer and Hile note that users sometimes find that collecting and entering data into the computer can take more time than the manual methods they used previously. Users of such systems are unlikely to be excited about using them unless they provide other benefits. Other crucial implementation variables identified by Hammer and Hile include the time and effort required for training staff, the quality of the documentation, and the availability of ongoing consultation. Failure to consider one or more of these issues has led to many unsuccessful applications.

In many cases developers of computer applications have not devoted sufficient effort to evaluating the quality of their applications (Farrell, 1984; Hofer & Green, 1985). Products are often marketed before adequate validity studies are completed, and software vendors may be unwilling or unable to provide users with sufficient information to evaluate their products (Farrell, 1989b). In other instances, software is developed by computer "hackers" and distributed through informal networks without adequate testing or documentation (Farrell, 1984). This has led to serious concerns about the quality of computer applications, particularly in the area of assessment. In some instances computer versions of established tests have been marketed before it has been determined that they have the same reliability and validity as the original tests (Hofer & Green, 1985). In other instances tests have been developed specifically for the computer, without the publication of any data on reliability or validity (Moreland, 1985). Developers of many computer-based test interpretation programs have been criticized for failing to provide any empirical support for their decision rules (Matarazzo, 1986; Skinner & Pakula, 1986). Although it is important to evaluate all mental health services, it is particularly important to evaluate computer applications, because they have the capability of being implemented on such a large scale. For example, whereas one human expert who makes poor diagnostic decisions will have a negative impact, one computerized expert system implemented in several statewide hospital systems will have many more negative impacts. The lack of information about the quality of many computer applications has made it difficult for practitioners to incorporate these applications into their practice.

Developers of clinical computer applications have often had difficulty obtaining the financial support needed to complete their work. The proper development, implementation, and evaluation of clinical computer applications can be a daunting task. The process requires a long-term commitment that continues beyond the development stage. This includes providing documentation and ongoing user support, controlling access to qualified users, and updating applications to reflect developments in the scientific literature. Such efforts do not come cheap, and developers often find it difficult, if not impossible, to obtain needed financial support. Commercial development of software for a market as limited as psychologists is rarely profitable (Schneider, 1991). Federal funding is also limited, although individuals have achieved some success by developing applications directed at high-priority content areas and by pursuing funding under the Small Business Research Initiative program (Schneider, 1991). Limited funding also suggests the need for greater collaboration and sharing of resources among software developers.

Developers of clinical computer applications also need greater recognition for their efforts. Considering the level of effort required, the development of computer applications is not adequately rewarded (Flynn, 1990; Monnickendam & Cnaan, 1990). Promotion and tenure committees need to recognize the contributions of university-based researchers to the development of computer applications. Incentives also need to be provided for practitioners who participate in the development and field testing of these applications (McCullough et al., 1986).

Issues for the Mental Health Field

As the preceding sections illustrate, both practitioners and developers of clinical computer applications face serious obstacles. To overcome these obstacles, the mental health field needs to take a more active leadership role. A number of issues must be addressed, including the establishment of standards for the development and appropriate use of computer applications, the development of mechanisms for disseminating information about applications, the development of programs for training practitioners in the responsible use of computer applications, and the continued development of a scientific knowledge base to provide a foundation for future developments in this area.

Repeated calls have been made for the mental health field to establish standards governing the evaluation and appropriate use of computer-based applications (Hartman, 1986; Hofer, 1985; Matarazzo, 1986; Skinner & Pakula, 1986). Many practices related to the use of clinical computer applications come under general guidelines governing professional practice and standards for specific areas such as psychological testing (Farrell, 1984; Kramer, 1985). However, computer applications pose some unique legal and ethical problems that require more specific standards governing their use. For example, developers of computer-based test administration programs need to be concerned about the possible influence of irrelevant factors such as computer literacy on performance (Hofer, 1985). Erdman et al. (1985) suggest the need for appropriate screening measures when computerized self-help programs are not supervised by clinicians. If such programs are not targeted appropriately, they may prevent some individuals from obtaining needed help and could make their problems worse. Concerns have also been raised about the unregulated use of computer-based test interpretation programs by individuals who lack sufficient knowledge about test interpretation (Matarazzo, 1986). These are just a few of the many concerns that need to be addressed by standards for responsible use of computer applications (Hartman, 1986; Hofer, 1985; Matarazzo, 1986; Moreland, 1985; Zachary & Pope, 1984). It is important that mental health professionals, rather than computer experts, the government, or third-party payers, take a leadership role in the development of such standards (LaMendola, Glastonbury, & Toole, 1989; Matarazzo, 1986; Skinner & Pakula, 1986). Past experience with such efforts highlight the difficulty that lies ahead. For example, in 1986 the American Psychological Association published specific standards governing the use of computer-based test interpretations. However, the APA was recently prevented from distributing these standards because certain provisions in them run counter to Federal Trade Commission requirements (Schlosser & Moreland, 1993).

There is also a need to establish mechanisms for evaluating and disseminating information about clinical computer applications. As previously noted, practitioners interested in using computer applications often find it difficult to obtain evaluative information about the applications they are interested in. There is a need for critical examinations of software conducted by independent reviewers. Such reviews would enable potential users to determine the extent to which vendors' claims about software are justified. In order for such a system to work, developers of computer applications must be willing to submit their applications for review. This has often been a problem. For example, many developers of computerized test interpretation software have been unwilling to make their decision rules and interpretive libraries accessible for review (Skinner & Pakula, 1986). In my own experience as software review editor for the journal *Behavioral Assessment,* I found that few developers of behavioral assessment applications were willing to submit their products for review. If practitioners insist on documentation that software meets standards, we may hope that the market will dictate that software developers provide such information.

Practitioners will not be able to take make effective use of computers until they acquire some basic computer skills. A major initiative is needed to develop programs to train practitioners in the use of computers (Hammer & Hile, 1985; Schoech & Arangio, 1979). These programs need to focus on practical issues and should provide experience with relevant applications. No single program will meet the varying needs and proficiency levels of all practitioners; programs will need to be tailored to specific groups. Ultimately, this training must be incorporated into graduate programs. In addition to basic computer skills, practitioners may also need familiarity with technical aspects of computer hardware, including programming, artificial intelligence (Hartman, 1986), and information and decision theory (Mutschler, 1990). Professions within the mental health field will need to establish the minimum proficiency to be required of practitioners.

A final issue to be addressed by the field is the development of the scientific basis that will be required for developing further computer applications. The development of a computer application demands a very detailed understanding of the specific application. Computer-based test interpretation systems require empirically valid rules for linking responses to interpretive statements. As

Butcher (1987) notes, few psychological tests have sufficient foundations of valid empirical information to support generalizable test inferences. Expert systems can be developed only where actual expertise exists (Gingerich, 1990b). The use of computer-based interventions requires the capability of selecting the most appropriate intervention for a specific client. Computer technology has advanced to the point where many things are technically possible, but we lack the substantive knowledge to take advantage of them. Lanyon and Johnson (1980) suggest that mental health service delivery is essentially in a pretechnological phase:

> Individually provided services are emphasized. There are relatively few tools or structured procedures. Standardization is lacking. The treatment process is seldom characterized by specific knowledge of cause and effect or ability to estimate the probability of success. Well defined categories for disorders and for treatment are lacking. The major process for training is the apprenticeship system, and the importance of a scientific base tends to be de-emphasized in favor of "experience." (p. 18)

The use of computer applications in mental health is on the verge of entering a new stage. We now have sufficient experience in developing clinical computer applications to have a basic understanding of the issues that need to be addressed before computer applications can be routinely implemented. As Hedlund (1987) notes, the major issues that need to be addressed do not relate to the technology itself, but rather to how the technology will be used. Over the next decade advances in technology will provide the tools for increasingly sophisticated applications. Travis (1987), for example, suggests that dramatic progress in miniaturization will lead us to consider computers a part of our clothing. Butterfield (1988) suggests that computers may eventually be developed with the ability to "see, smell, and sense temperature changes, in addition to noting changes in voice intonation and stress levels" (p. 29). Virtual reality systems that use technology to create artificial realities (Davis, 1991) could provide opportunities for mental health professionals to assess clients' behavior in simulations of relevant situations under controlled conditions. These are just a few samples of the exciting opportunities that are likely to present themselves. Whether we in the field of mental health will embrace this technology and use it to maximum effectiveness or reluctantly have it foisted upon us by outside parties remains to be seen.

References

Agras, W. S., Taylor, C. B., Feldman, D. E., Losch, M., & Burnett, K. F. (1990). Developing computer-assisted therapy for the treatment of obesity. *Behavior Therapy, 21,* 99-109.

American Psychological Association. (1986). *Guidelines for computer-based tests and interpretations.* Washington, DC: Author.

Angle, H. V., Ellinwood, E. H., Hay, W. M., Johnsen, T., & Hay, L. R. (1977). Computer-aided interviewing in comprehensive behavioral assessment. *Behavior Therapy, 8,* 747-754.

Bloom, B. L. (1992). Computer-assisted psychological intervention: A review and commentary. *Clinical Psychology Review, 12,* 169-197.

Butcher, J. N. (Ed.). (1987). *Computerized psychological assessment.* New York: Basic Books.

Butcher, J. N., Keller, L. S., & Bacon, S. F. (1985). Current developments and future directions in computerized personality assessment. *Journal of Consulting and Clinical Psychology, 53,* 803-815.

Butterfield, W. H. (1988). Artificial intelligence: An introduction. *Computers in Human Services, 3*(1-2), 23-35.

Carroll, J. A., Greist, J. H., Jefferson, J. W., Baudhuin, M. G., Hartley, B. L., Erdman, H. P., & Ackerman, D. L. (1986). Lithium information center: One model of a computer-based psychiatric information service. *Archives of General Psychiatry, 43,* 483-485.

Davis, D. B. (1991). Reality check. *Computer Graphics World, 14*(6), 49-54.

Elwork, A., & Gutkin, T. B. (1985). The behavioral sciences in the computer age. *Computers in Human Behavior, 1,* 3-18.

Erdman, H. P., Klein, M. H., & Greist, J. H. (1985). Direct patient computer interviewing. *Journal of Consulting and Clinical Psychology, 53,* 760-773.

Farrell, A. D. (1984). When is a computerized assessment system ready for distribution? Some standards for evaluation. In M. D. Schwartz (Ed.), *Using computers in clinical practice: Psychotherapy and mental health applications* (pp. 185-189). New York: Haworth.

Farrell, A. D. (1989a). The impact of computers on professional practice: A survey of current practices and attitudes. *Professional Psychology: Research and Practice, 20,* 172-178.

Farrell, A. D. (1989b). Impact of standards for computer based tests on practice: Consequences of the information gap. *Computers in Human Behavior, 5,* 1-11.

Farrell, A. D. (1991). Computers and behavioral assessment: Current applications, future possibilities, and obstacles to routine use. *Behavioral Assessment, 13,* 159-179.

Farrell, A. D., Camplair, P. S., & McCullough, L. (1987). Identification of target complaints by computer interview: Evaluation of the Computerized Assessment System for Psychotherapy Evaluation and Research. *Journal of Consulting and Clinical Psychology, 55,* 691-700.

Flynn, J. P. (1990). Issues in the introduction of computer and information technology in human services. *Computers in Human Services, 6,* 21-33.

Flynn, J. P., & Kuczeruk, T. (1984). Computer-assisted instruction for the private practitioner. In M. D. Schwartz (Ed.), *Using computers in clinical practice: Psychotherapy and mental health applications* (pp. 395-416). New York: Haworth.

Gingerich, W. J. (1990a). Developing expert systems. *Computers in Human Services, 6,* 251-263.

Gingerich, W. J. (1990b). Expert systems: New tools for professional decision making. *Computers in Human Services, 6,* 219-230.

Goldfried, M. R., & Kent, R. N. (1972). Traditional versus behavioral assessment: A comparison of methodological and theoretical assumptions. *Psychological Bulletin, 77,* 409-420.

Greist, J. H., Klein, M. H., Erdman, H. P., & Jefferson, J. W. (1983). Clinical computer applications in mental health. *Journal of Medical Systems, 7,* 175-185.

Greist, J. H., Klein, M. H., & Van Cura, M. (1973). A computer interview for psychiatric patient target symptoms. *Archives of General Psychiatry, 29,* 247-253.

Hammer, A. L., & Hile, M. G. (1985). Factors in clinicians' resistance to automation in mental health. *Computers in Human Services, 1*(3), 1-25.

Hartman, D. E. (1986). On the use of clinical psychology software: Practical, legal, and ethical concerns. *Professional Psychology: Research and Practice, 17,* 462-465.

Hedlund, J. H. (1987). Mental health computing: Directions for research. In J. H. Greist, J. A. Carroll, H. P. Erdman, M. H. Klein, & C. R. Wurster (Eds.), *Research in mental health computer applications: Directions for the future* (DHHS Publication No. ADM 87-1468). Washington, DC: Government Printing Office.

Hedlund, J. H., Vieweg, B. W., & Cho, D. W. (1987). Mental health computing in the 1980s. In J. H. Greist, J. A. Carroll, H. P. Erdman, M. H. Klein, & C. R. Wurster (Eds.), *Research in mental health computer applications: Directions for the future* (DHHS Publication No. ADM 87-1468). Washington, DC: Government Printing Office.

Hedlund, J. H., Vieweg, B. W., Wood, J. B., Cho, D. W., Evenson, R. C., Hickman, C. V., & Holland, R. A. (1981). *Computers in mental health: A review and annotated bibliography* (DHHS Publication No. ADM 81-1090). Washington, DC: Government Printing Office.

Hile, M. G., Campbell, D. M., & Ghobary, G. (in press). Automation for clinicians in the field: The validity of a performance support system. *Behavior Research Methods, Instruments, and Computers.*

Hile, M. G., & Desrochers, M. N. (1994). Decision support in designing behavior treatments: The Mental Retardation Expert. *Computers in Human Behavior, 10,* 325-332.

Hofer, P. J. (1985). Developing standards for computerized psychological testing. *Computers in Human Behavior, 1,* 301-315.

Hofer, P. J., & Green, B. F. (1985). The challenge of competence and creativity in computerized psychological testing. *Journal of Consulting and Clinical Psychology, 53,* 826-838.

Hudson, W. W., Nurius, P. S., & Reisman, S. (1988). Computerized assessment instruments: Their promise and problems. *Computers in Human Services, 3,* 51-70.

Kramer, J. J. (1985). Epilogue: Why not standards for computer-based testing and test interpretation? *Computers in Human Behavior, 1,* 317-320.

Krug, S. E. (1988). *Psychware sourcebook* (3rd ed.). Kansas City, MO: Test Corporation of America.

LaMendola, W., Glastonbury, B., & Toole, S. (1989). Information technology for service planning and administration. *Computers in Human Services, 4,* 157-168.

Lanyon, R. I., & Johnson, J. H. (1980). Technology in mental health: A conceptual overview. In J. B. Sidowski, J. H. Johnson, & T. A. Williams (Eds.), *Technology in mental health care delivery systems* (pp. 17-24). Norwood, NJ: Ablex.

Lawrence, G. H. (1986). Using computers for the treatment of psychological problems. *Computers in Human Behavior, 2,* 43-62.

Matarazzo, J. D. (1986). Computerized clinical psychological test interpretations: Unvalidated plus all mean and no sigma. *American Psychologist, 41,* 14-24.

Mathison, K. S. (1987). Issues in research on clinical computer applications for mental health. In J. H. Greist, J. A. Carroll, H. P. Erdman, M. H. Klein, & C. R. Wurster (Eds.), *Research in mental health computer applications: Directions for the future* (DHHS Publication No. ADM 87-1468, pp. 79-88). Washington, DC: Government Printing Office.

McCullough, L., Farrell, A. D., & Longabaugh, R. (1986). The development of a microcomputer-based mental health information system: A potential tool for bridging the scientist-practitioner gap. *American Psychologist, 41,* 207-214.

Monnickendam, M., & Cnaan, R. A. (1990). Teaching information technology to human service students: Meeting the needs of the future. *Computers in Human Services, 7,* 149-163.

Moreland, K. L. (1985). Validation of computer-based test interpretations: Problems and prospects. *Journal of Consulting and Clinical Psychology, 53,* 816-825.

Mutschler, E. (1990). Computer assisted decision making. *Computers in Human Services, 6,* 231-250.

Nurius, P. S., & Nicoll, A. E. (1992). Capturing clinical expertise: An analysis of knowledge "mining" through expert system development. *Clinical Psychology Review, 12,* 705-717.

Olevitch, B. A., & Hagan, B. J. (1989). "How to get out and stay out": An educational videodisc for the chronically mentally ill. *Computers in Human Services, 5,* 57-69.

Reinoehl, R., & Hanna, T. (1990). Defining computer literacy in human services. *Computers in Human Services, 6,* 3-20.

Roid, G. H. (1985). Computer-based test interpretation: The potential of quantitative methods of test interpretation. *Computers in Human Behavior, 1,* 207-219.

Ruberg, L. F. (1989). Human services on cable: A case study of a data retrieval system designed for public access. *Computers in Human Services, 4,* 233-241.

Sampson, J. P. (1986). The use of computer-assisted instruction in support of psychotherapeutic processes. *Computers in Human Behavior, 2,* 1-19.

Schlosser, B., & Moreland, K. L. (Eds.). (1993). *Taming technology: Issues, strategies and resources for the mental health practitioner.* Phoenix, AZ: American Psychological Association, Division of Independent Practice.

Schneider, S. J., Walter, R., & O'Donnell, R. (1990). Computerized communication as a medium for behavioral smoking cessation treatment: Controlled evaluation. *Computers in Human Behavior, 6,* 141-151.

Schneider, W. (1991). Equipment is cheap, but the field must develop and support common software for psychological research. *Behavior Research Methods, Instruments, and Computers, 23,* 114-116.

Schoech, D. J., & Arangio, T. (1979). Computers in the human services. *Social Work, 24,* 96-104.

Schoech, D. J., Jennings, H., Schkade, L. L., & Hooper-Russell, C. (1985). Expert systems: Artificial intelligence for professional decisions. *Computers in Human Services, 1*(1), 81-115.

Servan-Schreiber, D., & Binik, Y. M. (1989). Extending the intelligent tutoring system paradigm: Sex therapy as intelligent tutoring. *Computers in Human Behavior, 5,* 241-259.

Skinner, H. A., & Pakula, A. (1986). Challenge of computers in psychological assessment. *Professional Psychology: Research and Practice, 17,* 44-50.

Stoloff, M. L., & Couch, J. V. (1987). *Computer use in psychology: A directory of software* (2nd ed.). Washington, DC: American Psychological Association.

Travis, L. (1987). Trends in information technologies and their implications for mental health research. In J. H. Greist, J. A. Carroll, H. P. Erdman, M. H. Klein, & C. R. Wurster (Eds.), *Research in mental health computer applications: Directions for the future* (DHHS Publication No. ADM 87-1468, pp. 54-64). Washington, DC: Government Printing Office.

Weiss, D. J., & Vale, C. D. (1987). Computerized adaptive testing for measuring abilities and other psychological variables. In J. H. Butcher (Ed.), *Computerized psychological assessment* (pp. 325-343). New York: Basic Books.

Zachary, R. A., & Pope, K. S. (1984). Legal and ethical issues in the clinical use of computerized testing. In M. D. Schwartz (Ed.), *Using computers in clinical practice: Psychotherapy and mental health applications* (pp. 151-164). New York: Haworth.

CHAPTER 21

Mental Health Service Delivery in the Age of Managed Care

E. CLARKE ROSS

COLETTE CROZE

What Is Managed Care?

Managed care has been characterized as "one of the most significant changes to our nation's health care financing and delivery system in recent years" (Davis, Collins, & Morris, 1994, p. 178). And one of the nation's most senior state mental health commissioners has observed that managed care "is probably one of the most complicated topics of the day. It's a profound change—a shift in the whole way of organizing health and mental health care" (Surles, 1991, p. 4).

But what is managed care? In a guidebook prepared for state legislators, the following definition is provided:

> Managed care is a term that describes health care systems that integrate the financing and delivery of appropriate health care services to covered individuals by arrangements with selected providers to furnish a comprehensive set of health care services, explicit standards for selection of health care providers, formal programs for ongoing quality assurance and utilization review, and significant financial incentives for members to use providers and procedures associated with the plan. (National Conference of State Legislatures, 1994, p. 2)

But what is it? Some of the leading thinkers on managed care have used more succinct phrases in attempts to define it:

- Negotiated quality for a negotiated price (Dyer, 1992, citing Boland, 1991)
- Capitated prospective payment to preferred providers based on a performance contracting system; whereby capitation is an upper limit on the payment, prospective whereby the provider assumes financial risk for the treatment of illness, preferred whereby providers must demonstrate quality and accessibility, and performance whereby the provider must earn the reimbursement (Dyer, 1992)
- "The core managed care technology-utilization review and selective contracting" (England & Vaccaro, 1991, p. 130)
- "A payer-driven, outcome-oriented, consumer-sensitive behavioral healthcare market" (National Community Mental Healthcare Council, 1993, sec. 1, p. 1)

From a management and policy perspective, managed care's "idea is to make sure that the right people are getting the right services at the right time" (Surles, 1991, p. 5).

To help explain better what managed care really is, it might be useful to present a discussion of managed care within a historical context of changing financing and service arrangements and then summarize some operational forms of managed care.

Managed Care as Public Policy: Historical Context of Mental Health Service Delivery

It is the judgment of several leading psychiatrists who have thought about and practiced clinical care that "managed care is the inevitable consequence of forces that have been building over the past half century. This era is only part of a long process of change" (Schreter, Sharfstein, & Schreter, 1994, p. xiii). Most historians would agree with the following historical summary of the changing locus of responsibility for the delivery of public mental health services: historic reliance on state-owned and -operated inpatient facilities where total care and living needs were managed; advances in medications and psychotherapy in the 1940s–1950s; the community mental health centers (CMHC) movement in the 1960s–1970s; and the increasing use of state general revenue as match for federal Medicaid dollars in the 1980s and 1990s. These movements and trends have significantly expanded public mental health services, but "these expansions occurred without regard to the cost of the services provided" (Schreter et al., 1994, p. xiii).

The shares of total state government budgets devoted to Medicaid rose from 8.1% in FY 1987 to 18.4% in FY 1993. In FY 1993, 39.6% of all federal money coming into state budgets was used for Medicaid, up from 26% in FY 1987. In July 1994, the National Association of State Budget Officers observed that "Medicaid spending is threatening the ability of decision makers to use the budget as a tool for implementing public policy," that Medicaid is now "the single most important cost factor for states," and that "Medicaid has passed higher education as the second largest category of state spending" ("Medicaid," 1994, pp. 15-16). A similar expenditure escalation has occurred in private industry as it pays for the cost of medical care for its employees where health care costs are now equal to corporate after-tax profits. Thus there is growing emphasis, in both the public and private sectors, on effectiveness and efficiency. "Seen in this light, managed care involves accountability for every dollar spent" (Schreter et al., 1994, p. xiii).

In May 1996, of an estimated 181.4 million Americans with health insurance, approximately 68.4% (nearly 124 million) were enrolled in some type of specialty managed behavioral health program ("68% of Insured," 1996).

These trends have resulted in "distress and distrust." These tensions have long been with us, but managed care has increased the tensions. More than two decades ago, Robert Alford (1975) wrote about the competition between "dominant structural interests, the professional monopolies" and "challenging structural interests, the corporate rationalizers." The dominant structural interests are those interests "served by the structure of social, economic, and political institutions as they exist at any given time." These groups, such as organized medical and professional guilds, attempt to use existing institutions to protect and reinforce the logic and principle of professional monopoly over the production and distribution of health services. Conflicts occur within these groups, but none challenges the principle of professional monopoly; these groups all share an interest in maintaining autonomy and control over the conditions of their work. Fee-for-service payment is their preferred source of reimbursement.

Alford's challenging structural interests are bureaucratic organizations, such as hospitals, managed care organizations, and public health agencies, that must tailor professional services to meet not only the health needs but the social needs of society. Their objective is to maintain and extend the control of their organizations over the work of the professions. They cannot achieve their organizational goals without the professions, but they also cannot manage their social mission or financial situation without controls over the professions. Alford also articulates a third category of health groups, the unserved and underserved population groups, which he terms "repressed structural interests." Their desire is to maximize the responsiveness of health professionals and bureaucratic organizations to their concerns for accessible, high-quality health care.

One of the leading current textbooks on managed care and mental health is titled *Allies and Adversaries* (Schreter et al., 1994). It summarizes the distress, distrust, and clashes between "clinicians-psychiatrists, psychologists, psychiatric nurses, and social workers—who feel they know what their patients need, especially with regard to quality and quantity" and "reviewers—an industry whose product is cost savings to those who pay for the care." In an era of limited resources, the clash has intensified. Regardless of their positions on the issue, to function both clinically and financially, those concerned with mental health policy and services will have to understand the forces at work (Schreter et al., 1994, pp. xiii-xiv).

> Over the last decade there has been a monumental debate in health policy about whether the direction of health and mental health care services should be shaped by the invisible hand of the market, the guiding hand of professional planning and peer review, or the controlling hand of governmental regulation and utilization review. (Dorwart, 1990, p. 1088)

Forms of Managed Care

"Although the term health maintenance organization was coined in the 1970s, the concept of prepaid health services dates back to the early 1900s. . . . World War II accelerated the expansion of prepaid health plans, as Kaiser Industries expanded the Kaiser Permanente health plan, established in 1938" (Davis et al., 1994, p. 179). These early prepaid plans were predominantly operated by not-for-profit organizations using either a "staff model HMO," which employed full-time salaried physicians, or a "group model HMO," which contracted with a medical group practice (Davis et al., 1994). By the 1950s, "individual practice association, IPA, model HMOs" developed, in which HMOs contract with a group of physicians to care for HMO members. These physicians are in private practice, not part of a group. Also during this period, "network model HMOs" developed, in which private practice physicians became part of networks of providers but were not part of actual "groups" (Davis et al., 1994, p. 180; National Conference of State Legislatures, 1994, p. 7). HMOs predominate in the managed care business, closely followed by preferred provider organizations (PPOs). In a PPO, a payer negotiates discounted rates for services directly with selected providers. Beneficiaries covered by the PPO may use providers outside the selected network, but there are out-of-pocket incentives to use preferred providers (National Conference of State Legislatures, 1994, pp. 6-7).

A new form of managed care is the exclusive provider organization (EPO). Here beneficiaries must seek services only from participating providers. Services rendered by unaffiliated providers are not reimbursed. The EPO practitioner has greater responsibility to the payer than does the PPO provider (National Conference of State Legislatures, 1994, p. 7). The most recent form of managed care to come into increased use is the point-of-service (POS) plan. If a beneficiary goes to a provider affiliated with the HMO or PPO, the care is covered. If the beneficiary goes to a provider outside the network, reimbursement may be significantly reduced. This model is designed to allow beneficiaries to consult with providers outside the plan's network (National Conference of State Legislatures, 1994, p. 8).

These four models—HMOs, PPOs, EPOs, and POSs—are predominantly private sector models. They are being used in the public sector, both for state government employees and through Medicaid waiver programs.

In the public mental health sector, the past decade has witnessed a focus on "organized systems of care." These systems strive to use a centralizing fiscal authority to allocate resources under a fixed budget (a form of global budget), frequently through an allotment formula, an administrative mechanism for coordinating the use of existing resources, a focus on providing the most appropriate clinical services to a patient or group of clients (by discouraging inpatient services and encouraging community, non-24-hour, services), and a focus on continuous management of conditions over time (frequently through case management strategies) (Goldman, 1991; Hogan, 1991).

"Managed behavioral healthcare has come about largely because our previous way of doing things failed to solve fundamental problems related to the cost, quality, access, and outcomes of care" (Freeman, 1995, p. x). Managed behavioral health care has gone through a number of phases. The first phase was prior authorization, the second phase was utilization review, and a third phase is utilization management—the matching of services, needs, and benefits and the use of second opinions (Bobbitt, 1995). Ron Geraty (1996) has characterized managed care in two stages: "Just Say No" and "Beyond Just Say No." The Just Say No stage of health care delivery was characterized by open, large networks of providers and no real provider behavioral change from its fee-for-service, no-outside-accountability philosophy, with the role of the managed care organization being utilization review (saying no). The Beyond Just Say No stage of health care delivery is characterized by smaller networks of providers, demonstrated quality and outcomes, provider discretion and understanding of payer expectations, no significant reliance on utilization review, and interdisciplinary and integrated service delivery.

Capitation Methodology

"Today's managed care systems may soon become dinosaurs, many health analysts predict. They say that the next generation of managed care—capitated systems in which physicians manage the costs and assume the risks of caring for a population—is on its way" (Moran, 1994, p. 8). A capitation payment is an established monthly payment to a provider in exchange for a defined set of medical or behavioral services to an identified individual. According to the American Psychiatric Association (1995), the keys to successful capitation are as follows:

- Clear definition of eligible members
- An idea of what constitutes a sufficient volume of covered members
- An understanding of whether the amount of services promised is manageable
- A definable scope of services
- A view of potential cost shifting across provider groups
- A plan to control consumption
- Commitment to fair negotiations
- Reasonable links between capitated population and providers
- Actuarially sound basis for adjusting capitation rates

Risk management challenges for successful capitation programs include the following (American Psychiatric Association, 1995):

- Inadequate population base (a critical mass is necessary for stability)
- Risk sharing (the greater the risk sharing, the less the capitation approach transfers risk)
- Catastrophic cases (individual stop loss; aggregate stop loss)
- Reserves and margins (IBNR [incurred but not reported] claims; contingency reserves [percentage of expected medical expenses in 1 year])
- Operational issues
  o Tracking and managing member eligibility status
  o Customer service department's provision of high-quality and accurate information to members
- Management information systems

Managed Care as a Focus on Outcomes: Quality Versus Cost

In God we trust; everyone else must supply outcome data.
     —U.S. Health Care

Cost is the driver—delivery is the key.
 —American Managed Behavioral Healthcare Association

Payers—both public and private—are capping budgets and restraining costs. Payers—both public and private—are fixing costs and using competition to obtain the best service array at the least cost. Given fixed budgets, outcomes and performance are the keys to service delivery under managed care. At the moment, three "report cards" are at the center of attention in managed behavioral health care: the National Committee for Quality Assurance's Health Plan Employer Data and Information Set (HEDIS), the American Managed Behavioral Healthcare Association's PERMS, and the Center for Mental Health Services's MHSIP.

The National Committee for Quality Assurance is an independent nonprofit organization established by the HMO industry to improve managed care plan performance through both accreditation and HEDIS. Because HEDIS is a comprehensive set of indicators applicable to all full-service HMO services, its behavioral health indicators are few: ambulatory follow-up after hospitalization for major affective disorders, inpatient utilization, ambulatory services utilization, and readmission rates for major affective disorders (National Committee for Quality Assurance, 1995a, 1995b).

Among the concepts and approaches underlying managed behavioral health care are these three: documented performance by managed care companies and providers as the basis of continued business; positive clinical outcomes and consumer satisfaction as bases for such documented performance; and the management of innovative and comprehensive service delivery networks to deliver individualized, appropriate, and flexible service arrangements (Ross, in press). Given these premises, in 1994 the American Managed Behavioral Healthcare Association (AMBHA) was established by organizations specializing in the management of mental illness and addiction disorders. AMBHA operates with two primary purposes: to promote parity for mental illness and addiction disorders in health plan benefit coverage and to promote open competition for health plan management based on documented performance in the areas of positive clinical outcomes and consumer satisfaction (Ross, in press).

In a study of AMBHA members conducted by Foster Higgins that included 48 million covered lives, quality of care was routinely measured and monitored (AMBHA, 1994). The study found the following:

- People enrolled in AMBHA member companies who sought treatment were double the norm compared with non-managed insurance plans.
- A total of 82% of enrollees rated their access to care as satisfactory to excellent.
- More than 90% of the patients rated their satisfaction with their network providers as satisfactory to excellent.

In September 1995, AMBHA published *PERMS 1.0: Performance Measures for Managed Behavioral Healthcare Programs*. The 18 AMBHA members will collect data on 75 million enrollees. The data elements are described below.

The standards use three classifications of indicators: access to care, consumer satisfaction, and quality of care. In the area of access to care, the actual indicators are as follows:

- Overall penetration rate (percentage of the enrolled population actually provided services)
- Penetration rate by age, diagnostic category, treatment setting, and clinician type
- Outpatient, inpatient, and intensive alternatives to inpatient utilization
- Cost data for persons with severe and persistent mental illness
- Structural issues such as call abandonment rate, on-hold time, and call answer time

In the area of consumer satisfaction, the actual indicators are as follows:

- *Access:* satisfaction with the time interval to the first appointment
- *Intake:* satisfaction with the intake worker
- *Clinical care:* satisfaction with the therapist
- *Outcome:* self-assessment of outcome
- *Global satisfaction:* rating of overall satisfaction

The quality of care, or quality of the clinical management process, is measured on three dimensions: efficiency, effectiveness, and appropriateness. Efficiency is measured using the following question: "Is the clinical management maximizing positive outcome while minimizing resource utilization?" The PERMS measures (a) follow-up status from a psychiatric inpatient discharge and (b) follow-up status from an inpatient substance abuse detoxification discharge.

Effectiveness is measured using the question, "Is the clinical management process providing the desired results?" The PERMS measures (a) ambulatory follow-up after hospitalization for major depressive disorder and (b) treatment failure for substance abuse.

Appropriateness is measured using the question, "Is the clinical management process providing an accepted standard of care?" The PERMS measures (a) availability of medication management for individuals with a diagnosis of schizophrenia, (b) family visits for children age 12 and under, and (c) appropriate utilization of resources for adults with an adjustment disorder.

In April 1996, the Center for Mental Health Services published *MHSIP: Consumer-Oriented Mental Health Report Card* (U.S. Department of Health and Human Services, 1996). CMHS is now looking for pilot test sites. The CMHS report card data elements include the following:

- Priority concerns related to *access*
  o Quick and convenient entry into services
  o A full range of service options
  o Cultural and linguistic access
  o Financial barriers

- Priority concerns related to *appropriateness*
  o Voluntary participation in services
  o Services that promote recovery
  o Services that maximize continuity of care
  o Consumer involvement in policy development, planning, and quality assurance activities
  o Adequate information to make informed choices
  o Application of best practice guidelines

- Priority concerns related to *outcomes*
  o Increased access to general health care
  o Minimal negative outcomes from treatment
  o Reduced psychological distress
  o Increased sense of personhood
  o Reduced impairment from substance abuse
  o Increase in productive activity
  o Capacity for independent community living

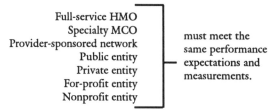

Figure 21.1. Public Accountability

    o Increase in independent functioning

    o Reduced involvement in the criminal justice system

    o Participation in self-help activities

    o Minimal recurrence of problems

    o Positive changes (in areas for which treatment is sought)

    o Increased natural supports and social integration

- Priority concerns related to *prevention*
  - o Information provided to reduce the risk of developing mental disorders
  - o Interventions designed to reduce the risk of developing mental disorders

A premise of managed behavioral health care companies is that any organizational entity claiming to manage behavioral health care must demonstrate accountability for the services it renders by using the same national measures and expectations. Every organizational entity—profit or nonprofit, public or private, full-service HMO or specialty behavioral health care program—must meet the same expectations and use the same measures (Ross, in press). Figure 21.1 represents an attempt to illustrate this advocacy point.

Public Sector Managed Mental Health

Whether in response to Medicaid reform or as a continuation of efforts to improve the public mental health system, a significant and growing number of states are becoming involved in managed mental health care. The variety in managed care models mirrors states' diverse approaches to mental health financing and service delivery and also reflects the variation in Medicaid policies and practices from one state to another. State mental health agencies' managed care efforts vary on a number of dimensions, the most significant being governance structure, benefits and provider network management, and payment methods. Although governance of mental health systems change might logically fall to the state mental health agency, when Medicaid cofunds a significant portion of the public system, the state Medicaid agency also determines public policy for mental health. In some states the Medicaid agency has assumed the role of "primary public payer" for mental health services, in other states the mental health agency retains control, and in yet another version, some states are collaborating in establishing program parameters. Although the commercial managed behavioral health care market has begun to merge benefits management with provider network management, many state mental health agencies are reluctant to contract for these functions in combination. They prefer, instead, to separate benefit management from the provision of service so that there is a somewhat external review of treatment. Finally, there are significant variations in payment methods states are using for managed mental health care, with models ranging from full capitation to case rate, to a combination of the two. The review below of specific states' initiatives covers each of these managed care design considerations.

With 24 states' public mental health systems currently affected by Medicaid reform efforts, several states have dramatically altered their public mental health systems through the initiation of managed care. Arizona has the longest-standing Medicaid-managed care program, and behavioral health was added in 1990; Utah has been conducting a demonstration of Medicaid-managed mental health care since 1991; Massachusetts initiated its Medicaid-managed Mental Health/Substance Abuse Program in 1992; Washington began to award contracts for managed mental health care in 1993 and completed statewide implementation by the end of 1994; Tennessee's TennCare program, which began in January 1994, includes almost all public mental health services in a statewide managed care system; and Oregon initiated managed mental health care for 25% of the state's population in January 1995.

Arizona

Arizona is unique among the states because it entered the Medicaid program in 1980 through a research and demonstration waiver from the Health Care Financing Administration and created the Arizona Health Care Cost Containment System (AHCCCS) as the state's medical assistance system to administer a managed care program for all Medicaid recipients. Through an intergovernmental agreement, the Division of Behavioral Health Services (DBHS, the state mental health agency) has managed the behavioral health "carve-out" since 1990, when these benefits were first covered. This Medicaid benefit was originally available only to adults with serious mental illness (SMI) and children with serious emotional disturbance (SED); Arizona's Medicaid program now covers AFDC recipients as well. DBHS establishes policies, develops the benefit design and scope, determines performance expectations and payment methods, and contracts with the vendors who administer the program.

Arizona's behavioral health services are administered through five regional behavioral health authorities (RBHAs), which are private, nonprofit corporations covering six geographic regions. Most do not deliver direct services, although the urban RBHAs do clinical case management (staffed by psychiatrists, social workers, and nurses), and some rural RBHAs deliver some services because providers are scarce. DBHS mandates a continuum of care focused on home- and community-based services; each RBHA chooses the providers with whom it contracts and the methods it uses.

Arizona originally financed behavioral health services through two single case rates—one for adults and one for children—once a person had been determined eligible, both financially (through a check against the Medicaid file) and clinically. Eligibility determination was done by the RBHA, using a definition based on diagnosis and functioning and that covered most mental illnesses. The behavioral health benefit package was and continues to be broad and includes "all medically necessary" transportation, counseling, in-home services, partial hospitalization, day treatment, inpatient hospitalization, and residential services. After using the case rate approach for 3 years, the DBHS made the transition to capitated contracts in 1996.

Utah

In 1991, Utah implemented a capitated mental health demonstration involving three community mental health centers, covering more than half of the state's Medicaid population, using a prepaid mental health plan approach. The state Medicaid agency had received Health Care Financing Administration approval of a freedom-of-choice waiver, which made it possible for the agency to contract with these CMHCs. Initiated as a response to dramatic growth in inpatient psychiatric spending, the demonstration originally financed only inpatient treatment on an at-risk basis, and outpatient services (a comprehensive, unlimited package) continued with fee-for-service payments. In January 1994, the CMHCs assumed full risk for inpatient and outpatient services, except for treatment provided to foster care children. Inpatient services for this group are provided on an at-risk basis; outpatient services are reimbursed through fee-for-service payments. The state has recently begun to implement plans to move to full capitation for all 11 CMHCs statewide.

Massachusetts

In January 1992, in response to continuing and accelerating spending increases, the Massachusetts Division of Medical Assistance entered into a contract with Mental Health Management of America (MHMA) to develop and operate a managed mental health program for about 375,000 Medicaid recipients as part of the broader Medicaid initiative called MassHealth Managed Care. MHMA managed the program until 1996, when the original contract expired and a new vendor was chosen through a competitive procurement.

Within MassHealth, Medicaid recipients have two choices for service delivery. They can either enroll with a health maintenance organization and receive all of their services through the HMO (including mental health and substance abuse) or they can enroll in the Primary Care Clinician Program and receive comprehensive mental health and substance abuse services through the Mental Health and Substance Abuse Program (MH/SAP). Operating as a prepaid health plan to deliver these benefits, the Managed Behavioral Healthcare Organization (MBHO) receives a capitated payment for each enrollee and is fully at risk for the provision of all "medically necessary" services. Although MBHO is prohibited by contract from directly providing any services, it conducts utilization review, performs case management and quality assurance, and handles all claims processing, and it has developed an extensive statewide network of providers from both the public and private sectors. An evaluation of the first 2 years of MHMA's management conducted by Brandeis University showed that spending was reduced by 22%, access increased by almost 5%, inpatient hospitalization decreased, and outpatient treatment was expanded (Callahan & Shepard, 1994).

Washington

Washington's public mental health system is administered by the Mental Health Division (MHD), with services delivered through 14 county-based regional support networks (RSNs), which were legislatively authorized in 1979 to cover the state's 39 counties.

Within the framework of the state's comprehensive health care reform under its Health Services Act of 1994, Washington has received Health Care Financing Administration approval for a freedom-of-choice waiver to contract with prepaid health plans (PHPs) that are administered by each RSN after they apply for PHP designation. As of February 1996, all 14 RSNs have received PHP designation.

Although the mental health system may eventually be fully integrated with the comprehensive health plans required by the Health Services Act, mental health's managed care implementation is being administered by the MHD, which intends to phase in financial risk and capitated payments. The benefits package includes the full range of outpatient community mental health rehabilitation services now available under the Medicaid state plan. PHPs must demonstrate the ability to cover all services, meet the needs of persons who are seriously and persistently mentally ill, and provide 24-hour services, 7 days a week. Qualified applicants for PHP contracts include anyone who is licensed or certified by the MHD and who can also be certified as a limited health care provider by the Office of the Insurance Commissioner. Currently, only RSNs have contracts. The PHPs oversee the provider network and are at full risk for service delivery; there is no stop loss provision in the contract, but the PHP can terminate its agreement with the MHD with 60 days' notice. PHPs can choose to receive a non-risk-based contract for children, because the state is uncertain about projected service utilization for this group.

Payments to PHPs are made monthly on a capitated basis, and financial (spending) reconciliation is made against three levels or "tiers" of capitated rates, with rates varying by RSN and actuarially determined based on historical service utilization data. Individuals served in the "base rate year" were placed in one of three tiers based on actual service utilization:

1. Persons with no more than 15 standardized service hours
2. Persons with more than 15 standardized service hours but fewer than 80 standardized hours (day treatment excluded)
3. Persons with more than 80 standardized service hours

Tier 1 capitation rates are allocated for all enrollees, regardless of service utilization. Payment rates for Tiers 2 and 3 are linked only to those enrollees who have been diagnosed as eligible for those tiers. Tier 2 persons are those who are chronically mentally ill adults or seriously emotionally disturbed children, or are at risk of becoming such, and for whom ongoing support is medically necessary to ensure stable community living. Tier 3 eligibles must meet these criteria plus additional indicators of potentially high service use. Statewide, total payments for service expenditures must not exceed 99% of the previous spending for outpatient rehabilitation services.

Statewide implementation was scheduled for completion by July 1995.

Tennessee

In November 1993, Tennessee received Health Care Financing Administration approval for a research and demonstration waiver to expand Medicaid coverage to previously uninsured populations using a totally managed care approach. Almost all publicly supported mental health services are included in the state's TennCare program, including services provided under the auspices of the Department of Mental Health. TennCare provides a basic mental health component of the physical health benefit and offers an expanded and unlimited benefit for adults with severe and persistent mental illness (SPMI) and children with serious emotional disturbance. These groups of enrollees must also receive case management.

Under the first TennCare plan, managed care organizations (MCOs) were to provide all covered services and receive a single capitated premium per enrollee per year plus a case rate for adults with SPMI and children with SED. Although TennCare began with fully integrated management of physical and mental health through the MCOs, the state revised that plan to require the MCOs to subcontract with specialty mental health networks for services to adults with SPMI and children with SED. In January 1996, the state issued a request for applications from MBHOs with whom the state would directly contract. Five MBHOs were approved for contracts and have consolidated into two joint ventures that began operation on July 1, 1996.

Oregon

In 1992, Oregon passed comprehensive legislation to reform the state's health care system through the Oregon Health Plan, which will achieve universal access to health care using a combination of public and private insurance plans. Following that action, the state requested and received a waiver of Medicaid requirements so that it could implement the plan. Under the umbrella of this waiver, the state then requested and received an additional waiver to develop prepaid mental health plans administered by the Mental Health and Developmental Disability Services Division (MHDDSD) beginning in January 1995. Mental health services are financed through a capitated arrangement, with 25% of the state's population covered. During this phase-in period, the MHDDSD will compare fee-for-service payment with capitated managed care, test the full integration of physical and mental health service, and measure the impact of mental health services on the use of physical health care. By July 1999, all state-funded mental health services will be prepaid and capitated.

Mental health managed care organizations (MHMCOs) were selected through a request for proposal process and then assumed responsibility for the provision of the full range of mental health services, including the first 30 days of inpatient care. Because of this, MHMCOs are required to have the financial capacity to assume full risk for service delivery. Because the state intends to integrate mental and physical health care eventually, only community mental health programs or their designees or comprehensive health plans were eligible to become MHMCOs.

Concluding Comments: Appropriate Applications of Managed Mental Health Care

Historically, public mental health agencies have attempted to offer adequate arrays of services under fixed budgets (a form of global budget). Private sector providers have attempted to prescribe what is in the patient's best clinical interest, regardless of cost, using fee-for-service arrangements, until the patient's insurance is exhausted. At that point, the patient has been transferred to the public mental health system. Today, both the public and private sectors are attempting to manage care in an effort to deliver appropriate care that meets the patient's clinical needs under a fixed budget. Though systems and benefits designers emphasize "outcomes," tensions are exacerbated by a lack of consensus in the mental health field regarding the efficacy of treatment interventions. Given this lack of consensus, more and more attention is being given to practice standards, treatment guidelines, and performance measures. An added complication of managed mental health care is the situation of involuntarily committed patients. Coercion is placed on the patient and, when combined with a fixed capitation, greater stress results (Petrila, 1994).

Programs must be put in place to assist patients, providers, and systems managers and designers to deal with these tensions. Practice standards, treatment guidelines, and performance measures should be helpful in reducing stress and tension in both patients and providers. Ultimately, for managed care and mental health services to work for the benefit of persons in need, society must create a "seamless" system. We simply have to get away from the notion that a person is a privately insured individual, and then when his or her benefits

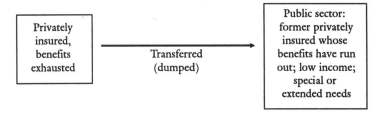

Figure 21.2. Predominant (Status Quo) Private-Public Model

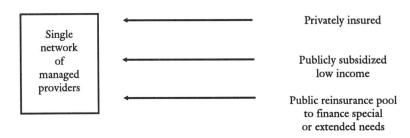

Figure 21.3. Alternative Model

are exhausted the individual becomes a public sector—that is, frequently second-class—citizen. We have to move away from the status quo model depicted in Figure 21.2 and toward an alternative model such as that pictured in Figure 21.3.

We conclude with the observations of medical ethicists Philip Boyle and Daniel Callahan (1995):

> Our contention is that managed care is inevitable, but this need be no more morally troubling than the present fee-for-service mental health system. If anything, attempts to manage care are or could be less morally doubtful. . . .
>
> To the extent that managed mental health care is making, and continues to make, good-faith attempts to curb abuses, rectify ethical problems, and address treatment effectiveness issues, it should prove superior in the whole to fee-for-service medicine. (pp. 11, 20)

References

Alford, R. (1975). *Health care politics: Ideological and interest group barriers to reform.* Chicago: University of Chicago Press.

American Managed Behavioral Healthcare Association. (1994). *Managed behavioral healthcare quality and access survey report.* Washington, DC: Foster Higgins.

American Managed Behavioral Healthcare Association. (1995). *PERMS 1.0: Performance measures for managed behavioral healthcare programs.* Washington, DC: Author.

American Psychiatric Association. (1995). *Actuarially determined capitation rates for mental health benefits.* Washington, DC: Author.

Bobbitt, K. (1995). Utilization management: Some practical advice. In M. Freeman & G. Zieman (Eds.), *The complete capitation handbook* (pp. 161-174). Tiburon, CA: CentraLink.

Boland, P. (1991). *Making managed health work.* New York: McGraw-Hill.

Boyle, P. J., & Callahan, D. (1995, Fall). Managed care and mental health: The ethical issues. *Health Affairs,* pp. 7-22.

Callahan, J. J., & Shepard, D. S. (1994). *Evaluation of the Massachusetts Medicaid Mental Health/Substance Abuse Program.* Waltham, MA: Brandeis University, Heller School for Advanced Studies in Social Welfare.

Davis, K., Collins, K. S., & Morris, C. (1994, Fall). Managed care: Promise and concerns. *Health Affairs,* pp. 179-185.

Dorwart, R. A. (1990). Managed mental health care: Myths and realities in the 1990's. *Hospital and Community Psychiatry, 41,* 1087-1091.

Dyer, R. L. (1992, July 14). *The many faces of public managed care in state mental health systems.* Paper presented at the summer meeting of the National Association of State Mental Health Program Directors.

England, M. J., & Vaccaro, V. (1991, Winter). New systems to manage mental health care. *Health Affairs,* pp. 129-137.

Freeman, M. (1995). Foreword. In M. Freeman & G. Zieman (Eds.), *The complete capitation handbook.* Tiburon, CA: CentraLink.

Geraty, R. (1996, January 25). [Remarks made at the conference of the Institute for Behavioral Healthcare, Behavioral Healthcare Delivery System Integration].

Goldman, H. (1991, June 17). *Perspectives on managed care in the public sector.* Paper presented at the 40th National Conference on Mental Health Statistics, National Institute of Mental Health.

Hogan, M. (1991, June 17). *Perspectives on managed care in the public sector.* Paper presented at the 40th National Conference on Mental Health Statistics, National Institute of Mental Health.

Medicaid: The elephant on the budget bus; controlling Medicaid costs; Can states solve the Medicaid problems? (1994, August). *State Policy Reports,* pp. 9-24.

Moran, M. (1994, October 21). Managed care: The next generation. *Psychiatric News,* pp. 8-13.

National Committee for Quality Assurance. (1995a). *HEDIS 2.5.* Washington, DC: Author.

National Committee for Quality Assurance. (1995b). *Medicaid HEDIS.* Washington, DC: Author.

National Community Mental Healthcare Council. (1993). *Managed care readiness in behavioral healthcare.* Rockville, MD: Author.

National Conference of State Legislatures. (1994). *What legislators need to know about managed care.* Denver, CO: Author.

Petrila, J. (1994, October). *Legal and ethical issues in managed care.* Speech delivered at the winter meeting of the National Association of State Mental Health Program Directors.

Ross, E. C. (in press). Managed behavioral health care premises, accountable systems of care, and AMBHA's PERMS. *Evaluation Review.*

Schreter, R., Sharfstein, S., & Schreter, C. S. (1994). *Allies and adversaries: The impact of managed care on mental health services.* Washington, DC: American Psychiatric Press.

68% of insured in managed behavioral health. (1996, May). *Open Minds,* p. 12.

Surles, R. (1991, August). Making the most of managed care for people with mental illness. *OMH News* (New York State Office of Mental Health), pp. 3-5.

U.S. Department of Health and Human Services, Center for Mental Health Services. (1996). *The MHSIP: Consumer-oriented mental health report card.* Washington, DC: Government Printing Office.

CHAPTER 22

Looking Ahead

Issues to Be Resolved

JAMES W. CALLICUTT

TED R. WATKINS

Each of the preceding chapters has presented and discussed important current issues related to mental health policy and practice in the United States. Also, some of the authors include content that draws on research and practice in other countries, thereby reflecting an international perspective. In this concluding chapter, we further highlight some of the critical issues facing the mental health field and offer our observations as to how we think they will be, or should be, addressed.

Bruce Jansson (1993), a scholar and historian of American social welfare policy and services, notes, "Profound ambivalence toward the victims of social problems has existed in American society since the colonial period" (p. 2). He characterizes the expression of this "paradox of punitiveness and generosity" as the "reluctant welfare state." Broadly, the health and mental health systems fall under the rubric of social welfare. In this context, today we are witnessing fervent political and philosophical debates charged with rhetoric reflecting the ideological positions of elected officials (as well as those seeking office) and their constituencies. Frequently the topics so hotly argued include issues of welfare, health, and mental health policy. These debates are likely to continue into the next century.

Two fundamental American values, the value of the individual and the value of the collective (group), are involved in virtually all aspects of these debates, which eventually result in legislation, regulations, and judicial decisions affecting the mental health arena. Although at times these values, when pushed to extremes, are competing, they clearly are not mutually exclusive. Ideally, they are complementary. With regard to mental health policy, an appropriate equilibrium is needed. Again, ideological positions in the political arena often translate into passionate rhetoric providing resistance to, and sometimes precluding, the negotiation and compromise required to achieve reasonable balance. This, then, is the backdrop against which the following presentation is to be viewed.

The question of the predominance accorded the identified patient (individual) vis-à-vis the family (collective) is discussed both by Cassandra Simon in her chapter on psychoeducation and by Brian Shannon in his chapter dealing with the impacts of the courts on the care of the mentally ill. In their discourses, these authors underscore as concerns the potential oppositional nature of the wishes, desires, and/or needs of the individual and those of the group, and the order of professional responsibility to the individual and to the group. Resolution of these issues requires a tempered dialogue that reflects the complementary values of the individual and the group. Once again, this is a dynamic equation that will remain in process, never finally, statically resolved.

As Shannon points out, decisions about if and when to hospitalize persons with schizophrenia or other major mental illnesses against their will continue to be a major issue. Similarly, controversy continues about if and when a person with a major mental illness should be given medication against his or her will. Opposing views tend to be represented by, on one hand, mental health professionals (and family members), who emphasize the concept of the responsibility to provide treatment, and, on the other hand, civil libertarians and groups of former patients, who emphasize the protection of individual rights, including the right to refuse treatment. At this time, the civil libertarians' position has carried the day and is in the ascendancy relative to practice, although Isaac and Armot (1990) elegantly contend that both psychiatry and the law have abandoned the mentally ill. In our view, the pendulum seems due to swing back toward increased commitment to the principle of the right to receive treatment at some expense to commitment to the principle of the right to refuse treatment.

We move now to another set of issues directly related to mental health funding for services and research designed to advance knowledge about the causes, treatment, and prevention of mental illness. As E. Clarke Ross and Colette Croze explicate in their chapter on managed mental health care, and as most mental health service providers well know, managed care is a fact of life across the entire spectrum of mental health programs and services. Although disagreement exists as to whether it is good for mental health clients (Corcoran & Bernstein, 1994), its current impact on the organization and provision of services is incontestable. In our opinion, the extension and further implementation of managed care arrangements, fundamentally driven by cost containment priorities, will generate additional conflicts among funding sources, service providers, and consumers. Although the need to control the costs of services is undeniable, we anticipate the occurrence of a "corrective" action as a consequence of providers' and consumers' reactions to the problems affecting them as a result of managed care. In this regard, we foresee providers organizing, both formally and informally, to develop their own databases and striving to reassert more control over their own service provision. One public program psychiatrist/administrator has observed that managed care is only a temporary blip on the screen in terms of the long-range picture (R. Denny, personal communication, March 12, 1996). How the adjustment will be achieved is dependent on interacting political, social, and economic factors; we underscore here the predicted influence of the mental health provider community in alliance with consumers and their advocates.

Recent advances in mental health research are summarized in the separate chapters by David Millard and William Wilson. Millard, educated in both social work and psychiatry, draws extensively in his review of social science research on the work of Brown and Harris (1978), who describe vulnerability factors and provoking agents. Wilson, also a psychiatrist, reviews contributions from neuroscientific research. At this time there is consensus that there are potent biological bases in mental illnesses that respond favorably to biochemical intervention. Schizophrenia and bipolar disorders are two examples of such major mental illnesses.

Clearly, neuroscientific research should receive adequate funding, as should social research. Dramatic discoveries in research in the neurosciences appear to have impacts on funding priorities, with greater emphasis given to neuroscientific research than to social research. However, important findings from social research can provide direction and focal points for intervention, and potentially prevention, as, for example, when identified vulnerability patterns are subject to being diminished. Our point here is that mental health research in the social sciences should not be sacrificed on the expectation that research in the neurosciences will yield all the relevant answers. Organizations such as the National Alliance for the Mentally Ill and the National Mental Health Association should continue to join forces in supporting funding for research on both of these fronts, as we discuss in Chapter 9.

In terms of coverage, insurance programs, both public and private, have discriminated against people with mental illnesses when compared with coverage provided for people with physical illnesses. Here, too, professional associations, advocacy organizations, and consumer groups should campaign to obtain both equity and parity for mental health insurance coverage in comparison with physical health coverage.

Another troubling point is raised by John McNeil and Robert Canon in their chapter on mental health services to the elderly: One in seven health care dollars (about $100 billion annually) is spent on the care of persons with Alzheimer's disease. We anticipate that research in the neurosciences will ultimately provide a measure of relief from this health care crisis as keys to the etiology and possibly the prevention of this devastating disease are discovered.

Returning again to managed care, as it flourishes we will see further movement toward the privatization of mental health services. Christian Molidor refers to an aspect of this trend toward privatization in his chapter on mental health services to children and adolescents. We expect that state mental health agencies and quasi-public agencies such as local mental health centers will be pressed, perhaps by legislative or other policy mandates, to contract out more and more services, and that for-profit agencies will successfully compete for some of these contracts. This is occurring in other areas of social welfare; for example, private corporations are contracting for and operating correctional facilities and programs that were formerly operated by government agencies.

In this context, Charles Turnbo and Donald Murray's chapter in this volume focuses on a number of critical issues germane to the intersection of the criminal justice system and the mental health system. These authors note the staggering number of persons in prison for drug offenses. Further, they assert that as a result of deinstitutionalization of the mentally ill, the criminal justice system increasingly has become the destination of developmentally disabled and mentally ill persons. This is another example of de facto policy being at great variance with de jure policy, as James Callicutt mentions in Chapter 1.

Turnbo and Murray also underscore the potential for suicide among prisoners, especially when they are first incarcerated. In reaction to this startling fact, we are convinced that the hard-nosed approach of incarcerating virtually all drug offenders is not sound social policy. This "tough on crime" stance may win votes and have powerful popular appeal, but it has a greater "feel-good" outcome for those promoting it than it has a desired impact on crime rates. The consumption of limited economic and human resources for imprisonment, taken with the fact that there are nearly a million persons currently in U.S. state and federal prisons, is cause for reexamining this growth industry. Other approaches, including the judicious expansion of effective community-based drug and alcohol treatment programs, should be considered. Furthermore, competent evaluation and classification of offenders should screen out of the criminal justice system those persons for whom more appropriate services can be delivered by the mental health system. Developing the optimal interface between the mental health and criminal justice systems is an ongoing process that merits serious and concerted effort on the part of professionals within the two systems as well as the legislative bodies involved in funding those systems.

Increased attention should also be paid to the mental health needs of veterans and immigrants and refugees. Recognition of the commonality of severe emotional trauma in contributing to post-traumatic stress disorder (PTSD) among these "special populations" may well lead to improved interventive technologies in the overall treatment of PTSD.

The chapters authored by Theresa Mulloy on women's issues and James Martin on political aspects of mental health evaluation and treatment highlight the significance of political processes as they directly affect mental health policies and services aimed at women, gays and lesbians, and minorities of color. Jansson (1993) provides an informative discussion on how persons in these categories, which he classifies (along with other identified minorities) as "outgroups," typically have been victims of discrimination and oppressive treatment in the United States. With leadership and pressure from professional associations, advocacy organizations, and consumers, mental health policies should be forged and services structured that will enhance protection and strengthen those most vulnerable and at high risk of experiencing mental or addictive disorders. This includes the provision of humane and effective services to those persons who experience serious mental illness, focusing on their being sustained within their families and communities.

In conclusion, the contributors to this volume identify and discuss a wide array of topics, issues, and sobering problems affecting mental health policy and practice. Still, we are persuaded that the future, despite all of the uncertainty we now see, holds the promise of new technologies to benefit mental health service users. These technologies include sophisticated computer applications (as discussed by Albert Farrell in Chapter 20) as well as interventive technologies based on neuroscientific and social research findings. Also, we are struck by the enthusiasm and optimism we encounter on the part of executives and program managers as they perceive exciting career opportunities for mental health professionals in the years ahead. They link these opportunities to the concomitant provision of more effective services to mental health consumers.

Finally, in this context, it is appropriate for the fundamental values of the group and the individual to provide the nexus for forging national mental health policy. Emerging mental health policy and practice in the United States should reflect, and be responsive to, the changing needs, demands, stresses, and challenges of our pluralist society.

References

Brown, G. W., & Harris, T. (1978). *Social origins of depression: A study of psychiatric disorder in women.* London: Tavistock.

Corcoran, K., & Bernstein, C. A. (1994). Is managed care good for mental health clients? In S. A. Kirk & S. D. Einbinder (Eds.), *Controversial issues in mental health* (pp. 240-251). Boston: Allyn & Bacon.

Isaac, R. J., & Armot, V. C. (1990). *Madness in the streets: How psychiatry and the law abandoned the mentally ill.* New York: Free Press.

Jansson, B. S. (1993). *The reluctant welfare state* (2nd ed.). Pacific Grove, CA: Brooks/Cole.

Name Index

Abreu, J., 246
Ackerman, D. L., 332
Ackerman, N., 275
Adar, H., 149
Addington v. Texas, 51
Adler, W. N., 276, 279
Agras, W. S., 332
Aigun, J. R., 90
Albrecht, J. W., 222, 223
Alford, R., 348
Algera, G., 196, 201
Allen, D. B., 245
Alterman, A. I., 312, 313, 315
Alvarez, R., 141, 248
American Managed Behavioral Healthcare
    Association, 352
American Nurses Credentialing Center, 78
American Psychiatric Association, 5, 33, 35, 37,
    38, 90, 95, 109, 167, 178, 199, 210, 211,
    212, 221, 232, 290, 291, 350, 351

American Psychological Association, 79, 178
Anderson, C. M., 131, 133, 137, 140, 204
Anderson, R. E., 4
Andijo, E., 247
Andreasen, N. C., 90, 93
Angel, R., 173
Angle, H. V., 329
Appelbaum, O., 149
Appelbaum, P. S., 62, 65
Appleton, W. S., 130, 131
Arangio, T., 329, 341
Arkansas Blue Cross & Blue Shield, Inc. v. Doe, 63
Armat, V. C., 51, 54, 66
Armor, V. C., 363
Armstrong, D., 200
Arnold v. Department of Health Services, 54
Ashbaugh, J. W., 43
Atay, J. E., 7, 8, 9, 10, 11, 13, 14, 70, 71
Atkins, D. R., 246
Atkinson, J. M., 131

Attneave, C. L., 249
Audini, B., 126, 127
Axinn, J., 209

Bachrach, L., 26, 204
Bachrach, L. L., 182, 184, 189, 190, 193
Back, K., 150, 152, 154
Bacon, S. E., 330
Bae, Y., 80, 81
Baer, M. A., 243
Baily, R., 183
Baker, F. M., 241
Bakker, Jim, 303
Barber, M., 204
Bardill, D. R., 76
Barker, R., 5
Barnett, B., 120
Barry, P. D., 222
Barter, J. T., 132
Bastani, B., 27
Baudhuin, M. G., 332
Bayer, R., 33
Bayer, T., 140
Bebbington, P. E., 111, 112
Beecham, J., 127
Beers, Clifford, 20
Begley, S., 263
Beiser, M., 249
Beland, F., 83
Belcher, J., 185
Benedek, E. P., 43
Benes, F., 90
Benjamin, M. P., 171, 175, 177
Benson, D. H., 61
Bentley, K. F., 137, 138, 140
Bentovim, A., 120, 121
Berkowitz, R., 121, 131, 135, 137
Bernheim, K. F., 130, 133
Bernstein, C. A., 3, 363
Bernstein, E., 203, 206
Bernstein, G. A., 261
Bernstein, J. G., 90
Berren, M., 182, 184, 193
Berry, G. W., 36
Bettelheim, Bruno, 122
Bevilacqua, J. J., 4
Bickman, L., 166
Bieber, I., 34, 41
Bieber, T. B., 34, 41
Bierce, Ambrose, 211
Bigelow, D. A., 202
Biggerstaff, M. A., 75
Binder, R. L., 203
Binik, Y. M., 335
Birley, J. L., 131
Bland, R., 156
Blank, A. S., 224

Blank, A. S., Jr., 212, 229
Blankertz, L., 69, 75, 77, 78, 79, 81
Blankertz, L. E., 325
Blazer, D. G., 288, 289
Bleuler, Eugene, 95
Blevins, G. A., 316
Bloom, B. L., 246, 334
Bloom, F. E., 89
Bloom, J. D., 251
Blumenthal, R., 141
Bobbitt, K., 350
Boehnlein, J. K., 164, 167
Boland, P., 347
Bond, G. R., 154, 159
Borkman, R., 153
Borkman, T., 160
Borus, J. F., 197
Boswell, J., 38
Boudewyns, P. A., 222, 223
Bourdon, K., 5
Bourgeois, P., 25
Boyd, J. H., 198
Boyd, J. L., 135, 137, 138
Boyle, P. J., 360
Brady v. Hopper, 58
Brakel, S. J., 56, 57
Brant, M., 263
Brawman-Mintzer, O., 223
Bray, D. W., 81
Bray, J. H., 261, 262
Brewer v. Lincoln National Life Insurance Co., 64, 65
Brickman, A. L., 293
Brittain, J., 189
Brizendine, L., 19
Brock, T. F., 281, 282
Brod, H., 259
Brodal, P., 89
Brody, D., 14
Brody, E., 173
Bromet, E. J., 83
Brooks, A., 52
Broskowski, A., 3
Brown, G. W., 116, 117, 119, 120, 121, 125, 131, 364
Brown, P. J., 228
Buckley, R., 202
Bucsela, M. L., 228
Burke, J. D., 112
Burke, J. D., Jr., 198
Burnam, M. A., 245, 246, 247
Burnett, K. E., 332
Burnett, S., 27
Burstein, A. G., 81
Bush, C., 186
Butcher, J. N., 330, 342
Butler, R. N., 291
Butterfield, W. H., 342

Butz, J. M., 17
Bybee, D., 187
Byler, W., 249
Byrd, K. R., 263

Caballero, I. L., 247
Cadden, J. J., 36
Callahan, D., 360
Callahan, J. J., 357
Callicutt, J. W., 4, 8, 11
Calvert, W. E., 222, 223
Campbell, D. M., 334
Camplair, P. S., 331
Caplan, G., 118
Caplan, P. J., 35
Carillo, C., 244, 245, 246
Carlin, J., 238
Carnevale, G. J., 222
Carpenter, W. T., 136
Carrion, P. G., 204
Carroll, J. A., 332
Carter, S., 4
Carter, W., 166
Cartwright, S. A., 243
Casas, A., 246
Castaneda, D., 152
Caton, C., 185
Cawlson, T. W., 69, 75, 77, 78, 79, 81
Chafetz, L., 186, 193
Chamberlain, J., 77
Chambon, A., 148, 152, 153
Checkoway, B., 29, 203
Chesler, P., 42, 43
Chiaramonte, J. A., 226
Cho, D. W., 329, 330, 336
Chrisman, N. J., 172
Christie, K. A., 198
Christison, C., 289
Christison, G., 289
Clancy, T., 178
Clery, P. D., 173
Cnaan, R. A., 149, 325, 336, 340
Cohen, C., 185
Cohen, E., 187
Cohen, J., 313, 315, 316, 318, 324
Cohen, N., 189
Cohen, N. L., 186, 193
Cohen, S., 252
Cohler, B. J., 141
Coid, J., 189
Collins, K. S., 346, 349
Comer, D. R., 262
Conaway, L., 245
Coner-Edwards, A. F., 242
Conger, J., 33
Congress, E., 173, 177
Connolly, J., 126, 127

Connolly, N. K., 292
Conrad, P., 33, 38, 39
Cook, J., 183
Cook, J. A., 141
Cooney, B., 69, 75, 77, 78, 79, 81
Cooper, J. R., 89
Cooperman, A., 131, 132, 136, 140
Corcoran, K., 3, 363
Costantino, G., 141
Couch, J. V., 330, 337
Council on Social Work Education, 72
Cournos, F., 198, 202
Courtois, C. A., 259, 261
Cox, A. J., 6
Cox, E. O., 147, 151
Coyle, S., 80, 81
Crocker, J., 46
Croughan, J., 111
Cullen, F. T., 205
Cummings, J. L., 290, 293, 295, 296
Cutler, D., 19, 22, 23
Cutler, D. L., 314, 315, 316

Dain, H. J., 34, 41
Dana, R. Q., 316
Daniel, G., 90
Davidson, L., 25
Davis, D. B., 342
Davis, J., 318, 319, 320
Davis, J. W., 130
Davis, K., 346, 349
Davis v. Watkins, 53
Dawson, M. E., 37
Day, R., 206
Decker, J., 252
DeCosta, Jacob, 211
de Girolamo, G., 166
De Graaf-Kaser, R., 154, 159
de Gruy, F. V., III, 14
De La Cancela, V., 36, 43, 44
Delgado, M., 177
DeMoll, L. E., 76
Dennis, D. L., 198
D'Ercole, A., 264, 265
Desrochers, M. N., 333, 334
De Titta, M., 82, 83
Dial, T. H., 69, 75, 77, 78, 79, 81
Dickstein, L. J., 259
DiClemente, C. C., 323
Dince, P. R., 34, 41
DiNitto, D. M., 314, 315, 317, 320, 322
Dix, Dorothea, 18
Doane, J. A., 37, 138
Dobyns, H. F., 249
Dolan, M. P., 166
Dolgin, D. L., 248
Donovan, D. M., 323

Dorwart, R. A., 349
Drake, R. E., 312, 315, 318
Drellich, M. W., 34, 41
Drope v. Missouri, 59
Dube, K. C., 166, 206
Duberman, M., 40
Dubin, W. R., 205
Dufort, F., 83
Dumont, M., 183, 189
Duncan, S. F., 259
Dworkin, R. J., 198
Dyer, R. L., 347

Eagle, P. F., 186
Eaton, W., 43
Ebedien-Vries, R., 121
Eberlein-Fries, R., 131, 135, 137
Edgerton, R. B., 246
Edinberg, M. A., 289, 294
Edwards, R., 249
Eisenberg, L., 197
Eisendorfer, C., 293
Ellinwood, E. H., 329
Ellsberg, Daniel, 39
Elwork, A., 328
Employee Retirement Income Security Act of
    1974, 65
Endler, N., 22
England, M. J., 347
English, J. T., 24
Epstein, C. F., 260
Equitable Life Assurance Society v. Berry, 64
Erdman, H. P., 331, 332, 336, 337, 338, 340
Erdman, K., 59
Ernberg, G., 206
Evans, K., 313, 315, 318, 319, 324, 325
Evenson, R. C., 329
Ex parte Lewis, 59
Ezekiel, J., 59, 60

Fabiszewski, K. J., 290, 291, 292
Fairbank, R. L., 215, 217, 219, 220, 221, 222,
    223, 225, 226, 228
Falloon, I. R. H., 131, 135, 137, 138
Farrell, A. D., 331, 332, 336, 337, 338, 339, 340
Feichter, M., 189
Feit, M., 252
Feldman, D. E., 332
Felton, B. J., 198
Fenton, W. S., 83
Fentress, C., 130
Fenyo, A., 127
Fernando, S., 36
Figley, C. R., 225, 226, 227
Findlay, S., 63
Fine, S., 164, 166, 179

Fink, P. J., 205
First, R., 189
Fisher, D. B., 27, 28
Fitsimones, T., 316
Flattau, P. E., 81
Flores, J. L., 246
Flores, L. P., 223
Flynn, J. P., 334, 338, 340
Flynn, L. M., 59, 60
Flynt, Larry, 303
Fogel, B. S., 296
Forslund, M. A., 249
Foster Higgins, 352
Foucha v. Louisiana, 61
Fox, J. C., 69, 75, 77, 78, 79, 81
Fox, R., 79
Frampton, J., 132
Francell, E. G., 207
Frank, R., 4, 6, 7
Frank, R. G., 65
Franklin, C., 131, 132, 136, 140
Franks, D. D., 7
Freddolino, P., 189
Freedman, E., 325
Freeman, M., 350
Freeman, W. B., 131
Freud, Sigmund, 95, 196, 211, 266, 268
Friedel, F., 211
Friend, D. M., 130
Fromm, Lynette "Squeaky," 303
Fujino, D. C., 246, 247
Furino, A., 296
Furumoto, L., 266

Gaes, G., 303
Gallup, P., 223
Galt, John, 18
Ganesan, S., 164, 166, 179
Gannon, L., 268
Garcia-Peltoniemi, R., 166
Garrett, G., 187
Gartner, A., 14
Gaw, A. C., 239
Gearing, M. L., 166
Gebhard, P. H., 34
Gebhart, J., 206
George, L. K., 288
George, W. H., 301
Geraty, R., 350
Gerber, L., 174
Germanson, T., 198
Ghobary, G., 334
Gibbs, J. T., 281
Giddens, A., 108
Gilderman, A. M., 135, 137
Giller, E. L., Jr., 222
Gingerich, W. J., 333, 338, 342

Ginsberg, L., 69, 75, 77, 78, 79, 81
Ginsberg, M., 69, 75, 77, 78, 79, 81
Gitlin, M. J., 196
Glaser, F. B., 198
Glastonbury, B., 341
Godinez v. Moran, 59
Goffman, E., 205
Gold, S. N., 262
Goldberg, D., 107, 109, 110, 111, 115
Goldberg, J. D., 4, 14
Goldfinger, S., 189
Goldfried, M. R., 331
Golding, J. M., 245, 246, 247
Goldman, H., 130, 350
Goldman, H. H., 21
Goldstein, G. S., 249
Goldstein, M. J., 134, 137, 138
Goldstein, M. Z., 83
Gong-Guy, E., 239
Goode, W. J., 120
Gordon, J. R., 301, 302
Gorski, T. T., 313, 314, 315, 316, 318, 322
Gott, W., 186
Gottfredson, G. D., 81
Gottlieb, G. L., 296
Gove, W., 282
Gowen, N., 186, 189, 190
Grady, D. A., 215, 216
Graham, S., 79
Graham, S. R., 258, 271
Grant, R. W., 184
Gray, G. J., 210
Green, B. F., 339
Green, H. J., 250
Greenberg, G., 252
Greenberg, H., 252
Greene, B., 45, 197, 207
Greenlee, R., 189, 222, 225, 226
Greenwald, D. P., 131
Greenwood, E., 83, 150
Greist, J. H., 329, 331, 332, 336, 337, 338, 340
Griffith, E., 25, 241
Grob, G. N., 3, 6, 20
Grossman, L., 177
Gruenberg, E. M., 24, 25, 30
Grunberg, J., 186
Guerrero, C. C., 247
Guido, J., 198, 202
Gussow, Z., 152
Gutheil, T. G., 37
Gutkin, T. B., 328

Haas, A. P., 211, 222
Hagan, B. J., 334
Hagman, G., 177
Hahn, S. R., 14
Haldeman, D. C., 41, 42

Hall, G. Stanley, 266
Hall, M., 45
Hall, Z. W., 89
Hallam, A., 127
Halpern, A., 35
Halpern, D., 37, 46
Halpin, S., 186, 189, 190
Hammer, A. L., 336, 338, 339, 341
Hanes, L. D., 17
Hanna, T., 338
Hansen, J. C., 136, 137, 138, 140
Hanusa, B. H., 83
Harmless, A., 225
Harris, T., 116, 117, 119, 120, 121, 125, 364
Harris, V. W., 249
Harrison, P. A., 322, 324
Hartley, B. L., 332
Hartman, D. E., 340, 341
Harvey, P. D., 90
Hatfield, A. B., 132, 139, 140, 142
Haulotte, S. M., 290, 291, 292
Hawk, Kathleen M., 310
Hay, D., 22
Hay, L. R., 329
Hay, W. M., 329
Hazel, K. L., 43
Healy, William, 275
Hearst, N., 221, 222
Hedlund, J. H., 329, 336, 330, 336, 342
Heinrichs, D. W., 136
Helzer, J. E., 111
Henderson, A. S., 107, 111, 119, 121
Hendin, H., 211, 222
Henry, J., 169
Herman, S. E., 43
Hetherington, E. M., 261, 262
Heyding, R., 186
Hickman, C. V., 329
Hidalgo, H., 33
Hile, M. G., 333, 334, 336, 338, 339, 341
Hill, R. B., 241
Hilliard, A., 242
Hinckley, John W., Jr., 58, 61, 303
Hippocrates, 195
Ho, M. K., 142, 237
Hoagwood, K., 5
Hofer, P. J., 339, 340, 341
Hoffmann, F. L., 282, 283
Hoffmann, N., 322, 324
Hogan, M., 350
Hogan, W., 20
Hogarty, G., 140, 204
Hogarty, G. E., 131, 133
Hoge, M. A., 25
Hohnecker, L., 262
Holland, R. A., 329
Hollingsworth, E. J., 21, 22
Holmes, T., 115

Holmes, T. M., 14
Hooker, E., 34
Hooper-Russell, C., 333
Hooyman, N. R., 290, 293, 295
Hopkins-Kavanagh, K., 170
Hough, R. L., 215, 217, 219, 220, 221, 222, 223, 225, 226, 228, 245, 246, 247
House Committee on Criminal Jurisprudence, 61
Howard, A., 81
Howenstein, R. A., 25
Hu, L., 246, 247
Hudson, B. J., 131
Hudson, C. G., 6
Hudson, W. W., 330
Hughes, D., 262
Hughes, D. C., 288
Hughes, E. C., 83
Hughes, R., 69, 75, 77, 78, 79, 81
Hulley, S. B., 221, 222
Hurry, J., 111, 112
Hutchinson, R. L., 222, 223
Huxley, P., 107, 110, 111, 115
Hyer, L., 222, 223

Immigration and Naturalization Act of 1980, 165
Indian Health Service, 253
In re Oakes, 50
In re Richard Roe III, 56
Iodice, J. D., 130, 132
Isaac, R. J., 51, 54, 56, 57, 66, 363
Isaacs, M. R., 171, 175, 177
Israel, B., 29
Israel, B. A., 203

Jablensky, A., 206
Jackson v. Indiana, 59
Jansson, B. S., 362, 365
Jarvik, L. F., 295
Javna, C. D., 131
Jefferson, J. W., 332, 336, 337
Jenkins-Hall, K., 36
Jennings, H., 333
Jensen, G. F., 249
Johanns, K. P., 40
Johnsen, T., 329
Johnson, A. B., 23
Johnson, H. C., 132
Johnson, J. G., 14
Johnson, J. H., 342
Jones, E. E., 36
Jones, K., 124
Jones, M., 276
Jones, S., 131
Jones, W., Jr., 174
Jordan, B. K., 215, 217, 219, 220, 221, 222, 223, 225, 226, 228

Jordan, C., 142
Jung, J., 312, 316
Jutagir, R., 292

Kadushin, A., 275
Kaha, A. S., 260
Kane, T. J., 76
Kanter, J. S., 131
Kaplan, H. I., 197, 198, 200
Kaplan, K. O., 69, 75, 77, 78, 79, 81
Karger, H. J., 281, 284
Karno, M., 245, 246, 247
Kass, F., 189
Katz, S., 189
Katz, S. E., 22, 23, 24, 25
Keefe, R. S. E., 90
Keefe, S. E., 245, 246
Kelleher, K., 14
Keller, L. S., 330
Kellert-Cecil, H., 204
Kelly, G., 174
Kelly, W. E., 210
Kemberling, S. R., 249
Kennedy, (President) John F., 21
Kent, R. N., 331
Keopraseuth, K., 142
Kiesler, C. A., 4, 6
Kim, S., 164
Kingston, W., 120, 121
Kinsey, A. C., 34
Kinzie, J. D., 164, 167, 239
Kirk, S., 25, 28
Kirk, S. A., 5, 37, 38, 281
Kiyak, H. A., 290, 293, 295
Klein, M. H., 329, 331, 336, 337, 338, 340
Klein, Melanie, 275
Kleinman, A., 166, 172, 197
Klerman, G. L., 37
Knapp, M., 127
Knickman, J. R., 265
Koh, K., 290
Kohout, J., 69, 75, 77, 78, 79, 80, 81
Kopeikin, H. S., 134, 137
Korman, M., 79
Kornbeth, S. J., 131
Kort, G. A., 248
Korten, A., 206
Koustogeorgopolou, V., 127
Kovacs, A., 79
Koyanagi, C., 6, 21
Kraeplin, Emil, 95
Kramer, J. J., 340
Kramer, M., 243
Kreisman, J., 141
Kroenke, K., 14
Kronemeyer, R., 41, 42
Krug, S. E., 330, 337

Krupinski, J., 166
Kuczeruk, T., 334
Kuhlman, T. L., 3
Kuipers, L., 121, 131, 135, 137
Kulka, R. A., 215, 217, 219, 220, 221, 222, 223, 225, 226, 228
Kunin v. Benefit Trust Life Insurance Co., 63, 64
Kurtz, L. F., 147, 148, 149, 152, 153, 156, 157, 158
Kutchins, H., 5, 37, 38, 281

Labonte, R., 30, 202
LaCoursiere, R. B., 49, 50, 51, 54, 55, 56, 57
Ladd-Franklin, Christine, 266-267
Laing, R. D., 66
Lamb, H., 130
Lamb, H. R., 184, 189, 193
LaMendola, W., 341
Landrum-Brown, J., 242
Lane, Homer, 122
Lane, J., 249
Langford, W., 186
Lantz, J., 222, 225, 226
Lanyon, R. I., 342
Larsell, O., 20
Lasch, C., 33
Lasch, K. E., 290, 291, 292
Lavell, J., 166, 167
Lawrence, G. H., 334
Lawrence, R. E., 126
Leaf, P. J., 43, 83
Lebowitz, B. D., 294
Lecca, P. J., 12, 129
Leda, C., 223
Le-Doux, C., 178
Lee, E., 130, 132, 135, 169, 176, 177
Leff, J., 121
Leff, J. P., 131, 132, 135, 137
Lefley, H., 17, 24, 28, 29
Lehman, A. F., 130, 133
Lemberg, R., 148, 151
Leng, N. R. C., 291
Lenge, A., 120
Lennon, T. M., 71, 72, 73, 74, 75
Leon, C., 206
Leonard, J. H., 17
Lessard v. Schmidt, 50, 51, 52, 53
Leukefeld, C., 184, 189
Leung, P. K., 239
Leventhal, G. S., 147
Levin, H., 209
Levine, I. S., 264
Levy, S. J., 313, 315, 316, 318, 324
Lewellen, A., 142
Lewis, J. A., 316
Lewis, M., 277
Lewis, R. A., 259

Lewis, R. L., 252
Liberman, R. P., 135
Lieberman, M. A., 152, 153, 158, 159
Lieberman, R. P., 37
Lin, A., 131
Lin, E., 166
Lin, T. Y., 164, 166, 179
Link, B. G., 205
Linzer, M., 14
Loch, B. E., 14
Locke, B. Z., 198
Loftus, E. F., 263
Logan, S., 242
Longabaugh, R., 331, 340
Longres, J. F., 280
Loring, J., 40
Losch, M., 332
Lubach, J., 282
Lubove, R., 20
Luchetta, T., 268
Luke, D., 159, 160
Lum, D., 236
Lutterman, T. C., 13
Lynch v. Baxley, 52
Lyon, E., 156
Lyons, B., 177
Lyons, J., 183

Mace, N. L., 291
Madara, E. J., 147
Madonia, M. J., 131
Maglothin, M. A., 261
Maheux, B., 83
Major, B., 46
Makarenko, 122
Malakie, B. B., 136, 137, 138, 140
Malgady, R. G., 141
Manderscheid, R. W., 5, 7, 8, 9, 10, 11, 13, 14, 43, 70, 71, 281, 282
Manning, N. P., 123, 124, 125, 126
Manson, S. M., 251
Marcias, R. F., 244
Marcos, L., 189
Marcus, E., 120
Marder, S. R., 37, 201
Marks, E., 3
Marks, I. M., 126, 127
Marlatt, G. A., 301, 302, 323
Marmar, C. R., 215, 217, 219, 220, 221, 222, 223, 225, 226, 228
Marmor, J., 34
Marsela, A., 206
Marshall, B. D., Jr., 37
Marshall, V., 134, 137
Martin, C. W., 34
Martin, J. A., 322, 324
Martin, M., 184, 193

Martinez, C., 246, 248
Mason, M., 27, 29
Mason, M. A., 281
Mason, P. H., 211, 212, 221, 222, 225
Mastrianni, X., 282, 283
Matarazzo, J. D., 340
Mathew, L. J., 295
Mathison, K. S., 336
Mathura, C. B., 243
Maton, K. I., 147
Matsakis, A., 212, 222, 225
May, J. H., 288
May, T., 108
McCarthy, D., 227, 301
McCausland, M. P., 275
McCullough, L., 331, 340
McDermott, J. F., 172
McDowell, E. E., 288
McGarrick, R. G., 24
McGill, C. W., 130, 132, 135, 137, 138
McGuire, T., 4, 6, 7
McIntosh, J. L., 249, 289
McKinnon, K., 198, 202
McLaughlin, B., 155
McNamee, G., 126
McNeil, D. E., 203
McNeil, J., 131, 132, 136, 140
McQuaide, S., 166, 168
Mechanic, D., 6
Meibach, R. C., 201
Mellman, T. A., 223
Meltzer, H. Y., 27
Menninger, W. W., 24, 195, 199
Merwin, E. I., 69, 75, 77, 78, 79, 81
Messina, J. J., 130
Metropolitan Life Insurance Co. v. Massachusetts, 65
Meyer, I., 198, 202
Meyer-Bahlburg, H., 198, 202
Meyers, Adolph, 20
Meyers, R. E., 249
Milanes, F. J., 223
Milburn, N., 264, 265
Milkowitz, D. J., 138
Miller, L., 189
Mills, M. J., 22
Mills, P. D., 136, 137, 138, 140
Mills v. Rogers, 56
Miranda, M. R., 247
Mirotznik, J., 205
Mitchell, Martha, 39
Mollica, R., 166, 167
Monnickendam, M., 336, 340
Moore, N., 156
Moore, Sara Jane, 303
Moos, R. H., 125
Morales v. State, 59
Moran, M., 350

More, W. W., 82, 83
Moreland, K. L., 330, 338, 339, 341
Morishima, J. K., 170, 173
Morris, C., 346, 349
Moss, H. B., 135, 137
Mossman, D., 185
Mowbray, C., 187
Mowbray, C. T., 43
Moxley, D., 189
Muijen, M., 126, 127
Mullins, L., 242
Munoz, R. F., 246, 247, 248
Murphy, T. F., 41, 42
Murray, D. W., 301, 306
Mutschler, E., 341
Myers, J. K., 243
Myers, M. F., 259

Nagi, S. Z., 249
Nardacci, D., 189
Narrow, W., 5, 14
National Association of Social Workers, 178
National Committee for Quality Assurance, 351
National Community Mental Healthcare Council, 347
National Conference of State Legislatures, 346, 349
National Institute of Mental Health, 150, 154
National Institute on Drug Abuse (NIDA), 314, 315, 316, 321, 322
National League for Nursing, 76, 77
National Research Council of the National Academy of Sciences, 212, 214
National Science Foundation, 80
Needleman, R., 140
Neighbors, H. W., 243
Neilson, J. A., 206
Nemeroff, C. B., 90
Nernez, G., 165
Newman, T. B., 221, 222
Nezu, A. M., 222
Nguyen, D. S., 166
Nickel, E. J., 313, 314, 316, 317, 321, 322
Nicoll, A. E., 333
Nicolosi, J., 41, 42, 44
Niederehe, G., 294
Noble, J. H., 59, 60
Norris, C., 303
Nuckols, C. C., 315
Nuechterlein, K. H., 37
Nurius, P. S., 330, 333

Oberst, G., 169, 176, 177
O'Connell, B., 158
O'Connor v. Donaldson, 51, 52,54
O'Donnell, R., 335
Oetting, E. R., 249

Office of Minority Mental Health, 249
O'Hare, T., 314, 315, 317, 325
O'Keefe, A. M., 62
Okin, R. L., 197
Olatawura, M., 206
Olevitch, B. A., 334
Olmedo, E. L., 197
Orley, J., 167
Orlin, L., 318, 319, 320
Osher, F. C., 318
Oskamp, S., 81
Ott, J., 228, 229

Padilla, A. M., 245, 248
Paines, Lewis, 211
Pakula, A., 339, 340, 341
Pandey, R. S., 261
Pardie, L., 268
Paredes, A., 251
Parker, G., 120
Parron, D. L., 44
Patterson, E. T., 166
Pavlov, Ivan, 275
Peck v. Counseling Service of Addison County, 58
Pederson, J., 138
Pelissier, B., 301
Penick, E. C., 313, 314, 316, 317, 321, 322
Penk, W. E., 166
Pepper, B., 205, 312, 313, 314, 315, 318, 319, 323
Perlin, M., 185
Perlin, M. L., 50, 51, 52, 53, 54, 55, 57, 58, 59, 60, 61
Peterson, G., 22
Peterson, T. L., 33
Petrila, J., 359
Pettigrew, T. F., 120
Pfafflin, S. M., 81
Phillips v. Lincoln National Life Insurance Co., 64
Piaget, Jean, 275
Pickett, S. A., 141
Pinderhughes, E., 242
Pinel, Phillipe, 196, 274
Pion, G. M., 69, 75, 77, 78, 79, 81
Pitta, P., 141
Pleck, J. H., 259
Plotkin, A., 156
Pomeroy, W. B., 34
Poole, D. L., 146, 154, 155
Pope, K. S., 341
Post, F., 289, 290
Poussaint, A. F., 242, 243
Powell, B., 40
Powell, T. J., 147, 148, 151, 153, 155, 156, 157, 158, 159, 160
President's Commission on Mental Health, 147, 245
President's Commission on Veterans' Pensions, 213

Prichard, J. W., 90
Prochaska, J. O., 323
Pugliesi, K., 35, 36

R. A. J. v. Miller, 53, 56
Rabins, P. V., 291
Rae, D., 5
Rae, D. S., 14
Rahe, R. H., 115
Raie, D. S., 198
Ramos, R. A., 247
Randolph, C. A., 223
Randolph, L., 83
Rappaport, J., 159, 160
Ratcliff, K. S., 111
Razani, J., 135, 137
Read, M. R., 313, 314, 316, 317, 321, 322
Reagan, (President) Ronald, 58, 61
Realmuto, G. M., 261
Red Horse, J. G., 252, 254
Redick, R. W., 7, 8, 9, 10, 11, 13, 14, 70, 71
Regier, D., 5
Regier, D. A., 4, 14, 198
Reid, W., 27, 29
Reider, R., 83
Reiger, D., 112
Reiger, D. A., 243
Reinoehl, R., 338
Reisman, S., 330
Reisner, R., 57, 58
Reiss, D. J., 131, 133, 204
Reiter, M., 156
Rennie v. Klein, 55, 56
Repotosky, J., 315
Revans, R. W., 123
Rheaume, Y. L., 290, 291, 292
Rhodes, K., 268
Ricord, Elizabeth, 267
Riesser, G. G., 28
Riessman, F., 14
Rife, J., 189
Rifkin, A. H., 34, 41
Riger, S., 260, 262
Riggins v. Nevada, 59
Roback, G., 83
Robbins, L. N., 111
Roberts, L., 159, 160
Roberts, W. R., 166
Robinowitz, C. B., 82, 83
Robinowitz, R., 166
Robins, L. N., 243
Robitscher, J., 33, 39
Rochefort, D., 184
Rochefort, D. A., 3, 18, 19, 20, 22, 23
Rog, D., 264
Rogers v. Okin, 55, 56
Rogler, L. H., 141

Roid, G. H., 333
Rosen, P., 186
Rosenberg, S. R., 312, 315
Rosenhan, B. S., 282
Rosenheck, R., 223
Rosenthal v. Mutual Life Insurance Co., 63
Rosewater, L. B., 35
Ross, A. O., 198
Ross, C., 159
Ross, E. C., 352, 354
Roth, R. H., 89
Roybal, Edward R., 295
Ruben, D. H., 127
Ruberg, L. F., 335
Rubin, J., 63
Rubonis, A., 166
Ruggeri, M., 126
Ruiz, D. S., 240
Ruiz, R., 141
Ruiz, R. A., 245, 248
Rumbaut, R. G., 243
Rupp, A., 5
Russo, N. F., 197
Ruth, A., 183
Rutter, M., 118, 119
Ryglewicz, H., 312, 313, 314, 315, 318, 319, 323

Sabatini, A., 189
Sacco, W. P., 36
Sadock, B. J., 197, 198, 200
Salazar, A. A., 248
Salmon, Thomas, 22
Sampson, J. P., 334
Sanankone, P., 170
Santiago, J., 182, 184, 193
Santos, J. L., 249
Sartorius, N., 206
Satel, S., 189
Saunders, B. E., 76
Scarborough, E., 267
Schatzberg, A. F., 90
Schilling, R., 147
Schimmel, D. J., 302
Schinkke, L., 147
Schkade, L. L., 333
Schlenger, J. A., 215, 217, 219, 220, 221, 222, 223, 225, 226, 228
Schlosser, B., 330, 341
Schmidt, A., 303
Schmidt, L., 313, 316, 317, 318, 319, 321, 325
Schneider, J. W., 33, 38, 39
Schneider, S. J., 335
Schneider, W., 340
Schoech, D. J., 329, 333, 341
Schorske, B., 28
Schreter, C. S., 347, 348, 349
Schreter, R., 347, 348, 349

Schroeder, P., 281, 282
Schulz, A., 29, 203
Schutt, R., 187
Schwartz, M. S., 123
Scott, W. J., 38, 211, 212
Scurfield, R. M., 224
Segrist, D., 268
Seidman, B., 83
Selley, C., 221
Servan-Schreiber, D., 335
Shannon, B. D., 61, 65
Sharfstein, J., 59, 60
Sharfstein, S., 347, 348, 349
Sharfstein, S. S., 37, 62
Sharkey, J., 3, 8
Shay, J., 211, 224
Shays, Daniel, 211
Sheikh, J. I., 293
Shenoy, R. S., 135
Shepard, D. S., 357
Sheppard, M., 43
Sheridan, M., 186, 189, 190
Sherwood, R. J., 222, 223, 224, 225
Shinn, M., 265
Shires, B., 135
Shore, J. H., 18, 19, 20, 21, 22, 196, 251
Showalter, E., 36
Sibulkin, A. E., 4, 6
Silk-Walker, P., 249, 252, 253
Silverman, P. R., 14, 148, 151, 153, 154, 155, 156
Simon, C., 131, 132, 136, 137, 138, 140, 142
Simpson, G. M., 135, 137
Skinner, B. F., 275
Skinner, H. A., 339, 340, 341
Slagg, N. B., 183
Sledge, W. H., 25
Sloane, P. D., 295
Slobogin, C., 57, 58
Snowden, L., 178
Snyder, K. S., 131
Socarides, C. W., 34
Sokoloff, N., 238
Solomon, B. B., 44, 45
Sommer, B., 152
Sommer, R., 152
Sonnenschein, M. A., 9, 281, 282
Sotomayor, G. M., 36, 43, 44
Southwick, S. M., 222
Spaniol, L., 138
Spelman, E. V., 260
Spiro, H., 22
Spitzer, R. L., 14
Spring, R. L., 49, 50, 51, 54, 55, 56, 57
Spurlock, J., 242
Stanton, A. H., 123
State ex rel Hawks v. Lazaro, 52
Staton, J., 69, 75, 77, 78, 79, 81
Stein, T. S., 259

Steinman, R., 148, 152
Stephens, K. S., 179
Stephens, P., 169
Stiffarm, L. A., 249
Stillon, J. M., 288
Stoddard, F. J., 37
Stoesz, D., 281, 284
Stoller, A., 166
Stoloff, M. L., 330, 337
Stone, A. A., 54
Storey, C., 178
Strand, P., 174
Stratton, R., 251
Strauss, J. H., 249
Straznickas, K. A., 203
Streiber, J., 59, 60
Stromgren, E., 206
Struening, E., 205
Sturgeon, D., 121
Sturt, E., 111, 112
Sue, D., 236, 237
Sue, D. W., 236, 237
Sue, S., 170, 173, 245, 246, 247, 252
Sugar, J. A., 197
Sullivan, J. M., 313, 315, 318, 319, 324, 325
Surles, R., 346, 347
Surles, R. C., 21, 23
Susser, E., 189
Swann, A., 204
Swinomish Tribal Mental Health Project, 249, 250, 251, 252, 253
Szasz, T., 4, 45, 66, 196

Takahashi, R., 206
Takeuchi, D. T., 246, 247
Tanay, E., 225
Tansella, M., 126
Tarail, M., 76
Tarasoff v. Regents of University of California, 57, 58, 59
Taube, C. A., 4, 14
Taylor, C. B., 332
Taylor, R., 150, 152, 154
Teichner, V., 36
Tennant, C., 111, 112
Teplin, L. A., 198
Tessler, R. C., 198
Texas Criminal Justice Policy Council, 59
Texas Department of Mental Health and Mental Retardation v. Petty, 51
Texas Penal Code, 61
Thoits, P., 173
Thompson, J. W., 249, 252, 253
Thompson, K., 185
Thompson v. County of Alameda, 58
Tidwell, B. J., 241
Toole, S., 341

Toomey, B., 185
Toprac, M., 27, 29
Torrey, E. F., 3, 50, 54, 56, 59, 60, 130, 131, 183, 245
Tracy, G., 152
Tran, T. V., 167
Traunstein, D., 148, 152
Travis, L., 342
Tseng, W. S., 172
Tuason, V. B., 322, 324
Tuckman, H., 80, 81
Turner, F. J., 291
Tyhurst, L., 166
Tyler, R., 153, 154, 158

U.S. Commission on Civil Rights, 237
U.S. Congress, 209
U.S. Department of Commerce, Bureau of the Census, 214, 240, 244, 245, 249, 286
U.S. Department of Health and Human Services, 165, 215, 216, 217
U.S. Department of Health and Human Services, Center for Mental Health Services, 353
U.S. Department of Veterans Affairs, 209, 210, 211, 213, 214-215, 216, 217, 218, 220, 224, 232
U.S. Department of Veterans Affairs, National Center for Posttraumatic Stress Disorder, 225
U.S. Senate, 295
Uba, L., 236, 238, 239
UNESCO, 168
Ussher, J., 36, 42

Vaccaro, V., 347
Vale, C. D., 330
Van Cura, M., 329
Van der Kolk, B. A., 166
VanDevanter, L. M., 228
Vandiver, V., 25, 28, 142
Vaughn, C. E., 131, 132
Vega, W. A., 243
Vieweg, B. W., 329, 330, 336
Viola, J., 227
Volicer, L., 290, 291, 292
Vranick, D. A., 141

Wade, J. C., 36, 44
Wakefield, J. C., 39, 40
Walker, R. D., 249, 252, 253
Wallace, L., 166
Wallach, M. A., 318
Wallerstein, N., 203, 206
Walter, R., 335
Wasmer, D., 183
Watkins, T. R., 76

Watson, John B., 266, 275
Weatherly, R., 147
Weaver, J. L., 245
Webb, D. K., 314, 315, 317, 320, 322
Webb, W. L., 275
Weber, R., 251
Weclew, R. V., 245
Weinberger, D. R., 90
Weinrich, J. D., 41
Weisaeth, L., 166
Weiss, D. J., 330
Weiss, D. S., 215, 217, 219, 220, 221, 222, 223, 225, 226, 228
Weissenberger, G., 49, 50, 51, 54, 55, 56, 57
Weitzman, B. C., 265
Wells, K. B., 245, 246, 247
Wenger, A. F. Z., 172, 175, 177
Westermeyer, J., 315
White, A., 189
White, M. S., 135
White, T. W., 302
Wich, M. J., 319
Wicherski, M., 80, 81
Wig, N., 206
Wilbur, C. B., 34, 41
Wilks, R., 172
Willetts, R., 151
Williams, C., 14
Williams, C. M., 225
Williams, J. B. W., 14
Williams, M. E., 292
Williams, P., 109, 152
Williams, T., 225
Williams, W., 152
Wills, David, 122
Wilson, W., 20

Windermuth, V. A., 69, 75, 77, 78, 79, 81
Windle, C., 171, 178, 246
Wing, J. K., 111, 112, 131
Winograd, C. H., 295
Witkin, M. J., 7, 8, 9, 10, 11, 13, 14, 70, 71
Wodarski, J. S., 130, 132
Wohlford, P., 80
Wolfe, J., 228
Wolfe, S. M., 59, 60
Wolkind, S., 118
Woo, D., 238
Wood, J. B., 329
Woodman, N. J., 33
Woods, M. G., 222, 223
Wood-Siverio, C., 135, 138
World Health Organization, 109
Worthington, C., 243
Wu, I., 171, 178, 246
Wyatt v. Stickney, 52, 53, 54
Wylie, M. S., 28
Wynne, L. C., 206
Wyshak, G., 166, 167

Yates, A., 249
Yehuda, R., 222
Yoder, J. D., 260
Youngberg v. Romeo, 55
Yu, M., 142, 169, 174

Zachary, R. A., 341
Zane, N., 246, 247
Zeiner, A., 251
Zimmerman, M., 29, 203
Zipple, A. M., 138

Subject Index

Addiction, biopsychosocial model of, 301
Addiction Intervention With the Disabled, 322
Addiction Severity Inventory Index, 321
Adjustment disorders:
  among immigrants and refugees, 167-168
Adolescents:
  acting out behavior in immigrant/refugee, 164, 166, 168
  alcohol abuse/dependence in, 198
  anxiety disorders in, 198
  drug abuse/dependence in, 198
  emotional withdrawal in immigrant/refugee, 168
  homeless, 189
  major depression in, 198
  mentally ill, xiii, xvi
  runaways, 189
Advocacy groups, 14, 146, 149-150
  as goal-oriented, 149
  as instrumental, 149
  as monitoring system, 149, 155

  as social movements, 155
  development of, 149
  future of, as mental health service, 156
  future research topics concerning, 159-160
  mental health professionals' view of in-service decisions, 152
  mental-health related, 147
  political activities of, 158
  purpose of, 149, 150
  view of mental health professionals, 153
Affirmative therapists, 45-46
Affirmative therapy:
  for gays/lesbians, 44-45
  for minorities, 45-46
African Americans, 235, 240-241, 244
  culturally sensitive mental health approaches for, 141
  demographics of, 240-242
  depression in female, 197
  diagnosis and treatment of mentally ill, 243-244

family structure of, 242
  females' use of drug therapy, 197
  overdiagnosis of schizophrenia in, 243
  racism and oppression as stressors for, 241-242
  underdiagnosis of affective disorders in, 243
  utilization of mental health services by, 242-244
  values of, 241
Alcohol abuse:
  among adolescents, 198
  among immigrants and refugees, 166
  See also Alcoholism; Substance abuse
Alcoholics Anonymous, 148, 153, 156, 305
Alcoholism:
  in elderly, 293
  males versus females with, 197
  panic disorder and, 198
  See also Alcohol abuse
Alcohol Research Center Intake Interview, 321
Alliance for the Mentally Ill, 130
Alprazolam (Xanax):
  for anxiety, 104
Alzheimer's disease, 291, 292, 295, 364
  as cause of death in elderly, 290
  as incurable, 292
  as progressive, 291
  diagnosis of, 292
  Down's syndrome and, 291
  in elderly, 290
  previous head injury and, 291
  thyroid dysfunction and, 291
  versus multi-farct dementia, 292
American Managed Behavioral Healthcare
  Association (AMBHA), 351
  PERMS, 351, 352-353
  primary purposes of, 352
American Medical Association, 82
American Nurses Association, 78
American Psychiatric Association (APA), 64, 83
  declassification of homosexuality as mental
    illness by, 32-33
  diagnosis of psychopathology in women, 35
  low ethnic representation in, 178
  1972 convention, 34
  recognition of PTSD as diagnostic category,
    231
  Work Group to Revise *DSM-III,* 35
American Psychological Association, 330
  as accrediting body for psychologists, 78
  declassification of homosexuality as mental
    illness by, 33
  low ethnic representation in, 178
  1991 annual meeting, 258
  standards for computer-based test interpretation,
    341
Amitriptyline (Elavil):
  for depression, 102
Antianxiety medications, 104-105. *See also*
  Diazepam; Alprazolam

Antidepressant medications, 102-104
  atypical, 103
  for elderly depressed patients, 289
  monoamine oxidase inhibitors (MAOI), 103
  selective serotonin uptake inhibitors (SSRIs),
    102-103
  tricyclic (TCAs), 102, 103
Antidepressant treatments, somatic:
  bright light, 103
  electroconvulsive therapy (ECT), 22, 103-104,
    289
Antipsychiatrists, 66
Antipsychotic medications, 100-102, 290
  for bipolar disorder, 100
  for schizophrenia, 38, 100
  side effects of early, 101
  side effects of newer, 101
  See also specific antipsychotic medications
Antisocial personality disorder:
  males versus females with, 197
  substance abusers with, 316, 322, 325
Anxiety disorders, 5, 199
  among immigrants and refugees, 166
  as most common mental disorders, 196
  as treatable, 293
  in elderly, 293
  in females versus males, 197
  primary symptom of, 293
Arizona Health Care Cost Containment System
  (AHCCCS), 355
Arkansas Blue Cross & Blue Shield, 63, 65
Asian Americans, 235, 236-237, 240
  cultural conflicts as stressor for, 237-238
  culturally sensitive mental health approaches for,
    142, 177
  model minority myth as stressor for, 237, 238
  needs for services, 238-239
  racism as stressor for, 237
  utilization of services by, 239-240
  See also Immigrants and refugees
Autism, 64

Battered women's shelters, 188
Biochemistry:
  and etiology of mental illness, 87
  and treatment of mental illness, 87
Biopsychosocial model of mental illness, 200-202,
  206, 207
  general systems theory and, 200
Bipolar affective disorder, 95, 98, 206, 364
  as neurobiological disease, 62, 63, 66, 207
  as severe mental illness, 199
Brain structure, basic, 90-91. *See also* Neurons;
  Neurotransmitters
Bupropion (Wellbutrin):
  for depression, 103
Bureau of Indian Affairs, 251

Buspirone (Buspar):
  for anxiety, 105

Capitation systems, 350-351
  key to successful, 350
  risk management challenges for, 351
Case management services, 4, 11, 21
  for elderly mentally ill, 296
  See also Medicaid
Center for Mental Health Services, MHSIP, 351,
    353-354
Chicago Orthogenic School, 122
Child/family guidance clinics, 11, 20
Child psychiatry:
  behaviorism and, 275
  ecological approach, 275-276, 280
  history of, 275
  perceptual/sensorimotor systems and, 275
  psychoanalysis and, 275
  See also Children, psychiatric treatment of
Children:
  homeless, 188-189
  mentally ill, xvi
  prevalence of mental illness in, 5-6
  psychological/behavioral disturbances in
    war-affected, 168
  See also Adolescents; Children, psychiatric
    treatment of
Children, psychiatric treatment of:
  and privatization of hospitals, 280-284
  elements of treatment approaches, 276-279
  family therapy, 279, 280
  group therapy, 279, 280
  insight-oriented therapies, 279-280
  short-term intervention, 279
  See also Milieu therapy; Psychodynamic therapy
Child Welfare Act of 1978, 250
Chlorpromazine (Thorazine), 100
  for psychotic disorders, 196
  for severe depression, 196
Civil Rights Acts, 267
Clozapine:
  for schizophrenia treatment, 27, 100, 101
  side effects of, 101, 102
"Combat fatigue," 211
Committee on Mental Health, World Health
    Organization:
  public policy recommendations, 21
Community-based care, 4
  underfunding of, 4, 54
Community-based mental health services, funding
    practices and, 24
Community-based programs, philosophy of, 19
Community mental health centers, 11, 12, 13, 356
  funding of, 12
  increase in number of, 8, 12, 25
  psychiatrists in, 71

  psychologists in, 71
  registered nurses in, 71
  social workers in, 71
Community Mental Health Centers Act (1963), xii,
    12, 21, 248, 295
  amendments to, 12
  psychoeducation and, 129
  purpose of, 129
Community mental health programs, 23
Computer-based mental health assessment
    applications:
  adaptive testing, 330
  clinical decision making and, 332-334
  conducting clinical interviews and, 330-331
  interviews, 330
  objective personality tests, 330
  recording behavioral variables and, 330, 331-332
  recording physiological variables and, 330
  self-report inventories, 330
  tests, 330
  See also Computer technology, mental health
    practice and
Computerized Assessment System for
    Psychotherapy Evaluation and Research
    (CASPER), 331
Computer technology, mental health practice and,
    xvi, 366
  administering psychological tests, 329
  assigning psychiatric diagnoses, 329
  conducting interventions with clients, 329,
    334-335
  developer issues and, 338-340
  expert system construction, 333
  interactive video, 334-335
  interpreting psychological tests, 329, 330, 333
  interviewing clients, 329
  issues affecting, 336-340
  keeping treatment notes, 329
  making treatment suggestions, 329
  mental health field issues, 340-342
  practitioner issues and, 336-338
  scoring psychological tests, 329, 330
  skills training/education, 334, 335
  See also Computer-based mental health
    assessment applications
Consumer groups, 14
Cottage plan, Illinois State Hospital (Kankakee),
    18
Counseling/therapy, short-term, 11
County mental hospitals, 13
  decrease in, 282
  psychiatrists in, 71
  psychologists in, 71
  registered nurses in, 71
  social workers in, 71
Cranial surgery, 22
Crime Bill, 1994, 301
Criminal justice system:

as destination of developmentally disabled, 298, 364

as destination of mentally ill, 298, 364

deinstitutionalization of mental health clients and, 299, 364

increasing use of prison sanctions for offenders and, 299

Criminal offenders, female:
    mothers, 307
    parenting programs for, 307
    pregnant, 307
    substance-abusing, 306
    See also Incarcerated mentally ill

Criminal offenders, transitional care programs for, 301-302. See also Incarcerated mentally ill

Cultural competence, definition of, 175

Culturally sensitive mental health approaches, 141, 175
    for African Americans, 141
    for Asian Americans, 142, 177
    for Hispanics, 141, 142, 177
    See also Immigrants and refugees, mental health program development/service delivery for

Culture-congruent care modality, 175

Dallas County Mental Health Mental Retardation, 190

Day programs, 23
    educational, 22
    Fountain House, 22
    growth-oriented, 22
    inpatient transition, 22
    rehabilitation, 22
    social clubs, 22

Decarceration, 124

Deinstitutionalization, 4, 23, 54, 130
    decrease in inpatient services and, 8
    de jure policy of, 12
    failure of, 130
    homeless mentally ill and, 4, 184-185

Dementia:
    as old-age disorder, 290
    diagnosis of, 292
    in elderly, 290
    multi-infarct type, 290, 291, 292
    prophylactic measures for, 292-293
    symptoms of, 290-291
    See also Alzheimer's disease

Dementia praecox, 95. See also Schizophrenia

Department of Veterans Affairs, 212-217
    as national system, 213

Department of Veterans Affairs medical centers, 12-13, 226
    average per psychiatric patient cost, 213
    criticism of, 214
    inpatient care in, 8-9
    mentally ill patients in, 210

psychiatrists in, 71

psychologists in, 71

registered nurses in, 71

social workers in, 71

See also Department of Veterans Affairs Readjustment Counseling Service (Vet Centers)

Department of Veterans Affairs mental health services, utilization of, 217

Department of Veterans Affairs Readjustment Counseling Service (Vet Centers), 215-217, 226, 231
    location of, 216
    mission of, 216
    number of, 216
    treatment modalities offered by, 216
    Vietnam vet interview guide used by, 224

Depression, 98, 199
    age of onset, 198
    among immigrants and refugees, 164, 166, 167
    antidepressant medications and, 98, 102
    as neurobiological disease, 62, 66
    as second most common mental disorder, 197
    female versus male rates of, 197, 288
    HPA activation as response to stress of, 98
    in African American women, 197
    in alcoholic women versus alcoholic men, 198
    in elderly, 288-289
    prevalence rates of, 288
    serotonin levels and, 98
    suicide risk from, 288
    thyroid hormone levels and, 98

Diagnosis, politics and, 32-40

Diagnostic and Statistical Manual of Mental Disorders (DSM), 33, 231
    and psychiatry's changing view of homosexuality, 33-34
    first edition, 33, 211
    fourth edition, 5, 95, 97, 109, 167, 199, 289, 291, 313
    post-traumatic stress disorder diagnosis in, 37-38
    second edition, 33, 38, 211
    third edition, 33, 35, 37, 38, 111, 229
    third edition revised, 33, 35, 39, 210

Diagnostic Interview Schedule (DIS), 111, 243, 321

Diathesis-stress model of mental illness, 132

Diazepam (Valium):
    for anxiety, 104

Domiciliary Care for Homeless Veterans, VA, 224

Drug therapy, African American females' use of, 197

Dual diagnosis:
    definition of, 313
    of mentally ill homeless, 192
    of mentally ill veterans, 214

Dual Diagnosis Assessment form, 319

Dual disorder, 313
    biopsychosocial aspects of, 314-315

diagnostic criteria for, 321
diagnostic interviews for, 321
incidence of, 315-317
recent research developments concerning, 321-322
subtypes, 313-314
treatment expense of, 316-317
See also Dual-disordered individuals
Dual-disordered individuals:
controversies about, 317-319
increasing numbers of, 316
numbers of, 315
policy recommendations concerning, 324-325
recent developments in treatment of, 319-321
requiring outreach, 319
treatment recommendations for, 322-324
See also Dual disorder
Dual Recovery Anonymous, 321

Educational systems, mental health services in, 15
Education for psychiatrists, 82-83
coursework, 82
licensing/certification, 83
psychiatric residents, 82-83
training in residence, 82
Education for psychologists, 78-81
areas of specialization, 78
clinical psychology, 78
counseling psychology, 78
faculty, 80-81
internships, 80
licensing/certification, 79
practicum training, 80
program emphasis, 79-80
school psychology, 78
students, 81
Elderly, xvi
anxiety in, 293
barriers to service utilization for, 294
degenerative disorders in, 288
dementias in, 288, 290-293
depression in, 288-289
Medicaid as necessity for, 295
mental health public policy and, 294-296
paranoia in, 288
paranoid disorders in, 289-290
polypharmacy and, 293
schizophrenia-like symptoms in, 289-290
service delivery to, 294
substance abuse in, 293
suicide among, 288-289
utilization of mental health services by, 294
See also Alzheimer's disease; Dementia
Emotional disorders, age and, 197
Empowerment of clients, 45
Epidemiological Catchment Area Studies, 111, 243, 293

Exclusive provider organization (EPO), description of, 349
Expressed emotion (EE), 121-122
components of, 131
critical comments, 131
hostility, 131
overinvolvement, 131

Family-blaming theories, 130
Family therapy, 11
brief focal, 120
in psychiatric treatment of children, 279, 280
Farm of St. Anne, 18
Federal Bureau of Prisons (BOP), 300, 306, 309, 310
employee assistance programs, 307-308
employee development/human resources management programs, 309-310
mental health professionals' staff services, 307-310
transitional care programs, 301-302
treatment programs, 302-307
Victim Assistance Program, 308-109
Federal Correctional Institution (Butner, North Carolina):
residential sex offender treatment program, 303-304
Florida Mental Health Institute, 155
Fluoxetine (Prozac):
for depression, 102

Gamblers Anonymous, 305
Gay/lesbian:
affirmative therapy for, 44, 45
reparative therapy for, 44
See also Homosexuality
General Health Questionnaire, 109-111
Good Chemistry program:
as psychoeducational group therapy, 320
"Gross stress reaction," 211
Group therapy, 11
in psychiatric treatment of children, 279, 280

Halfway houses, 24, 124
Haloperidol (Haldol), 100
Health Care Financing Administration, 355, 356, 357, 358
Health care reform, failure of national, xi
Health maintenance organizations (HMOs), 351, 356
domination of in managed care business, 349
group model, 349
individual practice association model, 349
network model, 349
staff model, 349

Health promotion model, 28
Health Services Act of 1994 (Washington State), 357
Hispanics, 235, 244-245, 248
    aftercare/rehabilitation for, 248
    cultural barriers to treatment of, 247-248
    culturally sensitive approaches for, 141, 142, 177
    diversity of, 244
    emergency services for, 248
    high-stress indicators of, 245
    high use of non-mental health services by, 245-246
    language barriers to treatment of, 246
    mental health assessment and diagnosis of, 247-248
    needs for mental health services, 245
    service delivery to, 247-248
    use of inpatient services by, 248
    utilization of mental health services by, 245, 247
    veterans, 221
HIV positive/AIDS mentally ill, 25
Homeless Chronically Mentally Ill program, VA, 224
Homeless mentally ill, xii, xvi, 4, 25, 125, 198
    as challenge to mental health professionals, 185, 193
    assessing numbers of, 183-184
    deinstitutionalization and, 184-185
    difficulty in treatment of, 185-189
    dual diagnosis of, 192
    elderly schizophrenics, 295
    establishing rapport with, 186
    establishing trust with, 186
    funding for treatment of, 189
    nontraditional forms of treatment for, 186
    physical needs of, 187
    schizophrenic, 192
    sexually transmitted diseases among, 187-188
    shelterization of, 186-187
    substance abuse among, 187, 192
    veterans, 223-224
    vulnerability of, 193
    with dementia, 192
    with severe antisocial personality disorders, 192
    See also Homeless mentally ill, Dallas response to treating; Homelessness
Homeless mentally ill, Dallas response to treating:
    achievable expectations in, 191
    case management in, 192
    clients with antisocial personality disorder, 192
    clients with bipolar disorders, 192
    clients with major affective disorders, 192
    Community Outreach Coalition, 190-193
    establishing client trust, 190
    goal of, 190
    initial treatment team, 190
    medication compliance in, 191-192
    number of clients, 192

    psychiatric examinations, 190
    schizophrenic clients, 192
    shelter-based clinics in, 190, 192
    staff consistency in, 191
    treatment team flexibility in, 191
Homelessness, 182-183
    as state of disaffiliation from society, 182
    complexity of, 193
    essence of, 182
    isolation of, 183
    prevalence of U.S., 182, 183-184
    See also Homeless mentally ill
Homosexuality:
    as illness, 39
    as personality disorder, 33
    as sexual deviation, 33
    criminalization of, 38-39
    critiques of nonmenclature changes concerning, 34
    ego-dystonic, 33, 34
    politics and diagnosis of, 32-34, 365
    prevalence of, 34
    psychiatric profession's change in classification of, 32-34, 39
    psychoanalysis as treatment for, 34
    removal of from DSM-III-R, 33, 34
    societal views of, 38
    See also Affirmative therapy
Hospitals. See specific types of hospitals
Hybrid organizations, 147
Hydrotherapy, 22

Illinois Department of Mental Health, 170, 171, 173
Imipramine (Tofranil):
    for depression, 102
Immigrants and refugees, xvi
    acculturation of, 170
    acting out behavior among young, 164, 166, 168
    adjustment of to United States, 169-170
    aid to, 178
    as traumatized groups, 164
    bereavement among, 169-170
    "boat people," 168
    Bosnians, 165, 168
    Cubans, 165, 169
    culture shock among, 170
    Ethiopians, 165
    family violence among, 164
    fear of persecution among, 165
    frequent diagnoses of, 164
    Haitians, 165, 169
    Laotians, 168
    marriage dissolution among, 164
    psychiatric disorders of, 164, 166, 179
    racial/ethnic discrimination against, 164, 165
    reduced economic status of, 164, 165

reduced social status of, 164
Salvadorans, 168, 169
Southeast Asian, 165
Soviet Jews, 165
underemployment among, 174
unemployment among, 174
war-affected children, 168
See also Immigrants and refugees, mental health
program development/service delivery for;
Immigrants and refugees, underutilization of
mental health services by; Refugee at-risk
status
Immigrants and refugees, mental health program
development/service delivery for:
critical elements in, 174-178
culturally competent intervention and, 175-177,
179
staffing and, 177-178
Immigrants and refugees, underutilization of
mental health services by:
cultural barriers and, 171-173
financial costs and, 174
geographic location and, 173
lack of insurance coverage and, 174
language barriers and, 173-174
obstacles/barriers and, 171-174
Incarcerated mentally ill, xii-xiii, 25, 59-61, 198,
300
forensic programs and, 303
HIV/AIDS counseling programs for, 304-305
hospice programs for, 302
mental health programs for special needs
populations of, 305-307
prosocial values development programs for, 304
self-help groups for, 305
sex offender treatment programs for, 303-304
special needs populations, 305-307
substance abuse programs for, 300-301
Suicide Prevention Program, 302-303
See also Criminal offenders; Federal Bureau of
Prisons (BOP)
Indian Freedom of Religion Act, 250
Indian Health Service (IHS), 253
Inpatient services, 7-10
decrease in, 8
deinstitutionalization movement and, 8
in county hospitals, 8
in private psychiatric hospitals, 8
in state hospitals, 8
length of stay, 8
reason for decrease in, 9
Insane asylums, 18
Institute for Juvenile Research, 275
Institute on Alcohol, Drugs and Disabilities, 322
Institutionalism, 122
Institutional racism:
of mental health profession, 36
Interactional theories, 130

International Classification of Disease (ICD-10),
109
"Irritable heart," 211

Joint Commission on Mental Illness and Health, 21
Judge Baker Clinic (Boston), 20
Junior Republics, 122
Juvenile courts, 20

Kinsey studies, 34

Law, mental health and, 65-66
competence to stand trial, 60
criminal law and, 59-61, 66
discrimination by insurers against mentally ill,
62-63
insanity defense, 61
insurance issues, 62-65, 66
involuntary commitment issues, 49-52, 65, 363
judicial challenges to insurance limits, 63-65
offender diversion, 61
potential liability of mental health professionals,
57-59, 66
right to refuse treatment, 55-57, 65
right to treatment, 52-54, 65, 363
Lithium:
for bipolar disorder, 38, 104
Lithium Information Center:
as information service, 332
Little Commonwealth, 122
Living Free Program, 304
Managed care, xii, 14
concepts/approaches underlying, 351-352
definition of, 346-347
focus of on outcomes, 351-354
forms of, 349-350
funding shifts to, xvi
in public mental health sector, 350
movement, 271
organized systems of care as, 350
phases of, 350
private-sector models, 349
See also Capitation systems; Exclusive provider
organization (EPO); Health maintenance
organizations (HMOs); Managed mental
health care, public sector; Point of service
(POS) plan; Preferred provider organizations
(PPOs)

Managed care organizations (MCOs), 358
Managed mental health care, 363-364
appropriate applications of, 359-360
Arizona's, 355-356
Massachusetts's, 355, 356-357

Oregon's, 355, 358-359
public sector, 354-359
Tennessee's, 355, 358
Utah's, 355, 356
Washington's, 355, 357-358
Massachusetts Alliance for the Mental Ill, 7
Massachusetts Division of Medical Assistance, 356
MassHealth Managed Care, 356
McNeil Pharmaceuticals, 100
Medicaid, 24, 347-348, 358
    as creator of case management services, 21
    as funder of general hospitals, 23
    as funder of specialty outpatient clinics, 23
    as necessity for elderly, 295
    expenditures, 6
    for medication, 27
    managed mental health and, 354-355
    mental health services and, 6
    reform efforts, 355
Medicalization of deviance, 38
Mental disorder:
    definition of, 5
    issues in definition of, 39-40
    major forms of, 5
    politics and concept of, 37-39
    See also specific mental disorders
Mental health agencies, freestanding, 13-14
    outpatient departments of, 11, 14, 24
    psychiatrists in, 71
    psychologists in, 71
    registered nurses in, 71
    social workers in, 71
Mental health care approaches:
    community-based, 17-18
    history of U.S., 18-23
    institutional, 17
    shift in, 18
Mental health expenditures, 6-7
    by payment source, 7
Mental health managed care organizations
    (MHMCOs), 359
Mental Health Management of America (MHMA),
    356, 357
Mental health policy, 3
    de facto, 4
    de jure, 4, 12
    mental health service system and, 3-4
Mental health professionals:
    primary care clinicians as, 14
    private practice offices of, 11, 14
    view of patient advocacy groups in service
        decisions, 152
    view of self-help groups in service decisions,
        151-152
    See also specific types of mental health professionals
Mental health professions, core:
    nursing, 69, 84
    psychiatry, 69, 84

psychology, 69, 84
social work, 69, 84
See also Education for psychiatrists; Education
    for psychologists; Nurses, registered; Nursing
    education; Psychiatrists; Psychologists; Social
    work education; Social workers
Mental health service organizations, number of, 7,
    11
Mental health services:
    funding sources, 6-7
Mental health service system, 3
    fragmented, 4
    mental health policy and, 3-4
Mental Health Study Act of 1955, 21
Mental hygiene movement, 22
    occupational therapy and, 22
Mental illness:
    epidemiology of, 196-198
    Hippocrates' description of, 195-196
    historical perspectives on, 196-197
    overview of, 195-199
    view of as illness, 196
    view of as unnatural, 196
    See also specific mental illnesses; Mental illness,
        severe/persistent
Mental illness, etiology of:
    biopsychosocial model, 200, 206, 207
    criticism of models of, 200
    social causation model, 200
    social selection theory, 200
    stress-diathesis model, 200
    theories, 199-202
Mental illness, severe/persistent, 195, 199
    disabilities associated with, 197
    HIV/AIDS and, 198, 201
    medical/medication noncompliance and, 201
    substance abuse and, 201
    traumatic head injury and, 201
    tuberculosis and, 201
    See also Delusional disorders; Mentally ill,
        severe/persistent; Mood disorders;
        Schizophrenia
Mentally ill, severe/persistent, 199
    as heterogeneous group, 199
    community integration problems of, 202, 206
    community issues confronting, 203-205
    health care problems of, 202, 206
    health promotion through education for,
        202-203
    HIV/AIDS risk for, 202
    individual issues confronting, 202-203
    professionally guided self-help groups and, 203
    psychoeducational approaches and, 203
    societal issues confronting, 205
    stigma problems of, 202, 205, 206
    unrealistic expectations about employment, 204
Mental Retardation Expert (MRE):

as computerized decision support/expert system, 333-334

Milieu therapy:
confrontation function of, 276, 278
education function of, 276, 279
problem-solving function of, 276, 278
safety and control function of, 276-277
social reintegration function of, 276, 277-278
structure function of, 276, 277
support function of, 276, 278

Minorities, mentally ill, xvi
inappropriate service of, 44
politics and diagnosis of, 36-37, 365
politics and treatment of, 43-44, 365
underservice of, 44
See also specific minority groups

Mood disorders, 5
brain control systems and, 90
decreased serotonin levels and, 98
genetics and, 98
neurobiological basis of, 97-99
See also Bipolar affective disorder; Depression

Mood-stabilizing medications, 104. *See also* Lithium; Valproic acid

Mutual aid groups, 14

Nafazodone (Serzone):
for depression, 103

Narcotics Anonymous, 305

National Alliance for Research in Schizophrenia and Depression, 154

National Alliance for the Mentally Ill, 49, 149, 154, 155, 160, 364

National Association for Mental Health, 146, 149

National Association of Social Workers (NASW), 75
credentialing programs, 75
low ethnic representation in, 178
Public Social Policy Statement on Gay Issues, 33

National Center for Posttraumatic Stress Disorder, VA, 225

National Coalition on the Mentally Ill in the Criminal Justice System, 298

National Committee for Quality Assurance:
Health Plan Employer Data and Information Set (HEDIS), 351

National Depression and Manic-Depressive Association, 154, 160

National Home for Disabled Volunteer Soldiers, 213

National Institute of Mental Health, 19
supporting establishment of self-help groups, 154

National Institute of Mental Health Epidemiologic Catchment Area (NIMH-ECA) Project, 197
findings, 197
major goal of, 197

National Institute on Drug Abuse, 301

National Mental Health Act (1946), 19

National Mental Health Association (NMHA), xii, xiii, 154, 364

National Mental Health Consumers Association, 154

National Vietnam Veterans Readjustment Study (NVVRS), 219, 223, 228
findings of, 219-220, 221, 222, 225
purpose of, 219

Native Americans, 235, 249, 254
acting out/violent behavior among, 252
alcoholism among, 249, 251-252, 253
barriers to service delivery for, 252
child welfare practices as stressors for, 249-250
delinquency among, 249
demographics of, 249
depression among, 251
disability among, 249
diversity among, 249
drug abuse among, 249
educational practices as stressors for, 250-251
infant mortality rate among, 249
introduction of alcohol as stressor for, 250
poverty among, 249, 253
religious persecution as stressors for, 250, 253
service delivery to, 253
suicide rates among, 249
teen pregnancy among, 249
unemployment among, 249, 253
utilization of mental health services by, 252

Neuroleptics, 26. *See also specific neuroleptics*

Neurons, 90-91, 92
postsynaptic, 91
presynaptic, 91
principal parts of, 91

Neuroscience technology, 92-94, 364
computerized axial tomography (CT/CAT scan), 93, 96
functional MRI (fMRI), 94
magnetic resonance imaging (MRI), 93, 94, 96
positron emission tomography (PET), 93-94, 97
single photon emission tomography (SPECT), 93, 94
xenon regional cerebral blood flow monitoring, 93, 96

Neuroscientific research, mental illness and, 89

Neurotransmission, 91

Neurotransmitter degradation:
depression and, 92
monoamine oxidase (MAO) and, 92
schizophrenia and, 92

Neurotransmitters, 91-92
dopamine, 92
norepinephrine, 92, 98
serotonin, 92, 98

Neurotransmitter system anatomy, 92

Nurses, registered, 69
in community mental health centers, 71

in county hospitals, 71
increase in, 70
in freestanding outpatient psychiatric clinics, 71
in nonfederal general hospitals, 71
in state hospitals, 71
in VA hospitals, 71
Nursing education:
  clinical specialist certification, 78
  curriculum content areas, 77
  degree program emphasis, 76-77
  faculty, 77-78
  licensure/certification, 78
Nursing homes, 24

Occupational systems, mental health services in, 15
Omnibus Budget Reconciliation Act of 1981, 12
Oregon Health Plan, 358-359
Organic mental disorders, 5
Organizational systems, mental health services in, 15
Outpatient services, 8, 11-12
  at private psychiatric hospitals, 13
  increase in, 8
  settings, 11
  treatment options, 11
Outreach programs, state hospital, 11

Panic disorder, male alcoholics with, 198
Paranoid disorders:
  in elderly, 289-290
Parenting skills groups, 305
Parents Anonymous, 153
Partial care, 8, 22, 23
Patient advocates, 24
Patient management teams, 24
Patients:
  characteristics of, 23
  extended care population of, 24
  increased numbers of severe, multiple-need, 24-25, 26
  underserved populations, 23
Personality disorders, 5. See also Antisocial personality disorder
Phobias:
  among immigrants and refugees, 166
Play therapy, 275
Point of service (POS) plan, description of, 349
Politics:
  concept of mental disorder and, 37-39
  diagnosis of homosexuality and, 32-34, 365
  diagnosis of minorities and, 36-37, 365
  diagnosis of "women's madness" and, 35-36, 365
  treatment of homosexuality and, 40-42, 365
  treatment of minorities and, 43-44, 365
  treatment of women and, 42-43, 365
Posttrauma groups, 305

Post-traumatic psychosis, 164
Post-traumatic stress disorder (PTSD), 105
  abundance of studies on, 232
  as family disorder, 225
  chronicity of, 167
  definition of, 99
  diagnosis of in DSM-III, 37-38, 221
  diagnosis of in DSM-III-R, 221-222
  encountering veterans, 223-224
  essential features of, 167
  eye movement desensitization and reintegration (EMDR) therapy for, 227
  neurobiological basis of, 99
  psychosocial/neurological causes of, 90
  RISE intervention model for, 227
  symptoms of, 99, 222-223
  treatment regimes, 226-227
  See also Post-traumatic stress disordered clients; Veterans, mentally ill
Post-traumatic stress disordered clients:
  as challenges for practitioners, 229-230
  female veterans, 221, 228-229
  Hispanic veterans, 221
  identifying, 224
  immigrants and refugees, 164, 166-167, 365
  male veterans, 221
  therapeutic goals for, 225-226
  veterans, 219-229, 365
  See also Post-traumatic stress disorder (PTSD)
Preferred provider organizations (PPOs)
  description of, 349
Prepaid health plans (PHPs), 357
Present State Examination (PSE), 111
  ICD and, 111
Primary Care Evaluation of Mental Disorders (PRIME-MD), 14
Private insurance, 24
Professionalism
  attributes of, 83, 150
  cognitive/intellectual component of, 83, 150
  collectivity orientation and normative/service component of, 83, 150
  monopolistic component of, 83, 150
Psychiatric classification, 94-95
  for advancement of political agenda, 38-39
  for purpose of financial reimbursement for services, 37-38
  for rationalization for therapeutic interventions, 38
  See also Diagnostic and Statistical Manual of Mental Disorders; International Classification of Disease (ICD-10)
Psychiatric Diagnostic Interview-Revised, 321
Psychiatric hospitals, private, 280-284, 364
  and increase in number of hospitalized adolescents, 281
  and increase in number of hospitalized children, 281

increase in, 13, 281
insurance payers and, 282-283
length of stay and, 283
number of, 281
outpatient services at, 13
revenues of, 281
unethical professional behavior and, 281, 282
Psychiatric outpatient clinics, freestanding, 13, 14
decline in, 14
Psychiatric social work, profession of, 20
Psychiatric units, general hospital, 13, 17, 24
increase in, 13
Psychiatrists, 11, 69
decrease in, 70
in community mental health centers, 71
in county hospitals, 71
in freestanding outpatient psychiatric clinics, 71
in nonfederal general hospitals, 71
in state hospitals, 71
in VA hospitals, 71
malpractice claims against, 57
Psychoanalysis, 123
Psychodynamic therapy:
for treating children, 279
Psychoeducation:
communication in, 132
criticisms of, 143
culture and, 140-142
definition of, 129, 131-132
duality present in, 139
early history of, 129-130
families as primary benefactors of, 140
family and, 130-131
for dually diagnosed individuals, 320
future research on, 143
group approaches to, 137-138, 320-321
idiographic approaches to, 138-139
issues, 139-140
potential for family blame in, 140
problem-solving in, 132
program components, 132
research and, 136-139
uniqueness of, 142
Psychoeducation models, 132-136
Anderson and Associates' diathesis-stress model, 133-134, 137
Bernheim's supportive family counseling framework, 133
Carpenter and Heinrichs' model, 136
Falloon and Associates' behavior therapy model, 135, 137-138
Goldstein and Associates' crisis-oriented program, 134, 137
Leff and Associates' model, 134-135, 137
Mills and Associates' education/skills acquisition model, 136, 138
Shenoy and Associates' Schiz-Anon model, 135-136

Simon's education/skills acquisition model, 136, 138-139
Psychologists, 11, 24, 69
in community mental health centers, 71
in county hospitals, 71
increase in, 70
in freestanding outpatient psychiatric clinics, 71
in nonfederal general hospitals, 71
in residential treatment centers, 71
in state hospitals, 71
in VA hospitals, 71
Psychopharmacology, 92, 98, 99-105
definition of, 99, 196
Psychosis, 5
Psychosocial rehabilitation program model, Fountain House as, 22
Psychotropic medications, 8, 11, 55
problems associated with, 55
Public Citizens Health Research Group, 49
Public mental health systems, privatizing, xii
Public policy, mental health, 20-21
controversy concerning, 21
disjointed, 24, 26, 29
emphasizing health education practices, 24
emphasizing health promotion, 24

Quarterway houses, 24

Racial bias:
in diagnosis of mental disorders, 36
in treatment of mental disorders, 43-44
Rational Recovery, 148
Reagan administration, 12
Recovery, Inc., 148
Refugee, definition of, 165. *See also* Immigrants and refugees
Refugee at-risk status, psychosocial factors and, 168-169
deprivation in homeland, 168
escape experiences, 168
refugee camp experiences, 169
trauma in homeland, 168
Residential treatment centers, 13
increase in number of, 13
psychologists in, 71
social workers in, 71
Richmond Fellowship, 124
Risperidone (Risperdal), 101
for schizophrenia treatment, 100

Schedule for Affective Disorders and Schizophrenia, 321
Schizophrenia, 206, 364
abnormal parenting view of, 90, 96
as neurobiological disease, 62, 66, 90, 96, 207

as severe mental illness, 199
dopamine neurotransmitter system and, 97
genetic factor and, 96
key features of, 95
neurobiological basis of, 95-97
neurological soft signs and, 96
prevalence of, 95
untested psychological explanations for, 96
Schizophrenia Research Foundation, 154
Schizophrenics, deinstitutionalized chronic, 295
    homeless, 295
Seasonal affective disorder, bright light treatment
    and, 103
Self-help groups, 14, 147-149
    advantages of, 153
    as expressive, 148
    definition of, 147
    for criminal offenders, 305
    future of as mental health service, 156
    future research topics concerning, 159-160
    members of, 146
    mental health professionals' view of in service
        decisions, 151-152
    mental-health related, 147
    number of, 146
    professional overinvolvement in, 157-158
    sharing of experience in, 148
    similarities of to mental health professionals,
        153-154
    versus support groups, 148
    ways of helping members, 148-149
Self-help movement, 147
    functionalist explanation for, 152
    See also Self-help groups
Sertraline (Zoloft):
    for depression, 102
Service-delivery strategies, mental health:
    assertive community treatment, 25
    case management, 25
    new financing strategies, 25-26
    use of local mental health authorities, 25
    See also Services, mental health
Servicemen's Readjustment Act of 1944, 213
Service needs, unmet:
    clinical therapy services, 26, 28
    family caregiver intervention, 26, 28
    housing, 26
    medication, 26-27
    open-ended community support services, 26, 27
    short-term hospitalization access, 26, 29
Services, mental health, 21-23
    fragmented, 25-26
    See also Service-delivery strategies, mental health
Sexpert, 335
Sexually/physically abused mentally ill, 25
Sexual orientation conversion, 41
    predatory nature of, 42
    questioning ethics of, 42

syntonic therapy and, 41
"Shell shock," 211
Social causation of mental illness, 107, 112-117,
    200
    earlier life experience factors, 112-113
    epidemiological research and, 107-108
    family interventions and, 120-122
    genetic factors, 112-113
    particular situation factors, 114
    precipitating factors, 115-117
    predisposing factors, 115, 116
    social support and, 119-120
    social theory and, 108
Social policy, mental illness and, 107, 124-127
Social prevention of mental illness, 117, 118-119
Social psychiatry, 107
    questionnaires for research in, 109-111
    standardized interviews for research in, 111-112
    See also Social causation of mental illness; Social
        policy, mental illness and; Social treatment of
        mental illness
Social Readjustment Rating Scale, 115-116
Social selection theory of mental illness, 200
Social treatment of mental illness, 107
    in institutions, 122-124
Social work education:
    Council on Social Work Education (CSWE)
        accreditation, 71
    curriculum content areas, 72-73
    degree program emphasis, 72
    degree programs, 71
    faculty, 74-75
    licensure/certification, 75
    students, 75
    voluntary credentialing programs, 75
Social workers, 11, 24, 69
    in community mental health centers, 71
    in county hospitals, 71
    increase in, 70
    in freestanding outpatient psychiatric clinics, 71
    in nonfederal general hospitals, 71
    in residential treatment centers, 71
    in state hospitals, 71
    in VA hospitals, 71
    professional roles/functions of, 76
    See also Psychiatric social workers
Sociologists, 24
Somatization:
    among immigrants and refugees, 166
State Comprehensive Mental Health Services Plan
    Act of 1986, 21
State hospitals, 13
    as antitherapeutic facilities, 19
    as custodial, 18
    closings of, 17
    decrease in, 282
    downsizing of, 17
    first U.S., 18

number of, 13
occupational therapy in, 18
professional psychiatric community and, 19
psychiatrists in, 71
psychologists in, 71
registered nurses in, 71
social workers in, 71
State mental health agencies (SMHAs), 6
Stress-diathesis model of mental illness, 200
Substance abuse:
    age and, 197
    as cause of mental disorder, 312
    as coexisting disorder in seriously mentally ill, 312
    as form of self-medication, 315, 317
    as result of mental disorder, 312
    as third most common mental disorder, 197
    in elderly, 293
    in males versus females, 197
    major depression and, 198
    schizophrenia and, 198
    See also Dual disorder
Substance-abusing mentally ill, xvi, 25
    homeless, 187, 192
    with antisocial personality disorder, 316
    See also Dual-disordered individuals
Systems theory, 123

Technology. *See* Computer-based mental health assessment applications; Computer technology, mental health practice and
TennCare program, 358
Theories of care, mental health:
    biological, 19, 20
    community, 19, 20
    custodial, 19
    mental hygiene, 19, 20
    moral, 19, 21-22, 30, 275
    social-environmental, 19, 20
    somatic, 19
Therapeutic community, 123
Third-party payment, diagnostic labels and, 37-38
"Transient situational disturbance," 212
Treatment
    extended supportive, 11
    politics and, 40-46
    See also specific types of treatments
Tuberculosis-suffering mentally ill, 25

U.S. Department of Health and Human Services, 183

VA initiative "stand-down," 224
Valproic acid:
    as mood stabilizer, 104

Venlafaxine (Effexor):
    for depression, 103
Veterans, mentally ill, xvi, 209, 210
    assessment of, 224-225
    dual diagnosis in, 214
    female, 228-229
    homeless, 223-224
    requirements of for mental health services, 231
    Vietnam-era hospitalized, 214
    World War II-era hospitalized, 214
    See also Department of Veterans Affairs; Department of Veterans Affairs medical centers; Department of Veterans Affairs mental health services; Department of Veterans Affairs Readjustment Counseling Service (Vet Centers); Post-traumatic stress disorder (PTSD); Post-traumatic stress disordered clients; Veterans' programs; War, traumatic effects of
Veterans Administration (VA), 213. *See also* Department of Veterans Affairs
Veterans Bureau, 213
Veterans groups, 305
Veterans' programs:
    first phase of, 212-213
    second phase of, 213
    third phase of, 213

War, traumatic effects of, 209-212. *See also* Post-traumatic stress disorder; Veterans, mentally ill
War neurosis, 22, 211
War Risk Insurance Act of 1917, 213
Widow to Widow program, 14, 147, 148
Women:
    anxiety in, 36
    as primary clients of mental health service systems, 261
    as selectors of future services for families, 261
    depression in, 36
    eating disorders in, 26
    erroneous borderline personality disorder diagnosis of, 36
    erroneous schizophrenia diagnosis of, 36
    inappropriate psychopathologizing of, 43
    involuntary hospitalization of, 43
    late luteal phase dysphoric disorder (PMS) in, 35
    paraphilic rapism in, 35
    politics and diagnosis of psychopathology in, 35-36, 365
    politics and treatment of, 42-43, 365
    self-defeating personality disorder in, 35
    See also Women, psychology of; Women as mental health service providers; Women as mental health service recipients
Women, psychology of:
    development of, 259-260

gender-biased human behavior research and, 260
Women as mental health service providers, 265-272
    entering the mental health field late, 268-270
    failing to mentor other women, 270-271
    history of, 265-267
    issues related to, 268-272
    underrepresentation in mental health
        administration, 268

women's intuition and, 271-272
Women as mental health service recipients, 259-265
    false memory controversy and, 262-263
    homeless mentally ill, 263-265
    issues related to, 261-265
    sexual harassment and, 261-262

About the Authors

James W. Callicutt, Ph.D., is Professor and Associate Dean in the School of Social Work at the University of Texas at Arlington. After receiving his M.S.S.W. degree, he held social work positions in mental health settings in Tennessee and Massachusetts. Following his doctoral studies at Brandeis University, he began his long association with the University of Texas at Arlington, where he has served as Associate Dean, Interim Dean, and Professor. As a consultant for community mental health centers in Eastern Maine and in Texas, he obtained federal funds for mental health and substance abuse boards. His previous book, *Social Work and Mental Health* (coauthored with Pedro Lecca), and numerous articles and reviews reflect his long commitment to mental health studies.

Robert L. Canon, Ph.D., is currently Lecturer and Computer Resources Consultant at the School of Social Work, University of Texas at Austin. He has conducted research on validation therapy, an intervention for geriatric dementia patients, and consumer satisfaction with social service programs. He also has social work practice experience in the area of chemical dependency, mental health, child welfare, and home health services.

393

Colette Croze, M.S.W., is Project Director for the National Association of State Mental Health Program Directors in Washington, D.C.

Albert D. Farrell, Ph.D., is Professor in the Department of Psychology at Virginia Commonwealth University. The focus of much of his research has been computer applications in mental health. In collaboration with Dr. Leigh McCullough, he developed the Computerized Assessment System for Psychotherapy Evaluation and Research (CASPER). He has also conducted studies of the effectiveness of prevention programs directed toward high-risk youth and research on risk and resiliency factors related to drug use and other problem behaviors among urban adolescents. He formerly served as software review editor for the journal *Behavioral Assessment,* and currently serves on the editorial boards of four journals.

R. Duane Hopson, M.D., practices psychiatry with children and adolescents at the Holiner Psychiatric Group in Dallas, Texas, following a long association with Timberlawn Mental Health Services. Additionally, he provides psychiatric care to homeless mentally ill persons through an innovative and aggressive outreach program in Dallas.

Robin Kennedy, M.A., is a doctoral student in the School of Social Work at the University of Texas at Austin.

James I. Martin, Ph.D., is Assistant Professor of Social Work at the University of Texas at Arlington. His research focuses on social work issues relating to gay men and lesbians, especially HIV prevention. He also writes on the development and application of clinical self-psychology to social work practice and research. He was formerly Director of Social Work at Hartgrove Hospital in Chicago. He received his M.S.W. degree from the University of Michigan and his Ph.D. from the University of Illinois at Chicago.

John S. McNeil, D.S.W., is Professor and holder of the Louis and Ann Wolens Centennial Chair in Gerontology in the School of Social Work at the University of Texas at Austin. He has extensive experience as a clinician as well as approximately 20 years' experience as a social work educator. He has published extensively in professional journals and has contributed to a number of books and monographs as author or editor. His current research interests center on bereavement.

David W. Millard, M.A., M.B.Ch.B., F.R.C.Psych., is currently Consultant in Old Age Psychiatry at Rivendell Assessment Centre, Radcliffe Infirmary, Oxford, England. For many years he held a faculty position in the Department of Social and Administrative Studies, University of Oxford, England.

Christian E. Molidor, Ph.D., received his master's in social work at Loyola University and his doctorate at the Jane Addams School of Social Work, the University of Illinois at Chicago. His research and clinical experience have focused on adolescent issues, including psychiatric hospitalization of adolescents, gang violence, and teen dating violence. He is currently Assistant Professor in the School of Social Work at the University of Texas at Arlington.

Theresa Bruno Mulloy, Ed.D., has been Executive Director of Pecan Valley Mental Health Mental Retardation Regional Center since its inception in 1977. Her initial degrees were in education and psychology, and she has taught at the elementary and university levels. She has more recently added an M.B.A. degree to her credentials.

Donald W. Murray, Jr., Ed.D., is Regional Psychology Services Administrator for the Federal Bureau of Prisons. He has represented that agency on the National Institute of Corrections' National Task Force on Substance Abuse Strategies, and has been expert witness and technical adviser before the House Select Committee on Narcotics Control and Abuse and the House Subcommittee on Crime and Criminal Justice. He has published extensively and has produced films in the areas of substance abuse and corrections.

David H. Price, M.A., M.S.S.W., is a retired U.S. Army Colonel. He is a readjustment counselor and advocate for veterans who have war-related post-traumatic stress disorder. He is a prolific writer of training materials and articles for social work journals and military publications, and he speaks nationally on issues related to mental health and military service.

E. Clarke Ross, D.P.A., is the Executive Director of the American Managed Behavioral Healthcare Association. He is also Adjunct Associate Professor of Health Services Administration at the University of Maryland. His doctorate is from George Washington University. His specialization is public finance and public policy. He has taught for Troy State University, European Region, and has worked for the United Cerebral Palsy Association.

Brian D. Shannon, J.D., is Professor of Law, Texas Tech University School of Law. He volunteers as a member of the boards of directors of the Lubbock (Texas) Regional MHMR Center and the Texas Council of Community MHMR Centers, and is President of the Llano Estacado Alliance for the Mentally Ill. Additionally, he has served on the board of the Texas Alliance for the Mentally Ill and of Advocacy, Inc. He chaired the latter organization's Mental Illness Protection and Advocacy Advisory Council. His is coauthor of the Texas Alliance for the Mentally Ill's *Texas Criminal Procedure and the Offender With Mental Illness: An Analysis and Guide*.

Cassandra Simon, Ph.D., is Assistant Professor of Social Work at the University of Texas at Arlington. She has a master's degree from Louisiana State University and a doctorate from the University of Texas at Arlington. Her research has focused on the development of psychoeducation as a means of assisting persons with mental illness and their families, and on issues relating to cultural diversity.

Charles Turnbo, M.S.W., is Vice President of Correctional Systems, Inc. He previously was Regional Director, South Central Region, Bureau of Prisons, U.S. Department of Justice. In that capacity he made major contributions to the professionalization of prison mental health services. His master's degree in social work is from Louisiana State University.

Vikki L. Vandiver, Dr.P.H., M.S.W., is Assistant Professor, Graduate School of Social Work at Portland State University, Oregon. Her research is in the areas of cross-cultural mental health policies and services, with active projects in Cuba, Mexico, Canada, and Portugal. She also is involved in research on clinical/policy issues for vulnerable populations affected by schizophrenia or traumatic brain injury. She has published in the areas of managed care, family psychoeducation, and services for ethnic populations. She chairs the board of a community mental health center and serves on two other boards affiliated with the Indochinese community and the local Brain Injury Association.

Ted R. Watkins, D.S.W., is Associate Professor in the School of Social Work at the University of Texas at Arlington. His practice experience has included clinical social work in a rural mental health center, administration and psychotherapy in a residential treatment center for adolescents, and administration in an urban comprehensive mental health center, all in Pennsylvania, and clinical administration in a large family service agency in Texas. He has also maintained a private practice in clinical social work with individuals and families and has been a consultant to numerous organizations that provide services to substance abusers. His doctorate is from the University of Pennsylvania School of Social Work. At the University of Texas at Arlington he has taught at the undergraduate, master's, and doctoral levels, and has served as Director of the Criminal Justice Degree Program; Director of the Bachelor of Social Work Program; Chair of the Department of Sociology, Anthropology and Social Work; and Graduate Adviser for the M.S.S.W.

Program. His current scholarship focuses on the interface of mental health and substance abuse problems and services.

William H. Wilson, M.D., is Associate Professor of Psychiatry at the Oregon Health Sciences University, School of Medicine, Department of Psychiatry, in Portland, Oregon. He has written extensively in the area of neuroscientific research in mental illness.

Muriel Yu, Ph.D., is Associate Professor in the School of Social Work at the University of Texas at Arlington. Her extensive career in mental health has ranged from clinical practice to statewide planning and administrative roles in Oklahoma. Since joining the faculty at UTA she has done a considerable amount of research and writing on issues affecting Asian Americans, immigrants, and refugees, substance abuse, and cultural diversity. She continues clinical practice on a part-time basis.